WILLIAM WORDSWORTH

THE EARLY YEARS
1770–1803

Oxford University Press, Amen House, London E.C.4

GLASGOW NEW YORK TORONTO MELBOURNE WELLINGTON
BOMBAY CALCUTTA MADRAS KARACHI
CAPE TOWN IBADAN NAIROBI ACCRA SINGAPORE

WORDSWORTH IN 1804, FROM A DRAWING BY HENRY EDRIDGE

WILLIAM WORDSWORTH

A BIOGRAPHY

THE EARLY YEARS
1770–1803

BY

MARY MOORMAN

OXFORD
AT THE CLARENDON PRESS
1957

PRINTED IN GREAT BRITAIN

To

BRENDA RITCHIE

in thankfulness for a
precious friendship

PREFACE

Wordsworth once described his poet's soul as

> A Rock with torrents roaring, with the clouds
> Familiar, and a favourite of the stars.

To share, however imperfectly, in his life, has seemed to me indeed like treading a high mountain-range where precipices often block the path entirely, although we find, as he himself said, that someone has planted many of the crevices with flowers. Any poet's life must take us into high and dangerous places, though with some, as with Coleridge, poetry appears as only one among many activities and achievements, and where this is so a biographer may content himself with saying little about those cloud-familiar heights of poetry. But there are poets to whom poetry is their calling and their choice, and they desire to make it the whole business of their lives. This was pre-eminently so with John Keats, and also with Wordsworth. In middle life indeed, with a family to bring up, he was fain to become a Distributor of Stamps, and his interest in politics became embarrassingly keen. But no life of Wordsworth could be constructed out of these activities. His poetry is itself the chief justification for a biography: it is of the mind and soul of the author of *Lyrical Ballads* and *Poems in Two Volumes* and *The Prelude* and *The Excursion* that his biographer must write and that those who care for him will wish to read.

He has had plenty of critics and interpreters, and it does not appear that his poetry is in any danger of attracting less attention in this generation than in those that are past. Wordsworth is still necessary to us. Some of the critics have rightly made a biographical approach to his poetry; among them H. W. Garrod and the great editor, Ernest de Selincourt, who was also the biographer of Dorothy Wordsworth. Upon the whole, however, Wordsworth has been unfortunate in his biographers. His nephew, Christopher Wordsworth, who compiled *Memoirs of William Wordsworth, Poet-Laureate, D.C.L.*, in 1850–1, accomplished a strictly limited task. He aimed simply at writing 'a biographical commentary' on his uncle's works, though he also printed a number of letters, and added some of the 'Fenwick Notes'—Wordsworth's own notes on his poems dictated to Isabella Fenwick, many of which contain biographical matter of importance. But he suppressed or omitted a great deal in the early part of the story. William Knight, whose three-volume biography of Wordsworth appeared in 1889, was inaccurate and impercipient. His editions of the *Letters of the Wordsworth Family* (1907) and Dorothy's *Journals* (1897) suffered from omissions and mistakes which the labours of more recent scholars have fortunately to a large extent repaired.

The first person to write a biographical study of Wordsworth with understanding and scholarship was the Frenchman, Emile Legouis, whose book, *La Jeunesse de Wordsworth, 1770–1798*, appeared in an English translation in 1898. Based on a study of *The Prelude* and of Wordsworth's early poems, *An Evening Walk* and *Descriptive Sketches*, it showed for the first time the true character and importance of his visit to France in 1791–2; and many years later, after the discovery of the love affair with Annette Vallon, Legouis told that story with admirable insight in *William Wordsworth and Annette Vallon* (1922).

In 1916 G. M. Harper, an American scholar, published his *William Wordsworth, his Life, Work and Influence*, in two volumes, later reprinted, with additions, as one. This work was curiously marred by undue emphasis on the picture of Wordsworth as a 'lost leader' of the democratic and liberal cause, and added little to what was already known of him. But the time when a full biography of Wordsworth could be written had scarcely then arrived. It was not until Professor de Selincourt had published the early text of *The Prelude* (1926) and brought out his six-volume edition of the *Letters of William and Dorothy Wordsworth* (1935–9) and his complete text of Dorothy's *Journals* (1941) that it became possible to study Wordsworth's life with some hope of understanding and completeness. His work on the poems was continued after his death by Miss Helen Darbishire, whose own writings on Wordsworth are valuable alike to the critic and the biographer.

In recent years Wordsworth, in common with many other departed great ones, has had to undergo study by what may be described as the psycho-analytical school of writers. Modern psychological knowledge is a useful aid to human studies of any kind, but psychological evidence is only one kind of evidence among many; it is very easily misinterpreted, and can be misleading when it results in the distortion or neglect of relevant facts. Biography cannot be reduced to an analyst's case-book, nor is it possible to make Wordsworth's life, poetry, and personality fit into a preconceived psychological pattern.

I have treated *The Prelude* (which must be the chief textbook of any student of Wordsworth) as a reliable guide in all that concerns the 'growth of his own mind', valuable also but not unerring from the point of view of biographical detail. Wordsworth's memory was perfect in recalling the scenes and experiences that had most deeply affected or impressed him, but he was not concerned with chronological exactitude, so that he describes events sometimes without dating them, or with a date that is inaccurate or which he himself subsequently altered. Sometimes he seems to unite into one story events which took place at different times, as in the first part of the first Book, and in Book VI he describes himself as witnessing an event which he could not possibly have seen—the military occupation of the Grande Chartreuse. But these are not matters which in any way invalidate *The Prelude* as a biographical source of high importance. Wordsworth himself said that in writing it he 'had nothing to do but describe what he had felt and thought; therefore could not easily be bewildered', and we must take it at not less than his own valuation.

I have brought the present volume down to the end of 1803, when Wordsworth had been married just over a year and Coleridge was about to depart to the Mediterranean. I hope to complete the story in a second volume. My aim has been to make full use of the material provided in the letters, journals, and poetical texts, with whatever else of additional information can be discovered or used. I cannot claim to have found out many new facts about Wordsworth; on the whole, what were mysteries before, such as what he did in Paris in 1792 and whether he returned thither in 1793, are mysteries still. Perhaps the most important new discovery is his acquaintance with Godwin in 1795, revealed in Godwin's diaries. For the rest, some new light on his school-days, on the Racedown and Alfoxden periods, and on his winter in Germany is about all that can be claimed, and for most of that I am indebted to the kindness of other people.

To Miss Helen Darbishire, chairman of the Dove Cottage Trustees, I am deeply grateful both for permission to use the Dove Cottage Papers and for her patience, help, and forbearance during the past eight years. Next to her I would thank Mrs. Rawnsley of Allan Bank, Grasmere, whose hospitality, interest, and assistance on many points connected with the Grasmere period have been invaluable and unfailing. Lady Pinney, of Racedown, Dorset, has put the Pinney Papers at my disposal and also made me welcome many times at Racedown. To Mrs. Ross of Sawrey and the Reverend Sam Taylor of Cartmel I am indebted for much help over the problems of Colthouse and Hawkshead, and to Mr. L. Brownson and the Trustees of the Hawkshead School Library for permission to examine it and 'Ann Tyson's Ledger'. Mr. Roy Hudleston, Mr. Tom Gray (then Librarian of Tullie House, Carlisle), and the City Librarians of Halifax, Bristol, and Norwich, and Mr. Sharpe France, Archivist of the Lancashire Record Office, have all generously assisted my researches and answered my questions whenever possible. I am deeply grateful to Miss Margaret Crum for the loan of her valuable unpublished monograph on Basil Montagu. Others who have put their knowledge and help at my service are the late Sir Ralph Wedgwood of Leith Hill Place, Miss Joanna Hutchinson, Dr. J. R. MacGillivray of Toronto, Mr. H. M. Margoliouth, Mr. A. W. Stockwell, and Mr. J. Dearden. Their special assistance has been acknowledged, where necessary, in the footnotes.

Three American scholars have been particularly kind in furnishing me with new material which they are using in their own researches; they are Professor Lewis Patton of Duke University, Mr. David V. Erdman, and Mr. B. R. Schneider. My thanks are also due to the Librarian of Duke University for permission to quote from the Abinger MSS. there.

I owe a very great debt to two friends, both of them poets, whose faith in the venture has meant much to me, and who have helped me with imaginative advice and criticism in the writing of the book—Mr. Robert Gittings of Chichester and Miss Margaret Cropper of Burneside, Westmorland.

There is a natural pleasure in thanking my father, Dr. G. M. Trevelyan, for his encouragement and interest, and my cousin Pauline Dower for her painstaking criticisms of style and punctuation. I owe much also to the patience and conscientious interest of my father's secretary Miss Ruth Jones, who has typed almost the whole of the book, and to Miss Helen Read, Miss Phœbe Johnson, and Mrs. Kirkbride, who have been so ready to assist me in my visits to Dove Cottage and its Library.

M. M.

Chichester
September 1956

NOTE. Professor E. L. Griggs's *Collected Letters of Samuel Taylor Coleridge* (1955) unfortunately appeared only after my book had gone to press and I have consequently been unable to make the use of it which I should have wished.

CONTENTS

LIST OF PLATES

LIST OF ABBREVIATIONS IN FOOTNOTES

D.W., W.W.,
R.W., J.W. = Dorothy, William, Richard, and John Wordsworth.

M.H. = Mary Hutchinson.

S.H. = Sara Hutchinson.

S.T.C. = Samuel Taylor Coleridge.

J.P., J.M. = Jane Pollard (later Jane Marshall).

D.C.P. = Wordsworth Letters and Papers at Dove Cottage, Grasmere.

E.L. = *The Early Letters of William and Dorothy Wordsworth*, edited by E. de Selincourt, 1935.

M.Y. = *The Letters of William and Dorothy Wordworth, The Middle Years*, edited by E. de Selincourt, 2 vols., 1937.

L.Y. = *The Letters of William and Dorothy Wordsworth, The Later Years*, edited by E. de Selincourt, 3 vols., 1939.

Grosart = *The Prose Works of William Wordsworth*, edited by A. Grosart, 3 vols., 1876.

S.T.C. i & ii = *The Letters of Samuel Taylor Coleridge*, edited by Ernest Hartley Coleridge, 2 vols., 1895.

U.L. = *Unpublished Letters of Samuel Taylor Coleridge*, edited by Earl Leslie Griggs, 2 vols., 1932.

D.W.J. = *The Journals of Dorothy Wordsworth*, edited by E. de Selincourt, 2 vols., 1941.

P.P. = The Pinney Papers at Racedown, Dorset.

P.W. = *Wordsworth's Poetical Works*, in 5 vols., edited by E. de Selincourt and H. Darbishire, Oxford University Press, 1940-9.

B.L. = *Biographia Literaria*, by S. T. Coleridge.

A.P. = *Anima Poetae* (extracts from Coleridge's note-books), 1895.

Prel. = *Wordsworth's Prelude*, edited by E. de Selincourt, 1928.

E.W. = *An Evening Walk*.

D.S. = *Descriptive Sketches*.

L. = *La Jeunesse de Wordsworth*, by E. Legouis, 1895. (English translation 1898: *The Early Life of William Wordsworth*.)

A.V. = *William Wordsworth and Annette Vallon*, by E. Legouis, 1922.

Harper = *William Wordsworth, his Life, Work and Influence*, by G. M. Harper, 2 vols., 1916.

Cottle = *Early Recollections chiefly relating to the late Samuel Taylor Coleridge*, by Joseph Cottle, 2 vols., 1837.

Lamb = *The Letters of Charles and Mary Lamb*, edited by E. V. Lucas, 1935.

Lowes = *The Road to Xanadu*, by J. Livingstone Lowes, 1927.

T.P. = *Thomas Poole and his Friends*, by Mrs. Henry Sandford, 2 vols., 1888.

E.K.C.   = *Coleridge*, by E. K. Chambers, 1938.

C.W.A.A.S. = *Transactions of the Cumberland and Westmorland Antiquarian and Archaeological Society.*

M.L.R.   = *Modern Language Review.*

N. & Q.   = *Notes and Queries.*

P.M.L.A.   = *Publications of the Modern Language Association of America.*

R.E.S.   = *Review of English Studies.*

T.L.S.   = *Times Literary Supplement.*

I

FAIR SEED-TIME, 1770-9

What seest thou
In the dark backward and abysm of time?
The Tempest

In the cold winter of 1798 in Germany, William Wordsworth, then aged twenty-eight, began to survey the landscape of his own life. The first object which attracted him as he gazed into the past was a river. He beheld it as a source of beneficence and peace, and hailed it as an influence stretching back even beyond the gates of conscious memory, a presence which

loved
To blend his murmurs with my nurse's song . . .
And from his fords and shallows sent a voice
That flowed along my dreams.

The river was the Derwent, flowing past the ruined walls of Cockermouth Castle in Cumberland, past the terrace-walk at the foot of his father's garden, on under the bridge, and away through the fields beyond. Cockermouth stands at the confluence of the Derwent and the smaller river Cocker which gives its name to the town. But Wordsworth always speaks of the Derwent, whose voice was for him a constant undertone of calm. Even in babyhood it had, he believed, given him

A foretaste, a dim earnest, of the calm
That Nature breathes among the hills and groves.

The sound of running water was always among the most precious to him of all the multitudinous sounds which reached his sensitive ears from the mysterious universe. He often felt it almost as part of his own being, and lovingly he thanked the Derwent for this first gift of 'ceaseless music' from his steady-flowing stream. It was such delight as this that caused him afterwards to see the human spirit as something 'exquisitely fitted' from birth to 'existing things', and to declare that there was, even in 'our dawn of being', a

bond of union betwixt life and joy.

At five years old he was bathing in that stream, or in the small mill-race that ran off from it, and rushing about naked in his father's fields, which bore the curious names of Sand Air and St. Leonard's, below the bridge, where in July and August 'groves of yellow ragwort' almost hid the grass, and were like trees to his small body as he leapt about amongst them. And after the bathing and the leaping there came, sometimes, for William, moments of a strange stillness, when in the sunset radiance he, a little naked boy,

> stood alone
> Beneath the sky . . .

filled with a mysterious happiness which he could not understand.[1]

As the Derwent was a constant, dependable source of freedom and pleasure out of doors, remembered afterwards as a composing power on the passionate little boy, so, within the handsome, double-fronted house in the High Street, with its spacious panelled rooms and marble fire-places, his mother, Ann Wordsworth, bestowed upon her brood, for the short time that she remained with them, the priceless gift of a peaceable and tranquil love, that sustained and cherished them without ever interfering with their pleasures or dominating them with schemes and activities of her own. When he wrote long afterwards his description of her,[2] he sought a comparison in the world of nature. But neither the dove nor the pelican—those overworked emblems of motherhood—did he choose. Mrs. Wordsworth's influence is compared to that of a hen with her chickens:

> Behold a parent hen amid her brood
> Though fledged and feathered and well-pleased to part
> And straggle from her presence, still a brood,
> And she herself from the maternal bond
> Still undischarged: yet doth she little more
> Than move with them in tenderness and love
> A centre to the circle which they make.

She had no nervous dread of calamity to her children; she did not expect too much of them; she

> Was not puffed up by false, unnatural hopes
> Nor selfish with unnecessary cares.

---

[1] *Prel.* I, ll. 269–300.   [2] Ibid. V, ll. 246–90.

Their life was free and unoppressed—full of little festivals. At
Eastertide they went with the other children of the town to the
'catechising' at the Parish Church, quite a solemn event when
the children appeared in new clothes with flowers in their
button-holes. Wordsworth never forgot his mother fastening
his nosegay for him, and ever afterwards the sight of those
flowers evoked for him 'her countenance, phantom-like'—floating up on the waves of association out of the abysm of time.[1]

Wordsworth in after years gave, in *The Prelude*, the most
exalted importance to the relation of the infant to its mother,
regarding it as the archetype from which springs the happiness
of the child's intercourse with the universe.

> For him, in one dear Presence, there exists
> A virtue which irradiates and exalts
> Objects through widest intercourse of sense.
> No outcast he, bewildered and depressed;
> Along his infant veins are interfus'd
> The gravitation and the filial bond
> Of nature, that connect him with the world.[2]

He could not have written thus if there had not remained with
him a profound conviction of the beneficence of his own mother's
care. She it was who first introduced him to 'Nature'—and when
her own presence was withdrawn, he stood safely, though a
little solemnly, in that universe which she had trusted and in
which she had felt so perfectly at home. Soon he learnt to transfer to Nature the affection, the faith, the 'religious love' which
he had felt for his mother. Wordsworth's maternal conception
of Nature echoes throughout his poetry—she was

> The anchor of my purest thoughts, the nurse,
> The guide, the guardian of my heart, and soul
> Of all my moral being . . .
> Surely I was led by her.

His awe and fear of Nature in him was never hideous or terrible,
but rather a source of strength and love. Doubtless this had
its analogy in his desire for his mother's approval—his consciousness sometimes of her disapproval. Those 'low breathings'

[1] *Prel.* V, ll. 246–60. *P.W.* iii, p. 395, *Ecclesiastical Sonnets,* Pt. III, XXII, *Catechising.*
[2] *Prel.* II, ll. 238–44. This passage and what precedes and follows it is one of those most frequently rewritten and revised in the various *Prelude* texts. Words-worth evidently looked upon it as of primary importance.

that followed him over the dark moors when he stole the wood-cock; his sudden awe of the 'huge peak' that gazed down at him when he was rowing in the stolen boat on Ullswater—how could Nature have so spoken to his conscience without some human experience at the heart of all? His mother, he tells us, once rebuked him for going to a church service with no more exalted motive than the acquisition of a penny.[1] He never forgot the tiny incident.

He afterwards thought that his mother's quiet virtues, and her benign trust in the good providence of God and Nature, were drawn partly from

the times
And spot in which she lived—

times tranquil indeed compared with those in which he passed his youth and early manhood—but more from an inward grace, that inexplicable benignity of heart which is the possession of some unsophisticated and humble souls.

Ann Wordsworth was the daughter of William Cookson, a linen-draper. She had been born in the little red sandstone market town of Penrith in east Cumberland. 'The town', said Anne Radcliffe, the novelist, who visited it in 1794, 'consisting chiefly of old houses, straggles along two sides of the high north road, and is built upon the side of a mountain, that towers to great height above it, in steep and heathy knolls, unshaded by a single tree.' Such appeared Penrith Beacon before its afforesta-tion with conifers. 'Penrith,' she continues, 'despite its many symptoms of antiquity, is not deficient in neatness. The houses are chiefly white, with door and window cases of the red stone found in the neighbourhood. Some of the smaller have over their doors dates of the latter end of the sixteenth century. The town lies . . . spreading prettily along the skirts of the mountain, with its many roofs of blue slate, among which the church rises near a dark grove.'[2] Ann's father lived over his shop in the market square.[3] His ancestry was nonconformist, but he had chosen to conform, was often church warden, and owned property in the town. He was by birth, and by the trade he pursued, identified with the life and interests of a small country town, but Words-

---

[1] *Mem.* i, p. 9.   [2] *Observations during a Tour in the Lakes, 1796.*
[3] The shop, now Arnison's, is still a draper's store, but has been rebuilt.

worth says of his line of business that 'it was very different from what it now is'; meaning that it was not then considered in any way mean or degrading. The snobbery which regarded 'trade' as contaminating was not yet so strong as it soon afterwards became; and there was nothing remarkable in William Cookson marrying Dorothy Crackanthorpe, who came of an ancient country family, and was born at Newbiggin Hall, just over the border in Westmorland, of a long line of squires who had played their part as warriors, sheriffs, and knights of the shire there since the reign of Edward III, and had built up from the six-teenth century a considerable estate. Dorothy Cookson, having survived her brothers, became heiress to these lands, and her son, Christopher Crackanthorpe Cookson (Wordsworth's 'Uncle Kit'), on entering into this inheritance in 1792, dropped the name of Cookson and, as Mr. Christopher Crackanthorpe, went to live at Newbiggin Hall.

Ann Cookson's marriage to the young attorney, John Words-worth of Sockbridge, man of business or 'law-agent' to Sir James Lowther, the chief land-owner and political magnate of the district, took place in 1766, when she was but eighteen and he twenty-five. He took her to live in a large house in the wide main street of Cockermouth, on the other side of the county. It is by far the most stately and pretentious house in that little town to this day, and none of the Wordsworth children ever again lived in so fine a mansion, except Christopher who in-habited the Master's Lodge at Trinity College, Cambridge, as Master from 1820 to 1841. Built in 1745 for one John Lucock, who was Sheriff of Cumberland, the house in Cockermouth had been bought by Sir James Lowther as a residence for his man of business, whom he wished to have living permanently there to look after his increasing financial and political interests through-out West Cumberland.

Sir James Lowther was one of the richest land-owners in the north of England, and his wealth was used in the acquisition of political power. He did not aspire, it seems, to high ministerial office, which he never held; he loved rather to influence politics indirectly through the control of borough and county representa-tion in Parliament. He eventually had in his 'interest' no less than nine seats in the House of Commons.[1] As a youth of

---

[1] They were: the two seats for Westmorland: two for Cockermouth, one each

nineteen he had, by inheritance, become immensely rich. Three or four great family properties devolved one after another upon him, including not only the great estates at Lowther near Penrith, but the town and harbour of Whitehaven with its valuable coal-mines, and various properties in and around the little borough of Cockermouth. In 1756, when he was still only twenty, he completed his control of Cockermouth by buying up the remaining burgage tenures from the Earl of Egremont; and thenceforward it was a 'Lowther' pocket-borough. In 1774 he similarly acquired the freeholds in the district known as the Seignory of Millom, between the Duddon Sands and White-haven, thus gaining control of the county representation in that area. He himself sat as member for one of the Cumberland county seats. John Wordsworth was made coroner of Millom, a post which gave him the political surveillance of the area in his mas-ter's interests. Both there and at Cockermouth his business was to see that the freeholders remained faithful in their political allegiance and voted properly at election time. At elections a considerable expenditure on drink and other favours was of course necessary, to which the accounts of Mr. Wordsworth bear their testimony.

Sir James Lowther married a daughter of Lord Bute, the tutor of George III and the successor of Chatham as Prime Minister in 1763. But he by no means always supported the Tory or 'Royal' cause in Parliament. He went his own way. In one instance his patronage had an interesting sequel: the younger Pitt first entered Parliament as member for Lowther's seat in the two-member borough of Appleby. Lowther was too fond of pushing his own ambitions ever to be popular: he was over-bearing and dictatorial to his parliamentary nominees; unswerv-ing in his struggles for power with the great Whig interests in his own neighbourhood, those of the Dukes of Portland and Norfolk; his business methods were unusual, and he would engage in endless litigation rather than acknowledge a debt—as the Wordsworths later found to their cost. He was perhaps more hated than he deserved, but he certainly took no pains to be liked.

In the house in the High Street at Cockermouth the Words-worths' five children were born. The eldest, Richard, a cautious,

at Appleby and Carlisle and one of the Cumberland county seats: two at Haslemere in Surrey.

unadventurous child, became a lawyer and was throughout his life the adviser to his brothers and sister in their business affairs. William and Dorothy followed next in age, William being born on April 7th 1770, and Dorothy on December 25th 1771. For some reason, William was not baptized until after the birth of Dorothy. The two received baptism on the same day. Next to them came John, the shy, silent boy who was to be the beloved companion of William and Dorothy in their early Grasmere days, and whose death by shipwreck in 1805 was so bitter a blow to them. He had been, said William after his death, 'from his earliest infancy of most lonely and retired habits: my Father in allusion to this part of his disposition used to call him Ibex, the shyest of all beasts'. (This, incidentally, is the only remark of John Wordsworth's about any of his children which has been recorded.) But this brother John was more than shy and retiring, he was 'a silent poet', and nourished secretly a love of Nature and poetry which found no outward expression save in his fellowship with William and Dorothy whom he adored and who alone understood him. At the end of the family came Christopher, born in 1774, a scholarly and industrious boy, who stuck closely to the beaten track which led to distinction and authority in the academic world.

It is difficult to form a vivid picture of John Wordsworth the father, for no personal description of him was ever given by William. This is perhaps an indication that they were never very intimate. A busy man, hard-working and unsparing of himself he certainly was, an admirable steward of Sir James Lowther's interests. For eighteen years, from 1765 until his death in 1783, John Wordsworth served his strange master with zeal and fidelity. His devotion made him reserved with his neighbours: he took little part in the life and affairs of Cockermouth; he was regarded as the representative of a man more feared than loved. 'It is indeed mortifying to my Brothers and me', wrote Dorothy to Jane Pollard four years after his death, 'to find that amongst all those who visited at my father's house he had not one real friend.' Those who owed John Wordsworth money for legal business frequently failed to pay, and his financial position was indeed an extraordinary one. There is no evidence that he ever received any payment for his services from his employer. Inquiries set on foot after his death revealed that there had never been any agreement between the baronet and his agent as to payments or reimbursements for expenses. A debt had accumulated amounting to over £4,000 which became the subject of endless dispute between Lowther and the guardians of the Wordsworth children, and was at length discharged by Lowther's successor in 1802.

Fortunately for his family, John Wordsworth had a small estate of his own at Sockbridge, just to the north of the road between Penrith and Pooley Bridge. This farm estate had been purchased early in the century by his father Richard Words-worth, who had come into Westmorland after the break-up of the family estate at Falthwaite in south Yorkshire 'through embarrassment arising out of suretyship and speculation in mines', and there was fortunate in obtaining the post of 'law-agent' for the Westmorland properties of the Lowther family. He was besides Receiver-General for the county of Cumberland and Clerk of the Peace. When the Pretender's highlanders passed through the district in 1745 he retired into Patterdale with the public moneys and documents in his care.

His elder son, Richard, who should normally have inherited the Sockbridge property, had for some reason—probably con-nected with his marriage[1]—incurred his father's displeasure and been disinherited. By old Richard's will, the Sockbridge estate was left to John, the younger son and father of William, though with a life interest to the widow, Mrs. Richard Wordsworth.[2] Richard the younger eventually became Collector of Customs at Whitehaven, where he often entertained his brother's children from Cockermouth. On the death of John Wordsworth, he became, with their maternal uncle Christopher Crackanthorpe Cookson of Penrith, their legal guardian.

John Wordsworth acquired besides some small properties in Cockermouth and Ravenglass, but all this together with Sock-bridge can have brought in but a moderate income. On that, and on the credit of his unpaid claims on his employer, he and his growing family continued to live comfortably enough for

---

[1] He married in 1751 Elizabeth Favell, his cousin, of Ackworth in Yorkshire.

[2] In 1765 Mrs. Wordsworth resigned her interest in the property to her son John in return for an annuity of £50 to be paid to her by him. She died in 1773, and was buried beside her husband at Barton Church, near Sockbridge. A memorial to them may still be seen in the church. She was the daughter of John Robinson of Appleby.

several years, with a liveried manservant besides a female staff;[1]
but they did not keep a carriage, partly no doubt because the
state of the roads made driving almost impossible. John Wordsworth rode about the country on horseback on his master's
business.

Mr. Wordsworth probably had little time to bestow on his
children, being ceaselessly engaged on Lowther's business and
often away from home. Yet William owed him one great debt.
He cared for English poetry, and it was he that taught his son
William to learn by heart 'large portions of Shakespeare, Milton
and Spenser'.[2] His library was at his sons' disposal at all times,
and William—the most voracious reader in the family—soon
found in Fielding's novels, *Gil Blas*, *Don Quixote*, and *Gulliver*
a world of endless delight opened up to him. As long as his
father lived, the chief pleasure of the holidays was always the
meeting again with these unchanging friends. He would take a
volume of Spenser, or the little abridged copy of the *Arabian
Nights* with him on his fishing expeditions and forget rod, line,
and fish sometimes for hours together as he lay on the warm,
dry stones of the river. The old fairy-tales of England, the *Nights*,
and later on tales of travel, romance, and adventure were his
favourites. Such was his passion for the *Arabian Nights* that
when he discovered from his school companions that his little
collection was

> but a block
> Hewn from a mighty quarry,

and that there were really four large volumes full of similar
matter, he could scarcely believe it, and forthwith set about in
partnership with one of his friends, 'hoarding up and hoarding
up', from his slender funds, to buy the precious work. They
persevered for several months, but in the end 'firmness failed'.
He ever afterwards maintained that early acquaintance with such
literature accustomed his imagination to strange and even terrifying sights, so that he was not the victim of panic or horror
when he met them in real life. Thus, in the very first week of
his school-days at Hawkshead, shortly after his ninth birthday,
rambling along the shores of Esthwaite, he watched the recovery

[1] *D.C.P.*
[2] *Mem.* i, p. 34.

of the body of a drowned man from the water, and even when
the dead man

> bolt upright
> Rose with his ghastly face,

he says he felt a thrill of awe instead of 'soul-debasing fear', for
had he not seen such sights before with his 'inner eye',

> among the shining streams
> Of fairy land, the Forests of Romance?[1]

Few children, perhaps, would be so quick as young William
Wordsworth to correlate an actual horror with fairy-tale disasters, but Wordsworth always insisted that fear played a
powerful and beneficent part in developing his imaginative
powers and opening up his 'visionary' faculties. Throughout his
life he continued to recommend a diet of fairy tale and heroic
legend as the best reading for children. He could not bear the
'instructive' stories of the *Sandford and Merton* kind, which
became at that time fashionable, and were calculated to turn
children into walking encyclopaedias, responding mechanically
and correctly to every question put by their omniscient papas.
So he exclaims in *The Prelude* at the end of a long description
of such an infant prodigy,

> Oh! give us once again the Wishing-Cap
> Of Fortunatus, and the invisible coat
> Of Jack the Giant-killer, Robin Hood,
> And Sabra in the forest with St. George!
> The child, whose love is here, at least doth reap
> One precious gain, that he forgets himself.[2]

Romance came to Wordsworth likewise from the folk-talk
and traditions of his own country-side. Cockermouth lies in the
country which Westmorland people sometimes call 'back o'
Skiddaw': its affinities are with the Solway Firth and Carlisle
and the Border country rather than with the Lake District. To
the child William Wordsworth, Criffel and the Scottish shore
of the Solway was as familiar a landscape as Skiddaw or the
Ennerdale fells. And something of the balladry and folk-lore of
Scotland and the Border was woven into the pattern of his childhood. 'I own', he wrote once to Allan Cunningham, 'that since

---

[1] *Prel.* V, ll. 450–81.   [2] Ibid., ll. 341–6.

the days of childhood, when I became familiar with the phrase,
"They are killing geese in Scotland and sending the feathers to
England" (which every one had ready when the snow began
to fall), and when I used to hear, in the time of a high wind, that

> 'Arthur's bower has broken his band,
>   And he comes roaring up the land;
> King o' Scots wi' a' his power
> Cannot turn Arthur's bower',

I have been indebted to the North for more than I shall ever be
able to acknowledge '[1]

The finding of the dead man in Esthwaite was not the first
occasion on which the world of event had been invested for him
with a peculiar richness and significance. The little Wordsworths were accustomed to spend almost as much time at their
mother's home at Penrith as at Cockermouth. While at Penrith
he learnt to ride, and with James the groom in attendance used
to go out on to the moorlands of Penrith Beacon. On one of these
expeditions a strange experience befell him, the first of many
intimations that he received of the 'modifying' powers of his
own mind.

He was riding with James on the eastern side of Penrith
Beacon, being, if his own statement is accurate, only five years
old,[2] when he somehow became separated from his 'encourager
and guide' and found himself alone on the moorland. Uncertain
where he was, he dismounted and led the pony downhill till he
came to a hollow, where he found an old mouldering post of
wood driven into the ground, and at the foot of it some letters
carved in the turf—'T. P. M.' The post was a gibbet-post, and
the initials apparently stood for 'Thomas Parker Murdered'. He
was on the scene of a murder committed some ten years before,
commemorated in the fashion of the times by the gibbeting of
the murderer on the spot where he had committed the crime.
The body had disappeared, but even so he recognized what he

---

[1] _L.Y._ i. 707, p. 128. W.W. to Allan Cunningham, Nov. 23rd 1823.

[2] It is possible that he was a little older as Wordsworth occasionally ante-dates
events, e.g. his first going to school, _Prel._ I, ll. 310–11. But the incident must have
taken some time before he went to Hawkshead. In a rejected version of this
passage he says that it occurred in 'the twilight of rememberable life', 'while I was
yet an urchin'. _Prel._ XII, p. 437, app. crit.

was looking at, having heard the story, and at once fled up the
hill again, half-faint with terror,[1] till he reached a little tarn
close to the beacon summit, and there saw a girl, carrying on
her head a pitcher, forcing her way with difficulty against the
wind. Long afterwards he thus described his sensations on
seeing her:

> It was in truth
> An ordinary sight; but I should need
> Colours and words that are unknown to man
> To paint the visionary dreariness
> Which while I looked all round for my lost guide
> Invested moorland waste and naked pool,
> The beacon crowning the lone eminence,
> The female and her garments vexed and tossed
> By the strong wind.

The whole landscape had suddenly become transformed into
'something rich and strange', under the influence of the fear
which his unexpected encounter with the gibbet had stirred up
within him. What he saw was 'visionary', although he saw no
objects other than those 'naturally' present to his eyes. Child as
he was, he seemed to have entered another world, one wherein
every object was strengthened and clarified with strange intensity, so that he never forgot it. Nor did he want to forget it,
in spite of the terror and loneliness which had inspired it. Rather
it became the earliest of those 'spots of time' that were to be so
frequent with him, to which he looked back as 'worthy of all
gratitude', bestowing 'a vivifying virtue', refreshing and 'repairing' his mind in times of distress or anxiety. His spirit had not
been crushed but strengthened by the intensity of the emotion it
had undergone, and when many years afterwards he returned to
the spot under contrasting circumstances in company with Mary
Hutchinson, in the days of their early love, the contrast only

---

[1] *Prel.* XII, ll. 246–7. The 1850 text makes his sensations clearer than that
of 1805. Speaking of the letters in the turf he says:

> A casual glance had shown them and I fled
> Faltering and faint and ignorant of the road.

1805 has:

> Faltering and ignorant where I was, at length
> I chanced to espy there characters inscribed
> On the green sod: forthwith I left the spot.

made the memory of his trance more precious, and each experience enhanced the other.

> So feeling comes in aid
> Of feeling and diversity of strength
> Attends us, if but once we have been strong.[1]

This is the only incident recorded in *The Prelude* of which the
setting belongs to Penrith. William was not happy in his grandparents' house. They and his Uncle Kit were not sympathetic
towards the aspirations of high-spirited children: the atmosphere
was one of respectability and decorum without culture or good
nature among the 'grown-ups'; hence William, who had, as he
afterwards admitted, 'a stiff, moody and violent temper', was
pretty often in collision with authority. Punishment only increased his defiance, and the lack of imaginative sympathy produced fits of angry depression. Once he says that he retired in
furious anger to an attic and contemplated killing himself with
some foils that lay there. With his Uncle Kit he was particularly
unfriendly, and the hostility between them continued to the end
of his uncle's life. It became more bitter after the death of Mr.
John Wordsworth, for then, the Cockermouth household being
broken up, the boys were obliged to spend most of their holidays
at Penrith immediately under their uncle's eye.

Whitehaven, the home of their other uncle, Richard Wordsworth, was only ten miles from Cockermouth. It was then a
flourishing port of nearly ten thousand inhabitants, with its
wealth lying in coal-mines, a ship-building industry, the Irish
coal-trade, and the importation of tobacco from Virginia. In the
tonnage of shipping cleared from the 'five principal ports' of
England in the year 1780, it is astonishing to find Whitehaven
coming second to London, far ahead of Liverpool, Newcastle,
and Bristol. All this prosperity had been built up in the early
part of the century by Sir John Lowther and his son Sir James.
They employed an architect to design the town, so that it
remains the earliest example of 'town planning' in the country.
It had a theatre in which classical tragedies were sometimes
produced by a local schoolmaster; there were three parish

---

[1] This incident is recorded in *Prel.* XII, ll. 208–71 in close connexion with
another of the same kind—'waiting for the ponies' at Hawkshead. *Prel.* XII,
ll. 272–389. See p. 69 below.

churches, and the Lowthers had a mansion on the outskirts of the town.

Richard Wordsworth, as Controller of Customs there, was mainly concerned with the importation of tobacco. He had a large family of nine children, with whom their Cockermouth cousins often stayed. The eldest, Richard, was a solicitor, already grown up and married when William Wordsworth was a child; the second, John, went to sea, and as Captain John Wordsworth he supervised the sea-going career of his much younger cousin, the shy John of Cockermouth.

The coast at Whitehaven is high, rising into great cliffs and headlands, the port lying in a hollow beneath steep hills. It was while descending 'from the top of the high ground down which the road then descended abruptly' that as little children William and Dorothy first saw and heard the sea. Dorothy burst into tears at the sight, a circumstance which (said William in old age) 'was often mentioned among us as indicating the sensibility for which she was so remarkable'.[1] William was never attracted to ships and sea-voyaging, in spite of his love of wandering and of books of travel. But at Whitehaven he listened with 'mysterious awe' to tales of storms and shipwrecks and conceived a veneration for mariners as men of action which later found perfect expression in his love for his sailor brother John. In Cockermouth too, sea-shells, large and small, were common playthings among the children, and William early learned the game of holding their hollow side to his ear and hearing within all that was passing in the waters whence they came.[2] Long afterwards this pastime wove itself into the most famous of his dreams—that one in which he beheld the Arab rider with the stone in one hand and in the other a 'shell of a surpassing brightness', which, when the dreamer put it to his ear, gave forth

> A loud prophetic blast of harmony,
> An Ode in passion utter'd, which foretold
> Destruction to the children of the Earth
> By deluge, now at hand.[3]

Regular schooling did not really begin for William until he went to Hawkshead Grammar School in the early summer of

[1] *P.W.* iv, p. 395.   [2] Ibid., pp. 397–8.
[3] *Prel.* V, ll. 95–98.

1779. But long before that he had learnt to read, perhaps from his mother,[1] and he had attended for at least a few months in 1776 and possibly for longer the grammar school at Cocker-mouth, a small building in the churchyard, now pulled down. It was not, it seems, a school of very eminent quality. The Rev. Mr. Gillbanks who taught the children and performed the church duties at Cockermouth for nearly thirty years while Sir James Lowther impropriated the tithes of the living, was not successful as a teacher and the Wordsworth boys did not stay long under his care.[2] But at Penrith, where so much of their time was spent, there was a better school for small children.

It was a dame school, kept for the children of the 'upper classes' of the little town, by an old lady called Mrs. Ann Birkett,[3] whose ways were even then those of an older and vanishing England. She was insistent that her scholars should keep the country festivals of Shrove Tide, Easter, and May Day with all due rites. So at Easter the boys climbed to the top of Penrith Beacon, then quite unenclosed, to roll their pace eggs, while on May Morning the girls brought their dolls to school and hung them from the school window in garlands of flowers. In book-learning the dame was 'no bad teacher but indifferent to method'. Besides the Bible—from which they learnt by heart —she nourished them somewhat strangely on the *Spectator* brought to school by the little Hutchinsons, whose fortunes were to be so closely linked with those of the Wordsworths. Mary Hutchinson, the eldest girl of the family, was but a few months younger than William Wordsworth, who was one day to be her husband. They were the children of John Hutchinson who had a tobacco business in the town, and had come from the county of Durham where his father farmed a small estate at Whitton. Their mother was Mary, the daughter of John

---

[1] 'The heart
And hinge of all our *learnings* and our love.'
Ibid., ll. 257–8.

[2] Wordsworth says he learnt more Latin in a fortnight from the usher at Hawkshead than he had learnt at Cockermouth in two years.
In the family accounts is the following entry:

1776. Oct 13 Richard, 1 year	1. 10. 0
Oct 22 William, half a year	15. 0
Paid Mr. Gillbanks	2. 5. 0

This is the only entry of payment for schooling at Cockermouth.

[3] *Mem.* i, p. 33. Mary Wordsworth's Memoirs (in MS. *D.C.P.*).

Monkhouse the post-master of Penrith—'the most gentlemanly man, both in looks and manner', said Wordsworth in after years, 'that I ever knew in Penrith'. He had married Margaret Richardson of Nunwick Hall on the Eden, thus linking his 'town' blood with one of the considerable country families in exactly the same way as William Wordsworth's grandfather, William Cookson, had done, when he married Dorothy Crackanthorpe. The Monkhouses had lived at Penrith at least since the beginning of the eighteenth century, and memories of the 'Great Rebellion' of 1745, when the Pretender's highlanders slept on straw in the kitchen, were handed down in the family. John Monkhouse possessed a small estate of his own at Sebergham where his grandchildren used to spend their summer holidays. Thus in quaint and simple schooling, in close contact with the country and all country doings, though living in the little market towns, the children of John Hutchinson and John Wordsworth passed their earliest years with little enough to trouble them.

It was in the main a play-time world, and none played together in it more joyously than William Wordsworth and his sister Dorothy, twenty-one months younger than himself. Their elder brother Richard, cautious and slow of temperament, was never much of a playmate for the more adventurous William. But

> The Blessing of my later years
> Was with me when a boy,

ready, then as always, to go with him anywhere. She reciprocated, even as a tiny girl, with exquisite delight every sight and sound of beauty or interest in the outdoor world. And it was out of doors that almost all their pleasures lay. At Cockermouth there was the garden stretching down to the river, with its terrace and quickset hedge of privet and roses, that hedge in which they watched day by day the hedge-sparrow's 'bright blue eggs together laid'. Dorothy, through all her life the most tender and delicate lover of all wild things, was in a state of quivering eagerness:

> She looked at it and seemed to fear it,
> Dreading, though wishing, to be near it:
> Such heart was in her, being then
> A little Prattler among men.[1]

---

[1] *P.W.* i, p. 227, *The Sparrow's Nest*. The hedge has now disappeared.

Or, in their father's fields beyond the river, and in the 'green courts' of the old castle they rushed about after butterflies, William, 'a very hunter', thinking only of the chase, Dorothy checked by a more sensitive consciousness of possible harm to loveliness:

> But she, God love her! feared to brush
> The dust from off its wings.[1]

And meanwhile, the world beyond the garden and the river was also beginning to draw him. Cockermouth lies in open, cultivated country, but the great mass of Skiddaw stands a few miles to the east, and other lower hills come nearer to the town. Over one of these neighbouring moorlands there stretched a road that could be seen from the back of the house in the High Street. It became to the child William a powerful symbol of the unexplored world. It was too far off for his childish walks and he had never trodden it. But it was precious as 'a guide into Eternity', 'an invitation into Space'. The spirit of the Wanderer was already knocking at the door, and the road to Isel beckoned him on and beyond.

Closely connected with the desire to wander was an intense interest in tramps. These ragged vagabonds were clothed in his eyes with a romance and awe like that with which he invested 'the Mariner who sails the roaring sea'. They came thus early into the field of William's imagination, never to leave it. The Pedlar, the Discharged Soldier, the Leech-gatherer, the Beggar-woman, one after another the gaunt, solitary figures appear in the poems, objects always of reverence and awe. The more tragic 'strolling Bedlamites' he encountered too, in days of lax lunacy-laws, and was afraid, but never panic stricken.[2]

Another kind of awe, equally enduring, and equally fruitful, belongs to these early days. One of his favourite haunts at Cockermouth was, of course, the ruins of the castle, a few hundred yards up the river from his father's garden. There he scrambled up the old red walls after the wallflower's 'golden progeny', and there, descending into the dungeon, he found

---

[1] Ibid. i, p. 226, *To a Butterfly*. *D.W.J.* i, p. 123.

[2] It is perhaps worth recording that in a very early prose fragment written at school when he was about sixteen, Wordsworth describes a mad woman with eyes of 'a certain wild brightness'. *D.C.P.*

himself face to face with 'soul-appalling darkness'. The experience thrilled him: this then was what was meant when people
spoke of death! Long afterwards, returning in old age to walk
there once more, he makes the castle say:

> Not a blink
> Of light was there:—and thus did I, thy Tutor
> Make thy young thoughts acquainted with the grave![1]

'Acquainted with the grave' the young Wordsworths were
destined to be indeed, for in March 1778, while they were all at
Penrith, their mother died of 'a decline'. Apparently she had
been away on a visit to London, where she had slept in a damp
bed.[2] She probably died of pneumonia. William's last sight of
her was 'passing the door of her room', as she lay on her death-
bed—a sad enough last memory for a child to have of his mother.
Wordsworth never speaks of her loss in its personal effect upon
himself, but only as affecting the little family as a whole. They
were left, the five bairns,

> destitute, and as we might,
> Trooping together.

How vividly those seven words describe the bewildered isolation of childhood face to face with the utter unfamiliarity of
death.

Their father was stunned and inconsolable after her loss, and
it is evident that there was no member of the immediate family
who could or would take much interest in the children. Even
the comfort of 'trooping together' was soon denied them, for
in December Dorothy was taken away to Halifax by her mother's
cousin Miss Elizabeth Threlkeld, and never came back to
Cumberland during all the time that William was at school at

---

[1] *P.W.* iv, p. 23, *Address from the Spirit of Cockermouth Castle.* In *The Borderers*,
Act ii, l. 985, Marmaduke descends into a dungeon of a ruined tower with the
intention of killing Herbert: but he is prevented by the sudden sight of a star
shining through a crevice.

> 'Twas dark—dark as the grave . . .
> Upwards I cast mine eyes and through a crevice
> Beheld a star twinkling above my head—
> And by the living God I could not do it.

It is likely enough that Wordsworth had also thus seen a star.

[2] In *Prel.* V, ll. 260–2, Wordsworth seems to suggest that her illness was due
to the carelessness of some person.

Hawkshead. The 'trooping together' was ended as far as she was concerned, and the 'squandering abroad' of which she complained so bitterly afterwards was begun. Yet she was happy in her exile, well loved and cared for, growing up in Miss Threlkeld's big household of nephews and nieces, the children of her dead sister Mrs. Ferguson. Certainly she was happier than she would have been had she remained with the cross grandparents at Penrith, or perhaps in the motherless household at Cockermouth, for her brothers all departed to school at Hawkshead as they grew old enough and she would soon have been a lonely child for most of the year had she remained at home. Afterwards she regretted that long separation from her brothers, not because she was herself unhappy during those years, but because she was thereby 'put out of the way of many recollections in common with my Brothers, of that period of life, which, whatever it may be actually as it goes along, generally appears more delightful than any other when it is over'.[1]

It may be surmised that William's clashes with his grandparents and Uncle Kit grew worse from this time on. He hints at frequent punishments; 'chastisement' that only made him bitter and defiant. The incident of the contemplated suicide perhaps took place now; and that also of his attack on the family portrait in the big uncarpeted drawing-room upstairs. 'Dare you strike your whip through that old lady's petticoat?' he challenged his unadventurous brother Richard, as they were playing at tops. On Richard's declining, William exclaimed 'Then here goes!' and the sound of rending canvas no doubt soon brought irate grandparents hastening up the stairs. William was certainly the most passionate and difficult of the four brothers. Richard was cautious and law-abiding; John, shy and quiet; Christopher, probably, competent and ordinary. We know at least that Christopher was his Uncle Kit's favourite. But of William his mother had said that he was the only one of her five children about whom she felt any anxiety: he had such capacities for good or evil.[2]

Accustomed as we are to think of the childhood of William Wordsworth as unusually happy, thanks to his own celebration

[1] *E.L.* 240, p. 560. D.W. to Lady Beaumont, Christmas Day 1805.
[2] *Mem.* i, p. 9.

of his Hawkshead school-days in *The Prelude*, the unhappiness of his Penrith experiences tends to be forgotten or glossed over. He never complained of them in *The Prelude*, being rightly absorbed in describing joyous things; but Dorothy's letters of 1787 and 1788, when she was living with her grandparents and their father was likewise dead, sharply convey the unhappy atmosphere still persisting; and a hint that there were 'miseries' in these early days is contained in some lines of *The Prelude* in which he marvels at the mysterious synthesis that has come about in himself:

> Ah me! that all
> The terrors, all the early miseries,
> Regrets, vexations, lassitudes, that all
> The thoughts and feelings which have been infused
> Into my mind, should ever have made up
> The calm existence that is mine when I
> Am worthy of myself.[1]

His inborn love of wandering probably received some additional strengthening from the necessity of escaping as often as possible from the strictness and stupidity of the house in the market-place. There were already plenty of things in that outdoor world to hold his delighted attention and make him forget the 'miseries'.

In a rejected passage of the eighth book of *The Prelude*[2] Wordsworth has expanded in affectionate detail his favourite theme of the union of the child's imagination, through love and wonder, with the world of nature and the works of man. The detail of this passage must be largely autobiographical, and we may trace in the first part of it his own estimate of the growth of his 'mind' down to about the time of his departure for Hawkshead. The objects which attracted his attention in early infancy never ceased to arouse his joy throughout the whole of his life. Thus, first and earliest there is his love for

> a little rill
> Of water sparkling down a rocky slope
> By the wayside.

Then, a little later, when he has begun to 'stir about', he is fascinated by

> things of Nature's rarer workmanship,
> Her scatter'd accidents of sight and sound,

[1] *Prel.* (1805), ll. 355–361.   [2] *Prel.*, pp. 553–6.

and among these are

> the rainbow or the Cuckoo's shout,
> An echo, or the glow-worm's faery lamp,

those four faithful images that haunt his poetry to the end, each of which, as he acknowledges,

> When it hath pass'd away, returns again
> In later days.

Then Nature's wonders and man's alternate in the delight they can give—a ship, a bridge, a river

> that flows on
> Perpetually, whence comes it, whither tends,
> Going, and never gone;

a fish, a skylark

> native to the heavens
> There planted like a star;

and the valuable 'objects of fear', whose ministry was of such importance to him,

> lightning and the thunder's roar,
> Snow, rain and hail, and storm implacable.

The seasons, at first so mysterious, gradually become familiar, and just as the child is becoming almost too well acquainted with these outward sights, he learns to read, and a new world opens to him, that of romance. Here, all the illustrations are drawn from the *Arabian Nights*, proving how strong a hold that 'slender abstract of the Arabian Tales' from his father's library took on his imagination. Tales of travel and 'real' adventure follow these, and so a taste begins to develop for that which most strongly contrasts with nature; for the marvellous and the unusual:

> temples, grots,
> Statue and terrace sward and trim cascade.

It was when he had reached some such stage as this that William Wordsworth was transplanted from Cockermouth to Hawkshead, from the High Street of a market town to the heart of a wild and lovely country-side, there to make human friend-ships with cottagers and pedlars, and mental friendships with books and poets and most of all with the precious things of the lasting hills.

II

HAWKSHEAD I, 1779–83

There was a time when meadow, grove, and stream,
The earth and every common sight,
To me did seem
Apparelled in celestial light,
The glory and the freshness of a dream.
Ode: Intimations of Immortality from
Recollections of Early Childhood, 1802

HAWKSHEAD, at whose grammar school all the Wordsworth
boys were educated, is a miniature market town of quaint
appearance, whose prosperity was made many centuries ago by
the trade in wool and cloth and whose fame as a place of education was at its height at the end of the eighteenth century. It lies
to the south-west of the main axis of the great road from Windermere to Keswick, slung in a cradle-like valley high between
the deep troughs of Windermere on one side and Coniston on
the other. It is not, like Grasmere or Keswick, overshadowed by
the giant mountains; it nestles quietly among the modest fells
of High Furness. Coniston Old Man almost peeps over at it
from the west, reminding it of the near neighbourhood of great
company, but the Hawkshead fells themselves rise to little more
than a thousand feet. From the top of them may be seen to the
north and east the peaks of Langdale, and the long smooth
backbone of Helvellyn and Fairfield, while southwards the
country runs off in low ribs of hill with shallow valleys between
till it meets the sands of the Kent and Leven in Morecambe Bay.
Esthwaite, the lake at whose north-west corner Hawkshead lies,
fills the little vale almost from end to end. Its shores were
wilder in Wordsworth's boyhood than they now are: enclosure
of the eastern side began at the end of the eighteenth century
shortly after Wordsworth had left.[1] The woodlands of hazel and
birch and oak then spread more widely than they do now over
the fells around the lake, interspersed with

> barren rocks with fern and heath
> And juniper and thistle, sprinkled o'er.

[1] See W.W.'s note to *Lines left upon a seat in a Yew-tree, P.W.* i, p. 329.

One tract of fell was known as the 'Holly-park', being, says
Pennant, 'preserved entirely for sheep, who are fed in winter
with the croppings'. And all about these wild uplands, dwelt,
in 'too great plenty', the wild cat.[1]

The little lake has no striking features except the two green
promontories jutting out one from either shore, so aptly described by Wordsworth as 'ears'.[2] At the upper end, near the
hamlet of Colthouse where Wordsworth lived, is a round pool,
separated from the rest of the lake, known as the 'Priest's Pot'.
In Wordsworth's time it contained a floating island which has
now disappeared. In the lake were pike, trout, and perch, and
on it lived an unusually large pair of swans who became very
dear to Wordsworth. A road ran along both shores, and at the
lower end of the lake it passed through the villages of Sawrey and
Far Sawrey and down a steep hill to the ferry on Windermere.
Windermere itself, with its host of islands, its swans, and long
coast-line of wooded bays and promontories, was a beloved
playground for all the Hawkshead boys, and for Wordsworth
it became almost as dear as his own 'darling vale' of Esthwaite.

Hawkshead in the late eighteenth century was at the beginning of an almost imperceptible decline in importance and
prosperity. It had shared with the other lakeland villages in the
ramifications of the great cloth trade which flourished with Kendal as its centre from the fourteenth century onwards. Fulling
and dyeing, which had accompanied the weaving as subsidiary
industries, had ceased in the valleys by the end of the sixteenth
century, but spinning and weaving were still carried on in many
a cottage and small farm up and down the dales, a real family
industry. The bales of yarn and cloth, loaded on to the backs of
pack-horses, were taken from the farms along the narrow lanes
to Hawkshead or Ambleside to be sold, and down to the middle
of the eighteenth century regular teams of pack-horses left the
town each week for Kendal and the south. After that improved
roads led to the gradual replacement of the pack-horse by the
covered wagon of the carrier, but when Wordsworth was at
school and for long after goods could only be transported from
the dale farms by pack-horse, for the roads up the dales were still

---

[1] Pennant's *Tour in Scotland*, 1770.
[2] *Prel.* V, l. 433.

but rough lanes running between old stone walls, linking farm to farm along the lower slopes of the fells.

Home-spinning survived longer than home-weaving, and the Monday market at Hawkshead in Wordsworth's day was mainly a market for yarn. In the market-place was an outcrop of grey rock, where an old woman used to spread her 'huckster's wares' week after week for the delight of Wordsworth and his friends.[1] William, in his wanderings in the dales, made acquaintance with many a cottage interior where the whole family, young and old, took part in the processes of spinning and carding. Even the old grandfather, too infirm to help on the farm, carded wool. 'Often when a boy', wrote Wordsworth afterwards, 'have I admired the cylinders of carded wool which were softly laid upon each other by his side'.[2]

Besides the wool-marketing, all the district of Furness, being covered with coppice-wood of oak, ash, and hazel, had carried on cask-, hoop-, and basket-making from very early times. Hugh Tyson, the husband of Wordsworth's 'dame' at Hawkshead, was a joiner by trade, and made among other things the casks in which the 'charpots', full of freshly potted char from Windermere and Coniston were packed for export to London and other places. In the woods, too, when Wordsworth was a boy, might still be seen the circular stacks built of poles and thatched with turf, which, after slow burning, produced charcoal. Wordsworth loved the 'silvered wreaths of quiet charcoal-smoke'[3] that rose over the fallen woods. 'Bloomsmithies', or forges for smelting and manufacturing the iron-ore from the great mines near Ulverston had sprung up at the beginning of the eighteenth century in many places in Furness. By Wordsworth's time the Backbarrow Company had bought out most of the smaller forges and the great forge at Backbarrow on the Leven, founded in 1711, was the main site of the industry, producing guns, cannon-balls, and other implements of war for the Royal Navy.[4] The difficulty was to find sufficient wood to keep up the supply of charcoal, and

---

[1] *Prel.* II, ll. 41–46. In one manuscript of *The Prelude* her name is given but is illegible save for the first letter which is R. As, however, it must have been a name of one syllable, it was probably Ruth.

[2] *P.W.* iii, p. 422, note to *Miscellaneous Sonnets*, XIX.

[3] Ibid. i, p. 38. *E.W.* (1793), l. 430.

[4] The Backbarrow Forge is still working, though the 'Blue-mill' a little higher up the stream is a more conspicuous object to the passer-by on the road.

by the middle of the century charcoal was being shipped from Scotland, where the Furness iron-masters bought up woodlands.

High up on the slopes of Coniston Old Man and the fells of Langdale were slate-quarries. Wordsworth loved to watch the beautiful 'pale blue' slate brought down in panniers on the backs of pack-horse ponies, sure-footed creatures picking their way deftly along the narrow mountain paths. From Waterhead on Coniston it was shipped on barges to the foot of the lake.[1]

Although its importance as a market town was beginning to fade by the second half of the century, Hawkshead had more than a purely local reputation because of Archbishop Sandys' Grammar School, founded in 1585. It was, in Wordsworth's time and until the middle of the nineteenth century, a school remarkable both for its scholarship and for the free and happy life led by the boys. Its founder, Edwin Sandys, Archbishop of York in Elizabeth's reign, was born at Esthwaite Hall, half-way down the lake on its western shore, and throughout his busy, rather unattractive life, embittered as it had been by imprisonment and exile under Mary, he retained an affection for his native valley, for almost the last act of his life was the foundation of the little grammar school, which he endowed with sufficient property to give a free education to the boys of the neighbourhood. There were twelve 'charity boys' on the foundation who were clothed and boarded as well as taught free of charge; the other boys were sons of farmers, local gentry, clergy, and professional men. The school's reputation was so high that, by the time the Wordsworths came there, boys were sent to it from as far away as Carlisle, Ingleton, and Lancaster, and even Hawick and Edinburgh, as well as from the valleys and villages of the Lake District itself. If they came from outside the immediate neighbourhood, they paid a yearly 'cock-penny'[2] or entrance fee of

---

[1] For slate-quarrying see *E.W.*, ll. 156–67, *P.W.* i, p. 17. Pennant mentions two other ways by which the poorer people of the Hawkshead district added to their slender incomes: they caught eels 'in wheels' (that is, in some kind of circular cage), and they scraped the yellow *Lichen tartareus* from the rock and sold it at a penny a pound for the use of dyers.

[2] A 'cock-penny' originally meant a fee paid by a boy to the headmaster who, out of the money thus collected, offered a substantial money prize to the boy who owned the best fighting-cock! Cock-fighting was a popular north-country sport but as there is no reference to it either in *The Prelude* or *The Minstrels of Winandermere*, it was probably discontinued at Hawkshead by Wordsworth's time. The term 'cock-penny' meaning an entrance fee goes back at least to the seventeenth century.

about a guinea a year; otherwise they received their education free. The headmasters were graduates of Cambridge and in orders in the Church of England.[1]

In Wordsworth's time there were about a hundred boys in the school, and we read that 'the place is much resorted to by the families who visit their children in summer there'.[2] The boys, except the charity boys, were given an education which fitted them for the University; many of them went to Cambridge where a high proportion of them became wranglers or fellows of their colleges. Those boys who could not afford a university education and yet wished to enter the ministry of the Church, often became ushers in schools until such time as they were old enough to receive ordination. Wordsworth tells us that the number of such boys at Hawkshead school in his time, 'from the families of the humble yeomanry', was considerable. One of them, whose name was Pearson, intruded into Wordsworth's later life in a rather ludicrous way. He had become a very successful proprietor of a private school where he had begun as usher, though when he came to Hawkshead 'his manners were as uncouth as well could be'. Long afterwards, this person built on the shore of Grasmere lake a very ugly boat-house, 'peculiarly fitted', says Wordsworth, 'to mar the beauty and destroy the pastoral simplicity of the Vale'.[3]

Among the boys who went on to Cambridge in Wordsworth's time was Robert Greenwood of Ingleton, who lived to become Senior Fellow of Trinity College, a mad-cap youth whom Wordsworth afterwards compared to Yorick in *Hamlet*.[4] He was a flute-player and on one occasion, as we shall see, his playing gave Wordsworth an experience of deep delight.[5] Another boy, Charles Farish, was the son of the rector of wild Bewcastle in Cumberland; he became a wrangler, and in 1811 published a curious poem called *The Minstrels of Winandermere*, in which he celebrated the outdoor exploits of the Hawkshead school-boys with as much zeal, though in a very different style and

---

[1] Edwin Sandys had been a member of St. John's College, Cambridge, and the connexions of the school were with Cambridge and particularly with St. John's. See below, p. 90.

[2] Clarke's *Survey of the Lakes*, 1787.   [3] *P.W.* v, pp. 456–7.

[4] *E.L.* 15, p. 56. W.W. to W. Matthews, Aug. 13th 1791.

[5] See below, p. 36.

spirit, as did Wordsworth in the first two books of *The Prelude*. Two brothers, John Fleming and William Raincock, were sons of the rector of Ousby; John, the elder, had changed his name to Fleming on becoming heir to the estate of Rayrigg on Windermere which belonged to his maternal uncle, the rector of Bowness. With John Fleming, who was two years older than he, Wordsworth formed a passionate friendship of which a mutual love of poetry was the basis, but, though in later life they were neighbours, Fleming living at Rayrigg and Wordsworth at Grasmere, intimacy did not continue. 'We live', said Wordsworth in *The Prelude*, 'as if those hours had never been.' Another friend was John Spedding of Armathwaite Hall at the foot of Bassenthwaite. He came of a family long connected with Whitehaven and, like Wordsworth's family, with the business interests of the Lowthers. His grandfather, James Spedding, was sheriff of Cumberland, married one of the Irtons of Threlkeld, and bought the Armathwaite estate. In the years following his return from France, in 1793 and 1794, Wordsworth paid more than one visit to his old schoolfellow's home, while Dorothy became intimate with John's two sisters, Maria and Margaret.[1]

Some letters of John Spedding's sister Maria, written while Wordsworth was at Hawkshead to her friend and confidante Martha Irton, the step-daughter of the vicar of Hawkshead, Mr. Reginald Braithwaite, show that the world of these northern gentry, with whose sons Wordsworth associated, was very like that of their south-country contemporaries described in Jane Austen's novels.[2] The girls were high-spirited and rather boisterous, living for balls and lovers, regattas and house-parties. Mr. Braithwaite, the vicar of Hawkshead, had a great reputation for hospitality. He lived at Belmont, a substantial new villa, about a mile out of Hawkshead on the Ambleside road, commanding a view of the lake and village, and was evidently of a convivial temperament. 'His kindness and hilarity', says one old guide-book, 'providentially soften the gloom and rigour of the country.'[3] His step-son Edward Irton, himself the owner of

---

[1] *E.L.* 39, p. 112. D.W. to J.P., Apr. 1794. John Spedding, though destined for the University, seems instead to have entered the army. He was the father of James Spedding, the biographer of Francis Bacon.

[2] Rev. S. Taylor, 'A Lakeland Young Lady's Letters', *C.W.A.A.S.*, 1943.

[3] Walker's *Remarks*, p. 58.

estates in west Cumberland, was, as we shall see, a young man
of strong literary and antiquarian tastes and a friend and admirer
of Wordsworth's beloved schoolmaster, William Taylor.[1]

The school, like many other north-country grammar schools
at that time, excelled in the teaching of mathematics. When
Wordsworth went up to Cambridge he found himself so much
in advance of most of his fellow students in the knowledge of
Euclid that he was unable to resist the temptation to get 'into
rather an idle way'. Classical studies formed the whole of the
rest of the curriculum, and Wordsworth retained a love for the
Latin classics throughout his life.

The grammar school was not quite alone in supplying the
educational and cultural needs of the boys. There was a Mr.
Mingay, who is described as a dancing master in the Wordsworth family accounts, and in 1785 was paid £2. 18s. 6d. for
teaching the four Wordsworth boys to dance. William, as we
shall see, was a keen dancer in his school and college years.
Later, in 1789, two years after Wordsworth left the school,
Mr. Mingay seems to have tried to expand his dancing school
into a more ambitious establishment, calling itself 'Hawkshead
School and military Academy', and offering to board pupils
and teach them French, 'writing in all hands', merchant's
accounts, geography and the use of the globes, dancing, fencing,
and music.[2] The classical and mathematical subjects would
be learnt at the grammar school. What happened to it we do not
know, but it seems not to have survived for there are no further
records of it.

There was one boarding-house belonging to the school, in
the headmaster's house.[3] It is said to have accommodated as
many as sixty boys. The rest were lodged in the cottages of the
little town and its surrounding hamlets. It was one of the many
providential circumstances of Wordsworth's youth that he became an inmate not of the crowded school-house but of a joiner's
cottage in the tiny hamlet of Colthouse, half a mile east of the
town, close under the wooded side of Claife Height, down which
ran a swift little beck, that made its way—'boxed in a channel'
—through the cottage gardens and orchards, into the larger

---

[1] See below, p. 50.   [2] H. S. Cowper, *History of Hawkshead*, p. 500.
[3] This is the house immediately opposite the turn to Sawrey, close to the
school-house.

stream, called the Black Beck, which separates Hawkshead from Colthouse. The hamlet contains two houses of some pretension, and some half a dozen cottages, the remains of an ancient 'bloom-smithy', and, a little way up the hill above the rest of the hamlet, a meeting-house of the Quakers. To this humble place of worship, 'on very wet or very hot Sundays', Wordsworth's 'dame' Ann Tyson and her lodgers used to repair, because it was nearer than the parish church—the 'throned lady' sitting in her white glory on the hillside across the valley.[1]

'What I chiefly recollect', Wordsworth said afterwards of those meetings for worship, 'is that they were always telling God Almighty of His attributes, rather than seeking spiritual communion with Him for themselves.' This criticism at first seems out of keeping with what we in these days associate with Quaker meeting: but there is evidence to show that at this period local meetings were apt to be over-talkative and warnings were sometimes issued against 'too often repeating the high and holy Name or his Attributes'. As an indication of what the boy Wordsworth was thinking and feeling about religious worship, this memory is of value, for it shows that at Hawkshead worship in another sense than pure 'Nature worship' was playing its part in the education of his soul.

Colthouse was indeed something of a Quaker colony. Three farms in the hamlet—Townend, Tockhow, and Sikeside—were all in Quaker occupation, while in the cottages lived a carpenter and other folk who were also members of the Society of Friends. It was therefore not surprising that old Ann sometimes joined her neighbours in their worship although she was not a member of their society.[2]

As there were holidays only twice a year, at Christmas and in the summer, with sometimes a few days at Easter, the boys were almost like foster-children in these 'lowly cottages', and to the motherless Wordsworths Ann Tyson gave all she could of that sort of simple, unpretentious rustic affection and discipline that seems like the very quality of the country-side distilled into human terms. In her youth Ann had been in service with a

---

[1] *D.C.P.*, letter from J. H. Thorne to Stopford Brooke, 1890, reporting a conversation with Wordsworth. Hawkshead Church was whitewashed at this time. See *Prel.* IV, l. 21.

[2] I am indebted to Mrs. Ross of Sawrey for information about the Quakers.

family of the name of Knott, of Coniston: they were iron-masters, who had built a house on Loch Etive in Argyll, whither they transferred their iron-foundry when the supply of smelting charcoal began to fail in Furness. Thither Ann had gone with them as a girl, and many were the tales she told the boys in after years of the Highlands in the years between the 'Fifteen' and the 'Forty-five', 'tales half as long as an ancient romance'.[1]

In their early married life the Tysons, besides the joinery business, seem to have kept a small shop. They then lived in Hawkshead, for in the marriage registers they are described as of 'Town'. About 1773 the shop was apparently given up and it was perhaps then that they moved to Colthouse and made their living mainly by boarding boys.[2] Hugh Tyson, Ann's husband, the joiner, died in 1784 while William was still at school. After that, Ann continued alone until 1789, when she retired. They had no children of their own. The sensible arrangement by which brothers lodged together in the same house kept the four Wordsworth boys together as a family; they lived successively and together with the Tysons, though Christopher spent his last years elsewhere after Ann retired. There were several other boarders. It seems, from Wordsworth's tributes in *The Prelude*, that Ann was a woman who understood boys. According to Wordsworth's account she did not give them quite enough to eat,[3] but the evidence of her own butcher's bills scarcely bears out this mild criticism. Legs and shoulders of mutton and loins of veal seem to have been plentifully provided. The modest charge of twelve guineas a year for each boy for board and lodging, though it must of course be considerably multiplied to compare with modern values, left not much margin for luxuries. Each boy was in fact charged 'extra' for candles, coals, or peats, certain groceries such as 'lof shuger', 'resins', and tea. 'A bottle

---

[1] *D.W.J.* i, p. 309. The story of a lamb stranded in mid-stream, originally intended as an episode in *Michael* but eventually incorporated into *Prel.* VIII was one of Ann's stories, as was also that of the Jacobite and the Whig in *The Excursion*, Book VI.

[2] The evidence of the Tysons' account book (the property of the Trustees of Hawkshead school) shows accounts of joinery, the shop, and lodgers from 1747. M. Moorman, 'An 18th Century Account-Book', *C.W.A.A.S.*, 1952.

[3]   More than we wished we knew the blessing then
         Of vigorous hunger, for our daily meals
         Were frugal, Sabine fare.   *Prel.* II (1805), ll. 80–82.
This criticism is, however, omitted in 1850.

of wine' was once bought, not for the Wordsworths but for
their fellow-lodger Thomas Gawthorp. 'Cake' (spelt 'Kek') is
also a frequent item in the bills and doubtless signifies the
famous 'Hawkshead cake'—a sort of glorified mince-pie, made
in rounds eleven inches in diameter and nearly two inches thick.[1]
Ann insisted on the boys keeping their old clothes for their
nutting and fishing expeditions,[2] but laid no restraints on their
activities and put up with their noise and merriment withindoors
of a winter evening when, gathered round the peat-fire, they
played round after round of whist and loo with the immortal
pack of cards—that

> thick-ribbed army
> . . . husbanded through many a long campaign.[3]

There was about the Tysons' cottage an atmosphere of
security, simple comfort, and freedom that William revelled in
with gratitude and delight.

> A sanctity, a safeguard, and a love!

he called it afterwards;[4] it formed the gracious background of all
his wanderings and when he returned to it after long days and
evenings on the hills or in far valleys, fresh perhaps from the
ecstasy of some visionary experience, there was no awkward
adaptation to be made to an uncongenial environment as in his
grandparents' house at Penrith; all was accepted; no questions
were asked, and he could go to his bed beneath the little window
and hold delighted communings with

> The moon in splendour couched among the leaves
> Of a tall ash[5]

that stood beside the house, or listen in rapture to

> the roaring wind
> And clamorous rain,

or to the 'loud, protracted yelling' of the ice on Esthwaite
splitting with a noise like the howling of wolves

> along the Bothnic Main.[6]

---

[1] These details are supplied by the Tysons' account book.
[2] *Nutting*, ll. 9–14. *P.W.* ii, p. 211.
[3] *Prel.* I, ll. 414–535. The adjective 'thick-ribbed' was first employed by
Wordsworth in a very early poem, *The Convict*, written about 1795. It is there
applied to the walls of the Convict's dungeon.
[4] Ibid. I (1805), l. 527. (Omitted in the 1850 text.)
[5] Ibid. IV, l. 88.   [6] Ibid. I. ll. 538–43.

And in those happy hours between sleep and waking came the many-coloured waking dreams—creations of his busy 'fancy' working on the material supplied by his day-time adventures or by story books and fairy-tales.

> When in my bed I lay
> Alone in darkness, I have seen the gloom
> Peopled with shapes arrayed in hues more bright
> Than flowers or gems or than the evening sky.

Country fairs, huntsmen and hounds, files of soldiers 'mounting upwards', and sometimes an array of inexplicable grotesques, passed before him, melting into one another with 'instant, unimaginable change'.[1]

The boy who came to Hawkshead at Whitsuntide 1779 was already familiar with all the outdoor sports and adventures appropriate to his age that the neighbourhood of Cockermouth or Penrith could supply. Hawkshead enormously multiplied the variety of these pleasures and inconceivably enhanced their glamour, because of its mountain neighbourhood. Hitherto he had known the great mountains only as a child-traveller between Cockermouth and Penrith, passing under the smooth flanks of Skiddaw along the shore of Bassenthwaite. He had perhaps wandered as far as Ullswater from Penrith, or Crummock from Cockermouth. Now he had moved inwards towards the great 'hub' of the Lake District, with its precipices of ancient volcanic structure and 'rocks with torrents roaring', and its dales hollowed out by glaciers and loud with the voice of streams. Swiftly it all became his inheritance, both the high mountains and the softer country-side in which Esthwaite and Hawkshead lay.[2] Absolutely no restrictions seem to have been put on his movements out of school hours, either by the school authorities or by Ann Tyson. From his earliest days he was often out late at night, sometimes simply

> roving up and down alone
> Seeking I knew not what,

---

[1] *Prel.*, p. 521. An early fragment, not incorporated into the poem.

[2] 'From Hawkshead he was always looking inwards towards the volcanic crags.' Norman Nicholson, *The Poetry of Wordsworth*, introduction. Mr. Nicholson traces an analogy between Wordsworth's geological surroundings and the various types of his poetry.

—as when he discovered the drowned man's clothes in the first week of his arrival—sometimes bent on more exciting sport. In his first Hawkshead winter, before his tenth birthday, he would be out roaming over the neighbouring fells for 'half the night, with store of springes o'er my shoulder hung', setting snares for the woodcock who came in large numbers on winter migration to those uplands. On moonlight nights they ran about in the open; on the dark nights they retired to the woods.[1] By day he was an ardent birdsnester, 'a plunderer in the high places', not content till he had scaled great crags alone in search of the raven's eyrie; or he set forth in the 'heavenly days' of autumn, clad in the old clothes, 'more ragged than need was', that his Dame kept for such occasions, to reap the hazel harvest in the woods. In these sports he was at first as acquisitive and destructive as other boys. He stole woodcock from the traps set by others. In the hazel woods he

> dragged to earth both branch and bough with crash
> And merciless ravage,

and returned home 'exulting, rich beyond the wealth of kings'.[2] He was also a passionate fisherman. He tells us that he brought the love of fishing with him to Hawkshead, having already had good sport in the big River Derwent. The little streams near Hawkshead could not satisfy him, however, so while still quite a little boy he sought acquaintance with a grown-up fisherman who took him over the fells to the upper waters of the Duddon, where they spent a long and not very successful day, in pouring rain, until young William, quite worn out, could scarcely stagger home and was glad enough to ride pick-a-back on his kind companion's shoulders. The memory of this rather exhausting day caused him to regard the Duddon 'for many years with recollections of disappointment and distress'. But happier associations

[1] An interesting description of snaring woodcock on the Hawkshead fells is supplied by Pennant in his *Tour of Scotland* (1770) of which the first part consists of an account of the Lake District. 'See on the plain part of these hills', he says, 'numbers of springes for woodcocks, laid between tufts of heath, with avenues of small stones on each side, to direct these foolish birds into the snares, for they will not hop over the pebbles. Multitudes are taken in this manner in the open weather; and sold on the spot for sixteen pence or twenty pence a couple, and sent to the all-devouring capital by the Kendal stage.' Wordsworth's zeal in the chase therefore may have had some commercial incentive!

[2] *P.W.* ii, p. 211–12, *Nutting*.

were formed in later youth and the Duddon became one of his most beloved haunts.[1]

A poem written in 1800 for the *Lyrical Ballads* called *The Two Thieves* gives not only a little vignette of a Hawkshead village scene, but Wordsworth's note upon it shows that even in these early days he was capable of moralizing on what he saw. The poem describes a very old man, a harmless klepto-maniac, who, with his three-year-old grandson, pilfered about the village streets and yards. Wordsworth watched him, think-ing how 'we may, any of us, I, or the happiest of my playmates, live to become still more the object of pity than this old man, this half-doating pilferer'.[2]

All his life, as we know from his poems, Wordsworth was fond of questioning small children. He had, in fact, almost a scientific or experimental attitude towards children which was very characteristic of his generation, and it is interesting to find that he conducted experiments even in his boyhood at Hawks-head. One day, he tells us, he led a little boy of about his own age, the apprentice of a travelling conjuror, up to the top of Claife Height, overlooking Windermere Ferry. 'My motive', he says, 'was to witness the pleasure I expected the boy would receive from the prospect of the islands below and the inter-mingling water. I was not disappointed.'[3]

Though he loved to go on solitary rambles, he was quite as deeply involved in the gregarious pastimes—'the games con-federate'—of his schoolfellows. Of these, skating and boating were dearest to him. Windermere, with its ferry and countless islands, large and small, was the place for water-sports of all kinds. Boat-races could be held there and landings made on the various islands—'Windermere Island', that is, Belle Isle with its new mansion, 'round and high as Danish Tower', Lady-holme, with its ancient oratory, or the two tiny 'Lily-holmes', 'sown with lilies of the valley, like a field'—while the inn on the Bowness shore supplied strawberries and cream and a bowling-green where they spent hours at games, 'making the mountains

---

[1] *P.W.* iii, p. 504. Note to *The River Duddon.*
[2] The poem begins with an admiring reference to Thomas Bewick's woodcuts:

O now that the genius of Bewick were mine.

It was a favourite with Lamb who approved of its lenient attitude towards 'aberra-tions'. Ibid. IV, p. 447.
[3] Ibid. i, p. 329. Note to *Lines left upon a seat in a Yew-tree.*

ring'. The ferry which took them across was called the 'Great Boat' and in winter the ferryman often had a tough passage,

> Winning his way across the lake
> With battering Maul and iron crow—

heaving aside the great slabs of ice.[1] They skated after dark of a winter evening, while 'the cottage windows blazed through twilight gloom'[2] summoning them in vain to supper and whist, and kept up in summer a continual uproar far into the night, long after the villagers had retired to bed, playing endless games round the rock in the market square. And occasionally, at the beginning of term when money was plentiful, they would hire ponies from the innkeeper for expeditions as far afield as Cartmel Sands and Furness Abbey, returning by moonlight after an immense circuit made 'in wantonness of heart'. Even without ponies they often ranged as far as Ings Chapel to see the famous Italian marbles (with many an admonition from the ferryman not to break the windows), up Ill Bell and back through Kendal.[3]

Wordsworth as a small boy at Hawkshead was indeed no 'recluse': his life was one with that of his companions. He had perhaps a greater preference for solitary expeditions than most of the other boys, but it is clear that at this period the normal interests of the male child were strong in him; he was daring, adventurous, competitive, and acquisitive. When he went off alone it was in search of a buzzard's nest, a bag-full of nuts, or some woodcock snared by night; when he was with the others it was to excel as much as possible in noise and breakneck activities. His spiritual education in the 'religious love' of Nature grew through a series of 'visitations' which came often with startling suddenness in the midst of some sport, leaving him penetrated with an incommunicable fear or delight. These 'visitations' varied in character. Sometimes, 'though rarely', they were 'gentle', like an opening of the clouds, gradual or

---

[1] C. Farish, *The Minstrels of Winandermere*, 1811. The house still stands on Belle Isle. It was built about 1778 by a Mr. English and bought by Mr. Curwen to whose descendants it still belongs.

[2] *Prel.* I, l. 427.

[3] C. Farish, op. cit. Farish also mentions in his poem the following favourite amusements of the boys: coursing, chasing lapwings, swimming, ducks and drakes, crowning with flowers, and fly-fishing. It is clear that organized games as we know them now did not exist.

sudden 'as at the touch of lightning', revealing unsuspected
beauty and 'glory' in all he saw. At other times, and much more
frequently, there were 'severer interventions' which came when
he was engaged on enterprises that had an element of guilt or
stealth about them—like the 'low breathings' that seemed to
follow him across the moor when he was stealing woodcock
from other people's snares—or were connected in some way
with fear and the presence of death. Fear, as we have seen, had
already been a source of revelation to him—on Penrith Beacon
when he found himself by the gibbet and on his first ramble
around Esthwaite when he saw the drowned man. It was no
disintegrating and abject thing but, like 'the fear of the Lord' in
the Old Testament, an awe-inspiring and life-giving grace.

These moments could come upon him when he was in full cry
with his companions in some noisy sport; or when he was alone
in solitary places. If the various descriptions of them in *The
Prelude* are examined, it seems as though they were generally
apprehended in moments following upon excitement often produced by rapid motion or physical effort or after a sudden
relaxation of nervous tension. Thus, when he was climbing
alone on Yewdale Crags after the raven's nest, earth and air
seemed suddenly to acquire an unearthly quality, as had the
landscape that day on Penrith Beacon; though it was not
'dreariness' that brooded over them now but an infintely enhanced life and movement.

> Oh! at that time
> When on the perilous ridge I hung alone,
> With what strange utterance did the loud, dry wind
> Blow through my ears; the sky seemed not a sky
> Of earth, and with what motion moved the clouds!

A 'gentle visitation' occurred one evening, after a boisterous
afternoon at the inn at Bowness, when they rowed back towards
the western shore, steering to an islet where they landed one of
their crew, the flute-player, Robert Greenwood, and leaving
him there rowed off again quietly while he

> blew his flute
> Alone upon a rock.

The sudden cessation of all sound except that of the flute made an answering silence in Wordsworth's spirit, a silence like an august and beloved presence.

> Oh! then the calm
> And dead still water lay upon my mind
> Even with a weight of pleasure, and the sky
> Never before so beautiful, sank down
> Into my heart, and held me like a dream!

Sometimes in moments of tension and expectation he would himself create the silence in which the mystery of things spoke to him. Thus a favourite game with the boys was to blow

> mimic hootings to the silent owls

of an evening, to provoke them to respond. After his own halloos had died down and while he was waiting for the owls to reply,

> Then sometimes in that silence while he hung
> Listening, a gentle shock of mild surprise
> Has carried far into his heart the voice
> Of mountain torrents; or the visible scene
> Would enter unawares into his mind,
> With all its solemn imagery. . . .[1]

Both eye and ear, stretched to their utmost capacity, were then only the gateways to a more ineffable experience. It was his 'heart' that received the voice of the torrents; his 'mind' the imagery of the trees and lake and sky.

Again, during one of their wild rides on ponies far beyond their usual range, he was caught and held prisoner by the voice of a 'single wren' singing alone in the damp and gloom of the ruined nave of Furness Abbey.

> So sweetly 'mid the gloom the invisible Bird
> Sung to itself, that there I could have made
> My dwelling-place, and lived for ever there
> To hear such music.[2]

[1] *Prel.* V, ll. 381–6. The famous 'boy' who 'blew mimic hootings to the silent owls' on the shores of Windermere was of course Wordsworth himself, and not John Vickars or George Gibson, boys who died at the school during Wordsworth's time, as some people have tried to maintain. The early manuscript of *The Prelude*, in which 'I' stands in place of 'he' in the final version, has made clear (if there could ever have been any reasonable doubt about it) that he is speaking of himself. The boy's death is simply a disguise no doubt suggested by the death of John Vickars in 1782. The champion owl-mimic was, according to Wordsworth, William Raincock, the brother of his friend John Fleming.

[2] Ibid. II, ll. 125–6.

And the responsive mood awakened by the singing of the wren lasted while they 'scampered homewards' across the sands and over the moonlit fells.

Thus frequently there broke in upon his happy child-consciousness of 'giddy bliss', 'gleams like the flashing of a shield', messages as it were from the world of beauty that became more frequent and more intense as childhood advanced into adolescence, until they filled the whole of his inward life of feeling and he 'breathed with joy' in a continuous ecstasy of consciousness of the beauty of the universe.

Night and darkness, and the wet weather that is the lakeland-dweller's constant companion, were more favourable in calling forth this close interaction, or 'intertwining', as Wordsworth himself called it, of passionate feeling with the 'mighty world of eye and ear', even than days of bluest calm. And this remained true throughout his life.

> November days
> When vapour rolling down the valley made
> A lonely scene more lonesome;

summer nights by Esthwaite; the darkness of woods at noon; these frequently produced this 'intercourse', this blessèd 'fellowship'. In adolescence his perceptiveness in the presence of the more solemn or gloomy of Nature's moods often merged into visionary experience. And even in his earlier boyhood it raised his awareness of the natural world and its mysteries to a degree bordering on the visionary, and sometimes, when aided by a feeling of stealth or guilt already present, it produced in his mind a strange sense of being haunted by awe-inspiring mental images.

Skating by moonlight on a winter evening on Esthwaite or Windermere was one of the things which took him beyond the limits of normal experience. Skating was the one form of athletic exercise in which he excelled and he remained devoted to it all his life. Once at least, skating on Windermere,[1] in the

---

[1] The difficulty of locating exactly the scene of the skating is well known. The 'cottage windows' no doubt were the lights of Colthouse, but what about the 'icy crags' and 'cliffs'? Probably it is a compound memory of Esthwaite and the steep western shore of Windermere near the ferry. The bay into which he retired may well have been the bay beside the ferry. An old guide-book to the lakes, Walker's *Remarks*, describes the path over Claife Height to Windermere as 'steep, rocky and cut through stone precipices whose bottom is washed by the Lake, so that this

midst of the uproar made by the hallooing, shouting crowd of skaters, he was aware of other sounds, as though the nocturnal landscape itself were joining in the hue and cry:

> . . . every icy crag
> Tinkled like iron, while the distant hills
> Into the tumult sent an alien sound
> Of melancholy, not unnoticed. . . .

Or, turning aside out of the crowd into the silence of a bay, he would suddenly stop short, and as he sat back on his heels, the sensation of rapid motion, gradually sinking to stillness in his own excited frame, transferred itself to the wooded cliffs beside him, until he and they seemed to move together in the very movement of the earth itself.

> Yet still the solitary cliffs
> Wheeled by me, even as if the earth had roll'd
> With visible motion her diurnal round.[1]

On another occasion, when he was on his way back to Penrith for the summer holidays, he stayed for the night in Patterdale, close to the shores of Ullswater. Late in the evening, when the moon was up, he wandered down to the shore of the lake, and finding a boat tied to a tree, got in and pushed forth into the water. He sat facing the great mass of Helvellyn, and as he rowed farther out, he suddenly beheld a 'huge peak, black and huge', mounting above the horizon of the nearer mountains. By daylight it was just St. Sunday Crag, but now, by moonlight, and to his guilty mind (for he had after all no business to loose the boat) it became a symbol of that strange 'conscience' in Nature of which Wordsworth was aware on more than one occasion. That conscience had followed him with 'low breathings' when he stole the woodcocks: it had pleaded with him in silent reproach when he ravaged the hazel-bower. Now it rose up in a more threatening form and drove him, terrified, back to

approach to the Lake of Windermere terrifies while the view enchants!' The lake is very deep at the foot of the cliffs.

[1] *Prel.* I, ll. 458–60. These lines were written in Germany almost simultaneously with the 'Lucy' poems, in one of which occur the lines describing Lucy's absorption in nature after death:

> Rolled round in Earth's diurnal course
> With rocks and stones and trees.

[2] Ibid., ll. 357–400. From the 1805 text it is clear that this episode took place on Ullswater.

the shore. And for long afterwards his mind, waking or sleeping, was disturbed to its depths by the presence of

> huge and mighty forms which do not live
> Like living men,

moving constantly before his imagination, driving away all 'pleasant images of woods and fields', such as usually peopled it. Such an experience, entirely undivulged as it was to any human being, would perhaps have produced in some children dangerous results, but that strength which had already surmounted the 'visionary dreariness' of Penrith Beacon and the sight of the drowned man in Esthwaite again asserted itself, and when he came to describe the event years later in *The Prelude*, he completed it with the great burst of thanksgiving to the 'Wisdom and Spirit of the Universe' which had 'sanctified' his terror and linked him afresh with the essential joyousness of Nature.[1]

Wordsworth, in pondering afterwards upon his early delight in Nature, believed that it had begun, not directly, but as a result of what he called

> collateral interest
> And by extrinsic passion.

Through the ordinary sports and adventures of boyhood, Nature had, in course of time,

> Peopled my mind with beauteous forms and grand.

The events and pastimes which had given pleasure or aroused feelings of delight or wonder—hunting, climbing, skating, or boating—were the means by which he had discovered beauty, and the scenes in which these events took place were the first to 'people' his mind with their own images, made clear by the strength of association. But Wordsworth, though he was 'sedulous' in pointing out the connexion between these interests and the love of nature, avoided the pitfall of dogmatism in so delicate a matter. Association, important though it was, was not all; memory, however powerful in evoking 'tenderness of thought', was not Nature's only means of teaching him. There was another power working in or upon him. There were 'joys

---

[1] *Prel.* XIV, ll. 232–66.

of subtler origin'—'hallowed and pure motions of the sense',
moments of extraordinary happiness when

> my blood appeared to flow
> With its own pleasure and I breathed with joy.

These, he thought, were not aroused by association, or 'conscious
memory of a kindred sight', but were 'drunk in' as a bee sucks
honey from flowers, directly and almost unconsciously, from what
lay before his eyes. In this passive reception he was affected
particularly by two great sights—water and sky. A moonlit sea,
seen from some rocky headland; 'lines of curling mist' wreathing
themselves along the hillsides; the clouds reflected in the 'level
plain' of a lake's surface—these, he believed afterwards, had
yielded him 'a pure, organic pleasure'—that is to say, a pleasure
not due to association with any objects or events exterior to
themselves, but direct and immediate. By the time he was ten
years old, he says, this kind of delight was a not uncommon
experience with him.

Delight was thus drunk in quietly through the senses, or
came upon him suddenly in the midst of adventure or activity:
gradually it begot love of all he saw and fastened itself into his
memory of the scenes which had aroused it, so that his mind
was constantly 'peopled' with 'pleasant images', as vivid as the
external world itself. This was the marvellous gift of his school-
days to Wordsworth, which he was to carry with him all his life.
Nor was this all. As has been seen, the external world, ever since
the adventure on Penrith Beacon, frequently took on 'a dream-
like vividness and splendour' and appeared 'apparelled in
celestial light'. Then he walked untrammelled by barriers of
'here' and 'there'—even of 'I' and 'not I'—a spiritual being
moving in a world of spirit that was yet the familiar one of
Colthouse, Hawkshead, Windermere. As the school-years went
on it needed no external stimulus, such as fear or rapid movement, to throw him into this visionary state. An ordinary walk
from Colthouse to Hawkshead was enough to bring it on. It was
frequent and habitual. 'I was often unable', he said many years
later, 'to think of external things as having external existence,
and I communed with all I saw as something not apart from
but inherent in my own immaterial nature. Many times while
going to school have I grasped at a wall or tree to recall

myself from this abyss of idealism to the reality.'[1] It was this state that he described in *The Prelude* when he

> forgot
> That I had bodily eyes, and what I saw
> Appear'd like something in myself, a dream,
> A prospect in my mind.

At the time, he says, he was 'afraid of such processes'. Later, when they had ceased to take place, he came to value them and mourn their loss. They were, perhaps, a glimpse of ineffable origins—an earnest of a reality more intense than 'the light of common day'.

Two things are noticeable about the manner in which Wordsworth speaks of this visionary state. The first is his comparison of it to the state of dream: 'dream-like vividness and splendour' —'the glory and the freshness of a dream'.[2] There can be little doubt that Wordsworth's dreams were more than ordinarily vivid; that with him the dream-experience was no confused, ill-recollected jumble of impressions, but in its scenery an intensification of waking reality, or of the fairy-land of books,[3] just as the visionary experiences of the natural world were more intense and more lovely than its ordinary appearance to the 'bodily eye'. It is significant that where most of us would not venture to use a dream for a simile of great vividness and beauty, Wordsworth did not hesitate to do so—thus placing himself with Coleridge and De Quincey among the great dreamers, but without the fatal aid of opium.

These times of idealistic vision had affinity also with another strange boyhood experience—his 'intimation of immortality'. 'Nothing', he said in after years, 'was more difficult for me in childhood than to admit the notion of death as a state applicable to my own being.'[4] And this was not due simply to 'animal vivacity', but to 'a sense of the indomitableness of the spirit within me'. He would brood over the stories of Enoch and Elijah, and with daring egotism look forward not to death but

[1] *P.W.* iv, p. 463.
[2] Ibid., p. 279.
[3] The famous dream in *Prel.* V of the Arab rider, which so fascinated De Quincey, is the most detailed account we have of any of Wordsworth's dreams, but references to dream are frequent throughout his poetry, e.g. *P.W.* iii, p. 17, *Miscellaneous Sonnets*, XXVIII.
[4] *P.W.* iv, p. 463.

to translation. The total rejection of the idea of death at this period was, as he said, 'congenial' to the sensation of all things being in some manner inherent in, rather than external to, his own spirit.

It is one of the poetic gifts to gaze with intense delight at objects which to the ordinary observer are without particular significance. A poet, whether he writes verse or not, is one who 'gives to airy nothing' and to ordinary objects of sight or sound, a meaning or a beauty, not born of his own fancy, but apprehended by his imaginative or visionary faculty. In the poems of his maturity Wordsworth was inclined to attribute this power of observing beauty in its more humble or detailed aspects—a power which gave him vivid joy and underlay the imagery of all his greatest poetry—to his sister's companionship.

> She gave me eyes, she gave me ears,[1]

he testified, and in one passage of *The Prelude* he seems to suggest that the work of opening his eyes to the beauty of small things was all done under Dorothy's guidance at Racedown in 1795 and the following years.[2] But the power of detailed observation was of course born in him, and the evidence that he possessed and used it throughout his school-days, all the nine years when he saw nothing of Dorothy, is abundant and convincing. No doubt Dorothy did strengthen, stimulate, and reciprocate it by her own unclouded vision at a time when Wordsworth's own insight had been temporarily overlaid by personal unhappiness and mental distress. No doubt also such poems as *To a Butterfly* and *The Sparrow's Nest* are a tribute as just as they are lovely to one who, even in infancy, by the example of her own exquisite perception and gentleness, softened the hunting instinct in her brother and directed his attention to the work of observation. But the perception was there, indwelling him, and the gentleness also. At times they came into collision with the other side of his nature, his acquisitiveness and desire to assert power; sometimes they were defeated, but whether defeated or victorious, he was never left without the knowledge —the inward evidence—of their attractiveness and power. Thus,

---

[1] Ibid. i, p. 226, *To a Butterfly*.
[2] *Prel.* XIV, ll. 232–66.

after ravaging the hazel-bower, he felt a strong revulsion of contrition for the damage he had done as he gazed upon

> The silent trees and saw the intruding sky.[1]

Thus, too, crossing a little bridge over a beck, he saw a 'snow-white ram' lying on the bank of the stream, its image perfectly reflected in the pool below. He instinctively picked up a stone to throw into the pool and scatter the image, but something stayed his hand, and instead he went on his way with a kind of tip-toe reverence.[2]

'I would not strike a flower', he says, and if by chance his foot in passing kicked a tuft of 'meadow-lilies',[3] or broke a foxglove stem, he would check himself,

> Self-questioned, asking wherefore that was done.[4]

The gist of the testimony given by Wordsworth in the first two and in the eighth books of *The Prelude* is in fact that as a young boy, before the age of adolescence, he was learning to love Nature for herself, by way of various 'props' such as sports, adventures, and the pursuit of prey, with which his perception of the beauty and mystery of things was at first associated, but which soon ceased to be essential either to perception or delight. This is the meaning of that passage often misunderstood, in which he records that

> the props of my affection were removed
> And yet the building stood as if sustained
> By its own spirit,

and that

> I was left alone
> Seeking the visible world nor knowing why.[5]

---

[1] *P.W.* ii, p. 212, *Nutting.* It should, however, be observed that Wordsworth adds a cautionary line:

> unless I now
> Confound my present feelings with the past.

[2] *Prel.*, p. 562. An incident not included in *The Prelude.*

[3] Perhaps wild daffodils, called lilies in the north.

[4] Ibid., p. 592. These lines were not included in *The Prelude*, but were written as early as 1798, and are associated with *Nutting.*

[5] Ibid. II, ll. 276–80. *Harper*, i, p. 51, and A. Beatty, *William Wordsworth*, p. 218, make this passage refer to the death of his mother: it is, however, obvious from its context that this cannot be so; the reference is to a later period. See *Havens, The Mind of a Poet*, p. 324.

He did not seek in vain. Love, 'this most watchful power of love' (and we should note the adjective), was now in full possession of his being:

> All that I beheld
> Was dear to me . . .
> I loved whate'er I saw,

and every season now brought its full store of delight as knowledge increased and observation became more constant and rewarding. The exact age at which he became aware that Nature was to be loved for her own sake and without 'props' is nowhere specified, but it is probable that his fourteenth year (1783) was a year of revelation in which he became aware of a more intimate and personal love for all he saw. How personal and 'local' rather than general and vague that love was is shown by his choice of recollections. It was not so much a case of

> The spacious firmament on high
> And all the blue ethereal sky

demanding the homage of his soul either to itself or to its Maker: it was rather that

> Already I began
> To love the sun, a boy, I loved the Sun
> Not as I since have loved him, as a pledge
> And surety of our earthly life, a light
> Which we behold and feel we are alive;
> Not for his bounty to so many worlds
> But for this cause, that I had seen him lay
> His beauty on the morning hills, had seen
> The western mountain touch his setting orb,
> In many a thoughtless hour . . .

So too 'the moon was dear to me', because he watched her 'couched among the leaves' of the ash-tree outside his own little bedroom window, or would

> dream away my purposes
> Standing to look upon her while she hung
> Midway between the hills as if she knew
> No other region; but belonged to thee,
> Yea, appertain'd by a peculiar right
> To thee and thy grey huts, thou one dear Vale.[1]

And clouds, in their infinite variety of colour and form

[1] *Prel.* II, ll. 191–7. The 1805 text has 'my darling Vale'.

peopling the world of sky and mountain around him, early began and for ever continued to enthral him. In a passage of *The Prelude* which was not included in the final text, he tells how he

> with a curious patience of regard
> Laboured the subtle process to detect
> By which, like thoughts within the mind itself
> They rose as if from nothing, and dissolved
> Insensibly;

or watched wonderingly

> A lonely One upon the mountain top,

that seemed fixed by a mysterious law

> Crowning that regal hill.

The solitary cloud attracted him, as did solitary human beings, by suggesting some analogy with his own being. So likewise mist—which was but cloud come down to earth—gave him many a moment of ecstasy, besides the 'pure organic pleasure' he drank in from its 'silvery wreaths'. One sight especially he remembered from very early days—it was probably soon after his arrival at Hawkshead, for he was 'yet a very child'—and it remained with him until he saw in it, in adult years, a symbol of the ideal relationship of man, in his nobility and simplicity, perfectly fitted to his environment and reigning over it. He was walking through a deep, narrow valley, on a day when warm steamy mist, 'gentle and beautiful' covered the hillsides, pierced here and there by gleams of sun. Suddenly, directly above him, the mist parted, and he saw on a little shoulder of crag the figures of a shepherd and his dog;

> Girt round with mists they stood and looked about
> From that enclosure small, inhabitants
> Of an aerial island floating on.

With what joy and love did the child gaze at this sudden revelation of the princes of that secret world.[1]

---

[1] This episode was first put into verse by Wordsworth while he was still at school. It stands at the beginning of *The Vale of Esthwaite*, written chiefly in the years 1786 and 1787. See below, p. 61.

> And on yon summit brown and bare
> That seems an island in the air
> The shepherd's restless dog I mark
> Who bounding round with frequent bark
> Now leaps around the uncovered plain,
> Now dives into the mist again.

These affections, which now became the delight of his youth and soon formed the growing-point of his creative powers, he first consciously saluted during an evening picnic with his companions in the summer of 1783.[1] They had borrowed a boat and were resting in it under the big sycamore trees in front of an ancient mansion on the western side of the lake of Coniston. The branches drooped low over the water, making

> A gloom through which a boat might sail along
> As in a cloister.

Butter, a kettle, cups, and a chafing-dish had been supplied by friends at the Hall, and they lay, moored to the shore, looking up through the branches at the top of the hills opposite, which were already flushed with sunset light, the sun being 'himself unseen' and the lake and vale lying in shadow. Suddenly Wordsworth spoke—aloud it would seem—but whether aloud or silently it was with articulate consciousness of what he was saying.

> And there I said,
> That beauteous sight before me, there I said . . .[2]
> That in whatever region I should close
> My mortal life I would remember you,
> Fair scenes! that dying I would think on you,
> My soul would send a longing look to you:
> Even as that setting sun while all the vale
> Could nowhere catch one faint memorial gleam
> Yet with the last remains of his last light
> Still linger'd and a farewell lustre threw
> On the clear mountain tops where first he rose.

So he wrote of the event fifteen years later in the German winter, altering them again at a later date for inclusion in the eighth book of *The Prelude*. But long before that he had put his vow into poetic form. *The Vale of Esthwaite*[3]—the long poem

---

[1] *Prel.* VIII, ll. 458–75, and note, p. 563. The more detailed account given in the 'MS. V' version is of particular interest because it contains the information, 'It was then my fourteenth summer.'

[2] Note the emphasis produced by the repetition. In the final version in *Prel.* VIII, l. 458, he says:
> thus flowed my thoughts
> In a pure stream of words fresh from the heart.

[3] See below, pp. 61 ff.

composed during his last year at school—contains towards its close these lines:

> Yet if Heaven bear me far away
> To close the evening of my day, . . .
> My soul shall cast the wistful view,
> The longing look alone on you.
> As Phoebus, when he sinks to rest
> Far on the mountains of the west,
> While all the vale is dark between
> Ungilded by his golden sheen,
> A lingering lustre softly throws
> On the dear hills where first he rose.

These lines, recast and perfected, were published in 1815 under the title *Extract from the conclusion of a poem composed in Anticipation of Leaving School*, beginning:

> Dear Native Regions, I foretell.

The celebration of this episode in no less than four differing though closely related forms at periods varying from three to twenty-eight years afterwards shows how intense the experience was, although with characteristic honesty, he insisted

> These words
> Were uttered in a casual access
> Of sentiment, a momentary trance
> That far outran the habit of my mind.[1]

It was a moment of response—of fully conscious intellectual as well as emotional response—to the influence of his surroundings which were becoming 'habitually dear'. It was in some ways a forerunner of that infinitely more solemn moment five years later when, looking on almost the same landscape, but in the light of the rising, not the setting, sun, he became 'a dedicated spirit', conscious not of himself making vows, but rather that

> Vows were then made for me.[2]

And it was, above all, a symbol and parable of his own lifelong habit of thought and feeling. The past would always glow for him in brighter hues than the present; always he would be casting a 'longing look' on the shining landscape of his boyhood, and always he would see it lit with a glory that shone ever more radiantly the farther he retreated from it into 'the light of common day'.

---

[1] *Prel.*, p. 564.   [2] Ibid. IV, l. 341. See below, p. 110.

III

HAWKSHEAD II, 1783-7

Meanwhile, whate'er of beautiful or new,
Sublime, or dreadful, in earth, sea or sky,
By chance or search, was offer'd to his view,
He scann'd with curious and romantic eye.
Whate'er of lore tradition could supply
From Gothic tale, or song or fable old,
Roused him, still keen to listen and to pry.

BEATTIE, The Minstrel

IN the churchyard of Cartmel Priory in Furness there is a gravestone of grey slate bearing an inscription to the memory of William Taylor, son of John Taylor of Outerthwaite in that parish. William Taylor died in 1786 at the age of thirty-two. The inscription ends with four lines from Gray's *Elegy in a Country Churchyard*; they were placed there by his own wish, testifying how in his last hours he had turned to poetry for consolation and hope.

> His merits, stranger, seek not to disclose,
> Or draw his Frailties from their dread abode:
> (There they alike in trembling Hope repose)
> The bosom of his Father and his God.

Standing eight years afterwards beside the grave, in the summer of 1794, William Wordsworth saw again in one of his vivid moments of recollection that were almost like visions, the death-bed of his beloved young schoolmaster; how he had summoned Wordsworth and other boys to take leave of them, and how a few days earlier he had said to Wordsworth: 'My head will soon lie low.'

> Those words
> With sound of voice and countenance of the man
> Came back upon me,[1]

he said afterwards in *The Prelude*, for he had loved him and knew that he owed him much. Taylor was headmaster of Hawkshead

---

[1] *Prel.* X, ll. 541-3.

school from 1781 to 1786. A Fellow of Emmanuel College,
Cambridge, he was a man who inspired friendship and admiration, though he left no memorial behind him except the love of
his friends. Among these was George Dyer, the minor poet and
journalist, and friend and butt of Charles Lamb.[1] He has left one
of the few, the very few, remaining tributes, other than Wordsworth's own, to the memory of William Taylor. In his *Poems*,
published in 1801, is one, *The River Cam*, in which he celebrates
many departed Cambridge friends, among them Taylor, whom
he describes as 'the most intimate and highly esteemed of the
author's friends when at College; and if extensive learning, a
sound judgment, a modest demeanour and unblemished morals,
have a claim to respectful remembrance, William Taylor will not
soon be forgotten by him'.

From his youth Taylor had 'loved the poets'.[2] No doubt many
of his Cambridge friendships had had poetry as their currency,
and when he came to Hawkshead he continued to gather round
him those who would reciprocate his enthusiasm. There is
extant a volume of Chatterton's *Miscellanies in Prose and Verse*,
published in 1778, containing an inscription to Taylor from the
donor, Edmund Irton, which not only throws light on Taylor's
love of poetry but shows indirectly how enthusiastic was that
love—how likely such a disciple of the poets was to kindle and
feed the mind and taste of such a boy as William Wordsworth.
It was given to Taylor, says Irton, 'to mark my appreciation of
his luminous and pertinent reflections on the poets of our time,
and especially the unhappy boy whose genius is evident in many
of the pieces contained in this slender volume'.[3] A few years
later we find Wordsworth making quotations from Chatterton's poems in his schoolboy verse. How did he come by them?
The school library was not in these years very rich in English

---

[1] Wordsworth afterwards said that Dyer's *Life of Robert Robinson* was one of
the best biographies he knew. Dyer also wrote an illustrated *History of the University and Colleges of Cambridge*, 1812.

[2] *Prel.* X, l. 548.

[3] Edmund Irton was the young owner of Irton Hall in Cumberland, but his
mother had married secondly Mr. Reginald Braithwaite, the vicar of Hawkshead,
and brought her six children from Irton to Belmont, Hawkshead, where they also
owned Hawkshead Hall. Edmund was twenty when Taylor became headmaster of
the grammar school. He afterwards collected a large library at Irton Hall and was
also an enthusiastic archaeologist. For the inscription I am indebted to Mr. B. R.
Schneider, of Lawrence College, Wisconsin.

poetry, though it became so in the years immediately following
Wordsworth's departure for Cambridge. Nor had Wordsworth
the wealth with which to buy books of modern poetry freely.
Yet somehow or other Wordsworth while at school became
acquainted not only with the poets of the eighteenth century
whose fame has survived—Thomson, Gray, Collins, and Goldsmith—but also with Chatterton and Beattie, Miss Williams,
and Elizabeth Carter, and the 'gothic' and 'sentimental' school
generally. There can scarcely be a doubt that the means of his
knowledge was Taylor, and that the young headmaster freely
lent Wordsworth his own volumes of poetry, among them this
of Chatterton's. The importance to Wordsworth of having such
a man as his teacher and the guide of his reading during these
vivid years need not be dwelt on. Young, scholarly, poetic, kind,
no one could have been better fitted than he to be, all unknow-
ing, the tutor of a great poet in his happy youth.

What Taylor thought of his pupil's general way of living we
do not know, but he laid no restrictions on his wandering habits.
Following the normal course of a boy's growth, Wordsworth, in
his later years at Hawkshead, was less gregarious and more
withdrawn to solitary pursuits than he had been at first. Competitive sports ceased to interest him; they had done their work
in bringing him face to face with Nature, and it was with her
almost exclusively that for the next few years he had to do—
with her and the mysterious 'openings' that communion with
her brought to him. In so far as he made human friendships, they
tended to be of a sort congenial to his absorption in her. Already
as a little boy at Cockermouth he had felt an awed attraction to
the solitary figures who haunted the roads—tramps and discharged soldiers and even madmen. At Hawkshead he formed
an intimacy with a person who was to become an important
figure in his poetry, whom he made first into the 'Pedlar' of *The
Ruined Cottage*; who probably was the chief inspiration of the
'Matthew' poems; and who finally, having dropped his pack,
became the 'Wanderer' of *The Excursion*. This 'Packman' (to
give his local title) wandered round the neighbourhood, visiting
the distant farms and hamlets with his pedlar's pack of wares,
an honest Autolycus selling 'what maids lack from head to
heel'. He possessed a room, 'a fifth part of a house' in Hawkshead
which he used as a sort of base. Thither Wordsworth would

come and, leaning by the door, listen to his tales of his youth
as a shepherd boy in the Perthshire hills, when he was

> hir'd to herd cattle
> On a hill-side for forty pence a year;

still more to his old Scotch ballads of *Love-Gregory, William
Wallace,* and *Rob Roy.*[1]

The old man had been attracted to Wordsworth, he tells us,
'for his grave looks', and they became companions in many a
ramble:

> Many a time
> He made a holy day and left his pack
> Behind, and we two wandered through the hills
> A pair of random travellers,

Wordsworth becoming ever more deeply attracted to a character which had learnt 'to suffer with those whom he saw suffer'
without being embittered or depressed; serene and cheerful in
himself, with no self-pity, he had gathered a store of 'home-felt
wisdom' which he imparted to his young companion in many
a story and comment.

> He was alive
> To all that was enjoyed where'er he went,
> And all that was endur'd.

There was about him a freshness, a sympathy, an insight which
made an indelible impression upon Wordsworth's mind. There
can be little doubt that this good creature influenced more than
any other human being Wordsworth's own approach in later
youth to 'the mystery of man'. The Packman's virtues were
those which Wordsworth came to regard as the best of which
human nature was capable. Under the disguise of 'Matthew' he
is probably pretty closely described in the cycle of 'Matthew'
poems written in Germany in 1799, when Wordsworth's mind
was so completely possessed by the memories of his youth at
Hawkshead. Matthew, with his songs and his 'mother-wit', and
his 'wild ways' and 'fun and madness', his love of folk and his
ready tears, and his

> idle art
> Of teaching love and happiness

---

[1] *P.W.* v, pp. 406–7. This description of the Packman, found in an 'Addendum'
to *The Ruined Cottage,* is the most lifelike and detailed of the many versions.

certainly has more affinities with the old Packman than with the scholarly William Taylor, who has been over-hastily identified as Matthew's original.

The Packman's store of ballads and songs was certainly one of the things that made him attractive to Wordsworth; to love poetry and to love reciting it seems indeed to have been at this time a passport to his affections. When he wrote the fifth book of *The Prelude* Wordsworth said that he was 'thirteen years or haply less'[1] when he first became conscious of loving 'words in tuneful order',

> found them sweet
> For their own sake, a passion and a power.

But it was not until his sixteenth year that he began to attempt to write verse; meantime his love of poetry was reciprocated and shared by at least one of his school companions—John Fleming of Rayrigg on Windermere, of whom he wrote in the glow of youthful love,

> Friendship and Fleming are the same.[2]

The two used to wander round Esthwaite's shores in sunrise hours in summer, before school began, reciting to each other or learning new poems, in unclouded happiness of spirit. The friendship of Fleming was as perfect for adolescent companionship as was that of Taylor for teacher and guide. Like many a boyish friendship it lapsed in later years and they did not often meet, though Fleming lived at Rayrigg all his life, being curate of St. Martin's, Bowness, of which his uncle was the somewhat disreputable rector. The lines in *The Prelude* celebrating their friendship Wordsworth believed Fleming would have 'perused with joy', but he never saw them, for he died fifteen years before their publication.

If we inquire what poetry it was that Wordsworth and John Fleming read and repeated to each other in their wanderings around Esthwaite's shores, the answer is best ascertained from a study of Wordsworth's own youthful verse, which he wrote during his last two years at Hawkshead. He took no pains to hide his models, and one cannot but be struck with the range of his taste, from Milton, who then and throughout his life

[1] *Prel.* V (1805). In 1850 it was altered to 'twice-five years'.
[2] *P.W.* i, p. 16, *Vale of Esthwaite*, I, ll. 249–50.

exercised a paramount influence on his style, through Pope and Thomson to the 'gothic' and romantic school who were the moderns of his day. Later he readily admitted that

> full oft the objects of our love
> Were false, and in their splendour overwrought.[1]

This criticism would apply probably to such writers as Helen Maria Williams, for whom he formed an early veneration and to whom he addressed his first published poem.[2] But what did it matter? It was all part of that

> most noble attribute of man,
> Though yet untutored and inordinate,
> That wish for something loftier, more adorned
> Than is the common aspect, daily garb
> Of human life.

A new world had been opened to them, one in which

> images and sentiments and words . . .
> Kept holiday; a never-ending show
> With music, incense, festival and flowers.[3]

Many years later he spoke of the 'first poem from which he remembered to have received great pleasure'. It was, he said, the *Poem on Spring*, by Elizabeth Carter, the learned friend of Johnson and translator of Epictetus. There is, however, some difficulty here, for Miss Carter wrote no poem on Spring, though she did write several poems in the six-line stanza which Wordsworth afterwards employed in *Ruth* and other poems. He is probably confusing her with Lucy Aikin, afterwards Mrs. Barbauld. Her poems, published in 1773, contained an *Ode to Spring* and also a poem *On the Backwardness of the Spring in 1771*, either of which might well have caught Wordsworth's fancy.

But the overriding attraction was undoubtedly Milton.

> Among the hills
> He gazed upon that mighty orb of song,
> The divine Milton,

Wordsworth said of his 'Pedlar' in *The Ruined Cottage* in lines that are clearly autobiographical.[4] In the poetry written at Hawkshead and Cambridge, all of it highly derivative, the

---

[1] *Prel.* V, ll. 569–70.   [2] See below, p. 60.
[3] *Prel.* V, ll. 573–7, and 580–83.   [4] *P.W.* v, p. 383, app. crit.

number of borrowings and echoes from Milton far exceeds those from any other poet.

A poet with whom he became acquainted at school and who at once aroused his interest not so much for his style as for his matter was George Crabbe. Some considerable extracts from *The Village* were printed in the *Annual Register* in 1783, and these Wordsworth read, in a copy presumably borrowed from Taylor. Among them were those lines describing the horrid realities of poverty—the village workhouse and its population of human derelicts, among them 'the moping idiot and the madman gay'. This description, said Wordsworth long afterwards, 'struck my youthful feelings particularly—tho' facts, as far as they had then come under my knowledge, did not support the description; inasmuch as idiots and lunatics among the humbler classes of society were not to be found in Workhouses—in the parts of the North where I was brought up,—but were mostly at large, and too often the butt of thoughtless children'. He learnt the extracts there and then by heart and remembered them to the end of his life.[1] Crabbe and another poet-parson, John Langhorne, author of *The Country Justice*, did much to draw Wordsworth's attention in his youth to the tragedy of poverty and the heartlessness with which society generally treated it.[2]

There was one famous work which might well have played a great part in his early acquaintance with poetry, but which aroused nothing but disgust in him, in spite of its lavish use of mist, mountain, storm, and darkness. Even in his boyhood Wordsworth was never taken in by 'Ossian'. His revered Miss Williams praised it, and Wordsworth was eager enough generally to welcome what came from beyond the Border.[3] It was not so much its vague 'free-verse' that he disliked, but its insincerity and sham enthusiasm for nature.

Having had the good fortune [he wrote in later years] to be born in a mountainous country, from my very childhood I have felt the falsehood that pervades the volumes imposed upon the world under the name of Ossian. From what I saw with my own eyes I knew that

[1] Scott read these extracts at the same time and 'committed them most faithfully to memory'. *Life of Crabbe*, by his son.

[2] *L.Y.* iii. 1075a, p. 1376. W.W. to George Crabbe. junr·, 1834. For Langhorne see below, p. 101.

[3] Ibid. i, p. 128. See above, p. 10.

the imagery was spurious. In nature everything is distinct, yet not
defined into absolute independent singleness. In Macpherson it is
exactly the reverse; everything (that is not stolen) is in this manner
defined, insulated, dislocated, deadened—yet nothing distinct. It will
always be so when words are substituted for things.[1]

In 1785, when Wordsworth was fifteen, Hawkshead school
celebrated its bicentenary. The cleverer boys, including Wordsworth, were 'called upon' to write verses to celebrate the occasion, and Wordsworth produced over a hundred lines of heroic
couplet, in which the Spirit of Education, personified as a god-
dess, addresses the schoolboy on the subject of modern learning.
They are the first verses of Wordsworth's which have survived,
and were, he tells us, 'much admired, far more than they deserved, for they were but a tame imitation of Pope's versification
and a little in his style'. Their interest lies perhaps chiefly in the
light they throw on the intellectual 'climate' of the school. The
boys had been taught that the Reformation had paved the way
for 'Science' and 'Philosophy'.

> Science with joy saw Superstition fly
> Before the lustre of Religion's eye . . .
> No jarring monks, to gloomy cell confined,
> With mazy rules perplex the weary mind;
> No shadowy forms entice the soul aside,
> Secure she walks, Philosophy her guide . . .
> Britain, who thought to stain the field was fame,
> Now honour'd Edward's less than Bacon's name . . .
> Fair to the view is sacred Truth display'd
> In all the majesty of light array'd,
> To teach, on rapid wings, the curious soul
> To roam from heaven to heaven, from pole to pole,
> From thence to search the mystic cause of things
> And follow Nature in her secret springs.[2]

Although the lesson hours at Hawkshead may have been
almost entirely devoted to classics and Euclid, it is clear from
these verses that under Taylor the boys were made familiar with
the name of Francis Bacon and with the more experimental and
'scientific' approach to knowledge which had been gaining

---

[1] *P.W.* ii, p. 423, 'Essay Supplementary to the Preface' of *Poems*, 1815.

[2] *P.W.* i, p. 260. For the influence of Pope's *Dunciad* on Wordsworth's lines
see A. F. Potts, *Wordsworth's Prelude*, pp. 33–38.

ground during the last two centuries. We know that before he
went up to Cambridge Wordsworth had conceived a veneration
for the name of Newton which amounted to worship. Another
great figure, and a contemporary this time, with whose name
Wordsworth was acquainted at school was Sir Joshua Reynolds,
for one of his early poems, written in his last year at school,
begins:

> Reynolds, come, thy pencil prove,
> And waft me, waft me to my love.

There was therefore a background to their classical studies of
what is sometimes called 'general culture', from which Wordsworth drew not a little inspiration.

Wordsworth tells us that the bicentenary lines led directly
to his beginning to compose verses 'from the impulse of my
own mind'. Before that he had written some lines on 'The Summer
Vacation', which was a subject set by his master: he added of his
own accord some more on 'Return to School'. These verses have
not survived, but in his old age Wordsworth said that 'the first
voluntary verses' that he ever wrote 'were written after walking
six miles to attend a dance at Egremont'.[1] Egremont is just six
miles from Whitehaven, where he and his brothers always spent
the Christmas holidays. These 'voluntary verses' therefore may
be the 'Return to School' lines, and were probably written during
the Christmas holidays of 1784–5. Dancing was, as we have
seen, taught at Hawkshead by Mr. Mingay; it is curious to find
Wordsworth so enthusiastic a dancer at the age of fourteen.

From the summer of 1785 onwards he wrote fairly constantly.
About this time he was given (we do not know by whom) a
manuscript book in a brown leather cover, in which, he says,
he began to write verses, 'and so got into the habit of reducing
to shape the thoughts which had been vaguely haunting his
brain, like to body-waiting souls, which wandered by the
Lethean pools'.[2] This note-book was used by Wordsworth
throughout his time at Cambridge and for some time after: it
even contains rough drafts of verses written at Racedown in
1795. About ten poems and a fragment of a prose 'Tale' belong
to the Hawkshead days. Of these, two are love-poems, written

---

[1] Diary of Miss Serle, in the possession of Miss Bell at Ambleside.
[2] Aubrey de Vere to W. R. Hamilton, Jan. 1843; R. P. Graves, *Life of Sir
W. R. Hamilton* (1882), ii, p. 402.

in 1786, the first an imitation of Anacreon, the second called
Beauty and Moonlight, An Ode, Fragment.[1] The 'Mary' of this
poem may be Mary Hutchinson, whom he saw in summer
holidays at Penrith and with whom he was mildly in love in the
summer of 1788.[2] There is also a *Dirge Sung by a Minstrel,*[3]
written apparently to commemorate the death of one of his
schoolmates, and then re-cast (during his first year at Cambridge) to suit the death of a girl. *A Ballad,*[4] in which 'William'
is made responsible for the death of a deserted 'Mary', is dated
'March 23 and 24, 1787'; in it he repeats the words spoken by
his master William Taylor on his death-bed in the previous year.

> Heaven told me once—but I was blind—
> *My head would soon lie low;*

   The interest of these early poems is upon the whole less biographical than literary. Whether the 'Mary' of *Beauty and
Moonlight,* if she is not Mary Hutchinson, is the same girl who
dies broken-hearted in *A Ballad*; whether there was a girl at
Hawkshead with whom Wordsworth was a little in love, and
who perhaps died (though more probably from tuberculosis, one
suspects, than from a broken heart) are questions which it is
impossible to answer, and scarcely profitable to discuss. One
point is worth noting in the *Anacreon* verses: Grasmere is mentioned there for the first time in Wordsworth's poetry, in connexion with 'curling mist'—later dwelt on in *The Prelude* as a
beloved 'object'—and a cottage full of domestic bliss:

> The white mist curls on Grasmere's stream,
> Which, like a veil of flowing light,
> Hides half the landskip from the sight . . .
> The pathway winding through the dale,
> The cot, the seat of Peace and Love,
> Peeping through the tufted grove.

We know that Wordsworth on one of his rambles from Hawkshead came unexpectedly on Grasmere as he walked over the
pass from Langdale—the green neck of land between Silver
How and Loughrigg that was then called Hammarscar.

> Once to the brow of yon steep barrier came
> A roving school-boy; what the Adventurer's age

[1] *P.W.* i, pp. 261 and 263.   [2] See below, p. 114.
[3] *P.W.* i, p. 267.   [4] Ibid., p. 265.

> Hath now escaped his memory—but the hour,
> One of a golden summer holiday,
> He well remembers, though the year be gone.
> And with a sudden influx overpowered
> At sight of this seclusion, he forgot
> His haste, for hasty had his footsteps been
> As boyish his pursuits, and sighing said
> 'What happy fortune were it here to live'.[1]

So he wrote in 1800, looking across the lake to the 'steep barrier' from the windows of Dove Cottage. From that day forth Grasmere became

> a haunt
> Of pure affections shedding upon joy
> A brighter joy,

a memory that cheered his moods of youthful self-pity, and to which he constantly returned in thought. When he at last came to live at Grasmere he invoked that first visit and its emotions to justify his retirement from the world.

The chief interest, however, of the *Dirge* and *A Ballad* lies in their style and literary ancestry. They are strongly 'romantic' in tone: he is imitating not Pope, but the ballads, and Chatterton and Collins. The first verse of the *Dirge* contains a refrain lifted, with its antique spelling unchanged, from Chatterton's *Aella*:

> Mie love is dedde
> Gone to her death bedde,
> Al under the willow tree.

He hesitates not to speak of worms and knells and graves, 'wafts' or wraiths; the classical decorum of Pope is entirely thrown aside. By this time, of course, the 'romantic' movement in literature and art was well under way. Nourished on fairy-tales, ballads, and the *Arabian Nights*, Wordsworth had plenty of material ready to his hand, and his homage to the modern writers who dealt in horror, romance, and sentiment was paid in this last year at school to Helen Maria Williams, whose poems appeared in 1786. To her Wordsworth addressed a sonnet which he sent to the *European Magazine*: it was printed there—Wordsworth's first publication—in March 1787 over

---

[1] Ibid. v, p. 313, *The Recluse*, ll. 1–10.

the transliteration 'Axiologus'.[1] It seems to have been inspired
by her poem *To Sensibility*. A more 'horrific' poem of hers,
entitled *Part of an Irregular Fragment*, probably influenced the
long poem which he wrote during his last two years at school,
and which he called *The Vale of Esthwaite*. Lucy Aikin also
seems certainly to have contributed in no small degree to this
composition. Her *Miscellaneous Pieces* had appeared in 1773,
and among these curious essays, one of which was called *On the
pleasure derived from objects of terror*, was a fragmentary romantic
tale called *Sir Bertrand*, full of dungeons, ghosts, and blue
flames, which Wordsworth almost certainly knew and used.

But the strongest contemporary influence on the young Wordsworth was Beattie. The Professor of Philosophy at Marischal
College, Aberdeen, published the first part of his *Minstrel* in
1770, and the second in 1774. It became and remained one of
Wordsworth's favourite poems: its echoes are found even in the
poetry of his maturity, and in the years of stress after his return
from France, when he was struggling to prepare himself for his
life's work as a poet, it was to Beattie that he turned for refreshment and inspiration.[2]

'Young Edwin', the hero of *The Minstrel*, delights in graves,
ghosts, and clanking chains, but not only in them. He had also
the modern delight in Nature and solitude. Beattie's doctrine
that the beauties of Nature held something more than a purely
aesthetic value; that they

> Shall work thy soul's eternal health,
> And love, and gentleness and joy impart,

would have found already in Wordsworth a sympathetic assent,
and Edwin was in many ways a poetic creation after his own
image. The character of Edwin may indeed have had some direct
influence on Wordsworth's changes of activity and taste in his
later school-days. With some fervour Beattie portrays Edwin's
dislike of blood-sports:

> His heart, from cruel sport estranged, would bleed
> To work the woe of any living thing,
> By trap, or net; by arrow, or by sling:
> These he detested; those he scorn'd to wield.

---

[1] *P.W.* i, p. 269, *On Seeing Miss Helen Maria Williams Weep at a Tale of Distress.*
It was never reprinted by Wordsworth. He had never seen Miss Williams, and did
not do so until 1820 when they met in Paris.   [2] See below, p. 287.

Wordsworth, the hunter of woodcocks and ravager of the raven's eyrie, in his later boyhood turned as we have seen towards these gentler dispositions grounded in his increasing love for all he saw and his sense of the sacredness of living things.[1]

Edwin too was a being who as he grew up delighted most in those very severities of nature which were daily becoming dearer to Wordsworth:

> And oft the craggy cliff he loved to climb
> When all in mist the world below was lost.
> What dreadful pleasure! there to stand sublime
> Like shipwreck'd mariner on desert coast
> And view the enormous waste of vapour. . . .

No wonder Dorothy, writing to Jane Pollard in 1793, quoted part of the stanza beginning

> In truth he was a strange and wayward wight,
> Fond of each gentle, and each dreadful scene;
> In darkness and in storm he found delight,

and commented: 'That verse of Beattie's "Minstrel" always reminds me of him [William] and indeed the whole character of Edwin resembles much what William was when I first knew him—after my leaving Halifax'—that is to say immediately after William left Hawkshead in the summer of 1787, when he and Dorothy were re-united after their long separation.

Wordsworth's tastes and indeed the whole colour of his mind at this time are best studied in *The Vale of Esthwaite*, the poem of which some 560 lines survive, though it originally ran to over 1,000.[2] He described it as 'a long poem running upon my own adventures and the scenery of the country in which I was brought up'. Parts of it reappeared, dressed more decorously in heroic couplet, in *An Evening Walk*, the work of his Cambridge years. For *The Vale of Esthwaite* he chose the eight-syllable metre of *L'Allegro* and *Il Penseroso*, and their influence on much of the verse is strong in other ways. The *Vale* is partly a

---

[1] In his Cambridge days a poem by William Greenwood, a Fellow of St. John's, called *A Poem written during a shooting excursion on the moors*, and published in 1787 made a similar appeal to him and he quoted from it in *An Evening Walk*. It was partly an appeal to sportsmen not to shoot birds in the mating season.

[2] In the existing manuscript the figure '1000' appears in the margin at one point, obviously indicating the number of lines. The poem, as much of it as survives, is printed in *P.W*. i, pp. 270–83.

descriptive and partly a 'romantic' poem, somewhat of a medley of images—the natural alternating with the supernatural, so that the result is a curious kaleidoscope. Thus, white-robed Druids suggest a waterfall, and the waterfall in its turn a spectre seen in a dungeon.

> Why roll on me your glaring eyes?
> Why fix on me for sacrifice?

he asks the Druids.

> But he, the stream's loud genius, seen
> The black arch'd boughs and rocks between
> That brood o'er one eternal night,
> Shoots from the cliff in robe of white.
> So oft in castle moated round
> In black damp dungeon underground
> Strange forms are seen that, white and tall,
> Stand straight against the coal-black wall.

Or he describes himself walking at night in a storm—a favourite activity at all times of his life:

> While yelling loud the torrents white
> Shot through the gloom upon my sight,
> So in his hall in times of yore
> Alone a Baron, wandering o'er
> At midnight hour with melting gaze
> The holy forms of other days,
> Has mark'd slow creeping round the wall
> A gloom as black as funeral pall,
> And a tall ghost of ashy hue
> On every canvas met his view.

But in spite of the predominance of these spectral horrors in the poem, he releases himself every now and then from the 'gothic' image, and, as it were, comes up to breathe. Thus, a minstrel is imagined pestered by a 'grisly phantom' who insists on playing his harp for him. But Wordsworth's fancy

> Shot from wondrous dream to dream
> Till round, perhaps, the flickering dove
> Broke from the rustling boughs above,
> Or straggled sheep with white fleece seen
> Between the boughs of sombrous green,
> Starting wildly from its sleep
> Shook the pebble from the steep,

and sent it

> gingling downward shrill and slow.[1]

In these natural images of the pigeon and the sheep breaking cover there is a promise of the poetry which was to come, and when *The Vale of Esthwaite* is compared with *An Evening Walk*, written only a year or two later, we find that the 'gothic' passages have been dropped and the pictures of landscapes and rural incidents retained and added to by many hundreds more, described with all the accuracy possible in a style that still clung to the politest classical models. One such picture, described first in *The Vale* and afterwards—certainly no more vividly—in *An Evening Walk*, was, says Wordsworth, 'important in my poetical history'. He was, he says, in his fifteenth year, and while 'in the way between Hawkshead and Ambleside' he saw an oak-tree, its boughs and foliage outlined with intense clarity against the glowing sky of evening. As he gazed upon it he realized with a thrill that no poet known to him had ever described just that beauty and that strangeness. And if that were so, must not there be hundreds—nay, thousands—of natural sights and sounds yet uncelebrated in verse, waiting to be discerned, valued, and given shape and expression? 'I made a resolution', he says, 'to supply, in some degree, the deficiency.'[2] That resolution, so momentous for English poetry, had its earliest fulfilment in some of the images of *The Vale of Esthwaite*. But although in *An Evening Walk* description gained the upper hand of romantic gloom, it must not be supposed that the 'stock-in-trade of Gothic romance'[3] disappeared altogether from Wordsworth's poetry after his school-years. The poetry of all his early years down to the writing of the *Lyrical Ballads* in 1798 constantly tends to revert to it. His play, *The Borderers* (1796), is full of it; the

---

[1] 'gingling'—a dialect word. In the Yorkshire dales a 'gingle-hole' is a hole in the limestone rock down which stones, tins, or other things are thrown.

[2] *P.W.* i, p. 319, note to *E.W.* The lines describing the oak-tree in *The Vale of Esthwaite* are as follows:

> While in the west the robe of day,
> Fades, slowly fades, from gold to gray,
> The oak its boughs and foliage twines
> Mark'd to the view in stronger lines.
> While every darkening leaf between
> The sky distinct and clear is seen.

[3] De Selincourt, 'The Early Wordsworth' in *Wordsworth and Other Studies*, 1947.

early version of *Guilt and Sorrow* (1793–5) contains a long
passage about druids and human sacrifices; the woman deserted
by her lover, and the haunting of the pond by the ghost of
her dead infant, is the theme of *The Thorn*, written as late as
1798.

The strong attraction which the romantic and gloomy school
of poetry had for the boy Wordsworth arose naturally from the
deeper experiences of his spirit. He to whom the sight of a
mountain peak outlined against the night sky could bring visions
of

> Huge and mighty forms that do not live
> Like living men,

which haunted him sleeping and waking for days together, and
who listened to

> sounds that are
> The ghostly language of the ancient earth
> Or make their dim abode in distant winds,

needed some kind of articulation to relieve the pressure on his
imagination that might otherwise become intolerable. He could
not then describe, as he did later in *The Prelude*, what he
was himself undergoing. He probably never even considered
such experiences as the subject-matter of poetry. But the
druids, dungeons, and spectres of romanticism offered a useful
disguise.

Occasionally, however, even in these early days Wordsworth
plunges beneath the appearances of things in what he wrote, and
seems to be feeling after what was to be one of the supreme
achievements of his greatest poetry—the description of the
response of the imagination and the affections to Nature. Thus
he records:

> Lone wandering oft by Esthwaite's stream
> My soul has felt the mystic dream
> When Twilight, wrapp'd in dusky shroud
> Slow journeyed from her cave of cloud.

And in a somewhat more detailed attempt:

> Now holy Melancholy throws
> Soft o'er the soul a still repose,

> Save where we start as from a sleep
> Recoiling from a gloom too deep.
> Now too, while o'er the heart we feel
> A tender twilight softly steal . . .
> The heart, when pass'd the Vision by,
> Dissolves, nor knows for whom, or why.

Here is in fact a first attempt to describe in verse 'that blessed mood' that was to be one of his most precious experiences, when the life of the senses seemed to be temporarily suspended and the 'soul' to live in union with the life of the Universe.

In another poem written at this time he gives us a glimpse of the creative process itself as he was experiencing it at this time. We know that it was his lifelong habit to compose his poetry while walking out of doors, and that, as he did so, he often spoke his lines aloud,

> like a river murmuring
> And talking to itself.

In *The Prelude*, he describes how, while absorbed in 'the toil of verse' in these youthful days at Hawkshead, strong bodily sensations would take hold of him.

> Along my veins I kindled with the stir,
> The fermentation and the vernal heat
> Of Poesy.[1]

With him in these poetical rambles went a dog, a faithful red terrier,

> an attendant and a friend
> Obsequious to my steps early and late,

who trotted in front of him along the road and turned back whenever he saw a wayfarer approaching, so that William could compose himself, stop 'murmuring' and prepare for a friendly greeting, lest his soliloquies should arouse the suspicion that he was 'crazed in brain'. Among Wordsworth's schoolboy verses is an *Idyllium*,[2] written to commemorate this dog, who was drowned, apparently, not long before Wordsworth left

---

[1] *Prel.* IV, ll. 102–4. Dorothy uses the expression 'William *kindled* and began to write the poem', in her Journal for Mar. 17th 1802. *D.W.J.* i, p. 125.

[2] *P.W.* i, p. 265. See J. Jones, *The Egotistical Sublime*, pp. 17–22, for a full discussion of this poem.

Hawkshead. The first part of the poem is a deliberate imitation of *Lycidas*;

> Where were ye, Nymphs, when the remorseless deep
> Clos'd o'er your little favourite's hapless head? . . .

In the last lines, however, he reveals the presence in his mind of a faculty or power of perceiving images, and also the joy which that creative power gave him. Nowhere else in his poetry does he describe so clearly this most significant mental process; the little poem is therefore important for the glimpse it gives us of his interior life; the development of a growing power of vision which became the foundation of all that was greatest in his poetry. After reproaching the 'nymphs' for allowing the death of the dog, he thus recalls how on their walks together:

> If, while I gazed to Nature blind,
> In the calm Ocean of my mind
> Some new-created image rose
> In full-grown beauty at its birth,
> Lovely as Venus from the sea
> Then, while my glad hand sprung to thee,
> We were the happiest pair on earth.

The phrase 'while I gazed to Nature blind' has special significance, for it shows that he was now doing what became habitual with him—looking through or beyond the outward images that were the raw material of his vision into the mysterious depths of his own creative imagination, which was 'a calm Ocean', a receptive mirror in which he could perceive, with the clarity of a landscape emerging from a mist—the poetic image which had been eluding his intellectual search. It was the experience familiar to him from early childhood of the visionary capacity of his mind in certain circumstances, when everything seemed inferior to his own being, and

> all I saw
> Appeared like something in myself, a dream,
> A prospect in the mind,

but now it was kindling to creative life. It is perhaps in this early fragment that he comes nearest to showing us the link between the passive and the active, the receptive and the creative states of his inner life. When he wrote the passage about the dog in *The Prelude* he evidently turned to or remembered it, for the line about the image, rising like Venus from the sea, is repeated there with very little alteration.[1]

It might have been expected that Wordsworth, with all his intercourse with the common folk of the dales, and his own lifelong use in speech of dialect words and of a Cumberland 'burr', would have essayed at least in youth to write verse in the local speech. Ballads he already knew from his Border childhood, and he probably had access to Percy's *Reliques*.[2] His friend the Packman must have spoken and sung in dialect. Burns' *Poems, chiefly in the Scottish Dialect* appeared in 1786 and he read it with delight soon after publication,[3] but neither then nor afterwards did he attempt dialect verse. This must have been chiefly due to his adoration of English poetry, particularly Milton, and also to his training in the Latin classics which he loved scarcely less. 'Before I read Virgil', he said afterwards, 'I was so strongly attached to Ovid, whose Metamorphoses I read at school, that I was quite in a passion whenever I found him, in books of criticism, placed below Virgil. As to Homer, I was never weary of travelling over the scenes through which he led me.'[4] Some of his schoolboy and undergraduate verse consists of translations or imitations of the classics, both Greek and Latin, and what is not of these has its origins, as has been seen, with established English models. Wordsworth, in spite of his attachment to his 'own darling Vale' and all the landscape of the fells and dales, and to the shepherds and wandering packmen, does not seem ever to have thought of himself as a local minstrel, singing to his own people in their own tongue. He preferred, by education and by personal taste, to write in the language of his English predecessors.

The death of their father John Wordsworth, which occurred suddenly at Christmas 1783, was an event which deeply affected all the Wordsworth children, both outwardly in the changed circumstances of their lives, and inwardly in the new and closer relationships which it brought about between them and particularly

[1] *Prel.* IV, ll. 110–17.
[2] A copy of Percy is in the school library at Hawkshead but it was not there until some years after Wordsworth left.
[3] *E.L.* 4, p. 12. D.W. to J.P. Dec. 17th 1787. See below, p. 73.
[4] *P.W.* iv, p. 422.

between William, Dorothy, and John. On William himself it made an impression of peculiar importance, but this was not so much because he felt intense personal affection for his father, as because it set in motion imaginative experiences that helped forward his creative powers.

Among his other activities Mr. John Wordsworth was coroner of a district called the Seignory of Millom. He rode over to that remote corner of Cumberland, where the mountains meet the Atlantic, to conduct two inquests just before the Christmas of 1783, and returning home he lost his way in the darkness on Cold Fell and was obliged to spend a winter night shelterless on a fell side, with the result that he arrived home in the grip of mortal illness. It may be that he did not fight very hard for life, for since his wife's death he had not had much happiness. He died on December 30th, and on January 5th was buried in Cockermouth churchyard, 'on a snowy, windy day'.[1] His three elder sons attended the funeral. They had arrived from Hawkshead for the Christmas holidays to find their father already on his death-bed. Christopher was at Penrith, not yet having started his career at Hawkshead, and Dorothy was still with her mother's relations at Halifax.

Just before leaving Hawkshead this Christmas-time, William had had one of his moments of inexplicable intensity of vision and feeling, while waiting by the roadside for the 'little horse to bear me home'.[2] The boys were always fetched from Hawkshead by a servant of their father who came for them with led ponies.[3] On this occasion William had gone up to a point about a mile north of Hawkshead, 'an eminence' or ridge of rough ground whence he could command a view of the two roads, one

---

[1] *M.Y.* i, p. 165. D.W. to Catherine Clarkson, Dec. 1807.

[2] *P.W.* i, p. 279, *The Vale of Esthwaite*, l. 425. It is curious that in his account of the incident in this poem, Wordsworth implies that while waiting for the ponies he already knew of his father's death:

> Long, long upon yon naked rock
> Alone, I bore the bitter shock,
> Long, long my swimming eyes did roam
> For little horse to bear me home.

This, however, must be inaccurate for the boys always returned home before Christmas. *Prel.* XII, ll. 287–399, gives the correct version.

[3] The various manuscripts of *The Prelude* contain 'two horses', 'three horses', 'rough palfreys', and 'led palfreys'. There were three brothers at Hawkshead, but perhaps John may have ridden on the groom's horse.

from the Wrynose Pass and Little Langdale and the other from
Skelwith and Ambleside, down either of which the ponies might
be expected.[1] It was a cold, misty, raw day,

> stormy and rough and wild

(his favourite weather in fact) and he was excited and restless
with desire for home. For, happy though he was at school, the
terms were long and as the holidays drew near he suffered a
vivid nostalgia. So he sat down on the wet grass, in the shelter
of a stone wall, to wait in the mist and rain, alone, save that

> Upon my right hand was a single sheep,
> A whistling hawthorn on my left, and there,
> With these companions at my side, I watch'd.

His own solitude, the solitary objects isolated by the mist from
relation with the landscape, and his mood of feverish expectation, gave exactly the conditions favourable for creating an
intense visual impression on his mind; indeed the resemblance
of the whole episode to the ride on Penrith Beacon eight years
before is obvious, and Wordsworth himself associated the two
together in his mind when he recorded them side by side in *The
Prelude*. What followed only made the impression more intense.
The ponies came, the boys rode joyfully home, but found a
disturbed and anxious household. The shock of finding himself
in the near presence of death, with all the happy schemes of
holiday pleasure overthrown, produced at first in William a
strong religious mood of Job-like contrition and self-abasement:

> when I call'd to mind
> That day so lately passed, when from the crag
> I looked in such anxiety of hope,
> With trite reflections of morality
> Yet in the deepest passion, I bow'd low
> To God, who thus corrected my desires.[2]

He felt as though he were being punished for presumptuous
hopes and selfish wishes. No doubt also his father's death came
like a sharp rebuke to that daring conviction of his own immortality which had made his boyhood seem like that of a divine

---

[1] *Prel.* XII, ll. 293–5, and note pp. 595–6. The spot is probably near Borwick
Ground, between the road over Oxen Fell, leading to Little Langdale and the
Wrynose Pass, and the lower road to Skelwith and Grasmere.
[2] Ibid., ll. 311–16.

being. *The Vale of Esthwaite* is full of rather melancholy pro-
phecies of his own early decease:

> I soon shall be with them that rest,[1]

he exclaims, after describing his emotions as he followed his
father's coffin to the grave.

> Ah! may my weary body sleep
> In peace beneath a green grass heap,
> In Churchyard such at death of day
> As heard the pensive sighs of Gray.

But these gloomy reflections were not the only result of that sad
Christmas on his inward being. The mental picture of the 'wait
for the ponies' remained and, like the picture of the gibbet on
Penrith Beacon, it brought him not gloom and depression but
increasing inspiration and delight. It was 'a spot of time' etched
on his memory by the strength of the feelings which had filled
him both at the time and immediately afterwards, vivid, mysterious, pregnant with imaginative life:

> the wind and sleety rain
> And all the business of the elements,
> The single sheep and the one blasted tree,
> And the bleak music of that old stone wall,
> The noise of wood and water, and the mist.

To this picture, he tells us, he

> often would repair and thence would drink
> As at a fountain,

delighting in the strangeness and pathos of that lonely scene.
When he recorded it in *The Prelude* he believed that the recollection of it set his imagination stirring and nourished his
creative power, especially when 'the business of the elements'—
the rain on the roof at midnight or the wind rocking the trees
overhead—by association re-created the feelings of that day.[2]

The real loss sustained by the Wordsworth children in the
death of their father was perhaps less that of a beloved person
than of a happy home. Owing to his constant preoccupation with
business he was not intimately known to them, but at Cockermouth they had a home where they were entirely free and happy,

---

[1] From Milton, *Samson Agonistes:* 'And I shall shortly be with them that rest.'
[2] *Prel.* XII, ll. 326–end.

and now it was gone for ever. During the two or three following
years the contrast between life at Cockermouth and life with
their unloved grandparents at Penrith was bitter enough.
William voiced their desolation when he was lamenting his
father's death in *The Vale of Esthwaite*:

> With sighs repeated o'er and o'er
> I mourn because I mourned no more,
> Nor did my little heart foresee
> She lost a home in losing thee.

Mr. John Wordsworth died intestate and with his financial
affairs hopelessly involved. His employer, Sir James Lowther
(who became Earl of Lonsdale in 1784) owed him a sum
amounting to £4,700 for legal and political business which he
had transacted. Other people were also in his debt. His realisable
assets for finishing his children's education and starting them
in the world amounted to less than £3,000, enough with very
careful management to finish the boys' education and 'put them
forward in the world', though as the event proved, William and
Christopher had to receive assistance for their expenses at
Cambridge from their guardians, the uncles at Whitehaven and
Penrith.[1]

These two uncles, their father's elder brother Richard Wordsworth of Whitehaven, and their mother's brother Christopher
Crackanthorpe Cookson of Penrith, now became responsible for
the Wordsworth boys. Henceforward the short Christmas holiday of about a month was spent at Whitehaven with their uncle,
or near by at Branthwaite with his eldest son, their cousin
Richard the solicitor and his family. To this younger Richard
fell the task of winding up Mr. John Wordsworth's affairs; he
prudently removed to Branthwaite all the papers relating to the
Lowther debts with the note that they 'were thought proper to
be secured in some private place of safety'. He also removed to
Branthwaite Mr. Wordsworth's books and book-case, when all
the rest of the furniture of the house at Cockermouth was sold.
Perhaps William pleaded for his father's books; in any case it
must have greatly comforted him to feel that he would not be
separated from them entirely.

[1] *E.L.* 1, p. 4. 'We shall have I believe about six hundred pounds apiece if
Lord L. does not pay. It is but very little but it will be quite enough for my
Brothers' education.' D.W. to J.P., summer, 1787. But it was not 'quite enough'.

Nothing definite is known of the household at Whitehaven to tell us whether it was a congenial environment for the Wordsworth boys in general or in particular. In after years, however, the cousins remained on friendly terms[1] and the Whitehaven uncle who had been deeply attached to their father was certainly more kindly disposed to the orphans than the household at Penrith. Uncle Richard helped William financially when he was at Cambridge. £400 was advanced for that purpose, a debt which Wordsworth strove vainly for many years to get repaid to his heirs. It was not finally settled until 1813.[2]

The summer vacations from 1783 onwards were spent at Penrith, under the eye of the strict and disagreeable grandparents and of Uncle Kit. The atmosphere of this uncomfortable household has been conveyed to us, with artless art, by Dorothy, who returned from Halifax to Penrith in the summer of 1787 to live with her grandparents—a change which held no pleasures for her except the intense one of meeting her brothers in the summer holidays. She poured out in her letters to her Halifax friend Jane Pollard all her mortifications and those of her brothers at the hands of their relations.[3]

Many a time have William, John, Christopher and myself shed tears together, tears of the bitterest sorrow; we all of us, each day, feel more sensibly the loss we sustained when we were deprived of our parents, and each day do we receive fresh insults. You will wonder of what sort; believe me of the most mortifying kind, the insults of servants . . . James [the same James who had ridden with William over Penrith Beacon years before] has even gone so far as to tell us we had nobody to depend upon but my Grandfather, for that our fortunes were but very small, and my Brothers cannot even get a pair of shoes cleaned without James's telling them they require as much waiting upon as any *gentlemen*. . . . James happens to be a particular favourite with my Uncle Kit, who has taken a dislike to my Brother [William] and never takes any notice of any of us, so that he thinks while my Uncle behaves in this way he may do anything.

The eager girl, on tip-toe to meet again the brothers she had not seen for nine years, was kept waiting a week at the begin-

---

[1] A daughter of Richard Wordsworth of Branthwaite, another Dorothy, was much liked in later times by Dorothy and used to stay at Rydal Mount. *M.Y.* ii. 192, p. 580.

[2] *M.Y.* ii. 539, p. 698. W.W. to C.W., Jan. 12th 1816.

[3] *E.L.* 1–7.

ning of the holidays 'owing to the ill nature of my Uncle who would not send horses for them because when they wrote they did not happen to mention them, and only said when they should break up which was always before sufficient'. At last William himself hired a horse and rode over from Hawkshead to see what had happened. So it came about that William's first meeting with Dorothy took place before the return of the other boys; for two days at least she must have had him to herself. She was lonely, missing her Halifax friends, chafing at her grand-mother's strictness and her lack of freedom. The 'strange and wayward wight' who came into her life that day, however un-welcome he was to some members of the household, found a place prepared for him in his sister's heart at least, and she soon found that when William sat beside her talking, even a letter to her dear Jane had to be postponed, while every moment that could be stolen from work under her grandmother's eye was spent with him. As for William, the rediscovery of Dorothy after nine years 'separation desolate' was like 'a gift then first bestowed'.[1] Her companionship proved 'a joy above all joys', 'another morn risen on mid-noon', the crowning happiness of a happy boyhood—for William was really intensely happy in spite of Uncle Kit. Together they rambled about the country-side, loving especially the banks of the Eamont—the river that links Ullswater with the Eden—and the ruins of Brougham Castle that stood beside it, where they could live over again their earlier adventures in the castle of Cockermouth. They scrambled about it and lay on the top of the tower in the July sunshine, 'listening to the wild flowers and the grass' that then fledged the old walls with a beauty that a more careful generation has since not suffered to remain.[2] And together they read the volume of poems by a young Scottish poet, which had appeared in the previous year. It was called *Poems, chiefly in the Scottish Dialect;* it was published at Kilmarnock, and the name of the author was Robert Burns. Dorothy's friend Jane Pollard had already recommended

---

[1] *Prel.* VI, l. 203. Wordsworth appears from the context to place their meeting during his first long vacation in 1788, but it is clear from Dorothy's letters that it took place in 1787.

[2] Ibid., ll. 95–223, and corresponding 1805 text. Wordsworth states that the Eamont was 'hitherto unnam'd in Song', but in 1824 a long poem to that river appeared in *Tours of the British Mountains* by Thomas Wilkinson, the Quaker of Yanwath near Penrith.

it to her, and William had read and admired it; he now procured a copy from the Penrith book club and together they read
in it during their walks. It is almost impossible to over-estimate
the effect of Burns' poems on Wordsworth. His own poems
written many years after,[1] commemorating Burns's fame, bear
their own witness to the passionate quality of his regard, while,
as he said, 'familiarity with the dialect of the border counties of
Cumberland and Westmorland made it easy for me not only
to understand but to feel them'. The character, both in subject-
matter and in versification, of the poetry of his own mature
years is often drawn from Burns,[2] while Burns' proud claim that

> My Muse, tho' hamely in attire,
> May touch the heart,

became his own faith and doctrine. Long afterwards he declared
that Burns and Cowper, 'two great authors', together with
Percy's *Reliques*, 'powerfully counteracted the mischievous influence of Darwin's dazzling manner', and kept his imagination
free from 'the extravagance of the earlier Dramas of Schiller'.

It must have been now, or very soon afterwards, that Wordsworth added to *The Vale of Esthwaite* some lines celebrating his
affection for his sister—the first of many tributes to her. None
ever excelled these in strength of feeling.

> Sister, for whom I feel a love
> Which warms a Brother far above,
> On you, as sad she marks the scene,
> Why does my heart so fondly lean?
> Why but because in you is given
> All, all, my soul would wish from Heaven?
> Why but because I fondly view
> All, all that Heav'n has claimed, in you?

He was evidently receiving from Dorothy, besides a most
delightful companionship of mind, the tenderness and strength
of affection which he associated with the memories of his mother,
whom 'Heaven had claimed' nine years before. The brother and
sister were united almost as much by the sadness of their

---

[1] *At the Grave of Burns*, and *Thoughts suggested the Day Following*, etc., the
second and third of the *Memorials of a Tour in Scotland, 1803*. Neither was written
as early as 1803. See below, p. 593.

[2] e.g. the three 'Daisy' poems of 1802.

orphanhood as by the joy of mutual harmony of spirit and warmth of heart.

Dorothy took William's part in all the difficulties of the Penrith household, and his enemies became hers. 'I absolutely dislike my Uncle Kit', she wrote, 'who never speaks a pleasant word to one and behaves to my brother William in a particularly ungenerous manner.' The worst grievance was that when August came and the younger boys went back to school, Uncle Kit refused to allow William to remain at Penrith with his sister, and sent him back with the others to Hawkshead, although he had really left school and was about to go up to Cambridge.

William's early resentment of his uncle's authority unfortunately led to a settled hostility between the two which was never overcome. Christopher Cookson's marriage in 1788 to a Miss Charlotte Cust of Penrith did not improve the situation. She and her sisters, said Dorothy, were 'a mixture of ignorance, pride, affectation, self-conceit, and affected notability . . . so ill-natured too'. Worst of all, when the marriage took place, Uncle Kit, probably at the request of the Custs, allowed or encouraged his aged mother to present £500 to his bride, although he had the certainty of succeeding on his mother's death to the Newbiggin estate. William never forgave him. The £500, he considered, ought to have been bestowed on the orphaned grandchildren. Years after his uncle's death, he was still complaining to his brother Christopher of the 'injustice' they had received from him, and when Christopher Cookson, now Crackanthorpe, died unexpectedly at Newbiggin Hall in 1799, he would not pay a visit of condolence to his widow.[1]

It would, however, be unfair to suppose that Mr. Cookson was ill-disposed towards the children in a general way. He constantly helped and advised Richard in the management of the Sockbridge property; he assisted Christopher in his career at Cambridge, while Dorothy, to her own great surprise, received an unexpectedly kind welcome from him when she visited him at Newbiggin Hall in the spring of 1795. She charitably concluded that his faults were 'chiefly owing to his wife', and that 'when left entirely to the workings of his own mind I am sure he would always act well'.

[1] See below, p. 448.

Their uncle was, unfortunately for the Wordsworths, a supporter of the other great political chieftain and landowner of
the district, the Duke of Norfolk. He had, Dorothy complained,
said so many disrespectful things in public of Lord Lonsdale
that that nobleman was much incensed, and his inclination to
do justice to John Wordsworth's children would be, she feared,
by so much diminished. So the political rivalries of two great
factions played their part in the Wordsworths' story also.

The effect of this uncongenial atmosphere at Penrith was to
draw the orphans so closely together as a family that in after
years in spite of differences of temperament they never thought
of acting separately or selfishly where their interests as a family
were concerned. Richard, the eldest, left school in 1785 and
went immediately to London to become a solicitor: he was not
much at Penrith during that first summer of the reunion of the
brothers and sister. His habits of procrastination in business
(for he acted as their lawyer and financial adviser) often drove
William and Dorothy to exasperation; entreaties to him to
'bring my Uncle Crackanthorpe to a settlement', or 'let me
know what you have done respecting Robinson Wordsworth's
claims' are a constant theme in their letters to him to the end
of his life. He seldom paid them a visit though they were constantly inviting him, and it is clear that he thought their habits
to say the least of it Bohemian. But he was their eldest brother;
there was never any thought of not trusting Richard with their
affairs, and it was to Richard that William uttered the heart-
broken cry when John was drowned in a shipwreck: 'God keep
the rest of us together! The set is now broken.'

John was already in 1787 destined for service at sea with
the East India Company, having interest through his uncle at
Whitehaven and his cousin John Robinson. Even in these early
years we get glimpses of his unselfishness and his affectionate
admiration for William. 'John, poor fellow,' wrote Dorothy,
'says that he shall have occasion for very little' (of the money
available for educating the young people): '£200 will be
enough to fit him out, and he should wish William to have the
rest for his education.' William at this time thought that he
too would become a lawyer, but it would be 'very expensive',
and besides he had already begun to suffer from the acute headaches and pain in his side which beset him throughout his

creative years—a kind of tribute exacted by Nature in return for the intensity of imaginative and perceptive vision with which he was endowed.[1] So the four talked and lamented and planned in the mid-summer weeks of 1787, the conclusion of all being, for Dorothy, that her brothers were the most delightful boys, and so clever that once their education was completed and they were 'put forward in the world' there could be no doubt of their succeeding. 'And for me, while they live I shall never want a friend.'

At Penrith at this time 'another maid there was', who had already attracted William's interest and contributed to his pleasure. This was Mary Hutchinson. It was perhaps of her that he wrote in *Beauty and Moonlight* in elaborate and inappropriate similes in which the image is always that of some natural form accurately observed.

> 'Twas twilight and the lunar beam
> Sail'd slowly o'er Winander's stream.
> As down its sides the waters stray'd
> Bright on a rock the moonbeam play'd
> It shone half-shelter'd from the view
> By pendent boughs of tressy yew . . .
> So shines her forehead smooth and fair
> Gleaming through her sable hair.[2]

It should, however, perhaps be noted that Mary Hutchinson's hair was not 'sable' but brown.

Mary Hutchinson was at this time living at Penrith with two of her sisters, Margaret and Joanna, and her youngest brother George, under the care of her mother's sister, Elizabeth Monkhouse. For the Hutchinsons, like the Wordsworths, were now orphans, though they were more pleasantly placed in the world, having a most affectionate grandfather at Penrith, old John Monkhouse, and another equally well-disposed in Durham who eventually took them all under his roof. They were besides free from any complication like the Lowther debt. When Dorothy Wordsworth came to Penrith she at once renewed the friendship of her earliest schooldays with the Hutchinson sisters. They were the only girls there with whom she could be

---

[1] *E.L.* 2, p. 7. D.W. to J.P., Aug. 1787.
[2] *P.W.* i, p. 263.

really intimate and who could reciprocate her sorrows and her hopes. Later she said that 'in the absence of my brothers their company was the only agreeable variety that Penrith afforded'. Dorothy's affection for her brother William was from the beginning of so intense and intimate a quality that it might easily have become a sinister, consuming thing. But she knew no jealousy. If she disliked those who were opposed to him, those whom her brother loved she loved also, richly and unselfishly, sometimes to her own cost. With Mary Hutchinson she now formed a close friendship which accepted and survived all the dangers in which their common love for William might have involved them. This friendship between the two who most loved him was one of the many fortunate circumstances which make his life seem like one blessed by a benevolent Providence, Not indulgently, or excessively, but at critical periods and with wonderful appropriateness he received exactly what he most needed for his growth as a poet and his happiness as a man.

His love for Mary at this time was rather a happy experience of a new pleasure than a great passion. Indeed, even when he took her for his wife it was with a deep and secure affection rather than with a lover's fire. De Quincey said afterwards that she was 'neither handsome nor even comely', but her 'sweetness all but angelic' and her 'sunny benignity' more than made up for her physical plainness. Another quality, in a sense negative, may have impressed Wordsworth. She was a being quieter and less highly strung than Dorothy; peaceful rather than stimulating. She, and not (as is usually supposed) Dorothy, is described in the twelfth book of *The Prelude*, after those lines in which Wordsworth describes his own 'appetite' and 'greed' for Nature in the disturbed years after his return from France.[1]

> And yet I knew a maid
> A young enthusiast, who escaped these bonds;
> Her eye was not the mistress of her heart;
> Far less did rules prescribed by passive taste
> Or barren intermeddling subtleties

[1] *Prel.* XII, ll. 151–62. That Mary is meant is clear from a variant reading in which he says that 'her years ran parallel with mine'. Mary was born in the same year as Wordsworth; Dorothy not till nearly two years later. Besides, Dorothy's circumstances were not 'genial', nor could she be said to enjoy 'perfect happiness of soul'.

Perplex her mind; but, wise as women are
When genial circumstance doth favour them,
She welcomed what was given and craved no more;
Whate'er the scene presented to her view
That was the best, to that she was attuned
By her benign simplicity of life
And through a perfect happiness of soul.

Recalling afterwards the summer holidays spent wholly or partly at Penrith in 1788 and 1789, it is clear that he did not always remember whether his walks and rambles were with Mary alone or with Mary and Dorothy together.[1] The happiness they shared was that of vigorous and resilient youth, moving in a world where almost everything was a source of delight. William, the central figure of the trio, was above all happy in the possession of that visionary faculty whereby he saw 'into the life of things'. It was growing in intensity and interest during his last four years at school. No poet has ever endeavoured to describe and analyse so honestly the progress of his own poetic and imaginative life, and although allowance must be made for the more settled picture drawn by memory twenty years later, there need be no doubt of the main outlines found in the second book of *The Prelude*, for they are consistent with one another, and with the picture that emerges of Wordsworth in his early manhood before the encounter with the dark things of the world.

One of the most important developments in these last school-years was an increasing delight in the 'transitory' or seasonal qualities and appearances of things; having learnt to love his landscape and all that it contained, the changes that the seasons or the weather brought became of interest in themselves; the 'minuter properties' of things, their colour, shape, and texture were delightful to him and left upon his mind 'a register of permanent relations' to be recollected when the actual appearance was past. He had reached the stage when 'all knowledge is delight'.[2] With this sense of the beauty of all change came an awareness of the infinite 'differences', unnoticed unless sought

[1] e.g. *Prel.* XII, ll. 261–6, where he describes walking on Penrith Beacon with 'the loved one at my side'—a correction from the earlier text: 'those two dear ones, to my heart so dear'. In 1788 Dorothy was still at Penrith, but by 1789 she had gone to live in Norfolk with her uncle the Rev. William Cookson, rector of Forncett. Mary went to Durham in 1789, but we do not know in what month.
[2] Ibid. II, ll. 284–93.

for with the eye of love, in Nature: the variety of leaf, rock, and
sky that made up the mystery of the earth. Sense-perception was
now with him reaching its full development: it had upon it still
the dew of youth and innocence: it was not yet, as for a time it
later became, the 'lust of the eye' seeking only a kind of physical
pleasure: it was the source for him also of 'sublimer joy'. This
came to him through ear as well as eye, in darkness as well as
light. He had always loved nocturnal expeditions, and now it
seems he sought darkness and solitude in darkness in order to
listen to sounds that were almost beyond aural sense.

   Of all his senses, that of hearing seems to have brought to
Wordsworth the subtlest and most spiritual delight, whether
it was sound or silence that he 'heard'.

                    The ear hears not,
he wrote once,

                          and yet I know not how,
          More than the other senses does it hold
          A manifest communion with the heart.[1]

So in these Hawkshead days he tells us,

          I would walk alone,
          Under the quiet stars, and at that time
          Have felt whate'er there is of power in sound
          To breathe an elevated mood, by form
          Or image unprofaned; and I would stand,
          If the night blackened with a coming storm
          Beneath some rock, listening to notes that are
          The ghostly language of the ancient earth,
          Or make their dim abode in distant winds.[2]

Sometimes he expresses visual images in terms of sound. Thus
we find moonlight compared to 'a strain of music' which

          seemed to sink into his very heart.[3]

But perhaps the most illuminating of all his descriptions of the
power of sound as it affected him in boyhood are these lines
describing the sound of wind in some fir-trees:

          There was a spot,
          My favourite station when the winds were up,
          Three knots of fir-trees, small and circular,

[1] *P.W.* v, p. 343. Fragment, probably written in 1798.
[2] *Prel.* II, ll. 302–10.
[3] *P.W.* v, p. 341. Fragment, probably written in 1798.

Which with smooth space of open plain between,
Stood single, for the delicate eye of taste
Too formally arranged. Right opposite
The central clump I loved to stand and hear
The wind come on and touch the several groves
Each after each, and thence in the dark night
Elicit all proportions of sweet sounds
As from an instrument. 'The strains are passed',
Thus often to myself I said, 'the sounds
Even while they are approaching have gone by,
And now they are more distant, more and more.
O listen, listen, how they wind away,
Still heard they wind away, heard yet and yet,
While the last touch they have upon the sense
Is sweeter than whate'er was heard before,
And seems to say that they can never die.'[1]

Here we have a glimpse, not only of the extraordinary acuteness of Wordsworth's senses, but of how his mind seized upon his sensations, described them to himself and as it were extracted from them the last drop of delight and wonder. From this kind of communion, he declares, he drank the 'visionary power'. This, it seems, was an exalted state of feeling, independent of anything seen, whose chief characteristic was 'a sense of possible sublimity', of unattained majesty that called perpetually to his 'growing faculties'. It was a state of mind which recurred often during his youth, and about which he was not ashamed of being obscure. The thing itself was 'obscure', indescribable; yet he believed it to be of great importance, no mere projection of youthful egotism. Rather it was a perpetual invitation; a voice saying 'Come up hither'.

It seems that Wordsworth's mind at this time was both abnormally receptive and abnormally creative. The experience, already considered, of his mind becoming like the surface of a lake in which the exterior world was reflected with dream-like clarity, apparently often came upon him, particularly in the silence of his early morning walks when he stole out of Ann Tyson's cottage, 'before the vernal thrush was audible', and sat on a hill looking over the little vale as it lay 'quiet in an utter solitude'. But at other times this passive condition gave way to something more active and creative: he found that he possessed

---

[1] Ibid., p. 342.

'a superadded soul', 'a plastic power', 'a forming hand', through
which sometimes he gave to the natural forms around him a new
and more splendid life.

> An auxiliar light
> Came from my mind which on the setting sun
> Bestowed new splendour, the melodious birds,
> The fluttering breezes, fountains that ran on
> Murmuring so sweetly in themselves, obeyed
> A like dominion and the midnight storm
> Grew darker in the presence of my eye.[1]

Here was an experience with which Blake himself might have
claimed affinity, when he said he did not see the sun as 'a round
disc of fire something like a guinea', but as 'an Innumerable
company of the Heavenly host, crying "Holy, Holy, Holy"';
and his severe judgement of Wordsworth as 'the Natural Man
rising up against the Spiritual Man continually', might have
been proportionately modified.

This power in Wordsworth had a double quality. Usually it
was 'subservient strictly to external things'—spiritualizing and
glorifying them. But at other times it was

> Rebellious, acting in a devious mood,
> A local spirit of its own, at war
> With general tendency.[2]

Here, perhaps, we have a reference to that 'shy spirit' of fancy
and whimsical invention, a kind of lighter imaginative faculty,
from which Wordsworth usually in later years turned away as
being too capricious and almost frivolous, but at times in his
great creative period allowed to

> leap
> from hiding-places ten years deep,[3]

and which when he did so was responsible for some of his most
characteristic though not his greatest poetical productions, such
as *The Idiot Boy* and *The Waggoner* and the Prelude to *Peter
Bell*. The gayer spirit in Wordsworth should not be forgotten,
and here he confesses that it was with him from his earliest days
though he generally refused to give it rein.

The general result of the growth of the imaginative and

---

[1] *Prel.* II, ll. 368–374.   [2] Ibid., ll. 364–6.
[3] *P.W.* ii, p. 204, *The Waggoner*, ll. 211–12.

creative spirit in Wordsworth during these years was to fill him with a pure and intense reverence—'obeisance' and 'devotion' he calls it—for the mystery of Nature; 'religious love' was the quality of life with which he 'walked' with her. And with the 'obeisance' went also 'transport'—a joy that reached its climax as he perceived what seemed to him the unity of all life and his own unity with all that partook of 'the sentiment of Being'. As he looked back he remembered the very year in which this revelation came to him. It was his seventeenth, that is, the year 1786. He had become aware of Nature's 'infinite variety', of the beauty of her changing face. Now to that perception was added another and in some ways a contrasting one:

> In all things now
> I saw one life and felt that it was joy.[1]

He was careful afterwards to allow that the overwhelming sense he had of 'affinity' and of 'brotherhood' with 'all that moves and all that seemeth still' might have been the result of unconsciously transferring to 'unorganic natures' his own enjoyment of all things. Nevertheless, it was also perhaps 'the power of truth coming in revelation', and, whatever the secret of the mystery, the result was a state of ecstasy—'bliss ineffable'.

The power to receive into one's mind a landscape in such a manner that it was invested with the intensity of a dream; to bestow new splendour on the setting sun; and finally to share in the essential harmony of Being—these were no mean spiritual achievements for a lad of sixteen or seventeen years. No wonder he was happy. The grandparents at Penrith, Uncle Kit, and his uncertain future were only like the disagreeable figures and obstacles in his favourite fairy-tales whose discomfiture makes the fairy prince's progress more triumphant. With such faculties too, even sorrowful episodes like the premature parting with Dorothy in August lost their sting, for, if beloved landscapes could dwell in his memory and imagination with living intensity, so also could beloved persons, and she was no doubt often before him in all the ardour of her loving comradeship, as he prepared himself for Cambridge in the shortening September days, and watched the familiar fell-sides slowly undergoing their autumnal change from green to gold.

---

[1] *Prel.* II (1805), l. 430. These words were omitted in the 1850 text.

NOTE ON COLTHOUSE

It is thirty-five years since doubts began to be thrown on the traditional site of 'Wordsworth's cottage' in Hawkshead. It was Mrs. Heelis of Sawrey (Beatrix Potter) who first looked into the matter, at the time when she rescued 'Ann Tyson's Ledger' from one of her barns. Her letters to Mr. Gordon Wordsworth on the subject are among the Wordsworth papers at Grasmere.

She based her conclusions partly on an examination of the parish registers, from which she learnt that Hugh Tyson, husband of Ann, had died at Colthouse on February 28th 1784, while Wordsworth was still at school. (Ann's death there in 1796 had been previously known, but it had been assumed by Knight, Wordsworth's biographer, that she moved thither only in her last years.) Mrs. Heelis then began to re-read the early books of *The Prelude,* and came to the conclusion that it was impossible to believe that the cottage was in Hawkshead itself. In the first place Wordsworth's detailed description of the brook, 'boxed within *our garden*' cannot apply to any brook in Hawkshead. The brook there runs underneath one of the streets but not through any garden. At Colthouse the brook, descending through the wood from Claife Height, runs in an artificial channel through the garden of Holm Croft (a house built since Wordsworth's time), then free again, and then in a channel through the orchard of a much older cottage, called Green End Cottage, through part of the garden of Green End House itself and so to Pool Bridge where it joins the Black Beck.

Mrs. Heelis also noticed that Wordsworth speaks of the *walk* with Ann Tyson after his return from his first year at college, to meet their neighbours:

> She guided me;
> I willing, nay—nay wishing to be led.

This, as she says, would be much more natural if they lived outside the town.

We may add to these observations Wordsworth's own description in his note to the *Ode: Intimations of Immortality* of walking to school, and catching hold of 'a wall or tree' in the trances that overtook him. Had he lived at the traditional cottage he would not have passed any tree—scarcely indeed a wall—on his way to school, which would have been just round the corner.

He also speaks (in *Prel.* VIII, ll. 408–9) of how he could see, 'fronting our cottage',

> A smooth rock wet with constant springs
> Sparkling from out a copse-clad bank,

which, in the earlier text, he describes as

> An upright bank of wood and woody rock
> That opposite *our rural dwelling* stood.

No such wood or rock would be visible from the doorway of any cottage in Hawkshead town. On the other hand, Spring Wood at Colthouse may very aptly be so described.

From textual evidence alone therefore, it seems clear that his lodging was not in the town at all. The evidence of his conversation with Mr. Thorne, referred to in the text, about attending service at the meeting-house 'on very wet or very hot Sundays' clinches the matter. Although Wordsworth refers to it as a 'Presbyterian Meeting-house', this must be simply a slip of memory. There was never a Presbyterian *meeting-house* at Hawkshead, though there had been a Presbyterian *meeting* at Hawkshead Tower early in the eighteenth century. The old Friends' meeting-house at Colthouse was the only nonconformist place of worship in the neighbourhood of Hawkshead in Wordsworth's time.

Finally, we have the testimony of Wordsworth himself. His younger son Willy remembered being taken to Hawkshead by his father who 'pointed to a spot on the eastern side of the valley and out of the village altogether' as being the place where he had lived. Knight, to whom Wordsworth's son related this fact, did not even then see its significance.

Why the cottage in Hawkshead itself should ever have been thought to be the Tysons' is a mystery. The explanation is probably to be found in the fact that an ash-tree grew in its garden, which was identified locally as 'Wordsworth's ash-tree'. Also, it may have been a school boarding-house in those days.

The identification of the exact cottage at Colthouse is a tempting problem. The most likely existing house is Green End Cottage. It is a roomy place, quite large enough to accommodate six or eight boys, and the 'brook' runs 'boxed' through its orchard. There is no evidence that an older house stood on the site of Holm Croft which is nearer to the wood and now interrupts the view from Green End Cottage to the 'woody bank'. Other houses in the hamlet are farther from the brook.[1]

---

[1] See Knight's edition of *Wordsworth's Poetical Works*, iii, pp. 190–4, for Knight's information on the whole subject. Mr. Oliver de Selincourt, in an article in *R.E.S.*, Oct. 1945, 'Where was Ann Tyson's Cottage?' first called attention to the matter in print.

IV

ST. JOHN'S COLLEGE, CAMBRIDGE
1787–90

*Love Nature and Books; seek these, and you will be happy: for
virtuous friendship, and love, and knowledge of mankind must
inevitably accompany these, all things thus ripening in their due
season.*

WORDSWORTH to De Quincey at Oxford, March 1804

In the first week of August 1787, William returned to Hawkshead, with John and Christopher, and remained there for another
nine weeks, until his final departure for Cambridge. No doubt
much of this time was employed in copying and completing his
long poem, *The Vale of Esthwaite*. He placed two lines from
Beattie's *Minstrel* at the beginning, emphasizing the serious
character of the work:

> Adieu, ye lays that fancy's flowers adorn,
> The soft amusement of the vacant mind.

The brown leather note-book in which parts of it were copied
went with him to Cambridge.

In Ann Tyson's account-book there is an entry headed
'William Wordsworth Account' and dated August 5th 1787. It
was settled in the following January and clearly represents
William's expenses from August 5th during this last half-term
at Hawkshead. Besides the entry 'To 9 weeks Board 6s. 4d.,
Wm: £2. 17. 0', and 'Honney for William' (the latter twice
over), it records a purchase of velvet and silk, the velvet cost-
ing 5s. 6d. and the silk 4s. 9d., and 'To Robert Dixon for making,
1s. 10d.' No doubt this was for a velvet coat for evening wear
at Cambridge; the extremely moderate price is almost incredible as well as the tailor's charge.

Before leaving Hawkshead Wordsworth and three of his
schoolfellows who were also going to Cambridge presented two
books to the school library, which just now was being improved
and enlarged. The new headmaster, Bowman, seems to have
started the custom of making the boys themselves responsible

for the upkeep of the library. The boys who went on to the University were encouraged or required to present a book on leaving, and they usually clubbed three or four together to present some work of history, literature, or travel. How much choice was allowed them we do not know. Wordsworth, who described himself as 'of Cockermouth', with Robert Greenwood and Thomas Gawthorp (his fellow lodgers at Ann Tyson's), and a boy called John Millar, gave two books, Gillies' *History of Greece*, in four volumes, and Hoole's translation of Tasso's *Jerusalem* in two.[1] Wordsworth was probably responsible at least for the latter, for Tasso was a favourite with him all his life.

Early in October 1787 William finally left his 'darling Vale' and rode to Penrith where he stayed for three weeks. A change favourable to the young Wordsworths had taken place at his grandfather's house since he was there in July. His other uncle, William Cookson, the second son of his grandparents, a clergyman and a fellow of St. John's College, Cambridge, who had lately been tutor to three of the royal children, was staying there. He was a kind man, disposed to take an interest in his sister's children. He at once won Dorothy's affection by undertaking to teach her French and arithmetic, thus rescuing her from the incessant shirt-mending and other household tasks imposed by her grandmother. She sat in his room, 'where we have a fire', and he seemed as ready to let her write to Jane Pollard and to William as to learn her lessons. Such a change was unspeakably welcome to the lonely girl, and it was no passing kindness. Mr. Cookson had for several years past been engaged to Dorothy Cowper, the daughter of the vicar: when they married in the following October (1788) they took their niece to live permanently with them in their new home, Forncett Rectory, twelve miles from Norwich; it was a college living to which Mr. Cookson was preferred on relinquishing his fellowship. So the trying Penrith days, which had seemed to hold out no prospect of coming to an end as long as her grandmother lived, were over in nineteen months.

For his clever nephew William, Mr. Cookson was hopeful and ambitious. He had no doubt that William would easily

---

[1] These books may still be seen in the library of the old grammar school at Hawkshead.

obtain a fellowship; he would be ordained, and thus his independence would be assured and the problem of supporting him in life would be solved. He probably put this scheme before William when they met at Penrith; and William may well at this time have thought it preferable to his first idea of becoming a lawyer. But he was still living too vividly in his everyday experience to be much concerned about the future. Dorothy was much occupied in preparing her brother's Cambridge outfit of clothes; the days passed all too quickly; about October 23rd he set out for Cambridge with his cousin John Myers of Bampton, the son of his father's sister, bound like him for St. John's. It seems that Uncle William also accompanied them, to introduce his two nephews to his old college. They spent three or four days at York staying with John Myers' married sister. Thence, travelling by chaise, they made their way down the Great North Road. Wordsworth records one incident on the journey. When

> Southward two hundred miles I had advanced,

perhaps as the chaise entered Stamford or Grantham, he saw a prostitute and heard for the first time

> the voice of woman utter blasphemy.

The shock of such a sight and such a sound was tremendous.

> A barrier seemed at once
> Thrown in, that from humanity divorced
> The human form, splitting the race of Man
> In twain, yet leaving the same outward shape.

In his own dales, indeed, girls sometimes met with misfortune and love-children appeared; but if that happened it did not mean their banishment from the kindly farmsteads, or their degradation to a life of raucous ugliness. The pleasure of his first days at Cambridge was interrupted sometimes by the 'distress of mind' which ensued upon this sight, and by 'ardent meditation'. Soon he came to look on such things with 'a milder sadness', in which pity for the individual, and for the 'overthrow of her soul's beauty' was the predominating feeling. The experience undoubtedly helped to nourish his interest in the outcasts of society, and in time the sense of a 'split' in humanity faded and he realized that such people were not 'statues' but breathing realities, part of the living texture of society in which there could be no 'gaps'.[1]

The chaise rolled on,

over the flat Plains of Huntingdon,

through a landscape whose monotony under a grey autumn sky made a dreary impression on William. The curious outline of King's College Chapel at length broke the horizon as they proceeded along the Huntingdon Road; flat as this road had been they yet found themselves descending a hill to a still lower level: a student passed them in cap and gown and William stared at the strange figure till he was a hundred yards behind.

At length they crossed Magdalene Bridge, with the 'sleepy Cam' beneath it—how different from the Derwent, the Lowther, or the Brathay—and finally reached the Hoop Inn, just beyond the Round Church and hard by St. John's. Here the three travellers were provided with supper. It was October 30th 1787.

The College of 'the Evangelist St. John', which William Wordsworth entered as a sizar[2] on that evening held at this time a pre-eminent position among the Cambridge colleges. It had grown in numbers between 1765 and 1775 under the energetic mastership of Powell who had introduced a system unique then among the colleges of twice-yearly examinations in classics, Euclid, algebra, and Christian apologetics. These examinations were obligatory on all students. Even when the milder Chevallier succeeded him as Master, the system continued and St. John's was especially distinguished for the number of its undergraduates who became wranglers. Many students coming up from the great public schools found the Cambridge insistence on mathematics for those who coveted an honours degree a terrible ordeal, for the subject was seldom taught in such schools. Here, however, the north-country grammar schools led the way, and Wordsworth found himself in advance of most of his fellow students in his knowledge of Euclid. This proficiency he

---

[1] *Prel.* VII, ll. 382–7 and app. crit.

[2] A sizarship had by that time completely lost its connotation of servitude and was a considerable advantage to a poor boy as it enabled him to live in college on reduced terms.

afterwards blamed as one of the causes for his failure to work hard at his studies. There was no need for him to con his Euclid and he soon dropped mathematics altogether.

St. John's had associations with Hawkshead school, which, quite apart from Mr. Cookson's influence, made it natural for Wordsworth to become a member of it. Archbishop Sandys, the founder of the school, had been a Johnian, and when Wordsworth came up Edward Christian, who came from the neighbourhood of Cockermouth and had been headmaster of Hawkshead for one year (1781) during Wordsworth's time there,[1] was a resident fellow. He was a friend of Wordsworth's Uncle William, and Professor of Common Law in the University. A few years later he was engaged by the Wordsworths as their lawyer in the suit with Lord Lonsdale about the Lowther debt.[2] There were besides scholarships and prizes connected with the school. Thomas Braithwaite of Ambleside had bequeathed £250 in 1674 to the college to endow scholarships, preference to be given first to boys from the grammar schools of Kendal and Hawkshead. He had also given £30 towards the building of the third court at St. John's. William Wilson, who came up to St. John's from Hawkshead in 1770 was a benefactor both of his college and of his school with prizes in classical learning and he also endowed the Reading prizes in St. John's College Chapel.

When Wordsworth came up there were two boys from Hawkshead already at St. John's; his dear friend John Fleming of Rayrigg, who had come up in 1785, and William Penny, who came from the country at the foot of Coniston. As a freshman of his own year there was Thomas Holden Gawthorp who had lodged with him at Ann Tyson's. Two others, Thomas Maude and Thomas Jack, came up the following year. Among other Hawkshead boys who were senior to him at other colleges were Charles Farish, of Trinity and Queens', who afterwards wrote *The Minstrels of Winandermere*; Edward Joseph Birkett of Christ's (where he occupied Milton's rooms); William Raincock of Pembroke (Fleming's brother and the champion owlmimic), and Robert Hodgson Greenwood of Trinity, he who had 'blown his flute alone upon a rock' on Windermere, unconsciously giving Wordsworth one of his 'moments' of ecstatic

---

[1] There is no evidence that he ever actually resided at Hawkshead, and it is improbable that he did so.   [2] See below, p. 167.

vision and happiness. Nearly all these boys were clever, and rose to varying degrees of distinction as wranglers, or fellows of their colleges. Most of them became clergymen.

Wordsworth was thus by no means the only 'stripling from the hills' and 'northern villager' in Cambridge, and one of his amusements on coming up was to find some of these 'poor, simple schoolboys' already advancing towards academic distinctions and

> hung round
> With honour and importance.

References to Wordsworth at Cambridge from any outside source are very few: *The Prelude*, and various references in his own letters of later years, are about our only guides. There is, however, a brief but significant picture of him in a review of *An Evening Walk* (his first poem published in his name), in the *Gentleman's Magazine* for March 1794.[1] The reviewer, who is anonymous, speaks of having used Wordsworth's poem as a companion during a tour of the lakes, and then goes on:

> Of the author of this poem, the only knowledge I can boast is that of having seen him once or twice while I was his contemporary at Cambridge. The only time indeed, that I have a clear recollection of having met him, I remember his speaking very highly in praise of the beauties of the North; with a warmth indeed which at the time appeared to me hardly short of enthusiasm. He mentioned too, which appears also from the present poem, that he had received the whole of his education in the very bosom of the Lakes at a small seminary which has produced of late years in our University several names which have done it very considerable credit.

The description has some importance, for it shows that Wordsworth was not aloof and silent as is sometimes supposed, but that he talked about the Lakes almost with 'enthusiasm', the word being used in its eighteenth-century sense of extravagance,[2] and that he was proud of being a Hawkshead boy.

Of friends made in his own college, Robert Jones, the Welsh-

---

[1] Quoted in Elsie Smith, *An Estimate of William Wordsworth by his Contemporaries, 1793–1822,* 1932.

[2] Cf. Wordsworth's use of the word in his letter to Dorothy describing his tour in Switzerland in 1790: 'I am a perfect enthusiast for Nature in all her forms', *E.L.* 10, p. 34.

man, is the only one with whom he kept up a lifelong intimacy,[1]
for even John Fleming, though they were afterwards neighbours for years in Westmorland, did not fulfil the glad pledge
of Hawkshead days—'Friendship and Fleming are the same'.
Outside St. John's, Wordsworth's chief acquaintances seem to
have been mainly at Pembroke, the college of Fleming's brother
William Raincock. There Wordsworth got to know William
Mathews,[2] a London youth, the son of a worthy Methodist
bookseller in the Strand and brother of Charles Mathews the
actor. With him he carried on an intimate correspondence for
several years after leaving Cambridge, the earliest of his letters
that have survived; they shared at Cambridge an interest in
modern languages, including Italian, and the friendship would
no doubt have continued but for William Mathews' departure in
1800 for the West Indies where he speedily caught yellow fever
and died. Another friend at Pembroke was Thomas Middle-
ton, afterwards the first Bishop of Calcutta.[3] He had been at
Christ's Hospital where he had known Coleridge and Lamb. It
does not appear that he and Wordsworth ever met after their
Cambridge days. With two other Cambridge men, Basil
Montagu and Francis Wrangham, he became very intimate
after taking his degree, but he did not meet them while at
Cambridge.[4]

Wordsworth's tutor when he came up was Edward Frewen,
a friend and contemporary of his uncle and one of the eight
senior fellows of the college. Later he came under James Wood,
a brilliant mathematician of humble origins who eventually became Master of the college. Frewen procured for his pupil a
Foundress' scholarship within a week of his arrival, on the
strength no doubt partly of Uncle William's recommendation
and partly of Wordsworth's proficiency in Euclid. This must
have been a great financial help. Altogether William's college
life began auspiciously. He had cheap rooms high up on the
south side of the first court; the window of the 'keeping room'
or study looked out on to Trinity College Chapel; the bedroom
was a mere dark windowless closet, but Wordsworth used to

---

[1] See below, p. 130.

[2] See *Life of Charles Mathews*, by Mrs. Mathews, 1838, for an interesting
account of the Mathews family.

[3] *L.Y.* iii. 1846, p. 1228. W.W. to Basil Montagu, Oct. 1st 1844.

[4] See below, pp. 260, 267.

draw his bed to the doorway so that he could see the top of the chapel window under which stood the statue of Newton. And in this 'nook obscure' he lived for nearly four years 'as joyous as a lark'.[1]

Wordsworth's academic career was not distinguished. That he could have done well, if not brilliantly, in University examinations, and obtained a fellowship, can hardly be doubted; that he deliberately chose to spend his time doing other things is equally clear. At first all went well. In the college examination in December 1787 he was placed in the first class with his cousin John Myers, two men who became intimate friends of his, William Terrot and Robert Jones, and sixteen others. And again in the following June he was placed in the second class with four others. Thereafter, however, he followed a downward path. Three times in these examinations he is described as being 'distinguished in the Classic' or as having 'considerable merit in the subjects taken', but because he did not take the whole examination he was not placed. Mathematics formed part of every examination, and he simply failed to sit for these subjects. Why he did not take them is best explained in the context of his attitude towards university and college life as a whole. For Wordsworth in *The Prelude* is careful to record a sense of disappointment in what the University offered him, although he was at the same time aware that his own disposition, nourished on 'daily intercourse' with Nature's 'lovely forms', was 'ill tutor'd for captivity', for the daily occupation of steady reading. Books of course he loved, of his own choosing: but his passion for Nature had made him

> less prompt, perhaps,
> To indoor study than was wise or well
> Or suited to my years.[2]

Besides this restlessness and longing to be with 'lovely forms', he brought with him to Cambridge, as many an undergraduate with a romantic temperament has done since, an altogether too highly coloured picture of what he expected university life to

---

[1] *Corr. of Henry Taylor*, p. 123, quoting Miss Fenwick's letter describing her visit to St. John's with Wordsworth in 1839. In *Prel.* VI. l. 17, he refers to his room as 'my own unlovely cell'.

[2] *Prel.* III, ll. 354–71.

be like. Just as he had imagined London to be a 'golden city' full of wonders, so he had dreamt of Cambridge:

> I confess
> That, having in my native hills given loose
> To a Schoolboy's dreaming, I had rais'd a pile
> Upon the basis of the coming time,
> Which now before me melted fast away,
> Which could not live, scarcely had life enough
> To mock the builder.[1]

When faced with realities, he soon discovered that there were many things in his new surroundings in which he was not interested, and some which he disliked and despised. Among the latter was the custom of compulsory attendance twice a day at College Chapel. This from the first seems to have aroused Wordsworth's indignation, not because he disliked the services of the Church—there is no evidence that he did so—but because enforced attendance in an age which was largely free-thinking bred irreverence and insincerity.[2] The attack on 'compulsory chapel' in *The Prelude* is fiercest in the text of 1804, somewhat milder in that of 1805, and from that very little altered in the final text of 1850.[3] This, when we take into consideration Wordsworth's strong Anglicanism in his later years, is remarkable. It shows besides that he must have disagreed on this subject with his brother Christopher who become Master of Trinity College in 1820 and was a strong upholder of compulsory attendance.

Another distasteful, or at least unattractive, feature of academic life was the character of the senior members of the University. William knew that his Uncle William designed for

---

[1] *Prel.* III. (1805), ll. 433–9.

[2] This obvious truth did not escape me then,
Unthinking as I was. Ibid., ll. 432–3.

[3] Ibid., ll. 402–25, and 407–31. The 1804 MS. (M) has this admonition to the clergy:

> Wear not the vizard of the ancient time
> Upon a modern face, fling to the ground
> Thy monkish Caul; and run no more abroad,
> A greybeard Masquerader, dizen'd out
> In Superstition's cast-off garb; and jingling
> The holy Toy thou carri'st in thy hand
> A bell as noisy as a common Crier's
> Dull thoughted mockery!

him a career similar to his own—a fellowship following an honours degree, ordination, and eventually probably a college living. But he felt little interest in the fellows of his own college, and it does not appear that he established personal relationships with any of them, or with his tutors. At Hawkshead he had had, for a few decisive years, in William Taylor, a teacher and friend whom he had loved and revered. He found no one at Cambridge who in the least resembled him. The Master of St. John's, Chevallier, died in 1788, and, greatly to Uncle William's disappointment, young William refused to join in the custom of pinning Latin and English epitaphs to his coffin-pall, 'because', as he said afterwards, 'I felt no interest in the deceased person, with whom I had had no intercourse and whom I had never seen but during his walks in the College grounds.'[1] The fellows of the college—fifty-five in number— were almost all clergymen, and though some were men of learning, their fellowships were not attached to teaching or research, and the younger ones suffered from not having enough to do. The older fellows,

> men unscoured, grotesque
> In character, trick'd out like aged trees,

formed a curious contrast to the other old men with whom Wordsworth was familiar—people like his packman, and Hugh Tyson, and the shepherds of the fells. Of the others, the college officers seem to have been on the whole unpopular with the undergraduates, some of whom were constantly falling foul of college rules and discipline. The rest were mostly young or middle-aged clergymen, waiting until their appointment to the next college living, which would enable them to marry and settle in some country parish. They took no interest whatever in the undergraduates. It is not surprising that the life of a clergyman-don was not a prospect calculated to attract a youth like William Wordsworth, with his love of wandering and of the wild. No, already in his first year at St. John's he was conscious of what he afterwards called 'a strangeness in the mind', a feeling that he 'was not for that time nor for that place', that his destiny lay elsewhere than in a Cambridge Combination Room, though where it lay was as yet dark to him.

[1] *Mem.* i, p. 14.

Wordsworth also disliked, seriously and deeply, the whole atmosphere of competitive examinations. This dislike was, perhaps, the main obstacle in the way of his obtaining a fellowship, for the attainment of that status depended first of all on gaining a high place in the tripos. His objections to examinations arose from seeing what havoc the 'low and mean' passions, which competition engendered, wrought among the hard-reading men. He never altered his opinion on this point.

My wiser mind grieves now for what I saw,

he wrote in 1804. The spectacle of the really unpleasant pitch to which these 'passions' could be raised in the entrants for the tripos distressed him, and he turned from the company of the more ambitious men to find companionship among what he describes as 'unthinking natures' and 'pillowy minds'.[1]

Years afterwards he spoke with disapproval of 'emulation', and of his thankfulness that as a boy he was untouched by it. Competitive examination was evidently unknown at Hawkshead. He had, he said, only once felt envy there. 'It was when my brother was nearly certain of success in a foot race with me. I tripped up his heels. This *must* have been envy.' Once there, and once at Cambridge. 'This once was in the study of Italian, which I entered on at College along with ——. I was his superior in many departments of mind, but he was the better Italian scholar, and I envied him.' And he added, 'The annoyance this gave me made me feel that emulation was dangerous for *me*, and it made me very thankful that as a boy I never experienced it. I felt very early the force of the words "Be ye perfect as your Father in heaven is perfect."' The strength of his inward self-discipline and the power of his self-knowledge is here unexpectedly revealed. He knew what harmed the essential integrity of his spirit, and how to avoid it. If he had allowed himself to feel 'emulation' frequently, the sense of the communion between himself and the Universe, which was later the spring of his poetic power, would have been broken. And, unless his memory is at fault (these words were spoken in 1843) Wordsworth was more inclined even in youth than is sometimes thought to guide his conduct by meditation on the precepts of the New Testament.[2]

[1] *Prel.* III, ll. 507–8.
[2] *Grosart*, iii, p. 456. His fellow-student was probably Mathews.

Wordsworth's reference to learning Italian brings us to the question of how he employed himself during his years at Cambridge. We have seen that in the college examinations, after the first year, he did not take the mathematical papers. Yet he had been well-grounded at Hawkshead in mathematics; he was much farther advanced in Euclid than most of the other men, and he had conceived a romantic veneration for the name of Newton. He would doubtless have continued with mathematics and perhaps distinguished himself in them had not he felt the scorn and distaste which he did feel for the tripos competition. As it was, he considered that he knew enough mathematics for his own purposes. He cared indeed only for Euclid, not for algebra or arithmetic, and to Euclid he repaired, for reasons of his own, as he tells us on several occasions, both while he was at college and afterwards. Euclid, being the science of measuring the earth, had had a natural attraction at school for a boy whose eye loved to dwell on the forms of mountain peaks lifted into space, and who could even feel the rotation of the earth itself in the sensation produced by suddenly stopping himself in the midst of skating at night on Windermere. In *The Ruined Cottage*, the poem written at Racedown and Alfoxden in 1797 and 1798, and later forming the first book of *The Excursion*, Wordsworth ascribed to his 'Pedlar' many of the feelings and experiences of his own youth, among them the relation which he saw between the forms of nature and the symbols of geometry.

> While yet he lingered in the elements
> Of science, and among her simplest laws,
> His triangles, they were the stars of heaven,
> The *silent* stars; his altitudes the crag
> Which is the eagle's birthplace. . . .[1]

And so

> with these lonesome sciences

he continued to amuse the heavier hours

> Of solitude and solitary thought.

Geometry was in fact a relief and an occupation to a

> mind beset
> With images and haunted by itself.

---

[1] *P.W.* v, p. 384.

It was also something more—a framework for the conception of Deity, and from it he drew

> A pleasure calm and deeper, a still sense
> Of permanent and universal sway,
> And paramount endowment of the mind,
> An image not unworthy of the one
> Surpassing Life, which out of space and time
> Nor touched by welterings of passion, is
> And hath the name of God. Transcendent peace
> And silence did await upon these thoughts
> That were a frequent comfort to my youth.[1]

The calming effect of geometry continued long after his college days. In the unhappy years of conflict and mental turmoil after his return from France in 1793, he would turn to it as an escape from the torment of his thoughts.[2] Finally, in his dream about the Arab rider fleeing across the desert from 'the fleet waters of a drowning world', the two precious symbols borne by the mysterious rider denote the one Poetry, the other 'Euclid's Elements'.[3] It sometimes seems that Wordsworth in his poetry is apt to try to limit and even belittle the work of Science compared with Poetry, as for instance in *A Poet's Epitaph* and in some of his remarks in the preface to the third edition of *Lyrical Ballads*.[4] But the dream reveals, in the absolute equality between the two symbols, the importance in the imagination of Wordsworth of mathematical science at least.

Though Wordsworth at Cambridge 'never opened a mathematical book', and did not attempt to follow the ordinary course of university studies, he read for his own pleasure and interest a great deal, and more in his second and third years than in his first.[5] Having decided early in his career not to read for a fellowship, he could have followed what he calls 'a course of independent study', self-planned, but was withheld from doing so by fear of what his relatives would think and say. To have undertaken studies other than those expected of him seemed to him 'an act of disobedience', 'proud rebellion and unkind';[6] yet he was determined not to read for honours. Compromising with himself

---

[1] *Prel.* VI (1805), ll. 151–9.   [2] Ibid. XI, ll. 328–33.
[3] See below, pp. 250–1, and *Prel.* V, ll. 71–140.
[4] See below, p. 508.   [5] *Prel.* VI (1805), ll. 20–29.
[6] Ibid., ll. 29–41.

in a manner which he afterwards recognized as rather cowardly, he decided that it would offend his uncles less if he did nothing at all in the way of regular study than if he studied something other than the prescribed course. It was a curious decision, and as he said 'gave treacherous sanction' to his innate love of having his own way. He read at Cambridge therefore for his own pleasure and for nothing else, and when he came to assess his conduct in *The Prelude* his conclusion was that his decision was in the long run beneficial to his ultimate destiny.

> Yet who can tell,
> Who knows what thus may have been gained, both then
> And at a later season, or preserv'd;
> What love of Nature, what original strength
> Of contemplation, what intuitive truths,
> The deepest and the best, what keen research
> Unbiassed, unbewildered and unawed?[1]

We come then to the question of what Wordsworth actually read during his Cambridge years. Dorothy, writing to Jane Pollard in 1791, a few months after William had left Cambridge, begged her friend not to think that William had wasted his time. 'For he does read a great deal, and not only poetry, and other languages he is acquainted with, but history etc. etc.' Among the languages with which he was 'acquainted', she mentions, besides Latin and Greek, the modern languages, French, Spanish, and Italian. His knowledge of French and Spanish at this time was probably self-taught and confined to the grammar-book stage, but Italian he learnt thoroughly by becoming a pupil of old Agostino Isola, the Milanese, who had known Gray, the poet, well, and had taught Italian for him when Gray, as Professor of History, was responsible for the teaching of modern languages in the University. This charming and lovable man[2] had a real enthusiasm for his country's poetry. He had published an edition of Tasso's *Gerusalemme Liberata*, in 1787, and in 1778 a volume entitled: *Pieces selected from the Italian Poets by Agostino Isola (Teacher of the Italian Language) and translated into English Verse by some of the Gentlemen of the University.*

[1] *Prel.* VI (1850), ll. 35–41.

[2] Tributes to his character by Charles Lamb's friends George Dyer and Matilda Betham are to be found in an album which belonged to his granddaughter Emma Isola, the protégée of the Lambs and later the wife of the publisher Moxon. The album is now in Harvard College Library.

Wordsworth became possessed of a copy of this book, and afterwards transcribed into it his own translations of some of Metastasio's poems, made between 1802 and 1807. They are, as might be expected, better than those of Isola's other pupils.

Wordsworth's purpose in becoming a pupil of Isola was clearly to gain an entry into another literature. Italian was a highly poetic language with a rich and varied heritage of poetry, and Wordsworth's love of it was lifelong. He translated in the years of his poetic greatness from Michelangelo, Ariosto, Chiabrera, and Tasso, besides Metastasio, and read Tasso along with Spenser and Chaucer.[1] At Cambridge he loved the poetry so much that he made swift progress with the language, and Isola 'was fond' of him.[2]

Latin poetry he continued to read and enjoy, particularly the *Georgics* of Virgil, and in his early note-books are fragments of translation from Virgil, Horace, and Moschus. In the latter, abandoning translation, he describes a lark who

> Like a mountain stream
> Sings discontinuous all day long.[3]

But it was above all English poetry which he read and re-read. Milton and Spenser, already familiar, became more dear when read in the context of Cambridge. The poetry of his own day furnished him with Cowper's *Task*, and Rogers' *Pleasures of Memory*, both published in 1785. *The Task* he had probably read while still at school, for his description of the owl in *The Vale of Esthwaite* seems to be borrowed from it, though the debt is more clearly visible in his next long poem, *An Evening Walk*, written during his college vacations. Cowper, being, as Wordsworth once said, 'passionately fond of natural objects',[4] was always one of his favourite poets. Rogers' poem was on the subject of revisiting the scenes beloved by the poet in childhood, a theme dear also to Wordsworth. A lady-poet of an earlier generation, Anne, Lady Winchilsea, now also became known to him, and remained beloved all his life. Echoes from her exquisite *A Nocturnal Reverie* and from other poems of hers are found in *An Evening Walk*, and it seems not unlikely that the title of his poem and its twilight atmosphere were suggested by her,

---

[1] See *Prel.* IX, ll. 446–53.   [2] *Mem.* i, p. 14.
[3] *P.W.* i, p. 287.
[4] *E.L.* 130, p. 296. W.W. to John Wilson, June 1802.

though Collins and his great *Ode to Evening* were probably also in his thoughts.[1]

In *The Prelude* Wordsworth says that

> Beside the pleasant Mill of Trompington
> I laughed with Chaucer,

and it has hence been concluded that his knowledge of Chaucer, which was considerable, began at Cambridge. It seems probable, however, that his memory here is inaccurate. Texts of Chaucer were not easy to come by before 1795 when Dr. Robert Anderson's *Works of the British Poets* began to be published.[2] Wordsworth's brother John acquired a copy of this collection (which ran into many volumes and was not completed until 1807) and left it with Wordsworth in September 1800 at the end of his stay at Grasmere with his brother and sister. 'Through these Volumes', said Wordsworth afterwards, 'I first became familiar with Chaucer.'[3] This statement does not accord ill with another made late in life to Crabb Robinson. 'When I began to give myself up to the profession of a poet for life, I was impressed with a conviction that there were four English poets whom I must have continually before me as examples—Chaucer, Shakespeare, Spenser and Milton'; though perhaps 1800 is somewhat late to be regarded as a 'beginning' to his 'professional' labours. But in any case it is unlikely that his acquaintance with Chaucer at Cambridge was very profound.

And now in all probability Langhorne, who had been born in Westmorland, claimed Wordsworth's lifelong interest and affection. Echoes of Langhorne appear in the poetry even of Wordsworth's maturity,[4] but what attracted him chiefly now was *The Country Justice*, in which Langhorne, speaking from his own

---

[1] The debt to *A Nocturnal Reverie* will be found in l. 398 of the early text of *An Evening Walk*, *P.W.* i, p. 34. Another early poem in which he borrows an image from her is the sonnet, *Calm is all Nature as a resting Wheel* (ibid., p. 3) where the description of the horse feeding in the dark is based on a similar one in *A Nocturnal Reverie*.

[2] Modernizations of *The Canterbury Tales* were, however, current in the eighteenth century.

[3] *P.W.* iii, p. 460, note to *Yarrow Visited*.

[4] e.g. in *The Oak and the Broom* and *The Waterfall and the Eglantine*, based on Langhorne's *Fables of Flora*, in the use of the west-country term 'wilding' for crab-apple in the 'Matthew' poems (Langhorne lived most of his life in Somerset): and in the reference to Langhorne's ballad *Owen of Carron* in an unpublished verse of *She dwelt among the untrodden Ways*, *P.W.* ii, p. 30, app. crit.

experience, made an eloquent plea for the more humane treatment by magistrates of the various wrecks of humanity who came before them, beggars, gipsies, and homeless women. Without Langhorne Wordsworth would scarcely have approached so confidently the theme of his *Female Vagrant*, and now in his college years he drew partly on him for the figure of his Beggar-woman in *An Evening Walk*. Later he said of *The Country Justice* that it was 'the first poem, unless Shenstone's *Schoolmistress* be excepted, that fairly brought the Muse into the company of common life'.[1]

Life in Cambridge could not fail to arouse enthusiasm and interest in a boy of romantic temperament with a strong love for the mystery and charm of vanished centuries. At Cockermouth and Brougham Castle and in the ruins of Furness Abbey he had felt all the spell of antiquity in its 'Gothic' manifestations; the charm and melancholy of those remains of whose history enough was known to kindle the romantic imagination, and not enough to trouble it. In Cambridge the past was a more living reality; the buildings he lived in, the great names associated with them, carried the mind indeed back into the past, but without any breach of continuity with the present. There was something to him profoundly moving in the thought that Spenser and his own 'divine Milton' had been young scholars here like himself. They were henceforth 'the more beloved', less unapproachable in the isolation of their genius, more human.

Something of this more easy feeling was no doubt delighting him when he attended, soon after he came up, a wine-party in Milton's rooms at Christ's, then occupied by one of his Hawkshead acquaintances, Birkett. This, as is well known, was the one occasion on which the University or any other place saw Wordsworth the worse for liquor. The impression given by his description in *The Prelude* is that he toasted Milton's name again and again till he was dizzy; the earlier text, however, makes it clear that the toasts were all 'within my private thoughts', not uttered aloud, and therefore quite unsuspected by his companions. So sacred was the name of Milton to him! His intoxication would appear to have been extremely mild for he was sober enough to run, with surplice bundled under his arm, straight back to St. John's in time for evening chapel. Later, in a letter

[1] *L.Y.* ii. 1199, p. 829. W.W. to S. C. Hall, Jan. 15th 1837.

of good advice to young De Quincey at Oxford, he said that 'the manners of the young men were very frantic and dissolute' when he was at Cambridge, and college and university records bear this out. Two undergraduates were charged with the murder of a drayman during Wordsworth's first year. Drunkenness and riotous behaviour were common among the richer men, who then formed a large proportion of the undergraduate population, but Wordsworth and most of his friends were too poor to live extravagantly, though at Cambridge, as at Hawkshead, Wordsworth could be sociable enough. The equalitarianism of Cambridge life, where no differences of rank or wealth or university status affected the social intercourse of the students, even in that aristocratic age, was in many ways a happy prolongation of the freedom and fellowship of the little 'republic' of schoolboys and shepherds he had left behind at Hawkshead.

Sociability and wine-parties made no difference to the hidden life of imagination. He tells us in *The Prelude* that when he first came up to St. John's there was a short period of 'dazzle', very exciting and pleasant, in which he settled into his new life and surroundings with a zeal that scarcely left time for reflection, and then

> As if with a rebound my mind returned
> Into its former self.

The inward life of intense communion with Nature was taken up, with scarcely any break, in new surroundings, and he made the joyous discovery that his mind did not depend on mountain-landscapes and lakes for its inspiration. The 'level fields', the fens, and chalk hills to the east and south, with the 'blue concave' of sky overhead were almost as fruitful a theatre of vision and contemplation as the shores of Esthwaite or Windermere or the crags of Yewdale and Coniston. To them he would repair, to resume intercourse with the mystery of Being. He found that his change of surroundings made his mind more active; it was less dependent on local affections, more aware of 'universals', and of its own inner powers both of synthesis and discrimination.

> As if awaken'd, summon'd, rous'd, constrain'd,
> I look'd for universal things; perused
> The common countenance of earth and heaven,
> And, turning the mind in upon itself,
> Por'd, watch'd, expected, listen'd.

The 'one life' feeling continued in an even intenser form; nothing was dead, or isolated; the very stones, if they did not 'cry out', were endowed with 'moral life' and 'respired with inward meaning'. The 'visitings' too from a reality beyond the visible world continued, strange 'incumbencies' which came from

> the Upholder of the tranquil Soul
> Which underneath all passion lives secure
> A steadfast life.

From the security of this 'central peace' he became intensely sensitive to all the changes of Nature's moods, whether storm or calm, as a lake reflects every passing motion of the clouds. And he rejoiced continually in the possession of a private happiness as incommunicable to others as the happiness of a lover accepted by the beloved or of some soul who has seen the Beatific Vision.

> Unknown, unthought of, yet I was most rich—
> I had a world about me—'twas my own;
> I made it, for it only lived to me
> And to the god who look'd into my mind.[1]

Such were his ecstasies that he could not always restrain looks and gestures of delight when in the company of others. Some people, he says, thought him mad. Yet

> it was no madness—

but a vision of a truth more wonderful than that of the philosophers,

> which spake perpetual logic to my soul.[2]

He had as yet no desire—probably no thought—of recording such experiences in verse, any more than he had of describing them to another person. He desired to write poetry, but when he began to do so, it was of his outward, not his inward, vision that he wrote. And the first year of his undergraduate life passed away without adding anything material to his stock of verse. It was his first long vacation that broke the silence. As it was not usual then for undergraduates to 'go down' for the Christ-

---

[1] *Prel.* III (1805), ll. 141–4.

[2] 'Logic', the science of relationship in rational thinking, was used by him here of deliberate purpose. To him the relation of every natural object with others and of the whole natural world with the human mind was the chief delight of his meditations.

mas and Easter vacations, and as in any case he was two hundred miles away from any place that could receive him, he stayed in Cambridge until the end of the academic year in early June. He then travelled north alone, intent not on visiting first Penrith and Dorothy, but simply on returning to Hawkshead and Colthouse and Ann Tyson's cottage. On the way, however, he 'peeped' into Dovedale, and left in a note-book a fragment of a description of it in prose, minute in its visual detail, yet simple in style, curiously anticipatory of his sister's letters and journals. The fragment is as follows:

Cambridge to Hawkshead. June 8th.[1] Saw nothing particularly striking till I came to Ashburn. Arrived there on Sunday evening and rode over to Dovedale. Dovedale is a very narrow valley, somewhat better than a mile in length, broken into five or six distinct parts, so that the views it affords are necessarily upon a small scale. The first scene that strikes you on descending into the valley is the River Dove fringed with sedge and spotted with a variety of small tufts of grass hurrying between two hills, one of which about 6 years ago was clothed with wood; the wood is again getting forward; the other had a number of cattle grazing upon it—the scene was pleasing—the sun was just sinking behind the hill on the left—which was dark—while his beams cast a faint golden haze upon the side of the other.[2] The River in that part which was streamy[3] had a glittering splendour which was pleasingly chastized[4] by the blue tint of intervening pieces of calm water; the fringe of sedge and the number of small islands, with which it is variegated. The view is terminated by a number of rocks scattered upon the side of one of the hills of a form perfectly spiral.[5]

From Ashbourn he went directly north, by coach to Kendal

[1] Probably 1788. From *Prel*. VI, ll. 190–3, it would appear that his visit to Dovedale took place in his *second* long vacation (1789), not his first: it seems most likely, however, that his visit to his Uncle William and to Dorothy at Forncett Rectory near Norwich in 1789 took place at the beginning of the long vacation that year, not at its end; for reasons of distance and geography it could not very well have taken place in the middle. See de Selincourt's note, ibid., p. 608F (addenda to Notes). Thus, the 'June 8th' of his visit to Dovedale would mean June 8th 1788. Moreover, June 8th, 1788, was a Sunday.

[2] The similarity of this description to that in *The Vale of Esthwaite* and *Dear Native Regions* is striking. See above, p. 48.

[3] A word used by Coleridge; 'the streamy nature' of the associative faculty. *Anima Poetae*, p. 55. Wordsworth's meaning must be 'rapid' or 'rushing'.

[4] The meaning of this word is obscure, but in another manuscript it is clearly used in the sense of 'chequered'.

[5] Cf. *Prel*. VI, l. 193. 'Dovedale's spiry rocks.' Gray's *Journal* speaks of 'a towering crag that spired up to equal the neighbouring cliffs'.

where he spent the night; the next morning he set out to walk
across the six miles of moorland road to Windermere Ferry and
so back to his 'beloved Vale'. It does not appear that he had a
thought of seeking any other lodging than Ann Tyson's cottage.
He returned to it naturally as to his home. Ann welcomed him
with tears of pride, and would not be content until she had
herself led him across the fields to the little town, to show off
her fine young Cambridge scholar to neighbours and schoolboys.
William felt a little embarrassed on meeting his schoolfellows
again;

> my habiliments,
> The transformation and the gay attire

in which he appeared fresh from fashionable Cambridge and in
particular his powdered hair called forth no doubt some laughter
from the boys. At Colthouse every beloved detail in house and
garden offered itself to his home-coming mood; the 'broad stone
table' under the pine-tree, the brook dimpling down its paved
channel; most of all perhaps his own bed at night where once
more he lay down to watch and dream and at last to sleep. But
on that first evening there was more to do before he sought his
bed. About sunset-time he wandered out alone, except for a
terrier who followed him as of old, into the wood above the
hamlet and sat down, where he could see

> The long lake lengthen out its hoary line,

and there fell into an 'abstraction', while the grey skies darkened
and a cold wind took all outward comfort from the scene.[1] But
it was not the view that absorbed him, but what was happening
in himself. It seemed to him that he was receiving, without any
special sense of need, inward gifts of comfort and strength.

> A comfort seemed to touch
> A heart that had not been disconsolate:
> Strength came where weakness was not known to be,
> At least not felt; and restoration came
> Like an intruder knocking at the door
> Of unacknowledged weariness.

And in the sense of security which they brought, came 'glim-
mering views' of the creative power of the 'undecaying mind'.

[1] 'For cold and raw the air was, and untuned', *Prel.* IV, l. 145.

Truly, all things were becoming possible to him. Other hopes too, of a more homely nature, grew within him:

> milder thoughts, of love,
> Of innocence, and holiday repose;

Mary, Dorothy, a cottage perhaps by Grasmere; and farther away a heroic death,

> a peaceful end
> At last, or glorious, by endurance won.

And then, in the midst of the dream, he was recalled to the present by a curious noise close to him, 'a breath-like sound', something like the panting of a dog. Was it the dog? He looked round, but no living creature was near him; the dog had wandered away. Perhaps it was the wind in the hazel-trees, or perhaps something less usual. Had he who had felt the earth herself roll

> with visible motion her diurnal round

now heard Nature breathing?

William spent nine weeks of the vacation at Colthouse, weeks in which for the first time he was able to exercise comparison and judgement on himself and on his surroundings. He had been away into a different world; he had come back with affections as deep as ever for the same scenes and faces, but in some respects modified by contact with other scenes. In the first place his delight in the 'plain-living' human beings around him was greater than before; he was able more subtly to enjoy all old Ann's unselfconscious charm by contrast with the sophistication or the coarseness of university life. She was really dear to him; he knew it now all the more certainly for having seen other kinds of womanhood, for Cambridge contained some of a notorious kind. Lovingly he watched her daily proceedings—they were 'affectionate without uneasiness'; her weekly walk to church or meeting-house, clad in sedate black velvet bonnet and short mantle like a 'Spanish Cavalier's'. So he delighted in the look and actions of the shepherds and woodmen more than before; they had a beauty and a dignity unparalleled by anything he had seen afar.

And the great universe of earth and sky, so familiar and beloved, was dearer too. It is not easy exactly to determine from his later description[1] wherein he thought the difference lay, but the key to it lies in the word 'human-heartedness'. Hitherto he had rejoiced in his landscape as in an exclusively personal possession; it was to him a discovery of intense wonder and delight, unshared with others, and in which it had not occurred to him that others could share. He had been, he says, like an angelic being from another world discovering the earth for the first time. Now his increased interest in and love for the human occupants of his landscape began to show him that earth and sky were not his inheritance only but theirs as well. Jupiter might indeed be for ever 'my own belovèd star', but the heavenly bodies were all of them 'acquaintances of every little child', and in this faith he lived and wrought when the time came for him to be the poet of the human heart.[2]

An unexpected but perfectly natural accompaniment of this new 'human-heartedness' was a new interest in 'the lighter pleasures'. On his return to Hawkshead after a year in Cambridge he took to dancing with a will, partly because the country people whom he loved danced also, and he wanted to share their pleasures, and partly because, as he says, he wished the neighbourhood to know that he was something more of a 'man of the world', not simply

> A wild, unworldly-minded youth, given up
> To Nature and to books.

His clothes constantly reminded him that he was no longer a savage. He did not feel at ease in them, yet he did not discard them for his old, shabby attire, except no doubt when he went off rambling among the hills. All this was very natural, and in no way harmful, as very soon appeared, to his imaginative life, though in his later years he spoke of having been 'seduced' into frivolities and a 'vague, heartless chase of trivial pleasures'. Being a north-countryman, it was natural for him to attend both the village dance, held in a barn or loft, when the farmers' and dalesmen's sons and daughters gathered for a night of merriment to be followed by a day of toil in the hayfield or with the sheep

[1] *Prel.* IV, ll. 231–55.
[2] Havens, *The Mind of a Poet*, p. 360.

on the fells; and the country-house dance, in some well-lit and 'flower-decked room', to which the young gentlemen of the district—many of them like William Wordsworth under-graduates on vacation—came with their sisters and sweet-hearts. The dances were probably much the same in both, for the days of 'ball-room dancing' proper were still in the future, and the country dance in its many local varieties still held the field.[1] William during this first vacation attended at least one of each kind, and each became memorable to him, not for itself, but for what happened afterwards, as he made his way home across the fells.

The first was a 'promiscuous rout, a medley of all tempers', held probably at some farm two or three miles from Hawkshead. It lasted until far into the June morning, and as he made his way homewards at about four o'clock men were already going to work in field and shippon. He crossed some high ground and there the full beauty of the morning broke upon him. Far to the south he could see the gleaming stretches of Morecambe Bay, while the great mass of the Coniston and Langdale fells stood transfigured—

> Grain-tinctured, drenched in empyrean light,[2]

as the sun rose over Helvellyn. Their glory was all the more divine by contrast with the homely loveliness that lay beneath him in the fields—

> all the sweetness of a common dawn,
> Dews, vapours and the melody of birds.

His body, tired and excited by the hours of movement, readily exulted in the sudden solitude and allowed his mind to leap forward into full communion with the beauty around him. So it

[1] That this was so is clear from many references to the 'country dance' in the novels of Jane Austen. In the north it has had a continuous life.

[2] Does 'grain-tinctured' mean 'golden' (the colour of ripe grain), or, as sug-gested by Professor de Selincourt, crimson? Either colour might be true of a lake-land sunrise.

The scene of this incident has been the subject of many conjectures. Mr. Gordon Wordsworth favoured a point on the top of Hawkshead Moor, after coming up from Coniston. But it is also possible that the view was from the top of Latter-barrow Crag, between Colthouse and Windermere. In this case the dance might have been at High Wray. Another possibility is some farm to the south of Esth-waite, at Grizedale or near Satterthwaite, as the scene of the dance, the viewpoint being a height known as Sans Keldin, or possibly one rather farther to the east, above the south-west shore of Esthwaite.

had been on many another occasion, after skating, rowing, climbing. What happened now was beyond any detailed description, and perhaps not in essence very different from what had been the constant experience of his youth, though he felt it now with a new intensity.

> I made no vows but vows
> Were then made for me; bond unknown to me
> Was given that I should be, else sinning greatly,
> A dedicated Spirit.

This 'moment at sunrise' was not a conscious acceptance by Wordsworth of his vocation as a poet. The bond was 'unknown', and the interpretation put upon it in *The Prelude* is, as this one word shows, the fruit of time. Indeed, even in *The Prelude* he does not state that the 'dedication' was to poetry or to any specific work or calling, though it has always been assumed that this is what he meant. And no doubt in fact his determination to make the writing of poetry the work of his life became from this time forward more fixed. Certainly it was during this vacation that he began to write *An Evening Walk*, a poem both in form and content far more mature than *The Vale of Esthwaite* and more likely to achieve publication. But the 'moment' in itself and at the time was simply another of those 'gentle visitations' whose chief characteristic was delight. And it was, in spite of its glory, a purely 'natural' experience, not one of those strange dream-like processes when the outward appearances of things became invested with a vividness derived from the state of his own emotions. It was not another 'Penrith Beacon'. Its benediction was direct and immediate and, like so much that happened to Wordsworth, it and the feelings it engendered became a part of his imaginative life, his 'poetic memory', that could be evoked at will years after the experience itself was over and gone.

> On I walked
> In blessèdness which even yet remains.

'Even yet'—that is to say in the spring of 1804.

The other memorable event of this vacation happened shortly before his return to Cambridge in October.[1] Again he was

---

[1] The incident is described in *Prel.* IV, ll. 370–469, and is one of the earliest descriptions to be written down, the manuscript belonging probably to 1798. See below, p. 365.

returning home alone from a dance, weary with the 'toil' of pleasure. But in every other way this was a contrast to the morning ecstasy in June. It happened by moonlight, and its significance lay partly in its strangeness, partly in its 'human-heartedness', not in its sensitiveness to natural glories. The dance this time had been held in some gentleman's house on the shore of Windermere, very probably Rayrigg, the home of John Fleming and William Raincock. The evening had been a very gay one, for it was the regatta season; they danced till late in a room ablaze with lights. He returned alone over the ferry in the dead of a moonlit night, and as he climbed the hill between the two Sawreys he was aware of a slackening through his whole being that made him quietly conscious of the objects about him—the road (which was wet) gleaming like a river in the moonlight; the noise of the beck on his left. He was tired; his senses drank in the silence and unbroken solitude, finding in them

> A restoration like the calm of sleep
> But sweeter far.

Once more his mind became luminous, this time with a succession of mental pictures that rose

> As from some distant region of my soul
> And came along like dreams—

images perhaps of lovely scenes and places soon to be woven into poetry. He felt 'animal delight' and a quiet satisfaction in himself as they came and went—and then suddenly he was called to full attention by a presence a little in front of him on the road. There, leaning against a milestone by the roadside, every feature distinct in the moonlight like a figure in a Bewick woodcut, was the 'Discharged Soldier'.

> He was of stature tall,
> A span above man's common measure tall,
> Stiff, lank and upright:
> A man more meagre as it seemed to me
> Was never seen abroad by night or day.

Poor fellow, he was but one of many wandering the roads of England then—survivors from the American War, dismissed to find their way home, if they had homes, as best they could.

For some time Wordsworth watched him from the shelter of a hawthorn bush, fascinated and a little frightened by his ghastly thinness, his utter isolation in that strange moonlight world. It became clear that the man was suffering; he uttered low groans and talked to himself with 'a murmuring sound of dead complaint'. At length, moved as much by compassion as by curiosity, Wordsworth came forward and hailed him. The man told him his 'soldier's tale' quietly and simply, but he was feeble of body and without a lodging for the night. Wordsworth looked back at the roofs of Far Sawrey; not a light twinkled there; all were asleep. But his knowledge of the country-side came to his aid; he had friends among the woodmen and charcoal-burners; and without more ado he led the soldier through a wood across a field, to the door of a cottage where he knew he could count on a welcome at any hour. As he went he questioned his companion, as he did so many of his chance acquaintance throughout life, from the little girl in *We are Seven* to the 'Leech-gatherer on the lonely moor'. What battles had he fought in? What diseases had he suffered in the 'Tropic Islands'—isles of death as they then were? He felt his curiosity rebuked—and again we are reminded of the Leech-gatherer—by the man's courteous but strangely indifferent replies,

> as of one
> Knowing too well the importance of his theme,
> But feeling it no longer.

They reached the cottage and the stranger was kindly received. But before leaving him Wordsworth suggested to him that it was better to ask for help than to 'linger in the public ways', and received the strange and somewhat disconcerting reply:

> my trust is in the God of Heaven
> And in the eye of him that passes me.[1]

The resemblance between the Discharged Soldier and other figures that haunt Wordsworth's poetry is clear. The Old Cumberland Beggar, the Old Man Travelling, the Female Vagrant, the Sailor's Mother, above all the Leech-gatherer, all share a like pathos of solitariness, helplessness, and uncomplaining dignity of speech. They are of a somewhat different quality

---

[1] D. G. James, in *The Romantic Comedy*, p. 82, points out the kinship between Wordsworth's description of the Discharged Soldier and Keats's description of Moneta in *The Fall of Hyperion*. Both are examples of romantic 'strangeness'.

from the more independent wanderers like the Packman and the Waggoner. Their appeal is to our pity, though never to our condescension, and they themselves always have the last word, literally and morally, in every conversation. Some of them were figures of invention rather than experience; others like the Leech-gatherer and the Discharged Soldier had physical reality and no doubt did speak and act much as Wordsworth represented them.

The meeting with the Discharged Soldier marked a new step in Wordsworth's experience and moral progress. Not only were the circumstances memorable; the contrast between the gay, thoughtless scene he had left and the stark poverty and helplessness of a fellow-countryman who had been fighting and suffering on the other side of the world and was now homeless and hungry under the autumn moon; but the thing itself, the fact of there being such a person in the world, in need of his help, at the mercy of his charity, was awful, disturbing. As he walked home to Colthouse, his heart was quiet because he had left the man in comfort, but the image of him remained, having a powerful effect on his approach to 'the problem of humanity' in the years to come.

During the later weeks of this vacation Wordsworth visited his guardian-uncles at Penrith and at Whitehaven.[1] At Penrith were his sister and his sweetheart, Mary Hutchinson, and with them again he roamed the country-side, particularly the Beacon, in great happiness of spirit; revisiting the scene of his early encounter with the old gibbet, and finding that the recollection of that adventure, far from diminishing, rather enhanced 'the spirit of pleasure and youth's golden gleam' which now was 'scattered' over

> the waste
> Of naked pools, and common crags that lay
> Exposed on the bare fell.

[1] Ann Tyson's Ledger records the item 'Horsehire 1s. 6d.' in the account for this vacation; this would almost certainly be to ride to Penrith. *Prel.* IV does not record a meeting with Dorothy, but the references in *Prel.* XI, l. 317, to walks with her and Mary *together* must refer to this summer, and not to 1789, for in that year Dorothy had already left Penrith for Forncett. In the careful accounts kept by the uncles of their expenditure on behalf of their wards, the item: 'Oct 5. Share of washing at Whitehaven', in the account for 1788 of William's expenditure, proves his visit there.

Now, apparently, he was first seriously attracted by Mary.

> Another maid there was who also shed
> A gladness o'er that season, then to me
> By her exulting outside look of youth
> And placid under-countenance, first endeared.

But it was with Dorothy that he still had the closest unity of spirit. With her he climbed about in the ruins of Brougham Castle, and there, lying in some high window-embrasure, they looked forth

> And gathered with one mind a rich reward
> From the far-stretching landscape,

or simply

> Lay listening to the wild flowers and the grass.

There to her in all likelihood he confided his plans and hopes for a new poem. For when *An Evening Walk* was published four and a half years later it bore the title *An Evening Walk. An Epistle; in Verse Addressed to a young lady, from the Lakes of the North of England*, and its opening lines recall how:

> Far from my dearest friend, 'tis mine to rove
> Thro' bare grey dell, high wood, and pastoral cove.

He left Penrith probably about the middle of September and spent some weeks at Whitehaven. At the beginning of October 1788 he returned to Hawkshead, and we may imagine him leaving the high-road at Cockermouth, and taking his way along Buttermere, over the Honister Pass, and down Borrowdale to Keswick, and so on by Grasmere, Rydal, and Windermere to Hawkshead, a ramble which roughly corresponds to his own description in the opening lines of *An Evening Walk*. The two or three weeks that remained of the vacation were spent at Hawkshead mainly in writing his new poem, but also, as we have seen, in fun and dancing, until the time came for him to return to Cambridge. In an early note-book belonging to this time occurs the question—inserted among fragmentary jottings of verse and prose—'Shall I ever have a name?' His veneration for poetry, and awe of poets, which had hitherto held him back in 'instinctive humbleness', was beginning to thaw, thanks to the new 'human-heartedness' which Cambridge was giving him. There was a good deal of romantic scribbling entering various note-books, concerned mainly with storms, ruined castles, and madmen. But *An Evening Walk* was not of a romantic character at all; it was descriptive and almost topographical and written in 'heroic couplet'—a poem in fact of a classical type familiar to all readers of poetry. The eighteenth century was indeed the century in which 'landscape' came into its own, in all the arts, poetry, painting, architecture, gardening. It was the century in which guide-books began to be written for the service of tourists, with a marked emphasis on 'the picturesque'. With some of these guide-books Wordsworth was familiar[1] and when he wrote *An Evening Walk* he placed himself deliberately among the writers of the 'landscape' school.

An Evening Walk makes no attempt to describe more than his outward eye saw; it deals neither with the processes of his imagination nor the feelings of mystical union with the 'Spirit of the Universe'. Its mood is one of pleasant 'melancholy', engendered by revisiting the scenes of his childhood. The sun was gilding, for William, 'the dear hills where first he rose'; already he was seeing his boyhood as a time of careless bliss contrasting with the heavy cares, the doubtful prospects of the present.[2]

> Fair scenes! with other eyes than once, I gaze
> The ever-varying charm your round displays,
> Than when, erewhile, I taught, a happy child,
> The echoes of your rocks my carols wild . . .
> In youth's wild eye the livelong day was bright,
> The sun at morning and the stars at night,
> Alike, when first the vales the bittern fills,
> Or the first woodcocks roam'd the moonlight hills.[3]

[1] Gilpin's *Guide to the Lakes* appeared in 1789 and was among Wordsworth's valued possessions. West's *Guide* came out in 1778 and James Clarke's *Survey* in 1787. Wordsworth must have studied this very soon after publication, for ll. 175–90 of *An Evening Walk* (1793) are taken straight from it with a footnote of acknowledgement.

[2] In an early note-book occurs the following prose fragment: 'Human life is like the plate of a dial, hope brightens the future, Reflection the hour that is past, but the present is always marked by a shadow.' In *An Evening Walk* this sentiment is turned into verse as follows:

> Alas! the idle tale of man is found
> Depicted in the dial's moral round;
> With Hope Reflection blends her social rays
> To gild the total tablet of his days;
> Yet still, the sport of some malignant power
> He knows but from its shade the present hour.

[3] *P.W.* i, p. 5, *E.W.* (1793), ll. 17–26.

An Evening Walk, as is well known, is from one point of view almost an anthology of borrowings and adaptations from the landscape-poets, from Milton to Beattie.[1] Wordsworth when he published the poem called attention to some of the borrowings in footnotes, showing that they were deliberately made, and that he intended his poem to be in part a tribute to the poets whom he loved and towards whom he had felt almost a religious awe. But afterwards he valued *An Evening Walk* not for its borrowings, but for that in it which was his own. 'There is scarcely an image in it', he said in his old age, 'which I have not observed.' If the poem was in literary form a memorial to his love of the poets, it was in content and in imagery a celebration of the landscape of his school-days and of everything in it which had given him delight. The oak-tree with the setting sun behind it on the Ambleside road, the swans on Esthwaite, the shepherd calling to his dog on Dunmail Raise, the quarry-men with their laden pack-horses on the giddy slopes of Coniston Old Man and Lingmoor, the smoke from the charcoal-burners' fires, the voices of the mountain streams growing clearer as twilight hushes the sounds of day, the moon rising over Claife Height; every sight, every sound that he associated with his 'darling Vale' and the neighbouring fells finds a place in *An Evening Walk*. 'The plan of it', he also said, 'has not been confined to a particular walk or an individual place; a proof (of which I was unconscious at the time) of my unwillingness to submit the poetic spirit to the chains of fact and real circumstance.' This 'unwillingness' of Wordsworth's should be borne in mind in interpreting his later work, especially *The Prelude*, which is often chronologically inexact. The 'landscape' there is Wordsworth's mental and poetic growth and all that had fed it. In *An Evening Walk* it is all that at the age of nineteen he had learned to love.

Just as the setting sun had lit up 'the dear hills where first he rose', and given William a symbol of his mind's constant 'backward look'—so at the end of *An Evening Walk* he makes the rising moon, as she

> flings her light
> Far to the western slopes with hamlets white

---

[1] *L.*, pp. 133–47, enumerates many passages in which more or less direct borrowings are made. After his stay in France Wordsworth added a passage, ll. 129–38, from the French writer Rosset, author of *L'Agriculture. ou les Géorgiques Françaises*.

the pledge of a precious future hope which even now

> decks for me a distant scene
> (For dark and broad the gulph of time between)
> Gilding that cottage with her fondest ray,
> Sole bourn, sole wish, sole object of my way,

where he and Dorothy ('my friend') would pass 'golden days' till called to a tranquil death. Why was it now with Dorothy, not with Mary, that he was looking forward to setting up house? The brother and sister must already have been planning during this vacation that ideal existence together in pastoral simplicity which for a few years they were in fact allowed to realize. Nor was it just an idle dream, an 'escape', a fantasy. With their future so uncertain, the 'Lowther debt' unpaid and perhaps never to be settled, anything like a home for William must be a matter of speculation for some time to come. How could he contemplate marriage, or think of asking Mary Hutchinson to enter the cottage at Grasmere or anywhere else in sober earnest? But there was one whom he might ask, who herself asked no better than to step some day over that threshold and who thrilled to the prospect of poverty with William. 'Neither absence nor Distance nor Time can ever break the Chain that links me to my Brothers', Dorothy wrote to Jane some five years later; and of all the brothers one must always hold pride of place in that eager heart. 'At the conclusion of the Evening Walk', she went on in the same letter, 'I think you would be pleased with those lines "Thus hope first pouring from her blessed horn" etc. etc. You would espy the little gilded Cottage in the Horizon, but perhaps your less gloomy imagination and your anxiety to see your Friend placed in that happy situation might make you overlook the dark and broad Gulph between.'[1]

Into the peaceful landscape of *An Evening Walk* Wordsworth introduced one significant human group—a Beggar-woman and her two children, who after suffering privations of heat and cold are overtaken by a storm in which the two infants perish. In 1794, when he was revising *An Evening Walk* at Keswick, he turned this passage into a description of an actual tragedy which had occurred two years previously on Stainmore, the wild moor-

---

[1] *E.L.* 28, pp. 84, 86, D.W. to Jane Pollard, Feb. 16th 1793. *An Evening Walk* and *Descriptive Sketches* had been published a month before this letter was written.

land road that links the Eden valley with the North Riding of
Yorkshire, when 'a poor woman was found dead with two children whom she had in vain attempted to protect from the storm
in the manner described'.[1] The introduction of the Beggar-
woman was bad for the poem from a poetical point of view,
for the sixty lines he gives to her are the weakest in it, but she
is nevertheless an important figure, for she is the forerunner of
The Female Vagrant, The Mad Mother, and many another lonely
and unfortunate figure who became as characteristic of his poetry
as 'rocks and stones and trees'. His natural attraction to the
ragged vagrant world no doubt moved him to describe her, and
his admiration for Crabbe's *Village* and Langhorne's *Country
Justice* encouraged him to introduce a figure of forlorn destitution into his poem. The Beggar-woman of *An Evening Walk*
is also a first indication of Wordsworth's early 'pacifism' and
hatred of the suffering caused by war, for she has a husband who
has perished in the American war,

> Asleep on Bunker's charnel hill afar.[2]

When at length he returned to Cambridge at the end of
October, leaving the fells in all the loveliness of a mild autumn,

> Clothed in the sunshine of the withering fern,[3]

he says that he was

> not so fond
> Or eager, though as gay and undepressed
> In spirit as when I thence had taken flight
> A few short months before.

His homesick longings satisfied, he was glad enough to return
to college life. In this second year he thought much of being a
poet, of leaving

> Some monument behind me which pure hearts
> Would reverence,

---

[1] *P.W.* i, p. 29; Wordsworth's own note to the revised passage, which, however,
he did not make use of when he republished *An Evening Walk* in 1849.

[2] An alteration by 'erratum' in the first edition which originally had 'Minden's
charmed plain'—a direct borrowing from Langhorne's

> Cold on Canadian hills and Minden's plain.

[3] This line was added to *The Prelude* in a late revision. There are several attempts
to describe the coming-in of this autumn, in 'mild magnificence', in the various
manuscripts of *The Prelude.*

but still he dallied in reading and thinking about poetry rather than settled to compose it.

> I loved and I enjoyed, that was my chief
> And ruling business, happy in the strength
> And loveliness of imagery and thought.[1]

He did indeed write one poem at Cambridge, which reflects the same quietly melancholy mood in which he had begun *An Evening Walk*. Walking one evening just after sunset beside the Cam, the rosy waters in front of him and the darkening scene eastwards brought up once more his frequent mood of dread of the future. 'The following gloom' would overtake him and blot out the glow of the present. And he was oppressed already with a thought that came often in his more mature years —the thought of 'mighty poets in their misery dead'. Collins's sad life and death came vividly before him, Collins to whose lovely Odes he was indebted for much of the imagery of his early poems. But this poem[2] contained another thought—more profound and more suggestive of the undercurrents of his mind:

> O glide, fair stream, for ever so
> Thy quiet soul on all bestowing,
> Till all our minds for ever flow
> As thy deep waters now are flowing.

It was almost like a first statement of his future theme, that our successive days are rounded and governed by

> A motion and a spirit that impels
> All thinking things, all objects of all thought,
> And rolls through all things.

The Derwent, the Cam, the 'sylvan Wye'—how often did running water, river water, bring to William Wordsworth his most fruitful thoughts and feelings; how often did movement, whether of flowing water or a 'vital breeze', seem the essential image to express the subtlest and deepest experiences of his spirit.

His colloquies with Nature continued undisturbed. He found an ash-tree in the Backs under whose ivied branches he would stand at night, by moonlight, 'foot-bound' for hours, gazing up into it as he had gazed into the ash outside his bedroom-window at Colthouse. He was more withdrawn into himself and into poetry, less 'dazzled' by the social life of the University, than in

---

[1] *Prel.* VI (1805), ll. 77–79.   [2] *Remembrance of Collins. P.W.* i, p. 41.

his first year. Looking back on this time from the maturity of his fully developed taste, he criticized what he called his 'outward taste in books'—his fondness for 'classic niceties' and elegant turns of phrase, such as he was making use of in *An Evening Walk*. His 'inner knowledge'—that which came to him for instance while contemplating the ash-tree—was something altogether apart, 'sequestered' from this literary veneer. Yet the inner life did affect his reading and gradually gave him a standard of judgement. For because what came to him in times of solitude and contemplation was of the nature of real insight 'into the life of things', his mind became able to distinguish the real from the false in literature. So he declared that in spite of the mistakes of youthful taste

> the books which then I loved the most
> Are dearest to me now.

Shakespeare, Spenser, Milton, Chaucer—they had learnt to utter the very truths that he was learning from the ash-tree and all his commerce with 'living nature' and with her human representatives; they spoke with 'the loving voice', and in the end they taught him to speak with that voice also.

Early in November William had the pleasure of welcoming Dorothy to Cambridge for a day's visit. She was accompanying her Uncle William and his bride, Dorothy Cowper, on their wedding journey from Penrith to Forncett in Norfolk, which was to be her home for the next seven years. Full of delight at her sudden and quite unexpected release from the disliked life at Penrith, her day in Cambridge was a memorable one.

The buildings [she said] added to the pleasure of seeing my Brother very well and in excellent spirits delighted me exceedingly; I could scarcely help imagining myself in a different country when I was walking in the college courts and groves; it looked so odd to see smart powdered heads with black caps like helmets, only that they have a square piece of wood at the top, and gowns, something like those that clergymen wear; but, I assure you (though a description of the dress may sound very strange) it is exceedingly becoming.

When June came round again—June 1789—he went off first on a visit to the Cooksons and Dorothy at Forncett—a visit that remains shadowy and indeed somewhat uncertain as to date, for all Dorothy's letters for that year have been unfortunately lost and we should not know about it at all save for a brief reference to it in one of her letters to Jane Pollard in the following year. He found his sister happy in the freedom of country life, and the activities of a well-run parish, in which she assisted her uncle in visiting 'the poor', besides starting, in this very summer, a little Sunday school in which she taught nine little scholars— 'one very bright, some very tolerable, and one or two very bad' —in reading, spelling, and learning by heart 'prayers hymns and catechisms'. When at the following Christmas William Wilberforce came to Forncett to visit his old Cambridge friend, he was so much impressed with Dorothy's good works that he gave her ten guineas a year 'to distribute in what manner I think best among the poor', and also Mrs. Trimmer's *Oeconomy of Charity* and 'a little treatise on regeneration' for her own edification. However, Dorothy was in no way overburdened with parochial cares; she was revelling in not having too much to do, in not being constantly watched and harassed, as she had been at Penrith. 'I have leisure to read, walk and do what I please', she wrote to Jane; and William's visit could not have come at a happier time. It was to be the last he paid there for nearly eighteen months.

From Forncett he went north, making 'peeps into Yorkshire dales' on his way; probably looking at Fountains and Jervaulx, for he speaks of 'making quest for works of art'—and no 'work of art' would be so likely to attract him as a ruined abbey. It may have been now that he spent some time with Tom Hutchinson, Mary's brother, at Sockburn-on-Tees in Durham. A strange statement, in a letter written in the last year of his life, says that 'for many years before our several marriages' Wordsworth was Tom's 'sole companion': 'we two out of a large family left by our parents, lived together'.[1] As it stands, this assertion is impossible to accept, and as the manuscript of the letter is missing it is possible that something has been omitted or misread. The times when Wordsworth could have been Tom's 'sole companion' are limited, for Mary Hutchinson and her youngest brother George are supposed to have joined Tom at Sockburn in the year 1789, though there is some uncertainty about the date. Wordsworth may well, however, have gone to Sockburn

---

[1] *L.T.* iii. 1661, p. 1324. W.W. to E. Moxon, July 7th 1849.

during this vacation, when Mary was still at Penrith and Tom alone with his old uncle at Sockburn. Tom at this time was sixteen years old.[1]

August and the first part of September were apparently spent mainly at Whitehaven or in its neighbourhood. An entry in the family accounts dated September 16th, 'Gave servants for William, 3ˢ', betrays his presence there, and another on November 8th (after his departure for Cambridge) 'By washing for William, 8ˢ.'

From Whitehaven he could easily walk over to visit his cousins the Smiths at Broughton-in-Furness.[2] There he spent his days roaming the fells and the recesses of the Duddon: he visited the Swinside Stone Circle on the slopes of Black Comb, believing it to have been a haunt of druids. Long afterwards he spoke in _The River Duddon_ of these happy days, and of the cousins who were evidently dear to him:

> Whence that low voice? A whisper from the heart,
> That told of days long past, when here I roved
> With friends and kindred tenderly beloved:
> Some who had early mandates to depart,
> Yet are allowed to steal my path athwart,
> By Duddon's side: once more do we unite,
> Once more beneath the kind Earth's tranquil light,
> And smothered joys into new being start.[3]

By the middle of September he was at Hawkshead,[4] where he found old Ann intending to retire from business at the end of the year, so that his brother Christopher would have to find new lodgings, and he himself would no longer be able to command

[1] Mary in her Reminiscences dictated in old age says that she and George 'finally left Penrith in 1789' though she does not say whither they went or give the exact date of their departure. They had other uncles in Durham with whom they may have lived for a time.

[2] Mary, d. of Richard Wordsworth of Whitehaven, married John Smith of Broughton. She died in 1799. In his note to _The River Duddon_, he says he stayed with these cousins 'several times', 'during my College vacations, and two or three years afterwards, before taking my Bachelor's degree'. 'Before', must be a mistake for 'after'. He probably stayed there again in the summer of 1794 when he was visiting some other cousins at Rampside near Ulverston. See below, p. 257.

[3] _P.W._ iii, p. 255, _The River Duddon_, XXI.

[4] Entry in accounts: '1789. Sept. 16. Remitted to Hawkshead and stamp £6. 6. 6.' This would represent board at Hawkshead and expenses and journey-money for the rest of the vacation and for the autumn at Cambridge. He received no more money until Jan. 1790.

a home there. This must have been a blow to him, for with Dorothy and Mary gone from Penrith, there would now be no place in his own north country which could be a truly congenial resort for him. This consideration may well have played its part in his decision to go abroad in the following long vacation (1790). He stayed at Hawkshead for about a month and while there he continued and probably completed *An Evening Walk*. It was now a poem of nearly 450 lines, the fruit of wide reading as well as patient observation of landscape, by car as much as by eye. The last fourteen lines, describing the return across Windermere ferry by night, are a succession of what might well be called 'sound-pictures', which in spite of their literary indebtedness to Milton, Beattie, and above all Gray's *Journal of a Tour in the Lakes*, show the personal delight of the young writer in each individual sound and its associations:

> The song of mountain streams unheard by day,
> Now hardly heard, beguiles my homeward way.
> All air is, as the sleeping water, still,
> List'ning the aerial music of the hill,
> Broke only by the slow clock tolling deep,
> Or shout that wakes the ferry-man from sleep.
> Soon followed by his hollow-parting oar,
> And echo'd hoof approaching the far shore;
> Sound of clos'd gate, across the water borne,
> Hurrying the feeding hare thro' nestling corn;
> The tremulous sob of the complaining owl;
> And at long intervals the mill-dog's howl;
> The distant forge's swinging thump profound;
> Or yell in the deep woods of lonely hound.[1]

Altogether *An Evening Walk* was no inconsiderable achievement for an undergraduate of nineteen.

On the way back to Cambridge he called at Penrith, apparently only for an hour or two. His Uncle Kit wrote sourly to Richard on October 22nd: 'Your Bro. William called here on Friday last in his road to Cambridge, he looks very well. I should have been happy if he had favoured me with more of his company, but I'm afraid I'm out of his good graces.' In December he wrote again:

---

[1] Gray's *Journal* mentions the 'murmur of many waterfalls not audible in the daytime', and 'the thumping of huge hammers at an iron forge not far distant'.

'I am sorry to say that I think your Bro^t William very extravagant. He has had very near £300 since he went to Cambridge
which I think is a very shameful sum for him to spend, considering his expectations.'[1] The last phrase 'considering his expectations' seems an echo of the ungenerous reproaches levelled at
the Wordsworth children by the servants at Penrith some years
before, and goes far to explain William's dislike of the man.
And had William been extravagant? The statement is not quite
correct; the payments can be traced in the family accounts. By
the end of 1789 his uncles had paid over about £220 to 'nephew
William' at Cambridge. This included his keep, fees, and pocket
money, and on the whole it does not seem excessive, amounting
to a little more than a hundred a year. A much higher standard
of dress was required in Cambridge than in Cumberland; the
undergraduates wore silk stockings and velvet in the evening,
and had their hair powdered.[2] A wine-party was the common
mode of social intercourse. Apart from his Italian lessons with
Isola, Wordsworth did not apparently involve himself in courses
outside the usual college lectures. Yet two years after leaving
Cambridge, in June 1792, his tutor, the Rev. James Wood, was
paid £30 'on nephew William's account', showing that there
was money still owing for fees, and many years later still, in
1803, William begged his brother to settle a still outstanding
debt of £10 to his old tutor. But, whether or not he is to be
considered extravagant, the money advanced for his education
had to be found by his uncle Richard, for his father's estate was
not, after all, adequate. This meant that after Mr. Richard
Wordsworth's death, in 1794, his widow claimed a sum of £400
from William. This was the source of much annoyance and
distress.[3]

Of his third year at Cambridge we know little, but it was
during the Christmas vacation apparently that he paid his first
visit to London. It was memorable for two experiences, one of
which enables us to date the visit pretty accurately. Many years
afterwards, in conversation with Samuel Rogers, Wordsworth

[1] *D.C.P.*
[2] *Prel.* iii, ll. 37–39.

> Behold me rich in monies, and attired
> In splendid garb, with hose of silk, and hair
> Powdered like rimy trees, when frost is keen.

[3] See below, pp. 337–8.

spoke of his first acquaintance with the poems of the poet-parson, William Lisle Bowles. 'When Bowles's sonnets first appeared', he said, 'a thin quarto pamphlet entitled *Fourteen Sonnets*, I bought them in a walk through London with my dear brother who was afterwards drowned at sea. I read them as we went along, and to the great annoyance of my brother, I stopped in a niche of London Bridge to finish the pamphlet.' Bowles's *Fourteen Sonnets, Elegiac and Descriptive*, first appeared in 1789. John Wordsworth had returned from his West Indian voyage in the spring of that year, and sailed again in the *Earl of Abergavenny* (the ship in which he afterwards lost his life) in January 1790.[1] William probably came to London for Christmas in order to be with him before he sailed. Bowles's sonnets soon became famous among all lovers of the 'sentimental' style in poetry: Samuel Taylor Coleridge felt so much indebted to them that he addressed a sonnet to Bowles,[2] and when at Stowey in 1797 walked over to Donhead in Wiltshire to visit him. To Wordsworth, their graceful melancholy, dwelling on the memories of beloved places, at once made a strong appeal. Their kinship with his own attachment to familiar landscape was quite striking enough to bring him to a standstill and so try the patience of the chafing John, as he read in *To the River Wansbeck*, how the poet

> whene'er of pleasures flown
> His heart some long-lost image would renew,
> Delightful haunts! he will remember you:

or in *On leaving a Village in Scotland*, how

> a look back on thy hills I cast,
> And many a soften'd image of the past
> Pleas'd I combine and bid remembrance keep,
> To sooth me with fair views and fancies rude,
> When I pursue my path in solitude.

The other incident in this visit to London concerned Wordsworth's interior life. It was so impressive an experience that he afterwards described it in *The Prelude*—the curious sensation which had come over him as he was approaching the City on the top of the Cambridge coach. Hitherto his most vivid spiritual

---

[1] *E.L.* 8, p. 24. D.W. to J.P. Jan. 25th 1790.
[2] *S.T.C. Poems*, i, p. 84, *To the Rev. W. L. Bowles* (printed in the *Morning Chronicle*, 1794).

experiences had been in the presence of what he called 'natural
objects'—mountains, moonlit lakes, and stormy skies. But now
he was overcome by something ineffable while sitting

> With vulgar men about me, vulgar forms
> Of houses, pavement, streets, of men and things.

What he felt—or what he afterwards thought that he had felt—
was the accumulated weight of human history pressing down
upon him with almost physical force.

> A weight of ages did at once descend
> Upon my heart; no thought embodied, no
> Distinct remembrances; but weight and power,
> Power growing with the weight—

He broke off, unable to describe the indescribable, only adding
that what happened within him 'came and went as in a moment'

> And I only now
> Remember that it was a thing divine.[1]

At Cambridge, during this last year, there are continued
records of his being 'unplaced' in the terminal examinations. His
relatives and even Dorothy began to feel anxious about his
future. 'I am very anxious about him just now', wrote Dorothy
in the spring of 1790, 'as he will shortly have to provide for
himself: next year he takes his degree; when he will go into
orders I do not know, nor how he will employ himself; he must,
when he is three and twenty either go into orders or take pupils;
he will be twenty in April.' For by this time William had
indicated to his family that they must not expect him to sit for
the examination which could have procured him a fellowship.
His neglect of mathematics was now a settled thing for which he
had neither the inclination nor the time to make up. His Uncle
William must have been disappointed and probably vexed at
this collapse of his expectations. William himself was not without some twinges of conscience and forebodings of an unpleasantly difficult time ahead. He did not wish, to use the
language of *An Evening Walk*,

> to delve in Mammon's joyless mine—

---

[1] *Prel.* VIII (1805), ll. 692–709. 1850 has at the end
> Yet with Time it dwells,
> And grateful memory, as a thing divine.

to be obliged to earn his living by employment which would probably keep him tied to one place almost the whole year round. Perhaps it was partly the dread of such a necessity which made him all the more anxious to make the most of his present freedom, and to celebrate his last long vacation in a manner which would satisfy his deepest longings. He decided to go on a 'pedestrian tour' through France and Switzerland and see the Alps with his own eyes.

V

THE ALPS, LONDON, AND WALES

July 1790 – September 1791

I'll walk where my own nature would be leading:
It vexes me to choose another guide.

EMILY BRONTË

Switzerland was already part of the landscape of romanticism when Wordsworth and his college friend Robert Jones went on their 'pedestrian tour'. Artists visited it; guide-books and descriptions were being written about it. Mont Blanc had been climbed for the first time in 1787. Wordsworth was acquainted with some of the descriptions of Swiss and Alpine scenery. In this very year, 1790, his schoolfellow William Raincock gave Coxe's *Travels in Switzerland* to the school library at Hawkshead. Wordsworth probably knew the book; he certainly used the French translation of it by Ramon de Carbonnière when he wrote *Descriptive Sketches* two years later. In 1786 Moore's *Travels in France, Switzerland and Germany* had been given by Fletcher Raincock and Edward Birkett. Wordsworth doubtless read this before he left Hawkshead. He was of course familiar with Thomson's *Liberty*, and its stately praise of Switzerland and the 'rough, laborious people' who were supposed to dwell in her. He also knew Gray's letters in which he describes the dangers of travel in the Alps and the beauties of the Grande Chartreuse. No doubt Gray's description determined him to include the Grande Chartreuse in the tour. All this, however, only helped to sustain his native appetite for 'mighty forms', which was the real spring of his desire to see Europe's highest mountains.

Wordsworth wrote two poetical accounts of his walking tour, separated in composition by some twelve years. They are *Descriptive Sketches*, written in France in the late summer and autumn of 1792, and the second half of the sixth book of *The Prelude*, begun on March 29th 1804. In *Descriptive Sketches* he gave, in the formal style and metre of *An Evening Walk* and with even more literary borrowings and fewer passages of intimate observation and truth of detail, a rather patchy picture of his wanderings, interspersed with romantically conceived descriptions of Swiss châlet-dwellers, and ending with a fierce political panegyric in praise of revolutionary France. It does not in any way reflect the real mood and spirit of the walk, for it affects to represent him in a melancholy frame of mind, whereas it is clear from his letter to Dorothy written from Switzerland, and from his references to the walking tour in later life, as well as from the account of his spirits in *The Prelude*, that although occasionally subject to fits of melancholy, Wordsworth never enjoyed any experience more. All that can be said for *Descriptive Sketches* as a record of the tour is that it mentions and describes rather more places than are treated in *The Prelude*, though it sometimes alters the order in which they were visited. Poetically it is weak and stilted in style, though it contains some phrases which he rightly thought worthy of being used again in *The Prelude*—'the torrents shooting from the clear blue sky', for instance, and the 'black, drizzling crags'.[1] Human types, such as the 'Grison gypsey' and the chamois-hunter are introduced as foreground figures in the landscape, to heighten the romantic effect, much as the Beggar-woman and her children are introduced into *An Evening Walk*.

The sixth book of *The Prelude* is even less a guide-book to the walk than *Descriptive Sketches*. It mentions but five scenes or incidents and says nothing at all of the tour after he and his companion left the Italian lakes. But, like the rest of *The Prelude*, it gives a poetic account of the things which left the deepest impression on him, which remained for one reason or another most vividly in his memory, which caused the keenest delight or the profoundest awe, or which, as he pondered over them, took on new and unexpected significance. Its fresh and buoyant description of the 'mood' of the walk, and particularly of France as he and Jones passed through it, take the place of the artificial melancholy and borrowed descriptions of the *Sketches*. And there is one other remarkable difference. *Descriptive Sketches* represents

---

[1] In *The Prelude* the torrents and crags make part of the scenery of the Simplon Pass. In *Descriptive Sketches* the 'torrents' are on the steep shores of Como (where, however, there are few waterfalls) and the 'crags' are placed in the valley of the Reuss. *Prel.* VI, ll. 629–32. *D.S.* ll. 249 (1793) and 130 (1793), 113 (1849).

the walk as a solitary undertaking of Wordsworth alone—
although he dedicated it openly on publication to his companion,
Robert Jones. But the account in *The Prelude* is a 'we-document'
throughout, and in that way is much more 'historical' than
Descriptive Sketches.

The last two long vacations had been spent in rambling about
Cumberland, Westmorland, Derbyshire, and Yorkshire in solitary enjoyment, and dearly did Wordsworth love this kind of
holiday. But for so unusual an undertaking as a tour through
Switzerland he felt that a companion would be desirable. There
was a certain amount of risk and danger in it, and two heads
would be better than one. Besides, there was his family, and
particularly Dorothy, to consider. It happened that among his
friends at Cambridge there was a spirit as eager for this kind of
adventure as himself.

Robert Jones, the Welshman, 'fat and roundabout and rosy',
as Dorothy described him many years later, was the chosen
companion of the great enterprise. With no other of his college
acquaintance did Wordsworth form so intimate a friendship.
In some respects their boyhood environment had been curiously
similar. Both were sons of country lawyers; both were educated
at country grammar schools;[1] both grew up in the neighbourhood of great mountains, and early learnt to love walking
among mountains better than any other pastime. Jones, like
Wordsworth, did not take an honours degree, but he gained a
fellowship in his college, and in time was appointed to a college
living in Oxfordshire. He had none of Wordsworth's hesitation
about a clerical life. Their friendship indeed was not an intellectual and spiritual reciprocation, but rather had its origins in the
attractions of contrast. Physically and mentally they amused,
pleased, and probably puzzled one another. Wordsworth had
a spare, somewhat awkward, figure; his face was long and his
expression usually grave, and he looked much older than his
years; and though not unsociable his manner was reserved, like
that of one who was holding in check feelings and enthusiasms
that he well knew might get the upper hand of his control.

---

[1] Jones went to Ruthin Grammar School and entered St. John's at the same time
as Wordsworth. 'Wordsworth and Wales', by D. Myrddin Lloyd, in *National
Library of Wales Journal*, vol. vi, No. 4, winter, 1950; and 'Wordsworth's Welsh
Friend', by T. H. Bowen in *English*, vol. viii, No. 43, spring, 1950.

Robert Jones was different in looks and ways: a being who did not know what it meant to repress or restrain any part of his cheerful, open-hearted, sweet-tempered nature. Many years afterwards Wordsworth described him as 'a most affectionate man, and, I verily believe, the best-tempered Creature imaginable; to me, who am apt to be irritable in travelling, an inestimable qualification'.[1] He could not have chosen a more desirable companion for a three months' trip in foreign lands with very little money and no previous knowledge of where they were going.

In the years immediately approaching, Jones was to be Wordsworth's host in Denbighshire on two occasions, and to introduce him to Snowdon and north Wales. He himself stayed with the Wordsworths in a later period both at Grasmere and Rydal Mount. But this tour was 'the golden and sunny spot' in Jones's life for ever, and Dorothy almost always referred to Jones as 'my brother's companion in his pedestrian tour in Switzerland', as though that had bound them together in a friendship that became indissoluble.[2]

It was Wordsworth who first broached the plan to Jones, as is clear from the early texts of *The Prelude*. Their acquaintances at Cambridge prophesied disaster to such a scheme. 'Pedestrian tours', on such a scale at least, were then unknown among 'gentlemen', who if they went abroad at all did so generally as tutors to some nobleman's son making the 'grand tour'. Wordsworth and Jones may be regarded as the pioneers of the great company who, from their day to the hikers and ramblers of our own, have claimed the right to walk for pleasure over hill and dale. Wordsworth wisely refrained from informing his Uncle William of their intention before they started. If many even of their friends at Cambridge thought it a mad scheme, how much more would the staid uncle? He would almost certainly have forbidden the journey altogether. William likewise said nothing to Dorothy until after he had reached France. He wished to spare her alarm, and, besides, to have told her while not telling their uncle would have placed her in a very difficult position.

---

[1] *L.T.* i. 169. W.W. to C.W. 1825. The poem called *A Character*, which Wordsworth in old age said was descriptive of Jones, is now thought to be about Coleridge. See *R.E.S.*, Dec. 1952.

[2] *L.T.* ii. 569. D.W. to Catherine Clarkson, 1831.

Dorothy was grateful. 'I confess', she wrote to Jane in October, 'that had he acquainted me with his scheme before its execution I should (as many of his other friends did) have looked upon it as mad and impracticable.'

The walkers left London on foot on July 11th and slept the first night at Shooter's Hill. William deliberately avoided seeing his brother Richard while he was in town, as he knew he would disapprove. They had very little money: 'twenty pounds in our pockets' is William's statement, and it was to last them three months.[1] They crossed from Dover on July 13th and found themselves plunged into the festivities of the great 'Federation Day' of the French Revolution which was still in its happy, confident, and fraternal stage. On the same day, but by a different boat, Miss Helen Maria Williams the poetess also crossed to France. She made her way straight to Paris, there to feast her enthusiastic eyes the following day on the inspiring spectacle of the Champ de Mars converted into a vast amphitheatre to accommodate half a million people; on the performance of High Mass at the 'autel de la Patrie' in the centre; on the king, the queen and the little dauphin seated in a pavilion composed of the national colours at one side of the amphitheatre; on La Fayette ascending the altar and taking the oath which was then repeated by the king; on the processions of deputies and national guards and children and soldiers. She remained in Paris throughout the stormy years to come, often at the risk of her life, never giving up her faith in the ultimate triumph of liberty. But her young admirer, the Englishman, William Wordsworth, would scarcely have been deflected from his predetermined route even had he known her to be in Paris. He and Jones cut right through the westward-streaming crowds in an inexorable southerly line. It was not that they were indifferent. Wordsworth was careful afterwards to record their delight in the delight of France. Like that of most Frenchmen too at that time, it was a purely heartfelt joy in hope and liberty, uninstructed by any formulated revolutionary doctrine, unembittered by any political passion.

---

[1] The family accounts contain the following items for this year relating to William:

Jan. 19 Expenses and Pocket Money	6.	1.	8
Mar 8 Remitted	37	–	–
May 24 „	25	–	–
Oct 19 „	30	–	–

The English students knew that the Bastille had been destroyed the previous summer and that the French king had abandoned absolutism and become a constitutional monarch. Most English-men approved these events;[1] and Wordsworth and Jones found that as Englishmen they were instantly popular with the enthusi-astic French—for was not England the home of liberty? Their appearance created mirth but never led to unpleasantness—for after all were not all Englishmen a little mad? 'Our appearance', wrote William, 'is singular. Our coats which we had made light on purpose, are of the same piece; and our manner of bearing our bundles, which is upon our heads, with each an oak stick in our hands, contributes not a little to that general curiosity which we seem to excite.' Elsewhere he says that they carried 'each his needments tied up in a pocket-handkerchief'—which to some extent explains the otherwise puzzling statement about carrying them on their heads. They were delighted with the treatment they everywhere received. The natural 'cheerfulness and spright-liness' of the French was enhanced by their joy in the Revolu-tion: 'the whole nation was mad with joy', wrote William to Dorothy from Switzerland.[2] He then proceeded to compare the disposition of the Swiss very unfavourably with that of the French. The Swiss he found already spoilt by 'perpetual inter-course with strangers'—for Switzerland was already a tourist resort. He admitted indeed that he and Jones 'had little to do but with innkeepers . . . and had we had time to insinuate our-selves into their cottages we should probably have had as much occasion to admire the simplicity of their lives as the beauties of

[1] Cowper, *The Task*, Book V, gives a typical English opinion of the Bastille before its fall:

> There's not an English heart that would not leap
> To hear that ye were fallen at last.

[2] Twelve years later, when he found himself once more at Calais under very different circumstances, with Bonaparte proclaimed Consul for life, and all hope and faith gone from the people after years of war and tyranny, he recalled the intoxicating atmosphere of those days of 1790 in a sonnet which contained the strange expression

> A homeless sound of joy was in the air,

and also

> The senselessness of joy was then sublime.

Dorothy, using the word 'homeless' in her *Recollections* of the Scottish tour of 1803, defined it as meaning 'without lasting abiding-place for the mind'. It is doubtless in this sense that Wordsworth used it.

their country.' In France, on the other hand, not only were they not imposed upon, but 'that politeness diffused through the lowest ranks had an air so engaging that you could scarce attribute it to any other cause than real benevolence.'[1]

The young men took about a month to pass through France. As they proceeded southwards they fell in with the crowds of *fédérés* returning from the Federation Festival. It was a triumphal march indeed; they were received as brothers everywhere by the crowds, and frequently on arrival at some town they stayed up all night to join in the revels, dancing in the streets after dining at communal tables in the open air.

> Round and round the board we danced again.[2]

The walk itself was accomplished with tolerable speed, covering on an average over twenty miles a day. They arrived at Châlons-sur-Saône, three hundred miles from Calais, on July 27th, after a fortnight's steady walking. They kept chiefly to the main roads, where the noise of the wind rustling in the endless avenues of elm-trees formed a pleasant accompaniment to Wordsworth's more thoughtful moods. It was very hot, and they approached the wooded country between Dijon and Montbar with 'an influx of chearing sensations as refreshing as a water-spring in a desert'.[3] At Châlons-sur-Saône they decided to vary their mode of travel for a day or two, and joined a company of returning *fédérés* on a boat that brought them down the Saône as far as its junction with the Rhône at Lyons. It was an uproarious journey, for the Frenchmen were in a state of wild excitement and joy. But in the intervals of merry-making Wordsworth watched the shores as they floated past,

> Reach after reach, succession without end
> Of deep and stately vales.

Every now and then a church spire coming into view

> Spake with a sense of peace, at intervals
> Touching the heart amid the boisterous crew
> By whom we were encompassed.

At Lyons they set forward once more on foot, and turning this time eastwards, they reached on August 4th a place that left

---

[1] *E.L.*, p. 35. W.W. to D.W., Sept. 6th 1790.
[2] *Prel.* VI, 1. 466.   [3] *D.W.J.* ii, p. 314.

THE GRANDE CHARTREUSE

an ineffaceable impression on Wordsworth's mind—the monastery of the Grande Chartreuse. As already pointed out, in planning their route Wordsworth must have deliberately included this place, for he would have known it by description from the letters of the poet Gray—a favourite volume with him as it contained also Gray's *Journal of a Tour in the Lakes*. Gray and Horace Walpole had visited the Chartreuse in 1739, and Gray's record of it was of exactly the kind to attract and excite Wordsworth.[1] Besides, his own love for such places as Furness Abbey made him eager to see a monastery that was still unruined and inhabited, and the situation of the Chartreuse in its remote mountain sanctuary satisfied the deepest cravings of his romanticism. They approached it by 'the narrow road that ran for six miles through the gorge of the river which thundered over its rocky bed two hundred feet below, while above them the cliff walls rose perpendicularly, crowned with yew trees, to meet the distant sky'.[2] Wordsworth saw with wonder that to the summits of some of these peaks crosses had been fixed, often in spots that looked inaccessible. They emerged at length into the valley-head where lay the great monastery, a seventeenth-century building covering several acres, for it had been rebuilt and enlarged after a fire in 1676. They stayed two days as guests of the monks, glad enough, after the noisy journey down the Rhône, to taste of the Carthusian silence, and to rest body and mind 'in an awful Solitude'. Having looked round on all things they departed in the direction of Aix.

They must have been among the last visitors to the monastery,[3] for already the shadow of tragedy hung over it. In February of that year the National Assembly had passed a decree dissolving the religious Orders and absolving all monks and nuns from their vows. Further, the Civil Constitution Bill, which was to bring upon the Church in France so much confusion and suffering, had just been passed by the Assembly in July, but as yet the monasteries had not been forcibly closed, and

[1] Mason's *Life and Writings of Mr. Gray*, 1775. Toynbee, *Correspondence of Gray, Wapole, West and Ashton* (1915), i, pp. 246, 259.
[2] *La Grande Chartreuse, par un Chartreux*, 1888, p. 9.
[3] *Prel.* VI, p. 196.

> The last, we two perchance the very last
> Of strangers destined to repose their limbs
> Within those modest walls.

the oath to the constitution had not been put to the parochial clergy. The whole fate of the Church in France was thus still fluid and uncertain in August 1790: much was threatened; little yet actually altered. At the Chartreuse all that had happened was that in February the Secretary of the local Commune had come and had taken an inventory of the valuables.[1] Why then does Wordsworth say in *The Prelude* that as he and Jones approached, the peace of the woods was disturbed by the flash of arms, and

> military glare
> Of riotous men commissioned to expel
> The blameless inmates?

This statement is followed by a long passage in which he hears the voice of Nature pleading 'from her Alpine throne' for the continuance of an institution so venerable and so saintly, while he himself joins his own petition to hers, on the score not only of the 'faith and meditative reason' of the inhabitants, but of the 'imaginative impulse' provided by the grandeur of those encircling mountains. At the same time he exclaims

> Honour to the Patriot's zeal,
> Glory and hope to new-born Liberty!

Only let patriotism reverence holiness and beauty.

All this was not in the first text of *The Prelude*. It was added an some unknown date, but probably not earlier than 1808, and perhaps at the suggestion of Coleridge. The first text as Wordsworth completed it in 1804 says nothing about any visitation by armed men. There can be no doubt that in August 1790 there was no 'flash of arms' anywhere near the Chartreuse. But nearly two years later, in May 1792, the exact event took place which Wordsworth has placed in 1790. Four hundred soldiers were quartered on the monastery for five months. Most of them behaved with scant respect to the monks or buildings; it was a kind of 'dragonnade', and ended, in October 1792, in the expulsion of the monks, some of whom found refuge in other houses of their order beyond the borders of France, while others endured imprisonment, deportation, and death at the hands of revolutionary tribunals. During the summer when all this was

---

[1] *La Grande Chartreuse, par un Chartreux*, 1888. This book contains a detailed contemporary account by one of the monks of what happened at the Chartreuse during the French Revolution.

happening, Wordsworth was in France, torn between his love for Annette Vallon, whose upbringing was Catholic and Royalist, and his new-found enthusiasm for the doctrines of the Revolution, taught him with innocent assurance by the gallant and high-minded Beaupuy. It was under these circumstances that he heard of the dissolution of the Chartreuse, and immediately afterwards wrote in *Descriptive Sketches* an account of the event, which was sympathetic in feeling towards the victims of the assault.

> The cloister startles at the gleam of arms,
> And Blasphemy the shuddering fane alarms;
> Nod the cloud-piercing pines their troubled heads,
> Spires, rocks and lawns a browner night o'erspreads,

with more in the same style. The passage added to *The Prelude* is little more than a rewriting and expansion of the lines in *Descriptive Sketches*.[1]

From the Chartreuse William wrote to Dorothy, a letter which unfortunately has not survived; after that the pace of their tour was so rapid that he did not write to her again for a month, when he addressed a letter to her from 'Keswill, a small village on the Lake of Constance', on September 6th. 'My spirits', he wrote gaily, 'have been kept in a perpetual hurry of delight by the almost uninterrupted succession of sublime and beautiful objects which have passed before my eyes during the course of the last month.' No one could blame him and Jones for extravagance. 'You will be surprized', he said, 'when I assure you that our united expenses since we quitted Calais, which was on the evening of the 14th of July, have not amounted to more than twelve pounds. Never was there a more excellent school for frugality than that in which we are receiving instructions at present. I am half afraid of getting a slight touch of avarice from it.' He was delighted with their feats of endurance and speed. 'We have', he says, 'met with little disasters occasionally: but, far from depressing, they rather gave us additional resolution and spirits. We have both enjoyed most excellent health; and we have been this some time so inured to walking,

---

[1] Legouis supposed that Wordsworth and Jones *did* encounter soldiers at the Chartreuse, but that they were engaged on a 'domiciliary visit' only. But it appears certain that no military visits took place this year, and no official visits at all during August. *L.*, p. 111.

that we are become almost insensible of fatigue. We have
several times performed a journey of thirteen leagues ⌈'thirty-
nine miles you know', explained the proud Dorothy to Jane
Pollard⌉ over the most mountainous parts of Switzerland without any more weariness than if we had been walking an hour
in the groves of Cambridge.' They slept at a different place every
night, except at Chamounix and Glarus, at each of which they
spent two nights. But William's estimate of distances is puzzling: it does not seem that they ever came near accomplishing
as much as thirteen leagues in a day; their usual distance was
more like fifteen or twenty miles. They walked sometimes
together, sometimes apart, and once, on Como, through mis-
adventure, spent the night apart.

After leaving the Chartreuse they crossed Savoy—then part
of the dominions of the King of Piedmont—and entered Switzerland at Geneva. From Martigny they doubled back into Savoy
in order to see Chamounix and its glaciers and Mont Blanc.
The mountain disappointed them, but not so Chamounix with
its 'motionless array of mighty waves'—and Wordsworth's
heart 'leap'd up' at his first sight of Swiss châlets in 'an aborigi-
nal vale'; brown, tent-shaped structures, so different from the
solid, stone farmsteads of his own dales. It leapt again thirty
years afterwards when he recognized the same spot with
Dorothy. 'Now', he said to her, 'I find that my remembrance for
thirty years has been scarcely less vivid than the reality now
before my eyes!'[1] On returning into Switzerland they made for
the Simplon Pass, for they wanted to see the Italian lakes. It was
the Simplon and the lake of Como which remained the most
memorable 'spots' of the entire walk for Wordsworth—the one
for its terrifying grandeur and for the strange incident that
occurred in crossing it; the other for its gracious beauty. Nature
in one place showed him her 'severer' glory—in the other she
gave him one of her 'gentler visitations'.

'Crossing the Alps' is the subject of a famous description in
The Prelude,[2] and it is there both because of the feelings which it
aroused at the time, and of the strange moment of illumination

---

[1] *D.W.J.* ii, p. 280. Dorothy's *Journal of a Tour on the Continent in 1820* is often
helpful in filling in and clarifying incidents in the tour of 1790, for she, William,
and Mary covered some of the same ground, though in the reverse direction.
[2] *Prel.* VI, ll. 562–616. *D.W.J.* ii, pp. 260–1.

which occurred fourteen years afterwards while he was in process of describing the event. Wordsworth and Jones joined a band of muleteers[1] up the Simplon Pass to the inn at the top. Here they lunched, and the muleteers went on, leaving the Englishmen to follow. They descended to the edge of the stream where the road apparently ceased. There was no sign of the others and the only route seemed to be a steep, almost perpendicular footpath, straight up the opposite mountain-side. After some hesitation they crossed the stream, then unbridged, and began to mount the path, climbing eagerly, but becoming more and more astonished that they did not overtake the muleteers. Presently a peasant met them coming down the path, which really led only to a mountain-village. He wondered to see them in such a place, and with kind concern explained to them that they ought to have continued downward by the bed of the stream and then along its banks, for all their upward climbing was now at an end—'they had crossed the Alps'. It was some time before the peasant could make himself understood:

> We questioned him again and yet again—

partly because of the difficulty of language, partly because their eager spirit of upward-climbing, upward-looking endeavour and desire to reach 'the top' was unwilling to be turned back.[2] 'Dull and heavy slackening' followed, and Wordsworth felt 'a deep and genuine sadness'—far different from the 'dejection taken up for pleasure's sake' in which he occasionally indulged during the walk. Why was he suddenly so sad? It was not until fourteen years later, when he was meditating this puzzling experience for inclusion in the 'poem on my own life', that in an intense moment of imaginative vision he saw the reality of which his depression that day had been the symbol.

> Imagination! lifting up itself
> Before the eye and progress of my Song
> Like an unfathered vapour; here that Power
> In all the might of its endowments, came
> Athwart me; I was lost as in a cloud,
> Halted, without a struggle to break through.[3]

[1] *Prel.* VI, l. 564. 'Travellers' in 1805 text.

[2] 'The ambition of youth was disappointed at these tidings; and they remeasured their steps with sadness.' *D.W.J.* ii, p. 260.

[3] *Prel.* VI (1805), ll. 525–30. The earlier text makes it clearer than the later that this whole experience occurred during the writing of *The Prelude*.

He entered into the cloud, and found that it was a dazzling darkness, a silence full of language. The vivid recollection of the scene, the recapturing not simply of the circumstances, but of the emotions of that moment, brought him beyond them, face to face with their true meaning. He saw something new about human life with a clarity he had never known before. He had entered the world of vision. This was the message:

> Our destiny, our being's heart and home,
> Is with infinitude, and only there;
> With hope it is, hope that can never die,
> Effort, and expectation, and desire,
> And something evermore about to be.

That was why he had felt such sadness at being turned back from the summit. His habit of intense meditation on experience had at length brought this reward. He felt the process to be mysterious, but he was too truthful an observer of mental processes not to make some attempt to describe it.

> In such strength
> Of usurpation,[1] when the light of sense
> Goes out, but with a flash that has revealed
> The invisible world, doth greatness make abode,
> There harbours, whether we be young or old.

Sixteen years after he wrote these lines, in 1820, Wordsworth found himself once more at the scene of the original incident. He, Dorothy, and Mary, were making their way up the Simplon on foot from the Italian side. A fine new military road had lately been made 'by Buonaparte', and the old track by which William and Robert had walked was now deserted. Mary and Dorothy, a little way ahead, noticed a wooden bridge spanning the stream below them and a path leading from it straight up the mountain-side to a small hamlet. As they were looking at it William joined them and at once recognized the path as the very one from which he and Jones had been turned back thirty years before. The bridge was of more recent date. 'It was impossible for me to say', wrote Dorothy, 'how much it had moved him when he discovered it was the very same which had tempted him

---

[1] 'Usurpation'—because the whole inward being was 'usurped' by the visionary suprarational faculty of the imagination.

in his youth. The feelings of that time came back with the freshness of yesterday, accompanied with a dim vision of thirty years of life between. We traced the path together, with our eyes, till hidden among the cottages, where they had first been warned of their mistake.'[1]

Having regained the river-bank Wordsworth and Jones continued downwards through the Ravine of Gondo, and here Wordsworth saw and felt Alpine majesty and Alpine terror in its most forbidding form. 'The impressions of these hours of our walk among the Alps', he told Dorothy, 'will never be effaced.' And, comparing that walk with the shores of Como where they arrived soon afterwards, he said: 'It was impossible not to contrast that repose, that complacency of spirit, produced by these lovely scenes, with the sensations I had experienced two or three days before, in passing the Alps. At the Lake of Como my mind ran through a thousand dreams of happiness, which might be enjoyed upon its banks. . . . Among the more awful scenes of the Alps, I had not a thought of man, or a single created being; my whole soul was turned to him who produced the terrible majesty before me.' The weather suited the landscape; it was wet and wild—the river roared at their feet, a raging torrent. 'Our path', wrote Dorothy afterwards when passing through the same ravine, 'was between precipices, still more gloomy and awful than before (what must they have been in the time of rain and vapour when my brother was here before —on the narrow track instead of our broad road!). Skeletons of tall pine-trees beneath us in the dell, and above our heads— their stems and shattered branches as grey as the stream of the Vedro, or the crags strewn at their feet.'[2]

But the scene with its wild splendours, which to some minds might simply have conveyed chaos and desolation, brought to William that solemn sense of the 'one life' which often came upon him in his contemplative moments. It lay in his imagination fructifying, and nine years afterwards, when he was in Germany with Dorothy, he wrote the description which eventually found its place in *The Prelude*.

> The immeasurable height
> Of woods decaying, never to be decayed,
> The stationary blasts of waterfalls,

[1] _D.W.J._ ii, p. 261.   [2] Ibid., p. 259.

And in the narrow rent at every turn
Winds thwarting winds, bewildered and forlorn,
The torrents shooting from the clear blue sky,[1]
The rocks that muttered close upon our ears,
Black drizzling crags that spake by the way-side
As if a voice were in them, the sick sight
And giddy prospect of the raving stream,
The unfettered clouds and region of the Heavens,
Tumult and peace, the darkness and the light—
Were all like workings of one mind, the features
Of the same face, blossoms upon one tree.[2]

Toward evening, half-stunned with the rigours of their walk, they reached a strange building with 'a lofty gable front, step-like on each steeply-sloping side',[3] eight stories high, 'a dreary mansion, large beyond all need';[4] the ancient Hospice or Spittal of the Simplon, built in the thirteenth century by the Knights of St. John. The night they spent there was not a good one. He and Jones lay in

High and spacious rooms, deafened and stunned
By noise of waters, making innocent sleep
Lie melancholy among weary bones.

Thirty years later he once more passed by the place, accompanied by Dorothy and his wife. Dorothy, referring in her Journal to her brother's stay there in 1790, says that it was 'an awful night' that he and his companion spent there, and that they were 'unable to sleep for other causes' besides the noise of the stream. She may be referring to the unwelcome accompaniments of hostel bedding, but she adds: 'I now regret not having the courage to pass the threshold alone. I had a strong desire to see what was going on within doors for the sake of tales of thirty years gone by; but could not persuade W. to accompany me.' What were the 'tales of thirty years gone by'? And why was William unpersuadable? Something more than the roaring of the stream and uncomfortable beds seems needed to account for his nervousness in this forbidding place.

Como was paradise after these purgatorial experiences. They followed the footpath—there was as yet no driving-road—along

---

[1] This line, lifted from *Descriptive Sketches*, forms there part of the description of the shores of Como. In the Simplon, when Wordsworth and Jones were there, the sky was neither clear nor blue.   [2] *Prel.* VI, ll. 624–37.
[3] *D.W.J.* ii, p. 258.   [4] *Prel.* VI, l. 645.

the western shore, through the chestnut woods that then clothed
the steep banks, from the foot of the water to its head,

> Winding from house to house, from town to town.

It was often roofed with vines, and from this shelter they watched
the brilliant green and gold reflections of the hill-sides in the
water. 'We entered upon this path about noon,' he told Dorothy,
'and, owing to the steepness of the banks, were soon unmolested
by the sun, which illuminated the woods, rocks and villages of
the opposite shore. The lake is narrow, and the shadows of the
mountains were early thrown across it. It was beautiful to watch
them travelling up the side of the hills for several hours, to
remark one half of a village covered with shade, and the other
bright with the strongest sunshine.'[1] The human occupants of
these Italian woods pleased Wordsworth who observed in
them a 'softness and elegance' contrasting with the 'austere-
ness' of the Swiss. The peasants were usually away from their
cottages, working up the mountains on their lofty pastures, but
the girls were pretty and gracious and not above a little light
flirtation, and once, turning aside alone into the woods, he came
to a little cabin at whose door an old man sat playing on a
primitive violin, while

> Beneath an old-grey oak as violets lie
> Stretch'd at his feet with stedfast, upward eye,
> His children's children join'd the holy sound—
> A Hermit—with his family around.[2]

At the northern end of the lake one of their 'little disasters'
overtook them—they became separated in the woods by a violent
thunderstorm,[3] lost their way and spent the night wandering.
Jones finally arrived at Chiavenna, and Wordsworth at Samo-
laco. At Gravedona they spent a night which was memorable
for other reasons. They were awakened in the middle of the
night by the chiming clocks of the little town, speaking

> In fashion different from ours,[4]

[1] This description is repeated in *D.S.* (1793), ll. 102–7. Cf. his description of
Dovedale, above, p. 105.

[2] *D.S.* (1793), ll. 172–5. To D.W. he wrote: 'It was with pleasure I observed
at a small Inn on the Lake of Como, the master of it playing upon his harpsichord
with a large collection of Italian music beside him.' *E.L.* 10, p. 36.

[3] For the reason of their separation see *D.W.J.* ii, p. 244.

[4] *Prel.* VI, ll. 691–4. See Havens, *The Mind of a Poet*, p. 430, for the explanation
of their mistake.

and thinking dawn was near, they went out into the woods intending to see the lake at the loveliest and stillest moment of the day. The moon shone on the water, 'like an uneasy snake', and soon they were lost in the woods, and were obliged to sit down on a rock and wait for day, which was yet far distant. It was a wakeful and uncomfortable night, but lovely in Wordsworth's memory, and when he wrote *The Prelude* he took it for the last picture from that mental treasure the walk left with him.

> On the rock we lay
> And wished to sleep but could not, for the stings
> Of insects, which with noise like that of noon
> Fill'd all the woods; the cry of unknown birds,
> The mountains, more by darkness visible
> And their own size, than any outward light,
> The breathless wilderness of clouds, the clock
> That told with unintelligible voice
> The widely-parted hours, the noise of streams,
> And sometimes rustling motions nigh at hand. . . .[1]

From Chiavenna they turned north again into Switzerland by Splügen, turning down the valley of the Reuss[2] into the Canton of Uri, where the legend and romance of Swiss patriotism broke upon them in the passionate narrative of the boatman who rowed them down the lake past the places connected with the exploits of William Tell. Wordsworth was moved as he listened to the half-understood tale, and in *Descriptive Sketches* he placed Tell with Wolfe and Sidney and Claverhouse among those who have

> wrought with god-like arm the deeds of praise.

Here, too, they saw a particularly glorious Alpine sunset, which Wordsworth in *Descriptive Sketches* made a challenge

---

[1] *Prel.* VI (1805), ll. 641–50, and *D.S.* (1793), ll. 215–37 Dorothy, in her Journal of 1820, says that Gravedona was 'interesting to Mary and me for the sake of an adventure of our youthful Travellers recorded by my brother in the poem on his own life. They were parted in a thunder storm', &c. Actually the night of the thunderstorm (Aug. 22nd) is not recorded in *The Prelude*, which only mentions the warm, still night (Aug. 21st) in which they got up in the dark. *D.W.J.* ii, p. 244.

[2] 'It was after a time of heavy rains that my brother and his friend descended through the valley of Schöllenen, mists were driving over the crags. The River Reuss was swoln, and a hundred cataracts roaring down the precipices, that in the bright season of our passage were silent.' *D.W.J.* ii, p. 189.

to all the accepted standards of the picturesque.[1] His note, omitted in the revised text of 1849, on his own description reveals both the extent of his study of the picturesque (in such works as Gilpin's *Tours* and West's *Guide to the Lakes*), and his recognition of the futility of all such attempts to lay down rules for Nature's glories. Writing of the Alps he says:

> Whoever in attempting to describe their sublime features, should confine himself to the cold rules of painting, would give his reader but a very imperfect idea of those emotions which they have the irresistible power of communicating to the most impassive imaginations. . . . Had I wished to make a picture of this scene I had thrown much less light into it. But I consulted nature and my feelings. The ideas excited by the stormy sunset I am here describing owed their sublimity to that deluge of light, or rather of fire, in which nature had wrapped the immense forms around me; any intrusion of shade, by destroying the unity of the impression, had necessarily diminished its grandeur.

The setting sun did not yet appear in English landscape painting, otherwise Wordsworth might not have felt it so incumbent on him to distinguish so sharply between 'the cold rules' of painting and the word-picture inspired purely by 'Nature and the feelings'. The English water-colour artists like Francis Towne who were already enthusiastic admirers of the Swiss landscape were more concerned with the severity and ruggedness of mountain architecture than with the effulgence of sunlight and the transfiguring of landscape by its rays.

From Lucerne they went to the lake of Zürich and turned aside there to Einsiedeln, a shrine of healing to which pilgrims came 'from every corner of the Catholick world'.[2] Wordsworth in *Descriptive Sketches* made much of this place and of the

[1] *D.S.* (1793), ll. 336–47.

> Triumphant on the bosom of the storm,
> Glances the fire-clad eagle's wheeling form;
> Eastward, in long perspective glittering, shine
> The wood-crowned cliffs that o'er the lake recline;
> Wide o'er the Alps a hundred streams unfold,
> At once to pillars turned that flame with gold.
> Behind his sail the peasant strives to shun
> The west that burns like one dilated sun,
> When in a mighty crucible expire
> The mountains, glowing hot, like coals of fire.

[2] W.W.'s note to *D.S.* (1793), l. 655.

sympathetic feelings which the sight of the pilgrims and their simple faith aroused in his soul that had itself lost or rejected any such consolations:

> My heart, alive to transports long unknown,
> Half wishes your delusion were its own.

But this is the Wordsworth of 1792, troubled, bewildered by passionate love, by concern for humanity, by the indoctrination of his mind with revolutionary fervour. In 1790 he was much less self-conscious and sophisticated, and probably more truly in sympathy with the real pathos of the scene. In his revision of the poem at the end of his life he cut out all reference to himself, thereby perhaps giving a truer impression of the feelings of 1790.[1]

Having reached the lake of Constance they stopped at Keswill where Wordsworth began his long letter to Dorothy, and then proceeded to Schaffhausen to see the famous Falls of the Rhine, where 'the whole stream falls like liquid emeralds—a solid mass of translucent green hue',[2] though Wordsworth was somewhat disappointed: 'I had raised my ideas too high.' From here they turned southwards again and back to Lucerne, and so up into the very heart of the high Alps, to Grindelwald and Lauterbrunnen. Here Wordsworth was in some danger of being drowned while crossing a rapidly rising stream to look at a waterfall.

On my return I found the difficulty of recrossing the stream much increased and being detained among the large stones in its channel I perceived the water swell every moment which with the dizziness of sight produced by the dashing of the foam placed me in a position of considerable danger. Returning down the valley, from a bridge under the arch of which about two hours before for the sake of shade we had retired, to eat our dinner, we observed such a quantity of water rolling over our late resting-place as would have swept us away before it.[3]

Thence they made their way to Basle where they arrived on

---

[1] *D.S.* (1793), ll. 644–79: (1849), ll. 540–69.

[2] *D.W.J.* ii, p. 90.

[3] *D.C.P.* Fragment in an early note-book. The rapid rising of the streams is compared with the similar behaviour of 'the rivers in Peru' when the sun melts the snow. This is not the only indication in the early note-books that he was familiar with some description of South America, probably Ovalle's account of Chile, which he could have read in a translation.

September 21st.[1] Having still some money left, they determined
to invest it in the purchase of a 'little Bark',[2] in which they
floated down the Rhine until they reached Cologne. Thirty
years later Wordsworth celebrated the delight of that voyage in
a sonnet written when he was travelling up the Rhine with Mary
and Dorothy. Dorothy, after re-creating for herself the picture of
the two friends with their 'freight of happiness' slipping past
tower and town, entered it in her Journal:

> The confidence of Youth our only Art,
> And Hope gay Pilot of the bold design,
> We saw the living landscapes of the Rhine,
> Reach after Reach, salute us and depart;
> Slow sink the Spires,—and up again they start!
> But who shall count the Towers as they recline
> O'er the dark steeps, or on the horizon line
> Striding, with shatter'd crests, the eye athwart?
> More touching still, more perfect was the pleasure,
> When hurrying forward till the slackening stream
> Spread like a spacious Mere, we there could measure
> A smooth free course along the watery gleam,
> Think calmly on the Past, and mark at leisure
> Features which else had vanished like a dream.[3]

At Cologne they left the river, sold the boat, and turned
westwards into Belgium. And here they came once more face
to face with the great events of the time. They

> crossed the Brabant armies on the fret
> For battle in the cause of Liberty.[4]

The Belgians had risen against the Emperor Joseph II in
January, and were now offering a rather confused allegiance to
his successor, Leopold, who was trying, with the encouragement
of Great Britain, to quiet his subjects with fair promises backed
by the threat of force. Wordsworth and Jones looked at it all as
they had looked at the Federation festivities, sympathetically but
'with no intimate concern'. Looking back in 1804 on himself as
he was in that time of the beginning of Europe's revolutionary

---

[1] It is not quite clear whether they visited Berne or not. It does not appear in
their list of stopping-places for the night, yet William tells Dorothy that he is
finishing his letter to her at 'Berne, on the 16th September'. They may have passed
through it without sleeping.   [2] *D.W.J.* ii, p. 57.
  [3] This sonnet was afterwards rewritten as No. 12 of *Ecclesiastical Sonnets*,
Part III. It was not improved in the process.   [4] *Prel.* VI, ll. 764–5.

tumults, he saw that he was in truth too happy—his imagination
too full of the glory that was revealed daily to his senses—to
be much concerned with man as a political animal.

> I seem'd to move along them, as a bird
> Moves through the air, or as a fish pursues
> Its sport, or feeds in its proper element;
> I wanted not that joy, I did not need
> Such help; the ever-living universe,
> Turn where I might, was opening out its glories,
> And the independent spirit of pure youth
> Called forth, at every season, new delights
> Spread round my steps as sunshine o'er green fields.[1]

By the peculiar strength of Wordsworth's powers of recollection and re-creation, these 'new delights' formed a permanent
enrichment to his mind and spirit. The Swiss tour became
something more than a pleasant memory: it was another door
through which he entered more deeply into communication with
'the ever-living universe'. To Dorothy he revealed something
of the process by which this was brought about.

I am a perfect enthusiast in my admiration of Nature in all her
forms [he wrote to her], and I have looked upon, and as it were con-
versed with, the objects which this country has presented to my view
so long, and with such increasing pleasure, that the idea of parting
from them oppresses me with a sadness similar to what I have always
felt in quitting a beloved friend. . . . Ten thousand times in the course
of this tour have I regretted the inability of my memory to retain a
more strong impression of the beautiful forms before me; and again
and again in quitting a fortunate station,[2] have I returned to it with
the most eager avidity, in the hope of bearing away a more lively
picture. At this moment, when many of these landscapes are floating
before my mind, I feel a high enjoyment in reflecting that perhaps
scarce a day of my life will pass in which I shall not derive some
happiness from these images.

Here Wordsworth is proclaiming unconsciously the mental and
imaginative process from which in after years so much of his
greatest poetry was to flow. From 'emotion recollected in tranquillity' in this manner sprang *Tintern Abbey* and *I wandered*

---

[1] *Prel.* VI, ll. 770–8.
[2] 'Station', i.e. viewpoint. It is the word used in all the guide-books to 'the
picturesque'.

lonely as a Cloud and *To the Cuckoo* and *The Solitary Reaper* and all the best of *The Prelude,* and numberless images throughout his poetry. The vivid manner in which a landscape would lie engraved upon his memory, and the swiftness with which he could recall it before the 'mind's eye' were indeed faculties of which he had been conscious since childhood, but the Swiss tour gave them a new stimulus, and strengthened his faith in their creative powers.

When he spoke to Dorothy of the sadness he felt at 'quitting a beloved friend' Wordsworth could scarcely have had another than Dorothy herself in his mind. A more acute awareness of what Dorothy meant to him was the other legacy of the Swiss tour. She had been his invisible companion all through this eventful holiday. 'I have thought of you perpetually', he wrote to her; 'and never have my eyes burst upon a scene of peculiar loveliness but I have almost instantly wished that you could be for a moment transported to the place where I stood to enjoy it.' He knew that in Dorothy he possessed someone who was not only at all times able and eager to reciprocate and to participate in every feeling of delight and wonder, but one to whom he could communicate his own delight with an absolute certainty of having it not only understood but enhanced. She made loveliness more lovely by the spontaneity and purity of her own delight in it.

To this 'dear, dear Sister' William now desired to hasten, for he was not due at St. John's for the completion of his residence until November, and he hoped to go to Forncett as soon as he reached England. For some reason the visit was postponed until December. Was it on account of his uncle's displeasure at his 'truant disposition'? There is nothing to tell us so, yet he was evidently in some anxiety as to how his uncle would receive him. As it is, we do not know where he went on first returning to England. The two friends crossed from Calais on or about October 10th. They probably went straight to Cambridge, and William stayed there until early in December. He then went to Forncett where he stayed for six weeks.

It was a time of most blessed companionship, and one that Dorothy looked back upon with the tenderest recollection, for, though neither of them knew it, another long period of separation lay ahead, and they did not see each other again for more than three years. But now, day after winter day, they grew together in walks and talks. 'You may recollect', she wrote to Jane in the following May, 'that at that time the weather was uncommonly mild; we used to walk every morning about two hours, and every evening we went into the garden at four or half past four and used to pace backwards and forwards till six.'[1] Two years afterwards she again described this walking up and down; it was only the 'always unwelcome' summons to tea (then taken after dinner, which was at about three) that stopped their perambulations; 'nothing but rain or snow prevented our taking this walk. . . . Ah! Jane! I never thought of the cold when he was with me.' And after he went away she continued to walk there alone, because it 'will always be dear to me from the remembrance of those long, long conversations supported by my brother's arm'. This visit of William's indeed was memorable for what it revealed to her of her brother's affection for her. Hitherto she had perhaps thought or felt less of his love for her than of hers for him; now it burst upon her with delightful conviction that she was indeed dear to him in no common fashion. 'The last time we were together', she told Jane in 1793, referring to this time, 'he won my affection to a degree that I cannot describe: his attentions to me were such as the most insensible of mortals must have been touched with, there was no pleasure he would not give up with joy for half an hour's conversation with me.' A little earlier in the same year she had drawn for Jane's benefit a comparison between William and their youngest brother Kit, now eighteen and about to enter on his highly successful career at Cambridge. All her description of William is drawn from her recollection of him as he had behaved to her in that Christmas visit two years before.[2]

Christopher [she wrote] is like William. He has the same traits in his character but less highly touched, he is not so ardent in any of his pursuits but is yet more particularly attached to the same pursuits which have so irresistible an Influence over William, which deprive him of the Power of chaining his attention to others discordant to his feelings.

---

[1] *E.L.* 12, p. 46. D.W. to J.P., May 1791. The Rectory and its garden at Forncett remain scarcely changed to this day.
[2] Ibid. 28, p. 83. D.W. to J.P., Feb. 16th 1793.

(Christopher in fact was prepared to work at mathematics!) Then she goes on:

Christopher is steady and sincere in his attachments; William has both these virtues in an eminent degree; and a sort of violence of Affection if I may so term it which demonstrates itself every moment of the Day when the Objects of his affection are present with him, in a thousand almost imperceptible attentions to their wishes, in a sort of restless watchfulness which I know not how to describe, a Tenderness that never sleeps, and at the same time such a delicacy of manners as I have observed in few men.

What did they talk about in those 'long, long conversations'? About the Swiss tour, no doubt, for its scenes and incidents became almost as familiar to Dorothy as they were to William. But the subject which most engrossed them was that of their own future. To live together in some humble dwelling was the 'central point of all their joys'. During the next three years, Dorothy dreamed out her longings in visions that increased in intimate detail. At Halifax she and Jane Pollard had often planned a cottage life together; in these years Dorothy renewed the theme, but now she and William were the host and hostess; Jane was to pay a long visit, 'at least a year', and all was to be harmony and peace. Thus she describes their snug pursuits on a winter evening:

When I think of winter I hasten to furnish our little Parlour. I close the Shutters, set out the Tea-table, brighten the Fire. When our Refreshment is ended I produce our Work, and William brings his book to our Table and contributes at once to our instruction and amusement, and at intervals we lay aside the Book, and each hazard our observations upon what has been read without the fear of Ridicule or Censure.[1]

Two things are of interest in this day-dream of Dorothy's. One is that the scene of these homely revels has now become 'my little Parsonage'. Dorothy at any rate was thinking of William's future in terms of the Church and its ministry. Her pleasant life at Forncett, her school and other charities, her liking for her uncle and aunt, had by this time given her a decided taste for parsonage life. The prospect of keeping house in one had no terrors for her. Could she have been sure that her brother felt the same pleasure in such a prospect her mind

[1] E.L. 28, p. 84. D.W. to J.P., Feb. 1793.

would have been more at ease. But William, though he made as yet no open rejection of the idea of taking orders, showed no enthusiasm. To him, ordination meant 'vegetating on a paltry curacy';[1] and even the ultimate hope of an independent parsonage promised too static, too immovable a life for him whose blood craved liberty to wander or to settle like the birds of the air. As he said in old age, 'the struggle between my conscience and my impulses would have made life a torture'.[2] For the present he hesitated, procrastinated, and in any case he was not yet of age.

Dorothy's parsonage is also, it should be noted, her own; she is its mistress. Mary Hutchinson, for whom William four years before had provided in his poems a cottage in Grasmere, is nowhere in the picture. This may be because, for financial reasons, marriage was out of the question for William, but it is also more than possible that Dorothy believed that the glow of love that William had felt for Mary was no longer of serious moment. She and Mary and William had spent two summers together at Penrith in 1787 and 1788 very pleasantly, but, if William's later account of his feelings is a true one, Mary had awakened in these years a delightful, but transitory, affection.

> She was a *Phantom* of delight
> When first she gleamed upon my sight:
> A lovely Apparition, sent
> To be *a moment's* ornament.

The characteristic of apparitions is that they come and go: and the story of the next few years justifies us in thinking that between 1789 and 1797, when Mary paid a long visit to William and Dorothy in Dorset, her image became dimmed.

In the same conversation in which he spoke of the 'struggle between his conscience and his impulses', he also made a surprising admission. He would, he said, have liked to enter the army. He had read books of military history and strategy, and thought he had 'a talent for command'. But he dreaded being sent to the West Indies, which were then indeed more fatal to British soldiers than any human enemy, before the study of hygiene and tropical medicine had begun. His wish could not

[1] *E.L.* 16, p. 58. W.W. to W. Mathews, Sept. 23rd 1791.
[2] *Grosart*, iii, p. 451.

be gratified. In a letter to Lord Lonsdale, written in 1812, he speaks rather obscurely of 'the circumstances in which my youth was placed, that threw great difficulties in the way of my adopting that profession to which I was most inclined, and for which I was perhaps best qualified'. His meaning is probably that there was no money available for the purchase of a commission. Wordsworth, if he thought he had 'a talent for command', would hardly have been content to enter the army as a poor private soldier, as Coleridge did when he fled from his Cambridge duns.

Wordsworth's desire for a military career is not so surprising as at first appears. His fundamental patriotism, bred from his reading of history and heroic legend, was as yet undisturbed by the French Revolution. That the disturbance was only temporary is shown by his deep concern for national defence and his joining the volunteers after the resumption of the war with France in 1803, and by his detestation of Bonaparte. Wordsworth was the author of *Poems dedicated to National Independence and Liberty* as well as of *Lyrical Ballads*. He loved the soldierly virtues, and his veneration for the French soldier Beaupuy was perhaps to no inconsiderable degree tinged with an affectionate envy.

On January 27th 1791 Wordsworth took his degree of Bachelor of Arts at Cambridge. His cousin John Myers also took his at the same time, and so did Robert Jones; all three took simple B.A.s without honours. But Jones was very soon afterwards elected to a Welsh fellowship at St. John's, where, however, he did not reside until several years later, preferring to live in his father's house in Denbighshire. As for Wordsworth, he knew at least where he wanted to go, if not what he wanted to do, and proceeded immediately to London, where for four months he lived in an obscurity which remains almost complete as far as his outward circumstances are concerned. We do not know where he lived or with whom he associated. But it is clear from a hint in the seventh book of *The Prelude* that he did not live with his brother Richard—who as yet had no chambers of his own—or with any friends. In all probability he took cheap lodgings:

> it pleased me my abode to fix
> Single in the wide waste, to have a house
> It was enough (what matter for a home?).

And indeed except for his brother, he knew scarcely anyone in London. William Mathews of Pembroke, his most intimate Cambridge friend, was now teaching at a school in Leicestershire.

Wordsworth had very little money,[1] and so could not afford—and was careful not to incur—the expense of entertaining others; his own amusements had to be confined to the cheapest shows, or simply to that which indeed he more than most people was perfectly content in doing—wandering about the streets by himself and observing the flow of the life of the great city round him. He had not come to London to seek a fortune or a job; so he sought no introductions to persons of position or quality. He was, he says,

> Though self-willed,
> From dangerous passions free.

In other words he did what he liked without endangering either his purse or his morals. In short he 'filled an idler's place'; neither the vigorous activity of Londoners nor their ceaseless pursuit of pleasure could lure him away from his own peculiar way of passing the time, which he summed up as

> living cheerfully abroad
> With unchecked fancy ever on the stir
> And all my young affections out of doors.[2]

What took Wordsworth to London at this moment was really his romanticism, or more accurately his romantic curiosity, and as usual with him this had its origins far back in childhood. At Hawkshead school there was a boy—'a cripple from his birth'—who once went on a visit to London. On his return Wordsworth tells how he gazed at him with awe and almost with disappointment that there was not some bodily change in him; that he had not brought back some 'beams of glory' with him from the capital.[3] Instead his answers to Wordsworth's eager questions

> Fell flatter than a cagèd parrot's note,
> That answers unexpectedly awry.

---

[1] On Jan. 28th his guardians remitted him the sum of £60. His Cambridge tuition fees were not all paid until after he had left college: £30 was paid to James Wood in 1792, but a bill was still outstanding in 1803 for £10. 15s. 3½d. On May 19th 1791 he received £20, and on Nov. 10th, just before leaving for France, £40, a total of £120. *D.C.P.*

[2] *Prel.* VII, ll. 74–76.   [3] *Prel.* VII (1805), l. 103.

All the pageantry that Wordsworth's fancy had conjured up about the sights and shows of London town were apparently invisible to this youth, and instead one most disturbing piece of information emerged which was a sad puzzle to Wordsworth:

> how men lived
> Even next-door neighbours, as we say, yet still
> Strangers, not knowing each the other's names.

To a boy growing up in a country-side where every cottage fireside was a home, and every face familiar and friendly, such isolation was unbelievable. And when he at length went there to see for himself, though he no longer expected to find the streets paved with gold, and though the unromantic George III occupied the throne, his expectations retained enough of their childhood glamour to invest many things with a glow of delight and to add interest even to what was disappointing. Yet we have only to read the account of London in the seventh book of *The Prelude* and compare it with that of the Swiss tour in the sixth, to feel that something is missing. Here is Wordsworth, interested, enjoying himself, storing up vivid scenes and incidents to be 'frequent day-dreams' afterwards, yet it is Wordsworth unmoved, save very occasionally, in his imagination. It was not that London was incapable of moving him—that he could only 'see into the life of things' when he was among mountains and valleys. On the contrary, it was the sight of that city in the stillness of an autumn dawn that drew from him years afterwards words that are still like a cry of aching wonder and delight:

> Earth hath not anything to show more fair. . . .

And two years before, when he had first come up from Cambridge on the top of a stage-coach, the immense significance of London descended on his soul like a physical weight.[1] But when he came to live in it day after day, and week after week, it was to him something remote from his own being, detached and only half-real; something moreover transient, unstable, and for ever slipping away:

> The comers and the goers face to face,
> Face after face; the string of dazzling wares
> Shop after shop. . . .

[1] Ibid. VIII, ll. 543–59. See above, pp. 124–5.

In the only contemporary description he has left us of his time in London—one sentence in a letter to William Mathews written in June—he makes use once more of his favourite image of a swift-flowing river:

> I quitted London about three weeks ago, where my time passed in a strange manner; sometimes whirled about by the vortex of its *strenua inertia,* and sometimes thrown by the eddy into a corner of the stream where I lay in almost motionless indolence.

The essential truth of this description is borne out by *The Prelude* accurately enough. London had plenty of quiet back streets and corners, away from the roar of the traffic,

> Still as a sheltered place when winds blow loud,

into which he could escape 'as from an enemy'.

But there were times when as he walked along the streets he felt with oppressive vividness the sad isolation of all these souls from one another and from himself—

> the face of every one
> That passes by me is a mystery.

And from there it was easy to pass into the dream-like state of contemplation that was familiar to him in moments of deep emotion:

> the shapes before my eyes became
> A second-sight procession, such as glides
> Over still mountains, or appears in dreams;
> And all the ballast of familiar life
> The present and the past; hope, fear, all stays,
> All laws of acting, thinking, speaking man
> Went from me, neither knowing me nor known.[1]

Once more intensity of thought and feeling had brought him to the threshold of vision. It did not fail him. Suddenly the throng among which he had become lost in trance became real, vivid, and incarnate in a single figure—a blind beggar standing against a wall, wearing on his breast a label, with the story of his life written upon it. 'My mind', says Wordsworth,

> turned round
> As with the might of waters,

[1] *Prel.* VII (1805), ll. 600–6. Cf. the passage in the second book, where
> what I saw
> Appeared like something in myself, a dream,
> A prospect in my mind.   II, ll. 348–52.

fastening itself in wonder and immovable attention on this strange symbol of humanity. He stared at the label and found in it

> a type
> Or emblem of the utmost that we know,
> Both of ourselves and of the universe,
> And on the shape of that unmoving man,
> His steadfast face and sightless eyes, I gazed
> As if admonished from another world.[1]

Why did Wordsworth use the word 'admonished' to describe the effect upon him of this experience? Incidents such as these were always something more to him than simply meetings with picturesque unfortunates. The Discharged Soldier, the Blind Man, the Leech-gatherer taught him prophetic and symbolic lessons; they gave food for moral reflection; above all they ministered to self-criticism and humility. In the blunter language of Hamlet, Wordsworth might have exclaimed after one of these meetings: '"What should such a fellow as I do, crawling between earth and heaven?"—I, with my idleness and indecision, my absorption in my own feelings and my own tastes.' Yet he did not feel called upon to rush into philanthropic activity on their behalf, as many of his evangelical contemporaries would have done. His life remained outwardly as idle, as isolated, as before. But in the more vivid mental life the images of these people lived on undimmed, and the emotions they had aroused lived also, to be brought forth in the fullness of time into the immortality of great poetry, to witness to the pathos, the dignity, and the mystery of man.

During his stay in London, Wordsworth listened to debates in the House of Commons. He was probably admitted into the House by John Robinson, the member for Harwich, who had formerly represented the borough of Appleby, and whose aunt, Mary Robinson, had married Wordsworth's grandfather, Richard Wordsworth, to whom Robinson had as a young man been articled as clerk. He was thus a first cousin of Wordsworth's father. Sir James Lowther had made him his agent for his Lowther estates and also secured his election for the borough of Appleby in 1764. Ten years later Robinson and his patron

----

[1] Ibid., ll. 637–49.

quarrelled violently over American affairs, and Robinson refused to obey Lowther's instructions to vote with the Whig
opposition. In that year he gave up all connexion with Sir James
and with Appleby, and became member for the government
borough of Harwich. He bought Wyke House at Isleworth,
where he lived with his family; we may surmise that Wordsworth visited him there. He was kindly disposed towards the
children of John Wordsworth and actively helped the younger
John in his career at sea.

In the House Wordsworth heard Pitt speak. *The Prelude*
tells us how the name of Pitt was one which

> from childhood we had heard
> Familiarly, a household term, like those,
> The Bedfords, Glosters, Salsburys, of old
> Whom the fifth Harry talks of.[1]

In the Cockermouth days it would of course have been the elder,
not the younger, Pitt whom the Wordsworth boys took into
their talk and games along with Shakespeare's men of war.
Burke also he heard, prophesying in his rather grim old age
against all that was coming to pass in the world. The laudatory
invocation of Burke in *The Prelude* was not written until 1820,
after Wordsworth's political opinions had become in many
respects like Burke's. But there is no reason to suppose that
the young Wordsworth of 1791, whose opinions were quite
unfixed, although he carried in his mind such happy pictures of
the new France, heard Burke's oratory without admiration, or
that there is much exaggeration in his description of his feelings:

> could a youth and one
> In ancient story versed, whose breast had heaved
> Under the weight of classic eloquence,
> Sit, see and hear unthankful, uninspired?[2]

Through Mr. Robinson Wordsworth could doubtless, had he
so wished, have seen something of the social life of London at
this, its most brilliant period. Though poor, he still possessed the
velvet coat and silk stockings which he had worn at Cambridge.

---

[1] *Prel.* VII, ll. 495–8. See also *Monument of Mrs. Howard in Wetheral Church*,
note, where he says that he had seen Pitt 'on his own ground' at Cambridge, as
well as in the House of Commons. *P.W.* iv, p. 409.
[2] *Prel.* VII, ll. 540–3.

But he had no interest in the great, and desired nothing that they had to give. He was, as he says,

> by personal ambition unenslaved,

and cared little as yet for public affairs or for those who carried them on. The passages of *The Prelude* which describe what he did see of the life of the great world—the fashionable preachers, the lawyers, and even the House of Commons—contain a flavour of somewhat heavy satire and lack the freshness and spontaneity of the descriptions of 'half-rural Sadler's Wells', and the varied life of the streets by day and night. We cannot escape the feeling that Wordsworth was trying here to write of what he thought afterwards should have interested him rather than recollecting with vividness and accuracy his real feelings.

So, alone and quietly happy, he wandered about the streets; alone he found out cheap places of amusement such as Sadler's Wells, a remote theatre in Islington that has grown famous again in our day. Long before, when he was a little boy at Hawkshead, he had sometimes seen a play performed in a barn by a strolling company. Nothing gave him keener delight, not only because of what he actually saw on this rustic stage, but also because of a certain snug and intimate satisfaction at being shut off from the 'real' world and inside one of romance and fantasy. Out there through a crack in the barn wall he could see the sunshine on the haycocks; but here he was safe—safe from the dangers and difficulties of reality—enjoying all the luxury of 'escape'. Something of the 'gloss' of these early days still hung over him as he watched popular tragedies, acrobats, clowns, and pantomimes—for Sadler's Wells made no pretensions to be 'high-brow', and retained much of its old character of a place of popular entertainment. It was licensed only for musical and pantomimic shows, not for stage plays, and it was these

> singers . . .
> Clowns, conquerors, posture-makers, harlequins,

that Wordsworth watched there, as he says, 'with ample recompence'.[1] At the more regular theatres he shed copious tears in

---

[1] Ibid. (1805), ll. 495–515. For the entertainments at Sadler's Wells see Allardyce Nicoll, *History of Late XVIIIth Century Drama*, 1927.

sympathy with the pathetic scenes on the stage. But these emotional disturbances usually

> Passed not beyond the suburbs of my mind.

Only occasionally, he says, was he touched in his dearest faculty, the imagination. Sometimes a performance of Shakespeare 'rose to ideal grandeur', or by force of the contrast of bad acting, caused him to see his own musings on Shakespeare in a fresh and vivid light, and so

> recognise
> As at a glance the things which I had shaped
> And yet not shaped, had seen and scarcely seen,
> Had felt and thought of in my solitude.

In London as in his own country Wordsworth often preferred to take his solitary walks at night, and in bad weather:

> at late hours
> Of winter evenings, when unwholesome rains
> Are falling hard, with people yet astir,
> The feeble salutation from the voice
> Of some unhappy woman, now and then
> Heard as we pass.[1]

Once, lingering about the doors of a theatre, he saw a sight which his imagination seized and fed upon as it had seized upon the blind man. It was a little boy, scarcely more than a baby, a harlot's child,

> in face a cottage rose
> Just three parts blown,

sitting on the refreshment-bar of the theatre, while all the riff-raff of the place, 'the wretched and the falsely gay', played with him, and

> oaths and laughter and indecent speech
> Were rife about him as the songs of birds
> Contending after showers.

It was indeed a scene exactly calculated to appeal to the heart of Wordsworth as he stood aloof, gazing at the strange scene with those eyes lit, perhaps, as De Quincey so often saw them afterwards, with 'an appearance the most solemn and spiritual that it is possible for a human eye to wear'.[2]

---

[1] *Prel.* VII (1805), ll. 635–40.
[2] *Prel.* VII, ll. 334–65. De Quincey, *Recollections of the Lake Poets.*

Towards the end of May Wordsworth left London for Wales,[1] where he spent nearly four months with Robert Jones at Plas-yn-Llan, the 'house by the Church' at Llangynhafal, not far from Ruthin, where Jones was living with his father and sisters. It seems that the visit to Wales was planned as part of a longer tour to the north, during which he hoped to visit Dorothy's beloved 'Aunt Rawson' at Halifax. He had seen this lady—his mother's cousin—in town and no doubt received an invitation from her then.[2] In fact, however, there was no northern visit this year; the early autumn saw him once more in Cambridge and before Christmas he was in France. In Wales he was happy enough. 'Who', as Dorothy gaily said to Jane, 'would not be happy enjoying the company of three young ladies in the Vale of Clwyd without a rival?' It was, however, more the charms of 'mountains, rivers, woods and rocks' that kept Wordsworth in Wales that summer. Jones took him for a three weeks' 'pedestrian tour' of north Wales, of which the itinerary is roughly outlined in the letter he prefixed to *Descriptive Sketches* when he published it early in 1793, dedicating it to Robert Jones. There he apologizes for not having celebrated the Welsh mountain scene in poetry: 'The sea-sunsets which give such splendour to the vale of Clwyd, Snowdon, the chair of Idris, the quiet village of Beddgelert, Menai and her Druids, the Alpine steeps of the Conway, and the still more interesting windings of the wizard stream of the Dee, remain yet untouched.' Was this because Wordsworth himself remained 'untouched' by their beauty? When he revisited north Wales more than thirty years later, he admitted that 'I had seen these things long ago but either my memory or my powers of observation had not done them justice.' And in the *Guide to the Lakes*, which he published in 1822, before his return to north Wales, he expressed the opinion that the 'Concentration of interest' and unity of the central part of the Lake District, 'gives to the country a decided superiority over the most attractive districts of Scotland and Wales, especially to the pedestrian traveller'.

Yet he has left us one magnificent memorial of that tour, in

---

[1] *E.L.* 12 and 13, pp. 45 and 48. D.W. to J.P., May 23rd 1791, and W.W. to W. Mathews, June 17th 1791.

[2] Ibid., p. 45. D.W. to J.P., May 1791. 'Aunt Threlkeld' was now married to Samuel Rawson, a rich mill-owner of Halifax, and so became 'Aunt Rawson'.

the description of the midnight climb from Beddgelert to the summit of Snowdon to see the sunrise.[1] This he wrote in March 1804 as the opening to the fifth book of *The Prelude*, though it was later transferred to the beginning of the last book (Book XIV), where it now stands. We hear nothing in it of the sunrise, only of the strange moonlight landscape that revealed itself when at length the moon emerged from the

> close, warm, breezeless summer night,
> Wan, dull and glaring, with a dripping fog.

The description of the ascent gives us a little picture of Wordsworth climbing a mountain which is rememberable:

> with forehead bent
> Earthward, as if in opposition set
> Against an enemy, I panted up
> With eager pace, and no less eager thoughts.

Because he was looking down he did not see the moon appear; but he was conscious of 'a light upon the turf'. When at length he looked up, he found that they had emerged above the mist which now lay below them lit up by the moon:

> A hundred hills their dusky backs upheaved
> All over this still ocean; and beyond,
> Far, far beyond, the solid vapours stretched,
> In headlands, tongues and promontory shapes
> Into the main Atlantic. . . .

Not far from the 'shore' of this strange sea at their feet was 'a blue chasm',

> a rift— . . .
> A fixed, abysmal, gloomy, breathing-place,

from out of which

> Mounted the roar of waters, torrents, streams
> Innumerable, roaring with one voice.

It is not surprising that this wonderful spectacle at once began to become in Wordsworth's mind a symbol and image of some-

---

[1] De Selincourt would date the incident in 1793, during his second visit to Wales, but it seems more natural to include it in the 'pedestrian tour' in which Beddgelert and Snowdon are both mentioned. The description in *Prel.* XIV should be compared with *D.S.* (1793), ll. 495–505, where a similar scene, but by daylight, of a valley filled with mist out of which ascends the sound of 'unnumbered streams', is recorded. This is the only passage in *D.S.* to which Wordsworth himself refers in his note on the poem. *P.W.* i, p. 324.

thing greater. 'A meditation rose in me', he says, as soon as the vision had 'partially dissolved', and it seemed that the moonlit world of mountain and mist had been

> the emblem of a mind
> That feeds upon infinity, that broods
> Over the dark abyss, intent to hear
> Its voices issuing forth to silent light
> In one continuous stream. . . .

The image brings *Kubla Khan* forcibly to the mind:

> And from this chasm, with ceaseless turmoil seething
> As if this earth in fast thick pants were breathing,
> A mighty fountain momently was forced. . . .

It is as though to each poet, as he brooded 'over the dark abyss' of his experience of the mystery of things, there came an intimation of the sources of creative power.

His idleness at this time was almost complete, both in reading and writing. He tells William Mathews in August that his 'incursions into the fields of modern literature' have been confined to *Tristram Shandy* and two or three papers of the *Spectator*, while his failure to bring with him his Italian and Spanish grammars made further acquaintance with these languages impossible. Nevertheless, he remained cheerful. 'I have not in addition to all this to complain of bad spirits. That would be the devil indeed. I rather think that this gaiety increases with my ignorance, as a spendthrift grows more extravagant the nearer he approximates to a final dissipation of his property'.[1]

As for poetry, it is impossible to say with certainty whether he wrote any at all during 1791. If the fragmentary lines about the woman seeking shelter while crossing a desolate heath really belong to this year, they show that his mind was already at work on a theme that was to absorb him much in the years after his return from France, and that the meeting with the 'friend' to whom the disasters afterwards described in *The Female Vagrant* had happened had already taken place.[2] Possibly also

---

[1] *E.L.* 15, p. 56. W.W. to W. Mathews, Aug. 1791.

[2] *P.W.* i, pp. 292–5. *Juvenilia*, XVI. In his note to *Guilt and Sorrow* Wordsworth says that 'much of the Female vagrant's story was composed at least two years before' the writing of *Salisbury Plain* of which it formed a part. If this is correct, he was already working on the story in 1790 or 1791. The lines about the

the long 'fragment of a Gothic Tale', in Spenserian stanza, belongs to this year. In the latter occurs an incident later incorporated into *The Borderers*—that of a blind man led into a ruined castle by a youth who contemplates murdering him. It contained also one line that, lifted from this early fragment and used again forty years later in the sonnet *Mutability*, was to take its place among the most haunting of Wordsworth's images:

The unimaginable touch of time.

Wordsworth's good spirits were useful this summer not only to himself. Mathews was in need of comfort and advice. Unable to live at home because of his hatred of the dregs of the religious world who haunted his father's house and took advantage of that good man's honesty and gullibility, he had left London and was teaching in a school in Leicestershire. Here, however, he soon became discouraged and depressed, and Wordsworth's letters to him are chiefly an attempt to cheer him up. They are the earliest letters of Wordsworth that have survived, with the exception of his letter to Dorothy from Switzerland in the previous autumn. Montagu's glowing tribute in later years to Wordsworth's powers as a comforter and guide to a mind in distress receive corroboration from these letters, which are among the most pleasing that he wrote. Thus he writes in August:

I think the fatigue which you undergo is a sufficient apology for that depression of spirits which disposes you to look on the dark side of things. But were you released from this irksome toil, take my word for it, you would find that you had been regularly though unconsciously advancing (in knowledge). As to the idea of the decay of your mental powers, you may easily get rid of it by reading Pope's description of the cave of spleens in the *Rape of the Lock*.

He wishes he had known in time Mathews's wish to join him and Jones in their tour of north Wales. 'Such an excursion

woman contain another tribute to Wordsworth's favourite creature, the glow-worm, already celebrated in *An Evening Walk*.

I saw, safe-sheltered by the viewless furze,
The tiny glow-worm, lowliest child of earth,
From his green lodge with undiminished light
Shine through the rain. . . .

would have served like an Aurora Borealis to gild your long Lapland night of melancholy.'[1]

In September Mathews seems to have proposed to Words-worth to join him in a drastic way out of his trouble—namely, to give up seeking a regular livelihood and to take to the roads as a tramp. Wordsworth's comments on this scheme are charac-teristic, for there was much in it with which he could sympathize, but his sturdy north-country caution and feeling of obligation to his family made his reaction sharply unfavourable. He says:

I take it for granted that you are not likely to continue long in your present employment, but when you leave it how you can put into execution the plan you speak of I cannot perceive. It is impossible you can ever have your father's consent to a scheme which, to a parent at least, must appear wild even to insanity. . . . I do not think you could ever be happy while you were conscious that you were a cause of such sorrow to your parents when all that they will know of you is that you are wandering about the world without perhaps a house to your head.

He continues significantly:

I cannot deny, were I so situated as to be without relations to whom I were accountable for my actions, I should perhaps prefer your idea to your present situation, or to vegetating on a paltry curacy.

That curacy, which his own relations designed for him, was a wretched, cramping thing in his eyes, and he goes on:

Yet still there is another objection which would have influence upon me, which is this. I should not be able to reconcile to my ideas of right, the thought of wandering about a country without a certainty of being able to maintain myself. . . . I see many charms in the idea of travelling, much to be enjoyed and much to be learnt. So many that were we in possession of perhaps even less than a hundred a year apiece, which would amply obviate the objection I have just made, and without any relations to whom we were accountable, I would set out with you this moment with all my heart. . . . But this is not the case; therefore, for my own part, I resign the idea.

---

[1] This curious phrase is anticipatory of a more famous one—that in which he prays for the 'dear child of Nature'—who is Dorothy—

> an old age serene and bright
> And lovely as a Lapland night.

It is possible he had read Scheffer's *History of Lapland*, referred to in a note in Beattie's *Minstrel*, Book I, st. 59.

His final advice, when we consider his own total idleness and disinclination to settle to any profession, is amusing:

What then is to be done? Hope and industry are to be your watchwords and I warrant you this influence will secure the victory. In order to defend yourself from the necessity of being immured for the future, in such a cell as your present, determine to spare no pains to cultivate the powers of your mind, and you may be certain of being able to support yourself in London. You know there are certain little courts in different parts of London which are called bags. If you stumble into one of them there is no advancing, if you wish to proceed on your walk you must return the way you went in. These bags of Life are what every man of spirit dreads, and ought to dread. Be industrious and you never need get your head into them, let hope be your walking staff and your fortune is made.

Wordsworth's protest was evidently of some use, for in his next letter he writes: 'I am very happy to hear you had given up your travelling scheme, that your father had consented to your changing your situation and that in consequence your mind was much easier.' And he adds, 'I am happy to find my letter afforded you some consolation. There are few reflections more pleasing than the consciousness that one has contributed in the smallest degree to diminish the anxiety of one's friends.'[1]

Not long after writing this letter Wordsworth was faced with the necessity of dealing with proposals from his own relations about his uncertain future. His cousin John Robinson wrote early in September offering him the curacy of Harwich, with the reversion of the living in prospect.[2] 'I thought it best', says Wordsworth, 'to pay my respects to him in person, to inform him that I was not of age.' This could, one feels, have been done equally well by letter, but Mr. Robinson was a person of some worldly consideration. Perhaps his guardians or Uncle William had urged him to pay the visit. He repaired therefore to London, where probably an indefinite arrangement was come to about the curacy; there can be no doubt Wordsworth did not want it, but he was well aware that ordination was almost the

---

[1] *E.L.* 16, 18, pp. 58, 60–61.

[2] The Rev. William Cowper, vicar of Harwich, was a brother of his aunt, Mrs. William Cookson. He got into debt and had to fly to Holland to escape his creditors. At this period he was in Holland and resigned the living shortly afterwards.

only way open to him of earning a living. Eighteen months, however, were yet to pass before he would be of age to take orders.

In August 1791 the long-standing lawsuit brought by the administrators of John Wordsworth's estate came on for trial at Carlisle Assizes. If it succeeded, and Lord Lonsdale was forced to pay the accumulated debt that was claimed, William would be in possession of something approaching the £100 a year which, meagre though it was, would just enable him to live without a profession, for it was estimated that about £5,000 would be divided between the five Wordsworth children.[1] The story of the lawsuit is a vivid illustration of how in those days a really determined man who was also very wealthy could hold up the processes of law and evade the pronouncements of justice.[2]

On August 30th 1786 Richard Wordsworth of Branthwaite, William's cousin and his father's executor, delivered at Lowther Hall a bill for £4,625. 3s. 7d., most of which consisted of charges for legal work undertaken by Mr. Wordsworth on behalf of his employer. Lord Lonsdale took no notice of it and in January 1788 he was summoned to appear at the assizes. He ignored the summons and at length the sheriff's officers arrived at Lowther Hall with orders to make a distraint upon him for £5,000. Upon that he instantly appeared, but, as the time of the assizes had now gone by, he had gained time. 'His principle', said Richard of Branthwaite, 'has been delay from the first moment until now, and still will be if possible.' Lord Lonsdale then took the initiative, filed an Exchequer Bill and obtained an injunction for a stay of proceedings which enabled him to hold everything up for nearly three years. At length, in February 1791, the defendants (now the administrators) obtained a final order dissolving the injunction, and ordering Lord Lonsdale to pay £4,000 into court. This, of course, Lord Lonsdale had no intention of doing, but the way was now cleared for the hearing of the main cause at the Carlisle Assizes. In the meantime the administrators had succeeded in getting a commission of inquiry to sit at Whitehaven to determine whether there had in fact ever

---

[1] E.L. 2, p. 7. D.W. to J.P., Aug. 5th 1787.
[2] The papers relating to the lawsuit, with Gordon Wordsworth's notes, are among the Dove Cottage Papers at Grasmere.

been an agreement between Lord Lonsdale and John Wordsworth, as his Lordship claimed. In December 1790 the Master
of the Court declared that he was satisfied there had never been
any agreement, only that 'Mr. Wordsworth was to be paid for
all law business as other gentlemen were paid'. A report to this
effect was eventually signed on February 23rd 1791.

The spring and summer of 1791 were filled with preparations
for the trial at Carlisle Assizes. Some idea of the magnitude
of the case may be gained from the volume of documents involved. Richard Wordsworth of Branthwaite had sent up to
London, two years before, three large packing cases containing
altogether 1,830 folios. There were all kinds of difficulties connected with the trial. Upwards of two hundred witnesses had to
be summoned to Carlisle by the administrators and their expenses paid. Some came from as far away as Yorkshire. The
sheriff's books were searched for 'the residences of several free-
men who received large sums from Intestate [that is, Mr. John
Wordsworth] on Defendant's [Lord Lonsdale's] account'. This
gives a glimpse of Lord Lonsdale's political methods at election
times. One of the chief witnesses was William Arnott, who had
been clerk to Mr. Wordsworth, and was now employed by the
Lowther interest. He was subpoenaed, but succeeded for a month
in evading service.

Lord Lonsdale retained a large number of counsel; the administrators employed four, of whom the chief was Edward
Christian, a Fellow of St. John's College and Professor of Law
at Cambridge. He was engaged no doubt because he was a
Cumberland man; he came from Moorland Close, two miles
outside Cockermouth, and was a brother of Fletcher Christian,
the leader of the famous mutiny on the *Bounty*, which by this
time had disappeared into the South Seas. Edward Christian
was somewhat of a character in Cambridge. He was youthful
and inexperienced, and no one in Cambridge ever took him very
seriously.[1] Dorothy speaks of him as 'a very clever man' but too
young to have much authority: he was a friend, she said, of her
Uncle Cookson and 'knows my brother William very well'.

The case came on in August. No account exists of its progress,
but it apparently lasted a week, as Richard Wordsworth sent

[1] Gunning: *Reminiscences of Cambridge*, i, p. 220, says that he died in 1823, 'in
the full vigour of his *incapacity*'.

in a bill for seven days' attendance. The result was a victory for the administrators and Lord Lonsdale was ordered to pay. But the amount to be paid was referred to an arbitrator,[1] and the proceedings dragged on in London all the winter, with the examination of many more witnesses, and in the end no conclusion was reached. The affair simply petered out. Probably the administrators felt they could no longer afford to run up bills. Richard Wordsworth of Branthwaite drew up a bill amounting to nearly £1,000 for the expenses of the trial, and in order to meet the expenses of witnesses a mortgage had to be surrendered. Thus only a barren victory had been gained after six years of fighting. Nothing further was done until the death of Lord Lonsdale in 1802 opened new possibilities. The story then proceeded without further difficulty to a happy ending for the Wordsworths.

The 'affair with Lord Lonsdale' overshadowed the youth of the Wordsworths, giving to their lives an atmosphere of uncertainty and frustration. Dorothy felt keenly the disagreeableness of 'living upon the bounty of one's friends', however kind.[2] As for William, he was deeply galled by what he considered the unscrupulous use of aristocratic power. He, too, thirsted for independence, however modest, for that hundred a year which would enable him to free himself from the threat of the 'paltry curacy'. The great unresolved dilemma of his youth may well have contributed towards his admiration for the independent small farmers who formed the backbone of the population of the Lake District, and who play so large a part in his poetry. Poverty he did not mind, but independence was an essential part of human dignity. The humiliations he endured in boyhood in his grandfather's house at Penrith, and Uncle Kit's ungracious behaviour, were all to be attributed ultimately to his dependent position. He went on his way uncomplaining but by no means indifferent to the harsh circumstances which his father's employer forced upon him and his brothers and sister.

In the meantime his Uncle William had insisted on his returning temporarily to Cambridge, where we find him established at the end of September, and intending 'by the advice of my Uncle William' (says Dorothy) 'to study the Oriental languages'.

[1] *E.L.* 19, p. 63. D.W. to J.P., Dec. 7th 1791.
[2] Ibid. 48, p. 141. D.W. to J.P., Sept. 1795.

This would have meant a course of private tuition in Hebrew and Arabic as preparation for the life of a learned clergyman. It was not a plan which commended itself to William. 'What must I do among that immense wilderness', he wrote to Mathews, 'I who have no resolution, and who have not prepared myself for the enterprise by any sort of discipline amongst the Western languages? who know little of Latin and scarce anything of Greek. A pretty confession for a young gentleman whose whole life ought to have been devoted to study.'[1]

Something of the force of this objection William evidently succeeded in impressing upon his uncle, for this letter was written from Brighton on November 23rd while he was waiting for a wind to carry him to France! He had now in fact succeeded in obtaining his guardians' permission to spend some months in France, to perfect his knowledge of French, with a view to getting a situation on his return as a travelling tutor to some wealthy youth. Only if this scheme failed would he revert to the 'Oriental languages'. We can see in all this a strong attempt to break through the net which he felt closing round him—the net of ordination. A travelling tutorship was possible without taking orders.

At Brighton he was detained for four days waiting for a wind, but their tedium was relieved by making acquaintance with Mrs. Charlotte Smith, whose *Elegiac Sonnets* he had bought and read while at Cambridge, retaining for them a considerable admiration throughout his life. This lady was at present living at Brighton, having separated from her spendthrift husband, and was seeking to support by her pen the numerous children of her marriage. Her first novel, *Emmeline*, had appeared in the previous year. She received William kindly, and gave him a letter of introduction to Miss Helen Maria Williams, who had been living in Orleans, the very city of France to which he was now making his way. Miss Williams had, however, left it just before he arrived. On Saturday, November 27th, he crossed over to Dieppe. Nearly thirteen months were to pass before he set foot again in England, months full of excitement and disaster both for himself and for the country in which he had taken refuge from the difficulties which had faced him in his own.

[1] *E.L.* 18, p. 61. Nov. 23rd 1791.

VI

FRANCE, 1791–2

The fire-ship is Old France.
THOMAS CARLYLE

WORDSWORTH landed at Dieppe on November 28th, proceeded to Rouen where he took the 'diligence' and arrived in Paris on Wednesday, November 30th. He remained there until the following Monday, December 5th, when he went on to Orleans, which he had selected as a convenient city in which to study French.

Wordsworth in 1791 was very little more politically-minded, or less ignorant of the causes and history of the great Revolution, than he had been when he had passed through France in the previous year on the flood-tide of the Feast of Federation. He had, he said, read some of the 'major pamphlets of the day', but with only a detached interest. He wandered about Paris much as he had wandered about London, looking at the human shows, but, as he himself confessed, he was roused to greater emotion by 'the painted Magdalene of Le Brun'[1] in the Carmelite Convent than by the ruins of the Bastille. In them, indeed, he sat for a while in the winter sunshine, 'glad—could living man be otherwise?', at the destruction of such a symbol of tyranny, yet 'affecting more emotion than I felt'.

Le Brun's 'Magdalene' is one of the most extreme examples of the exaggerated treatment of sentiment in baroque art. We may wonder that Wordsworth could be moved by such histrionics, but he was a true child of the eighteenth century in his disposition to admire the 'softer emotions'. He was throughout his life easily moved to tears, and his first published poem had been addressed to Miss Helen Maria Williams 'weeping at a tale of distress'. His eye was quite untrained in the judgement of art; it simply followed his feelings. Later, he held the view

---

[1] *Prel.* IX, ll. 77–80. This picture was really a portrait of Louise de la Vallière, Louis XIV's mistress who eventually took the veil. It was a famous sight for visitors to Paris. It is now in the Louvre.

that painting, like poetry, should 'ennoble human nature',[1] and
something of this feeling may have been present in his mind as
he gazed upon the Magdalene.

In Paris he visited the Legislative Assembly, having been
furnished while at Brighton with an introduction to one of the
deputies probably by Mrs. Smith.[2] It would be gratifying to
know who this person was, but there is little clue. It has been
suggested that it may have been Brissot himself,[3] but Wordsworth later denied this. Wordsworth himself says he was 'introduced by a member of whose acquaintance I shall profit on
my return to Paris', and it is therefore reasonable to suppose
that it was a member of the 'Girondin' group, for it was certainly with these that he associated during his second stay in
Paris.[4] The Girondins, the sentimentalists among the revolutionaries, lived largely in a world of dangerous idealism which
was soon to bring them to destruction after they had plunged
their country into war. In no political group was the heady influence of Rousseau so clearly traceable. In Buzot's description
of himself in youth we have a perfect picture of the romantic,
virtuous 'child of nature'. In some respects it is like a caricature
of Wordsworth himself in boyhood, with the homely, matter-
of-fact influences of Hawkshead Grammar School and Ann Tyson
left out.

My head and heart [he says] were filled with Greek and Roman
history and . . . I . . . lived on the study of their virtues. As a boy I
almost ran wild. My passions were tight-packed in a fervent and sensitive heart. But their violence and excess were turned inwards. . . .
I always had a horror of debauchery. . . . I made acquaintance early
enough with misfortune; but only to become more attached to virtue,
in whose consolations alone I found relief. With what pleasure I can
still remember that happy period of my life, now gone beyond recall—
the day when I wandered silent across the mountains and woods of my
native place, reading with delight something of Plutarch or Rousseau
. . . or the times when, seated on the flowery turf, under the shadow
of branching trees, I gave myself up in sweet melancholy to recalling
the pleasures and pains that had influenced my early days.[5]

[1] *E.L.* 177, p. 402. W.W. to Sir G. Beaumont, July 20th 1804.
[2] Ibid. 20, p. 66. W.W. to R.W., Dec. 19th 1791.
[3] *T.L.S.*, Jan. 29th 1931. See below, p. 202, n.
[4] *Mem.* i, p. 77.
[5] Hérissay, *F. Buzot*, 1907, pp. 20–21. Buzot, *Mémoires sur la Révolution Française*, 1823, pp. 2–3, Buzot was a native of Evreux in Normandy whither he

Whether or not Wordsworth was personally acquainted with Brissot or Buzot, he would naturally find friends among men who read his old favourite, Plutarch, enjoyed solitary reflection, and shunned the coarser pleasures. There was enough here to attract him, though the deepest passion of his life—his love of Nature—would have been incomprehensible to these Frenchmen, whose interest in 'Nature' was philosophical rather than empirical. Wordsworth would never have read a book while walking across country.

Wordsworth says that he visited both the Assembly and the Jacobin Club, and that there he

> saw the Revolutionary Power
> Toss like a ship at anchor, rocked by storms.

But in thus describing the scene he is really speaking of his memories of the far stormier sessions of the Convention a year later, when again he was in Paris after the September massacres and the fall of the king, at the time of Robespierre's rise to a dominating position and the discomfiture of the Girondins. The debates during the first few days of December 1791 mainly concerned the revolt of the negroes in St. Domingo and the measures taken by the French Government there to restore order. The French settlers were royalists; they were using the revolt, so it was said, to undermine the position of the mulattos to whom rights had been granted by decree of the Assembly; therefore no troops should be sent to the aid of the white settlers except under guarantees that they would not be used against the mulattos. Brissot was the chief protagonist of the mulattos in these debates; he was known as a champion of coloured peoples and an opponent of slavery—a member of the society called 'Amis des Noirs'. He succeeded, in the teeth of fierce opposition, in gaining his point about the troops. Wordsworth just missed the debates about the *émigrés*, and Brissot's speeches advocating an immediate war 'of peoples against kings' as a means of national regeneration and a proof that the country was 'worthy' of liberty.[1]

Wordsworth did not linger in Paris. On Monday December

had returned from Paris in the autumn of 1791 having been made President of the Criminal Tribunal at his birthplace. He was not therefore in Paris during Wordsworth's visit.

[1] Allery, *Brissot de Warville*, pp. 232, 599.

5th he departed southwards, and reached Orleans on the 6th. Orleans had been until the Revolution a popular resort of young Englishmen desirous to learn, if not French, at least French manners.[1] Its aristocratic families were numerous and through its duke it was connected with the royal family; it had public libraries in many of its churches and monasteries; a university and a famous medical school; and an Académie Royale des Sciences, of which Benjamin Franklin was an honorary associate. During the middle of the century it had been largely rebuilt, with new walls, quays, gates, a new Gothic façade to the cathedral, and a fine new bridge of nine arches spanning the Loire, replacing that which had witnessed the entry of Joan of Arc. Joseph Jekyll, who had stayed there fifteen years earlier, found it 'one of the cleanest, neatest and finest towns of its size we have seen', superior in many respects to Paris. Since the Revolution, however, the aristocratic families—or at least their male members—had departed for Turin or Coblentz, unable to endure a life shorn of privileges. The monasteries and nunneries were rapidly being closed and turned into public institutions of various kinds. There were no young English gentlemen; Wordsworth found himself the only Englishman in the city.[2] Over the town the winds of the Revolution were blowing, as over every town in France. A society of 'Friends of the Constitution' was in ardent correspondence with the Jacobin Club in Paris. It demanded the renaming of certain streets and squares with revolutionary names, and this process began during the autumn of 1791. Orleans became also the seat of the newly created 'Haute Cour Nationale', set up after the Flight to Varennes to try and punish with death those accused of crimes against 'national honour', but it did not begin to function until the following year. Political prisoners were, however, being sent to Orleans to await trial there. But what was most significant of changed times and ominous for the future was the steady drift to the frontiers of the young men, some to join Condé and the *émigrés*, but many more to enrol under Lafayette in the

---

[1] *Correspondence of Mr. Joseph Jekyll*, 1894.

[2] Except for 'a Mr. Foxlowe', who had set up a cotton factory in the city and to whom Wordsworth introduced himself. *E.L.* 20, p. 67. W.W. to R.W., Dec. 19th 1791. Mr. Foxlowe was a supporter of the Revolution, and while the National Assembly was at Versailles he had galloped to Paris with the news of the king's coming to the Maison de Ville. Helen Maria Williams, *Letters*, vol. ii.

army which in the course of the next year, after its early
humiliations, was to carry the Revolution triumphantly over the
borders of France into Belgium and Germany and Savoy. This
volunteering had begun in Orleans in October and was to continue throughout Wordsworth's stay. Both there and during the
summer at Blois he was to watch the departure of the young
'patriots' with a beating heart. Their very enthusiasm made
them seem so many

> Arguments sent from Heaven, that 'twas a cause
> Good, pure, which no one could stand up against.[1]

Yet at first Wordsworth lived more among royalists and con-
servatives than among revolutionaries.

He took lodgings with a M. Gellet-Duvivier, a hosier in the
Rue Royale. Here he was assigned a 'very handsome apartment
on the first floor' for thirty 'livres' per month, about one pound
at the current rate of exchange; this, with board at fifty livres,
he considered 'extremely reasonable'. He had come to France
with twenty pounds, which he had cashed in Paris; this was to
last him until the following September when he wrote to his
brother Richard for a 'note' for a further twenty.[2]

In the same house in the Rue Royale lodged 'three officers
of the Cavalry and a young gentleman from Paris'.[3] Their host,
M. Gellet-Duvivier, was a bitter and rather unbalanced opponent
of the Revolution; he was to pay for his outspokenness with his
life in less than two years' time.[4]

Wordsworth had also received from Mrs. Charlotte Smith
an introduction to Miss Helen Maria Williams, but, as has
been seen, she had already left Orleans and had returned to
Paris a day or two before Wordsworth's arrival, and he felt
'considerable disappointment' at missing one whom he had long
admired from a distance. She was still a warm supporter of the

---

[1] *Prel.* IX, ll. 262–87. Miss Williams, describing the departure of a contingent
from Orleans during this autumn, says: 'They were drawn up on the Place du
Martroi and after affectionately embracing their friends . . . they ordered by way
of cordial the reviving air of *Ça ira*, and marched off singing in chorus.' *Letters,*
vol. ii.

[2] *E.L.* 20, p. 66. W.W. to R.W., Dec. 19th 1791.

[3] Ibid.

[4] *A.V.*, pp. 42–45. Gellet-Duvivier was guillotined at Paris together with nine
others accused from Orleans on July 13th 1793. There seems to be no doubt that
by that time he was insane.

Revolution, and her letters from France form a vivid and enthusiastic commentary on the day-to-day progress of events. Her
robust revolutionary patriotism was untempered by any fears
for the direction in which affairs were drifting. 'Living in France
at present', she said, 'appears to me somewhat like living in a
region of romance'. She rejoiced in the self-sacrifice of the work-
men who gave up their wages to equip men for the frontiers, and
in the cheerfulness of the poor peasants who worked to the strains
of *Ça ira*. In considering Wordsworth's response to the French
scene, it has to be remembered that he also daily witnessed scenes
like these, scenes of the most genuine and heartfelt enthusiasm,
such as could scarcely fail to move his sympathy more than the
complaints and recriminations of the royalist bourgeoisie and
cavalry officers.

Wordsworth had come to Orleans for the purpose of learning
French, but he told his brother he was not going to engage a
master, owing to the expense. He seems to have relied on
picking it up in ordinary conversation, and it was perhaps for
this purpose that he frequented for a while 'routs, card-tables',
and the meetings of various societies,

> Polished in arts and in punctilio versed.[1]

These meetings were exclusively aristocratic in tone, and all
political discussion was forbidden in them 'with scrupulous care',
for the position of all such societies, however unpolitical their
purpose, was becoming increasingly suspect. Patient research
in the records of Orleans has failed to throw much light on
these obscure clubs;[2] the well-known Académie Royale des
Sciences can scarcely be meant, for that was a genuine scientific
body, and besides, many of its members were active revolutionaries. Wordsworth's societies must have met in private
houses. After a while he ceased to attend such gatherings, finding their atmosphere unreal and remote, and withdrew

> Into a noisier world—

the world of the revolutionary clubs, and the clash of opinions
passionately held and fiercely defended.

In the house in the Rue Royale he had to listen to the talk of
the cavalry officers, who like almost all the officers of the old

---

[1] *Prel.* IX, l. 117.   [2] *Harper*, i, p. 152.

army of France, were bitterly opposed to the Revolution. Being
of necessity aristocrats—for no one could hold a commission in
the French army before the Revolution unless he was of noble
birth—they had suffered through the abolition of their privileges; their attitude was resentful and nostalgic; they would
not accept the changed society which had been thrust upon
them. Wordsworth was again thrown among these military
gentlemen when he migrated to Blois in the Spring; his description of them in *The Prelude* covers both groups.[1]

After a fortnight in Orleans he wrote to Richard a brief and
detached description of his surroundings. 'We are all perfectly
quiet here', he assured his brother, 'and likely to continue so;
I find . . . all the people of any opulence aristocrates and all the
others democrates—I had imagined there were some people of
wealth and circumstance favorers of the revolution, but here
there is none to be found.'[2] There is a slight note of disappointment here, or at least of surprise.

The Prelude describes in greater detail his feelings and his
impressions. He lived at first much as he had lived in London,
perfectly content to be a spectator:

> Amused and satisfied, I scarcely felt
> The shock of these concussions, unconcerned,
> Tranquil, almost, and careless as a flower
> Glassed in a green-house, or a parlour shrub
> While every bush and tree, the country through,
> Is shaking to the roots.[3]

This aloofness he explains by his ignorance of what was really
going on; he was like one who

> had abruptly passed
> Into a theatre, of which the stage
> Was busy with an action far advanced.[4]

If he remained an 'unconcerned' spectator at first, it was not
from lack of interest, but simply because, as yet, he had met with

---

[1] In *The Prelude* he makes no distinction between what happened at Orleans and
what happened at Blois—mentioning neither city by name and including both
under the title of 'a pleasant town, washed by the current of the stately Loire'.
[2] *E.L.* 20, p. 66. W.W. to R.W., Dec. 19th 1791.
[3] *Prel.* IX, ll. 85–90.
[4] Ibid., ll. 93–95.

nothing that touched his inner being. If that were to happen, all would indeed be changed. Now he lay like a becalmed ship;

> all things were to me
> Loose and disjointed, and the affections left
> Without a vital interest.[1]

The affections! Now, as always, they were the key to his spiritual and moral being. When his heart was touched, his imagination would spring to life, and he would 'kindle' in sympathy. Only too soon—alas for that amused detachment with which he was surveying the scene—more than one 'vital interest' was to seize on his 'affections' and he would move out into stormy and dangerous seas.

We do not know precisely when or where Wordsworth first met Annette Vallon, but it was certainly in Orleans, not in Blois, for she and she alone could have supplied him with a motive strong enough to make him leave Orleans after less than three months for Blois which was her home.[2] Fifteen years earlier, young Joseph Jekyll had made exactly the same migration, but that was because Orleans was then so full of English that he found it impossible to learn French there. No such reason could apply to Wordsworth. Their first meeting probably took place at the house of André Dufour, a magistrate's clerk, for it was to the Dufours that Annette returned in the autumn from Blois, and in their house that Caroline, her child and William Wordsworth's, was born in December 1792. Wordsworth had spoken in his letter to Richard soon after his arrival in Orleans of another family with whom he had at first wished to take lodgings, but their charges were too high. He found them, he says, 'very agreeable', and formed the habit of passing some of his evenings there.[3] The presence of Annette may well have been one of the attractions. It was quite natural for her to be staying in the city, for her brother Paul, who afterwards so narrowly escaped the guillotine, and for whose sake Annette herself became so deeply involved in the royalist cause, was then a lawyer's clerk in Orleans. At home, in Blois, her mother had married again, and as she had several sisters her presence at home might not have been considered at all times necessary.

---

[1] *Prel.* IX., ll. 105–7.

[2] He had already been many weeks in Blois when he wrote to William Mathews thence on May 17th 1792. *E.L.* 24, p. 74.   [3] Ibid. 20, p. 67.

Having met, she and Wordsworth rapidly became lovers, and when Annette returned home, probably in March, she was already with child by him.

What sort of girl was Annette Vallon that she could arouse such a storm of passion in William Wordsworth? A good deal is known about the home she came from. She was the sixth and youngest child of the late surgeon of the Hôtel Dieu at Blois— an ancient charitable institution where the sick poor were nursed by a religious sisterhood. Her father had been the fourth in successive generations of his family to hold this position, and her two eldest brothers were now jointly succeeding him there. Her mother's second husband was likewise a surgeon. She herself was educated at one of the many convents in the religious city of Blois. Though she and all her family were strong Catholics, and she herself later a prominent member of the royalist 'resistance movement', there is nothing to indicate that they were from the beginning violently opposed to the Revolution. She had two much older cousins, Charles and Claude Vallon, who were priests; both of them took all the oaths required of them by the Civil Constitution of the Clergy, and one of them, who was curé of the parish of S. Saturnin in Blois, celebrated mass in the cathedral after the election of the popular Grégoire as Bishop of Blois under the procedure laid down by the Civil Constitution. Like many of the best clergy in France they welcomed the new order, because it seemed to them to be founded on justice and common sense; later, however, when under the Convention pressure was put on the clergy to give up their ministries, they made a firm and successful stand against any such surrender.[1] Nevertheless, the progress of the Revolution bore hard on Annette's family; the dissolution of the Sisterhood of the Hôtel Dieu, where her brothers worked, in 1793, would naturally have aroused her resentment; above all the treatment of her brother Paul at Orleans in the same year turned her into a passionate and active royalist. It is, however, improbable that she was taking any particular interest in politics at the time she fell in love with William Wordsworth. By nature this young woman

---

[1] *A.V.*, pp. 9–10. It is probably of these men that Wordsworth was thinking when he told Professor Reed, his American friend, that 'he had known many of the abbés and other ecclesiastics and thought highly of them as a class; they were earnest, faithful men'.

—she was twenty-five in 1791—was tender-hearted, easily moved to tears, unsophisticated, finding her interests entirely in those whom she loved. We should indeed know very little of her character were it not that, by the strangest of chances, two of her letters, one to William and one to Dorothy Wordsworth, written in March 1793, after William's return to England and after the outbreak of war between England and France, were confiscated in the post by the Blois police. One hundred and thirty years later they came to light in the archives of the Department of Loire-et-Cher. They reveal with a touching fidelity and freshness the heart that had captivated Wordsworth and melted all his reserve. As we read them we feel we are in the presence of a girl who embodied almost to perfection one side at least of Rousseau's 'child of nature'. Here is Marianne Dashwood in all the exuberance of her 'sensibility', but without Marianne's literary romanticism or her delight in blasted trees, wet weather, and hill-top walks. Annette, indeed, cared nothing for art or poetry or 'Nature' in the sense of the world of earth and sky—her interests were 'pure womanly'. Her soul craved for one thing only—a home with her lover and her child. There is not a word of blame or reproach throughout the letters, and the self-pity is of such a simple kind that it cannot be called selfish. Caroline, their child, was three months old when these letters were written, and it is she rather than herself that Annette makes the centre of every appeal, as when she exclaims:

Come, my love, my husband,[1] and receive the tender embraces of your wife, of your daughter. She is so pretty, poor little thing, so pretty that the affection I have for her will drive me mad if I do not have her continually in my arms.[2] She grows more like you every day. I seem to be holding you in my arms.[3] Her little heart often beats against my own; I seem to feel her father's; but why, Caroline, are you so insensible? Why does not your heart stir when your mother's is beating so? O my beloved, soon it will be stirred when I shall say to her: 'Caroline, in a month, in a fortnight, in a week, you are going to see the most beloved of men, the most tender of men.' Then my

---

[1] Annette called herself 'Madame William' or 'Veuve Williams' for the rest of her life.

[2] For the first months of her life Caroline lived apart from her mother, near her, under the charge of a nurse.

[3] The portrait of Caroline in vigorous middle age does indeed bear a strong resemblance to some of the portraits of Wordsworth. It is reproduced in *A.V.*

Caroline's heart will be moved, she will feel her first emotion and it will be of love for her father.

And to Dorothy—who as was to be expected had at once written affectionately to Annette as soon as William informed her of what had occurred—she wrote:

> I cannot be happy without him, I desire him every day, but I shall have plenty of reasons for submitting to the lot which I must undergo. I often call to my aid that reason which too often is weak and powerless beside my feelings for him: no, my dear friend, he will never picture justly the need I have of him to make me happy; mastered by a feeling which causes all my unhappiness, I cherish always his dominion over me, and the influence of his dear love on my heart which is always concerned with him. His image follows me everywhere; often when I am alone in my room with his letters I think he has entered. . . . Ah my dear sister this is my continual state; emerging from my mistake as from a dream I see him not, the father of my child; he is very far from me. This scene is often repeated and throws me into extreme melancholy.

Annette's letters are those of a girl who not only loves but knows herself beloved. For William, this passion for Annette was a far more devastating thing than his schoolboy love for Mary Hutchinson. Wordsworth in his life loved a few people deeply and fervently—Dorothy, his brother John, his daughter Dora—Mary his wife, Coleridge. And for Annette he felt all the worship of a great first love, even if it is admitted that probably the attraction was felt at first more on her side than on his. Yet, when the winds of war blew them apart, his love for Annette failed to survive enforced absence; it became first a source of sorrow and self-blame, and then gradually faded into a

> memory of what hath been
> And never more can be.

Was this due to blameworthy callousness on Wordsworth's part, or to some flaw, unrecognized at first, in the beloved object which time and absence gradually revealed? Annette, warm-hearted and affectionate though she was, undoubtedly lacked certain qualities which were essential if his love for her was to be permanent. There was in her nothing that could have 're-ciprocated him' (to use Coleridge's phrase) in all the deepest springs of his being; in his exploration of the human spirit, in his

visionary experience of the natural world. The other people—
men and women—to whom he gave his love, were all of them
in different ways beings from whom he drew inspiration in the
great business of his life, which was to be a poet. He must soon
have realized that Annette could not do this—indeed, that she
had no conception that such a world even existed as that in
which he lived and thought. This, and not merely absence, or
difference of nationality or religious upbringing, must have been
the real cause of their estrangement. Letters like the one quoted
above, charming though they were, could not permanently
satisfy anyone as intent as Wordsworth on the things of the soul.

The history of their love must remain largely conjectural,
for even if we regard *Vaudracour and Julia* as a disguised account
of it, the disguise is so complete that very little that can be regarded as 'historical' can be gleaned from it. And nowhere else
did Wordsworth leave any trace of his thoughts or feelings
about it. Annette's letters to him, which arrived at irregular
intervals and by underground routes during the years of war,
and again in numbers during the interval of peace in 1801–2,
have entirely disappeared, and must either have been destroyed
by Wordsworth himself or by the members of his family after
his death. For in 1850 Wordsworth's surviving family decided
to suppress all reference to the affair and forbade his first biographer, his nephew Christopher, to make any mention of it.[1]
We are therefore left with those few facts which the researches
of Legouis and Harper brought to light thirty years ago, with
what can be made of some of the passages of *Vaudracour and Julia*,
and with what we know of Wordsworth's movements in 1792.

Vaudracour and Julia originally formed part of the early text
of *The Prelude*. This tale of two hapless French lovers, the youth
an aristocrat, the girl a bourgeoise, prevented from marrying
by the laws and customs which under the old régime forbade the
mingling of classes, was a well-known one in France at that
time, and was evidently repeated by 'democrates' as an example
of the kind of injustice from which the Revolution had delivered

---

[1] It is clear from a letter of Christopher Wordsworth to Wordsworth's son-in-
law Edward Quillinan, dated Mar. 21st 1851, that Christopher wished to tell the
story in his *Memoirs*, and had even done so in a passage which was, however,
suppressed before publication. His reasons for wishing to make the matter public
were that in any case 'the truth will out', and that it had been mentioned to him
in a public street in London. Other counsels, however, prevailed. *D.C.P.*

the country. Wordsworth says that he learnt it from his 'patriot friend', Michel Beaupuy, 'and others'. Certain features of the story were sufficiently akin to Wordsworth's entanglement with Annette for him to be able to use it as a disguise for his own story. Yet, having included it, he eventually withdrew it from his 'autobiographical poem' and published it separately, with many additional lines, in 1820. The final text of *The Prelude* contains only the barest outline of it.[1] Wordsworth has been assailed by many critics, first, for not telling the story directly, as an important personal experience, and also for omitting from 'the poem on his own life' a story which, however disguised and distorted, is the only account he has left us of the shattering impact of early love. But here, obviously, we have to take into account the long gap of years that separated his love for Annette from the writing of *Vaudracour and Julia*. There were many reasons why he could hardly have told the story in the first person—there were his wife's feelings to be considered, and, should the poem ever be published, Annette's also. And as one writer has said: 'After ten years perhaps the whole episode came to seem so much a dream, a story which belonged so little to his present self, that it was truer to relate it in terms of fiction.'[2] And if it was so remote, how much had it had to do, after all, with 'the growth of a poet's mind'? More, no doubt, than he thought, yet less, certainly less, than the great imaginative experiences of childhood; less than the solitary wanderings in mountain country and in London streets; less even than the sight of France in revolutionary turmoil. Indeed, in his own view, it might—probably did—seem that the whole episode had been more of a set-back than a process in poetic growth. It had plunged him into anxiety, perplexity, and self-reproach, which grew worse when, after his return to England, the outbreak of war made any hope of their marriage more remote than ever. He was forced to sit, reading those heart-wringing letters of 'poor Annette', as Dorothy called her, and face to face with the bitter thought that he was himself now a guilty party in a tragedy that might end, for Annette, as it had ended for those girls whose voices had haunted him in London streets and round the doors of theatres. It was not indeed, he knew, quite so bad

---

[1] *Prel.* IX, ll. 553–85. The 1805 text contains the full story, ll. 554–933.
[2] Peter Burra, *Wordsworth*, p. 44.

as that, but it came near to being so. It was a distasteful, a harrowing memory, the bitterest experience of his life; yet it had
begun in an ecstasy of passionate beauty. As the years passed,
he was able to retrieve something from the wreck. *Vaudracour
and Julia* as he published it in 1820 contains lines of intensity of
feeling second to none that he wrote, in spite of the weakness of
the poem as a whole; and these lines were most of them added
about the time when the poem was revised for publication, that
is, quite late in Wordsworth's poetic life, at a time when it is
usual to suppose that he had practically ceased to write great
poetry. There is for instance the image of the birds—clearly
reminiscent of the lines in *The Recluse* about himself and Dorothy
on their winter walk from Yorkshire to Westmorland in 1799.[1]
The lovers were

> Strangers to content if long apart,
> Or more divided than a sportive pair
> Of sea-fowl, conscious both that they are hovering
> Within the eddy of a common blast,
> Or hidden only by the concave depth
> Of neighbouring billows from each other's sight.

And there is the description of the streets of the town at night
when the lovers contrive their secret meeting—surely a direct
transcription of those intoxicating nights at Blois when Wordsworth stole from his lodging to some rendezvous with Annette.

> Through all her courts
> The vacant City slept; the busy winds
> That keep no certain intervals of rest,
> Mov'd not; meanwhile the galaxy display'd
> Her fires, that like mysterious pulses beat
> Aloft—momentous but uneasy bliss!
> To their full hearts the universe seemed hung
> On that brief meeting's slender filament!

Then there is the lovely simile of the dandelion seed and the
broken bough in the river, which is like a reflection of a more
tragic image—that of Paolo and Francesca blown about in the
unrelenting winds of Hell.[2]

---

[1] *P.W.* v, p. 319, *The Recluse*, ll. 152–70. See below, p. 457.
[2] *Inferno*, V, ll. 31–33.

> La bufera infernal, che mai non resta
> Mena gli spirti con la sua rapina;
> Voltando e percotendo li molesta.

> Have you beheld a tuft of wingèd seed
> That, from the dandelion's naked stalk
> Mounted aloft, is suffered not to use
> Its natural gifts for purposes of rest,
> Driven by the autumnal whirlwind to and fro
> Through the wide element? Or have you marked
> The heavier substance of a leaf-clad bough
> Within the vortex of a foaming flood
> Tormented? by such aid you may conceive
> The perturbation of each mind.

Wordsworth and Annette meant from the first to marry; of that Annette's letters and Wordsworth's anxiety leave no doubt. In *Vaudracour* there is a curious passage which seeks to account for their anticipating marriage. There seems no good reason for including so strange a passage in the poem if it had no personal reference. The story of Vaudracour and Julia was intelligible enough without it.

> This state was theirs till, whether through effect
> Of some delirious hour, or that the youth
> Seeing so many bars betwixt himself
> And the dear haven where he wished to be
> In honourable wedlock with his love,
> Without a certain knowledge of his own,
> Was inwardly prepared to turn aside
> From law and custom, and entrust himself
> To Nature for a happy end to all. . . .[1]

In 1820 Wordsworth altered the first lines of this passage as follows:

> So passed the time, till, whether through effect
> Of some unguarded moment that dissolved
> Virtuous restraint—ah speak it, think it not!

Most of Wordsworth's biographers have shown a preference for the first of the two alternative causes—a 'delirious hour'— but surely we must, if we are to take any of *Vaudracour* autobiographically at all, accept however reluctantly Wordsworth's own confession, and believe that the lovers came to a deliberate agreement to 'entrust' their cause to 'Nature', in the hope that such a proceeding would hasten, not delay, their eventual marriage.

---

[1] *Prel.* IX (1805), ll. 594–602.

For well might Wordsworth see 'many bars' between himself and marriage with Annette. He had no money and no prospect of a profession, except the distasteful one of taking orders, which would not be made any easier if he proposed to marry a French Roman Catholic. Uncle William would certainly oppose such a marriage very strongly, and his opinion would weigh with the guardian uncles in Cumberland. On Annette's side, too, there might well be objections to her allying herself with an obscure and penniless English Protestant. To cut through the difficulties of reality by becoming husband and wife in all but name, and from that situation to challenge all opponents, was their rash decision.

William's plans for the future are revealed in a letter he wrote to Mathews from Blois on May 17. 'It is at present', he says, 'my intention to take orders in the approaching winter or spring.[1] My uncle the clergyman will furnish me with a title. Had it been in my power I certainly would have wished to defer the moment.' This is the nearest William ever came to taking orders willingly. Less than a year before he had hastened to tell Mr. Robinson that he was not of age for ordination; now necessity was forcing him to seek to anticipate the normal date. He had another slender hope of adding to his income. He wished to enter into some sort of literary partnership or venture with Mathews.

You have still [he says] the hope that we may be connected in some method of obtaining an independence. I assure you I wish it as much as yourself. Nothing but resolution is necessary. . . . Your residence in London gives you, if you look abroad, an excellent opportunity of starting something or other. Pray be particular in your answer upon this subject. [He then speaks of taking orders.] But though I may not be resident in London, I need not therefore be prevented from engaging in any literary plan, which may have the appearance of producing a decent harvest. . . . You say you have many schemes. Submit at least a few of them to my examination. Would it not be possible for you to form an acquaintance with some of the publishing booksellers of London, from whom you might get some hints of what sort of works would be the most likely to answer?

We shall hear more of these literary schemes after the lapse of two years, when they reappear in a more political form, and

---

[1] *E.L.* 24, p. 75. Although William would not reach the normal age for ordination until April 1793, it was sometimes anticipated at this period. N. Sykes, *Church and State in the XVIIIth Century.*

when all hope of marriage with Annette had of necessity been abandoned. At present he had no political faith to advertise— only an overriding and haunting need to earn a livelihood.

Annette returned to her home in Blois in the early spring of 1792 and thither Wordsworth followed her.[1] He remained there probably until about the middle or end of September, when, again accompanying or following Annette, he returned to Orleans. Their child was born there on December 15th.[2] But Wordsworth departed at the end of October for Paris. That Annette's child should be born at Orleans and not at her own home, Blois, is probably an indication of her family's displeasure at what had occurred. In fact, when her state became known, it appears that the Vallons were very angry. Afterwards, when she returned to Blois with Caroline, she was not allowed to keep the baby at home; it was put out to nurse, and she visited it daily, a privation which grieved her sorely, and which she attributed wholly to the fact that she was not married.[3]

That summer of 1792 at Blois was one of the decisive seasons of Wordsworth's life. In it, and because of it, he ceased to be simply a 'stripling from the hills'—an observer and recorder of events that left him personally unmoved—and became passionately concerned for the human catastrophe that was shaking all France. A double tension racked him: he was deeply and anxiously in love, and he was also becoming a proselyte of the Revolution. In *The Prelude* we are only given one side of the picture—the story of his 'conversion' by Beaupuy: of the pathetic complexity of those summer months he tells us nothing, save in *Vaudracour and Julia* in an almost impenetrable disguise. And it may well have seemed to him at the time that the two ecstasies

---

[1] In the same letter to Mathews he says: 'Your last reached me just at the moment when I was preparing to quit Orleans; . . . since my arrival day after day and week after week have stolen insensibly over my head', indicating that he had been perhaps as much as two months in Blois when this letter was written.

[2] On her tombstone the date of Caroline's birth is given as Dec. 6th 1792 (*A.V.*, p. 113) but in the baptismal register it is stated that she was 'born the same day' as her baptism, which was on Dec. 15th. Harper, *Wordsworth's French Daughter*, pp. 28–29. See below, p. 209.

[3] *A.V.*, p. 130. Annette, in her letter to Dorothy, looks forward to the day when, having become William's wife, she will 'rejoice in having [Caroline] always with' her. 'I will then myself give her the care that I am jealous of her receiving from other hands.'

belonged to two separate planes of being; that the self which
sought rendezvous by starlight with Annette was scarcely the
same self as that which woke to passionate political life under
Michel Beaupuy's teaching. However this may have been, it is
easy to see how the emotion and anxiety engendered by Annette,
and the discomfort and distress of her family's anger, made him
turn with relief to one who could give him, with all the warmth
of friendship and sympathy, access to a totally different world,
in which his private anxieties sank to insignificance, and he
breathed freely in an atmosphere of hope, of purpose, of infinite
possibilities.

In Blois he again lodged in a house with some 'military
officers'. They were of the Bassigny Regiment, four companies
of which had arrived in the town in August. The Colonel of the
Regiment, who had left to join the *émigrés* in June, as soon as
he heard of the king's flight, had been arrested by the citizens
of Tours and conducted out of the town; the other officers,
though with one exception royalists, had taken the new Military
Oath of loyalty to the Constitution. But most of them were only
waiting opportunities to join the *émigré* forces beyond the
Rhine. For them the Revolution was a call, not to a new world,
but to the reinstatement of the old. They 'were bent upon undoing what was done'. Wordsworth listened with astonishment
and cautious politeness to their wild talk; they tried to enlist
his sympathies, but he would not commit himself to them, for
he knew that his world and theirs had no common frontier.

War had been declared in April against Austria, and had
begun badly enough for the revolutionary armies. In his letter
to Mathews in May, Wordsworth referred to the murder of
General Theobald Dillon by his own soldiers and went on:

The approaching summer will undoubtedly decide the fate of France.
It is almost evident that the patriot army, however numerous, will
be unable to withstand the superior discipline of their enemies. But
suppose that the German army is at the gates of Paris, what will be the
consequence? It will be impossible to make any material alteration in
the Constitution, impossible to reinstate the clergy in their antient
guilty splendour, impossible to give an existence to the *noblesse* similar
to that it before enjoyed, impossible to add much to the authority of
the King: Yet there are in France some (? millions)—I speak without
exaggeration—who expect that this will take place.

These observations from a youth just twenty-two seem remarkably penetrative and just.

Wordsworth was by nature and upbringing what he would
have called 'a democrate'; royalty meant nothing to him outside
the world of heroism and fancy; his boyhood had never brought
him into contact with 'the great',[1] with the one exception—most
important indeed—of his family's connexion with Lord Lonsdale,
who, by refusing to settle the debt question, was keeping him and
his brothers and sister out of their just inheritance. Privilege,
whether of wealth or birth, had nothing to say to this country
boy, taught in an obscure grammar school, and brought up among
plain village folk who had given him their own broad-vowelled
speech and a love of simple things and homely ways. Cambridge,
in its own way 'something . . . of a Republic', had done nothing
to destroy his inborn habit of estimating people on their merits.
His early reading—Plutarch, Milton, Shakespeare—had likewise fostered it, and over all were those 'familiar presences of
awful Power', Nature, and the God of Nature, to whom his
soul had given its homage in such completeness that there was
little room for other allegiances. And the memory of his trip
the previous summer, with Jones, was not without its influence.
Then he had seen Revolution in its happiest mood, and felt the
warmth of a new human fellowship. Now, seeing the joy on the
faces of the young men as they gathered, full of 'faith and fire'
to march to the frontiers, he felt that these children of the
Revolution were in themselves its best justification. In fact, to
Wordsworth what had happened seemed both natural and right.
What was done could not, in his opinion, be undone, even if it
were desirable to undo it—and he was certain that it was not.

Meanwhile his poet's eye observed these disappointed men
of the old régime with an intensity that might have embarrassed
some of them had they suspected it. In *The Prelude* long afterwards he described the officer whose face

> endowed by Nature with her fairest gifts
> Of symmetry and light and bloom, expressed,

[1] *Prel.* IV, ll. 218–22.
> It was my fortune scarcely to have seen
> Through the whole tenor of my school-day time
> The face of one who, whether boy or man,
> Was vested with attention or respect
> Through claim of wealth or blood.

> As much as any that was ever seen,
> A ravage out of season, made by thoughts
> Unhealthy and vexatious.

Every day the arrival of the newspapers from Paris threw this man into a state of feverish agitation:

> while he read
> Or mused, his sword was haunted by his touch
> Continually, like an uneasy place
> In his own body.

And it was not only among the officers that there was this bitter uneasiness.

> The soil of common life was, at that time,
> Too hot to tread upon.

Families were divided or united by their political opinions; it may well be that among Annette's relatives Wordsworth saw opinion hardening. Her clerical uncles were more favourable to the Revolution than her brothers and sisters. During this summer revolutionary fanaticism became noticeably more provocative and fantastic. The club known as the 'Friends of the Constitution' became more and more a dominating influence in the town, supported by the enthusiastic bands of volunteer troops who constantly passed through on their way to the frontier and were entertained by the club in riotous fashion. In July the club decided to abolish the use of 'vous' at its own meetings, basing its decision on the supposed usages of Republican Rome, 'persuadé que l'on n'avait jamais dit "vous" au Brutus et autres grands hommes de l'antiquité'. Soon, it became unsafe to use 'vous' in the relations of common life, and the titles 'monsieur' and 'madame' were forced to give way to 'citoyen' and 'citoyenne'. Tradesmen were ordered to supply the volunteers with uniforms and other necessaries free of charge. These were the sort of provocations that irritated the bourgeoisie of Blois and of all the cities of France at this time. And in the excited state of men's minds all due sense of the relative importance of people and things was lost.

> Carra, Gorsas—add
> A hundred other names, forgotten now,
> Nor to be heard of more; yet, they were powers,

> Like earthquakes, shocks repeated day by day,
> And felt through every nook of town and field.

Wordsworth, whose previous ideas of history and of revolutions were taken from Plutarch, was disgusted at the complaints and petty passions which seemed to him to smudge the progress of great events. To himself he exclaimed:

> What a mockery this
> Of history, the past and that to come!
> Now do I feel how I have been deceived
> Reading of Nations and their works, in faith,
> Faith given to vanity and emptiness:
> Oh! laughter for the page that would reflect
> To future times the face of what now is!

There is even, in his repudiation of the views of the royalists, a bitterness that betrays some personal memory—something more than a mere polite disagreement. The cause of the Revolution seemed one

> which no one could stand up against
> Who was not lost, abandon'd, selfish, proud,
> Mean, miserable, wilfully depraved,
> Hater perverse of equity and truth.

Such a passage, left unimpaired in the final text of *The Prelude*, would scarcely have been written if Wordsworth had not come to feel in some deeply personal way the goodness of the new order as contrasted with the old. His 'affections' in fact, found 'a vital interest', and woke to a passionate concern with all that was befalling France, through his association with that knight-errant of the Revolution, Captain Michel Beaupuy. His love for Beaupuy and reverence for his character made him love the things that he loved and hate the things that he hated. Seeing, too, the way in which his friend was treated as an outcast by the royalist society of Blois and by his brother-officers in the regiment, deepened his indignation against those who wanted to 'undo what was done'.

The portrait given in *The Prelude* of Beaupuy is exactly borne out by all that is known of him from other sources.[1] When he met Wordsworth he was thirty-five years old. He and all his

---

[1] All that is known about Beaupuy has been collected by Bussière and E. Legouis in their monograph, *Le Général Michel Beaupuy*, 1891.

family, though aristocrats, were enthusiastic supporters of the new order. He came from Mussidan, in Périgord, his family being originally of Périgueux, where they had risen from bourgeoisie to noblesse. His father, now dead, had been steward of some royal estates, and lord of Montpon. His mother, to whom all her five sons were deeply devoted, was descended from Montaigne, and it was she who brought up her family on the Encyclopedists and nourished in them a hatred of arbitrary power. The four elder sons, Nicolas, Michel, Louis-Gabriel, and Pierre-Armand, all entered the army,[1] Michel at the age of sixteen. Their military obligations did not prevent them from taking an active part in their country's affairs. Indeed, as we read the story of this band of brothers, we can see that Miss Williams and others were not exaggerating when they said that the Revolution raised men's natures to heroic levels of unselfishness and sacrifice. Michel, Louis-Gabriel, and Pierre-Armand all took part in 1789 in drawing up the *cahier* of grievances against the royal power which the States-General was to discuss; they steadily resisted the demand for new powers for their own order, the nobility, after the fusion of the three estates, and Michel in particular was singled out at a meeting of the Estates of Périgueux as one who for his patriotic zeal had been rewarded by the praise of 'all good men, of that of his three brothers (philosophers and warriors), and by the joy of his mother, who, like the noble Spartans, mingles the zeal of her country with the virtues of her sex'. The eldest brother, Nicolas, who was Lieutenant-Colonel of another regiment, threw up his commission and was elected deputy of the Dordogne for the Legislative Assembly, where he was zealous in promoting the creation of volunteer battalions for the war with Austria. Pierre and Louis-Gabriel remained in Périgueux to promote the patriot cause there. Michel, after thus assisting in the political activities of his own Estates, rejoined his regiment, where he faced all the ostracism and scorn which his brother-officers meted out to him for his actions and opinions. He knew that he would soon be called upon to fight for the new order he had helped to create. Without resentment and without self-pity, Michel Beaupuy endured his isolation.

---

[1] The youngest brother became a priest, but after the Revolution resigned his orders and was elected mayor of his native town of Mussidan.

A meeker man,

says Wordsworth,

> Than this lived never, nor a more benign,
> Meek though enthusiastic. Injuries
> Made *him* more gracious, and his nature then
> Did breathe its sweetness out most sensibly
> As aromatic flowers on Alpine turf,
> When foot hath crushed them.[1]

At Blois he alone of all the officers attended the meetings of the revolutionary club—the 'Friends of the Constitution'—and occasionally spoke at them.[2] Wordsworth may well have attended these meetings also, for in February two Englishmen had been granted permission to do so.[3] With his letter of introduction to a deputy and to Miss Williams, he would find little difficulty in joining such circles, and indeed we have his own word that he did so when he says that he forsook the royalist salons for 'a noisier world'. It may have been thus that he first became acquainted with Beaupuy.

Such a man as Beaupuy, in such a situation, needed above all things a friend, and in Wordsworth, thirteen years younger, he found both a friend and a pupil. As for Wordsworth, the impact of Beaupuy upon his life was something that he never forgot or regretted, and which became all the brighter in his memory when the high hopes for mankind, which they both had cherished crumbled as the years passed by. Their brief friendship lasted but four months; in July Beaupuy left Blois with his regiment, and there is no evidence of correspondence. But of the four individuals mentioned in *The Prelude* as having influenced Wordsworth's life for good, Beaupuy is one.[4] Perhaps the key to Wordsworth's admiration for the French soldier is to be found in those lines in which he speaks of him as

> one whom circumstance
> Hath call'd upon to embody his deep sense
> In action, give it outwardly a shape.

[1] *Prel.* IX, ll. 292–8.
[2] *Harper*, i, p. 168. The record of one of his speeches, delivered on Jan. 22nd 1792, shows him pleading for moderation in judgement and for less political distrust.
[3] Ibid., p. 155. Their names have not been preserved, and as February seems an early date for Wordsworth to be already in Blois, it is improbable that he was one of them.
[4] The other three are William Taylor, Dorothy, and Coleridge.

Beaupuy was a man of action, and as such he brought to his talk a quality which Wordsworth had never met before—the quality of action inspired by purpose. We have seen how in early youth Wordsworth wished to enter the military profession because he thought he had a talent for command. Just as he loved heroic themes in literature, so the heroism of such a soldier as Beaupuy stirred his heart. In the same way his own brother John was endeared to him not only because he was 'a silent poet', but because of his fine seamanship. And in spite of his own statement that *The Happy Warrior*[1] was in some sense a memorial to Nelson, and also that it was inspired by his brother's memory, it is impossible not to feel that one image that rose before his 'inward eye' in writing it was that of Michel Beaupuy.

Throughout the few months of their acquaintance they walked and talked endlessly through the

> wide forests of continuous shade
> Lofty and over-arched, with open space
> Beneath the trees, clear footing many a mile.

From *The Prelude* the substance and subjects of their discourse can be gathered, and also the exalted spirit in which it was conducted. It was of these days that Wordsworth wrote

> Oh pleasant exercise of hope and joy! . . .
> Bliss was it in that dawn to be alive
> But to be young was very heaven.[2]

They found from the first much common ground of sentiment. Beaupuy loved the poor with almost a Franciscan love. Wordsworth had also found among poor people much to wonder at and admire; they were already becoming for him types of poetic significance. In France he saw a new kind of poverty, far more bitter to contemplate than anything his northern dales could show—a half-starved and long-depressed peasantry. To Beaupuy the sight of the 'hunger-bitten girl' listlessly guarding her heifer in the lane was a challenge which drew from him the words "Tis against *that* that we are fighting!' And together they looked forward to a golden age in which poverty and 'cruel power' would be abolished and a healthy and responsible democracy would bring in 'better days to all mankind'.

---

[1] Written in the winter of 1805–6.   [2] *Prel.* XI, ll. 105–109.

They spoke much of the corruption and heartlessness of royal courts:

> A light, a cruel, and vain world, cut off
> From the natural inlets of just sentiment.[1]

What would Wordsworth have thought had he known that Dorothy was at this very moment with her uncle and aunt at Windsor, where she was in raptures over the condescension of the kindly king, George III?[2] With Beaupuy he rehearsed the great events of 'ancient story', remembering only the moments when justice had triumphed and 'error passed away'. Here, that handbook of all good democrats, a favourite with Wordsworth since his boyhood, Plutarch's *Lives*, was their text. And then came 'dearest themes'—'man and his noble nature'. Here no doubt Wordsworth described his dealings with lakeland shepherds and farmers who fitted ideally into Beaupuy's picture of man as Rousseau had conceived him.

They also spoke of the 'aspirations of our own minds'—and here Wordsworth must have talked of poets and perhaps of his own poetic hopes. But finally every conversation came round to the world in which they were living—to the spectacle of France,

> A people risen up
> Fresh as the morning star;

to the heroisms and sacrifices of the common people, and the great reforms which the Revolution had already effected, especially the abolition of arbitrary arrest by 'lettres de cachet'. And hence, perhaps, arose the telling of the tale of *Vaudracour and Julia*.

Wordsworth, when he 'became a patriot', did not cease to be a romantic who cast many a 'longing, lingering look behind'. Beaupuy, probably, held no regrets for the past which the Revolution had destroyed. One of the earliest achievements of the National Assembly had been the Dissolution of the Monasteries—accomplished in England 260 years before. In this summer of 1792 the decrees relating to the monasteries were put into effect. It was now that the Grande Chartreuse was

---

[1] Cf. *D.W.J.* i, pp. 62–63. Oct. 2nd 1800. 'We had a pleasant conversation about the manners of the rich', &c. See below, p. 475.

[2] *E.L.* 26, p. 79. D.W. to J.P., Oct. 16th 1792.

subjected to a military occupation, which began on May 10th
and lasted until October when the monks were finally expelled.
Wordsworth felt its fate so deeply that he lamented it in
Descriptive Sketches, written in this very summer and early
autumn while he was still in France.[1] And in their walks they
once came upon a ruined monastery,

> a roofless Pile
> And not by reverential touch of time
> Dismantled, but by violence abrupt.

Wordsworth's gothic romanticism was outraged.

> In spite of those heart-bracing colloquies,
> In spite of real fervour, and of that
> Less genuine and wrought up within myself—
> I could not but bewail a wrong so harsh,
> And for the Matin-bell to sound no more
> Grieved, and the twilight taper and the Cross. . . .[2]

It is doubtful whether Beaupuy could follow him here, any more
than he could into that fairy-land into which Wordsworth's
fancy often strayed, peopled by the heroes and heroines of
Tasso and Ariosto. The sight of Francis I's palaces—Blois,
Romorentin, Beauregard, Chambord—softened

> the bigotry,
> So call it, of a youthful patriot's mind.[3]

But the palaces moved him less than the ruined monastery.

At the end of July this intercourse, so momentous and so
memorable for Wordsworth, came to an abrupt end. Beaupuy's
regiment left the Loire for active service on the Rhine. Beaupuy
himself marched at the head of the grenadiers. His two brothers,
Pierre and Louis-Gabriel, left Périgueux at the same time with
the first battalion of volunteers from the Dordogne, of which
Louis-Gabriel was the commander, Pierre serving under him
as a simple foot-soldier. Wordsworth never saw Michel again.
In *The Prelude* he says that he

> perished fighting in supreme command
> Upon the Borders of the unhappy Loire

---

[1] See pp. 135–6 above.   [2] *Prel.* IX, ll. 470–5.
[3] Ibid., ll. 498–9. The distance of some of these châteaux from Blois throws light
on the length of some of their walks. Romorentin is twenty-five miles away.

in the Vendéan Civil War of 1793. How Wordsworth came to make such a statement is a mystery. For Beaupuy, having been made a General, was killed in the battle of the Elz, on the Rhine front, fighting not against 'his fellow-countrymen' but against the Austrians, in November 1796. He did serve for a time in La Vendée and was wounded, but recovered. His brother Pierre, however, died fighting in the Vendéan War, and it seems that whoever told Wordsworth must have been confusing the two brothers. But when and how did Wordsworth receive this incorrect news? There seem only two possible answers to that question. He may have learnt it from Annette either in a letter, or when they met once more in Calais in 1802; or he may have heard it during his secret journey to France in September 1793—if indeed he really undertook that risky venture.[1]

Beaupuy's departure left Wordsworth again very much to himself, for meetings with Annette were now probably difficult owing to the hostility of her family when her state could no longer be concealed. He employed his leisure in writing *Descriptive Sketches*. He finished it in Orleans in October 1792 just before his final departure for Paris and England. It was by far the longest and most ambitious poem he had yet attempted. In form and metre it was still a conventional 'landscape poem', founded on the roamings and musings of a solitary traveller. But it was nearly twice as long as *An Evening Walk*, and Wordsworth evidently wrote it with the intention of immediate publication on his return, for on September 3rd he told Richard that he would 'be in town during the course of the month of October' and that he hoped to stay some time in London 'to see about my publication'. His return was in fact delayed for two months, but the first thing that claimed his attention when he reached London at Christmas was the publication of his two poems, *An Evening Walk* and *Descriptive Sketches*.[2]

Something has already been said of *Descriptive Sketches* in its relation to the Swiss tour and to *The Prelude*. Its merits as a poem are few, for it lacks much of the spontaneity and accurate observation of *An Evening Walk*, is more disfigured by

---

[1] For the return to France in 1793 see p. 239 below.
[2] See below, p. 216.

awkwardnesses of style, and especially, towards the end of the poem, by unnatural personifications of abstract qualities. The mood of the poem is sombre, reflecting Wordsworth's troubled state of mind. The hero is not the cheerful, companionable youth who set out two years before with Robert Jones to explore Switzerland, but a solitary and dejected young man, at enmity with himself.

> Me, lured by hope her sorrows to remove,
> A heart, that could not much itself approve,
> O'er Gallia's wastes of corn dejected led. . . .

In later years Wordsworth made many alterations and improvements in it without changing its essential character. He must have loved it in spite of its faults, for though written in dejection it was a memorial of one of the happiest episodes of his life. In 1820 he republished it with alterations and some omissions, and in 1836 with many more. In its original form, like *An Evening Walk*, it was too rich in borrowings from other poets. Did Wordsworth take many volumes of English poetry to France with him, or was his memory so well stocked that quotations came as he needed them? It is not only his favourite poets who are laid under contribution, but such works as Addison's *Cato* and Smollett's *Ode to Leven Water*. But the chief literary source is a French book—Ramond de Carbonnière's 'interesting observations annexed to his translation of Coxe's Tour in Switzerland'—as Wordsworth himself describes them in a footnote. Ramond's Coxe had appeared in 1781, but almost certainly Wordsworth had not read the book before 1792. Its descriptions of the Swiss châlet-dwellers were idealized under the influence of Rousseau—they were the representatives of primeval man. This picture Wordsworth incorporated into *Descriptive Sketches* when he described the Swiss as moving about their world with

> eye sublime and surly lion-grace,
> The slave of none, of beasts alone the lord.[1]

It in no way represented his feelings and observations in 1790, for then he had found the Swiss mercenary and 'imposing' by comparison with the French. But now his whole outlook on man had undergone a change—or rather, all that he had ever wanted

---

[1] *D.S.*, ll. 531–2.

to believe of man's nature, and what his youthful experience of
north-country shepherds taught him about it, had received a
tremendous stimulus from the atmosphere in which he lived in
France. Ramond furnished him with human material which
fitted in with his own mood. Many of the descriptive parts of
the poem too were lifted almost bodily from Ramond's work.[1]

From the virtues and hardships of the Swiss he went on to
celebrate the achievement of France and the new mood of hope
which 'Freedom' seemed to have spread over the face of Nature
herself. This part of the poem is Wordsworth's salute to the
new French Republic, proclaimed on September 20th 1792.

> Methought from every cot the watchful bird
> Crowed with ear-piercing power till then unheard, . . .
> The measured echo of the distant flail
> Winded in sweeter cadence down the vale.

And he finished the poem with an impassioned prayer that God
would grant

> to Freedom's waves to ride
> Sublime o'er Conquest, Avarice and Pride . . .
> And grant that every sceptr'd child of clay
> Who cries, presumptuous, 'here their tides shall stay',
> Swept in their anger from th'affrighted shore,
> With all his creatures sink—to rise no more.

Descriptive Sketches in fact reflects pretty faithfully the eschato-
logy of the children of the Revolution—their faith in man's
nature set free from oppression; their readiness to face war on
behalf of their ideals; their hope of the swift advent of a new
golden age. And in spite of the failure of these hopes and the
changes in his own political outlook, Wordsworth refused
afterwards to change essentially the political and humanitarian
content of _Descriptive Sketches_. He shortened it, cutting out the
literary borrowings and the personifications, but he did not
alter its message. The most he would do to modify the ending
was to introduce a few lines of warning:

> All cannot be: the promise is too fair
> For creatures doomed to breathe terrestrial air.

---

[1] See the Appendix to _L._ where he enumerates the parallel passages. Another
French poet to whom W.W. refers in the last footnote to _Descriptive Sketches_ is the
Abbé Delille, who wrote _Inscription en vers pour Moulin Joli_ in which, says Wordsworth, he 'pathetically deprecates' the outrages made by 'false taste' on the banks
of the Seine. For Delille's influence on _The Reverie of Poor Susan_ see _L._, p. 143.

at its baptism.[1] This was as far as it was possible to go in
legalizing his relationship with Annette without actually marrying her. His intention probably was to make a stay of a few
weeks in Paris, and then return to England to deal with his
personal and financial problems, but Paris so enthralled him that
in the end it was only the cutting off of funds from home that
induced him to return.

Wordsworth arrived in Paris on October 29th, the very day
on which the Girondin Louvet made his accusations against
Robespierre in the Convention.[2] Walking out early the next
morning, into the arcades of the Palais Royal, he found them
crowded with people, eager for copies of Louvet's speech which
was being loudly cried by the news-vendors—'Denunciation of
the crimes of Maximilien Robespierre': one was thrust into his
hand as he appeared on the scene. This was his introduction to
the Paris of the Republic. The king and his family were prisoners
in the Temple, the Tuileries stood empty and was being slowly
prepared to house the Convention. In the Place du Carrousel,
where the fighting had taken place on August 10th, the guillotine had been erected and had already had its victims. Nine
émigrés caught with arms in their hands had been executed there
only two days before. Over all brooded the memory of 'those
September Massacres' in the prisons; to Wordsworth's imagination a source of much anxiety and horror. At night, when he lay
down to think but not to sleep in his attic bedroom at the top
of a large 'hôtel'[3] he 'felt and touched them, a substantial dread'.
All his detached indifference to his surroundings, which had
been his mood a year ago, and which lingered even for the first
few hours of his return to Paris, was soon gone, and he

felt most deeply, in what world he was.

Lying sleepless under his 'high and lonely' roof, he was filled

[1] Harper, *Wordsworth's French Daughter*, 1921. *A.V.*, p. 25. Wordsworth is
described in the register as 'William Wordsworth, Anglois'.
[2] *Prel.* X, l. 83.
[3] J. R. MacGillivray, in a letter to *T.L.S.* Jan. 29th 1931, suggested that he
stayed in the same house as Brissot, basing his conjecture on the places mentioned
in *Prel.* X, ll. 49–57, all of which lay close by. This suggestion was also made in
Barron Field's unpublished 'Life' of Wordsworth, but Wordsworth himself wrote
in the margin against this statement: 'A mistake. There is much mistake here
which I should like to correct in person.' Unfortunately he never did correct it.

with gloomy forebodings that these were only the beginnings
of sorrows.

> The earthquake is not satisfied at once.

At times, the whole world seemed to rock with the terrible curse
of Macbeth:

> I seem'd to hear a voice that cried
> To the whole city, 'Sleep no more!'

Fear—fear of the future and horror of the past—was making
Paris

> Defenceless as a wood where tigers roam.

He had indeed entered Paris at perhaps the most critical of
all the great moments of the Revolution. Louvet's speech,
accusing Robespierre of aiming at a dictatorship and of having
instigated the September massacres, caused a momentary reaction against the Jacobins, even in the Paris sections; resolute
political leadership on the part of the Girondins could have saved
the situation. But they took no united action, and Robespierre's
reply in the Convention on November 5th more than re-established him in popular favour and left the Girondins uncertain
and divided. This first week of November 1792 therefore really
decided the victory of the Commune and of the Jacobin extremists. The Girondins made the great political mistake of
despising the Commune and population of Paris and of allowing
it to fall under the influence of Marat, Danton, and the dema-
gogues of the Jacobin Club. In due time, Paris took its revenge.

People were already demanding that the king be brought to
trial. Wordsworth thought Louis guilty:[1] he had besides little
sympathy with thrones and crowns. The sinister figure of Marat,
the most hated and also the most feared of all the figures on that
formidable stage, dominated Paris. Every night the newsboys
cried his *Journal* in the arcades of the Palais Royal. Wordsworth
often doubtless found a copy thrust into his hands with the
recommendation: 'Journal par Marat, l'Ami du Peuple! Com-
bien voulez-vous, Citoyen anglais? Vous prendrez deux ou
trois, n'est il pas vrai, mon cher Milor?'[2]

Wordsworth saw it all clearly enough now. 'With my proper

---

[1] See below, p. 227.
[2] *Journal of Dr. John Moore*, 1793, ii, p. 400.

eyes'[1] he says he saw what was happening in 'the fierce metropolis'; the exploitation of its passions by unscrupulous dema-
gogues. He saw also and deplored the 'indecision' of 'those
whose aim seemed best'—of the genuine revolutionaries, Brissot, Roland, and the Girondins. He not only saw it; he felt a
deep and passionate concern about it. Beaupuy had indoctrinated
him with the belief in the 'reasonableness' of human nature. By
'patient exercise of reason' men became 'worthy of liberty', and
weakness lay only in 'mistrust and want of hope'. Now, as he
watched the extinction of reason by party strife and the unscrupulous desire for power, 'I could almost have prayed', he
says, for heavenly intervention; for a 'gift of tongues' on those
worthy to receive it, or for outside helpers to do

> For France what without help she could not do,
> A work of honour—

namely, the deliverance of her government from the threat of
tyranny and mob rule. Wordsworth's dislike of 'the mob' and
those who exploited and led it was a powerful sentiment in his
later years, turning him more and more towards political conservatism; it originated in his Paris days. His loathing of the
Jacobins was acquired at first hand, in the midst of the fears and
hatreds which they had aroused, and with the memory of the
September massacres always in the background. It was increased
in the following year by the slaughter of the men he most admired. His faith in the Revolution and the ultimate triumph of
'reason' remained, however, as yet unshaken. From

> the least fear about the end of things
> I was as far as angels are from guilt.

He mused on 'remedies', and fell into the fallacy of longing for
a benevolent dictatorship. If only there could emerge some 'one
paramount mind', which would be able to 'clear a passage for
just government' whatever opposition it met with, the Revolution would be safe. He held to this belief even when the 'one
paramount mind' had proved to be Bonaparte's, whom he could
never regard as anything but a tyrant. It was a

> Creed which ten shameful years have not annulled,[2]

he said in *The Prelude* in 1804—a line which was, however,
omitted from the final draft of the poem.

---

[1] *Prel.* X, l. 124.   [2] *Prel.* X (1805), l. 179.

How far was Wordsworth involved with the Girondin party
in this autumn of 1792? And what was his connexion, if any,
with the 'English Jacobins' and radicals who lived in or were
visiting Paris? The most careful researches have brought little
to light. His own vague hints in *The Prelude*, that if it had not
been that funds were cut off by his uncles in England, thus forcing him to return home, he would have 'made common cause
with some who perished'—that is to say, with Brissot, Roland,
and their friends—is the only information we have from Wordsworth himself about his French associates. His nephew and
biographer says that he was 'intimately connected' with the
Brissotins, but gives no particulars.[1] Research has failed to
reveal any further knowledge. And, when we take into consideration his self-confessed unfitness for political intrigue, his 'lack
of eloquence' and of familiarity with the French language, it is
unlikely that he could have been of much practical use to those
whom he wanted to help. The fact that he was still dependent
on funds from England shows that he was unable to get work
in Paris by which to support himself. Journalism no doubt would
have been his choice—but his command of French was not
nearly fluent enough for such work.

Of his relations with the English a little more is known.
Among the young English supporters of the Revolution then
in Paris was James Watt, the son of the great engineer. He had
come over in the previous December, and as the anonymous
'Constitutional Whig' had been received by the Jacobin Club
with enthusiastic applause at their session of December 18th.[2]
He remained in Paris, and in April 1792, with Thomas Cooper,
presented fraternal greetings to the Jacobin Club from the Constitutional Club of Manchester, and with Cooper marched, carrying the British flag and a bust of Algernon Sidney, the Whig and
Republican martyr, in the procession of April 15th, when Paris
turned out to fête some released mutineers who had been condemned to the galleys two years before. With this young
enthusiast Wordsworth did associate. Many years later James
Muirhead, the biographer of Watt the engineer, visited Words-

---

[1] *Mem.* i, p. 77.
[2] Aulard, *Société des Jacobins*, vol. iii. Carlyle, *Essays*, vol. vi. This was one of
the occasions when the Jacobin Club displayed what Carlyle calls 'a touch of the
moral-sublime'.

worth at Rydal Mount, bringing a letter of introduction from
James Watt the 'Constitutional Whig'. Wordsworth told Muirhead how he was in Paris 'at the time of the Revolution in 1792
and 1793[1] and so was "pretty hot in it" but he "found Mr Watt
there before him and quite as hot in the same cause".' He gave
Muirhead 'many details of their early friendship and frequent
meetings'—which one wishes Muirhead had recounted in detail.[2]
Watt, in common with Wordsworth, was horrified at the September massacres, and spoke his disgust so publicly that eventually he was denounced by Robespierre as a spy of Pitt's. He
was obliged to leave Paris immediately to escape Robespierre's
vengeance.[3]

   Watt is the only Englishman with whom we can say with any
certainty that Wordsworth associated while in Paris. Tom
Paine, Helen Maria Williams and her friend John Hurford
Stone were all there, yet he has left us no word of any of them.[4]
It seems indeed as though he never used his letter of introduction
to Miss Williams. She lived in the Rue Helvétius, and gave
parties every Sunday for English people in Paris and for French
political leaders and journalists. It would have been natural for
Wordsworth to have introduced himself. Yet in 1814 Miss
Williams, on first hearing some of Wordsworth's poems recited
by Crabb Robinson, said that she 'had never heard of him before'.
And in 1820 when the Wordsworths were in Paris and at length
visited her, they appear to have met as strangers.

   Again, did Wordsworth attend the dinner at White's Hotel
on November 18th, which the English Jacobins held to celebrate
the victories of the Republican armies? No list of the guests has
survived. Monro, the agent of the British Embassy, who kept an
eye on the English during that autumn and winter, makes no
mention of him. It is possible that Wordsworth found most of
the English unacceptable as companions. He did not make
friends easily, and many of them seem to have been quarrelsome,
discontented people, unlikely to have attracted his interest.

   [1] Are these dates an indication that he *did* return to Paris in 1793, or is his
memory again at fault? See below, pp. 238 ff.
   [2] 'A Day with Wordsworth', *Blackwood's Magazine*, 1927.
   [3] Muirhead, *James Watt*, pp. 492–3.
   [4] Stone was in Orleans in Sept. 1792 staying with the manufacturer Foxlowe,
whom Wordsworth knew (see above, p. 174, n.); he may therefore have met
Stone there. Letters of J. H. Stone, loc. cit.

Another Englishman in Paris in this autumn of 1792 whom Wordsworth afterwards knew well was James Losh, of Woodside, near Carlisle. He was older than Wordsworth by some seven years, and in Carlisle had been a member of the 'patriotic' (that is, republican) club there. This club had enjoyed the doubtful honour, some years before, of a visit from Marat himself, when he was practising medicine in Newcastle, and there was afterwards a tradition in the Losh family that Losh, when threatened by 'sans-culottes' in the streets of Paris because of his long hair ('Aristocrate! quelle belle tête pour la lanterne!') had appealed to Marat for protection.[1] There is, however, no evidence that Wordsworth met this fellow Cumbrian in Paris; the first record of their meeting is in London in 1795.[2]

But, though Wordsworth's movements in Paris are obscure and his companions also, there seems no doubt that it was in these six weeks that he read political literature intensively and that some of it made upon him an unexpectedly lasting impression. It was not Rousseau and Montesquieu so much as the political writers of his own country, the Puritan publicists of the seventeenth century, whom he studied, and whom he came to venerate as models of wisdom and virtue. Ten years later, when his thoughts were again turned to France through revisiting it to see Annette in the summer of 1802, he wrote a sonnet celebrating the English Republicans:[3]

> Great men have been among us; hands that penned
> And tongues that uttered wisdom—better none:
> The later Sidney, Marvell, Harrington,
> Young Vane and others who called Milton friend.
> These moralists could act and comprehend:
> They knew how genuine glory was put on;
> Taught us how rightfully a nation shone
> In splendour: what strength was, that would not bend
> But in magnanimous meekness. France, 'tis strange,
> Hath brought forth no such sons as we had then . . .

It is a matter of some interest to speculate when it was that Wordsworth acquired a detailed knowledge of the political writings of the Puritans. He would not have been taught to

[1] Lonsdale, *Worthies of Cumberland*, vol. iv. Essay on James Losh.
[2] See below, p. 263.
[3] *P.W.* iii, p. 116, *Poems dedicated to National Independence and Liberty*, XV.

venerate them in boyhood; at Cambridge he was absorbed in poetry. In 1794, however, we find him proposing to include Algernon Sidney in a series of articles for the periodical he and William Mathews were proposing to launch together,[1] and the influence of Harrington is traceable in his unpublished political tract, the *Letter to the Bishop of Llandaff*, which he wrote early in 1793, immediately after his return to England.[2] It is therefore an almost inescapable conclusion that he read these writers while he was in France, and nothing would in fact have been easier. Since the beginning of the century editions of Harrington's writings had been appearing in French translations; after the outbreak of the Revolution the bookstalls of Paris were stocked with Milton's *Areopagitica*, Ludlow's memoirs, and Harrington's *Oceana*, along with accounts of the trial and execution of Charles I. The Girondins were the group most strongly influenced by the English republicans, for they were the idealists and theorists of the Revolution, bringing to the work of constitution-making a moral enthusiasm not unlike that of the English, though untouched by their biblical fervour. Algernon Sidney was regarded by them as the martyr of the republican cause; his bust, as we have seen, was carried in procession through the streets of Paris in the spring of 1792. In the dark days of 1793, when the Girondins were writing their political testaments in prison as they awaited their summons to the guillotine, some of them compared their fate with his.[3]

There is nothing surprising in Wordsworth's absorption in these writers at this time, especially after his indoctrination by Beaupuy. What is surprising is that ten years afterwards they should still have had such a hold over him. For by that time his faith in republican France was shattered. Another twenty years after that, however, and we find him writing sonnets deprecating the Puritan rebellion as a terrible excess of 'headstrong will', and celebrating the martyrdom of Laud.[4]

By the middle of December Wordsworth had run out of funds, and no more money was forthcoming from England. His guardians no doubt disliking this prolonged absence in a country

---

[1] See below, p. 256.   [2] See below, pp. 226 ff.

[3] Z. Fink, 'Wordsworth and the English Republican Tradition', *Journal of English and German Philology*, 1948. H. T. Parker, *The Cult of Antiquity and the French Revolutionaries*, 1937.

[4] *P.W.* iii, pp. 383–4, *Ecclesiastical Sonnets*, Part II, XLIV and XLV.

that was in such a state of disturbance, must have indicated to
him that he could expect no more unless he returned. Had he
ever received the £20 for which he had asked Richard in
September? Probably he had, but he may have given some of it
to Annette, and Paris was more expensive than Orleans. There
was nothing for it but to return home. The exact date of his
return we do not know, but on December 22nd Dorothy wrote
that he was in London and that she was hearing from him
frequently.[1]

Perhaps the last news that he received in Paris was that of the
birth of his daughter, Anne-Caroline, at Orleans on December
15th. She was baptized in the church of Ste Croix on the day of
her birth, Mme Dufour and Annette's brother standing as god-
parents, while M. Dufour represented her father.[2] Probably,
however, Wordsworth had returned to England a few days
earlier. Dorothy's letter gives the impression that he had already
been in England for some days, and the time required for the
journey must be taken into account. At least three days under
most favourable weather conditions would be required to reach
London from Paris, and a letter to Forncett would probably take
two. Legouis pictures him lingering in France much more for
Annette's sake than for the Revolution's, and gently accuses him
of suppressing in *The Prelude* his real motive for delay.[3] Yet we
should be cautious how we interpret the meagre facts.

The refusal of the uncles to sanction a longer stay in Paris
was most unwelcome.

> Reluctantly to England I returned,
> Compelled by nothing else than absolute want
> Of funds for my support—[4]

His political awakening, grim though it had been, had not terrified him. As the storms in his own mountains brought him in
childhood a fear that was strangely mingled with delight, so

---

[1] *E.L.* 27, p. 82. Fragment of a letter to an unknown correspondent.

[2] Harper, *Wordsworth's French Daughter*, where the record of the baptism is
given.

[3] *A.V.*, pp. 25–26.

[4] *Prel.* X (1805), ll. 190–2. In the revised text he decided to change this
passage to

> Dragged by a chain of harsh necessity,
> So seemed it—now I thankfully acknowledge
> Forced by the gracious providence of Heaven.

now the roar of revolutionary Paris held him fascinated. All his
emotions, too, were keyed up to a high pitch of political—almost
religious—expectation and hope. He went back to England, but
with desire and intention of an early return.

Had the voice of what Wordsworth afterwards called 'the
gracious providence of Heaven' not spoken thus in the avuncular
summons, Wordsworth would have bade a long—perhaps an
eternal—farewell to England, for the war, which began in
February 1793, would have made return difficult, if not impossible. He himself thought that he might have perished in the
Terror—

> a poor, mistaken and bewildered offering,—

though this is unlikely, as very few Englishmen were actually
guillotined, though almost all were at one time or another
imprisoned.[1] But his growth towards his poetic maturity would
have been irretrievably damaged. The next three years show
clearly enough how dangerously near he came to a mental state
inimical to the writing of poetry—at least the kind of poetry
which was to be his gift to man. In the process of his recovery,
Dorothy was to play an indispensable and decisive part, and
'preserve him still a poet'. If he had been trapped in France all
communion with her would have been cut off. Without Dorothy,
and without living communion with earth and sky, in the blood-
stained turmoil of the Paris of 1793, William Wordsworth as
we know him might have perished indeed.

[1] See below, p. 241.

VII

IN TIME OF WAR, 1793–4

All changed: changed utterly:
A terrible beauty is born.
w. b. yeats, Easter, 1916

THE year which followed his return to England is the most obscure period in that which lies between Wordsworth's departure from Cambridge and his settlement with Dorothy in the west of England. His inward state of mind is clearer than his outward movements, for we have the long narrative poem, *Salisbury Plain*—altered and published many years later as *Guilt and Sorrow*—and the unpublished *Letter to the Bishop of Llandaff*, to throw light upon it. But no letters have survived, and we must depend on the references to him in Dorothy's letters to Jane Pollard, and to occasional entries in the family accounts, to trace his movements. And there are no letters even of Dorothy's for the latter half of the year 1793. The obscurity covering that autumn is almost total, and it is to this period that the secret return to Paris belongs—if indeed it was ever made. At least there is no *alibi* for the period in question.

On returning to England William lived with his brother Richard who was now in chambers of his own in Staple Inn.[1] He probably continued to reside there during the whole of his seven months' stay in London, though it must have been at times an uneasy partnership, for Richard had scant sympathy with William's political views which just now were at their fiercest and most inconvenient. However, the brothers, as Dorothy said, 'never quarrelled', although they had few tastes in common.

The first problem that meets us in surveying Wordsworth's return to England is the length of his stay in 'the vast city'. Why did he not seek once more his native hills, and why did

---

[1] 'William arrived back, he is with me.' R.W. to Christopher Crackanthorpe Cookson, 1792, n.d. *D.C.P.*

he not go to see Dorothy at Forncett? *The Prelude* supplies a
hint towards an answer to the first question. After remarking
on the length of his absence from England, he says:

> A patriot of the world, how could I glide
> Into communion with her sylvan shades
> Erewhile my tuneful haunt? It pleased me more
> To abide in the great City.[1]

For the moment, Man was in the ascendant in his mind. He had
seen a revolution in process; and, haunted by its memories and
painfully anxious for its success, he could not withdraw himself
from such contact as was possible with what he had reluctantly
left behind. He must seek the company of those, the 'ingenuous
youth' who felt as he did and who shared his horror of the
war with France when it began in February and his view that
it was the work of 'a few weak men' in the Government, who
had misled the nation with their panic fears. He must read the
newspapers and pamphlets that poured from the press; he
might contribute something himself to the unceasing war of
words.

Meanwhile Dorothy was having a difficult time at Forncett.
It was two years since she had met her brother: they longed for
a meeting, but it was not to be. He was kept away by the anger
and disapproval of Uncle William when the Annette affair was
revealed. 'The prejudices of my two Uncles against my dear
William' were a source of much concern to Dorothy during this
spring and summer.[2] In June she wrote to Jane that William
would certainly come to Forncett to visit her 'if it be but for one
day', if there was any prospect of his 'making an engagement
which would take him out of England or confine him to one
spot for some time', such as a tutorship or teaching post, but
'he has never received an invitation from my Uncle and can have
no possible inducement but the pleasure of seeing me'.[3] Something very serious must have occurred to change Uncle William's
good will into such disapproval. It is unlikely that William
aired his republicanism to his conservative uncle, but he was

---

[1] *Prel.* X, ll. 242–5. These lines were added by Wordsworth after the completion of the 1805 text.
[2] *E.L.* 31, p. 97. D.W. to J.P., July 1793. By 'my two Uncles' she means
Mr. Cookson and Mr. Christopher Crackanthorpe.
[3] Ibid., D.W. to J.P., July 10th 1793.

obliged to tell all who had legal or financial control over him
about his obligation to Annette Vallon. Mr. Cookson was his
patron where ordination was concerned; in May of the previous
year (1792) his uncle had offered him a title for orders which
William had accepted—undoubtedly because he felt it was the
only way in which he could provide Annette with a home.[1]
Mr. Cookson at that time of course knew nothing about Annette.
What seems to have happened in the spring of 1793 is that
Mr. Cookson, when he found out the true state of the case,
withdrew his offer, or at least made it conditional upon his
nephew's giving up his absurd project of marrying a French-
woman who was a Roman Catholic.[2] When William refused to
comply, his uncle must have made it pretty clear to Dorothy
that his favourable opinion of William was entirely changed.
So the prospect of ordination was finally given up, not so much
through William's own action as through that of his uncle. No
doubt he felt relief at the thought that he need no longer enter
a profession which was distasteful to him, but it made the task
of earning a living more difficult than ever. Henceforward he
made some attempts—none of them successful—to obtain a
travelling tutorship.[3]

The breach with his uncle probably took place in the month
of March, for Annette, in her one surviving letter to her un-
wedded lover, dated March, in which she enclosed one to
Dorothy, says: 'I beseech you, my darling little one, to pass on
this letter to my dear sister whom I love with all my heart, and
to charge her to say nothing to your uncle; it would be a painful
fight that she would have to sustain. But you think it necessary.'[4]

Whether Dorothy was the first to inform her uncle, or whether
William himself wrote to him, we do not know. She would not
have shrunk from the task if William had asked it of her, but
it is to be hoped he had regard to Annette's merciful appeal. The
effect of the communication, however it was made, was virtually
to forbid him to come to Forncett. As a result, the longing of
the brother and sister to see one another became so acute that

---

[1] See above, p. 186.
[2] Mr. Cookson may also have taken a serious view of William's having become
the father of a child. He was a close friend of Wilberforce and other Evangelicals
who were leading the revolt against the prevailing laxity in such matters.
[3] *E.L.* 30, p. 92. D.W. to J.P., June 16th 1793.
[4] *A.V.*, p. 126.

they began in the summer to make elaborate and secret plans for a meeting at Halifax in the autumn, whither Dorothy had at last obtained permission to go and visit 'Aunt Rawson', Jane Pollard, and all her early friends. She was now twenty-one, but she still felt herself bound to act only in obedience to the uncle and aunt with whom she had made her home. To Mrs. Cookson she had become an almost indispensable companion, nurse-maid, and helper,[1] with the ever-increasing family of children—whom she dearly loved—making constant demands on her time and her affection. But William was the overriding consideration; so, with many cautions to secrecy she informed Jane Pollard that when she came to Halifax William was determined to come thither at the same time; his movements would probably by then have brought him into north Wales, whence it would be easy to cross into Yorkshire. But her uncle must not know that their meeting had ever been premeditated. Hence not even Mrs. Rawson, who was friendly to William, and who had invited him to Halifax when she met him in London in the earlier part of the year,[2] must be told of this part of the plan: William's arrival must appear to be quite unexpected. And then her longing for a meeting with the brother who was all to her overflowed, and she indulged in the luxury of describing his appearance, and quoting from his letters to her. Sitting out of doors on a summer evening she writes:

I am willing to allow that half the virtues with which I fancy him en-dowed are the creation of my love, but surely I may be excused! he was never tired of comforting his sister, he never left her in anger, he always met her with joy, he preferred her society to every other pleasure when we were compelled to be divided. . . . In the first place you must be with him more than once before he will be perfectly easy in conversation; in the second place his person is not in his favour, at least I should think not; but I soon ceased to discover this, nay I almost thought that the opinion which I first formed was erroneous. He is however, cer-tainly rather plain than otherwise, has an extremely thoughtful countenance, but when he speaks it is often lighted up by a smile

[1] 'As I am head nurse, housekeeper, tutoress of the little ones or rather super-intendent of the nursery, I am at present a very busy woman.' There were at present four little Cooksons including a new-born baby. E.L. 31, p. 96. D.W. to J.P., July 1793.

[2] Ibid., p. 94. The Rawsons were Unitarians, and probably less likely to dis-approve of William's political views than Mr. Cookson, while his withdrawal from Anglican orders would not disturb them.

which *I* think very pleasing—but enough, he is my Brother, why should *I* describe him? I shall be launching again into panegyric.

In the same letter we catch a glimpse of the passionate affection which William felt for the one being who thoroughly understood him, for Dorothy in the fullness of her heart repeated to Jane several passages from William's letters to her.

How much do I wish [he had written in June] that each emotion of pleasure and pain that visits your heart should excite a similar pleasure or a similar pain within me, by that sympathy that will almost identify us when we have stolen to our little cottage! I am determined to see you as soon as ever I have entered into an engagement (i.e. as a tutor): immediately I will write to my uncle and tell him that I cannot think of going anywhere before I have been with you. Whatever answer he gives me I certainly will make a point of once more mingling my transports with yours. Alas! my dear sister how soon must this happiness expire, yet there are moments worth ages.

A little later, when they were scheming to meet in Halifax, he wrote: 'Oh my dear, dear sister, with what transport shall I again meet you, with what rapture shall I again wear out the day in your sight. I assure you so eager is my desire to see you that all obstacles vanish. I see you in a moment running or rather flying to my arms.'[1]

How was it possible for Dorothy and William, feeling for one another what and as they did, to contemplate sharing their 'little cottage' with another, and that other Annette? Yet this, apparently, is what they planned to do, and Dorothy, who would have had the most to sacrifice, was the foremost with the plan. She, looking on Annette simply as a creature whom William loved, had at once taken the French girl to her heart with enthusiastic pity and tenderness; Annette would some day join herself and William in the 'little cottage', and they would all live happily together. Such seems to have been her proposal, to judge from Annette's reply:

When we are there, Oh sister, how happy we shall be! And you, my dear [meaning William], do you desire that day as ardently as your Annette? When you are surrounded by your sister, your wife, your daughter, who will breathe only for you, we shall have but one feeling, one heart, one soul, and everything will depend on my dear Williams. Our days will flow along quietly. I shall at last

---

[1] *E.L.* 31, p. 99. D.W. to J.P., July 10th 1793.

enjoy the calm which I cannot feel except with you, in telling you *out loud* that I love you.

She poured out her sympathy too for all Dorothy's anxieties:

If you feel so tenderly for my lot, I share equally the unpleasantness of yours. You have no one to whom you can freely confide the painful state of your soul and you are obliged to stifle the tears which your feelings draw from you. O my dear sister, how unhappy I am to know you are so on my account; never, no never, can I recompense you too much for all you suffer for my sake. My beloved shares my gratitude— he had indeed told me—this dearly beloved one—that he had a charming sister, but how is the picture he drew of your soul inferior to what I see in your letter! No, my dear Williams, you had not told me enough.[1]

Meanwhile, in London, two volumes, of small quarto size, had been published by Joseph Johnson, a bookseller and publisher in St. Paul's Churchyard. They were *An Evening Walk*, published at two shillings, and *Descriptive Sketches*, which cost three. *An Evening Walk* was described as *An Epistle, in Verse. Addressed to a Young Lady, from the Lakes of the North of England. By W. Wordsworth, B.A. of St. John's Cambridge.* The young lady is, of course, Dorothy. *Descriptive Sketches. In Verse. Taken during a Pedestrian Tour in the Italian, Grison, Swiss, and Savoyard Alps*, was prefaced by two Latin quotations, the first from Lucretius: 'Loca Pastorum deserta atque otia dia': the second from Virgil's *Georgics*; 'Castella in Tumulis— Et longe saltus lateque vacantes'. The Castella, Wordsworth believed, were the 'summer hamlets' in the Alps described in the poem.[2] Scarcely a month elapsed between Wordsworth's return and their appearance; later he said that it was 'with great reluctance that I huddled up these little pieces for the press, but as I had done nothing at the University I thought these little things might show that I could do something'.[3] The pressing need for money was no doubt likewise a consideration. By the middle of February Dorothy and Christopher, who was staying there, had together prepared at Forncett 'a bulky criticism', which unfortunately has not survived. But in a letter to Jane

[1] *A.V.*, p. 129.
[2] *D.S.*, l. 428, W.W.'s own note to this line.
[3] *E.L.* 40, p. 116. W.W. to W. Mathews, May 23rd 1794.

she sums up her feelings. Her criticism is more remarkable for
its severity than for its partiality—surprisingly perhaps, but at
this period Dorothy longed anxiously for her brother to be
admired, and feared that the peculiarities of his style would
prevent his being so. She was probably also influenced by
Christopher's comments. Thus she says:

> The poems contain many passages exquisitely beautiful, but they
> also contain many Faults, the chief of which are Obscurity, and a too
> frequent use of some particular expressions and uncommon words,
> for instance *moveless*, which he applies in a sense if not new, at least
> different from its ordinary one; by moveless when applied to the Swan
> he means that sort of motion which is smooth without agitation; it is
> a very beautiful epithet but ought to have been cautiously used, he
> ought at any rate only to have hazarded it once, instead of which it
> occurs three or four times.

When many years later the poems were reprinted Wordsworth
removed 'moveless', and the other word to which Dorothy had
objected, 'viewless', altogether from the text. The poems in
general suffered, Dorothy thought, from not having been previously subjected to 'the inspection of some friend' before their
publication, and her brother agreed with her in this regret.
When he next prepared a poem for publication—*Salisbury Plain*
in the year 1796—he submitted it to the voluminous and enthusiastic criticism of Coleridge, whose suggestions were so
numerous that publication was indefinitely delayed.

It was during this summer of 1793 that *An Evening Walk* and
Descriptive Sketches were seen and read by Coleridge. During his
first long vacation, Coleridge paid one of his rare visits to his
native country, Devonshire, and at Exeter was present at a
meeting of a literary society where the poems were read aloud.
'Seldom, if ever', he wrote many years afterwards, 'was the
emergence of an original poetic genius above the literary horizon so evidently announced.' And he went on to compare the
'harshness and acerbity' of the style of *Descriptive Sketches*, and
the 'words and images all aglow' 'with those products of the
vegetable world, where gorgeous blossoms rise out of a hard
and thorny rind and shell'.[1]

This is the judgement of Coleridge's maturity, but it differs

[1] *B.L.*, ch. iv.

little from that of his youth. In a note to his own *Lines written at Shurton Bars* (1795) he explains that the expression 'green radiance', as a description of the glow-worm's light, 'is borrowed from Mr. Wordsworth, a Poet whose versification is occasionally harsh and his diction frequently obscure; but whom I deem unrivalled among the writers of the present day in manly sentiment, novel imagery and vivid colouring'.

The first review of *An Evening Walk* appeared in the *Critical Review* for July 1793. It complimented Wordsworth on possessing 'that merit which a poetical tale most values, new and picturesque imagery'. A much more severe reviewer castigated *Descriptive Sketches* in the same paper in August, and complained of 'harsh and prosaic' lines, 'ill-chosen images', and 'feeble and insipid descriptions'. In October the *Monthly Review* came down very heavily on both poems, ending with advice which was by no means inappropriate: 'There are passages in his poems which display imagination, and which afford hope for the future: but, if he can divest himself of all partiality, and will critically question every line that he has written, he will find many which, he must allow, call loudly for amendment.' By far the most appreciative notice was that by the anonymous Cambridge man which appeared in the *Gentleman's Magazine* in March 1794, although it was dated in the previous September. The author's description of his meeting with Wordsworth at Cambridge has already been quoted.[1] At the end of his review he expressed his hope that Wordsworth would eventually 'restore to us that laurel to which, since Gray laid down "his head upon the lap of earth" and Mason "declined into the vale of years" we have had so light pretensions'.[2]

Wordsworth's publisher, Joseph Johnson, was a north countryman of dissenting origins, well known for his business connexions with poets, scientists, and people of a liberal and critical turn of mind. He published all the scientific works of Priestley, and had given Cowper's *Task* and Darwin's *Economy of Vegetation* to the world. He was generous and considerate to his young clients. 'Perhaps few men of his means', says one of his friends, 'have done more substantial services to persons

---

[1] See above, p. 91.
[2] For the reviews see Elsie Smith, *An Estimate of William Wordsworth by his Contemporaries, 1793–1822*, pp. 7–16.

whose merits and necessities recommended them to his notice.'[1]
He was also the editor of the *Analytical Review*. He was a
bachelor, and kept a hospitable table and fireside, which is perhaps why it has been conjectured—and stated almost as though
it were ascertained fact—that Johnson introduced Wordsworth
to some of the leading radicals of the day; even that he met
William Godwin, whose *Political Justice* was published by
Johnson in February 1793, 'at Johnson's table or in his shop'.[2]
We now know that Wordsworth did not meet Godwin before
the early spring of 1795.[3] Doubtless he did meet in Johnson's
bookshop some of the obscure younger radicals whom he mentions without naming in *The Prelude*; but his acquaintance
with James Watt must have been sufficient introduction to such
circles without depending on his publisher. He is strangely
reticent, in all his later reminiscences, about his London associates, seldom mentioning any of them by name. The only person
whom he ever named as a personal acquaintance was a Mr.
Nicholson of Cateaton Street, Holborn, with whom he formed
a habit of supping on Sunday evenings, and going afterwards
with him to 'sit under' Joseph Fawcett, the minister of a dissenting chapel in Old Jewry, whose sermons were attracting large
audiences. Nicholson was not, as Harper supposes, William
Nicholson, the friend of Holcroft and Godwin. That Nicholson
lived not in Cateaton Street but in Red Lion Square. Wordsworth's
host was Samuel Nicholson, a haberdasher.[4] He may well have
been a friend of Johnson's.

Of Joseph Fawcett we have a description in the life of Robert
Bloomfield, the author of *The Farmer's Boy*, who some years
before had sat under him to learn classical English and to gain
'enlarged notions of Providence'. 'His language', we are told,
'was just such as *The Rambler* is written in; his Action like a
person acting a Tragedy; his Discourse rational, and free from
the Cant of Methodism.'[5] This latter virtue perhaps was attractive to Wordsworth, who was at no time influenced by evangelicalism. At this very time John Newton was preaching at St.

---

[1] Obituary notice by J. Aikin in the *Gentleman's Magazine*, Dec. 1809.
[2] Harper, i, p. 212.
[3] Godwin's Diary makes this certain. See below, pp. 262–3.
[4] I am indebted for this identification to Mr. A. B. Stockwell, of Colorado
University, who searched the Holborn Rate-books.
[5] *The Farmer's Boy*, by Robert Bloomfield, preface.

Mary Woolnoth, not far from the Old Jewry, but the young Wordsworth, in spite of his sympathies with the anti-slavery movement, did not go to hear 'the old African blasphemer'. There was too much of personal unreserve in evangelicalism for his cautious temperament.

Fawcett later, in 1795, published a poem which was a fierce satire against war and which, said Wordsworth afterwards, 'had a good deal of merit, and made me think more about him than I should otherwise have done'. But his chief importance in the Wordsworth story is that he furnished Wordsworth with some of his 'copy' for the character of the Solitary in the *Excursion*.[1]

Wordsworth's mind in the months following his return dwelt ever more and more intensely and unhappily on the political situation. It absorbed almost all his attention, and deepened and emphasized his anxiety about Annette. How powerful was this absorption can be seen from the contents and structure of the later books of *The Prelude*. As a story *The Prelude* may be said to be fairly continuous (though with 'Retrospects' and interruptions) down to the news of the death of Robespierre in 1794, in Book X. The next three books are given up almost entirely to 'reflections on the French Revolution', as they occurred to Wordsworth at the time (though modified and compared with the maturer views of 1804 and 1805 when the poem was written), or to reflections on his own reactions to the political events, particularly the outbreak of war, and on the inward condition of his mind and spirit which were thrown by these events into a severe and prolonged state of crisis and suffering. The amount of space given up to this subject is itself a measure of the profundity and enduring power of the shock administered to what he calls his 'moral nature' by the conflict between the land of his birth and of all his early loves and that in which he had seen what to him was almost a redemption of mankind.

We shall never understand Wordsworth's feelings unless we

---

[1] See Wordsworth's note to *The Excursion*, *P.W.* v, p. 375. M. Ray Adams, 'Joseph Fawcett and Wordsworth's Solitary', *P.M.L.A.* 48, 1933, has shown that Wordsworth was mistaken in thinking that Fawcett sank into a state of moral disintegration and misanthropy as a result of the war and the failure of the Revolution.

realize that for him the French Revolution was the cause, not simply of a people struggling to be free, but of mankind, and that his vision of man was something deeply precious to him. In France he had seen what he believed and hoped would prove the coming of a new and better age for the whole human race. In this he was, of course, not alone; Tom Paine and Priestley, Godwin and Gilbert Wakefield, the younger writers, Coleridge, Southey, and Thelwall, and a host of 'philosophers', poets, and pamphleteers before and after them, were convinced of the evils of monarchy and aristocracy, and of salvation through the light of 'reason' dawning on superstition and tyranny. Wordsworth differed from the 'Painites' not in opinions nor in ideals, but in his psychological approach, his personal vision. Priestley and Godwin and many of the English Jacobins sprang from the world of English nonconformity, with its long history of exclusion by statute from the universities and from the government of the country. For them the French Revolution meant the defeat of an old hereditary enemy—the tyranny of Church and State. Tom Paine was partly of Quaker origin, a born agitator, republican, and disturber of things as they are. But Wordsworth, coming from his free world of shepherds and farmers and Cambridge students, had no inherent grievance against society. True, he had an inborn dislike of 'the great' who were great by reason of birth or wealth only, and this dislike had been sharpened by what his family had suffered and was still suffering at the hands of Lord Lonsdale. For him the Revolution—seen first in its most joyous moments in the summer of 1790 and then through the eyes of Beaupuy—was the coming into being for all men of what was already his own precious heritage—freedom and equality between man and man. Because he knew what these blessings meant, and because his poet's temperament gave him imaginative sympathy with those who had them not, he held on to his belief in the Revolution in spite of the growth of the darker elements, confident that in the end all would be well. His faith in France was stronger than any particular philanthropic enthusiasm. When he first returned to England he seems to have associated with some of the Abolitionists, and from them he heard the story of the grievous disappointment of the previous spring, when the Bill for the gradual abolition of the slave trade which Pitt had supported and which had passed the Commons was thrown out by the Lords.[1] He was less disturbed by this setback than some of his friends, for he regarded slavery and the slave trade as only one of the evils associated with the old order.

> I brought with me the faith
> That, if France prospered, good men would not long
> Pay fruitless worship to humanity.
> And this most rotten branch of human shame,
> Object, so seemed it, of superfluous pains,
> Would fall together with its parent tree. . . .[2]
> Such was my then belief, that there was one
> And only one solicitude for all.[3]

But this and every other hope was shattered by the events of February. In Paris Wordsworth had felt deep anxiety about the course France was following; but that was as nothing to the agony of mental conflict into which he was thrown by the outbreak of war.[4]

> What then were my emotions, when in arms
> Britain put forth her free-born strength in league,
> Oh, pity and shame! with those confederate Powers!
>   . . . No shock
> Given to my moral nature had I known
> Down to that very moment; neither lapse
> Nor turn of sentiment that might be named
> A revolution, save at this one time.[5]

The early text of *The Prelude* contains some lines following upon these, which reveal even more intimately the nature of this 'shock'.

> 'Twas not conceal'd with what ungracious eyes
> Our native Rulers from the very first
> Had looked upon regenerated France,
> Nor had I doubted that this day would come.
> But in such contemplation I had thought
> Of general interests only, beyond this
> Had never once foretasted the event.
> Now had I other business for I felt

---

[1] *Prel.* X, ll. 245–62.   [2] Ibid., ll. 257–62.
[3] Ibid. (1805), ll. 228–9.
[4] France declared war on England on Feb. 1st.
[5] *Prel.* X, ll. 268–72. This revised text is even stronger in expression than that of 1805.

> The ravage of this most unnatural strife
> In my own heart; there lay it like a weight
> At enmity with all the tenderest springs
> Of my enjoyments.[1]

'The tenderest springs of my enjoyments'! It is only when we consider where lay these 'springs', and what the words 'enjoyment' and 'joy' meant for Wordsworth, that the extremity of the suffering he was undergoing can be realized. How often in these London days must there have swept over him, as over his own *Poor Susan*, visions of his 'own darling vale' of Hawkshead, steeped in billowy mist in the silence of morning, or dreaming in moonlight glory under winter stars. There were the fells too, with their innumerable voices, of waterfalls and winds, of sheep, and shepherds with their dogs; with summits swept by clouds or 'grain-tinctured, drenched in Empyrean light'. Pictures such as these, which often enough have sent other English poets to die gladly for England when they have felt no anxiety about the justice of her quarrel, were now, for Wordsworth, a source of acutest pain. For all that beauty, and all that happy intercourse of nature and man with which his inner being was bound up, which for him *was* history, and patriotism, and happiness, was being flung into what he believed to be a wellnigh diabolical warfare. Were his dalesmen, or his schoolcompanions, to fight against Beaupuy and those young volunteers of France? This was the 'unnatural strife' that he felt ravaging his own heart, throwing him 'out of the pale of love', forcing him to violent revaluation of all his dearest ties.

> What had been a pride
> Was now a shame; my likings and my loves
> Ran in new channels, leaving old ones dry.[2]

Hitherto his love for his homeland had marched step for step with his new love for France and for humanity; now they were torn violently apart, and it seemed as though there were nothing for it but to substitute completely the new for the old.

His memories of his own past seemed now 'perfidious', he could hope only for a total separation between 'the man to come' and 'him who had been'; thus reversing his ultimate doctrine that 'the child is father of the man' and all existence linked in

---

[1] Ibid. (1805), ll. 243–54.   [2] *Prel.* XI, ll. 183–5.

an harmonious relationship. Even his faith in history and poetry, and in the heroic figures of legend, faltered and almost failed.

> an emptiness
> Fell on the Historian's page and even on that
> Of Poets . . . their rights
> Seemed mortal and their empire passed away.[1]

One painful and bitter consequence ensued upon this state of mind; he found it impossible to rejoice in English victories; rather, he felt his joy—a fierce, unhappy joy it must have been—

> When Englishmen by thousands were o'erthrown,
> Left without glory on the field.[2]

This refers to the defeat of Hondeschoote on September 8th 1793, when he was staying once more with Robert Jones at Plas-yn-Llan. To this visit must also belong the description of his being unable to join in the prayers for victory in the village church service. Joseph Fawcett, the radical and pacifist, would not have offered prayers for victory at his chapel in Old Jewry. Nor would Wordsworth normally have attended a church service. But when staying with his Welsh friend, who was now ordained, he would have gone with him.

Wordsworth's sufferings were probably unique in their peculiar depth and passion, but he insists that he was one of a large company:

> Not in my single self alone I found,
> But in the minds of all ingenuous youth,
> Change and subversion from that hour.

And again, he speaks for a whole generation of young men when he exclaims

> Oh! much have they to account for who could tear,
> By violence, at one decisive rent,
> From the best youth in England their dear pride,
> Their joy, in England.[3]

And among them he is surely including his friends of the years immediately ahead—Montagu, Losh, and, above all, Coleridge.

[1] See for the whole passage, *Prel.* X (1805), ll. 42–95.
[2] Ibid., ll. 286–7.
[3] Ibid., ll. 266–8, and ll. 300–3.

Such a state of conflict demanded relief either through sympathetic contact with a kindred mind, or through literary or poetic creation. Wordsworth did not easily make friends. In London he had met no one to whom he could unburden himself, for among the Jacobins there was no English Beaupuy, no one who could appeal to his 'moral being'. Instead he took up his pen and wrote one of the most eloquent political pamphlets of that generation.

The opportunity came through the appearance on the bookstalls of London, a few days after the execution of Louis XVI on January 21st, of a reprint of a sermon preached some years before by Richard Watson, Bishop of Llandaff, on the subject of *The Wisdom and Goodness of God in having made both Rich and Poor*. To the sermon was now added an appendix, written after Louis' death, containing severe strictures on the behaviour of the French, and a bland eulogy on the excellence of the British constitution, of British justice, and of the laws then regulating the condition of the British poor. The bishop was a countryman of Wordsworth's, being the son of the headmaster of Heversham Grammar School, where he had been educated and whence he had proceeded to Cambridge. There he had risen rapidly, being first Professor of Chemistry and then of Divinity. Of neither subject did he know much, but he had good abilities, and gained more reputation as a chemist than as a theologian. On becoming a bishop he did not trouble his diocese with his presence more than once in three years, and lived, after his retirement from Cambridge, in the old mansion of Calgarth Park on the shores of Windermere. He rebuilt it suitably, according to the taste of the time. In churchmanship and politics he was 'liberal' rather than 'high', and for a time this prevented his preferment in the Church. But, after giving qualified support to the progress of the French Revolution down even to the declaration of the Republic, he was startled by the execution of the king into writing his complacent defence of the 'British way of life'. It contained indeed some curious statements. 'The Poor', he said, 'possess a ninth part of the landed rental of the country' —because at the time of writing they were supported to that extent out of the rates. Injustice in a British court of law was a virtual impossibility. Parliamentary reform was unnecessary; the Constitution provided as much liberty and equality as was

necessary or desirable: 'peasants and mechanics' should have
nothing to do with legislation. As for the French, their treatment
of the king and of the clergy, and the means by which their
republic had been established, had caused him to 'fly with terror
and abhorrence from the altar of liberty'.

Wordsworth's tormented spirit seized on this document.
Some time during this unhappy spring he composed a reply.
Why he did not also publish it is a question to which we have
no certain answer. But the most likely explanation is that Johnson, when Wordsworth presented it to him for publication (as
he probably did), strongly advised him to keep it quiet. For
Johnson, though a friend of radicals, was no party politician.
When, a few years later, he was sent to prison for selling (not
publishing) a pamphlet of Gilbert Wakefield's—itself a reply
to another effusion of Watson's—men of all parties thought he
had been unfairly treated. Certainly he was not the sort of man
to assist a young writer to get into difficulties with Government.
And there were passages in Wordsworth's document which
might have drawn upon him unpleasant attention.

To begin with, it was entitled *A Letter to the Bishop of Llandaff on the Extraordinary Avowal of his Political Principles . . .
by a Republican.*[1] It was largely an attack on monarchy, and on
the constitution of 'King *and* Lords *and* Commons . . . who have
constitutionally the right of enacting whatever laws they please,
in defiance of the petitions or remonstrances of the nation'. But
the interest of the *Letter* lies, not so much in the views which it
expresses, as in the tone of personal passion in which they are
expressed. Legouis was right in saying that Wordsworth's
pamphlet breathes 'an almost religious fervour', and reflects the
'puritan austerity of his temperament', the austerity that is the
rein of deeply felt passion.[2] It is the fruit not only of the year in
France, but of his wanderings and watchings in London, and
along English roads and by-ways, of his musings on poverty,
suffering, and war. He writes as a disciple of the old English
Republicans and the Declaration of the Rights of Man,[3] but he

---

[1] The *Letter,* and Watson's appendix, were published in 1875 by A. Grosart in
the first volume of his *Prose Works of William Wordsworth.*

[2] *L.,* p. 232.

[3] In the *Letter* he quotes from the *Contrat Social,* ch. i; from Racine's *Athalie* on
the downfall of kings; from the Declaration of the Rights of Man, and from the
speech of Bishop Grégoire at the Convention. The influence of such writers as

feels as the writer of *The Ruined Cottage* and *The Female Vagrant* was to feel in the immediately ensuing years.

At the beginning, we see the result of his stay in Paris in the autumn, when public interest centred on the question of the king's guilt, and of his trial. He had then become convinced that Louis' guilt was deep, and so he deplored the 'idle cry of modish lamentation which has resounded from the Court to the cottage', at his execution. He allows compassion—but not apparently mercy—for one who has been forced into 'an unnatural situation, which requires more than human talents and human virtues and at the same time precludes him from attaining even a moderate knowledge of common life'. Fervently did Wordsworth pray, quoting Racine, that 'neither by the hands of his priests nor of his nobles' would 'his posterity be raised to the rank of his ancestors'.

Monarchy, for Wordsworth, was better dead, because from the system associated with it arose those social evils which disgraced the nation. And so the rest of the *Letter* is a repudiation of the bishop's smug satisfaction with things as they are. His contempt for the social grandeur of royalty and aristocracy and the sycophancy it bred—no imaginary evil in those days: his own family sense of injury at the hands of a member of the British aristocracy: his keen eye for the sufferings of the poor—all find here their voice, often edged with sarcasm.

'I congratulate your Lordship', he says, 'upon your enthusiastic fondness for the judicial proceedings of this country. I am happy to find you have passed through life without having your fleece torn from your back in the thorny labyrinth of litigation. . . . Your Lordship cannot, I presume, be ignorant of the consuming expense of our never-ending process, the verbosity of unintelligible statutes, and the perpetual contrariety in our judicial decisions.' Wordsworth here speaks as the exasperated plaintiff of the Lowther lawsuit.

Hereditary nobility, and all titled state, seemed to him unjustifiable and dangerous—breeding insolence and flattery. Nobility was bad also because 'it binds down whole ranks of men to idleness', and 'the languid tedium of a noble repose', whose only relief was 'gaming, or the tricking manœuvres of

Harrington and Milton is also distinctly traceable, and is quite as strong as that of Rousseau. See above, p. 207.

the horse-race'. And he saw an even worse consequence. 'Does your Lordship shudder', he asks, 'at the prostitution which miserably deluges our streets? You may find the cause in our aristocratical prejudices.'

Poverty was destroying marriage, and driving the poor to 'that promiscuous intercourse to which they are impelled by the instincts of nature, and the dreadful satisfaction of escaping the prospect of infants . . . whom they are unable to support'. These evils could and should be overcome in a juster society, and he even hoped 'that the class of wretches called mendicants will not much longer shock the feelings of humanity'. Yet would Wordsworth, the poet of beggars and wayfarers, have alto-gether endorsed what Wordsworth the radical here demanded? All this is strange doctrine from one who lived to lament the Reform Bill of 1832 and to be the deferential political adviser of a great Tory landowner. But Wordsworth was always a de-fender of the poor, and even in his conservative old age he could kick at a fence raised by some noble encloser across a right of way, and say with half a smile to Crabb Robinson: 'I have no respect for the Whigs, but I have a good deal of the Chartist in me.'

So, in the *Letter*, war is wicked because it results in 'giving up to the sword so large a portion of the poor, and consigning the rest to the more slow and painful consumption of want'. War, as a disaster involving the poor in misery, had already appeared in *An Evening Walk*, whose Beggar-woman was the widow of a soldier killed in the American war. Soon, he made both the characters of *Salisbury Plain*, the vagrant woman and the sailor who commits the murder, victims of what would now be called an 'imperialist war'. Wordsworth was never a pacifist in the sense of holding a conviction that fighting is at all times wrong. He had seen nothing wrong in the young men of France gather-ing to defend their frontiers, or in the generous patriotism of Beaupuy. Ten years later, when England was threatened with invasion, his sonnets were a trumpet-call to arms. But in 1793 this siding with the 'coalesced Kings' against the French Republic was an outrage of which the poor were the first victims.

It is of course easy to criticize the illogicalities of Words-worth's objections to the war. The French Republic had invaded the Netherlands and broken international treaties. It was

engaged in forcing its not always welcome, and invariably expensive, assistance on 'all nations struggling to be free'. From
being a defending it was rapidly becoming an aggressive power.
The dangers of its policy did indeed reveal themselves slowly to
Wordsworth, but not until several years had passed of unrelieved anguish of mind for him—not until young Bonaparte
had carried the war over the sacred frontiers of republican
Switzerland. Now and for several years to come he could see
in government policy nothing but the 'unhappy counsel of a few
weak men'[1] who had thrust the country into a war of which he
felt persuaded there could be no speedy end. He believed too that
Government was the instigator of 'anti-Jacobin' disturbances
such as the destruction of Priestley's house at Birmingham, and
that it encouraged a war-fever in the population which would
never have arisen spontaneously. So he asks the Bishop:

> Left to the quiet exercise of their own judgment, do you think
> that the people would have thought it necessary to set fire to the
> house of the philosophic Priestley, and to hunt down his life like
> that of a traitor and parricide? that, deprived almost of the neces-
> saries of existence by the burden of their taxes, they would cry
> out, as with one voice, for a war from which not a single ray of con-
> solation can visit them to compensate for the additional keenness with
> which they are about to smart under the scourge of labour, of cold and
> of hunger?

Between the composition of the *Letter to the Bishop of Llandaff*
and the first version of the narrative poem *Salisbury Plain*,
lay probably not more than two or three months. Both these
compositions are the outcome of the same feelings, but it is
doubtful whether Wordsworth could have bent his mind to
poetry as long as he remained in London. Fortunately an event
occurred in the summer which once more freed the springs
of his imagination.

Among Wordsworth's school-acquaintance at Hawkshead
was a youth named William Calvert, the elder son of Raisley
Calvert, the steward of the Duke of Norfolk's properties at
Greystoke. His younger brother, Raisley, was to become, in the
course of the next year, the friend and benefactor in death of

---

[1] *Prel.* X (1805), l. 293. This line was afterwards omitted, but Wordsworth
never modified his general description of the war as both a tragedy and a blunder.

Calvert and Wordsworth were travelling in a 'whiskey' across Salisbury Plain when an accident occurred to their conveyance which brought their joint tour to an abrupt end and turned Wordsworth once more alone upon the roads of England. 'Mr. C.', says Dorothy, 'mounted his horse and rode into the North and William's firm friends, a pair of stout legs, supported him from Salisbury, through South into North Wales, where he is now quietly sitting down in the Vale of Clwyd.'[1]

The two or three weeks thus spent unexpectedly alone were productive both of immediate poetic achievement and of incidents that left in his imagination emotional impressions that ripened afterwards, when at last his genius was fully released. Not only *Guilt and Sorrow*, but *Tintern Abbey, Peter Bell*, and *We are Seven* have their remote origins in this long ramble. The journey into the west was a 'recall to Nature'. We have to remember that it was nearly two years since he had been alone with the English landscape. Coming in the midst of a period of conflict and doubt about the validity of his own experience, this tour brought him back once more to solitude and to all that had formerly given him his deepest delight. Would Nature still be to him what she had been? The answer was both 'yes' and 'no'.

He had, he tells us, in the midst of the 'eclipse' of so much that had formed his earlier inheritance, retained his delight in

> The life of nature by the God of love
> Inspired,[2]

and this was a true 'living sound', not a 'deaf echo' merely of what he had so deeply loved. But although his response was immediate and strong to what Nature offered him, there was a difference—or so he thought afterwards—between his feelings now, in 1793, and those of the days before the world darkened. To this summer journey over Salisbury Plain and into Wales must be assigned the curious description in the twelfth book of *The Prelude* of that restless, 'greedy' craving after Nature and the sights of Nature; that state which he described afterwards in *Tintern Abbey* as 'appetite'—quite different from the veneration and 'worship' which he had felt as a boy. In this state he says 'the eye was master of the heart'. A kind of lust for natural forms and sights possessed him, a

---

[1] *E.L.* 34, p. 105. D.W. to J.P., Aug. 30th 1793.
[2] *Prel.* XI (1805), ll. 99–100.

delight in his own powers of seeing rather than a worshipful
love of the thing seen.

> My delights
> Such as they were, were sought insatiably,
> Though 'twas a transport of the outward sense,
> Not of the mind, vivid but not profound.
> Yet was I often greedy in the chase;
> I roamed from hill to hill, from rock to rock,[1]
> Still craving combinations of new forms,
> New pleasure, wider empire for the sight.[2]

And it is this condition that he recalled five years later when
he returned to the same country in a very different mood. He
was, he says, then, in 1793,

> more like a man
> Flying from something that he dreads than one
> Who sought the thing he loved.[3]

And from what was he flying but from the torment of his own
thoughts and memories? Such a mood of restless craving is
surely no uncommon one with all those who have ever loved the
world of Nature and suffered in the world of man.

Yet this was not his only state of mind during that solitary
August. *The Prelude* tells in a passage too often neglected of the
experience that befell him as he was crossing Salisbury Plain.

> There on the pastoral Downs without a track
> To guide me, or along the bare white roads
> Lengthening in solitude their dreary line,
> While through those vestiges of ancient times
> I ranged, and by the solitude overcome,
> I had a reverie and saw the past.[4]

From what happened there, he says, he first began to hope that
he might achieve some 'enduring and creative' work, infused
with 'passion' or feeling from the 'forms of Nature'. It is usual
to suppose that Wordsworth did not contemplate any poem
dealing in universals until he began to compose *The Recluse*

---

[1] Cf. *To the Daisy*, written in 1802. *P.W.* ii, p. 135.

> In Youth from rock to rock I went,
> From hill to hill in discontent
> Of pleasure high and turbulent.

[2] *Prel.* XI (1805), ll. 187–93.   [3] *Tintern Abbey*, ll. 70–72.
[4] *Prel.* XII (1805), ll. 315–20.

at Racedown in 1797. But it is scarcely likely that he would have inserted the description of his reverie or vision on Salisbury Plain in this particular context unless he had regarded it as an important 'moment' in his creative life. The importance of the vision must not be judged entirely by the merits of the poem which was its immediate consequence, namely, the first version of *Guilt and Sorrow*. In that, gloomy realism rather than imaginative power is the prevailing tone. Although the vision of the human sacrifices and of the druids was included in the original version of the poem, in somewhat highly coloured language,[1] almost all of it was dropped from the published version in 1842, perhaps because, when he was writing the thirteenth book of *The Prelude* in 1805, Wordsworth realized that his mental experience during that time was of a truly poetic kind, and would therefore be more suitably included in his story of the 'growth of a poet's mind'.

The vision was different from those 'spots of time' recorded in *The Prelude*—the 'wait for the ponies', or the sunrise dedication—for it was a vision of man rather than of pure Nature. It is easy to see its psychological provenance. War, foreboding of woes to come, horror at acts of violence and cruelty,[2] had inevitably filled his mind with an image of man much more terrifying than the shepherd-kings who alone had peopled it before his stay in France. Now, in the solitude of the great spaces of Salisbury Plain, and within sight of Stonehenge and other memorials of the 'silent, vanished races', his mind produced day-dreams of the savagery of prehistoric man. The visionary state lasted, apparently, throughout the three days' wandering on the Plain, and consisted of three stages, the first two terrifying, the last—that of the druids seen as 'Teachers'—peaceful. In the first stage he

> Saw multitudes of men, and here and there
> A single Briton in his wolf-skin vest
> With shield and stone-axe, stride across the Wold;
> The voice of spears was heard, the rattling spear
> Shaken by arms of mighty bone, in strength,
> Long mouldered, of barbaric majesty.

---

[1] See *P.W.* i, pp. 103–4 in app. crit.

[2] It must be remembered that during the past month Robespierre had come into power in Paris and the 'Terror' was beginning in earnest.

At this point Wordsworth seems to have been overcome with fear, and in broad daylight prayed for night to shut the vision out.

> I called on Darkness—but before the word
> Was uttered, midnight darkness seemed to take
> All objects from my sight; and lo! again
> The Desert visible by dismal flames;
> It is the sacrificial altar, fed
> With living men—how deep the groans! the voice
> Of those that crowd the giant wicker thrills
> The monumental hillocks, and the pomp
> Is for both worlds, the living and the dead.[1]

But at other times these horrific visions gave place to a gentler 'waking dream', or 'antiquarian's dream', in which he saw the druids,

> with white wands
> Uplifted, pointing to the starry sky,

moving rhythmically to musical sounds, while the whole vast Plain

> Rejoiced with them and me in those sweet sounds.

The pattern of the reverie was indeed purely antiquarian, drawn from various literary sources. Human sacrifices probably never took place on Salisbury Plain, nor was it, more than anywhere else, a druid centre. But Wordsworth had been attracted to druids in early youth, and associated them with the stone circles that really belonged to an earlier age. For the druids themselves—as teachers of the mysteries of nature, astronomy, and of a supposed primitive faith, he felt all his life a sort of sympathetic admiration. He drew his knowledge of them partly from the classical writers and partly from the antiquarian writers of his own time.[2] It is significant that in two of the *Ecclesiastical*

---

[1] *Prel.* XIII, ll. 328–35. This part of the vision is recorded in an early draft of *Guilt and Sorrow*, *P.W.* i, p. 104, as that of 'a swain' who, 'far astray', sees 'gigantic beings', who 'with shield and stone-axe stride across the wold'. This and the line about the 'sacrificial altar fed with living men' were retained in *The Prelude*.

[2] Wordsworth could easily have read, while at Cambridge, William Stukeley's *Stonehenge, A Temple restor'd to the British Druids*, 1740, or Sammes's *Britannia Antiqua Illustrata*, 1677. Both these writers were referred to by William Hutchinson in his *History of Cumberland*, which was published in 1794 and contained lengthy descriptions of 'Long Meg and her daughters' and other Cumberland antiquities well known to Wordsworth. It seems indeed likely that the stanzas of *Guilt and*

Sonnets he speaks of them with respect,[1] and that in some dis-
carded passages of the third book of *The Prelude* he calls himself

> A youthful Druid taught in shady groves
> Primaeval mysteries.[2]

   The poem which he began to compose mentally in the intervals of reverie and wrote down during the next few weeks in its
first and least complicated form, revising and adding to it two
years later at Racedown, is practically the story of *The Female
Vagrant* which was printed in the *Lyrical Ballads* in 1798. His
own early name for the poem was *Salisbury Plain*, and there are
in it many lines and images which show how alert were his
bodily eyes during that 'visionary' journey. Wordsworth, even
in his most intense experiences of vision or dream, was never far
from earth. Such lines as

> Dreary cornfields stretched without a bound,
>
>   Winds that whistling near
> Sweep the thin grass,
>
> Desert lark on high, a wasted strain,
>
> The crows in blackening eddies homeward borne,
>
>   the bustard, of those regions bleak
> Shy tenant,

who

> Forced hard against the wind a thick, unwieldy flight,

bring before the eye and ear with a curious melancholy vividness
the landscape of which they are speaking. No wonder that
Coleridge, when he first read *Salisbury Plain* in the spring of
1796, thought that in it Wordsworth

>   had exercised
> Upon the vulgar forms of present things,
> The actual world of our familiar days,
> Yet higher power.[3]

Sorrow in which he describes the human sacrifices, as well as the lines in *The
Prelude*, owe something to Hutchinson. Hutchinson, *History and Antiquities of
Cumberland*, i, pp. 225–52. See also Wordsworth's note to *E.W.* (1793), l. 171.
   [1] *P.W.* iii, pp. 342–3.   [2] *Prel.*, p. 74.
   [3] *Prel.* XIII, ll. 355–8.

There are indications that the story itself may contain fragments of Wordsworth's own feelings on the Plain. The woman's
story of how her despair after her sufferings in America was
healed by beholding the calm of the Atlantic may reflect his
own sense of relief at being once more alone among the sights
and sounds of Nature however much his mind might be hurt
and troubled. The opening of the poem (which was afterwards
omitted) is certainly a reflection of his depressed and dis-
illusioned mood, as it compares the sufferings and privations of
'the hungry savage', who has never known any other life, with

> The thoughts which load the kindly spirit down,
> And break the springs of joy.

Wordsworth was suffering from just such a 'load', and, it can
scarcely be doubted, felt some of it lifted as a result of his three
days' sojourn on the Plain.

The story itself, he tells us, as far as the woman is concerned,
is a true one and was told him a year or two before by the
sufferer herself. When or how he met her is not revealed. As a
tragedy of poverty and war it fitted well with his present pre-
occupations.

He pursued his way through Bristol, and across the Severn
to the valley of the Wye, which he was afterwards to revisit
with such great poetic consequences. He was now in country
totally new to him. At Goodrich Castle he met the little girl
who became the pious heroine of *We are Seven*. Some such conversation must have taken place between them as is recorded
in the poem, for nearly fifty years later Wordsworth revisited
Goodrich and regretted that he could not find 'in the neighbouring hamlet traces of one who had interested me so much; but
that was impossible, as unfortunately I did not even know her
name'. He went up the Wye to the neighbourhood of Builth, where
he met a travelling tinker whom he afterwards made famous, as
far as 'countenance, gait and figure' were concerned, as 'Peter
Bell'. A curious description survives, in a rejected verse of the
poem, of their meeting.

> Now Peter do I call to mind
> That eventide when thou and I

> Over ditch and over stile
> Were fellow travellers many a mile
> Near Builth on the banks of Wye.
> Oh Peter who could now forget
> That both hung back in murderer's guize?
> 'Twas thou that wast afraid of me
> And I that was afraid of thee,
> We'd each of us a hundred eyes.[1]

That Wordsworth could be taken for a possible murderer is probably an indication that by this time, after perhaps a fortnight of wandering across country, in all weathers and with little money, he looked more like a common tramp than a gentleman on holiday. They walked together down the Wye from Builth to Hay, and Peter told him strange stories. The Wye left the most gracious images in his mind in spite of his 'greedy' mood. One suspects that after all that mood was not continuous—that the old filial delight was not far away. At any rate he was grateful enough to the Wye afterwards:

> oh! how oft—
> In darkness and amid the many shapes
> Of joyless daylight; when the fretful stir
> Unprofitable and the fever of the world
> Have hung upon the beatings of my heart—
> How oft, in spirit, have I turned to thee,
> O sylvan Wye! thou wanderer thro' the woods,
> How often has my spirit turned to thee![2]

From Hay Wordsworth struck north until he reached the hospitable roof of Robert Jones's father at Plas-yn-Llan in the vale of Clwyd. Here, at the end of August, he arrived, to rest and write down *Salisbury Plain*, and enjoy once more the company of Robert and his sisters.

We now enter upon a mysterious episode in Wordsworth's life—that of his possible but unproved return to France. If it took place at all, it must have been at the end of September or very early in October 1793, for all English people in Paris were placed under arrest by the middle of October, and Wordsworth could scarcely have escaped. From September to December a cloud of impenetrable obscurity lies over his whereabouts and

---

[1] *P.W.* ii, p. 530.   [2] *Tintern Abbey*, ll. 50–57.

his movements; we know only from a note in the family accounts that he must have been at Whitehaven at Christmas.[1] Dorothy's expectation of being in Halifax by the end of August had meanwhile been disappointed. She had to wait for an escort, her cousin Mr. Griffith, a business man of Newcastle, having promised to take her whenever he was free to call for her. On August 30th Dorothy wrote to Jane Pollard that 'you will certainly see both my brother and myself at Christmas', though with many cautions not to speak of it, for the meeting planned between her and William must not reach the ears of her uncle. She evidently now expected that her brother would not leave north Wales until she came into the north, for she told Jane that 'he is now [August 30th] sitting quietly in the vale of Clwyd where he will wait my arrival at Halifax and join me there'. This statement must mean that William had written to her expressing such an intention. If therefore he went to France at any time during the following month, it must have been unexpectedly; a sudden decision must have been taken, and probably nothing was said to Dorothy. A motive for so difficult and risky an undertaking is not very easy to find. Some will have it that it was a desperate attempt to reach and marry Annette.[2] But, if so, why did he go to Paris? On the whole, he is more likely to have gone for political reasons, to try to re-establish contact with his Girondin friends, though if this was so it was both a forlorn hope and an expedition beset with dangers, for the Girondins had by this time fallen on evil days and no longer had the slightest chance of controlling affairs. Robespierre and the Jacobin extremists were masters of the Convention.

The only important evidence of this visit to Paris is to be found in Carlyle's *Reminiscences*, and is a report by Carlyle of a conversation which took place in London between him and Wordsworth about the year 1840.[3] The passage is worth quoting in full:

He had been in France in the earlier or secondary stage of the Revolution; had witnessed the struggle of *Girondins* and *Mountain*, in particular the execution of Gorsas, 'the first *Deputy* sent to the Scaffold'; and testified strongly to the ominous feeling which that

---

[1] 'Dec. 26. 1793. Cash advanced to Nephew William. £20. 0. 0.' *D.C.P.*
[2] *A.V.*, pp. 34–36.
[3] Carlyle is not certain of the exact date.

event produced in everybody, and of which he himself seemed to retain something: 'Where will it *end*, when you have set an example in *this* kind?'[1] I knew well about Gorsas; but had found, in my readings, no trace of the public emotion his death excited; and perceived now that Wordsworth might be taken as a true supplement to my Book, on this small point. He did not otherwise add to or alter my ideas on the Revolution.

Now Gorsas was a Girondin deputy and journalist, and he was guillotined on October 7th 1793. After the Girondin deputies were expelled from the Convention on May 31st, he, with Pétion, Buzot, Louvet, and some others escaped to Normandy, where they made Caen the centre of a brief attempt to rally the departments against the dictatorship of Jacobin-dominated Paris.[2] But in Normandy the Girondins lacked popular support; there were too many cross-currents of royalist feeling to give them even a slender chance of victory, in spite of the defection of General Wimpfen to their side; the only direct result of their presence in Normandy was the murder of Marat on July 13th by Charlotte Corday who passed from Normandy into Paris through the Jacobin lines. But on the same day the Girondin troops suffered a reverse at Pacy; the Jacobins turned the murder of Marat to good account, and the Girondin leaders were declared outlaws on July 28th. They fled all over France, hunted and broken men, caught one by one in Robespierre's inexorable net; Gorsas alone with foolhardy courage slipped back into Paris after the decree of outlawry and was caught hiding there. He was executed immediately; the other Girondins who were already in prison—twenty-eight in number—followed him to the guillotine on October 31st.

Such was the state of Paris when Wordsworth re-entered it— if he ever came. The risks he ran can be measured to a certain extent by what we know of the fate of other English people in France at this time. A decree ordering the arrest of all foreigners was passed by the Convention on August 1st; it was not immediately put into force, but all over the country arbitrary arrests were frequently made; prisons were crowded with

---

[1] The inverted commas indicate Wordsworth's actual words.
[2] This was the 'federalist' revolt, involving Lyons, Marseilles, Bordeaux, and Toulon in anti-Jacobin risings, sometimes of considerable danger to the Government.

suspects; in Arras (Robespierre's town) and elsewhere execu-
tions were frequent;[1] the failure of the 'federalist' rising brought
about local reigns of terror in many cities of France.

Measures against foreigners in Paris became much stricter
about the middle of October. Between October 11th and 15th all
the English in Paris were arrested, and remained in prison for
varying lengths of time.[2] Whatever their previous political
records, scarcely any but saw the inside of the Luxembourg
or one of the many improvised prisons in former convents and
colleges. Most of them escaped execution; it is one of the few
redeeming marks of the Jacobin régime that it did not perpetrate
a general massacre of foreigners. But Helen Maria Williams,
John Hurford Stone, even Tom Paine himself, were placed under
arrest, and Paine, who was a deputy, only escaped execution by
a lucky accident. If Wordsworth had remained in Paris, he must
have joined them. If, therefore, he was present at the execution
of Gorsas on the 7th, he must have left Paris immediately
afterwards. There is indeed one rather dim piece of evidence that
he was warned of what was coming, and fled. Alaric Watts, the
journalist and art critic, later a friend of Wordsworth, relates
that an old 'republican', Bailey, used to tell him how he warned
Wordsworth that his life was in danger, whereupon Wordsworth 'decamped with great precipitation'.[3]

We are still faced with many practical difficulties in accepting
this story of Wordsworth's return to France. How, for instance,
was he financed? He may possibly have borrowed money from
Robert Jones;[4] if so, we have no record of its ever being repaid.
Then the difficulty of getting to France must have been great,
though Stone had succeeded both in leaving and returning to
France after the outbreak of war. Wordsworth's command of
French cannot have been such as to allow him to pass for a native
and it is difficult to see how he can have escaped arrest as a spy
of Pitt's even before he reached Paris, or, after leaving it, on

---

[1] *Un Séjour en France de 1792 à 1795,* translated by H. Taine, 1872. These are
the letters of an anonymous Englishwoman who was herself arrested in Sept. 1793.

[2] J. G. Alger, *Englishmen in the French Revolution,* 1889. See appendix E for a
list of English prisoners in the Paris prisons during the Terror.

[3] *Harper,* i, p. 379. It has proved impossible to trace the source of this story, as
Harper does not give his authority.

[4] Harper suggests he borrowed from Calvert, but he had parted from him six
or seven weeks before deciding to go to France.

his way back to the coast. Had he come in June or July, when the 'federalist' revolt was at its height, his chances would have been better.

Yet, in spite of all the difficulties, the conversation with Carlyle is hard to reject outright. Why should Wordsworth have spoken as he did of the obscure Girondin, Gorsas, and of the effect of his death, unless he had indeed been in Paris at the time?

It is reasonable also to ask whether any marks are left upon his mental life, which may be traceable to the strenuous experience of being nearly caught and imprisoned in Paris during the Terror. There are in *The Prelude* some indications of feelings and sufferings of an intensity which are, to say the least, more explicable if he had seen the guillotine at work, and lived even for a few days under the shadow of the Revolutionary Tribunal. There is, for instance, his statement that for months, nay years, after the outbreak of war, he suffered frequent nightmares about being brought to trial for his life, or about 'innocent victims sinking under fear'. In these dreams he heard himself pleading

Before unjust tribunals—with a voice
Labouring, a brain confounded, and a sense,
Death-like, of treacherous desertion, felt
In the last place of refuge—my own soul.[1]

These dreams have been explained as part of his 'guilt-complex' about Annette.[2] They are much more likely to have their origin in his conflict about the war, and the horrible realism of their form is more explicable if he had seen the Terror at work at first hand. Then there is his fierce loathing of Robespierre and the Jacobins which made him break forth into a sort of psalm of vengeful joy when at last they were overthrown.[3] They were the men who had butchered his friends, and he speaks of them as a man speaks who has escaped by the skin of his teeth a like fate.

Whatever may have been Wordsworth's movements in the autumn and winter of 1793–4, he certainly spent several weeks in Cumberland before finally joining Dorothy at Halifax in February 1794. Again her journey thither seems to have been delayed, for William was certainly at Whitehaven at Christmas,

[1] *Prel.* X, ll. 397–415.
[2] e.g. by H. Read, *Wordsworth*, 1950.
[3] See *Prel.* X, ll. 503–10, for his feelings about Arras, Robespierre's birthplace, and ibid. (1805), ll. 540–1, on the death of Robespierre.

not with her at Halifax, as she had hoped. On February 17th 1794 he told Mathews that he had 'quitted Keswick some time since' and had been 'moving backwards and forwards' before coming to Halifax.[1] 'Keswick' probably indicates that he stayed there with William and Raisley Calvert, at Windy Brow, the farm-house on Latrigg in which Calvert sometimes lived before he built Greta Bank. Wordsworth also now visited the Speddings[2] at Armathwaite, by Ouse Bridge at the foot of Bassenthwaite. John Spedding was an old schoolfellow, and the family had always shown him kindness.

Doubtless it was these visits to the Calverts and the Speddings which led to William and Dorothy borrowing Windy Brow in the spring for several weeks, and thus becoming intimate with the Keswick world. After spending six or eight weeks at Halifax with the Rawsons, they started out in April on the first of the many, many journeys which they were to make together during the next forty years. It must have been a day of ecstasy for Dorothy; she was at last to have William entirely to herself. They meant ultimately to visit their uncle at Whitehaven, but first they were to stay as long as they chose at Windy Brow, which Calvert had given up to their use. They went by coach to Kendal, and then, says Dorothy, 'I walked with my brother at my side, from Kendal to Grasmere, eighteen miles, and afterwards from Grasmere to Keswick, fifteen miles, through the most delightful country that ever was seen'. Every incident of that walk was long remembered. Eight years afterwards, when she came that way again with William and his bride, Mary Hutchinson, she remembered as they passed through Staveley what pleasure she had felt at first seeing it. 'I am always glad to see Staveley,' she wrote, 'the first mountain village that I came to with William, when we first began our pilgrimage together. Here we drank a bason of milk at a publick house, and here I washed my feet in the brook and put on a pair of silk stockings by William's advice.' To be footsore was almost a pleasure under such circumstances.

They approached Grasmere by the footpath along the western side of Rydal Water. 'I always love to walk that way,' she wrote afterwards, 'because it is the way I first came to Grasmere. . . .

[1] *E.L. 36*, p. 108. W.W. to W. Mathews, Feb. 17th 1794.
[2] Ibid., p. 112. D.W. to J.P., Apr. 1794.

It was just at sunset. There was a rich yellow light on the waters, and the Islands were reflected there.' After crossing the stepping-stones they must have mounted the road over White Moss Common and descended past the door of the very cottage which, five and a half years later, became their home. The night would have been spent at Robert Newton's little inn, just north of the church.

Sometime after they were settled at Grasmere, probably in 1801, Wordsworth wrote for Dorothy a sonnet: 'in recollection of that happy ramble, that most happy day and hour'. It described how they picnicked beside the tiny stream that descends from Wans Fell beside Dove Nest, and enters Windermere just north of Low Wood:

> For on that day, now seven years back, when first
> Two glad Foot-travellers through sun and shower,
> My Love and I came hither while thanks burst
> Out of our hearts to God for that good hour,
> Eating a traveller's meal in shady bower,
> We from that blessed water slaked our thirst.

When he revised the poem for publication in 1820, he cut out the description of the picnic, a loss which some may regret, though it is redeemed by the radiance of the last two lines:

> There is a little unpretending Rill
> Of limpid water, humbler far than aught
> That ever among Men or Naiads sought
> Notice or name!—It quivers down the hill,
> Furrowing its shallow way with dubious will:
> Yet to my mind this scanty stream is brought
> Oftener than Ganges or the Nile; a thought
> Of private recollection sweet and still!
> Months perish with their moons; year treads on year;
> But, faithful Emma, thou with me canst say
> That, while ten thousand pleasures disappear,
> And flies their memory fast, almost, as they,
> The immortal Spirit of a happy day
> Lingers beside that Rill, in vision clear.[1]

[1] *P.W.* iii, p. 4, *Miscellaneous Sonnets*, VI.

VIII

FRIENDS IN NEED, 1794–5

Wherefore Christian was left to tumble in the Slough of Despond alone . . . but I beheld in my dream, that a man came to him, whose name was Help, and asked him, what he did there?

THE PILGRIM'S PROGRESS

WILLIAM and Dorothy spent about six weeks at Windy Brow, experiencing the delights of rustic housekeeping, of Keswick's beauties, and above all of each other's company. 'Till my brother gets some employment he will lodge here', said Dorothy —not unpleased, perhaps, for the present, at the vagueness of their horizon. 'We please ourselves', she went on, 'in calculating from our present expenses for how very small a sum we could live. We find our own food, our breakfast and supper are of milk and our dinner chiefly of potatoes and we drink no tea.' One hopes that she forgot to mention bread and butter! Thus they were both still absorbed in the prospect of eventually living together. Windy Brow was the prologue to Racedown, and indeed to the whole of their lives together. The farmer and his wife were 'the most honest cleanly sensible people I ever saw in their rank of life—and I think I may safely affirm, *happier* than anybody I know'. They were, indeed, an embodiment of those rural virtues which William was soon to dwell on in his poems, and which really existed among the people of the dales. 'They are fond of reading and reason not indifferently on what they read', said Dorothy. She saw something, too, of the society of the neighbourhood. 'We have received great civilities from many very pleasant families, particularly from a Mrs. Spedding of Armathwaite.' This was the mother of William's old schoolfellow, John Spedding. Mrs. Spedding's two daughters, Maria and Margaret,[1] were 'women whose acquaintance I am very desirous of cultivating. They have read much and are amiable and engaging in their manners.' She and William spent three

---

[1] Maria died unmarried; Margaret married the Rev. Hurrell Froude, and was the mother of James Anthony Froude, the historian.

nights in this pleasant household, and Dorothy returned there later in the summer for a visit of several weeks.

While they were at Windy Brow Dorothy received from Mrs. Crackanthorpe of Newbiggin,[1] the disagreeable wife of her Uncle Kit, a letter reproving her for 'rambling about the country on foot' and living at Windy Brow in 'an unprotected situation'. Dorothy's reply to this ill natured attack is one of the delights of her correspondence. To the charge that she was not living as a respectable young woman should, she replied:

I affirm that I consider the character and virtues of my brother as a sufficient protection. . . . I am now twenty-two years of age and such have been the circumstances of my life that I may be said to have enjoyed his company for a *very few* months. An opportunity now presents itself of obtaining this satisfaction, an opportunity which I could not see pass from me without unspeakable pain. Besides I not only derive much pleasure but much improvement from my brother's society. I have regained all the knowledge I had of the French language some years ago . . . and I have now begun reading Italian.[2]

It is sometimes suggested that this little brush with Aunt Crackanthorpe was the origin of the poem *To a Young Lady who had been Reproved for Taking long Walks in the Country*, written several years later at Grasmere.

But Dorothy had other work to do at Windy Brow besides learning French and Italian. She began here her almost lifelong work of being her brother's secretary and copyist. She made a complete fair copy of *Salisbury Plain*, and on May 23rd William told Mathews that it was ready for the press, 'though I should certainly not publish it unless I hoped to derive from it some pecuniary recompence'. *An Evening Walk* and *Descriptive Sketches* had not brought in any hope of profit and he asked Mathews to call on Johnson and 'ask him if he ever sells any of those poems'. Meanwhile he began to revise and add to *An Evening Walk*, thereby beginning what became a permanent habit which cost him much weariness of body and mind and caused many an entry in Dorothy's journals—'William tired himself altering his poems'. He was dissatisfied with the way in which he had

---

[1] *E.L.* 39, p. 114. With regard to walking, Dorothy said that her friends ought to be glad that she 'had courage to make use of the strength with which nature had endowed her'.

[2] 'I have forwarded the Italian grammar, Tasso and Ariosto for you at Keswick.' R.W. to W.W., May 23rd 1794. *D.C.P.*

'huddled up those two little works' and published them with
so many imperfections. For the purpose of revising *An Evening
Walk* he cut up a printed copy and pasted the pages on to folio
sheets with wide margins for additional passages.[1] When he
finally revised the poem for republication in 1842 none of these
additions was retained. Yet some of them are of more than
academic interest. There is for instance the description of the
school-children at Grasmere playing in the churchyard—for
the school-house (now the ginger-bread shop) stood 'within the
churchyard's bound'. He and Dorothy must have watched the
scene when they stopped in Grasmere on their way to Windy
Brow. The new passage is reminiscent of his own strong sense
of immortality in childhood:

> Even now of that gay train who there pursue
> Their noisy sports with rapture ever new
> There are to whom the buoyant heart proclaims
> Death has no power o'er their particular frames.[2]

Of greater importance is a passage in which he dwells for the
first time on the mystical experience, showing thereby that the
doors of the spiritual vision remained open and that his unhappiness and the peculiar 'domination of the eye' which resulted
from it were not permanent states. He speaks of a 'hollow ghyll',
which can

> Sanctify the soul
> And on the morbid passions pouring balm
> Resistless breathe a melancholy calm;
> Or through the mind, by magic influence
> Rapt into worlds beyond the reign of sense,
> Roll the bright train of never ending dreams
> That pass like rivers tinged with evening gleams.

This stream can, he says, produce

> Harmonious thoughts, a soul by truth refined,
> Entire affection for all human kind,
> A heart that vibrates evermore, awake
> To feeling for all forms that Life can take,
> That wider still its sympathy extends
> And sees not any line where being ends.[3]

---

[1] The volume still exists in the Dove Cottage collection.
[2] *P.W.* i, p. 7, app. crit.   [3] Ibid., pp. 9–10, app. crit.

Whether or not the use of such a word as 'vibrates' indicates that he was reading Hartley's philosophy at this time, as one critic affirms,[1] there is no doubt that the 'bright train of never ending dreams', moving like sunset-lit rivers through the mind, is an image that only Wordsworth could have created. He added as he looked out over Derwentwater a loving description of Dorothy which must have caused those 'wild eyes' to glow with all their tenderest fires.

> Yes, thou art blest, my friend, with mind awake
> To Nature's impulse like this living lake,
> Whose mirror makes the landscape's charms its own
> With touches soft as those to memory known;
> While exquisite of sense the mighty mass
> All vibrates to the lightest gales that pass.[2]

No tribute in *The Prelude* is more beautifully conceived.

Finally, Wordsworth in these passages paid homage to Science. 'The harmonious doors of Science' have 'unbound celestial stores' to man and revealed the infinite variety of the universe and the limitless powers of man's mind. Later, Wordsworth became more cautious and critical in his approach to the science of his day.

All this argues a happier mood than some of his descriptions of himself in *The Prelude* about this time seem to imply. From them it is possible to gain the impression that from 1793 onwards for an unspecified period extending almost until his acquaintance with Coleridge in 1797, he was in a continually unhappy state of mind. And no doubt unhappiness or at least anxiety predominated. But here at Windy Brow, in the benign presence of his sister, and with the spring advancing to its perfection in fell and dale, 'a poet could not but be gay'—or nearly so, in spite of Pitt and Robespierre and the memory of Annette.

They left Windy Brow about the middle of May and proceeded to pay visits among their relations in West Cumberland. As they passed through Cockermouth on their way to Whitehaven, they paused to look again at the house in the High Street which had been their earliest home. Alas!—'all was in ruin, the terrace-walk buried and choked up with the old privot hedge which had formerly been so beautiful, roses and privot inter-

---

[1] Meyer, *Wordsworth's Formative Years.*
[2] *P.W.* i, p. 12, app. crit.

mingled—the same hedge where the sparrows were used to build their nests'.[1] The house was indeed tenantless.

Three years later Wordsworth wrote some lines which seem to be a remembrance of that visit. Characteristically, it is the River Derwent that he chiefly celebrates:

> Yet once again do I behold the forms
> Of these huge mountains, and yet once again,
> Standing beneath these elms, I hear thy voice,
> Belovèd Derwent, that peculiar voice
> Heard in the stillness of the evening air,
> Half-heard and half-created.

The resemblance of these lines to the opening of *Tintern Abbey* is remarkable.[2]

At Whitehaven they stayed with Mrs. John Wordsworth, the wife of their cousin, Captain John Wordsworth of the East India Company. She, said Dorothy, was 'a sweet woman' and Dorothy had her time at her own disposal. While they were there, their uncle and sometime guardian, Richard Wordsworth, the Collector of Customs, died. His death led within a few months to financial anxieties for his nephew William; for this uncle had administered that part of John Wordsworth's estate which had supported William, and it had not been sufficient to cover William's expenses at Cambridge. Richard Wordsworth's heirs, represented chiefly by his youngest son Robinson, soon put forward a claim of £460 which they said had been paid on William's behalf while at college. This was to be a source of worry to William and Dorothy for several years to come, after it was first put forward in 1797.[3]

Was it during this stay at Whitehaven that William had his strange dream of the Arab rider in the desert carrying the Shell and the Book of 'Euclid's Elements'—symbols of Poetry and Science, 'the knowledge that endures'—away from the destruc-

---

[1] *E.L.* 225, p. 516. D.W. to Lady Beaumont, Aug. 7th 1805.

[2] *P.W.* v, p. 340. The word 'half-created' he owed to Young's *Night Thoughts*, VI, l. 424: 'And half-create the wondrous world they see', and he used it again, with an acknowledgement to Young in a footnote, in the *Tintern Abbey* lines in 1798. It harmonized well with his own experience of the interaction of Nature and the creative faculty of the mind.

[3] It was finally paid by Richard Wordsworth in Dec. 1812. *M.Y.* ii. 539, p. 698. W.W. to C.W., Jan. 12th 1816. See below, pp. 337–8.

tion which seemed to be advancing towards them in the form of a great tidal wave?[1] It is of course impossible to fix its date with absolute certainty, but several features point to its taking place in this summer of 1794. In the first place the great under-current of anxiety and fear which runs through the whole dream places it unmistakably after his return from France; it is clearly a 'Revolution dream'. Then it took place in summer, beside the sea; it must therefore have been either in the Isle of Wight, the previous July, or now, beside the Whitehaven cliffs, or at Rampside in Furness where he stayed in August, unless we are to put it as late as 1798, in Somerset. But this is unlikely, as he says he was sitting 'in a rocky cave', and the coast near Alfoxden is open and flat. Wordsworth was not again beside the sea in summer in any other year. It is, however, one of the images in the dream itself which seems to incline the balance towards Whitehaven, and that is the shell, which Wordsworth put to his ear and so heard

> A loud prophetic blast of harmony;
> An Ode in passion uttered, which foretold
> Destruction to the children of the earth
> By deluge now at hand.

In a note to a poem written late in life[2] Wordsworth described how in childhood one of their games at Whitehaven was to hold sea-shells to their ears, so as to 'know from the sound whether the tide was ebbing or flowing'. The association of shells and their voices with this part of the coast—an association belonging to early childhood, his most vividly receptive period—was in all probability strong enough to have produced this strange image in his dream-mind.

Towards the end of June Dorothy went to stay with their cousins the Barkers at Rampside, on the Furness coast a few miles from where the town of Barrow now stands. Wordsworth, after escorting Dorothy from Whitehaven as far as Broughton-in-Furness, returned to Keswick,[3] and probably to Windy Brow. Here he stayed with Raisley Calvert, who was already ill with the consumption of which he died in the following January. Raisley

---

[1] *Prel.* V, ll. 56–165.

[2] *P.W.* iv, pp. 397–8, *Evening Voluntaries*, X, *Composed by the sea-shore.*

[3] *E.L.* 43, p. 125. W.W. to William Calvert, Oct. 1st 1794. This is apparently the best way of interpreting the rather obscure and vague notes of time in the letter.

had been at Magdalene College, Cambridge, for a short time in 1793, but had left it after a few weeks, telling his brother that college was a waste of time and that he would learn more by continental travel.[1] He had an independent income of about £100 a year and, as has been seen, the expectation of considerably more wealth when he reached the age of twenty-one. He had evidently formed an intimate friendship with Wordsworth either during the previous autumn (before Wordsworth went to Halifax) or while Wordsworth and Dorothy were at Windy Brow. Wordsworth had described his difficulties, his lack of money, his aversion to entering a regular profession, his fundamental sense of dedication to a great task. Raisley, moved by something in Wordsworth's manner and person to an ardent admiration, generously offered to 'share his income' with him. This offer was made before the Wordsworths went to Whitehaven.[2] Presumably therefore Wordsworth was partly supported by Raisley during the next few months. From the end of June until Raisley's death in January 1795, Wordsworth was constantly with him, except for a visit to Rampside in August, lasting about a month. During the latter part of the summer Raisley, aware that he was gravely ill, determined to make a will bequeathing a legacy to Wordsworth sufficient to enable him to live without a profession. As Raisley did not come of age until November, and died in January, he lived only just long enough to have personal control of the trust money left him by his father. Wordsworth later described to Sir George Beaumont Raisley's motives and intentions. 'I had had', says Wordsworth, 'but little connection' with Raisley Calvert, 'and the act was done entirely from a confidence on his part that I had powers and attainments which might be of use to mankind.'[3]

On October 1st Wordsworth wrote from Keswick to William Calvert who was an Ensign in the Duke of Norfolk's Regiment, stationed at Tynemouth Barracks, telling him that Raisley wished to go to Lisbon for his health, and suggesting that, if Calvert would find the money, he would accompany him and 'stay with him till his health is re-established'. Raisley, he said, had drawn up a will leaving all his property to his brother

---

[1] 'The Last of the Calverts', *Cornhill Magazine*, 1890. Venn, *Alumni Cantabrigienses*.   [2] *E.L.* 42, p. 119. W.W. to W. Mathews, June 1794.
[3] Ibid. 199, p. 450. W.W. to Sir George Beaumont, Feb. 20th 1805.

except for a legacy of £600 'to me, in case that on enquiry into
the state of our affairs in London he should think it adviseable'.[1]
The purpose of this bequest was 'to secure me from want, if not
to render me independent', and 'to enable me to pursue my
literary views or any other views with greater success'. But
there was one difficulty which Raisley with great wisdom insisted on having cleared up before the will was made secure.
The money advanced for William's education by his uncle at
Whitehaven would certainly, he said, be claimed from him by
the widow or her heirs; as it amounted to over four hundred
pounds, Raisley's generous aim would be entirely defeated. 'He
says', wrote William to his brother Richard in London on
October 10th, 'he would not leave his money to be seized immediately by people that he knows nothing of.' William therefore urgently requested Richard, 'as you have my welfare at
heart', to engage to pay the debt to his aunt himself, on the
understanding that William would repay him 'the moment I
am worth more than this six hundred pounds'. This letter[2] was
written in great agitation with many repetitions; William was
desperately anxious that the door to independence thus suddenly
opened should not be shut in his face. It was a lot to ask of
Richard, but it was not in any way an unreasonable request, for
Richard was the only one of the brothers who had independent
means, through his possession of the Sockbridge estate. He was
besides prospering in his profession. William did not ask in
vain. The brother with whom he had so little in common and
who was usually so dilatory and procrastinating, now that there
was a real crisis, did not fail him. He replied at once: 'I will
readily enter into the Bond you require . . . I am happy to
inform you that my Business encreases daily and that although
our affairs have been peculiarly distressing I hope that from the
industry of ourselves at one time we will enjoy more independence than we have yet experienced.'[3] Here Richard hinted
delicately at William's continued idleness! William replied with
gratitude only asking that the bond might be completed at once
so as to give Raisley no further excuse for delay, for 'he is so
much reduced as to make it probable he cannot be on earth

---

[1] By this Wordsworth means the state of his family's affairs with regard to
Lord Lonsdale. No steps were being taken at present to pursue the matter of the
debt.   [2] *L.Y.* iii, pp. 1329–30.   [3] *D.C.P.*

long'.[1] Raisley meantime had increased the legacy from £600 to £900—a substantial increase which was intended to enable William to provide something for the support of Dorothy as well as for himself.

The journey to Lisbon was abandoned, for Raisley's health could not bear the strain of travelling; during the autumn he grew more and more ill. In November Wordsworth wrote to Mathews that he had scarcely time to read, 'as I am so much with my sick friend, and he cannot bear the fatigue of being read to'. As for poetry: 'This is a country for poetry it is true; but the muse is not to be won but by the sacrifice of time, and time I have not to spare.' A month later they had moved to Penrith, for reasons connected probably with Raisley's illness, and there, on January 9th or 10th, Raisley Calvert died. He was buried at Greystoke, his early home, and Wordsworth, his task completed, departed immediately after the funeral for Newcastle, where Dorothy was staying with her cousins the Griffiths. By February he was in London.

The episode of Raisley Calvert's legacy took place at the same time that Wordsworth was renewing his acquaintance with his old Cambridge friend, William Mathews. Mathews, having given up thoughts of ordination (a decision which Wordsworth strongly approved) was now entered at the Middle Temple, but was also full of a scheme for launching a monthly periodical, to which he asked Wordsworth to contribute. In several long letters of the summer and autumn of 1794 Wordsworth discussed this proposal and also set forth, as an essential preliminary, his political views, for he could not, he said, in any writings of his 'ever admit of any sentiment which can have the least tendency to induce my readers to suppose that the doctrines which are now enforced by banishment, imprisonment etc. are other than pregnant with every species of misery'. This was written in May 1794, after Muir, Palmer, and the other Scottish reformers had been transported, and after Hardy, Thelwall, and Horne Tooke had been sent to the Tower to await their trials, which did not take place until the autumn. The Government had now suspended the Habeas Corpus Act, and was fully launched on the policy of repression which drew from

[1] *L.Y.* iii. 43*b*, p. 1331. W.W. to R.W., Oct. 20th 1794.

Wordsworth afterwards one of his bitterest strictures. He felt
even in 1804 too strongly to write at length about it. It was a

> Reality too close and too intense,
> And intermixed with something, in my mind,
> Of scorn and condemnation personal,
> That would profane the sanctity of verse.

The Government were

> Giants in their impiety alone,
> But in their weapons and their warfare base
> As vermin working out of reach.[1]

It was now that Richard thought it advisable to warn his
brother: 'I hope you will be cautious in writing or expressing
your political opinions. By the suspension of Habeas Corpus
the Ministers have great powers.'[2] To this warning Dorothy
replied: 'I think I can answer for William's caution about expressing his political opinions. He is very cautious and seems
well aware of the dangers of a contrary conduct.'[3] Dorothy was
quite right. Not only was William cautious; he was thinking and
feeling differently about reform and revolution than he had
thought and felt a year ago. He was as keen a republican as ever,
but, said he to Mathews: 'I recoil from the bare idea of a revolution.' This, from the man who had exulted with Beaupuy over
the events in France, approved of the execution of Louis, and
who, a year ago, had waved aside the usual objections to immediate abolition of monarchy with the metaphor: 'The Animal
just released from its stall will exhaust the overflow of its
spirits in a round of wanton vagaries; but it will soon return to
itself, and enjoy its freedom in moderate and regular delight.'[4]
Though still an enemy of his country's institutions, he now declared that the only remedy for abuses was education—the slow
and patient appeal to 'reason'. 'I know that the multitude walk
in darkness; I would put into each man's hand a lantern to
guide him.' The would-be reformer must constantly explain
and enforce these general principles of social order which are
applicable to all times and all places. For this, two things were

[1] *Prel.* X (1805), ll. 653–7. These lines were softened somewhat and the word
'vermin' was omitted in the published text.
[2] *D.C.P.* R.W. to W.W., May 23rd 1794.
[3] *E.L.* 41, p. 117. D.W. to R.W., May 28th 1794.
[4] *Grosart*, i, p. 11.

necessary—complete freedom of the press and the avoidance of all inflammatory addresses to the 'passions' of men.

Whence had this change arisen? A year of Robespierre on the other side of the Channel no doubt had had its effect, and if Wordsworth had really been in Paris in the previous October and seen the guillotine at work, his feelings might well 'recoil'. But the faith in reform by means of education and the appeal to reason alone shows that Wordsworth had not simply been 'put off'—he had wrestled with the problem and, still clinging to his original faith in mankind, he was approaching it from a different angle. The assisting influence in this change was almost certainly William Godwin. Nowhere in *The Prelude* does Wordsworth mention the famous treatise, *Political Justice*; though the passage in which he describes his attempt to solve all moral problems by the light of 'the human Reason's naked self', and of

> circumstances flash'd
> Upon an independent intellect[1]

is generally assumed to refer to his absorption in it. When he first read it it is impossible to say, but whereas the *Letter to the Bishop of Llandaff* shows no trace of Godwin's doctrines, the letter to Mathews of June 1794 certainly does. *Political Justice* severely condemned revolutions because they 'suspend the wholesome advancement of science and confound the process of nature and reason'. Reform can only be effective when it advances step by step with 'the illumination of our understanding'; 'the conviction of the understanding is a means fully adequate to the demolishing of political abuse'. Such teaching—offered in the lucid, yet eloquent English which makes Godwin's book so readable even today—might well seem a lighthouse in the raging sea of Wordsworth's perplexity. Hence the prospectus of 'The Philanthropist, a Monthly Miscellany', as he expounded it to Mathews in June, is an excellent example of the appeal to 'reason' in which he had now put his faith. It would not, of course, he reminded Mathews, have any sale among 'the mighty class of selfish alarmists' who supported the war and the Government. The clergy of the Church of England 'will turn from us'. Only the undergraduates at Oxford and Cambridge and the dissenting community generally would 'receive

---

[1] *Prel.* XI, ll. 232–44. Cf. *The Borderers*, ll. 1494–5.

with pleasure a work like ours'.[1] Still, it was worth trying. Politics should first be discussed, but, said Wordsworth, 'I should principally wish our attention to be fixed upon Life and Manners, and to make our publication a vehicle of sound and exalted Morality'. Here he would make his own principal contributions, and would also supply, on the lighter side of the paper, biographies of 'eminent men distinguished for their exertion in the cause of liberty'. His list of these worthies is of some interest: 'Turgot, Milton, Sydney, Machiavel, Bucaria.'[2] There should be reviews of works which recommend 'benevolence and philanthropy'; he could himself contribute criticism of 'Poetry, Painting and Gardening'. On poetry his views were decided; 'original communications' should not be encouraged, they were usually 'trash', but 'from new poetical publications of merit, and such *old* ones as are not generally known, the pages allotted to verse may generally be filled'. He wanted foreign correspondents and extracts from 'the French moniteurs' (newspapers): 'for while we expressed our detestation of the execrable measures pursued in France, we should belie our title if we did not hold up to the approbation of the world such of their regulations and decrees as are dictated by the spirit of Philosophy'—an interesting indication of his present views about the Revolution.

Probably owing to lack of financial backing, 'The Philanthropist' never appeared.[3] By November the scheme had been relinquished. But Wordsworth now thought of journalism as a possible career. He proposed coming to London as soon as he was released from attendance on Raisley, and asked Mathews, who was himself employed as parliamentary reporter on a new periodical which is not named, to find him employment on a newspaper. But he warned him that he could not act as reporter of parliamentary debates. 'I have neither strength of memory,

---

[1] Wordsworth's knowledge of the 'dissenting community' must have come partly from the Rawsons and their friends at Halifax who were Unitarians and liberals; partly from his London acquaintance, the publisher Johnson and his circle.

[2] Beccaria, the Italian reformer of the penal code. Turgot is classed by Tom Paine in *The Rights of Man* (1791) with Montesquieu, Voltaire, and Rousseau as one of those who by their writings had helped to stimulate 'a spirit of political enquiry' in France in the years preceding the Revolution.

[3] A magazine of extreme radical opinion called *The Philanthropist* did appear in Mar. 1795 and ran for six months, when Pitt's 'Gagging Acts' must have killed it. It was scurrilous in style and contained nothing which could have issued from the pen of Wordsworth.

quickness of penmanship, nor rapidity of composition'; he was besides 'subject to nervous headaches, which invariably attack me when exposed to a heated atmosphere, or to loud noises, and that with such an excess of pain as to deprive me of all recollection'. Seven years earlier, Dorothy had mentioned these headaches and the 'pain in his side'; they were to be an even worse annoyance in the creative years ahead, for they became closely associated with the act of writing.

The months spent at Keswick with Raisley Calvert were interrupted for a few weeks in August by a visit to his relatives the Barkers at Rampside, on the coast of Furness. Dorothy had stayed there in June, and William now spent a month there from about August 20th. We know little of the Barkers, but it would appear that he must have liked his cousins, and they him; otherwise he would scarcely have stayed there so long. Elizabeth, Mrs. Barker, was the eldest daughter of Uncle Richard Wordsworth of Whitehaven, and so a first cousin of William and Dorothy. She married in 1790, as his second wife, Francis Barker, a gentleman of small estate who lived in a house close to the sea-shore at Rampside; as he had no children the house was sold after his death in 1797, and in time became an inn. It is now completely rebuilt and is known as the Clarkes Arms Hotel.[1] Rampside was then a small health resort and shortly after Wordsworth's stay there became locally famous as the place where early experiments in vaccination were carried out. At Aldingham, a few miles farther along the coast towards Ulverston, lived the Baldwins, in the fine rectory beside the ancient church. Wordsworth seems to have become acquainted with them, for he said later of one of the daughters who married his friend James Losh: 'I know that Cecilia Baldwin has fine activity and spirit'.[2] Other society there can have been little in that remote country.

The coast there is not striking in its outlines; a mile or two inland lies Furness Abbey—scene of Wordsworth's wild schoolboy rides—and about a mile out from the coast is Peil Island with its magnificent ruined castle, built to keep off pirates from

---

[1] I am indebted for the identification of the house to Mr. J. Dearden, of Taynton, Gloucester.
[2] *E.L.* 75, p. 190. W.W. to James Losh, Mar. 11th 1798.

the Isle of Man, and once the headquarters of Lambert Simnel's army; beyond it is the long, flat ridge of Walney Island. And, all around, 'the lone and level sands stretch far away'—the sands of Morecambe Bay, dry at low tide, and in those days a busy thoroughfare for travellers crossing to and from the Lancaster side of the bay. To the north of the sands lie the hills, far back, a splendid encircling chain, with the long ridges of Whitbarrow and Cartmel running down to the mosses and the sea.

There, 'in a season of calm weather', dwelt William Words-worth in those 'summer weeks' of 1794. The *Elegiac Stanzas suggested by a Picture of Peile Castle*, written at the end of 1805, commemorate his stay.

> How perfect was the calm! It seemed no sleep;
> No mood, which season takes away, or brings:
> I could have fancied that the mighty Deep
> Was even the gentlest of all gentle things.

And the tenth book of *The Prelude* describes how while cross-ing the sands of the Leven estuary, from Holker to Alding-ham, close by the Island chapel of St. Catherine, that he heard by chance of the death of Robespierre. The same memory of the unchanging calm of the landscape pervades both descriptions. He had gone on a long ramble from Rampside, and had spent some time in the churchyard at Cartmel Priory where he found the grave of his 'honoured teacher', William Taylor,

> A plain Stone, inscribed
> With name, date, office, pointed out the spot,
> To which a slip of verses was subjoined,
> (By his desire, as afterwards I learned)
> A fragment of the Elegy of Gray.[1]

Moved by this discovery, Wordsworth returned across the sands at sunset in a particularly tender and receptive frame of mind. He looked back at the mountains through the Haver-thwaite gap and saw them with the sunset clouds

> In one inseparable glory clad,
> Creatures of one ethereal substance met
> In consistory, like a diadem

---

[1] *Prel.* X (1805), ll. 496–500. The early text is more detailed than that of 1850. The stone is still visible and answers exactly to Wordsworth's description.

> Or crown of burning seraphs as they sit
> In the empyrean. Underneath this show
> Lay, as I knew, the nest of pastoral vales
> Among whose happy fields I had grown up
> From childhood.

He thought gratefully of Taylor, saying to himself as he gazed:

> He loved the Poets and if now alive
> Would have loved me as one not destitute
> Of promise nor belying the kind hope
> That he had form'd when I at his command
> Began to spin, at first, my toilsome songs.[1]

Near at hand the sands presented a busy scene of

> Coaches, wains and travellers, horse and foot;

Wordsworth paused to watch them, and inquired of one of the horsemen coming from the eastern side 'If any news were stirring.' The man shouted a reply that rang through Wordsworth's soul: 'Robespierre is dead!'

It was a moment of tremendous emotional relief. For in Wordsworth's mind Robespierre and the Jacobins had spoilt the French Revolution. Their removal, he had fully persuaded himself, would once more enable the true ideals of the Revolution to be carried on. So great was his joy that he burst forth, as soon as his informant had passed on, into a paean of revengeful joy— a sort of Song of Deborah—shouted aloud to the great waste of sand.

> Great was my glee of spirit, great my joy
> In vengeance and eternal justice thus
> Made manifest,[2]

he wrote afterwards, and proceeded to welcome the 'golden times' that would now come 'out of the bosom of the night'.

> Elsewhere will safety now be sought and Earth
> March firmly towards righteousness and peace.

---

[1] Ibid., ll. 511–15.
[2] Ibid., ll. 540–1. The 1850 text is softened to

> Great was my transport, deep my gratitude.

But the earlier text probably preserves more accurately his real feelings.

Thus did he at once start building a new paradise on the ruins of the old.

The incident reveals vividly the intensity of the trouble that was seething in his mind, and also illustrates that description in the eleventh book of *The Prelude*, in which he tells how he strove to cure 'the wounds of mortified presumption' by adhering 'more firmly to old tenets'—that is, by reaffirming his faith in the ultimate triumph of right and liberty. He needed all that faith. For the fall of Robespierre, though it ended the Terror, did not end the aggressive advance of the French armies in Holland and on the Rhine. The French Government was bankrupt; unblushingly they admitted that their armies were living and had been living for months on the wealth of conquered countries. Such proceedings, said Wordsworth, made him

> With anger vexed, with disappointment sore,
> But not dismayed, nor taking to the shame
> Of a false prophet.

He clung to his faith with such intense and desperate strength that it seemed to become

> The very being of the immortal soul.

All this autumn man and his troubles outweighed nature and poetry in his mind. As he sat by the bedside of the dying Raisley, writing to Mathews, he made a curious statement, very significant of the trouble which tormented him. 'I begin', he said, 'to wish much to be in Town. Cataracts and Mountains are good occasional society, but they will not do for constant companions.' His third long sojourn in London—from February to August 1795—was in part an attempt to prove to himself that 'Cataracts and mountains will not do for constant companions.' It did not succeed.

In London he lived, not with his brother Richard, but with Basil Montagu, a young man living in chambers in Lincoln's Inn and studying law.[1] Although he later became a famous barrister and author, Montagu had not yet been called to the Bar; he took pupils, from whom and from most of his other friends,

[1] From a manuscript among the Pinney Papers at Racedown, Dorset, we know that in 1797 Montagu was living at 7 New Square, Lincoln's Inn. The probability is that this was also his address in 1795. I am very much indebted for information about Montagu to Miss Margaret Crum who allowed me to consult her unpublished thesis, 'Basil Montagu, Q.C., Literary Work and Literary Friendships'.

he constantly borrowed money; he was charming, warm-hearted, enthusiastic, and impulsive. He was the same age as Wordsworth and had been his exact contemporary at Cambridge, where he was sixth wrangler in the tripos in 1790; but they met now for the first time by chance, and, sharing a detestation of the war and the Government, were drawn together into an intimate friendship. Montagu was at this time both poor and unhappy. He was the acknowledged natural son of John, fourth Earl of Sandwich, by his mistress, Martha Ray, the singer. She had been shot dead many years before outside Covent Garden Theatre by a former lover, the Rev. James Hackman, rector of Wiveton in Norfolk, whom James Boswell is said to have accompanied to his execution at Tyburn in the mourning coach. Marrying imprudently in 1790, Basil Montagu offended his father and was obliged to support himself by taking pupils. In 1793 his wife died, leaving him with a two-year-old child, also called Basil.

Young Basil was now living rather miserably with his father, who was himself in no condition to make a small child happy; he was heart-broken at the death of his wife, and in his unhappiness had apparently reverted to wild habits and intemperance. It was then that he met Wordsworth. 'I consider', he said in his unprinted autobiography,[1] 'having met William Wordsworth the most fortunate event of my life.' Wordsworth found himself now called upon to act as counsellor and guide to the distraught Montagu, as he had done a few years earlier to William Mathews when he was in perplexity. 'He saw me', says Montagu, 'with great industry, perplexed and misled by passions wild and strong.[2] In the wreck of my happiness he saw the probable ruin of my infant. He unremittingly, and to me imperceptibly, endeavoured to eradicate my faults and encourage my good dispositions.'

The nature of Wordsworth's consolations is a question of some interest. Without taking too seriously Hazlitt's story that Wordsworth told a young law student at the Temple to 'throw away his books of chemistry and read Godwin on Necessity',

---

[1] The manuscript is at Grasmere in the Wordsworth Museum.

[2] Montagu means that although he was working hard at the law, he was also apt to revert to bouts of wild living, as in his Cambridge days. Some pages have been torn out of his Autobiography which probably describe in more detail these excesses.

it is undoubtedly in this year 1794–5 that we can trace in Wordsworth his closest attempts to follow the moral teaching of *Political Justice*. For that celebrated work could be used as a guide
not only to political and social, but to personal conduct. When
in the autumn of this year Wordsworth enlarged and completed
Salisbury Plain, he made his new character, the Sailor, as perfect
an example as he could of Godwin's theory that a man's good
dispositions may, under the pressure of external circumstances,
lead him into crime. Another of Godwin's doctrines he had
already explained to Mathews—the necessity of purely educational methods in furthering the cause of reform. It seems
reasonable to conclude that Godwin was still his guide in the
task he had now set himself with Montagu. For there was much
in *Political Justice* which could be applied to Montagu's state of
mind and which corresponded to Montagu's brief summary of
Wordsworth's methods. 'A tranquil and placid temper', said
Godwin, and 'intellectual tranquillity', would result from the
acceptance of the doctrine of 'necessity', and from recognizing
that 'all things past, present and to come' are 'links in an indissoluble chain'. Such a belief will assist a man 'to surmount the
tumult of passion', and to realize that only our subservience to
habit prevents us from achieving a completely detached attitude
to our own troubles and those of the world.[1]

We now know that in this spring and summer of 1795 Wordsworth was indeed under Godwin's influence in a far more direct
manner than simply by reading *Political Justice*. He was having
frequent personal contact with him. Nowhere in his letters
or other writings does Wordsworth give any indication that
he met Godwin in these early years, although some writers have
assumed that he did so as early as 1793.[2] The entries found in
Godwin's diaries[3] have now put the matter beyond doubt. Godwin, who was living in Somers Town, records no less than nine
meetings with Wordsworth between February and August 1795.
All except two of these were unaccompanied calls on Godwin by
Wordsworth, sometimes for breakfast, and must have been for
the purpose of tête-à-tête conversations. Unfortunately, Godwin
records only the fact of the meetings, not the nature of the

---

[1] *Political Justice*, Book IV, ch. vii.   [2] *Harper*, i, pp. 212, 267.
[3] These diaries form part of the Abinger Collection housed in the Library of
Duke University, N. Carolina, U.S.A.

discussions. But that Wordsworth returned again and again must surely show that he found Godwin's talk stimulating and acceptable, and we can imagine that his reasonings with Montagu gained greatly in interest and effectiveness as a result. Godwin was now at the height of his fame, as the author not only of *Political Justice* but of the philosophical novel *Caleb Williams*. As he himself remarked: 'If temporary fame ever was an object worthy to be cultivated by the human mind, I certainly obtained it in a degree that has seldom been exceeded.'

The first meeting took place at an evening tea-party in a large company consisting almost entirely of Cambridge men who were political liberals, more or less opposed to the Government and the war. Godwin's diary records it as follows: 'February 27, 1795: tea at Frend's, with Holcroft, Losh, Tweddell, Jones, Jonathan Raine, Edwards, Wordsworth, Higgins, French and Dyer.' Frend was the fellow of Jesus College, Cambridge, who, two years before, had been expelled from the University for advocating peace with France. Holcroft was Godwin's intimate friend. He had recently had success as a dramatist,[1] and along with Thomas Hardy and other radicals had been confined in Newgate in the previous autumn on a charge of high treason. He had, however, been released after the acquittal of Hardy. Losh is James Losh of Woodside near Carlisle, who had been in Paris at the same time as Wordsworth in the autumn of 1792. Soon afterwards they became closely acquainted in the west country and they remained lifelong friends. Tweddell of Trinity was a brilliant classic, notorious also for his political radicalism; a few years later he went out to Greece to pursue archaeological and artistic studies and died there. He was a close friend of Losh and he and Wordsworth were probably already acquainted, for they had been contemporaries at Cambridge.[2]

Jones is not Wordsworth's companion of the Swiss tour but a learned wrangler who was one of the tutors of Trinity and therefore may have been known at least by sight to Wordsworth. Edwards of Jesus was a friend of Coleridge and later helped him to launch his periodical, *The Watchman*.[3] Higgins,

[1] In *The Road to Ruin*, performed in 1792. Wordsworth described one of his later plays, *The Man of Ten Thousand*, as 'such stuff'. *E.L.* 54, p. 156. Mar. 21st 1796.
[2] *Remains of John Tweddell*, by R. Tweddell, 1816. *E.L.* 74, p. 190. W.W. to Losh, Mar. 11th 1798.
[3] Four letters from Coleridge to Edwards are included in *U.L.*, vol. i.

who was younger than Wordsworth, afterwards became a student of Celtic and biblical archaeology. He was a keen social reformer and founded an asylum for pauper lunatics near Wakefield.

Another member of this interesting company was George Dyer. This enthusiastic, but not very discriminating literary man of whom Lamb said that he had 'an utter incapacity of comprehending that there can be anything bad in poetry', had, as has been shown, known and loved William Taylor, Wordsworth's schoolmaster at Hawkshead, in their days at Emmanuel College, Cambridge.[1] As it is unlikely that Wordsworth had previously met him—for Dyer had not been living in Cambridge while Wordsworth was there—it may have been here that they discovered the link between them. Although they do not seem ever to have corresponded, Dyer was among those whom Wordsworth called upon in his visits to London in later years, when Dyer was totally blind, and Dyer once, in 1804 with Montagu, visited Grasmere.

It is impossible to say to which of this company Wordsworth owed his introduction to Frend's house. Tweddell or possibly Losh may have brought him, or he may have been invited through Montagu, who probably knew Frend. The character of the company, and Wordsworth's presence there, throws an unexpected light on that passage in the sixth book of *The Prelude*, where he speaks of the 'ingenuous youth' whom he met in London and who shared his horror of the war with France.[2] He is there describing the year 1793, but in *The Prelude* dates are often telescoped. We see him here a member of the liberal 'opposition', and it is a matter of some note that they were all Cambridge men.

Godwin must have attracted Wordsworth's admiration at this meeting, for on the very next day he notes: 'Wordsworth calls', evidently alone. On March 10th he called again, this time for breakfast, and there were further visits on March 25th, 28th, and 31st, on April 9th (another breakfast visit) and 22nd. After that Godwin was out of town for some weeks, but in July he called twice on Wordsworth. On August 15th he noted: 'Wordsworth and Mathews call', showing Wordsworth bringing his old friend William Mathews to meet the philosopher.

---

[1] See above, p. 50.   [2] *Prel.* X, ll. 266–8.

This acquaintance with Godwin was never relinquished by Wordsworth. On most occasions when he was in London throughout the following years, down to Godwin's death in 1836, Wordsworth called on him or was visited by him. In 1816 Godwin, returning from Scotland, spent a night at Rydal Mount. It is pleasing to find that, in the years when most of his old admirers dropped all acquaintance with him, Wordsworth did not do so, although by that time their political opinions had drifted far apart.

The conversations with Godwin, combined with the opportunities presented by Montagu's state of mind, were probably a blessing to Wordsworth in this uncomfortable and rather desolate period of his youth. He needed light in his mental distress: Godwin's lantern, though afterwards it seemed but a dark one, when he had learnt once more to follow his own imagination, was at least something which could be put to a practical test. In his ministrations to Montagu, Wordsworth did good to himself as well as to his friend. He needed to feel himself of use; to counteract the isolation and 'self-involution' (to use one of Coleridge's words) of the recent six months by concerning himself with the interests of someone else. We have seen how Montagu testified to the practical results of Wordsworth's teaching, and to the tactful manner in which it was offered.

Wordsworth, he says, endeavoured 'unremittingly but to me imperceptibly' to eradicate his faults. Here Wordsworth was acting as a good Godwinian. Godwin deprecated 'exhortations' and allowed only 'representation', or suggestion, of ideas to the reason. The 'necessarian' apostle 'would suggest motives to the mind, but he would not call upon it to comply, as if it had a power to comply, or not to comply. His office would consist of two parts, the exhibition of motives to the pursuit of a certain end and the delineation of the easiest and most effectual way of attaining that end.' From such a method 'real effects' might be expected, just as when one billiard ball is hit by another, it changes its position.[1]

Certainly in Montagu there were 'real effects'. He became an ardent disciple and friend of Godwin for a few years, and then turned against him in the general tide of reaction and repudiation which set in among many who had acclaimed him as a prophet.

[1] *Political Justice*, Book IV, ch. viii. Montagu's Autobiography, *D.C.P.*

But Montagu never wavered in his admiration for Wordsworth. He was one of those who thought, in early life at least, that he had a right, as a benevolent and enlightened human being, to live on money borrowed from his friends, and who became indignant if they asked for repayment. Wordsworth, however, who lent him part of Raisley Calvert's legacy in return for an annuity, was never treated in this manner. Him Montagu always endeavoured to pay as regularly as his extremely precarious circumstances would allow; rather than fail in his obligations to him he would disappoint and quarrel with all his other creditors. This is a curious illustration of the impression Wordsworth not infrequently made on his contemporaries. He was never popular, but by those who knew him he was revered, and felt to be a person somewhat apart, endowed with unusual powers and possessing a certain moral grandeur. Basil Montagu undoubtedly felt for him more than common affection and respect,[1] and to the end of their lives these two men remained friends. Wordsworth was aware of Montagu's exasperating habits, and indeed suffered severely from them in a great crisis, for it was through Montagu's blundering that the estrangement from Coleridge became so bitter. But he bore with all his eccentricities, and once described him as 'very kind, very humane, very generous, very ready to serve, with a thousand other good qualities, but in the practical business of life the arrantest Mar-plan that ever lived'.[2]

One person benefited without doubt from this sojourn of Wordsworth's with Basil Montagu, and that was little Basil. Wordsworth hated to see children unhappy, and realized that Montagu was in no fit state to bring up a child. It so happened that by the middle of the summer a plan was formed by which at last William and Dorothy were able to live together, and Basil was to go with them and grow up under Dorothy's care.

This great and beneficent change in the fortunes of the Wordsworths was made possible through the kindness of Montagu's young friends and pupils, John Frederick Pinney and Azariah. Their father was John Pretor Pinney, a rich West India merchant of Bristol, owner of the 'sugar-island' of Nevis. The younger brother, Azariah, had lived during the previous year, 1794, as a private pupil with Montagu and his friend

---

[1] See below, p. 439.   [2] *M.Y.* i. 338. W.W. to F. Wrangham, June 5th 1808.

Francis Wrangham, wrangler and scholar, who in 1793 had
been excluded from a fellowship at Trinity Hall on account of his
liberal opinions and was now, in 1795, curate of Cobham in
Surrey. There, Montagu had for a time lived with him and they
took pupils, all sons, like the Pinneys, of 'West Indians'. Early
in 1795 Montagu had returned to London and taken chambers
in Lincoln's Inn, but he and John Pinney, who was studying law
under Montagu's rather eccentric direction, frequently visited
Wrangham at Cobham, and when Wordsworth arrived he
joined them on these expeditions.[1] Thus was formed the friendship between Wordsworth and Wrangham which was of lifelong duration.

Old Mr. John Pinney had built himself a fine house in Great
George Street,[2] Bristol, and also rebuilt and furnished an old
family property called Pilemarsh Lodge in a fold of the North
Dorset hills. This house he renamed Racedown Lodge, and
described it to his friends as 'a lee-port in a storm'; for the
American war was then threatening his 'sugar' interests. As he
had not been called upon to retire to an economical rural solitude, however, Racedown was not much used by the family, and
his son, John Frederick, now took upon himself to offer it, rent-
free, to Wordsworth and his sister, for as long as they liked,
provided he and his brother might come there for shooting and
coursing from time to time, staying with the Wordsworths and
paying for their board. John Pinney had fallen, like Raisley
Calvert and Montagu, under Wordsworth's spell, and, without
being himself in the least interested in poetry, showed his admiration by opening up for the homeless north-countryman this
haven in the west. For Wordsworth, Racedown was indeed 'a
lee-port in a storm'.

Mr. Pinney approved the plan, though he was not told until
much later of one of its chief attractions, namely, that Wordsworth would pay no rent.[3] He immediately invited Wordsworth
to stay with him in Bristol until Dorothy could come down from
Yorkshire and, with little Basil, join her brother.

---

[1] *P.P.* For Wrangham, see Gunning, *Reminiscences of Cambridge.*
[2] It is now a municipal museum of Georgian furniture.
[3] In the following spring Mr. Pinney found out about the rent and threatened
to make Wordsworth pay, but the two sons pleaded with him and so 'at our earnest
desire he relinquished his intention'. *P.P.* and *R.E.S.*, Jan. 1932, 'Racedown and
the Wordsworths', by Bergen Evans and Hester Pinney.

The alacrity with which Wordsworth accepted the offer of
Racedown shows that he had not found it possible to live permanently in London. A home with Dorothy was still his most
earnest desire, and there had been an idea of her coming to
London and of their earning some kind of livelihood by 'writing
and translating'. This their wise Aunt Rawson thought a 'very
wild bad scheme',[1] far too uncertain, even with Calvert's legacy,
to support them securely. Nothing apparently had come of the
plan of joining the staff of a newspaper. He found probably that
it was impossible to settle to writing of his own choosing in the
confusion and discomfort of poor Montagu's London lodgings.
But Dorothy hoped that, if he could once have a stable home in
the country, he would 'have such opportunities of studying as
I hope will be not only advantageous to his mind but to his
purse'. He had, it appears, received an offer of ten guineas for
'a work which has not taken him up much time'. This is probably
a reference to the *Imitation of Juvenal*—a political satire which
he began writing in collaboration with Francis Wrangham
during this summer.[2] It was continued at Racedown, but never
finished. It was directed against the Government and the royal
family, and such parts of it as survive make one thankful that it
was never among Wordsworth's published works, for it has
little merit. He himself realized afterwards that satire was not
his calling, and when in 1806 Wrangham suggested publishing
their old lines, he wrote that he wished his own verses, which
were in Wrangham's possession, to be destroyed, as he had
quite determined to 'steer clear of personal satire'.[3]

Dorothy had been paying a round of visits to various friends
and relations in the north, including the Hutchinsons who were
now living in County Durham. She was at present with the
Rawsons at Halifax. She did not return to Forncett. This was
both a sorrow and a relief. She knew that her aunt needed her
(Mrs. Cookson was to be confined for the fifth time at Christ-

---

[1] E. de Selincourt, *Dorothy Wordsworth*, pp. 58–59.

[2] She can hardly be referring to *Salisbury Plain*, for this was still unfinished;
Wordsworth added to it in the first weeks at Racedown and told Wrangham in
November that he would publish it 'if I can get anything for it'.

[3] *M.Y.* i. 379, p. 72. W.W. to F. Wrangham, Nov. 7th 1806. Wordsworth's
lines are in his letter to Wrangham of Feb. 1797. *E.L.* 55, p. 156. This letter was
written in Feb. 1797, as its postmark proves and not, as printed, in 1796. See
P.W. i, p. 343.

mas), but even her busy life there did not satisfy her craving
to be 'doing something'. 'It is', said she, 'a painful idea that
one's existence is of very little use which *I* really have always
been obliged to feel.' Dorothy hated to be dependent; she had
felt keenly the absence of a real home, in spite of the kindness
of the Cooksons, who she said had been as kind as 'relations not
positively congenial in pursuits and pleasures . . . and with
separate and distinct views' could be. One need not ask the
nature of Uncle William's 'distinct views' on one subject very
near Dorothy's heart! To be mistress of a home of which William would be the master, and to have the care of children—this
was the answer to all her most fervent prayers. She felt humbly
confident that she could succeed in bringing up Basil. There was
a hope that a little girl—a natural daughter of their cousin Tom
Myers—would also be committed to her, but for some un-
explained reason this never took place.[1]

She was very hopeful about their financial affairs; events
proved that she had been too sanguine. Montagu was to pay £50
a year for Basil; this he did for the first two years and then
financial stringency brought the payments to an end. For nearly
a year, from September 1797 till July 1798, the Wordworths
supported Basil unaided. From Raisley Calvert's legacy Dorothy
expected an income of about £70 or £80. Half the capital, says
she, William intended to invest in a life insurance policy for
her, 'which will always make me comfortable and independent'.
This, however, was not done. The legacy was only gradually paid
over: £525 by the end of 1795; another £250 by the end of
1796; the remainder was not completely paid until August 1798.
Of the first £500 Wordsworth lent £300 to Montagu in the
autumn of 1795, and in January 1796 £200 to a friend of
Montagu called Charles Douglas, of whom nothing is known
except that he had 'very opulent relations'.[2] The £300 lent to
Montagu was secured on an annuity at 10 per cent. Douglas
paid 10 per cent. on his £200. Thus for the first three years after
Raisley's death, Wordsworth received only about £50 a year
from the legacy. He was obliged to borrow from Richard for
such things as the purchase of linen for Racedown. 'You should

---

[1] *E.L.* 48, p. 138. D.W. to Jane Marshall, Sept. 2nd 1795.
[2] *L.Y.* iii. 57a and 77a, pp. 1336–9. W.W. to R.W., May 7th 1797, and May
5th 1798.

have been repaid immediately if I had not been disappointed of
my settlements with Calvert', he wrote to Richard in May 1797,
'which has reduced my income much lower than I had reason to
expect'. When at last William Calvert paid over the full amount
of the legacy, Richard invested it in consols at 3 per cent.[1] Nothing more is heard of a separate investment on Dorothy's behalf,
or of a life insurance for her. One cannot help feeling that
William would have done better to have stuck to his first intention, and made a settlement on her, instead of handing over his
slender capital, even at high interest, to impecunious friends.
Montagu's affairs indeed became so precarious in 1798 that he
was threatened with jail for debt, and for about two years he
paid very little, if anything at all, to Wordsworth.

It is necessary to enter at some length into the financial
situation of William and Dorothy at this time, as it has sometimes been assumed that after the death of Raisley Calvert all
went smoothly with them. On the contrary, throughout the
Racedown and Alfoxden period they were obliged to practise
the strictest economy and to live as far as possible on the produce
of garden and orchard. It was besides a time of rising prices for
such things as tea and sugar—'our only luxuries', as William
said. When they went to Germany in the autumn of 1798 they
were obliged to borrow from Coleridge's patron, Josiah Wedgwood. The shadow of financial anxiety was constantly with them,
and if they had not both been ready to live in the simplest
possible manner they must have come to disaster.

Wordsworth left London about the middle of August[2] for
Bristol, where he stayed with the Pinneys. This visit to Bristol
is another link in the chain of 'necessary' incidents which assisted
his destiny at this time, for it was now that he first met Samuel
Taylor Coleridge. Whether it was, as Wordsworth thought in
old age, 'in some lodgings'—presumably Coleridge's lodgings
in College Street—or, as we read in the Farington Diaries, at
a political society at which Wordsworth spoke so eloquently
that Coleridge inquired who he was,[3] it is impossible to ascertain.
Wordsworth was not in the habit of speaking in public, though

[1] *D.C.P.*

[2] *L.Y.* iii, appendix, p. 1333. 'I stayed at Bristol at least five weeks.' W.W. to
W. Mathews, Oct. 24th 1795. He arrived at Racedown on Sept. 26th.

[3] *Farington Diary*, vol. vi, p. 36.

Coleridge at this time was both lecturing and speaking on political matters. It may be that the diarist confused the names, and that Wordsworth inquired who Coleridge was. Coleridge was in the midst of his estrangement from Southey over the idealistic scheme of 'Pantisocracy';[1] he was also on the eve of his marriage to Sara Fricker, Southey's sister-in-law, and was fast forming an enduring friendship with Thomas Poole, the tanner and farmer of Nether Stowey, who was to stand by him through so many storms. 'Coleridge', said Wordsworth, writing from Racedown on October 24th, 'was at Bristol part of the time I was there, I saw but little of him. I wished indeed to have seen more—his talent appears to me very great.'[2] He met Southey also and was impressed with his 'power of mind'; indeed, he thought more favourably of him now than he did a few months later, after reading the preface to his *Joan of Arc*, which he thought 'a very conceited performance' proving its author 'certainly a coxcomb'.[3]

Now also he probably met someone who was to play an indispensable part in the lives of both poets in the next three years —Joseph Cottle, the bookseller and publisher, the friend of both Southey and Coleridge. Cottle was doing a valuable service to Coleridge in offering to publish anything he might write, and thus helping to turn him from the absurdities of pantisocracy to the exercise of his real powers. In the following March he sent Wordsworth a copy of Southey's *Joan of Arc* and from then onwards became Wordsworth's adviser on all questions of publishing.

[1] 'Pantisocracy' was the name given by Coleridge, Southey, and their friends to their scheme for emigrating to the Susquehanna and starting a community based on the common ownership of land. Coleridge had come to Bristol in order to raise funds to buy a ship. Owing to Southey's defection in the summer of 1795 and also to lack of funds, nothing came of it.

[2] *L.Y.* iii. 48*b*, p. 1333. W.W. to W. Mathews, Oct. 24th 1795. Coleridge was with Thomas Poole at Stowey in the middle of September. The *Lines written at Shurton Bars*, which are dated September and which contain the quotation 'green radiance' from *An Evening Walk*, may have been written on the way to Stowey on Sept. 9th or 10th. In a note to the poem Coleridge says it was written 'before I had even seen Mr. Wordsworth, atque utinam opera ejus tantum noveram'. If this is so, their first meeting must have taken place just before Wordsworth left Bristol on Sept. 25th and after Coleridge returned to it.

[3] *E.L.* 54, p. 155. W.W. to William Mathews, Mar. 21st 1796. No doubt he disliked Southey's criticisms of his favourite writers, Virgil, Tasso, and Ariosto.

During this five weeks' stay in Bristol Wordsworth was visited once more by the creative spirit of poetry. For it seems impossible to assign to any other period the fifty-four opening lines of *The Prelude*, whose date and origin have been such a puzzle to Wordsworthian scholars.[1] There is no manuscript of them or of the following lines that is earlier than 1804, and it is now believed that the whole of this long passage at the beginning of the first book was not written down before 1803, although much of it must have been mentally composed long before. But Wordsworth's declaration that he uttered the opening lines

> Even in the very words that I have here
> Recorded,[2]

on 'that day'—the day on which he felt the sense of release and freedom—cannot be entirely disregarded. The 'day' must have been one shortly after his departure from London, for the lines celebrate his release from the 'bondage' of life in 'the vast city', which can only be London, and his return to country life, at least for a time:

> If not a settler on the soil, at least
> To drink wild water and to pluck green herbs.

These words may perhaps indicate the temporary nature of his tenure of Racedown. The passage goes on to celebrate his hopes of being able at last to compose 'a work of glory'. At no other time in his life did Wordsworth quit a city after a long period of poetic inactivity, or as he calls it, after 'a long-continued frost'. Hence the attempts to date the experience much later, in 1799, and to make the little town of Goslar in Germany do duty for the 'vast city', fall to the ground.[3] It may be objected that the lines in which he asks

---

[1] *Prel.* pp. xxi–xxxii. H. Darbishire, *Wordsworth*, 1950. H. W. Garrod, *Wordsworth*, 1927.

[2] Or, according to the later text,

> in measured strains
> That would not be forgotten, and are here
> Recorded.

Fragmentary jottings of some of the lines are in MS. JJ, written in Germany in 1798 or 1799. *Prel.*, p. 608E.

[3] His earliest biographer—his nephew Christopher Wordsworth—was responsible for this misleading statement. *Mem.* i, p. 143. It was repeated by Knight and first questioned by Hutchinson.

> What dwelling shall receive me? In what Vale
> Shall be my harbour? Underneath what grove
> Shall I take up my home?

are unsuitable to the autumn of 1795, because he then already knew that he was going to live at Racedown. But this is surely to be too particular. What he celebrated was a general sense of freedom from restraint, and of a return to congenial conditions of liberty and 'long months of ease and undisturbed delight' in Dorothy's company, in a house of his own, after the confinement and discomfort of Montagu's dismal chambers. It must be remembered too that financial as well as physical freedom was now beginning to be a reality. He had already received in August the first instalment—only £5—of Raisley Calvert's legacy, with the promise of a more substantial one in the near future. £250 was paid on September 25th, and a further £50 a month later. This must all have contributed to his new feeling of release.

We may conclude then that, one day while he was at Bristol, in August or September 1795, Wordsworth walked out into the open fields near the town and chanted aloud something akin to the opening lines of _The Prelude_. But there is more in them than an outburst in praise of liberty and hope. They contain also a description of the spirit of poetry—genius itself—at work within him. He had once or twice attempted something of the kind before, but never with such wealth of imagery and detail. Wordsworth often spoke of the experience of the creative spirit as a 'breeze'. In a passage not included in the text of _The Prelude_ he says that he frequently felt it in childhood. Addressing 'the Eternal Spirit' he says:

> O bounteous power
> In Childhood, in rememberable days
> How often did thy love renew for me
> Those naked feelings, which, when thou wouldst form
> A living thing, thou sendest like a breeze
> Into its infant being![1]

Now, in the experience recorded in _The Prelude_, the actual breeze blowing on his body seemed to have a real relationship to the 'creative breeze' within; it aroused and awakened it. Thus he speaks of the two 'breezes':

---

[1] _Prel._, p. 508. See also _P.W._ V, p. 128, _The Excursion_, IV, 600.

> Oh! there is blessing in this gentle breeze
> That blows from the green fields and from the clouds
> And from the sky: it beats against my cheek
> And seems half-conscious of the joy it gives.
> O welcome Messenger! O welcome Friend![1]

Of the breeze in his mind he says:

> For I, methought, while the sweet breath of heaven
> Was blowing on my body, felt within
> A corresponding, mild creative breeze,
> A vital breeze which travelled gently on
> O'er things which it had made and is become
> A tempest, a redundant energy,
> Vexing its own creation.[2]

Here is Wordsworth's most characteristic conviction of the living and spiritual character of natural phenomena. 'The experience', says a great critic, 'is not simply of the poet's own awareness of receiving pleasure; it is also of the breeze's awareness of giving pleasure.'[3]

The breath of the creative Spirit was full of hope for the future.

> 'Tis a power
> That does not come unrecogniz'd, a storm,
> Which, breaking up a long-continued frost
> Brings with it vernal promises, the hope
> Of active days, of dignity and thought,
> Of prowess in an honourable field,
> Pure passions, virtue, knowledge and delight,
> The holy life of music and of verse.[4]

Again he felt, as he had felt on former occasions, that he was 'singled out', 'consecrated', 'cloth'd in priestly robe'. As he poured out his hymn, in audible words, to the open fields around

----

[1] *Prel.* I (1805), ll. 1–5. The language of the earlier text is more vivid than that of 1850.

[2] Ibid., ll. 41–47. In the earliest manuscript are the variants:
> With lights and shades, and with onrushing power,
> With loveliness and power.   *Prel.*, p. 608E.

[3] Lascelles Abercrombie, *The Art of Wordsworth*, 1952.

[4] *Prel.* I (1805), ll. 47- 54.

him, he was conscious of an 'echo' in his mind, a sort of assurance of powers yet unused:

> To both I listened, drawing from them both
> A cheerful confidence in things to come.

The story of Wordsworth at Racedown during the next two years is the story of the manner in which that confidence was justified. But after the description of the breeze there follows in *The Prelude* a passage of some sixty lines which presents even more difficult problems. In these he tells how, when the initial outpouring had ceased, he went and lay down for a long time in a 'green, shady place', an oak-grove, and there thought about his situation, and of what lay before him. The passage is worthy of fresh consideration.

> 'Twas Autumn, and a clear and placid day,
> With warmth as much as needed from a sun
> Two hours declined towards the west; a day
> With silver clouds, and sunshine on the grass,
> And in the sheltered and the sheltering grove
> A perfect stillness. Many were the thoughts
> Encouraged and dismissed, till choice was made
> Of a known Vale, whither my feet would turn
> Nor rest till they had reached the very door
> Of the one cottage, which methought I saw.
> No picture of mere memory ever looked
> So fair; and while upon the fancied scene
> I gazed with growing love, a higher Power
> Than Fancy gave assurance of some work
> Of glory there forthwith to be begun,
> Perhaps too there performed. Thus long I mused
> Nor e'er lost sight of what I mused upon
> Save when amid the stately grove of oaks
> Now here, now there, an acorn, from its cup
> Dislodged, through sere leaves rustled, or at once
> To the bare earth dropped with a startling sound.
> From that soft couch I rose not, till the sun
> Had almost touched the horizon; casting then
> A backward glance upon the curling cloud
> Of city smoke, by distance ruralised;
> Keen as a Truant or a Fugitive,
> But as a Pilgrim resolute, I took,
> Even with the chance equipment of that hour,

> The road that pointed toward the chosen Vale . . .
> A pleasant loitering journey through three days
> Continued, brought me to my hermitage.[1]

It has been generally held that while lying in an oak-grove somewhere on the outskirts of Bristol Wordsworth thought fancifully of Racedown, and that, on the impulse of the moment, he forthwith paid it a solitary visit of inspection, alone and on foot.[2] Apart from the unlikelihood that he would have thus left his hosts the Pinneys for a week or more without any warning or explanation, there are other difficulties in this interpretation. First, there is the question of date. On September 16th we know he was in Bristol, for on that day he wrote a letter to his brother Richard, telling him that he was expecting Dorothy and little Basil Montagu 'in a week at farthest'.[3] He says nothing in the letter about having already visited Racedown. Then there is the evidence of Joseph Gill's Diary.[4] Gill was a broken-down relation of the Pinneys who lived at Racedown and was employed as caretaker and overseer of the house and grounds. He kept a diary to which he confided his manifold disagreements and arguments with the gardener, the neighbouring farmer, and most of his other neighbours. He also recorded carefully all arrivals at and departures from Racedown. Thus, when Wordsworth and Dorothy finally arrived on September 26th he noted: '26. At midnight arrived Mr and Miss Wordsworth.' There is no mention of an earlier arrival of Wordsworth alone.

The day-dream under the oak-tree is likewise difficult to explain if it is taken to refer to Racedown. The vision of a cottage in a 'chosen Vale' scarcely answers to the description the Pinneys must have given him of Racedown—a substantial house of two stories and an attic floor on the side of a hill, four hundred feet above the level of the sea.[5] In a rejected variant of this passage Wordsworth says that he saw in his dream 'its porch, its casements and its curling smoke'. Racedown then had no porch; and its windows were sashes, not casements. It may also be noted

---

[1] *Prel.* I, ll. 65–93, 106–7.

[2] Garrod, *Wordsworth*, p. 190.

[3] *L.Y.* iii. 48*a*, p. 1332.

[4] The diary is preserved at Racedown among the Pinney Papers.

[5] The correct name of the house at that time was Racedown Lodge, and this i·
the address the Wordsworths put on their letters.

that Wordsworth had not 'chosen' Racedown; it had been offered to him and he had accepted it. No: what Wordsworth is describing here is his favourite and oft-repeated dream—a cottage in a Lake District valley, and ever since he had first looked down into it as 'a roving school-boy', Grasmere had been his 'chosen Vale'. Quite possibly he may indeed have thought thus of his and Dorothy's cherished haven even when about to take up residence at Racedown, but, even if this is so, now that the walk to Racedown on a preliminary visit of inspection must be regarded as improbable, what are we to make of his statement that

> Keen as a Truant or a Fugitive,
> But as a Pilgrim resolute, I took,
> Even with the chance equipment of that hour,
> The road that pointed towards the chosen Vale?

Is it simply 'invention'? *The Prelude* is not an autobiography, and we know that it does contain incidents which did not occur exactly as described. Such is the description of the sight of armed men at the Grande Chartreuse in Book VI, and the visit to Bartholomew Fair in Book VII. Yet in both these cases Wordsworth is not 'inventing'. He is simply telescoping events which occurred at different times. It is perhaps possible that he is doing something of the same kind here. There was an occasion when he did set off towards 'the chosen Vale' in such a spirit, and that was when, in December 1799, he left the Hutchinsons' house in Durham to go, with Dorothy, to settle at Grasmere. It was winter and severe weather, but they walked from Wensleydale to Kendal, sleeping two nights on the road, and turning aside several times to look at waterfalls. He described the walk in a letter to Coleridge and in the fragment of *The Recluse* which is known as *Home at Grasmere*.[1] It was in fact

> A pleasant loitering journey through three days
> Continued,

like this walk in *The Prelude* although it took place in winter, not in autumn. Nor is it impossible that he should have woven a reference to Grasmere into his picture of an earlier time. For his opening of *The Prelude* was not written in any coherent form until 1803 when Wordsworth and Dorothy had been

---

[1] *P.W.* v, appendix A, p. 319. See below, pp. 453–7.

settled at Grasmere for more than three years. Its purpose was to describe to Coleridge how he came to be so long in settling down to write the 'work of glory' which he wanted to write and which Coleridge was always urging him to start. His attempts had been interrupted or, as he said, 'frustrated'. The lines which follow the description of the rest in the oak-grove and the walk to 'my hermitage' describe this frustration, and apply much better to the first two years at Grasmere than to Racedown. The description of the happiness of his daily life is certainly much more true of the former than of the latter.

> I spare to speak my Friend of what ensued—
> The admiration and the love, the life
> In common things; the endless store of things
> Rare, or at least so seeming, every day
> Found all about me in one neighbourhood,
> The self-congratulation, and from morn
> To night unbroken cheerfulness serene.

Certainly during his two years at Racedown, Wordsworth did attain to this 'cheerfulness', but it was not an immediate or sudden growth. By the time he reached Grasmere it had become a more habitual state of mind.

IX

RACEDOWN

September 1795 – June 1797

Many a green isle needs must be
In the deep, wide sea of Misery,
Or the mariner, worn and wan,
Never thus could voyage on . . .
SHELLEY

WHEN Wordsworth came to Racedown he was half-way through his twenty-sixth year. At his age Milton had already written the *Ode on the Morning of Christ's Nativity*, and was in the full flow of his genius. Wordsworth's poetic spring-time was slow in coming, harsh and raw like a north-country March. The 'visitations' he had had in youth in his communion with Nature had taught him to regard himself as a being set apart for some high purpose, some 'priest-like task'. Since Cambridge days or earlier he had been sure that this task must lie in the field of poetry, and he had started on a well-worn classical path—that of the landscape-poem. Then came the great crisis; the human tragedy breaking into the bright vision of his youth; the sharp suffering, and the desperate search for a philosophy that would make life possible again. A slow and painful adjustment had to be made; his poetry, when he could write at all, became peopled with the sad figures of suffering men and women; and for two years before coming to Racedown he wrote scarcely anything. But he could not lose sight of his poetic vocation: Raisley's faith in him, so boldly put into a solid deed of friendship by the legacy, strengthened his sense of responsibility. Yet it was long still before his genius was fully released. Even the visitation of the 'gentle breeze', while it reawakened all his enthusiasm and sent a torrent of energy and hope through his being, did not produce any startling poetic results. The first two months at Racedown were spent in revising and adding to *Salisbury Plain*. Then, after months of silence, he began his tragedy, *The Borderers*, his only dramatic venture, which, in

spite of Coleridge's opinion that it was 'absolutely wonderful',
was rejected for production in London and has, as far as is
known, never been produced on a stage. Moreover, both
The Borderers and *Salisbury Plain* continue to dwell on the
themes of human suffering and human sin which had been
troubling his spirit for the last three years; they are no new
prophetic song. His mind was still absorbed with 'moral questions', the conversations with Godwin in the spring fermented
in his mind, driving him to the creation of abnormal criminal
types—the Sailor in *Salisbury Plain*, Oswald in *The Borderers*.
But when, in the spring of 1797, he began to write in a different,
gentler strain, and made the serene old Pedlar the narrator in
The Ruined Cottage, we can see the 'breeze' beginning to do its
work. He was at length coming to terms with the human problem in his own original and poetic way. The story of Wordsworth at Racedown is the story of his reconciliation with Man—
partly through a 'return to Nature', and partly through two
precious human agencies. Dorothy cheered and fostered his
spirit and 'preserved him still a poet' by her own faith in him
and in the things they both loved: Coleridge loudly declared
his belief in his poetic genius. Before he left Racedown he had
begun to utter his own authentic good tidings.

It was here at Racedown that William and Dorothy Wordsworth were for the first time able to realize their dream of
living together, although four more years were to pass before
they came into possession of a home they could call their own.
The few weeks at Windy Brow in 1794 had been a most valuable
rehearsal, but now the play began in earnest. The two years
at Racedown are decisive in the history of Wordsworth's
recovery and in the development of his genius, and his own
ascription of praise for that recovery to Dorothy and 'Nature's
self' in *The Prelude* may be accepted at his own valuation. In
order to realize the difficulty of the task Dorothy set herself,
we have to remember the disturbed and unhappy condition of
his 'moral being' when they first arrived at Racedown: remorse
for Annette still a torment; faith in human nature only pre-
cariously balanced on theories which were really alien to his
nature; doubt about his own calling as a poet perhaps the most
acute torture of all. For two years before he came to Racedown
he had written scarcely any poetry. Yet he was living on

Raisley Calvert's legacy, that gallant wager with the future. Dorothy believed that her brother was a poet, and set about re-creating that belief in him. It is this part of her ministry which he chose to celebrate in speaking of this time when he was writing the eleventh book of *The Prelude* in 1804.

> Then it was
> That the beloved woman in whose sight
> Those days were pass'd, now speaking in a voice
> Of sudden admonition, like a brook
> That did but *cross* a lonely road, and now
> Seen, heard and felt, and caught at every turn,
> Companion never lost through many a league,
> Maintained for me a saving intercourse
> With my true self; for, though impair'd and chang'd
> Much, as it seemed, I was no further chang'd
> Than as a clouded, not a waning moon:
> She, in the midst of all, preserv'd me still
> A Poet, made me seek beneath that name
> My office upon earth, and nowhere else.[1]

The unobtrusive, yet decisive, character of Dorothy's companionship is here clearly seen; she could be sharp, 'sudden' in her encouragements; at other times she contented herself in being at hand if needed. Her own unsullied love of Nature was the key to her power over him; that, and her devotion to him. To bring him back again to his 'first love' was both her prayer and her task; she felt that the life he had been leading in London was not his true life; if once his communion with Nature could be restored, he would once more follow his true vocation. And this was what happened at Racedown.

> And lastly, Nature's self, by human love
> Assisted, through the weary labyrinth
> Conducted me again to open day,
> Revived the feelings of my earlier life,
> Gave me that strength and knowledge full of peace,
> Enlarged, and never more to be disturbed.

Wordsworth once wrote of Dorothy as one

> Whom I have loved
> With such communion, that no place on earth
> Can ever be a solitude to me,[2]

[1] *Prel.* X (1805), ll. 908–21 (XI, ll. 333–8).
[2] *P.W.* ii, p. 115, *Poems on the Naming of Places*, III.

and as

> The dear companion of my lonely walk,
> My hope, my joy, my sister, and my friend,
> Or something dearer still, if reason knows
> A dearer thought, or in the heart of love
> There be a dearer name.[1]

There is no need to quarrel with such expressions and try to read into them morbid implications. Theirs was a love that found its daily food in a thousand tiny incidents, the 'small miracles' of Nature, such as the glow-worm's light, and it was firmly based on the strongest ground of all, a common inheritance from earliest childhood of memories and associations that were entirely happy.

Racedown is a square-built house[2] lying beside the road from Crewkerne to Lyme, just where it begins to descend into a hollow before rising again to the hamlet of Birdsmoorgate. It stands high, with a long view westward; to the south beyond the hollow is a ridge of hill with woods and clumps of trees, while a high, bare down called Pilsdon Pen runs out eastward, ending in a great flat space enclosed by primitive earthworks. This hill, which is over nine hundred feet high, covered as it still is with furze and heath, must be very much as it was when William and Dorothy Wordsworth roamed over it. Dorothy was thinking of the ascent of this hill when she wrote two months after their arrival that from a point a hundred and fifty yards from the door they could see the sea, and it was perhaps from its summit that William 'saw the West India Fleet sailing in all its glory before the storm had made such dreadful ravages'. She was indeed delighted with their new country-side. Some of the hills reminded her of 'our native wilds'; the apple-orchards, often unenclosed, formed a pleasant feature of their walks: 'in some of our walks we go through orchards without any other enclosure than as a common field'. In a field close by the house was a small brick-kiln where bricks were made and sold locally. On the west and south of the house lay a 'pleasure-garden',

---

[1] *P.W.* v, p. 347, Fragment, composed about 1800.

[2] It was enlarged by additions early in this century, but the original house was left outwardly unchanged, and the bedroom and attic floors still remain exactly as they were.

kitchen garden, and orchard: in the garden were some statues, called by Joseph Gill 'images'; they must have been a curious sight, for they were painted and gilded.

It was in the garden at Racedown that Wordsworth had one day a visionary experience. The event is of interest because it was brought about by the one of his five senses which was least strong in him, least commonly the means of evoking vivid mental images—the sense of smell. There was there, he long afterwards related, a bed of stocks in full bloom. Quite suddenly one day he became aware of their scent. 'It was', he said, 'like a vision of Paradise.' But after a few moments the vision faded, and the sense that had awakened it sank into its usual torpor; he found himself standing outside Paradise. To many people the sense of smell is the most strongly evocative of all the senses; but it was not so with Wordsworth. On the one occasion when he knew its power he at once turned for a comparison to that sense which brought him most of his 'openings', the sense of sight—'it was like a vision'.

The garden was a source of constant anxiety to poor Joseph Gill, for the horses and cattle which grazed in the surrounding fields were always breaking into it. Several entries in Gill's diary show his rather helpless annoyance and concern. On September 30th 1795 he noted:

The Gardner has been all this day going round the kitchen Garden fences, and the fences towards the road, stopping the broken places to prevent Mr. Perkins cattle from continuing to break through, aforetime he would not do it at my ordering him . . . it was then too much trouble to him, nor would he fence in the young trees tho' many times repeatedly ordered to do it, nor weed the young fences, it is now too late to remedy the most of them.

On November 13th:

Old Jnᵒ Hitchcock's Stock still keep trespassing, two of his yearlings drove out of the pleasure garden this morning.

And on September 11th 1796:

Hawkins the carpenter being at work at Harlescombe I made him promise to come up and have some talk with Mr. Wordsworth and try if we cannot get what done that is necessary.

When at length 'S. Palmer the husbandman' was prevailed upon to mend the fences all round the house, his labour was to a

large extent wasted, for 'the fences are stolen and the horses
get out'. The fences were probably stolen by the poor of the
neighbourhood, whose poverty and consequent bad habits
distressed both William and Dorothy. Dorothy, with her memories of the well-cared-for poor at Forncett, for whom she had
opened her little school, now saw English poverty at its worst.
There was no village within two or three miles, and these poor
creatures lived about in scattered huts, 'shapeless structures (I
may almost say)', says Dorothy, 'of wood and clay, indeed they
are not at all beyond what might be expected in savage life'.
And William, looking on them with the eye of a Godwinian
student of social phenomena, remarked to Mathews: 'The
country people here are wretchedly poor; ignorant and overwhelmed with every vice that usually attends ignorance in that
class, viz. lying and picking and stealing etc.'[1] Wordsworth's
ballad of *Goody Blake and Harry Gill*, though written at Alfoxden and based on a story in Erasmus Darwin's *Zoönomia* which
he borrowed from Cottle,[2] is really a picture of the Dorsetshire
peasantry:

> Auld Goody Blake was old and poor,
> Ill fed she was and thinly clad;
> And any man who pass'd her door,
> Might see how poor a hut she had.
>
> .   .   .   .
>
> This woman dwelt in Dorsetshire,
> Her hut was on a cold hill-side,
> And in that country coals are dear,
> For they come far by wind and tide.[3]

Dorothy herself wrote 'You would be surprized to see what a
small cart full (of coals) we get for three or four and twenty
shillings'; this had to be fetched in the neighbouring farmer's
cart from Lyme, whither it had come by sea, and once or twice
the Wordsworths were obliged to borrow coal from their
nearest neighbours, the Pinneys of Blackdown,[4] friendly people
with whom they occasionally exchanged visits.

<hr/>

[1] *E.L.* 50, p. 149. *L.Y.* iii, p. 1334. W.W. to William Mathews, Oct. 24th
1795. The association of vice with ignorance is typically Godwinian morality.

[2] *E.L.* 62, p. 169. W.W. to Joseph Cottle, n.d., but probably spring 1798.

[3] It may be noted that 'Blake' is a local name in that district, while Wordsworth
probably borrowed the name 'Gill' from the author of the diary.

[4] *P.P.* Gill's Diary. May 1796 and Oct. 31st 1796.

The appearance of the interior of the house is known to us from the inventory of the furniture which old Mr. Pinney had had made. This inventory Wordsworth checked three days after his arrival, and signed it, remarking to Joseph Gill that he 'was now responsible for the whole'. All the extra silver, glass, and linen were kept by Gill in a locked room on the attic floor, to be doled out to Dorothy when there were visitors; he always carefully noted what was taken. The 'breakfast or common parlour' on the left of the front door was their favourite room; it contained a pianoforte, a mahogany sofa and armchairs, a Bath stove, a 'painted floor cloth', a picture of 'little St. Mark's Place in Venice' over the chimney, and—most important for the Wordsworths—two mahogany glass-door book-cases, filled with books, standing in the recesses on either side of the chimney. A complete catalogue of these books is among the treasures of Racedown. Among them Wordsworth noted particularly 'Machiavel, Boccaccio, Davila and several other italian Books'.[1] There was also a good deal of English poetry, though none later than Prior; the scientific works of Ray and Derham, and some theology of the dissenting and 'Broad Church' divines— for the Pinneys were of Puritan descent. And there was a Euclid. Was it here at Racedown, and from this old copy, dated 1696, that Wordsworth renewed his acquaintance with mathematics, drawing from them a steadying, abstract sort of comfort when the human problem oppressed him? The passage in which he describes this proceeding on his part is linked closely—in the 1805 text of *The Prelude*—with his first acquaintance with Coleridge, as well as with his debt to Dorothy.

> I . . . for my future studies, as the sole
> Employment of the enquiring faculty,
> Turned towards Mathematics, and their clear
> And solid evidence—Ah! then it was
> That thou, most precious Friend! about this time
> First known to me, didst lend a living help
> To regulate my soul, and then it was
> That the belovèd Woman in whose sight. . . .[2]

The final version of this passage explains more clearly why he

---

[1] *L.Y.* iii. 48*b*, p. 1335. W.W. to William Mathews, Oct. 24 1795.
[2] *Prel.* X (1805), ll. 902–16. The reference to Coleridge was entirely omitted in 1850, perhaps because he felt that it was somewhat premature.

found mathematics helpful. After saying that he refused merely to stop thinking:

> Such sloth I could not brook,
> (Too well I loved, in that my spring of life,
> Pains-taking thoughts, and truth, their dear reward)—

he tells how he

> turned to abstract science, and there sought
> Work for the reasoning faculty enthroned
> Where the disturbances of space and time . . .
> Find no admission.

Mathematics was one of the roads by which he was able to regain intercourse with unchanging universals. And he had great need of such help. The poetry he wrote in the first months at Racedown shows him intensely absorbed in a struggle to avoid complete mental chaos. There exist some fragments of blank verse belonging to this time, one of them headed *Incipient Madness*. After describing how he 'crossed the dreary moor' by moonlight, until he came to a deserted hut where he saw on the ground

> A broken pane which glittered in the moon,
> And seemed akin to life,

he thus describes the effect the sight had upon him:

> I found my sickly heart had tied itself
> Even to this tiny speck of glass . . .
>   Many long months
> Confirmed this strange incontinence; my eye
> Did every evening measure the moon's height
> And forth I went before her yellow beams
> Could overtop the elm trees on the heath,
> I went, I reach'd the cottage, and I found
> Still undisturbed and glittering in its place
> That speck of glass more precious to my soul
> Than was the moon in heaven.[1]

It was a symbol like the symbols of his dreams. All around was darkness, ruin; the silence of desolation; in the midst, drawing him back night after moonlight night, the precious, shining fragment of glass. It was no wonder perhaps that *The Ruined*

---

[1] *P.W.* i, pp. 314–15, and app. crit.

Cottage became the subject and title of Wordsworth's best work at Racedown.

He did not have a breakdown because Dorothy was at hand to help him and because he turned himself with deliberate effort towards those things which had helped him in earlier days— mathematics and poetry. Before he had been a month at Racedown he had begun to long for his old favourite, Beattie's *Minstrel*. This longing sprang from sights and sounds on a morning walk over the hills to Lyme. At Lyme—about eight miles from Racedown—lived a friend of his called Leader, of whom nothing is known except that he was also a friend of William Mathews. On October 23rd 1795 Wordsworth walked over to Lyme in the hope of seeing him but was disappointed, and returned to dinner.[1]

My walk over the hills [he told Mathews] was charming. I could hear the murmuring of the sea for three miles, of course I often stopped 'listening with pleasing dread to the deep roar of the wide weltering waves'. This from the Minstrel and has reminded me of a request I have to make to you, which is that you would accept of my edition of Cato's Letters,[2] and in return make me a present of that Vol: of Bell's forgotten poetry which contains The Minstrel and Sir Martyn.[3] I know you are possessed of it; so was I once, but one of my brothers valued it so highly as to deny himself the pleasure of returning it. You will write your name in it as presented to me. If you chuse to take the trouble of inserting my name in the Cato's Letters, here it is; you may cut it out and paste it in.

From W. Wordsworth
to
W. Mathews.

Wordsworth's wanderings by night and day made him an object of suspicion among the poor people of the country-side. He possessed, it seems, a small pocket telescope, with which they thought he bewitched the cattle, while his habit of speaking poetry aloud as he walked was extremely puzzling to them. More than a hundred years after he had left that country-side

[1] *L.T.* iii, appendix, p. 1334. *P.P.* Gill's Diary, Oct. 26th. 'Mr. Leader from Lyme to see Mr. Wordsworth.' I have been unable to trace this person.

[2] Wordsworth must mean the *Disticha Catonis*, maxims for use in daily life ascribed to the elder Cato and, with comments by Erasmus, often translated into English. They are sometimes referred to as 'Epistula'. No 'letters' of Cato exist.

[3] *Sir Martyn*, by Mickle, another Scotch poet who was a favourite with Wordsworth. See D.W.'s *Journal of a Tour in Scotland*. *D.W.J.* i, p. 443.

for ever, old people there still talked of their parents' memories of the strange young man from the north.[1]

Racedown was and still remains a lonely place: and Wordsworth felt at first very keenly the loss of his London friends. At Blackdown, about a mile away, lived some relations of the Pinneys, whom the Wordsworths found rather uninteresting: 'though they are very good, kind people', wrote Dorothy, 'they have not much conversation'. William wrote to Mathews when they had been a month at Racedown: 'We are both as happy as people can be who live in perfect solitude. We do not see a soul. Now and then we meet a miserable person in the wood or an accidental traveller.' And a few months later: 'Our present life is utterly barren of such events as merit even the short-lived chronicle of an accidental letter. We plant cabbages;[2] and if retirement in its full perfection be as powerful in working transformations as one of Ovid's gods, you may perhaps suspect that into cabbages we shall be transformed.' He begged his London friends to come and stay with them, but the distance kept all of them except Montagu from attempting it. He did not come until the spring of 1797, when he saw the miracle that Dorothy's wise management had wrought in his fretful little Basil.

It should not be forgotten that the Wordsworth's life at Racedown was shared by this little boy who was not three years old when he came to them. 'He is my perpetual pleasure', wrote Dorothy, after six months at Racedown. 'He is quite metamorphosed from a shivering half-starved plant, to a lusty, blooming, fearless boy. He dreads neither cold nor rain. He has played frequently an hour or two without appearing sensible that the rain was pouring down upon him or the wind blowing about him.' A year later she described how they had broken him of his habit of crying for everything:

Upon these occasions we used to tell him that if he chose to cry he must go into a certain room where he cannot be heard and *stay* till he chose to be quiet, because the noise was unpleasant to us; at first his visits were very long, but he always came out again perfectly

---

[1] I am indebted for this information to Lady Pinney of Racedown. The telescope is mentioned in *The Thorn*, written at Alfoxden.

[2] *P.P.* Gill's Diary, Mar. 17th and 24th 1796: 'Amusing myself with the Garden this week and the last, the weather being tolerably moderate. . . . Planted one bed Cabbage plants, 1 Bed pease.'

good-humoured. He found that this mode was never departed from, and when he felt the fretful disposition coming on he would say. 'Aunt, I think I am going to cry' and retire till the fit was over. He has now entirely conquered the disposition. I dare say it is three months since we have had occasion to send him into this apartment of tears.[1]

Basil had one other bad habit which was apparently not so easily cured. 'Basil', wrote Wordsworth to Francis Wrangham, 'is quite well, *quant au physique, mais pour le moral il-y-a bien à craindre*. Among other things he lies like a little devil.'[2] Basil's untruthfulness, however, became in time a source of admiration to Wordsworth. The little poem written at Alfoxden and published in *Lyrical Ballads* where it bore the extraordinary title *Anecdote for Fathers, showing how the Art of Lying may be Taught*, records a conversation between Wordsworth and young Basil. Many years afterwards Wordsworth told a correspondent who had been not unnaturally puzzled at the purport of the poem, that his intention was 'to point out the injurious effects of putting inconsiderate questions to Children, and urging them to give answers upon matters either uninteresting to them, or upon which they had no decided opinion'. Can it be that Basil's habit of giving false answers—which Wordsworth complained of at Racedown—was all along due in part to the necessity of defending himself against the poet's questions, and that at Alfoxden, after a particularly long catechism, Wordsworth at last realized that it was himself, and not Basil, who was to blame?[3]

The loneliness of their life at Racedown was interrupted at Christmas by the Pinney brothers, who came to stay for a week and returned again in February for a whole month.[4] They paid for their own board; so their visits were apt to be festive occasions. Joseph Gill's store-room was raided for wine-glasses and decanters. The Pinneys of Blackdown were entertained to what Dorothy described as 'a grand rout'—'and very dull it was except for the pleasure of talking about it afterwards'. The Pinney brothers were keen sportsmen, and Wordsworth

---

[1] *E.L.* 57, p. 165. D.W. to J.P. Mar. 19th 1797.
[2] Ibid. 53, p. 154. W.W. to F. Wrangham, Mar. 1796.
[3] *P.W.* i, p. 241, and note, and *L.Y.* i, p. 253. In 1845 Wordsworth cut out the subtitle and substituted a quotation from Eusebius: 'Retine vim istam, falsa enim dicam, si coges.' This made the purport of the poem rather clearer.
[4] Gill's Diary, Jan. 1st–6th and Feb. 10th–Mar. 6th 1796.

'relaxed the rigour of his philosophic nerves so much as to go a-coursing several times'.[1] Dorothy described their out-door activities: 'When the weather was fine they were out generally all the morning, walking sometimes; *then* I went with them frequently—riding sometimes, hunting, coursing, cleaving wood.' But the Pinneys were bookish young men as well. John Pinney took several books, including the writings of Algernon Sidney, the Whig hero, away with him when he left.[2] And it was the Pinneys who kept Wordsworth supplied with modern political literature. Louvet's Memoirs and those of Mme Roland were lent during the first winter, and Helen Williams's *Letters from France*—all these had a personal interest for Wordsworth. They also lent him *Lewesdon Hill*, a landscape poem about the country-side near Racedown, by a local poet-parson, William Crowe, the able and amusing public orator at Oxford. This poem was admired also by Coleridge,[3] who probably first read it when he came to Racedown. Wordsworth many years afterwards spoke of it as an 'excellent loco-descriptive poem'.

But the greatest service the Pinneys did for Wordsworth after he came to Racedown was to keep him in touch with Coleridge. Coleridge, with other Bristol radicals like Thomas Beddoes the doctor and physicist, was much disturbed this autumn by the new repressive measures of the Government. In October the mob which surrounded the king's coach shouting for 'peace' and 'bread' was made the excuse for two very severe new acts, the Seditious Meetings Act and the Treasonable Practices Act. The first of these forbade meetings of more than fifty persons unless permitted by the magistrates, and the second made it high treason to speak or write anything in criticism of the Constitution. While the two bills were still being discussed in Parliament, meetings were held everywhere to congratulate the king on his 'late escape', and counter-meetings in protest against the bills. Aza Pinney sent a lively account to Wordsworth of the doings in Bristol.[4] At a meeting convened to send a loyal address to the king, Coleridge and his friends had tried to move an amendment.[5] 'A great noise ensued but Coleridge's

---

[1] *P.P.* Letter of Azariah Pinney.　　　　　　　　　　　　[2] Ibid.
[3] *B.L.*, ch. i.
[4] *P.P.* A. Pinney to W.W., Nov. 26th 1795.
[5] Ibid. The account of this meeting, with a report of Coleridge's speech, is given in the *Star* for Nov. 23rd 1795, a London newspaper.

party were at length compelled to give up the point.' Then
Dr. Beddoes wrote a pamphlet condemning the two bills and a
meeting of radicals was held at the Guildhall to protest against
them. A petition was drawn up, and 'Coleridge voted that the
petition be presented by Fox and Sheridan, but willingly
acceded to Dr. Beddoes's opposition'—that they should be
presented by the members of Parliament for Bristol.[1] 'I would
like to know', said Aza to Wordsworth, 'your opinion of the
Convention Bill. I can almost anticipate it.' In the following
spring Coleridge began writing and publishing his short-lived
periodical, *The Watchman,* in direct defiance of the new acts,
for its confessed object was to secure their repeal. By publishing
The Watchman Coleridge was risking imprisonment. Fortunately it kept so few subscribers (in spite of Coleridge's can-
vassing tour of the midland and northern towns) that it died a
natural death before it could attract the attention of Government.
Through Aza Pinney copies reached Racedown, but no letters
survive to show what Wordsworth thought of it.

When the Pinneys returned to Bristol on March 6th 1796
they took with them the revised and enlarged manuscript of
Salisbury Plain. It was to be delivered to Cottle for publication,[2]
but with the request that he would first show it to Coleridge to
read and criticize. 'This', said John Pinney, 'Coleridge appears
to have done with considerable attention, for I understand he
has interleaved it with white paper to mark down whatever may
strike him as worthy your notice and intends forwarding it you
in that form.'[3]

That Wordsworth should have deliberately sought Coleridge's
assistance and criticism in this way is remarkable. His earlier
poems had been shown to no one. Unfavourable criticism he
disliked intensely, and praise he coveted with youth's appetite.[4]
Coleridge, however, had already expressed open admiration
for *An Evening Walk* and *Descriptive Sketches,* and Wordsworth

---

[1] The petition, with four thousand signatures, was presented by Lord Sheffield,
M.P. for Bristol. Sheffield was taken to task by Sheridan for not mentioning the
number of signatures. *Felix Farley's Bristol Journal,* Nov. 28th 1795.

[2] Wordsworth had intended sending it to Cottle in January, but for some reason
it was delayed till March. See his letter to Cottle of Jan. 7th 1796. *E.L.* 51, p. 149.

[3] *P.P.* A. Pinney to W.W., Mar. 26th 1796.

[4] In 1816 W.W. wrote to J. H. Reynolds: 'I remember when I was young in
the practice of writing praise was prodigiously acceptable to me and censure most
distasteful, nay even painful.' *M.Y.* ii, p. 758.

may have known this.[1] It seems that Wordsworth may already
have written to Coleridge during the autumn, for in January
he asked Cottle to convey his greetings and to say that he
'wished much to hear' from Coleridge.[2] From now onwards
certainly they were in active correspondence, for on May 13th
Coleridge, in a letter to Thelwall the radical, described Wordsworth as 'a very dear friend of mine, the best poet of the age'
And a letter from Lamb to Coleridge at the end of May proves
that there had been letters passing between the two poets
Coleridge had forwarded the manuscript of *Salisbury Plain* to
Lamb in London, and Lamb replied: 'I shall be too ill to call on
Wordsworth myself, but will take care to transmit him his
poem, when I have read it.' Was Wordsworth then in London
Not indeed at the end of May, but by the end of the first week in
June he was there, as an entry in Gill's diary proves: 'June 2nd
Wednesday. Mr. Wordsworth set out for London.' He
remained there for a month and did not return to Racedown
until July 11th.[3] Coleridge therefore must have known of his
journey and have told Lamb to expect him in London.

On his return journey from this expedition[4] it seems almost
certain that Wordsworth saw Coleridge in Bristol. For in the
fourth chapter of *Biographia Literaria*, Coleridge describes how
'in my twenty-fourth year'—that is, in 1796—Wordsworth
recited to him the poem about the Female Vagrant, and what an
effect the recitation—or reading aloud—produced on him. We
have no definite record of Wordsworth visiting Bristol in 1796
yet what more natural than that he should have taken this
opportunity of seeing Coleridge? One curious point, however
arises from Coleridge's reminiscence. He writes as though
when he heard Wordsworth's recitation, he was not previously
acquainted with the poem.

I was [he says] in my twenty-fourth year, when I had the happiness
of knowing Mr. Wordsworth personally, and while memory lasts
I shall hardly forget the sudden effect produced on my mind, by his
recitation of a manuscript poem, which still remains unpublished, but
of which the stanza and tone of style were the same as those of The
Female Vagrant, as originally printed in the first volume of the Lyrical

[1] Coleridge's *Poems* in which he quotes from *E.W.* were not published until
April this year (1796).

[2] *E.L.* 51, p. 149. W.W. to Cottle, Jan. 7th, 1796.

[3] *P.P.* Gill's Diary, July 11th 1796.   [4] See below, p. 296.

Ballads. . . . It was not however the freedom from false taste, whether as to common defects, or to those more properly his own, which made so unusual an impression on my feelings immediately and subsequently on my judgment. It was the union of deep feeling with profound thought . . . and above all the original gift of spreading the tone, the atmosphere . . . of the ideal world around forms, incidents and situations of which, for the common view, custom had bedimmed all the lustre.

Is it possible after all that he had not read it himself before sending it to Lamb? Although unlikely, such a thing is not altogether incredible, in view of Coleridge's constant failure to fulfil his own promises. But more probably Wordsworth's recitation so impressed him by its manner that it was like an entirely new revelation of Wordsworth's powers.

Soon after Coleridge received the manuscript of *Salisbury Plain*, his own first volume of poems *On Various Subjects* was published in Bristol by Cottle. It contained a long poem called *Religious Musings*, now seldom read. It was, however, admired by Wordsworth, as we know from Coleridge's letter to John Thelwall, who, being a strong atheist, had disapproved of it.

'But why so violent against *metaphysics* in poetry? . . . 'Some for each' is my motto. . . . My religious poetry interests the *religious*. . . . A very dear friend of mine, who is, in my opinion, the best poet of the age (I will send you his poem when published) thinks that the lines from 364 to 375 and from 403 to 428 the best in the volume,[1]—indeed, worth all the rest. And

---

[1] The first passage which Wordsworth admired was as follows:

> When on some solemn jubilee of Saints
> The sapphire-blazing gates of Paradise
> Are thrown wide open; and thence voyage forth
> Detachments wide of seraph-warbled airs,
> And odors snatch'd from beds of amaranth,
> And they that from the crystal river of life
> Spring on freshen'd wing, ambrosial gales!
> The favor'd good man in his lonely walk
> Perceives them, and his silent spirit drinks
> Strange bliss that he shall recognise in heaven.

In the last three lines Wordsworth no doubt marked an experience akin to that which had visited him when he found 'blessing in this gentle breeze'.
The second passage, which was much longer, described the Judgement day, and not so easy to recognize as appealing to Wordsworth's taste. But Coleridge's lines had a certain Miltonic glow about them which may well have aroused his admiration.

this man is a republican, and, at least, a *semi*-atheist.' Now this chance reference to Wordsworth is of importance, for it shows not only that Wordsworth was in possession of Coleridge's poems as soon as they came out, but that he had written to Coleridge about them at length and in detail, and that the two poets had exchanged views on religious matters as well as on politics.

Salisbury Plain, as Coleridge and Lamb read it, was a much longer and more complicated poem than that written two years earlier. The revision had been Wordsworth's first activity after arriving at Racedown, for in November he had written to Wrangham: 'I have a poem which I should wish to dispose of provided I could get anything for it. I recollect reading the first draught of it to you in London. But since I came to Racedown, I have made alterations and additions so material as that it may be looked on almost as another work. Its object is partly to expose the vices of the penal law and the calamities of war as they affect individuals.'[1]

The poem as it originally stood had already shown the 'female vagrant' as a destitute war-widow, but now, not only were several stanzas added describing her various sufferings after her return from America, but the 'traveller' to whom she related her story became himself a character with a tragic story. He is a sailor, who, after being kidnapped by the press-gang, is cheated of his earnings by the 'slaves of office', and in desperation robs and murders a traveller while on his way home, after which he escapes across Salisbury Plain where in due time he meets the 'female vagrant'.

The two unfortunates become fellow travellers, and eventually meet with the sailor's wife who, after leaving her home and wandering abroad, has fallen ill, and is now, in a dying condition, being sent back in a cart to her own parish by the overseers. The sailor just has time to ask her forgiveness before she expires. He then makes his way to the nearest town, gives himself up to justice and is hanged in chains, while 'women and children were by Fathers brought' to see the spectacle.

This gloomy story—which was somewhat softened in detail but not materially altered, in the published version of 1842[2]—

---

[1] *E.L.* 49, p. 145. W.W. to Francis Wrangham, Nov. 20th 1795.
[2] e.g. The sailor makes a Christian instead of a stoical end, and is not hanged i

was Wordsworth's commentary on Godwin's theory that criminals are made by circumstances, not by nature. The sailor's tragedy is, not that he committed a murder, but that he was by nature 'mild and good', and that his crime was the result of his treatment by Government and society. His kindness to the 'female vagrant', and to the child ill treated by its father whom he and the vagrant meet in the course of their wanderings, show that his essential nature is still unspoilt. Yet in the end this far from hardened criminal asks to be hanged as the only escape from the torments of conscience.

As the first-fruits of Wordsworth's retirement this revision of *Salisbury Plain* is scarcely the sort of work we should have expected from one who had just welcomed the 'gentle breeze' of creative genius rising up within him. It is the bitterest, most unsparing indictment of social injustice that he ever wrote; its tragedy is quite unrelieved.

The months in London had certainly deepened his loathing of the war. Moving entirely among radicals, he had read such things as Joseph Fawcett's deeply sarcastic poem *The Art of War* (to whose influence he later testified), with its fierce attack on war as nothing but murder 'hid in magnificence and drowned in state'. In the print-shops he had gazed, no doubt, at Gillray's brilliant cartoons of the sufferings war inflicts on the poor.[1] Poetically the poem was improved by the omission of some of the more spectacular descriptions of supernatural visions on Salisbury Plain, while some incidents are coloured with personal experience and the recollection of past emotion. Thus the sailor, on his flight across the Plain, encounters a gibbet with a body hanging on it.

> It was a spectacle which none might view
> In spot so savage, but with shuddering pain;
> Nor only did for him at once renew
> All he had feared from man, but roused a train
> Of the mind's phantoms, horrible as vain . . .

chains. The resemblance of Wordsworth's sailor to Hardy's heroine, Tess, is striking. The woman's story was published in *Lyrical Ballads*, 1798, as *The Female Vagrant*. See below, p. 369.

[1] Especially the series *John Bull's Progress* which appeared in June 1793. Gillray's earlier work had included *The Liberty of the Subject*, an attack on the press-gang.

As doth befall to those whom frenzy fires,
His soul which in such anguish hath been tossed
Sinks into deepest calm; for now retires
Fear, a terrific dream in darkness lost,
The dire phantasma which his sense had crossed,
The mind was still as a deep evening stream.

In this last wonderful line Wordsworth the poet seems suddenly
to look out at us, like the sun among storm-clouds, and the
whole passage, with its picture of stillness following intense
fear, takes us back far into a Cumberland childhood, when a
little boy, riding alone and astray among the fells, came face to
face with a gibbet, and, after a moment of panic, saw the world
under a strange new aspect of 'visionary dreariness', of indescribable mental intensity and power.[1]

His own unhappiness, and Dorothy's cheerful consolations,
are likewise reflected in the poem, where he describes how the
woman endeavoured to cheer the sailor's anguish:

She with affectionate and homely art
His peace of mind endeavour'd to restore:
'Come, let us be', she said, 'of better heart.'
Thus oftentimes the woman did implore
And still the more he grieved she loved him still the more.

Wordsworth's journey to London, at midsummer, 1796, was
undertaken mainly for financial reasons. The settlement of
Raisley Calvert's legacy had been a matter of importance to the
Wordsworths since the previous autumn, when the instalments
began to be paid over. By the end of October 1795 Wordsworth
had received £300. This sum he had immediately lent to
Montagu 'in a sort of irregularly secured annuity for which I
have received ten per cent.'[2] It was of course to Wordsworth's
advantage to get as high a rate of interest as possible for his
money, as it was all he had to live upon, and an annuity offered
the best terms. In January 1796, having received another £200
from Calvert, he lent it on similar interest, but not on annuity,

---

[1] See above, p. 11.
[2] See above, p. 269. *L.T.* iii, p. 1336. W.W. to R.W., May 7th 1797. In Aug.
1796 this loan was acknowledged in a bond signed by Montagu, Douglas, and
Francis Wrangham. The bond is among the Dove Cottage Papers. Richard
Wordsworth was somewhat uneasy about the loan, and urged his brother 'to
keep a close and regular account' and 'not to trust too much to memory'. *D.C.P.*

to a friend of Montagu's called Charles Douglas. While he was in London in July he received a note signed by both Montagu and Douglas promising to repay the £200 with interest at 10 per cent. on January 1st 1797. Instead, however, Montagu in December 1796 took over £100 of this debt; Douglas did not repay his £100 until four years later. Thus £400 of Calvert's legacy was in Montagu's hands by the end of 1796. Wordsworth also took out an insurance policy on Montagu's life at a premium of £7. 10s., which Montagu paid to Wordsworth annually, along with the interest on the principal.

These transactions with Montagu, as has been seen, proved somewhat rash. Montagu during the next few years was in no position to pay interest regularly, although he never willingly defaulted to Wordsworth; he repaid in the course of time all the arrears of interest on the original loan, but the principal remained in his hands until 1814, when it also was finally repaid.[1]

While in London Wordsworth again saw Godwin. With 'Pinney' (whether John or Aza Godwin does not tell us) he called on him 'after dinner' on June 7th and in the evening Godwin supped 'with Wordsworth at Basil Montagu's'. On the 18th they met again at Montagu's, 'Tobin' (either John or James Tobin of Bristol, friends of the Pinneys) and 'Stoddart' (John Stoddart, later a friend of Coleridge and brother-in-law of Hazlitt) being also of the party. On the 19th, a Sunday, Godwin again supped at Montagu's, 'with Wordsworth and Stoddart'. On the 28th they met once more,[2] at Stoddart's. Whether in these meetings Wordsworth began to find himself differing from Godwin's teaching on many important subjects cannot be said with certainty: but what is certain is that in the ensuing autumn Wordsworth began to write his tragedy, *The Borderers*, in which he clearly revealed the dangerous implications of much of the morality of *Political Justice*.

During William's absence in London Dorothy's main interest centred on the post office at Crewkerne, seven miles away.

---

[1] *M.T.* ii. 487, p. 566, and 497, p. 587. W.W. to R.W. Aug. 19th 1813 and Apr. 1st 1814. Coleridge, in a letter to Wordsworth in 1808, about Dorothy's anxieties for their financial affairs at that time, speaks of 'the fears which harassed you at Racedown', showing how difficult their situation was there and how uncertain their future. *E.K.C.*, p. 350.

[2] Godwin's Diary (see above, p. 262, n.).

She had now obtained the services of a charming country girl as maid, the devoted 'Peggy' who stayed with them until they left the west for ever and would even then have 'gone to the world's end' with them. Young Basil therefore could be safely left in Peggy's care, while Dorothy three times persuaded old Joseph Gill to accompany her on foot to Crewkerne to see if there were any letters from the absent brother.[1] Wordsworth returned just in time for the hay-making at Racedown. The weather in the second part of July was wet, but most of the hay was stacked before the end of the month, and in August Gill painted the outside of the house, and Wordsworth himself picked the first French beans. 'The Garden', says Gill, 'produces everything we have planted or sown in it very well this season.'

There is also in the Diary at this time an entry of some interest: 'Lent Mr. Wordsworth four sheets of gilt-edged paper —and the Entertainers from my Newspapers.' Earlier in the year, when the Pinneys were at Racedown, he had noted: 'F.P. [that is John Frederick Pinney] had . . . my Town and Country Magazines for Mr. Wordsworths etc amusement . . . F.P. had all the Letter paper and other loose writing paper out of the upper drawer of the desk.' Wordsworth had probably been complaining that paper was scarce, expensive, and difficult in any case to procure at Racedown; hence the turning out of the drawer. The absence of newspapers had been a source of annoyance to him from the beginning. In November he had asked Francis Wrangham to try and procure the *Morning Chronicle* for him free of charge: 'If it can be managed I should be much pleased, as we only see here a provincial weekly paper, and I cannot afford to have the 'Chronicle' at my own expense.'[2] Why Wordsworth should have thought that he could obtain this favour is not clear, but when he was in London in 1793 he had met the owner-editors, Grey and Perry, apparently at the House of Commons;[3] their reports of debates were by far the

---

[1] *P.P.* Gill's Diary, June 6th, 10th, 12th 1796. It was at this time too that Dorothy asked to be allowed to measure the distance from Racedown to Crewkerne with the 'perambulator' or way-wiser, one of the curiosities of Racedown. The perambulator was, however, sent away in the 'Millar's Cart' before her wish was fulfilled. Ibid. June 20th. During Wordsworth's absence John Pinney and his father came to Racedown and stayed two nights.

[2] The cost of a newspaper in 1797 was $4\frac{1}{2}d.$, including the stamp tax.

[3] *E.Y.* 45, p. 130. W.W. to William Mathews, Dec. 1794.

best, and theirs was the most influential opposition newspaper.

The 'provincial weekly paper' was no doubt the *Weekly Entertainer*, borrowed from Joseph Gill. It was published at Sher-
borne, and was the nearest approach to a literary periodical that
ever found its way to Racedown. It published contemporary
verse: Southey and Charlotte Smith were among its contributors.
To this magazine Wordsworth in the course of the next few
months contributed a letter and a poem. The letter appeared in
the issue of November 7th 1796 and ran as follows:

Mutiny on Board the Bounty
To the Printer

Racedown Lodge. October 23rd 1796

Sir.

There having appeared in your Entertainer (vide the 255th page
of the present vol.) an extract from a work purporting to be the production of Fletcher Christian, who headed the mutiny on board the
Bounty, I think it proper to inform you, that I have the best authority
for saying that the publication is spurious. Your regard for truth will
induce you to apprize your readers of this circumstance.

I am, sir,
your humble servant,
William Wordsworth.

This letter is apparently the only one that Wordsworth ever
wrote to the press, signed with his own name.[1] His interest in
the mutiny on the *Bounty* arose from his connexion with the
family of the leader of the mutineers, Fletcher Christian. This
man was the brother of Edward Christian, the Professor of Law
at Cambridge whom the Wordsworths had engaged some years
before as their advocate in the lawsuit with Lord Lonsdale.
The Christians, as has been pointed out earlier, had been
neighbours of the Wordsworths at Cockermouth, and for a year
or two Fletcher Christian and Wordsworth had been pupils
together at the Cockermouth Grammar School, though as
Fletcher was six years older than Wordsworth they cannot
have known each other well. The argument about the causes of
the mutiny on the *Bounty* had been going on for several years
in pamphlets, the point at issue being whether Captain Bligh

---

[1] He wrote several political letters and articles in the *Kendal Chronicle* and
Westmorland Gazette in later years, but they were signed anonymously as he was in
government employment at the time.

had provoked the mutiny by harsh conduct towards his crew. In 1794 Edward Christian initiated on his own account an investigation of the mutiny, and published the results in a pamphlet. Among those who assisted him in this investigation and signed the pamphlet with him were two of Wordsworth's close relatives, his uncle Canon Cookson of Forncett and his cousin Captain John Wordsworth of Whitehaven. His Cambridge Tutor, Frewen, also signed it, and several other people who were either fellows of St. John's or Cumberland friends of the Christians.[1] It is a curious instance of local loyalties rallying to the cause of a man who, whatever the provocation, was certainly guilty of a serious crime.

Bligh complained in reply that Edward Christian had 'vindicated Fletcher Christian's conduct at my expense', and presently, in 1796, there appeared a work entitled *Letters of Fletcher Christian*, which exonerated Bligh and put all the blame on Christian. Extracts from it appeared in the *Weekly Entertainer* in September 1796, and it was this publication to which Wordsworth took exception. The *Letters* were indeed obviously forgeries and did Bligh's cause no good. No further correspondence took place in the *Entertainer*. The incident is, from its connexion with Wordsworth, of considerable interest, for it shows him maintaining pride in his Cumberland origins in a way that is somewhat unexpected. No doubt he had seen a copy of Edward Christian's pamphlet. The matter was still being discussed two years later, when James Losh, whose brother John Losh had also been among its signatories, noted in his diary on April 3rd 1798: 'I explained the real state of Christian's mutiny to Southey and Barry who both seemed much struck by it.'[2]

Shortly after this episode Wordsworth sent a poem to the *Weekly Entertainer*. It appeared on November 21st 1796 and was entitled: *Address to the Ocean*,[3] and signed W.W. Its first line,

How long will you round me be roaring,

---

[1] C. S. Wilkinson, *The Wake of the Bounty*, 1953, pp. 70–74. The attempt in the latter part of this book to prove meetings between Wordsworth and Fletcher Christian in 1795 and 1797 is based on misconceptions of the facts, and inaccuracies which make it impossible to accept any such idea.

[2] Diary of James Losh, Tullie House, Carlisle.

[3] Some lines of it are in the brown leather note-book which he began to use at Hawkshead. On the alternate pages is a good deal of verse belonging to the years following his return from France.

is quoted, with acknowledgement, from a poem of Coleridge's
called *The Complaint of Ninathona*, an imitation from Ossian,
written in 1793 and published in his *Poems on Various Subjects* in
April 1796. Wordsworth's poem, though in the same metre, is
not Ossianic. It is the lament of a girl for her drowned lover—
'my Charles'—and is much more in the style of some of his
schoolboy verse than of *Salisbury Plain* or *The Borderers*.

In March 1797 appeared another, much longer poem, headed
Address to Silence: Read at a Literary Club, and signed W.C.
Part of this poem was copied by Dorothy years afterwards into
a note-book containing extracts from her brother's and other
poems; she called it: 'Passages taken from an Address to
Silence, published in the Weekly Entertainer.' A few words of
this manuscript are in Wordsworth's hand, and there is a
possibility that the poem is his work.[1] It is not, however,
except here and there, characteristic of Wordsworth's style,
being very much in the manner of Thomson, grand and dignified, while the scenery is partly arctic in character. If he wrote
it, we have to account for the difficulty of the signature in the
Entertainer, 'W.C.', and for the fact that it was 'read at a
Literary Club', for this club appears to have met at Tavistock,
more than fifty miles from Racedown. There was, however, at
least one line in it which Wordsworth afterwards made good
use of:

> Our noisy years are moments of thy life.

The phrase 'Our noisy years' was to find its final home in the
Ode: Intimations of Immortality. But whether or not the *Address
to Silence* is by Wordsworth, we know that he did attempt to
publish a poem in the *Entertainer* early in this year, 1797, for
Gill notes in his Diary: 'Jan. 1st 1797. Mr. Pinney of Blackdown to send Mr. Wordsworth's poem to The Entertainer.'
Unfortunately he does not tell us the name of the poem. No
other poem signed W.W. appeared in the *Entertainer*.

In the early autumn of 1796 Wordsworth began to write his
tragedy in blank verse, which he called *The Borderers*. The first
mention of it occurs in a fragment of a letter from Dorothy

---

[1] Miss Helen Darbishire from internal evidence believes the whole poem to be
by Wordsworth. See 'An Approach to Wordsworth's genius', in *English Studies
Today*, 1951. This view is challenged by F. W. Bateson, in *Wordsworth, A Re-
interpretation*, 1954, p. 136, n.

dated October 24th 1796. 'William', she says, 'is now ardent in
the composition of a tragedy.'[1] It was a work of great complexity
to which he devoted much energy and labour.

The Borderers is an indication both of his absorption in and
his reaction from Godwin's doctrines. In March 1796 he had
re-read *Political Justice*, in a copy of the new edition given or
lent him by Montagu.[2] He expected, he said, to find it 'much
improved', but thought the preface 'a piece of barbarous writing'. What he finally thought of it we do not know, but a year
later he told Wrangham: 'I do promise—not a Godwynian,
Montaguian, Lincolnsonian promise—that I will become a
regular correspondent.'[3] This seems to indicate some decline of
respect for the sage, who in his chapter 'Of Promises' had
concluded that promises 'stand in opposition to the genuine
and wholesome exercise of an intellectual nature'. *The Borderers*
was in some respects an exposure of the dangers of the doctrine
of 'intellectual man', when pushed to extremes, but in another
direction the play might be regarded as upholding one of
Godwin's cardinal precepts, that of 'benevolence', by creating a
character—Oswald—wholly devoid of it.

The Borderers is, like *Salisbury Plain*, a study in some
problems of criminal psychology. It was not, as first written,
intended to be acted, although, under pressure from Coleridge,
it was offered in the following year to the manager of Covent
Garden and returned as unsuited for the stage.[4] The play is
indeed quite unactable; a good deal of it is nearly unreadable
also. The blank verse is clumsy and abrupt except for some
passages where it suddenly bursts into great poetic splendour.
The story is entirely Wordsworth's invention and is extremely
complicated and difficult to follow. Like the story of *Salisbury
Plain* it has a strongly didactic aim, and to the end of his life
Wordsworth believed that on the whole the play successfully
illustrated that aim. When he revised it for publication in 1842
he wrote in the prefatory note:

. . . Not the slightest alteration has been made in the conduct of the
story, or the composition of the characters; above all in respect of the

---

[1] *Mem.* i, p. 96. The letter was probably written to Mary Hutchinson.
[2] *E.L.* 54, p. 156. W.W. to W. Mathews, Mar. 21st, 1796.
[3] Ibid. 55, p. 161. W.W. to F. Wrangham, Feb. 27th 1797. Montagu was very
unreliable in keeping his promises to visit Racedown.
[4] See below, pp. 350–1.

two leading Persons of the Drama, I felt no inducement to make any change. The study of human nature suggests this awful truth that, as in the trials to which life subjects us, sin and crime are apt to start from their very opposite qualities, so there are no limits to the hardening of the heart, and the perversion of the understanding to which they may carry their slaves.[1]

In *Salisbury Plain* he had drawn the picture of a man goaded to commit murder through poverty and hunger—the result of his treatment by Government and society. Except for this one act of desperation, his character is wholly benevolent. In *The Borderers* he presents us with a much more formidable kind of sinner; Oswald, the man in whom the springs of pity have been completely dried up; who, having once started on a career of crime, plunges on in reckless and deliberate wickedness; gratifying his love of power by leading into crime a young and unspoilt character by working on his credulity and innocence. Oswald is to Marmaduke what Iago is to Othello, persuading him to cause the death of the innocent blind man Herbert, the father of Idonea, the woman whom he loves. Oswald is not, like the sailor, the victim of an unjust social system. Indeed, *The Borderers* has no concern with social evils, just as it has no definite historical setting: the scene is the 'Border' where no king's writ runs; the root of Oswald's depravity is his vindictiveness and innate pride; his moral destruction of Marmaduke is unprovoked, except by the fact that Marmaduke once saved his life and Oswald dislikes being under an obligation to any man.

After completing his play Wordsworth wrote an essay of some length on the psychology of such people as Oswald.[2] In this essay Wordsworth traces the process by which vice and crime become attractive to 'a young man of great intellectual powers yet without any solid principles of general benevolence'. It has been maintained that in this essay Wordsworth is simply portraying his own state of mind after the 'crime' of his seduction and desertion of Annette. Such an argument is impossible to accept, if only for the reason that Wordsworth himself did not, on his return to England, embark on such a career of depravity as he describes in *The Borderers* and accounts for in

---

[1] *P.W.* i, p. 342.

[2] This remained undiscovered until 1934. It was published by Professor de Selincourt in his edition of Wordsworth's poetical works, *P.W.* i, p. 345.

the essay. Yet there are paragraphs in the essay which are almost certainly self-descriptive, whether or not Wordsworth was conscious of it. There is, for instance, the opening paragraph in which he sets before us the sort of individual who becomes the villain of his drama.

His master passions are pride and the love of distinction. . . . He goes into the world and is immediately betrayed into a great crime. That influence on which all his happiness is built immediately deserts him. His talents are robbed of their weight, his exertions are unavailing, and he quits the world in disgust, with strong misanthropic feelings. In his retirement he is impelled to examine the unreasonableness of established opinions, and the force of his mind exhausts itself in constant efforts to separate the elements of virtue and vice. It is his pleasure and his consolation to hunt out whatever is bad in actions which are usually esteemed virtuous and to detect the good in actions which the universal sense of mankind teaches us to reprobate. . . . His feelings are interested in making him a moral sceptic and as his scepticism increases he is raised in his own esteem.

Now some of these sentences almost exactly describe Wordsworth's own mental conflicts during the past three years. He, too, had had to question and revise his youthful moral principles; he, too, when he found men unlike what he had supposed, had had to wrestle with feelings which might easily have turned to misanthropy and 'moral scepticism'. And although his unhappiness was partly caused by seeing the betrayal of justice and liberty by those who should have upheld them— his own countrymen and the French Revolutionaries—there was in it an element of personal remorse: he too had been 'betrayed', if not into a 'great crime', at least into an act which brought suffering on someone he loved. Another paragraph perhaps throws some light on what he now felt about Annette:

There is a kind of superstition which makes us shudder, when we find moral sentiments to which we attach a sacred importance applied to vicious purposes. In real life this is done every day, and we do not feel the disgust. The difference is here. In works of imagination we see the motive and the end. In real life we rarely see either the one or the other: and when the distress comes it prevents us from attending to the cause. This superstition . . . appears to be one great source of our vices; it is our constant engine in seducing one another.

We are lulled asleep by its agency, and betrayed before we know that an attempt is made to betray us.[1]

If we compare these sentences with those lines in *Vaudracour and Julia* in which Wordsworth hints that his union with Annette was a deliberately planned and not a merely impulsive act,[2] we come near perhaps to seeing something of what he was thinking by this time about his unhappy love-affair. What had seemed at the time to be dictated by the best motives was now seen to be a 'betrayal'.[3]

But this must be the extent to which the preface to *The Borderers* is autobiographical. Wordsworth had indeed come to the brink of that inferno in which he placed Oswald, but he had drawn back. He had become neither an Iago nor a Macbeth. Rather, he had suffered as he makes Oswald's victim, Marmaduke, suffer. When Marmaduke awakes to the realization of how he has been deceived into causing the death of an innocent person, his remorse takes the form of accusing himself, not of weakness or folly in believing Oswald's lies, but of 'presumption' in judging an innocent man.

> I am the man,
> (Abused, betrayed, but how it matters not)
> Who, casting as I thought a guilty Person
> Upon Heaven's righteous judgment, did become
> An instrument of Fiends.

Rejecting both Christian penitence in a hermitage, and suicide, he condemns himself to perpetual exile:

> a wanderer *must I* go,
> The spectre of that innocent Man, my guide.
> No human ear shall ever hear me speak;

---

[1] Wordsworth's use of the word 'superstition' here is somewhat puzzling. What he appears to mean is: 'There is a superstition or prejudice to the effect that we always shudder instinctively when we are in the presence of hypocritical speech or behaviour. In fact, however, we do nothing of the kind, and hypocrisy in every day life—our own or other people's—is seldom recognised until too late.' I am indebted to Mr. D. V. Erdman for this elucidation of a difficult passage.

[2] See above, p. 185.

[3] In Nov. 1795 Wordsworth received a letter from Annette, one of several others which had not reached him. *E.L.* 50, p. 147. D.W. to J.P., Nov. 30th 1795. This may have helped to strengthen his inquest into cause and effect, and the hidden springs of conduct.

No human dwelling ever give me food
Or sleep, or rest: but over waste and wild
In search of nothing that this earth can give
But expiation, will I wander on—
A man by pain and thought compelled to live,
Yet loathing life—till anger is appeased
In Heaven, and Mercy give me leave to die.

The Borderers, though a tragedy unrelieved by any lighter tones or scenes, is shot through with gleams of poetic feeling and beauty that show how Wordsworth was advancing, as he wrote, towards his true vocation as the poet of nature and man. Nature in *The Borderers* is always a 'benevolent' influence. The sight of a star twinkling through a crevice above his head prevents Marmaduke from murdering Herbert in the dungeon of the castle.[1] The Beggar-woman, who, though succumbing to Oswald's bribes, remains 'benevolent' at heart and repents of her part in the tragedy, speaks in a way that reminds us of the many poems Wordsworth afterwards wrote about poor women —she is helpless and ignorant, but familiar with the ways of wild things, like poor Martha Ray in *The Thorn*.[2] Describing her poverty she says:

I'd rather be
A stone than what I am—But two nights gone
The darkness overtook me—wind and rain
Beat hard upon my head—and yet I saw
A glow-worm, through the covert of the furze,
Shine calmly as if nothing ailed the sky.

And here and there Marmaduke speaks Wordsworth's deepest experiences. Thus, alone in the wood on the edge of the moor, he muses:

Deep, deep and vast, vast beyond human thought,
Yet calm—I could believe that there was here
The only quiet heart on earth. In terror,
Remembered terror, there is peace and rest.

[1] Act II, ll. 989–91.
[2] There is an anticipation of Martha Ray also in Oswald's description of Clifford's deserted mistress:

Upon the self-same spot, in rain or storm
She paces out the hour 'twixt twelve and one—
She paces round and round an Infant's grave,
And in the churchyard sod her feet have worn
A hollow ring: they say it is knee-deep— . . .

And he sees Nature with a poet's eye:

> Hush!—'tis the feeble and earth-loving wind
> That creeps along the bells of the crisp heather . . .
> Here is a tree, ragged, and bent, and bare,
> That turns its goat's beard flakes of pea-green moss
> From the stern breathing of the rough sea-wind.

But the lines of greatest power are put into the mouth of the merciless Oswald. In trying to stiffen Marmaduke's resolution he bids him take refuge in action from doubt and perplexity which only bring suffering:

> Action is transitory—a step, a blow,
> The motion of a muscle—this way or that—
> 'Tis done, and in the after-vacancy
> We wonder at ourselves like men betrayed:
> Suffering is permanent, obscure and dark,
> And shares the nature of infinity.

Wordsworth himself knew something of that sort of suffering.

Oswald's great aim was to make Marmaduke repudiate conscientious scruple, pity, and remorse, and act as circumstances and 'reason' only direct.

> You have obeyed the only law that sense
> Submits to recognise: the immediate law
> From the clear light of circumstances, flashed
> Upon an independent Intellect.

These lines Wordsworth took up afterwards and repeated in *The Prelude*, when describing his own attempts to make 'reason' the rule of all conduct.[1]

The doctrine of ruthless self-interest is not Godwin's—who indeed recognized the necessity of 'benevolence', but based it on intellectual, not emotional, grounds. Ruthlessness was a fashionable theme in contemporary fiction and drama: Wordsworth owes as much to Mrs. Radcliffe and Schiller as he does to Godwin. Indeed *The Romance of the Forest* seems to have been lying beside him as he wrote, for he makes Oswald say:

> Murder! what's in the word!—
>   . . . If a snake
> Crawl from beneath our feet we do not ask
> A license to destroy him—

Prel. XI, ll. 243–44.

Mrs. Radcliffe's Marquis says: 'Self-preservation is the great law of nature: when a reptile hurts us, or an animal of prey threatens us, we think no farther but endeavour to annihilate it.'[1]

But Wordsworth was not simply reproducing contemporary fashions in villainy. He had before his eyes the sinister figures of Robespierre, Marat, and their kind, and the havoc their logic wrought with human happiness. They are the flesh-and-blood models from whom Oswald is drawn, as Wordsworth himself afterwards testified: 'During my long residence in France, when the revolution was rapidly advancing to its extreme of wickedness, I had frequent opportunities of being an eye-witness of this process (i.e. the progressive hardening of the heart), and it was while that knowledge was fresh upon my memory, that the Tragedy of *The Borderers* was written.'[2]

The winter had been a severe one: snow at Christmas made supplies of food difficult to obtain; Joseph Gill complained that he had to eat carrion meat 'of a cow that had died in calving'.[3] Prices were rising too;[4] Wordsworth, writing to Wrangham in February 1797, begged him to frank his letters and adds: 'I have lately been living on air and the essence of carrots, cabbages, turnips and other esculent vegetables, not excluding parsley, the produce of my garden.' Dorothy, writing to Richard in May, said: 'Pray take care of your old cloaths. They will be of great use at Racedown.' In the early spring two visitors came to Racedown; Basil Montagu and Mary Hutchinson. Mary was escorted by her sailor brother Henry, who was on his way to join his ship at Plymouth.[5] Mary stayed at Racedown till the beginning of June. Her company was most valuable to Dorothy, who had had no female companionship except Peggy Marsh's since she came to Racedown. On March 15th Basil Montagu arrived unexpectedly and stayed four days. It was a happy time:

---

[1] *L.* pp. 271–2. For other critical studies of *The Borderers* see Garrod, *Wordsworth*, pp. 86–93; de Selincourt, *Oxford Lectures on Poetry*, 1934; Meyer, *Wordsworth's Formative Years.*

[2] *P.W.* i, p. 342.   [3] *P.P.* Gill's Diary, Jan. 1797.

[4] 'Everything has been very dear for housekeeping this seasons: we can get no meat under 6*d.* and Tea and Sugar, our only luxuries, are rising.' *L.T.* iii. 57a p. 1337. W.W. to R.W., May 1797.

[5] Henry mentions the visit in the highly amusing account in doggerel verse of his own adventures: *The Retrospect of a Retired Mariner in Nine Cantos*, published at Stockton in 1836.

Montagu was very good company; William himself was more serene and cheerful than he had been for years. On the 19th he and Montagu went away together on a visit to Bristol, and Dorothy wrote to Jane:[1] 'You cannot imagine how dull we feel and what a vacuum his loss has occasioned. . . . William is as cheerful as anybody can be; perhaps you may not think it, but he is the life of the whole house.'

After a week in Bristol Wordsworth and Montagu went to Bath, where they saw much of Wordsworth's fellow Cumbrian James Losh of Woodside, near Carlisle, who was at present living in Bath for his health. He had been present at the gathering at Frend's rooms where Wordsworth first met Godwin; he knew Coleridge, Southey, and Cottle; and since August 1796 he had been in correspondence with Wordsworth.[2] His diary, in which he carefully noted all his social engagements and the letters he wrote to his friends, helps us to trace Wordsworth's movements during this and the following year. He was an ardent reformer and promoted while in Bath the cause of Unitarian Sunday schools. Wordsworth was under an obligation to him, for he had sent him, on the day after Wordsworth and Montagu had left Racedown, a parcel of magazines and political pamphlets. It contained the *Monthly Magazine* from March to December 1796; Coleridge's *Conciones ad Populum* in which he protested against the Government's 'gagging Bills'; Burke's *Letters on a Regicide Peace* and *Letter to the Duke of Portland*; Coleridge's *Ode on the Departing Year*, a political poem which had been published in pamphlet form; some sermons against atheism by Estlin, the well-known Bristol Unitarian who was a friend of Coleridge; and Thomas Erskine's *View of the Causes and Consequences of the Present War*.[3] These details are of interest

---

[1] *E.L.* 57, p. 165. Jane Pollard was now married to John Marshall, a mill-owner of Leeds.

[2] Now in the library of Tullie House, Carlisle. On the last page of the volume for the year 1796 he notes the following addresses: 'William Wordsworth, Racedown, Crewkerne, Somerset. ?T. C. Coleridge Adscombe near Stowey, Bridgewater. Robert Southey 8 Westgate Buildings, Bath. Mrs. Newton Cothay near Redcliffe ch(urch). Bristol.' In the autumn of 1796 Coleridge was still doubtful where to settle and was inquiring about a house at Adscombe. Mrs. Newton was Chatterton's sister. For Southey's and Cottle's generous assistance to her against the purloiner of her brother's letters, Herbert Croft, see *Cottle*, i, pp. 256–71.

[3] Erskine was the advocate who had defended Paine, Hardy, and Horne Tooke when they were tried for treason in 1794.

because such a parcel must have been sent at Wordsworth's own request; they show how strong his interest still was in political matters and how far he was from being a recluse at heart.[1]

With Losh, Wordsworth also visited his Cumbrian acquaintance Mrs. Spedding of Armathwaite, who with her two daughters Maria and Margaret, Dorothy's friends, were visiting Bath. And on March 27th he, Montagu, and Losh supped with Mr. and Mrs. John Wedgwood at Cote House, on the Downs outside Bristol.[2]

On his way back to Racedown—Montagu having returned to London—Wordsworth visited Coleridge at Nether Stowey, where he had been living since the end of December, in the dark little cottage that Thomas Poole had found for him. Coleridge was suffering from 'a depression too dreadful to be described', partly owing to the illness and departure of his queer young lodger, Charles Lloyd, and was in need of companionship. 'Wordsworth's conversation etc. roused me somewhat', he told Cottle. They talked of Southey's poems, which had just been published; neither of them could feel much enthusiasm. 'Wordsworth complains, with justice,' wrote Coleridge, 'that Southey writes *too much at his ease*—that he seldom 'feels his burthened breast

Heaving beneath th'incumbent Deity'.[3]

Indirectly here Wordsworth reveals something of the burden he himself felt when he was engaged in writing poetry.

They also discussed the writing and acting of tragedies. Sheridan had asked Coleridge to write a tragedy for production at Drury Lane, and Coleridge was already sketching out *Osorio*.[4] Wordsworth must have described *The Borderers* to him and probably now determined, with Coleridge's encouragement, to try after all to make it fit for presentation on the stage. By the end of May he had altered and shortened it for this purpose, for Dorothy wrote at that time: 'W. has nearly finished

---

[1] In April Losh noted that he sent another 'large parcel of pamphlets' to Racedown.

[2] John Wedgwood, the elder brother of Coleridge's benefactors Josiah and Tom, came to Bristol in 1797 and seems to have bought Cote House about midsummer. He may, however, have been already living in it as tenant for a few months before that.   [3] *U.L.* i, p. 71. S.T.C. to Cottle, n.d.

[4] *U.L.* i, p. 72. S.T.C. to Josiah Wade, Mar. 16th 1797.

a tragedy which he has good hopes of getting shown to Sheridan.' He had certainly had no thoughts of writing it for the stage when he began it in the previous autumn. The conclusion of this enterprise did not, however, take place until the following November.

The spring months following Wordsworth's return to Racedown—April and May 1797—were months of great and happy poetic activity. The 'winter of his discontent' had given way at last, and with his new cheerfulness and zest for life came also once more the 'creative breeze'. Dorothy, writing of the countryside in May, said: 'It has burst into beauty all at once, after the coldest spring I ever remember.' She might have written thus of her brother, whose May of life had begun at last.[1]

The Borderers was a sort of purgation. The poetry of this spring, though its theme is still the suffering and unhappiness of human kind, breathes a new spirit. It is 'the still, *sad* music of humanity' that he now bids us hear; its patience and dignity in misfortune, rather than its despair, at which he bids us look. In some respects, he is returning to the spirit in which he had written the story of the woman in *Salisbury Plain*. Suffering should be met in 'lowliness of heart', not in pride and resentment; and nothing should be allowed to stand between the sufferer and the compassion of his neighbours. The poems of this new spirit are *Lines left upon a Seat in a Yew-tree*, *The Ruined Cottage*, and *The Old Cumberland Beggar*. The two last concern poor and obscure people; the *Yew-tree Seat* deals with the problem of the disappointed intellectual. The origins of these poems, as well as their contents, are closely interwoven with scenes and events in Wordsworth's own life, some of them belonging to his boyhood, others to more recent days.

The *Yew-tree Seat* was apparently begun many years before at Hawkshead, though the work then cannot have progressed beyond the first seven lines, for the rest is obviously of later date.[2] Yet those seven lines contain one that has become famous:

---

[1] Sometime between March and June, however, they were all unwell. 'Poor Basil', wrote Dorothy, 'was very, very ill. I was afraid we should have lost him.' *E.L.* 58, p. 167, D.W. to R.W., May 28th 1797.

[2] Its full title is *Lines left upon a Seat in a Yew-tree, which stands near the lake of Esthwaite, on a desolate part of the Shore, commanding a beautiful Prospect.* It was completed before July 1797, when Coleridge read it to Lamb, and published in

> the curling waves
> That break against the shore, shall lull thy mind
> By one soft impulse saved from vacancy.

The poem then describes a gentleman of the country-side who, having gone forth into the world 'a favoured Being', became disgusted with the world's supposed neglect of his talents, and returned to Esthwaite's shores to become a sort of solitary. He is in fact a harmless edition of Oswald. In real life he was, Wordsworth tells us, the same man who built the 'Station' or gazebo on the top of Claife Height above the ferry on Windermere. This was a Rev. Mr. Braithwaite of Satterhow, who died in 1800. Shortly before his death he acquired some of the unenclosed land on the eastern shore of Esthwaite so that Wordsworth's favourite evening walk from Colthouse thereafter lost 'much of its charm'.[1] In the completed poem, he uses the phrase 'the holy forms of young imagination'—a use of the word 'imagination' which shows what significance it already had for him. The poem ends with an admonition which may be contrasted with the despairing end of *The Borderers*.

> True dignity abides with him alone
> Who in the silent hour of inward thought,
> Can still suspect and still revere himself
> In lowliness of heart.

The blank verse too has a purity, a serenity, about it which is wholly new. There are glimpses of the landscape that only Wordsworth could have given us—

> His only visitants a straggling sheep,
> The stone-chat or the glancing sandpiper.[2]

How far this misanthropic character resembled the flesh-and-blood Mr. Braithwaite we do not know. But Wordsworth has woven into it strands from his own experience, as he was soon to do with the 'Pedlar' of *The Ruined Cottage*:

> And, lifting up his head, he then would gaze
> On the more distant scene,—how lovely 'tis

Lyrical Ballads in 1798. There is no trace of any early version of it in any of the note-books used by Wordsworth while at school or at Cambridge.
    [1] *P.W.* i, p. 329. The yew-tree was apparently cut down about 1820 for fear of its poisoning cattle.
    [2] That 'line all alive' as Lamb called it, and he successfully begged Wordsworth to restore it after he had altered it for the edition of 1815.

> Thou seest,—and he would gaze till it became
> Far lovelier and his heart could not sustain
> The beauty, still more beauteous!

This is Wordsworth himself bestowing 'on the setting sun new splendour' and generally 'modifying' the landscape by the power of his own imagination.

The Old Cumberland Beggar—perhaps begun earlier than any of the other poems, for part of it is on a sheet of paper with the watermark 1795[1]—has likewise for its setting the scenery and customs of his boyhood. The country-side is that of Cockermouth; the beggar one of the fraternity of Edie Ochiltree[2] who 'confined themselves to a stated round in their neighbourhood' and were sure of alms at various houses. Wordsworth tells us that this old man was 'observed, and with great benefit to my own heart, when I was a child'. The reason for making him the subject of a poem was the 'war upon mendicancy in all its forms', now being carried on by the 'political economists'. All his life Wordsworth entertained strong views on the poor laws, as framed by 'utilitarian' legislators. In particular, he hated the workhouse as a cure for unemployment. To herd poor people together, especially old people, in such places was both an insult to their liberty and to the charity and kindness which they had a natural right to expect from their neighbours. Parish workhouses had increased during the century as a result of the act of 1722 authorizing their erection by the overseers of the poor; they were in many cases not 'work'-houses at all, but comfortless and unhealthy asylums for the aged, the sick, and for orphan children. Crabbe's famous description in *The Village* was no doubt in Wordsworth's mind when he pleads for his beggar:

> May never *House*, misnamed of *Industry*,
> Make him a captive!—for that pent-up din,
> Those life-consuming sounds that clog the air,
> Be his the natural silence of old age![3]

The poem is, as Lamb found it, 'too like a lecture';[4] the old man is treated too much as an 'exhibit'; yet, before Wordsworth

---

[1] Wordsworth says that it was begun at Racedown and completed at Alfoxden. *P.W.* iv, p. 445.   [2] In Scott's *Antiquary*.

[3] 'I could now convict some overseers of murder', wrote Hannah More of her visits to parish workhouses in Somerset in 1795. Chatterton, *Memoirs of Admiral Gambier*, i, p. 291.

[4] *Lamb*, i, p. 178. Lamb to W.W., Jan. 30th 1801.

begins moralizing about him, there is, in the descriptive part
of the poem an intimacy of observation, a tenderness, which was
new in poetry—or at any rate had its only counterpart in
Shakespeare—

> In the sun . . .
> Surrounded by those wild, unpeopled hills,
> He sat, and ate his food in solitude:
> And ever, scattered from his palsied hand,
> That, still attempting to prevent the waste,
> Was baffled still, the crumbs, in little showers
> Fell on the ground; and the small mountain birds,
> Not venturing yet to peck their destined meal,
> Approached within the length of half his staff.

But by far the most important poem completed during this
eventful spring was that which he called *The Ruined Cottage*,
and which after many alterations and additions became the first
book of *The Excursion*. It took its origins from those lines of
blank verse called *Incipient Madness* written probably very early
in the Racedown time.[1] These, besides describing Wordsworth
entering a ruined and deserted cottage on a moorland by moonlight, describe also the various seasonal visitants to the cottage
—glow-worms, birds, and the 'poor man's horse'; finally, an
incident, which may well be actual, of the baker's cart driving
past the cottage where a woman lives who is too poor to buy
bread.[2] A few lines of it were incorporated into *The Ruined
Cottage*; many others are of great personal interest. Thus,
when even the birds had deserted the place:

> I alone
> Remained: the winds of heaven remained: with them
> My heart claimed fellowship and with the beams
> Of dawn and of the setting sun that seemed
> To live and linger on the mouldering walls.

This, one feels, is Wordsworth as he was when he first came
to Racedown, absorbed in suffering; conscious of his isolation;
finding companionship only in the impersonal powers of nature.
But when he wrote *The Ruined Cottage* he had emerged from

---

[1] See above, p. 286.

[2] We know that a baker's cart came to Racedown, for Gill notes in his Diary
on June 20th 1796: 'Got the Perambulator packed up for the Bakers Man at Clapton
to take away in his Cart whether he will do it or not is a matter of doubt.' See
above, p. 298, n. 1.

this state of depression and could look objectively at the things of which he desired to treat. This objectivity he secured in the poem by the device of introducing a narrator other than himself to tell the story of Margaret. This was 'the Pedlar'—a kindly, gentle, detached observer, and a lover of the country-side through which he trod his endless rounds. The Pedlar became more and more the centre of Wordsworth's interest as the poem grew; next year when he resumed it he made him the recipient of his own youthful experiences of communion with Nature, so that whole sections of *The Ruined Cottage* are found at length incorporated in *The Prelude*. Eventually 'the Pedlar' became 'the Wanderer' of *The Excursion*.

The Ruined Cottage is a story of poverty, sorrow, and death; Margaret is very like 'the Female Vagrant' of *Salisbury Plain* except that she stays in her cottage instead of wandering about the world. War and unemployment are again the background of Margaret's personal tragedy. But it is told without bitterness or exaggeration; Margaret does not resent her sufferings, nor does the Pedlar resent them for her: we feel that Wordsworth also has ceased to resent them. Pity and sympathy are the emotions which Wordsworth wants to evoke; and the whole story is made lovely and vivid by the wealth of detail about the cottage, and its gradual decline from cheerful prosperity to complete ruin. The figure of Margaret is beautifully harmonious with her surroundings: in a fragment not incorporated in the final text he shows their essential unity:

> Her person and her face
> Were homely such as none who pass her by
> Would have remembered. Yet when she was seen
> In her own dwelling-place a grace was hers
> And Beauty, which beginning from without
> Fell both on her with sanctifying power.

We are reminded of the lines in *Three Years She grew*:

> grace that shall mould the Maiden's form
> In silent sympathy.

There are no horrifying incidents such as abound in the second version of *Salisbury Plain*. Wordsworth had learnt that such things arouse 'morbid' rather than benevolent passions in the reader, and he was convinced that poetry should aim at calling out and strengthening what he called 'the affections'—all the gentler, wiser, and kinder feelings of humanity. As he had said in the *Yew-tree Seat*, 'true knowledge leads to Love', and the knowledge revealed in *The Ruined Cottage* of human sorrow and the sufferings of the poor kindles our sympathy and respect rather than our indignation. Margaret, like the Old Cumberland Beggar, and like many of Wordsworth's characters in the years to come, makes her appeal and achieves her victory by her meek endurance, without hatred or any thought of revenge for her undeserved wrongs.

Long afterwards Wordsworth said that Margaret illustrated 'the character possessed in common by many women whom it has been my happiness to know in humble life'; he insisted, moreover, that 'several of the most touching things which she is represented as saying and doing are taken from actual observation of the distresses and trials under which different persons were suffering, some of them strangers to me and others daily under my notice'.[1] As we read of Margaret, we feel that Wordsworth has already moved a long way from the frame of mind in which he looked at the poor when he first came to Racedown, when he saw them as victims of 'ignorance' rather than as suffering individuals; while the indignation with which, in Beaupuy's company, he had watched the 'hunger-bitten girl' near Blois has likewise given way to a gentler feeling. Wordsworth was indeed fast ceasing to be a social reformer and was becoming the poet of the human heart.

The Ruined Cottage was written in fragmentary fashion and put together from a number of detached passages. Mary Hutchinson, who was at Racedown all the spring, took away with her a copy of the last forty-five lines which, Wordsworth said in after years, were in fact the first to be written of the whole poem.[2] This statement throws an interesting light on his methods of composition; he must have composed the story, or at least an outline of it, in his head first, and then written it down, not consecutively but in separate pieces, as his imagination prompted.

---

[1] *P.W.* v, p. 376, note to *The Excursion*.
[2] Ibid., p. 373, note to *The Excursion*, I. Here he says that they were written in "95 at Racedown'. They may indeed be earlier than this spring of '97—they correspond closely with ll. 871–916 of *The Excursion*, I.

Mary, with Dorothy, had shared in all the excitement of this creative spring, and taken her part in copying poems. It was she who made a copy of the first two cantos of a long ballad poem called *The Three Graves*, which was afterwards continued by Coleridge. She slipped easily and naturally into her place beside the brother and sister—the place which after a few more years she would occupy as William's wife. It is scarcely possible not to feel that William's happiness at this time was in part due to her presence, and that she helped to make him 'the life of the whole house'. She left Racedown on June 5th[1] and the very day after her departure another visitor appeared. Coleridge, unable any longer to do without the company of one whom he already regarded as 'the best poet of the age', arrived on foot from Taunton, where he had breakfasted with the Unitarian minister, Mr. Toulmin.[2] William and Dorothy were on the look-out for him. 'We both', said Wordsworth more than forty years afterwards, 'have a distinct remembrance of his arrival. He did not keep to the high road, but leaped over a gate and bounded down a pathless field by which he cut off an angle.'[3] The gate and the field over which he 'bounded' still invite the pilgrim to Racedown to cut off the angle of the road. There, in the high bloom of summer, with the scent of hay filling the air, the three met who in the years to come were together to create and share, to suffer and to love so much.

The immediate business which brought them together was poetry, and they at once set to work reading aloud each other's work. 'The first thing that was read after he came was William's new poem *The Ruined Cottage* with which he was much delighted; and after tea he repeated to us two and a half acts of his tragedy *Osorio*. The next morning William read his tragedy *The Borderers.*' So wrote Dorothy to Mary, adding also that description of Coleridge which still brings him before us as he first appeared to her in all the ardour of his friendship and happiness. 'His conversation teems with soul, mind and spirit. Then he is so benevolent, so good tempered and cheerful, and, like William, interests himself so much about every little trifle. His eye . . . speaks every emotion of his animated mind.'

[1] *E.L.* 59, p. 167. W.W. and D.W. to R.W., June 5th 1797.
[2] Philobiblon Society, *Miscellanies*, xv, p. 38. S.T.C. to Estlin.
[3] *L.T.* 1584. M.W. to Sara Coleridge, Nov. 7th 1845.

Their delight and satisfaction in each other's company was complete. To William and Dorothy, Coleridge was 'a wonderful man'.[1] To Coleridge, Wordsworth was 'a great man',[2] beside whom he felt himself to be 'a little man'—though without detracting from his estimate of himself. At Racedown he went on working at *Osorio,* with the intention of walking on from there to Shaftesbury, to show it to William Lisle Bowles, for whose sonnets he had had for many years such an ardent love. Such, however, was his happiness with the Wordsworths that he found it impossible to do without their company, and after three weeks at Racedown he persuaded them to return with him to the cottage at Nether Stowey. The visit to Bowles did not take place until September.[3] Although they did not know it, the Wordsworths when they went away with Coleridge were leaving Racedown for ever. Henceforward their destiny was linked inextricably with his. But Racedown always remained in Dorothy's memory with a special sentiment of affection. 'Racedown was the first home I had', she said a few years later, 'I think it is the place dearest to my recollections upon the whole surface of the island.'[4] It was natural that it should be so. For there she had watched and fostered her brother's slow recovery; had 'preserved him still a poet', by turning his eyes back to the things that had given him his primitive and most profound delight; and when his genius began to ripen she had been always at hand as his secretary and copyist. The quality of her ministry is extraordinarily subtle and unassuming; she never discussed her brother's state of mind in her letters; except for that one glad outburst, 'William is the life of the whole house', she gives nowhere any indication of his progress. This was perhaps because her concern for him was so absorbing and so tender a thing for her that to speak of it was impossible. She had her reward, for not only did William record his debt to her in *The Prelude,* but two lyrics commemorate in intimate fashion what 'his Love'

---

[1] *E.L.* 61, p. 168. D.W. to unknown correspondent (probably M.H.), June 1797. Cf. W.W.'s testimony in later life: 'Coleridge was the only wonderful man I ever knew.'

[2] *U.L.* i, p. 76. S.T.C. to Estlin, June 1797. At the end of this letter is a copy of the last thirty-seven lines of *The Ruined Cottage* which, says Coleridge, 'I have procured Miss Wordsworth to transcribe'.

[3] *E.L.* 66, p. 172. W.W. to Joseph Cottle, Sept. 13th 1797.

[4] The rest of this letter is lost. It is quoted in *Mem.* i, p. 94, and was probably written to Mary Hutchinson.

meant to him in these days. One is the poem in the 'Lucy' cycle, written in Germany in 1799,[1] in which he imagines, as he rides towards the house in the moonlight, that 'Lucy' is dead. The imagery of the uphill ride, and the approach to the house from the east as the moon sets, is true to Racedown. The whole poem, indeed, reads like a personal memory of a dear event.

> Upon the moon I fixed my eye,
> All over the wide lea;
> With quickening pace my horse drew nigh
> Those paths so dear to me.
>
> And now we reached the orchard-plot;
> And as we climbed the hill,
> The sinking moon to Lucy's cot
> Came near, and nearer still.
>
> In one of those sweet dreams I slept,
> Kind Nature's gentlest boon!
> And all the while my eyes I kept
> On the descending moon.
>
> My horse moved on: hoof after hoof
> He raised, and never stopped:
> When down behind the cottage roof,
> At once the bright moon dropped.
>
> What fond and wayward thoughts will slide
> Into a Lover's head!
> 'O mercy!' to myself I cried,
> 'If Lucy should be dead!'
>
> I told her this: her laughter light
> Is ringing in my ears:
> And when I think upon that night
> My eyes are dim with tears.

The other poem is *The Glow-worm*. It was written in the spring of 1802, when William was riding back to Dorothy after a visit to Mary Hutchinson, with whom he had just completed the arrangements for their wedding. His first and immediate thought even in that hour was for Dorothy, and he speaks as if

---

[1] *Strange Fits of Passion I have Known*, P.W. ii, p. 29.

to reassure her that the communion between them could never be changed. Writing to Coleridge and enclosing the poem, he said: 'The incident of this poem took place about seven years ago between Dorothy and me.'[1]

> Among all lovely things my Love hath been;
> Had noted well the stars, all flowers that grew
> About her home; but she had never seen
> A Glow-worm, never one, and this I knew.
>
> While riding near her home one stormy night
> A single Glow-worm did I chance to espy:
> I gave a fervent welcome to the sight,
> And from my Horse I leapt: great joy had I.
>
> Upon a leaf the Glow-worm did I lay,
> To bear it with me through the stormy night:
> And as before it shone without dismay;
> Albeit putting forth a fainter light.
>
> When to the Dwelling of my Love I came,
> I went into the Orchard quietly;
> And left the Glow-worm, blessing it by name,
> Laid safely by itself, beneath a Tree.
>
> The whole next day I hoped, and hoped with fear;
> At night the Glow-worm shone beneath the Tree;
> I led my Lucy to the spot, 'Look here!'
> Oh! joy it was for her, and joy for me![2]

[1] E. de Selincourt, *Dorothy Wordsworth*, p. 137. *P.W.* ii, p. 466, and W.'s note, p. 532.

[2] This and the previous poem both mention him riding a horse. A tradition existed at Racedown about fifty years ago that he had once ridden over to Lyme, forgot while there that he had a horse, and walked back! It is possibly to this incident that Aza Pinney refers in a letter of Mar. 1796: 'I am sorry for the Fate of poor Rosinante.' *P.P.*

X

ALFOXDEN, 1797–8

There did they dwell—from earthly labour free.
As happy spirits as were ever seen:
If but a bird, to keep them company,
Or butterfly sate down, they were, I ween,
As pleased as if the same had been a Maiden-queen.

WORDSWORTH, 'Stanzas written in Thomson's
"Castle of Indolence"', 1802

NETHER STOWEY, whither Coleridge drove Dorothy from
Racedown 'over forty miles of execrable road' one midsummer-
day in 1797,[1] is a long village, or perhaps more accurately a very
small country town lying along the road about five miles
westward of Bridgwater. Its houses and cottages are built out
of the brown local sandstone, and Coleridge's cottage stood at
the extreme western end of the village. In the road in front of
it ran a canalized brook—Coleridge's 'dear gutter of Stowey';
it may have reminded Wordsworth of his 'child of mountain
birth' in the garden at Colthouse. Behind the house, away from
the road, lay the large garden and orchard in which Coleridge
meant to perform so many agricultural wonders; it adjoined
that of his friend and devoted admirer, Thomas Poole, whose
house gave on to the main street of the town. A door had been
cut by Poole in the wall between, so that Coleridge could pass
at any time into his friend's garden and 'book-room' without
going round by the street.

Thomas Poole was a bachelor; with him lived his aged
mother, his enthusiastic secretary Thomas Ward, and a French
émigré abbé, Barbey by name, who earned a living in the neighbourhood by teaching French. Poole was a radical and a strong
opponent of the war, but his humanity and generosity were the

---

[1] The actual day of their arrival at Stowey is nowhere stated, but it was probably Sunday, July 2nd. Coleridge said on June 29th: 'I returned from Wordsworth's last night' (*U.L.* i, p. 78), but he had probably come back in order to
borrow Poole's 'one-horse shay' in which he fetched Dorothy. We know that the
Wordsworths stayed a fortnight at Stowey (*E.L.* 64, p. 170), and that they did not
move to Alfoxden before July 14th, the probable date being Sunday, July 16th.
See H. M. Margoliouth, *Wordsworth and Coleridge, 1795–1834*, p. 16.

greatest things about him; his practical help to Coleridge alone would make him notable, but he was the friend, counsellor, and assistant of all the neighbourhood. His tan-yard—the chief source of his wealth—stood close by the house. He was also a farmer, farming his own land. Not far away, at Over Stowey, lived his cousins, the John Pooles, whose political opinions were exactly contrary: Charlotte, their daughter, who kept a journal, must, one feeels, have kept her face in a continual pout of disdain at what she termed his 'democratick sentiments'. Wordsworth, recollecting years afterwards the impression this good man made on him, said:

I had frequent occasion to admire the course of his daily life, and especially his conduct to his labourers and poorer neighbours. Their wishes he carefully encouraged, and weighed their faults in the scales of charity. . . . After his death was found in his escritoire a lock of grey hair carefully preserved, with a notice that it had been cut from the head of his faithful Shepherd, who had served him for a length of years. I need scarcely add that he felt for all men as his brothers.[1]

Wordsworth and Dorothy spent a fortnight in the Stowey cottage with Coleridge, Sara, and the baby Hartley. This was the brief period of Coleridge's married happiness.[2] Sara, pretty, simple, and totally uncomprehending of the brilliant husband who had so unwisely allowed himself to think that he loved her, was struggling not in vain to make a pleasant home out of the 'miserable cottage' with its damp walls, dark rooms, and innumerable mice which Coleridge felt it would be unchivalrous to combat with traps. The cottage, which had but three bedrooms, must have been filled to capacity by the arrival of the Wordsworths, but a week later yet another visitor came. Charles Lamb—Coleridge's 'gentle-hearted Charles'—had obtained his week's holiday from the East India Company's office and came down on the outside of the mail coach. Shy, sensitive, diffident, he had scarcely recovered from the horror of his mother's death the previous year;[3] but in the glowing kindness

---

[1] *P.W.* iv, p. 447.

[2] Reynell, a young man who visited Coleridge this summer, says of the Coleridge household: 'I have seen domestic life in all its beauty and simplicity: affection founded on a much stronger basis than wealth—on esteem.' *Illustrated London News,* Apr. 22nd 1893.

[3] Mrs. Lamb was murdered by her daughter Mary in a fit of lunacy on Sept. 22nd 1796.

and enthusiasm of the Stowey household he felt a new impulse to life and hope. 'I could not talk much while I was with you', he wrote afterwards, 'but my silence was not sullenness, nor I hope from any bad motive, but in truth disuse has made me awkward at it. . . . It was kind in you all to endure me as you did.'[1]

Their talk ran chiefly on poetry. In the second edition of Coleridge's poems, which had just appeared, Lamb and Charles Lloyd, the banker's son from Birmingham who had been Coleridge's lodger in the first months at Stowey, had published some verses along with his. Now Lamb made Wordsworth's acquaintance, and that of his poems. He took a great fancy to the *Lines left upon a Seat in a Yew-tree*, which Wordsworth had probably just completed, and asked for a copy of it. 'I feel improvement', he wrote afterwards to Coleridge, 'in the recollection of many a casual conversation. The names of Tom Poole, Wordsworth and his good sister, with thine and Sara's, are become "familiar in my mouth as household words". You would make me very happy, if you think W. has no objection, by transcribing for me that inscription of his. I have some scattered sentences ever floating on my memory, teasing me that I cannot remember more of it.' And again, later on in the same letter, 'But above all, *that Inscription*!—it will recall to me the tones of all your voices—and with them many a remembered kindness to one who could and can repay you all only by the silence of a grateful heart.'[2]

The 'Inscription' seems to have impressed Coleridge too. To its teaching—that the true approach to criticism is by 'lowliness of heart'—is sometimes attributed Coleridge's confession to Southey in this very month: 'I am as much a Pangloss as ever, only less contemptuous than I used to be, when I argue how unwise it is to feel contempt for anything.'[3] But Dorothy also had contributed to this softening of Coleridge's critical temper. He had lately been writing reviews for the *Critical Review*; many years later he related how he had written

---

[1] *Lamb*, i, p. 112.   [2] Ibid.
[3] *S.T.C.* i, p. 224. S.T.C. to Southey, July 1797. The reference is to Dr. Pangloss in Voltaire's *Candide*. Cf. his letter to Thelwall in Dec. 1796, *S.T.C.* i, p. 198: 'Contempt must be always evil, and a good man ought to speak *contemptuously* of nothing.' By 1798 he was trying not only not to speak, but not to feel, contemptuously.

'some half a score or more of what I thought clever and epi-
grammatic and devilishly severe reviews . . . but a Remark made
by Miss Wordsworth to whom I had, in full expectation of
gaining a laugh of applause, read one of my judgments occasioned my committing the whole batch to the Fire'.[1] Charlotte
Poole's opinion, that Coleridge was 'clever, and a very short
acquaintance will unfold that he is extremely vain of it', was true
enough of him at this time. But Dorothy's charity and sense of
justice were as irresistible as her 'simple, ardent, impressive
manners'. The whole incident throws a vivid light on their talk
and doings in this fortnight's visit to Stowey.

Having brought the Wordsworths to Stowey, Coleridge
became very anxious to keep them near him. His triumphant
exclamation to Southey, in July, that 'I brought him and his
sister back with me and here I have *settled them*', is, however,
claiming for himself credit which really belongs to Thomas
Poole. He it was who negotiated for them the renting of
Alfoxden House, on the northern edge of the Quantocks about
four miles from Stowey; he it was who, in view of Wordsworth's precarious financial position, made himself security for
the rent. The circumstances were as follows.

Alfoxden House was standing empty and fully furnished at the
time of the Wordsworths' visit to Stowey. It belonged to a
family of the name of St. Albyn, who had possessed it since the
fifteenth century; its owner since 1781 had been the Rev. Lance-
lot St. Albyn, who was also incumbent of the family living of
Stringston. He had, however, recently died, leaving his widow
guardian of his son, a minor; they lived elsewhere; the estate
was let to a Mr. John Bartholomew who lived at Putsham, and
the agreement for letting Alfoxden House to the Wordsworths
was made between Wordsworth and Mr. Bartholomew with
Thomas Poole as witness.[2] It was Poole who, at Wordsworth's
request, when it was known that Alfoxden might be to let
introduced him to Mr. Bartholomew and who 'strongly recommended Mr. Wordsworth as a tenant'. Dorothy and William
had already, in a 'wander' by themselves during their first week

---

[1] *U.L.* ii, p. 407. S.T.C. to J. G. Lockhart, 1828. See also A. A. Watts, *Life of
Alaric Watts*, p. 247, where a similar incident is recorded as taking place while
Coleridge was 'in the Lake country'. But Coleridge wrote no reviews in his Keswick
days and the incident must belong to the Alfoxden period.

[2] *T.P.* i, pp. 225–6.

at Stowey, 'found out a sequestered waterfall in a dell formed
by steep hills covered with full-grown timber trees'. This was
the waterfall in Alfoxden Park. They had seen the house also,
'but without any more fixed thoughts upon it than some dreams
of happiness in a little cottage' (their old day-dream) 'and
passing wishes that such a place might be found'.[1] Then came
Lamb's visit, and Coleridge, obliged to stay at home in the
arbour in Thomas Poole's garden with a sore foot because 'dear
Sara had upset a skillet of boiling milk' upon it, wrote the
delightful lines, *This Lime-Tree Bower my Prison*, while the
Wordsworths took Lamb for a walk over the hills, and showed
him the Alfoxden 'dell'.

> Well, they are gone, and here must I remain,
> Lam'd by the scathe of fire, lonely and faint,
> This lime-tree bower my prison! They meantime
> My Friends, whom I may never meet again,[2]
> On springy heath, along the hill-top edge
> Wander delighted, and look down, perchance,
> On that same rifted Dell, where many an ash
> Twists its wild limbs beside the ferny rock
> Whose plumy ferns forever nod and drip,
> Spray'd by the waterfall.[3]

The rent for Alfoxden was to be £23 a year, rate and tax-
free. The agreement was signed on July 14th and the Wordsworths moved in immediately without returning to Racedown.
For a month they lived there with an old woman as a daily
servant; then in August William went back to Racedown to
fetch Basil and the faithful Peggy, and collect clothes and
books.[4]

Their new home was larger than Racedown; a charming
middle-sized country house about a hundred years old, 'with
furniture for a dozen families like ours', Dorothy said. Her

[1] *E.L.* 63 and 64, p. 170. D.W. to Mary Hutchinson, July 4th and Aug. 14th
1797.

[2] Because at this time their future was unsettled and Alfoxden as a residence had
not been thought of.

[3] The 'plumy ferns' are the Hart's Tongue, which still grow in magnificent
profusion all over the 'dell'.

[4] We know this detail only from the letter of Walsh, the 'Spy', of Aug. 16th
1797. See H. Eaglestone, 'Wordsworth, Coleridge and the Spy', in *Coleridge.
Studies by Several Hands*, 1934.

description, given in a letter to Mary Hutchinson in August, is
as true of it now as it was then:

In front is a little court, with grass plot, gravel walk, and shrubs;
the moss roses were in full beauty a month ago. The front of the
house is to the south, but it is screened from the sun by a high
hill which rises immediately from it. This hill is beautiful, scattered
irregularly and abundantly with trees, and topped with fern, which
spreads a considerable way down it. The deer dwell here, and sheep,
so that we have a living prospect. . . .[1] Exactly opposite the window
where I now sit is an immense wood whose round top from this point
has exactly the appearance of a mighty dome. In some parts of this
wood there is an undergrove of hollies which are now very beautiful.
In a glen at the bottom of the wood is the waterfall of which I spoke,
a quarter of a mile from the house. . . . Wherever we turn we have
woods, smooth downs and valleys with small brooks running down them
through green meadows, hardly ever intersected with hedgerows, but
scattered over with trees. The hills that cradle these valleys are either
covered with fern and bilberries or oak woods which are cut for charcoal.

Close by the house also stood a 'tall larch' which figures in
several of the poems written at Alfoxden, and also a gigantic
beech, which 'threw out arms which struck into the soil . . . and
rose again from it' so that they looked like enormous serpents.
When Wordsworth revisited Alfoxden forty-four years later,
the larch was still standing but the beech had disappeared.[2]

'Our principal inducement in coming here', as Dorothy
remarked, 'was Coleridge's society.' Just as Racedown must
always be precious as the first home of William and Dorothy
Wordsworth, so Alfoxden cannot be thought of apart from the
three for whom for one wonderful year it and its lovely surroundings became the home and playground; the centre of poetic
creation and scene of every dear personal tie. Coleridge spent
almost as much time at Alfoxden as at Stowey; he went there,
apparently, with the Wordsworths, when they moved in, 'for
change of air',[3] and indeed the spaciousness of Alfoxden must

---

[1] In her _Recollections of a Tour made in Scotland_, in 1803, Dorothy wrote o
Ferniehurst: 'It made me think of our walks at Alfoxden, and of _our own_ park . .
and the slim fawns that we used to startle from their couching-places among th
fern at the top of the hill.' _D.W.J._ i, p. 403.

[2] _P.W._ iv, p. 412. Note to _To my Sister_.

[3] _S.T.C._ i, p. 227. S.T.C. to Southey, July 1797. In this letter Coleridge say
that Wordsworth 'has commissioned me to offer you a suite of rooms in this place
which is called "Allfoxen" . . . and is very solicitous to know you'.

have been welcome after the darkness and stuffiness of the Stowey cottage. Sara Coleridge also was one of the party, for in spite of their poverty the Coleridges had a maid, 'Nanny', who could be left in charge of little Hartley. On the 17th July John Thelwall, the 'agitator' with whom Coleridge had been in correspondence for about a year, arrived on foot at Stowey, having walked from London.[1] He found Sara alone there, just returned from Alfoxden 'to superintend the wash-tub'. The next day he wrote his description of the household at Alfoxden, in a letter to his wife written from there.

'I slept at Coleridge's cot, and this morning we [that is himself and Sara] rose by times and came here time enough to call Samuel and his friend Wordsworth up to breakfast. Faith, we are a most philosophical party . . . the enthusiastic group consisting of C. and his Sara, W. and his sister, and myself, without any servant, male or female. An old woman, who lives in an adjoining cottage, does what is requisite for our simple wants.'[2] Three days later they all walked back to Stowey. Thelwall in his diary[3] noted the heads of their conversation. It ran on 'the moral character of Democrats, of Aristocrats.' Here Wordsworth could have supplied information from his memories of France, and Coleridge, in the full flow of his reaction from Godwinism, perhaps voiced his opinion that, with a few exceptions (Thelwall was one of them) 'the *Patriots* are ragged cattle—a most execrable herd—arrogant because they are ignorant, and boastful of the strength of reason, because they have never tried it enough to know its *weakness*'.[4] They spoke also of the 'pursuits proper to literary men—unfit for management of pecuniary affairs—Rousseau, Bacon, Arthur Young!'[5]

It can be seen from these brief records that mere railing at the Government and the war was not the subject of their political discussions. It was not that either Coleridge or Wordsworth was growing indifferent to political events. Rather, their

---

[1] *Monthly Magazine*, Aug. 1799, and following numbers, give extracts from a sort of journal entitled *A Pedestrian Excursion through Several Parts of England and Wales during the Summer of* 1797. Though anonymous it is certainly by Thelwall, but unfortunately after the first few days no more extracts are given.

[2] *T.P.* i, p. 233.

[3] Now lost. Extracts from it are given by Dykes Campbell, *Samuel Taylor Coleridge*, p. 73.

[4] *U.L.* i. 46, p. 81. S.T.C. to Josiah Wade, Aug. 1st 1797.

[5] J. Dykes Campbell, *Samuel Taylor Coleridge*, p. 73.

seen examining the Brook quite down to the Sea'. Among other suspicious circumstances about them was their habit of 'washing and mending their cloaths all Sunday', and their being 'frequently out upon the heights most part of the Night'.

The rumour therefore had got about that the Wordsworths were, not English Jacobins, but French spies. A combination of north-country accent and dark colouring—one remembers De Quincey's description of Dorothy's 'pronounced gipsy tan'—perhaps helped to float this legend, or it may have been Dorothy's breach of Sunday decorum. The details of their activities—the nocturnal walks, the note-books, and even the inquiries about the course of the brook—are all accurate enough, as Coleridge's own account of the affair testifies. For Coleridge was planning a long poem on a subject which should 'give equal freedom for description, incident and impassioned reflections on men, nature and society, yet supply in itself a natural connection to the parts and unity to the whole'. He thought he had found such a subject in a stream

traced from its source in the hills among the yellow-red moss and conical glass-shaped tufts of bent, to the first break or fall, where its drops become audible and it begins to form a channel; thence to the peat or turf barn, itself built of the same dark squares as it sheltered; to the sheepfold; to the first cultivated plot of ground; to the lonely cottage and its bleak garden won from the heaths, to the hamlet, the villages, the market town, the manufactories and the seaport. My walks therefore were almost daily on the top of Quantock, and among its sloping combes. With my pencil and memorandum-book in my hand I was *making studies*, as the artists call them, and often moulding my thoughts into verse, with the object and imagery immediately before my senses.

Like so many of Coleridge's projects, this poem, *The Brook*, was never finished. 'Had I finished it', said he, 'it was my purpose in the heat of the moment to have dedicated it to our then committee of public safety as containing the charts and maps with which I was to have supplied the French Government in aid of their plans of invasion.'[1]

As a result of these reports and of the complaints of some

---

[1] *B.L.*, ch. x. It is curious and interesting to find that Coleridge's account of the 'spy' affair, which has often been considered largely apocryphal, is borne out by the discovery of the Home Office correspondence.

country gentlemen in the neighbourhood, the Home Office sent a detective who took up his quarters in the inn at Stowey. Coleridge's account of how the spy used to lie behind the sand-dunes by the shore listening to him and Wordsworth discoursing about 'Spy Nozy' (Spinoza) and drawing conclusions therefrom that they were referring to him and his 'Bardolph nose', is hardly credible, though it throws an interesting light on Coleridge's pronunciation of the philosopher's name. Neither Coleridge nor Wordsworth had the slightest idea they were being watched[1] until 'a friendly medium'—probably Poole—warned Coleridge of the spy's presence in the village. Walsh, the spy, soon ascertained from the landlord of the Inn at Stowey that the inhabitants of Alfoxden 'are not French, but they are people that will do as much harm as all the French can do'. 'I think', commented Mr. Walsh, 'this will turn out no French affair but a mischiefuous gang of disaffected Englishmen.' From one Thomas Jones who lived at Alfoxden, Walsh learnt a few more details, very amusing to posterity but not of much importance to him. One thing was that 'on the Sunday after Wordsworth came, he Jones was desired to wait at table, that there were 14 persons at Dinner Poole and Coldridge were there, And there was a little Stout Man with dark cropt Hair and wore a White Hat and Glasses [Thelwall] who after dinner got up and talked so loud and was in such a passion that Jones was frightened and did not like to go near them since'. One would be inclined to doubt this story of so large a gathering at Alfoxden when the Wordsworths' poverty was such that they had to live on the simplest food themselves. The problem of food is solved, however, by the following letter from Coleridge to Poole,[2] dated July 1797, which almost certainly must refer to this occasion. It was evidently written from Alfoxden, and in anticipation of a large gathering.

My dear Poole, we have taken a fore-quarter of lamb from your mother, which you will be so good, according to your word, or (as the wit said to the Minister of State) *notwithstanding your promise,* to send over to The Foxes [evidently Coleridge's nickname for Alfoxden] to-morrow morning by a boy.

---

[1] See Coleridge's amusing account of his meeting with the spy on the road to Alfoxden, *B.L.*, ch. x.

[2] Printed in the *Illustrated London News*, Apr. 22nd 1893.

I pray you, come over if possible by eleven o'clock, that we may have Wordsworth's tragedy read under the trees.

                                                    S. T. Coleridge.

Poole probably arrived with a party of his Stowey neighbours for the reading of *The Borderers* in the morning, after which they sat down in the big dining-room with its three long windows looking towards the sea, to feast on the fore-quarter of lamb which Poole's mother had so generously provided. The party, besides the Coleridges, Wordsworths, Poole, and Thelwall, with perhaps other members of Poole's circle at Stowey, may also have included Montagu. A letter from his young friend Francis Tweddell, a brother of John Tweddell the artist and traveller whom Wordsworth had known at Cambridge, was addressed to him at Stowey and dated July 14th.[1] There is no mention of Montagu in Coleridge's letters at this time, and it is possible that he was in fact still at Bristol with the Pinneys and did not come to Alfoxden till August, for on August 16th Walsh the spy reported that 'two men came to Alfoxden House the night before last'—i.e. August 14th—and that 'the Woman Servant [Peggy] told Jones that one of the Gentlemen was a great Counsellor from London and the other a Gentleman from Bristol'. Jones was bribed to weed the garden and find out who they were, but at this point the correspondence of Walsh breaks off. The 'great Counsellor' is probably Peggy's version of Montagu, who lived in London and was supposed to be preparing for the bar, while the most probable identification of the 'gentleman from Bristol' is that it was John or Azariah Pinney. Soon afterwards Walsh seems to have decided that he had after all only found a mare's nest and departed from the neighbourhood. The only solid piece of information about Wordsworth which Jones elicited from Peggy was that 'her master was a Phylosopher'. This had been the Pinneys' nickname for him at Racedown. It would have pleased Coleridge.

There was thus a good deal of coming and going at Alfoxden during these summer months. To complete the tale of visitors, Tom Wedgwood, the brilliant, delicate brother of John and Josiah Wedgwood, came on September 15th and stayed for

---

[1] *P.P.* The letter urged Montagu to 'get money from Pinney and Wordsworth to pay Tweddell's debts. But Montagu certainly did not apply to Wordsworth for money at this time.

five days.[1] With him came a friend whom he refers to as ———n and who may be James Tobin, a scion of the Bristol firm of Pinney and Tobin who became intimate with both Wordsworth and Coleridge. Tom Wedgwood, who was making observations on the nature of Time, made the following note in his diary: 'Remarked to ———n on the 5th day at Alfoxden that the time had gone like lightning. He agreed with me.'

Wedgwood had never before met either Wordsworth or Coleridge, but he had heard of them and had his own plans and hopes in which he intended they should play a part. When he came to Alfoxden it seems probable that Coleridge was still away, visiting William Lisle Bowles; Wordsworth, writing to Cottle on September 13th, says: 'he set off a week ago;' but the date of his return is not known. Tom Wedgwood was rich, unmarried, and full of schemes for the reform and improvement of mankind. He had lately written a long letter to Godwin discussing the best way of using his wealth in the service of humanity. He decided to finance the education of a genius. The letter is a curious example of the fallacy which often beset the idealists of that age, that the human child, if educated with sufficient care, will become exactly what its teachers desire it to become. Such a belief was the outcome of the 'mechanistic' philosophy of Hartley, Paley, and the other Necessitarians, who failed to allow for the more incalculable elements of human behaviour. Tom Wedgwood's letter is a characteristic product of its generation.[2]

My aim is high [he writes]. I have been endeavouring some masterstroke which should anticipate a century or two upon the large-paced progress of human improvement. . . . Let us suppose ourselves in possession of a detailed statement of the first twenty years of the life of some extraordinary genius; what a chaos of perceptions! . . . How many opposing tendencies which have negatived each other. . . . How many hours, days, months have been prodigally wasted in unproductive occupation! How many false and contradictory ideas imprinted by authority!

---

[1] R. B. Litchfield, *Tom Wedgwood*, p. 51. B.M. Add. MSS. 35345, f. 83.

[2] I am much indebted for the text of this letter to Mr. David V. Erdman of Princeton, New Jersey, and to the Librarian of Duke University, N. Carolina. It is among the Abinger MSS. Mr. Erdman has also allowed me to draw upon his unpublished article: 'Wedgwood's Master Stroke: Coleridge, Wordsworth and the Fund', for some of the following observations and suggestions.

He then goes on to define 'genius'—'Rudiments, perhaps, are *distinct, vivid* primary and consequently *distinct, vivid* secondary ideas with *high* degrees of pleasure associated.' By 'primary ideas' he seems to mean sense impressions, and by secondary, the memory or mental impression arising from it, for he goes on: 'The practice should be to simplify and render intense the first affections of Sense, and secondly to excite those affections under every possible favourable circumstance of pleasure.' 'Sight and Touch' were in his view 'the two important senses; 'they must be taught together', and gradually educated. Then he begins to lay down suggestions for the actual method of education. It strikes one as grim in the extreme. 'Should not the nursery, then, have plain, grey walls with one or two vivid objects for sight and touch? Could not children be made to acquire manipulation sooner? Let hard bodies be hung about them so as continually to irritate their palms.' A difficulty, however, would soon arise—how must one undertake 'the gradual explication of Nature?' For 'impressions' must be neither too rapid nor too slow, or the budding genius would lose its balance. The solution which occurred to Wedgwood had at least the merit of simplicity: 'The child must never go out of doors or leave his own apartment.' And how deal with the child's 'strong desires' for further gratifications of his little senses? The only hope was to 'connect their chief pleasure with rational objects', and hence such frivolous recreations as 'romping, tickling and fooling' must be avoided, and a nice balance struck by the 'superintendent' between assisting in the attainment of his desires and leaving the little fellow to find his own way to them. Above all, idleness of mind was to be resisted; no time was to be allowed for solitary musing. 'In the best regulated mind of the present day, has not there been, and is not there some hours every day passed in reverie, thought ungoverned, undirected? How astonishingly the powers and produce of the mind would be increased by a fixed habit of earnest thought. This is to be given.'

And by whom was this school—or nursery rather—for geniuses to be run? Wedgwood envisaged a committee of 'philosophers', Godwin, Thomas Beddoes the physician, Holcroft, Horne Tooke, and himself, to decide on 'a plan', and then there would be a need for 'one, or two, superintendents for the practical part'. And for this important post 'the only persons that I know of as at all likely for this purpose, are Wordsworth and Coleridge'. Neither was at present known to him, but he had heard of Wordsworth, and thought he probably had 'many of the requisite qualities', 'and', he added, 'from what I hear of him, he has only to be convinced that this is the most promising mode of benefiting society, to engage him to come forward with alacrity'. Wedgwood had evidently heard of Wordsworth rather as the advanced reformer and improver of mankind, as he was in his London days, than as a poet who had retired to the country. Of Coleridge, Wedgwood spoke with somewhat more caution. 'The talents of Coleridge I suppose are considerable and, like Wordsworth's, quite disengaged. I am only afraid that the former [i.e. Coleridge] may be too much a poet and re-ligionist to suit our views.'

We do not know who it was who had spoken to Wedgwood about Wordsworth, but it was in all probability Montagu. He and Godwin had travelled together to Etruria to visit the Wedgwood family in June, for Montagu was then hoping to marry Sarah Wedgwood, the sister of Josiah and Tom. Tom was at Etruria at the time of Montagu's visit and no one was more likely than Montagu to speak with enthusiasm of Wordsworth as a teacher and guide. He would have been less concerned with Wordsworth's more recent activities, the change in his outlook and his absorption in poetry and 'Nature'.

It was with this fantastic scheme in mind that Tom Wedgwood visited Alfoxden in September. It is scarcely possible to suppose that he did not speak of it to Wordsworth; and that, if he did, Wordsworth did not make some fairly devastating comments. With some of the ideas that lay behind it he would have felt himself in agreement—with the importance, for instance, of sense-perception, though he would have surely put in a plea for the importance of the ear as well as the eye. But when it came to imprisoning a child indefinitely within a grey-walled nursery and depriving it of all contact with 'Nature', or apparently with any 'objects' not deliberately presented to it by its teachers, his amazement and perhaps his amusement must have been great. Playing round them as they talked was little Basil Montagu, whom for the past two years William and Dorothy had been teaching to grow up as a true 'child of nature'. He too, was learning from the evidence of his senses, but under circumstances how different from Wedgwood's little genius! 'Till a child is four years old', wrote Dorothy of their methods with him, 'he needs no other companions than the flowers, the grass, the cattle, the sheep that scamper away from him, when he makes a vain unexpecting chase after them, the pebbles upon the road etc.' Under such a régime, Basil had grown from a fretful, sickly infant into a good-tempered, active, healthy little boy. Alas for Tom Wedgwood's 'grey-walled nursery'!

But there are indications that Wedgwood's theories drew from Wordsworth more than verbal criticisms. In the fifth book of *The Prelude* is a long passage scornfully satirizing modern systems of education which make children into infant prodigies and divorce them from their true instructress, Nature. This passage is a very early one. It was written in its first form in Germany, in the late autumn of 1798, when William and Dorothy were at Goslar, and Coleridge at Ratzeburg. The last part of it, the lines beginning

> There was a Boy: ye knew him well, ye cliffs
> And islands of Winander,

was sent in a letter to Coleridge in December. In it Wordsworth described himself, and the ecstasies brought to his soul by blowing 'mimic hootings to the silent owls' by night on the shores of Esthwaite. Such joys were unknown to the little prodigies, for whom,

> In the corrected scheme
> Of modern days all error is block'd out
> So jealously, that wisdom thrives apace,
> And in our very boyhood we become
> Familiar friends with cause and consequence.
> Great feats have been performed, a smooth high-way,
> So they assert, has lately overbridged
> The random chaos of futurity . . .
>   or briefly, 'tis maintained
> We now have rules and theories so precise
> That by inspection of unwearied eyes
> We can secure infallible results. . . .

Then he speaks of the 'watchful men' who presided over the education of these prodigies, and how they lacked one thing:

they had no faith in—no knowledge of—that 'wiser Spirit'
which was all the time invisibly at work:

> A better eye than theirs, more prodigal
> Of blessings, and more studious of our good,
> Even in what seem our most unfruitful hours.

And he broke out into an impassioned address to his former
schoolmates who had shared that freedom:

> My playmates! brothers! nurs'd by the same years,
> And fellow-children of the self-same hills,
> Though we are moulded now by various fates
> To various characters, I do not think
> That there is one of us who cannot tell
> How manifold the expedients, how intense
> The unwearied passion with which Nature toils
> To win us to herself, and to impress
> Our careless hearts with beauty and with love.

One is tempted to think not only from the general character but
from some of the particular phraseology of this passage that one
contributory memory among the many which crowded his mind
during that autumn in Germany was that of Tom Wedgwood's
visit to Alfoxden and his unfolding of his plan. If Wedgwood
really suggested to Wordsworth that he should be himself one
of the 'watchful men', the passage becomes rich in irony.

Early in 1798 Coleridge, on a visit to the Hazlitts at Wem,
reported that 'Mackintosh and Tom Wedgwood had expressed
a very indifferent opinion of his friend Wordsworth', on which
he remarked to them—'He strides on so far before you that he
dwindles in the distance.' It is possible that Wedgwood's
'indifferent opinion' may have been partly due to Wordsworth's
criticisms of his scheme.

The Wordsworths' financial affairs were at present fairly
stable, for Montagu had not yet defaulted on Basil, and Wordsworth did not think it necessary to accept an offer from Cottle of
'accommodation'. There was, however, one very vexatious
matter which had begun to cause them anxiety before they left
Racedown. This was the demand being made upon them by their
cousin and former schoolfellow, Robinson Wordsworth, and
his mother, the widow of their uncle Richard Wordsworth of

Whitehaven, for money advanced while William was at College. These claims were, apparently, quite just, but unpleasantly made, and very difficult to meet. The request was for £250, and both William and Dorothy wrote urgently to their brother Richard on May 7th 1797: 'Do not fail to write to me upon this subject. . . . Could £150 or £200 be paid by way of pacifying them and showing that we have a disposition to be just!' As usual Richard was dilatory. In November they were still asking him what had been done.[1] It is very clear from the correspondence which survives that the last thing William and Dorothy wished was to quarrel with their cousins or to get out of paying what they regarded as a perfectly just claim.

Meanwhile Thelwall's visit and the general suspicions of the neighbourhood brought down upon the Wordsworths the wrath of Mrs. St. Albyn, the mother of the infant owner of Alfoxden. She was angry with Mr. Bartholomew for letting it to them, and Poole gallantly sprang to the defence of both Bartholomew and the Wordsworths. In a letter to Mrs. St. Albyn, dated September 16th 1797, he tried to do away with her suspicions.[2] The Wordsworths, he said, came of a most respectable family; the late vicar of Stowey, Dr. Fisher,[3] had known their uncle Canon Cookson very well. They were exemplary tenants, being a small household with but one child and an 'excellent female servant'. 'How different would be the case with a large family—full of careless servants, a run of idle company, hunting, breaking down fences etc.' As for Wordsworth, he 'is a man fond of retirement—fond of reading and writing'—Poole evidently did not think it expedient to mention the word 'poetry'—'and has never had above two gentlemen at a time with him'. Thelwall's visit had been purely fortuitous: 'No person at Stowey nor Mr. Wordsworth knew of his coming.' Once there indeed, 'surely the common duties of hospitality were not to be refused to any man'—a sentiment with which Mrs. St. Albyn probably would not have agreed. Finally, he begged her not to listen to calumnies. 'I will pledge myself in

---

E.L. 58, 59, 60, pp. 166–8. L.Y. iii, appendix, 57a. The claim seems to have been shelved, and was finally settled by W.W. and Richard Wordsworth in 1812. M.Y. ii. 539, p. 698, W.W. to C.W., Jan. 12th 1816.   [2] T.P. i, p. 241.

[3] Dr. Fisher was a Johnian and also a Canon of Windsor. He eventually became Bishop of Salisbury. He never resided at Stowey, where the duties were performed by the curate, Mr. Roskilley, S.T.C. i, p. 267.

every respect that you will have no cause to complain of Mr.
Wordsworth.' Whatever the effect of this letter, the Wordsworths' tenancy was not allowed to continue beyond midsummer 1798. In March Dorothy wrote that the house was let to the
Cruikshanks, a young couple at Stowey, friends of the Coleridges. Wordsworth afterwards rather petulantly denied that
what Coleridge called 'caballing long and loud' had driven him
from Alfoxden. Years afterwards, in the margin of Barron
Field's unpublished memoir of him, he wrote against a statement of this kind: '*Not the occasion* of my removal. Annoyances
I had none. The facts mentioned by Coleridge of a spy etc.
came not to my knowledge till I had left the neighbourhood.
I was not refused a continuance. I never applied for one.'[1] There
is indeed no evidence that they were unduly disturbed by
having to leave, though Dorothy says she had seldom quitted
any place with so much regret.[2] It was Coleridge and Poole
who were desolated. 'Whether we shall be able', wrote Coleridge,
'to procure him a house and furniture near Stowey, we know
not, and yet we must: for the hills and the woods, and the
streams, and the sea, and the shores, would break forth into
reproaches against us, if we did not strain every nerve to keep
their Poet among them. Without joking and in serious sadness
—Poole and I cannot endure to think of losing him.'[3]

For the present, however, all was well; the autumn and winter
passed without any further disturbances from Government or
among their village neighbours. The 'wonderful year' of their
comradeship went forward, becoming ever more productive of
poetry, until with midwinter and early spring both were almost
daily producing some verses of surpassing power.

During the first five months of their association little was
written by either, except that Coleridge completed his tragedy
Osorio, and Wordsworth, at Coleridge's entreaty, revised *The
Borderers* with a view to stage production. Coleridge was,
however, full of schemes of which *The Brook*—the preparations
for which had aroused the suspicions of the villagers—was the
most ambitious. He had already described to Cottle his plans

[1] It is probably true that he did not ask to have the lease extended, but that Poole,
on Coleridge's entreaty, did.
[2] *E.L.* 81, p. 193. D.W. to Mrs. Rawson, July 3rd 1798.
[3] *Biographia Epistolaris*, ed. A. Turnbull, 1911, i, p. 158. S.T.C. to Cottle,
pr. 1798.

for a gigantic poem on a Miltonic scale in which all modern scientific and historical knowledge would be included: 'Ten years to collect materials and warm my mind with universal science . . . the next five in the composition of the poem, and the last five in the correction of it.'[1] *The Brook* was probably an attempt at such an all-inclusive poem; there are some jottings in the note-books which obviously form part of it: but one of the miracles of this year of wonders was the abandonment—more accidental perhaps than deliberate—of these vast projects which could scarcely, Coleridge's temperament being what it was, have advanced beyond the note-book stage, and the production instead of *The Ancient Mariner* and *Christabel* and *Frost at Midnight*. The writing of a long 'philosophical poem' containing 'views of man, nature and society' was a burden which Coleridge transferred with enthusiastic confidence in 'the giant Wordsworth's' powers, to Wordsworth's shoulders, in the course of the following spring; for the long and complicated history of *The Recluse*—Wordsworth's never-completed 'philosophic song'— has its birth in this year of comradeship.[2]

Coleridge had recently described himself in a letter to Thelwall thus: 'the walk of the whole man indicated *indolence capable of energies*'. He knew himself to be 'sloth-jaundiced all', and although he had during the past two years produced a considerable amount of poetry, pamphlets, and reviews, the poetry was too heavily overshadowed by the influence of Milton to give more than a rather blotched and misty view of his real 'energies'. No one who reads his *Visions of the Maid of Orleans* (published much later under the title of *The Destiny of Nations*) can help agreeing with Cottle, who, on being asked by Coleridge for his opinion, answered that 'it was all very fine but what it was about I could not tell: . . . it was profuse, but detached splendour, and exhibiting nothing like construction'. Cottle's criticisms, combined with Lamb's and perhaps also Wordsworth's, to whom he sent the poem, although there is no record of what Wordsworth thought of it, induced him to abandon the idea of publishing it in the new edition of his poems which appeared in October. Coleridge was beginning to be aware of his own faults as a poet. In July 1797, just after the Wordsworths had come to Alfoxden

---

[1] *U.L.* i. 38, p. 71.   [2] See below, p. 359.
[3] *Lamb*, i, pp. 98–99. *Cottle*, i, pp. 229–30.

he poured withering scorn, in a letter to Southey, on his own
Pixies' Parlour and *Monody on the Death of Chatterton*. Here, he
said, 'all his powers of buckram' had been 'put on the stretch',
to the exclusion of natural emotion and good taste. 'Chasteness
and severity of diction' were lacking, and in his preface to the
new edition he said he had 'used his best efforts to tame the
swell and glitter both of thought and diction'.[1] Few things,
indeed, are more striking in English poetry than the change
in Coleridge's poetic style between the *Visions of the Maid of
Orleans* and *The Ancient Mariner*—that is to say during the
year 1797. True, he had shown, in *The Aeolian Harp*, written
two years earlier in the first happiness of marriage, that he
could write in another much purer style, full of delight in beauty,
tender and yet detached. And he had returned to this style in
July of 1797 with the beautiful *Lime-Tree Bower* lines. The
'Conversation Poem' as he called this kind of reflective, personal
poetry, achieved a wonderful perfection in the following winter,
when he wrote *Frost at Midnight*. It was a medium peculiarly
his own discovery,[2] the short blank-verse poem in which the
poet muses in solitude, ranging over present, past and future in
his mind. Wordsworth owed much to *Frost at Midnight* when
he came to write the *Tintern Abbey* lines.

Kubla Khan, The Ancient Mariner, and Christabel are even
more startling in their novelty; and all reach the perfection of
imaginative splendour. *Kubla* was written probably in October
1797; the *Mariner* and *Christabel* were the work of the winter
and spring. But it is doubtful whether life with Sara and Poole
at Nether Stowey would of itself ever have resulted in such a
harvest. The arrival of the Wordsworths had made Coleridge
happy, happier than he had ever been before, and for him,
happiness meant that 'equipoise of the intellectual and emotional
faculties' which was essentially creative in its result. Many
years later Wordsworth himself recalled in *The Prelude* Coleridge's happiness in these wonderful months:

> Beloved Friend!
> When, looking back, thou seest, in clearer view
> Than any liveliest sight of yesterday,

[1] *S.T.C.* i, pp. 222–3.
[2] Though Mr. House has shown that he owes much to parts of Cowper's *Task*.
Humphry House, *Coleridge*, 1953.

> That summer, under whose indulgent skies,
> Upon smooth Quantock's airy ridge we roved
> Unchecked, or loitered 'mid her sylvan courts,
> Thou, in bewitching words, with happy heart,
> Didst chaunt the vision of that Ancient Man,
> The bright-eyed Mariner, and rueful woes
> Didst utter of the Lady Christabel.

And a few lines later he speaks of

> The buoyant spirits
> That were our daily portion when we first
> Together wantoned in wild poesy.[1]

Coleridge needed above all things to be understood, for he, with consciousness most intense and penetrating, realized the essential solitariness of the human soul. 'The unspeakable comfort to a good man's mind, nay, even to a criminal to be *understood*—to have someone that understands one—and who does not feel that, on earth, no one does? The hope of this, always more or less disappointed, gives the passion to friendship.' Coleridge's sensitiveness about this necessity of being understood made him as has been well said 'a bad maker of allowances',[2] when he imagined that people failed him, or when they really did so; it underlay also his almost Pecksniffian declarations of his own charity and forgiveness towards those who had offended him. Now, however, he was rejoicing in total friendship. Loudly he proclaimed to his friends his love for Wordsworth. As a poet he had admired him ever since the publication of *Descriptive Sketches*. Then came acquaintance and with it an almost idolizing admiration.

'Wordsworth is a very great man, the only man to whom *a all times* and in *all modes of excellence* I feel myself inferior. . . . 'The Giant Wordsworth—God love him! Even when I speak in the terms of admiration due to his intellect, I fear lest those terms should keep out of sight the amiableness of his manners . . .' And in May 1798 he wrote to Estlin: 'I have now known him a year and some months,[3] and my admiration, I might say

---

[1] *Prel.* XIV, ll. 392–401, and 416–18.
[2] House, op. cit.
[3] This statement has often puzzled students. But I think Coleridge dates his re 'knowledge' of Wordsworth from Mar. 1797 when Wordsworth visited him Stowey. See above, p. 310.

my awe, of his intellectual powers has increased even to this
hour, and (what is of more importance) he is a tried good
man.'

In Dorothy too he found friendship of a new and rare beauty.
His description of her in a letter to Cottle in July is the earliest
we have: it shows how delicately he appreciated that peculiar
quality in her, which those of her own day would have called
'sensibility'.

> Her manners are simple, ardent, impressive. In every motion, her
> most innocent soul out beams so brightly, that who saw would say,
>> Guilt was a thing impossible in her.[1]
> Her information various. Her eye watchful in minutest observation of
> nature; and her taste, a perfect electrometer. It bends, protrudes, and
> draws in, at subtlest beauties, and most recondite faults.[2]

We have here the key to their relationship and indeed to
Dorothy's peculiar genius. Between Dorothy and Coleridge
there existed an affinity of perception in regard to the smallest
details of interest in the natural world; she perfected his
'eye', which was in danger of looking too much at the Miltonic
splendours of heaven. Dorothy's Journal, which she began to
keep in January at Alfoxden, is full of echoes of Coleridge's
poetry, even as he was then daily writing it, as it is also of her
brother's. Some have even surmised that her own descriptions
inspired his, and though this is probably not so, save perhaps
in one instance,[3] the impression given is of one experience of
delight mutually shared with great intensity and actuality; and
it is scarcely possible to avoid the conclusion that Dorothy's
reactions to the manifold events of Nature—the moon's
behaviour, the spring's delay, cobwebs in the sunshine, or the
last leaf of autumn twisting in the wind on a tree-top—gave
Coleridge keen delight and drew out and enhanced his imaginative observation. Coleridge has often been quoted as saying
that in these Alfoxden days he, William, and Dorothy were
'three people, but one soul'. The origin of this remark is not
distinctly traceable, though he did once say to Godwin of the

---

[1] This line is a quotation from Coleridge's *Visions of the Maid of Orleans*.
[2] *Cottle*, i, p. 252. An electrometer was an instrument for 'detecting the presence
and determining the kind of electricity in any body'.
[3] See below, pp. 355–7. The extent to which Coleridge and Dorothy repeat each
other has been examined in *Lowes*, pp. 171–6. See also House, op. cit., p. 123.

early days at Grasmere and Keswick: 'Though we were three persons, there was but one God.'[1]

While Dorothy quickened his outward delight in things, Wordsworth supplied a new kind of unitive and spiritualizing vision. In a letter to Thelwall, written on October 16th 1797,[2] Coleridge reveals something of the hunger and thirst in his soul, and we can see how of all men Wordsworth could have helped him here. 'Frequently', says Coleridge, 'all *things* appear *little*, all the knowledge that can be acquired child's play; the universe itself! what but an immense heap of *little* things? . . . My mind feels as if it ached to behold and know something great, something *one* and *indivisible*. And it is only in the faith of that that rocks or waterfalls, mountains or caverns, give me the sense of sublimity or majesty. But in this faith *all things* counterfeit infinity.' And then, breaking into verse, he writes:

> Struck with the deepest calm of joy, I stand
> Silent, with swimming sense; and gazing round
> On the wide landscape, gaze till all doth seem
> Less gross than bodily, a living thing
> Which acts upon the mind and with such hues
> As clothe th'Almighty Spirit where he makes
> Spirits perceive his presence! . . .

Now this is very much akin to the visionary experiences that Wordsworth had had in boyhood and was still enjoying, though Coleridge characteristically gives it a theological turn. It is scarcely conceivable that Wordsworth had not spoken of these experiences to Coleridge, especially as Coleridge, who never concealed anything that was passing in his mind, must have described to Wordsworth his longing for 'the One'.

As for Wordsworth, his debt to Coleridge was scarcely less great. Hitherto it was only with Dorothy that Wordsworth could feel at one, and even that unity had its limitations. Their companionship was as perfect as mutual affection and delight in 'this beauteous world' could make it. But Dorothy had not a creative intellect, and while believing profoundly in her brother's genius she could not advise, suggest, or criticize from an intellectual point of view. Wordsworth needed some other kind of reciprocation, something more challenging, masculine, and

---

[1] K. Paul, *William Godwin*, ii, p. 83. S.T.C. to Godwin, Nov. 1801.
[2] *S.T.C.* i, p. 228.

stimulating, someone who could disagree as well as encourage, someone with whom it was possible to have intellectual communion. Coleridge's loudly proclaimed admiration, his reiteration of his faith in Wordsworth's intellectual greatness, was most precious mental food. His affection and friendship were so genuine as to dismiss any possibility of his admiration being that of a flatterer. As Coleridge craved for understanding, so did Wordsworth for praise—the praise of a mind and spirit as full of genius as his own. Coleridge razed Wordsworth's defences on that day when he leapt over the gate at Racedown; while still remaining the somewhat silent and reserved north-countryman to others, in Coleridge's company he could be joyous, eloquent, enthusiastic, warm. 'His genius', said Coleridge, in May 1798, 'is most apparent in poetry, and rarely, except to me in *tête-à-tête*, breaks forth in conversational eloquence.'

It seems that after finishing the final version of *The Borderers*, probably in September or October, Wordsworth did not write much consecutive verse until the early spring. There was a pause, but one filled with hope and plans for the future.

Coleridge, William, and Dorothy passed even more of their time together. Sara Coleridge no longer formed one of their 'philosophical parties'. By September—after a miscarriage in July—she was again with child, which perhaps explains her withdrawal; but one cannot help feeling that more than that kept her away. She could not share their life. There is something almost startling in Coleridge's '*three* persons and one soul' (if that was what he did say) when one remembers her. There are signs that Dorothy at least was anxious to draw her in, for in the spring we both find Sara and Coleridge staying at Alfoxden, and later, when Coleridge was away, Dorothy spent a night with her at Stowey.[1] Certainly Dorothy, though increasingly despairing of her as a wife for Coleridge, always tried to keep on friendly terms with her. But in November the three twice left her entirely alone for more than one day at a time, while they went on 'tours' about the country-side.

In these expeditions great events in English poetry had their origins. The first walk was early in November to Lynton by

[1] *D.W.J.* i, p. 15. Apr. 13th 1798.

way of the coast, sleeping apparently one night at Porlock and
another at Lynton. This bit of country was already known to
Coleridge and became a favourite haunt of them all. He had
spent a day or two 'at a Farm House between Porlock and Linton a quarter of a mile from Culbone Church in the fall of the
year 1797'.[1] He had gone away from Stowey apparently because
he was unwell, and there at this remote spot had taken two
grains of opium 'to check a dysentery', and there had dreamed,
and beheld in his dream that vision that became *Kubla Khan*.
That must have been in late September or October 1797. The
expedition with the Wordsworths gave rise to a curious episode
which was also the first attempt at collaboration between
the two poets. Many years later, in 1828, Coleridge published
the fragment of what was intended to be a 'prose tale', on the
curious subject of the death of Abel. It was called *The Wanderings of Cain*.

    The Wanderings of Cain, Coleridge tells us in a preface, was
composed in 1798,

in concert with another . . . who was then residing at a small distance
from Nether Stowey. The title and subject were suggested by myself,
who likewise drew out the scheme and the contents for each of the
three books or cantos . . . which, the reader is to be informed, was to
have been finished in one night! My partner was to undertake the first
Canto, I the second: and whichever had *done first*, was to set about the
third. Almost thirty years have passed by, yet at this moment I cannot
without something more than a smile moot the question which of the
two things was the more impracticable, for a mind so eminently
original to compose another man's thoughts and fancies, or for a taste
so austerely pure and simple to imitate the Death of Abel? Methinks
I see his grand and noble countenance as at the moment when having
despatched my own portion of the task at full finger-speed, I hastened
to him with my manuscript,—that look of humorous despondency
fixed on his almost blank sheet of paper, and then its silent mock-
piteous admission of failure struggling with the sense of the exceeding
ridiculousness of the whole scheme—which broke up in a laugh: and the
Ancient Mariner was written instead.

    Now Coleridge, like Wordsworth, was never trustworthy
about dates, and for 1798 we must read 1797—because, as we
shall see, *The Ancient Mariner* was begun in the latter year.
Hazlitt tells us, in his account of his visit to Stowey the following

[1] *E.K.C.*, p. 162. Coleridge's note to the earliest manuscript of *Kubla Khan*.

summer, how Coleridge took him on that same walk to Lynton, and in the Valley of Rocks told him how he and Wordsworth 'were to have made this place the scene of a prose-tale, which was to have been in the manner of, but far superior to, Gessner's Death of Abel'. *The Death of Abel* was a German curiosity, written 'in a kind of loose poetry', and widely read in an English translation made by Mrs. Collyer.[1] Hence Coleridge speaks of 'imitating' it. For him, the queer stuff had certain attractions; for Wordsworth, none whatever. But the interest of the episode lies in that last half-sentence of Coleridge's apology—'the Ancient Mariner was written instead'.

Not much more than a week afterwards the three set out again on another tour. This time they started late in the afternoon of November 13th about four o'clock, 'towards Watchet', where they probably spent the night; the exact course of their tour is not known, but at some point they struck inland, and returned to Alfoxden by way of Dulverton.[2] 'The evening', says Dorothy (meaning the first evening), 'was dark and cloudy: we went eight miles, William and Coleridge employing themselves in laying the plan of a ballad, to be published with some pieces of William's.' Here we have the origin of the idea of the *Lyrical Ballads*, though Wordsworth, in his account, says nothing of any other 'pieces'; and attributes the origin of the most famous of all romantic poems to financial necessity. 'As our united funds were very small', he says, 'we agreed to defray the expense of the tour by writing a Poem, to be sent to the new Monthly Magazine set up by Phillips the bookseller and edited by Dr. Aikin. Accordingly we set off and proceeded along the Quantock Hills, towards Watchet, and in the course of this walk was planned the Poem of The Ancient Mariner.' He then goes on to describe his own part in its planning. It is not always realized how great was Coleridge's debt to Wordsworth for several of the most important incidents in his 'Old Navigator's' story.

[1] *Lowes*, pp. 255–7. *The Wanderings of Cain* is printed in *S.T.C. Poems*, i, pp. 285–92.
[2] The sources for this famous walk are (1) A fragment of a letter of D.W.'s dated Nov. 20th 1797, *E.L.* 69, p. 174; (2) W.W.'s note of 1843 to *We are Seven*, *P.W.* i, p. 360, but he dates it 'in the spring of 1798' and confuses it with the Lynmouth walk of the previous week; (3) Wordsworth's conversation with Alexander Dyce, in Coleridge's *Poems*, 1852, quoted *Lowes*, p. 223; (4) Coleridge's note to *The Ancient Mariner* in *Sibylline Leaves*, reprinted *S.T.C. Poems*, i, p. 196.

Much the greatest part of the story [he says] was Mr. Coleridge's invention; but certain parts I myself suggested, for example, some crime was to be committed which should bring upon the Old Navigator, as Coleridge afterwards delighted to call him, the spectral persecution, as a consequence of that crime, and his own wanderings. I had been reading in Shelvock's *Voyages* a day or two before that while doubling Cape Horn they frequently saw Albatrosses in that latitude, the largest sort of sea-fowl, extending their wings 12 or 13 feet. 'Suppose', said I, 'you represent him as having killed one of these birds on entering the South Sea, and that the tutelary Spirits of these regions take upon them to avenge the crime'. The incident was thought fit for the purpose and adopted accordingly. I also suggested the navigation of the ship by the dead men, but do not recollect that I had anything more to do with the scheme of the poem. . . . We began the composition on that, to me, memorable evening. I furnished two or three lines at the beginning of the poem, in particular:

> And listened like a three years' child;
> The Mariner had his will.

These trifling contributions, all but one (which Mr. C. has with unnecessary scrupulosity recorded) slipt out of his mind as they well might.[1]

The 'contribution' recorded by Coleridge in a note in *Sibylline Leaves* is the two lines at the end of the first stanza of Part IV.

> And thou art long and lank and brown
> As is the ribbed sea-sand.[2]

Wordsworth then describes their attempt at collaboration, which ended much as that over *Cain* had done, save that Coleridge went ahead on his own until the poem was completed. 'As we endeavoured to proceed conjointly (I speak of the same evening) our respective manners proved so widely different that it would have been quite presumptuous in me to do anything but separate from an undertaking upon which I could only have been a clog. We returned after a few days from a delightful tour, of which I have many pleasant, and some droll-enough recollections.'

One wishes that more of these recollections had been recorded. But what we do know is of more than incidental interest. The

---

[1] *P.W.* i, p. 361. Note to *We are Seven*.
[2] By 'trifling contributions' Wordsworth must mean the lines quoted, not the incidents in the story, which no one could call trifling.

most striking thing in Wordsworth's account is the nature of his contributions to the story of *The Ancient Mariner*. To Wordsworth, since his return from France, crime and the psychology of crime, its consequences and repercussions, both on the criminal and on his victims, had been a subject of absorbing interest, and had been indeed a favourite subject in his poetry. The second version of *Salisbury Plain* and *The Borderers* are both studies in criminal psychology. And since the spring he had been further interested by the kindred subject of a curse, and the effect which it could produce on the mind of the person cursed, even if that person were in fact innocent of any crime. In the spring at Racedown he had written part of a long ballad called *The Three Graves*, on the subject of a curse laid on an innocent person and its disastrous consequences. This ballad, we shall see, was continued by Coleridge but never completed.[1] And in *Goody Blake and Harry Gill*, written probably in the early spring of 1798, based on a story in Erasmus Darwin's *Zoönomia*, and included in the *Lyrical Ballads*, he shows his continuing interest in the theme. But all these poems speak of crime and curses from a purely psychological point of view; there is no element of the supernatural in them; he had even removed from *Salisbury Plain* the stanzas about the druids as being too fanciful for his stern realism. Yet now we find him recommending to Coleridge the story of a sailor who kills an albatross and his 'spectral persecution' by 'tutelary Spirits'. The probable explanation is that, remembering the Cain episode, he saw that Coleridge's imagination could handle things which his own would find unreal; in fact, that Coleridge could—in his own famous words —'procure for these shadows of imagination that willing suspension of disbelief for the moment, which constitutes poetic faith'. And so 'the Ancient Mariner grew and grew'—grew in length until it was far beyond the limits of a magazine poem; grew in strange and haunting beauty until it became one of the wonders of English poetry. It was nearly the end of March 1798 before Coleridge 'brought his ballad finished' to show William and Dorothy at Alfoxden.[2]

---

[1] See below, pp. 388–90.

[2] *D.W.J.* i, p. 13. Mar. 23rd. 'Coleridge dined with us. He brought his ballad finished. We walked with him to the Miner's house. A beautiful evening, very starry, the horned moon.'

Early in November 1797 Montagu came to Alfoxden for a visit which lasted about eight weeks.[1] He was in sore financial straits—even worse than usual. He had lost in September a chancery suit about a sum of money left him by his father, and, being still under the influence of Godwinian views of morality, now felt conscientiously unable to work at the law, the calling for which he had been originally trained. For the present he was unable to pay Wordsworth either the interest on his loan or the board and lodging fees for Basil. The Wordsworths took this inconvenient breakdown with great calmness; they never thought of parting with Basil, and in the following June Dorothy wrote to her Aunt Rawson: 'Notwithstanding Mr. Montagu (from having changed the course of his application to the law) has not been able to fulfil his engagements respecting Basil, we have lived upon our income and are not a farthing poorer than when we began housekeeping.'

The only means of a livelihood open to Montagu appeared to be teaching, and he came now to Alfoxden partly in the hopes of getting Coleridge to join him in a plan for taking pupils. Coleridge also was desperate for an income. Inevitably, as soon as Coleridge had anything to do with it, the scheme became 'singular and extensive' in character. The pupils were to pay £100 a year each and their board, for the privilege of being given a truly encyclopaedic course of study for three years by Montagu and Coleridge.[2] By January, however, Coleridge had tired of it, or felt its impracticability.

At the very end of November or early in December the Wordsworths went to London, leaving Montagu at Alfoxden in charge of Basil. Coleridge had obtained a promise from Harris, the manager of Covent Garden, that he would read *The Borderers*, and if he accepted it, put it in train for acting immediately, and in consequence of this the manuscript had been sent to London by post. 'It was sent', says Dorothy, 'to one of the principal actors in Covent Garden, who expressed great approbation, and advised William strongly to go to London to make certain alterations.' They went accordingly, but all was disappointment.

---

[1] In a letter dated Nov. 11th 1797 Dorothy speaks of him as in the neighbourhood. He may have stayed part of the time at Stowey. He did not accompany them on their tours. *E.L.* 67, p. 173.

[2] S.T.C.'s Letters to Estlin, *Philobiblon Society*, vol. xv.

'Our business was the play: and the play is rejected', said Dorothy, and added: 'Coleridge's play is also rejected.'[1] One senses the vexation behind these words. When they first sent the play, they had 'not the faintest expectation that it will be accepted', but the encouragement they had received must have raised their hopes. Wordsworth learnt a useful lesson from this failure. *The Borderers* had never been intended for the stage, and only Coleridge's enthusiasm had made him think it possible. Wordsworth had accordingly rewritten parts of it with a view to stage production, but without success. 'If ever', he wrote to James Tobin in the following March, 'I attempt another drama, it shall be written either purposely for the closet, or purposely for the stage. There is no middle way.' Wisely, he never did attempt another drama.

While they were in London they saw a good deal of Southey. Dorothy was repelled by what she thought his priggishness, and she rather scathingly described him to her Aunt Rawson as 'a young man of rigidly virtuous habits . . . much inferior to Coleridge'. She knew of his quarrel with Coleridge, which probably increased her distrust. Time and chance made him eventually the neighbour of the Wordsworths in the Lakes, and in days of sore trouble they learnt the value of his unselfish friendship. There was also a visit to Godwin, who noted in his diary on December 13th: 'Tobin and Wordsworth call.' During the year and a half since Wordsworth had last met Godwin, much had happened in Wordsworth's mind to shake his faith in Godwin's philosophy. Godwin was also much disapproved of by Coleridge. On the next two occasions when Wordsworth was in London, September 1798 and 1802, he did not call upon him, indicating perhaps that he preferred at present to avoid him. Later, however, the acquaintance was renewed.

It was now that one of his earlier poems, *The Convict*, appeared in the *Morning Post*, where it was printed on December 14th over the name 'Mortimer'. 'Mortimer' was the name given to Marmaduke in the more recent manuscripts of *The Borderers*, and no doubt, with his play much in his mind, Wordsworth affixed it to this poem because he also was or had been a 'Mortimer' in his self-deception and absorption in false doctrines. The poem was probably written in 1794 or 1795, for it

---

[1] *E.L.* 71, p. 175. D.W. to unknown correspondent.

is a pure exercise in Godwinism. Godwin had advocated the deportation of criminals to other lands where they could have a chance of rebuilding their lives, and in this poem Wordsworth tells the convict that

> My cure, if the arm of the mighty were mine,
> Would plant thee where yet thou wouldst blossom again.

It was printed, with some alterations, in the *Lyrical Ballads* in 1798, but never reprinted by Wordsworth.

The appearance, however, of this early poem in the *Morning Post*, at a time when he was already the author of other and very superior poetry, is curious. The explanation seems to be that Coleridge sent it in as part of his own contract with Daniel Stuart, the editor. Two other poems, also signed 'Mortimer', appeared in the same paper in April and May of the following year, 1798. They were a translation of Catullus, 'My Lesbia, let us love and live', and some lines 'written by a French prisoner as he was preparing to go to the Guillotine', beginning 'The hour-bell sounds and I must go.' Both these poems, together with another called *The Death of the Starling*, were included in 1836 in Coleridge's *Literary Remains*, and have been reprinted since in his collected poems. They are, however, all by Wordsworth, and are found among his early manuscripts. A sonnet, 'If grief dismiss me not to them that rest', also of early date, appeared in the *Post* on February 13th, 1798, over the signature W. W. Absorbed as he was in his new poetry in the spring of 1798, he seems to have given Coleridge a free hand with his old note-books.[1]

In the first week of January 1798 William and Dorothy returned to Alfoxden, but they spent nearly three weeks in Bristol on the way. At Alfoxden they found Montagu still in residence, but he left a day or two later, carrying a parcel of shirts for Richard Wordsworth in London—which, however, he contrived to leave behind at Stowey.[2] He went to Cote House and there met Sir James Mackintosh, a meeting fortunate both for himself and for the Wordsworths. For a friendship sprang up between Montagu and Mackintosh in which Mackin-

---

[1] For the poems see *P.W.* i, pp. 263, 306, and 308.
[2] *E.L.* 72, p. 175. D.W. to R.W., Jan. 6th 1798.

tosh's good sense and perseverance at length triumphed over Montagu's Godwinian 'principles'. By the end of the visit Mackintosh had persuaded Montagu to earn his living seriously as a barrister, so that his financial affairs gradually improved, and after about two years he was able to resume the payment of Wordsworth's annuity.

Meantime Coleridge, while at Shrewsbury, had received and accepted the noble offer by Tom and Josiah Wedgwood of a pension of £150 a year, deliberately made in order to prevent him entering the Unitarian Ministry and to enable him to go on working at literature. No gift in the world of letters has ever been more timely or was ever followed by a more immediate and brilliant harvest. For Coleridge, on returning to Stowey early in February,[1] rejoicing in his deliverance from the Unitarians, gave himself up to poetry with an intensity which was never to be repeated, and wrote, in the course of the next two months, *Frost at Midnight*, the first part of *Christabel*, *France: An Ode*, *Fears in Solitude*, and completed *The Ancient Mariner*. But the Wedgwoods, while they had not attached any conditions to the gift, were not themselves much concerned with poetry. Tom Wedgwood, as we have seen, had been somewhat suspicious, a few months earlier, that Coleridge was 'too much of a poet and religionist' to take part in his schemes for the improvement of the human race. Since that time, however, he had 'canvassed' Coleridge's past and present life to his own satisfaction, and had probably met and heard him talk at Cote House early in December.[2] It was Coleridge the philosopher and omniscient critic, rather than the poet, whom the Wedgwoods decided to enrich. 'I hope', wrote Wordsworth to Tobin on March 6th, referring to the pension, 'the fruit will be as good as the seed is noble.' He already knew something of Coleridge's weaknesses, of his procrastination and many unfulfilled schemes. One 'fruit' of the gift was the trip to Germany in which the Wordsworths shared. But some months were to pass before that took place. A spring was now at hand which was to be for

---

[1] The first mention of Coleridge in Dorothy's Journal is on Feb. 3rd: 'Walked with Coleridge over the hills.'

[2] It is difficult to fix an exact date for a first meeting between Coleridge and Tom Wedgwood. Coleridge was in Bristol in the first week of December. Hazlitt's reference to his remarks about Tom Wedgwood and Mackintosh indicate that he had already met them both before he went to stay with Hazlitt in Jan. 1798.

each of them a time of keen delight, and to give to English poetry a new and unfading life and glow.

On January 20th 1798 Dorothy began her Journal—or rather, the fragment of it that survives begins on that day. At Racedown at Christmas 1796 she had commissioned Joseph Gill to buy her a 'diary'—it cost 10*d.*;[1] whether it was the note-book used for the 'Alfoxden Journal', or whether she kept a journal at Racedown which has since been lost, there is no means of knowing. The manuscript of her Alfoxden Journal has been lost; we are therefore dependent on the defective and almost certainly incorrect text transcribed by Knight and first published in 1897. Yet how vividly, in spite of all the omissions, does this little fragment bring before us the daily doings of the three; their walks by day and by their beloved moonlight; their glad commerce with earth and sea and sky.

They met almost daily in to-and-fro walks, 'to Stowey over the hills', returning 'with Coleridge' for dinner and the rest of the day. Coleridge seems not infrequently to have stayed for a night or two at Alfoxden. 'Walked a great part of the way to Stowey with Coleridge. The morning warm and sunny', she says on February 4th. Coleridge, although he walked a great deal, sometimes preferred to sit and talk; we find such entries as 'Coleridge came after dinner, so we did not walk again.' On March 9th he and Sara both came for a stay of nine days: a sort of convalescence for Coleridge who had been prostrated with a violently inflamed tooth. Little Hartley also came, and in the first burst of warm spring weather 'we all passed the morning in sauntering about the park and gardens, the children playing about, the old man at the top of the hill gathering furze; interesting groups of human creatures, the young frisking and dancing in the sun, the elder quietly drinking in the life and soul of the sun and air'.[2] It was after this week of convalescence and change from his gloomy cottage that Coleridge wrote: 'my new and tender health is all over me like a voluptuous feeling'. Coleridge in his sufferings had already resorted to 'laudanum' to pacify the raging tooth as well as the violent attacks of internal pain, which, said Wordsworth long afterwards, 'some-

---

[1] *P.P.* Joseph Gill's Diary, Dec. 24th 1796.

[2] *D.W.J.* i, p. 12. Mar. 10th 1798. It has been suggested that 'the old man at the top of the hill' was 'Simon Lee' of Wordsworth's poem.

times caused him, when we walked together in Somersetshire, to throw himself down and writhe like a worm upon the
ground'.[1]

Meanwhile William was once more almost daily writing
poetry. He was above all engaged in blank-verse composition,
some of it of a fragmentary character, of which lines and phrases
and even whole passages are found incorporated into *The Prelude*
or *The Excursion*; some of it the expansion and completion of
The Ruined Cottage; some of it the beginning of what he meant
to make into a poem on 'Man, Nature and Society'. We can
trace in much of this verse two new patterns of thought which
were to absorb him more and more during the next seven years.
One is the highly original and daring attempt to put into words
the inward mental states which resulted from his intercourse
with the landscape around him. The other is the frequent retro-
spection into his own youth—particularly into his school-days
at Hawkshead and his experiences there with the mystery of
Nature. The two tendencies are intimately connected and often
overflow into one another. With this new outburst of poetic
life Dorothy had much to do. She shared not only her brother's
outward delight in the details and interest of a landscape, but
she possessed in no small degree the same powers of inward
contemplation and recollection of outward vision, and of entering
into a trance-like state beyond the consciousness of the senses.
Her Journal and William's fragmentary verse often record the
same incident or the same view, though it is he, not she, who
makes the deepest exploration of the mind's responses.

So we find Dorothy writing in her very first entry, on
January 20th: 'After the wet dark days, the country seems more
populous. It peoples itself in the sunbeams.' And William wrote
in the 'Alfoxden Note-book' of

> these populous slopes
> With all their groves and with their murmurous woods,
> Giving a curious feeling to the mind
> Of peopled solitude.[2]

And on February 1st Dorothy recorded: 'Full moon. She rose in
uncommon majesty over the sea, slowly ascending through the

---

[1] R. P. Graves, *Afternoon Lectures*, 1869, p. 299.
[2] *P.W.* v, appendix B, p. 341.

clouds.' William, perhaps as they 'sat with the window open an hour in the moonlight', wrote of

> solemn dreams,
> Dreams beautiful as the fair hues that lie
> About the moon in clouds of various depth,
> In many clouds about the full-orb'd moon.[1]

Their two favourite companions—the moon and the wind—haunt all about their writing almost antiphonally. The lines *A Whirlblast*,[2] which were published in 1802, describe the day—March 18th—when they 'sheltered under the hollies during a hail-shower. The withered leaves danced with the hailstones. William wrote a description of the storm.' And in the same manner on January 25th 'the clouds seemed to cleave asunder, and left her [the moon] in the centre of a black-blue vault. She sailed along, followed by multitudes of stars, small, and bright, and sharp.' This becomes blank verse of great splendour in William's *A Night-Piece*.[3]

A more ambitious fragment of his betrays how they shared more than the experience of the senses. He was now for the first time trying to put into words the central fact of his own inward life—that the senses are themselves capable of 'creation' —of re-creating and enhancing the beauty and significance of 'the thing perceived'. Speaking in the first person plural, he says:

> In many a walk
> At evening or by moonlight, or reclined
> At midday upon beds of forest moss,
> Have we to Nature and her impulses
> Of our whole being made free gift, and when
> Our trance had left us, oft have we, by aid
> Of the impressions which it left behind,
> Looked inward on ourselves, and learned, perhaps,
> Something of what we are.[4]

There is perhaps a hint of one of these happy 'trances' in Dorothy's Journal when on February 26th she describes how they 'Lay sidelong on the turf, and gazed on the landscape until it melted into more than natural loveliness'. On this occasion

---

[1] *P.W.* v, appendix B, p. 341.   [2] Ibid. ii, p. 127.
[3] Ibid. ii, p. 208.   [4] Ibid. v, p. 343.

Coleridge was with them. How his poetry too is shot through with the same descriptions of things observed in fellowship with Dorothy and William has often been remarked—the 'one red leaf, the last of its clan' in *Christabel*, which Dorothy noted on March 7th: the 'restless gossamers' of *The Ancient Mariner* observed on Quantock top on the day, early in February, when the whole heath was 'restless and glittering with . . . the waving of the spiders' threads'.[1] Most interesting of all perhaps is the description of the moon in *Christabel*:

> The thin gray cloud is spread on high,
> It covers but not hides the sky.
> The moon is behind and at the full,
> And yet she looks both small and dull.

The corresponding entries in Dorothy's Journal are for January 25th, 27th, and 31st, while Coleridge was still away at Shrewsbury. 'The sky spread over with one continuous cloud, whitened by the light of the Moon. . . .' 'The sky flat, unmarked by distances, a white thin cloud' . . . 'When we left home the moon immensely large, the sky scattered over with clouds. These soon closed in, contracting the dimensions of the moon without concealing her.' *Christabel* was not begun until early in April, as its references to the late spring, also recorded by Dorothy, clearly show; we are therefore faced with the probability that, in his description of the moon, Coleridge was actually drawing on Dorothy's Journal.

From February onwards until the middle of May Wordsworth's output of poetry was rapid and voluminous. It was all poetry which, although opinions both then and now differ about its merits, was highly original in language and feeling, possessing something which has come to be regarded as authentically 'Wordsworthian', and so as marking a new era in English poetic creation. In these three months he completed *The Ruined Cottage*; wrote all the poems, except *Tintern Abbey*, which in September he published in *Lyrical Ballads*; the whole of *Peter Bell*; and, most important of all in Coleridge's eyes, began what he intended to be a long poem, called *The Recluse*.[2]

---

[1] *D.W.J.* i, p. 7. Feb. 8th 1798.

[2] In the MS. called 'the Alfoxden Note-book', containing drafts for the completion of *The Ruined Cottage*, dating from the early months of 1798, occur some strange lines which seem to be a throw-back to the 'gothic' style of his earlier work,

although they contain a note of genuine though gloomy passion. They are, perhaps, a reminiscence of his last unhappy days with Annette, brought on by the disappointment and depression of the London visit and the rejection of the play.

> Away, away, it is the air
>   That stirs among the withered leaves;
> Away, away, it is not there,
> Go, hunt among the harvest-sheaves.
> There is a bed in shape as plain
> As from a hare or lion's lair
> It is the bed where we have lain
> In anguish and despair.
>
> Away, and take the eagle's eye,
>   The tyger's smell,
> Ears that can hear the agonies
> And murmurings of hell;
> And when you there have stood
> By that same bed of pain,
> The groans are gone, the tears remain.
> Then tell me if the thing be clear,
>   The difference betwixt a tear
> Of water and of blood.

P.W. iv, p. 357.

XI

THE PEDLAR, THE RECLUSE, AND LYRICAL BALLADS, 1798

Bards of Passion and of Mirth,
Ye have left your souls on earth!
JOHN KEATS

From January to March 1798—the first two months of the period of poetic creation—Wordsworth was engaged in writing blank verse. There were two main streams, which eventually united into one. The two were, first, *The Ruined Cottage*, expanded into a long poem of over nine hundred lines; and then the lines beginning 'On Man, on Nature and on Human Life' which eventually found their home, many years afterwards, as the 'prospectus' to *The Excursion*, of which *The Ruined Cottage* formed the first book. Both compositions were, by the beginning of March 1798, intended to form part of a long, comprehensive, and ambitious poem to be entitled *The Recluse; or Views of Man, Nature and Society.* There were, besides these two main compositions, many other fragments of blank verse, some of which were also intended for *The Recluse.* The additions to *The Ruined Cottage* may first be considered.

We do not know the exact form or length of this poem as it was first read to Coleridge at Racedown, but on March 9th 1798 Dorothy wrote an important letter about it to Mary Hutchinson who had been at Racedown when it was first composed. 'You desire me, my dear Mary,' she writes, 'to send you a copy of the Ruined Cottage. This is impossible for it has grown to the length of 900 lines. I will however send you a copy of that part which is immediately and solely connected with the Cottage. The Pedlar's character now makes a very, certainly the *most*, considerable part of the Poem.' She then copied out nearly four hundred lines, adding 'You have the rest to the end of Margaret's story. . . . I must request that you will not let this poem go out of your own hands, even into your brother Jack's.'

Even that part of the poem which was copied by Dorothy had grown and altered since Racedown. There is in it, for instance, an example of the way in which Wordsworth and Dorothy observed and described the same incident, the one in his poem, the other in her Journal. Dorothy writes in her Journal on February 4th: 'The moss rubbed from the palings by the sheep, that leave locks of wool, and the red marks with which they are spotted, upon the wood.' In *The Ruined Cottage* Wordsworth thus describes the stones of Margaret's threshold:

> With dull red stains discoloured, and stuck o'er
> With tufts and hairs of wool, as if the sheep
> That feed upon the commons thither came
> As to a couching place, and rubbed their sides
> Even at her threshold.

But the main change in the poem, as Dorothy says, concerns the 'Pedlar'. In the poem as read to Coleridge he and the narrator, 'I', had simply met as 'strangers'—this we know because in a letter to Estlin from Racedown Coleridge quotes some lines in which the Pedlar thus addresses the poet.[1] But now they are no longer 'strangers' but old acquaintances:

> I knew him. He was born of lowly race
> On Cumbrian hills.

The Pedlar is in fact compounded of Wordsworth's old friend the Packman of Hawkshead, and of Wordsworth himself. Almost all the spiritual experience of Wordsworth's boyhood is here attributed to him—the force of the impressions made on his mind by 'great objects' in nature, the brooding of the memory on those objects, the conviction of the existence of a 'mind' or life in inanimate nature; even an ineffable experience at sunrise when

> the clouds were touched
> And in their silent faces did he read
> Unutterable love. Sound needed none
> Nor any voice of joy: his spirit drank
> The spectacle. Sensation, soul and form
> All melted into him.

This is beyond doubt an early version of the 'dedication' experience at sunrise during his first long vacation, recorded in

[1] *U.L.* i, p. 76.

the fourth book of *The Prelude*. Even the Pedlar's early literary tastes are the same—fairy-tales and Euclid—while the Bible, of which we hear curiously little in the early books of *The Prelude*, plays a greater part:

> Ah! *then* how beautiful, how bright appeared
> The written promise.

Yet this too bears its own significant qualification:

> But in the mountains did he *feel* his faith,
> There did he see the writing.

And this follows close on some lines which throw much light on what Coleridge called Wordsworth's 'semi-atheism', and are indeed a more direct statement of Wordsworth's religious experience in youth than anything in *The Prelude*.

> In such access of mind, in such high hour
> Of visitation from the living God,
> He did not feel the God: he felt his works;
>
> .   .   .   .   .
>
> Such hour by prayer or praise was unprofaned,
> He neither prayed, nor offered thanks or praise,
> His mind was a thanksgiving to the power
> That made him; it was blessedness and love.[1]

This passage, with some significant softenings of the blunt statements, is to be found in the first book of *The Excursion*,[2] together with very many of the other lines about the Pedlar. Others again have been taken into *The Prelude*.[3]

The Ruined Cottage, as expanded and completed by Wordsworth at Alfoxden in February 1798 is therefore strongly self-descriptive and is most important as showing how his mind was being attracted to think about the experiences of his youth. In the next two years this tendency became a settled determination to write an autobiographical 'poem to Coleridge' as part of *The Recluse*.

The lines beginning 'On Man, on Nature and on Human Life', although there is no manuscript which can be precisely dated,[4] were clearly meant to be a prelude, preamble, or introduction to

---

[1] *P.W.* v, p. 382.   [2] Ibid., p. 15.
[3] e.g. ll. 238–56 of *The Ruined Cottage* are to be found in the 1805 text of *Prel.* II, ll. 416–34.
[4] The earliest copy seems to belong to 1798 or 1799.

a longer poem, for they contain a statement of what he wanted
to write about:

> Of Truth, of Grandeur, Beauty, Love, and Hope,
> And melancholy Fear subdued by Faith;
> Of blessèd consolations in distress;
> Of moral strength and intellectual Power;
> Of joy in widest commonalty spread;
> Of the individual Mind that keeps her own
> Inviolate retirement.

This last above all, the Mind of Man, was to be

> My haunt, and the main region of my song.

It is possible that it is to these lines, and not to those usually
called 'the preamble' which now stand at the opening of *The
Prelude,* that he refers at the beginning of the seventh book of
that work, written in the autumn of 1804.[1]

> Six changeful years have vanished since I first
> Poured out (saluted by that quickening breeze
> Which met me issuing from the City's walls)
> A glad preamble to this Verse: I sang
> Aloud, with fervour irresistible
> Of short-lived transport, like a torrent bursting
> From a black thunder-cloud, down Scafell's side
> To rush and disappear. But soon broke forth
> (So willed the Muse) a less impetuous stream
> That flowed awhile with unabating strength
> Then stopped for years.

If this is the case, the difficulty about the date of the 'preamble',
hitherto supposed to be 1795, disappears. Six years before 1804
brings us to 1798, and we may even venture to surmise that as
he and Dorothy left Bristol on that January morning to return
to Alfoxden,[2] William burst forth into some such strains, just
as three years earlier he had sung aloud in anticipation of his
new freedom at Racedown. As we shall see, this was a 'short-
lived transport'; but was continued a few months later in Germany, when he began to write the 'poem on his own life'. For
the germ of *The Prelude* is to be found in these early lines,

---

[1] H. M. Margoliouth, *Wordsworth and Coleridge* (1953), pp. 130–1.
[2] See above, p. 352.

where, after praying for 'a gift of genuine insight' into his theme, he goes on:

> And if with this
> I mix more lowly matter; with the thing
> Contemplated describe the Mind and Man
> Contemplating; and who, and what he was—
> The transitory Being who beheld
> This Vision; when and where and how he lived;—
> Be not this labour useless,—

words which suggest that Wordsworth envisaged writing *The Prelude* at the very moment when he thought he was going to write on more universal themes. But for the present we must look on these lines as a prelude or prologue to the work which he intended to call *The Recluse*.

The first mention of *The Recluse* by name is in a letter to James Losh dated March 11th 1798. 'I have written', he says, '1300 lines of a poem which I hope to make of considerable utility. Its title will be *The Recluse; or Views of Nature, Man and Society.*' To another friend he wrote in the same style a few days earlier, that he was engaged on a poem 'in which I contrive to convey most of the knowledge of which I am possessed. . . . I know not anything which will not come within the scope of my plan.'[1]

This description of *The Recluse*, and above all its sub-title, is almost identical with Coleridge's description in after years of his own unwritten poem, *The Brook*, the preparations for which had so alarmed the neighbourhood. This work, said Coleridge, was to 'give equal freedom for description, incident and impassioned reflections on men, nature and society'.[2] But Wordsworth, as we should expect of him, gives Nature pride of place.

Coleridge had indeed succeeded in persuading Wordsworth to attempt what he himself had projected in *The Brook*. Wordsworth, he believed, was that perfect combination of philosopher and poet which he—and the world—were waiting for. Admiration and affection united to make Coleridge declare loudly, 'Thou art the man'. Long afterwards he related what he remembered

---

[1] *E.L.* 75 and 74, pp. 190 and 188. W.W. to James Losh, Mar. 11th 1798, and James Tobin, Mar. 6th 1798.

[2] It is possible also that the sub-title owed something to Thelwall's 'Politico-Sentimental Journals' which appeared in 1793 with the title *The Peripatetic, or Sketches of the Heart, of Nature and Society.*

of their schemes:[1] 'The plan laid out and, I believe, partly suggested by me, was, that Wordsworth should assume the station of a man in mental repose, one whose principles were made up, and so prepared to deliver upon authority a system of philosophy. He was to treat man as man, a subject of ear, touch and taste, in contact with external nature, and informing the senses from the mind, and not compounding a mind out of the senses.'

Now in supposing that Wordsworth could ever 'deliver upon authority a system of philosophy' Coleridge was following a will-o'-the-wisp. Wordsworth was not a philosopher but a poet. Only Coleridge's enthusiasm could ever have persuaded him that he could undertake the task as Coleridge envisaged it. It is true that in a sense he was what Coleridge said he was: 'Spectator ab extra': but the field of his vision was primarily his own mental experience, with whatever understanding of 'Nature, Man and Society' arose out of that.

Coleridge goes on: 'Then he was to describe the pastoral and other states of society, assuming something of a Juvenalian spirit as he approached the high civilisation of cities and towns. . . . thence he was to infer, and reveal the proof of and necessity for the whole state of man and society being subject to and illustrative of, a redemptive process in operation showing how this idea reconciled all anomalies and promised future glory and restoration.'

Here we are somewhat nearer to Wordsworth's present and future achievements. Parts of *The Prelude* and *The Excursion* do reveal a 'Juvenalian spirit', and in *The Ruined Cottage* Wordsworth had taught something like a doctrine of redemption through the quiet acceptance of suffering. Both Margaret and the Pedlar have something to teach of the capacity of the human spirit to make something of its own misfortunes, and in *Hart-leap Well*, written two years afterwards, there is an approach towards the hope of a redeemed humanity. Coleridge at this very time was writing *The Ancient Mariner*, which is the story of the redemption of a human soul from a state of condemnation into one of humility and peace.

Returning to *The Recluse*, what did Wordsworth include in the

[1] *Table Talk*, &c., ed. T. Ashe, 1884, July 31st 1832. Quoted *P.W.* v, p. 364.

'1300 lines' from which he hoped so much? There was, first, *The Ruined Cottage*, which with its recent additions amounted now to 960 lines.[1] This, we know, he afterwards spoke of as 'part of' *The Recluse*, although he also considered publishing it as a separate poem called *The Pedlar*.[2] Eventually it became the first book of *The Excursion*, which again was 'a portion' of *The Recluse*. Besides *The Ruined Cottage*, we have, in March 1798, the 'glad preamble', 107 lines, and several other long blank-verse compositions from which we can take our choice for the rest. There was for instance *The Old Cumberland Beggar*, written at Racedown, very similar in pathos to the earlier parts of *The Ruined Cottage*, consisting of 197 lines in the printed text, but longer in its original form. There was also the description of the 'Discharged Soldier', later incorporated into the fourth book of *The Prelude*; the existence of some lines from it in an early note-book proves it to be of this early date.[3]

Having got so far, Wordsworth went no farther until the following winter in Germany, when he began to write the 'poem on his own life' which was to become *The Prelude* and which he was accustomed to describe as 'an appendix' to the unwritten *Recluse*. The rest of the spring and summer of 1798 at Alfoxden was spent writing short poems for a projected volume to be called *Lyrical Ballads*, and one narrative poem of considerable length—*Peter Bell*. *The Recluse* continued to haunt about his mind for the rest of his life, but except for one book called *Home at Grasmere*, written in the early spring of 1800, he never wrote any more of it. What was written already was included for the most part either in *The Excursion* or in *The Prelude*. It has been said that *The Recluse* was never in fact much more than 'a Prelude to the main theme and an Excursion from it'.[4] This is true, and must be accepted with thankfulness as being Wordsworth's own interpretation of his calling as a poet, and not Coleridge's.

The 'preamble' or prologue to *The Recluse* throws light on one aspect of his relations with Coleridge on which Coleridge felt some anxiety. Wordsworth did not share Coleridge's religious convictions. Coleridge's approach to the study of

---

[1] This is including the 'Addendum to MS. B', *P.W.*, v, pp. 400–4, 147 lines, and a passage of seventy-four lines (ibid., pp. 386–7, app. crit.) never incorporated into the complete text.

[2] See below, pp. 520–2.   [3] *Prel.*, pp. xxi and xxxiii.

[4] H. Darbishire, *Wordsworth*, 1950, p. 90.

human problems was avowedly theistic and what he called Christian—though his definition of 'the Christian religion' at this time would scarcely be accepted as an adequate description of the historic Christian faith.[1] He believed in God and in prayer and he read the Bible daily. In philosophy he had now added the idealism of Berkeley to the sensationalism of Hartley, and his two sons were called in turn after these sages. 'Hartley and Berkeley are his idols', said Reynell of him in the summer of 1797. He was intimate with several distinguished Unitarian ministers, such as Estlin at Bristol and Toulmin at Taunton. He preached frequently in Unitarian chapels, and pleaded eloquently with Thelwall against atheism and materialism. Coleridge, in his exuberance and unreserve, poured forth his feelings and opinions about all things in heaven and earth, both in his letters and in that never-ending stream of talk that was always fascinating, though not always readily comprehensible by ordinary human kind. But in conversation with Wordsworth on the subject of religion, Coleridge presently found that even he had better put a brake on his own eloquence.

On one subject [he wrote to Estlin in May 1798] we are habitually silent; we found our data dissimilar, and never renewed the subject. It is his practice and almost his nature to convey all the truth he knows without any attack on what he supposes falsehood, if that falsehood be interwoven with virtues or happiness. He loves and venerates Christ and Christianity. I wish he did more, but it were wrong indeed if an incoincidence with one of our wishes altered our respect and affection to a man of whom we are as it were instructed by one great Master to say that not being against us he is for us.

During his visit to Racedown Coleridge had shown Wordsworth some of Estlin's sermons and wrote to Estlin: 'He admires your sermon against Paine much more than your last; I suppose because he is more inclined to Christianity than to Theism, simply considered.' The 'Sermon against Paine' was one published in Bristol in 1796 with the title *Evidences of Revealed Religion and particularly Christianity, stated with reference to a Pamphlet called The Age of Reason*. It was an

[1] 'Now the religion which Christ taught is simply, first, that there is an omnipresent Father . . . and secondly that when we die we . . . shall continue to enjoy or suffer the consequences . . . of the habits we have formed here, whether good or evil. This is the Christian *religion* and *all* of the Christian *religion*.' *S.T.C.* i, p. 199. S.T.C. to Thelwall, Dec. 17th 1796.

extremely able and lucid defence of the early date and historicity of the books of the New Testament. 'Your last' was a discourse on *The Nature and Causes of Atheism*, mainly an exposition of the 'argument from Design' in Nature, and of the 'sense of religion' in man. Wordsworth may well have appreciated better the solid historical grounds on which Estlin met Paine's shallow objections than his more conventional arguments about the 'existence of God'.

To understand the 'dissimilarity of data' between Wordsworth and Coleridge on the subject of religion, we must bear in mind the intensity of Wordsworth's absorption in the interaction of the 'mind of man' with Nature. To him this was in itself a gospel and there was not, at present, much room for Coleridge's theological faith as well. The 'preamble' to *The Recluse* bears witness to the distinction. After saying that 'affecting thoughts', 'dear remembrances', and 'feelings of delight' often visit him while musing

> On Man, on Nature and on Human Life,

he declares his intention of celebrating these emotions in verse, praying only, with Milton, 'fit audience let me find though few'. The difficulty of the task is great, for it has no precedent and will lead him into entirely new paths.

> All strength—all terror, single or in bands,
> That ever was put forth in personal form—
> Jehovah—with his thunder, and the choir
> Of shouting Angels, and the empyreal thrones—
> I pass them unalarmed. Not Chaos, not
> The darkest pit of lowest Erebus,
> Nor aught of blinder vacancy, scooped out
> By help of dreams—can breed such fear and awe
> As fall upon us often when we look
> Into our Minds, into the Mind of Man—
> My haunt and the main region of my song.

Now not only does this by-passing of Jehovah and the heavenly choirs show Wordsworth aiming at something which he considered of as much importance to mankind as the theme of *Paradise Lost*, but it is also a sort of counter-cry to Coleridge in his *Religious Musings*, that flamboyant hymn in which the Book of Revelation, Habakkuk, *Paradise Lost*, Hartley and Berkeley are all laid under contribution, and the world is full of the divine 'diffusion'.

> But 'tis God
> Diffused through all that doth make all one whole;
> This the worst superstition, him except
> Aught to desire, Supreme Reality!

It concludes with a vision of the triumph of God.

> The veiling clouds retire,
> And lo! the Throne of the redeeming God
> Forth flashing unimaginable day
> Wraps in one blaze earth, heaven and deepest hell.

Wordsworth, on the other hand, found the earth as it was quite enough for him—or rather, the earth, 'this goodly universe', wedded to 'the discerning intellect of Man'. Heaven and Paradise were not metaphysical conceptions, but

> A simple produce of the common day.

The 'fitting' of the mind to the external world he finds 'exquisite', and (recollecting his experience of the 'living' universe) the converse of that process, the 'fitting' of the external world to the mind, is also exquisite, with the consequent

> creation (by no lower name
> Can it be called) which they with blessed might
> Accomplish.

This is an approach to reality very different from Coleridge's, though probably neither poet would say that their 'systems' were mutually exclusive. Coleridge's faith, though sincere and deep, was based on intellectual conceptions and clothed in images drawn from his voluminous reading. Wordsworth's was purely empirical, the result of inward experience of exceptional power, extending back to the earliest recesses of memory. To describe it was perhaps the most lonely adventure ever undertaken by the human mind.

When Dorothy sent the copy of *The Ruined Cottage* to Mary Hutchinson on March 9th she said of her brother: 'William was very unwell last week, oppressed with languor and weakness. He is better now. He gets up between seven and eight in the mornings and I dare say will continue it for he is fully convinced of the relaxing tendency of lying in bed so many hours. His faculties seem to expand every day—he composes with much more facility than he did, as to the *mechanism* of poetry, and his ideas flow faster than he can express them.'

Up to this first week of March 1798 he had been engaged entirely in blank-verse composition. From early March onwards, however, there was a change, and a large number of poems in short ballad metres occupied him during the spring months of March, April, and May. These poems formed the bulk of the volume called *Lyrical Ballads and A Few Other Poems* which Cottle accepted for publication in May. The two longest of them are *The Idiot Boy* and *The Thorn*; there are four other short ballads about characters in English rustic life—*Simon Lee, Goody Blake and Harry Gill, We are Seven,* and *The Last of the Flock.* There is *Anecdote for Fathers,* the study in child psychology of which the hero is young Basil Montagu; and there are two poems about deserted women—*The Mad Mother* and *The Complaint of a Forsaken Indian Woman.* There is that part of *Salisbury Plain* which concerns the Woman, under the title *The Female Vagrant,* the *Lines left upon a Seat in a Yew-tree,* and two early poems, *The Convict* and *Remembrance of Collins.* And there are four poems which are not ballads at all, but lyrics in which Wordsworth reveals his feelings and his faith: they are—*Lines written at a small Distance from my House* ('It is the first mild day of March'), *Lines written in Early Spring* ('I heard a thousand blended notes'), *Expostulation and Reply* ('Why, William, on that old grey stone'), and its companion poem, *The Tables Turned* ('Up! up! my friend and clear your looks'). Finally, added when the volume was already in the press, are the *Lines Written a few Miles above Tintern Abbey.*

Coleridge's contribution consisted of only four poems, but of these one was *The Ancient Mariner,* and it stood at the beginning of the volume. *The Nightingale,* one of the loveliest of his blank-verse 'conversation pieces', redolent in every line of the delights of that intoxicating spring, was fortunately substituted, just before the volume appeared, for *Lewti,* a love poem which had already appeared in the *Morning Post* in April and whose inclusion would have destroyed the anonymity of the volume which both poets wished to preserve, for Coleridge was widely known to be its author. Besides, *Lewti* is little more than an enlargement and transformation into what he calls a 'Circassian Love-Chant' of Wordsworth's youthful poem *Beauty and Moonlight*. Like *The Three Graves*, it is an example of a poem handed over by Wordsworth to Coleridge to finish. The other two poems by Coleridge are *The Foster-Mother's Tale* and *The Dungeon*, both extracts from Coleridge's tragedy *Osorio*. The latter shows strong signs of Wordsworth's influence and teaching.

The history of *Lyrical Ballads* is somewhat complicated, but its origins can be traced, like those of *The Ancient Mariner*, to the necessity of raising a little extra money with which to meet future expenses. Early in March the Wordsworths received the news that as from midsummer Alfoxden was let to the Cruikshanks of Stowey[1] and that they would therefore again be homeless. They thought of returning to Racedown, of a walking tour in Wales, or possibly of visiting the Hutchinsons at Sockburn.[2] But on March 9th the Coleridges came on a ten-day visit, and at once Coleridge began to propound another and more venturesome plan for both their households. The first we hear of the German plan is in a letter of Wordsworth to James Losh written on March 11th. 'We have a delightful scheme in agitation', he says. 'We have come to a resolution, Coleridge, Mrs. Coleridge, my Sister, and myself of going into Germany, where we purpose to pass the two ensuing years in order to acquire the German language and to furnish ourselves with a tolerable stock of information in natural science. Our plan is to settle, if possible, in a village near a University, in a pleasant, and if we can a mountainous country.'

Many modifications were to be made in this plan before it was finally put into execution, the chief being the dropping of Mrs. Coleridge from the party. The whole idea is much more characteristic of Coleridge than of Wordsworth; he told Poole that he regarded it as of high importance 'to my intellectual utility and of course my moral happiness'. Life at Nether Stowey, even with Wordsworth close at hand, was too narrow for the range and variety of his mental interests and particularly his

[1] *E.L.* 74, p. 188. W.W. to James Tobin, Mar. 6th 1798.
[2] Ibid. 73, p. 176. D.W. to Mary Hutchinson, Mar. 5th 1798, and 74, p. 188

quest for philosophical and metaphysical enlightenment. He wanted to learn German and to explore and assimilate the writings of German philosophers and theologians; above all to master the works of the inscrutable Kant.

The expenses of a sojourn in Germany would be considerable. Coleridge would be supported by the Wedgwood annuity, of which the first instalment was paid to him in this early part of March; but Wordsworth and Dorothy would have to acquire new funds. They had nothing to sell but poetry. Coleridge therefore now began a long correspondence with Cottle. The idea of publishing a joint volume of poetry had been mooted as early as the walk on which *The Ancient Mariner* had been conceived;[1] it had been set aside during Coleridge's absence in Shrewsbury and Bristol; now financial necessities made them take it up again. Coleridge, in an undated letter to Cottle which must, however, have been written from Alfoxden in March, says that he is 'requested by Wordsworth to put to you the following questions. What could you . . . and what would you give for—first, our two Tragedies, with small prefaces, containing an analysis of our principal characters?[2] . . . second— Wordsworth's *Salisbury Plain* and *Tale of a Woman*, which two poems, with a few others which he will add, and the notes, will make a volume.'

The Tale of a Woman must be *The Ruined Cottage*, which is nowhere else referred to by that title. Lamb, however, called it the story of Margaret' when he met it again years afterwards as Book I of *The Excursion*. That Wordsworth was considering publishing it is interesting. The copy made by Dorothy of the poem just before she wrote to Mary Hutchinson on March 5th when she sent her a copy of 'that part which is immediately and solely connected with the Cottage') had been written out neatly on fifty-two octavo sheets and stitched together.[3] It was prefaced, under the title, by a quotation from Burns' *Epistle to John Lapraik*:

> Give me a spark of Nature's fire,
> 'Tis the best learning I desire—

. . . . .

[1] See above, p. 347.
[2] An interesting point as it shows that Wordsworth meant at this time to publish as preface to *The Borderers* if the tragedy was published.
[3] *P.W.* v, p. 378.

My Muse though homely in attire
May touch the heart.

It was divided into two parts at line 452, and 'The End' written
after the line 'Last human tenant of these ruined walls'. *The
Ruined Cottage* was thus a poem complete in itself and ready for
publication.

Cottle says that he offered the two poets thirty guineas each
'for their two tragedies'. He also says that he visited Coleridge
at Stowey (apparently at the end of March or very early in
April 1798), and that Wordsworth then read him 'many of his
Lyrical Pieces', which Cottle, seeing in them 'a peculiar but
decided merit', offered to publish at his own risk.[1] What he
seems eventually to have proposed was the publication of
Wordsworth's long poems, *Salisbury Plain* and *Peter Bell*, in
one volume, and the shorter poems in another; nothing more is
said of *The Ruined Cottage* under any title. But Wordsworth was
'decisively repugnant and oppugnant' to publishing his own poems
in two volumes. He was determined on a joint, anonymous publication with Coleridge, for, wrote Coleridge, he and Wordsworth
'regard the volumes offered to you as to a certain degree one
work, in kind, though not in degree, as an ode is one work,
and that our different poems are as stanzas, good, relatively
rather than absolutely'. At the same time he explained that they
had decided not to publish their tragedies if they could raise the
necessary money for the German trip in some other way, either
by selling their poems, or, he added, 'we could procure the money
without selling the poems'. He probably had his benefactors the
Wedgwoods in mind. They would advance money to Wordsworth, as in fact they eventually did. He ended by begging
Cottle to come down again 'and we will go on a roam to Linton
and Linmouth'.[2] Wordsworth also wrote urging Cottle to come
'You will be pleased', he says, 'to hear that I have gone on
very rapidly adding to my stock of poetry. Do come and let me
read it to you under the old trees in the park.' This was written
on May 9th; Cottle's visit must have taken place before the

---

[1] *Cottle*, i, p. 309.

[2] Ibid. p. 313. This letter is undated but is probably about Apr. 12th.

[3] *E.L.* 76, p. 140. There is no record in Dorothy's Journal of any meeting with
Cottle, or visit from him, which is strange, but as the manuscript is missing
omissions in the published version cannot be checked.

end of May, for on May 31st Dorothy wrote to her brother Richard: 'William has now some poems in the Bristol press. . . . William has sold his poems very advantageously'—showing that the business had been successfully concluded. Cottle himself gives no definite dates, but his visit probably took place in the last week of May.[1] The poets took their publisher on their favourite tour to Lynmouth and the Valley of Rocks, and in the course of the visit the character of the volume he was to publish was finally determined. It was to consist of one volume only of poems by both poets. *Peter Bell* was not to be included, and there was to be only an extract from *Salisbury Plain*. *The Ancient Mariner* was to stand at the beginning, and Cottle took the manuscript of this poem back with him to Bristol. He agreed to pay thirty guineas for the copyright of the poems. In all these transactions Wordsworth insisted on publishing only jointly with Coleridge. Their life together during the past year no doubt made this arrangement seem a fitting climax; yet Wordsworth could, had he wished, have made a more striking appearance before the world if he had accepted Cottle's first suggestion. The explanation probably lies partly in his often-reiterated dislike of publishing; he told Cottle after the poems appeared that he only published them for the sake of the money they would bring. And in the end Cottle only paid ten of the thirty guineas before the departure for Germany: the journey was financed by the Wedgwoods.[2]

Both poets, against Cottle's advice, insisted on remaining anonymous. 'Wordsworth's name is nothing,' said Coleridge, 'and mine stinks.' The *Essay on Man*, the *Botanic Garden*, the *Pleasures of Memory*, he said, were published anonymously. They also refused to dedicate the volume to the Wedgwoods as Cottle suggested. It would, said Coleridge, be 'indelicate and unmeaning', for *Lyrical Ballads* was not the result of their benefaction. Finally, Coleridge gave Cottle some typographical hints—'18 lines to a page, the lines closely printed, certainly more closely printed than those of "Joan"; ("Oh, by all means, closer, *W. Wordsworth*")[3] equal ink, and large margins; that is beauty.'

Coleridge's remark about the volume being in effect 'one

[1] See below, p. 396.   [2] See below, p. 409.
[3] Added in W.W.'s hand and signed by him.

work', and the component poems as stanzas of an ode, shows how closely the two were working and thinking together. They had spent a great deal of time talking about poetic style and the kind of subjects with which modern poetry should deal. Coleridge afterwards described their proceedings.[1] The failure of the attempt to co-operate over *The Ancient Mariner* led eventually to a friendly agreement to write different kinds of poems while remaining faithful to two great general principles. There must be, in every poem, 'a faithful adherence to the truth of nature': and also 'the power of giving the interest of novelty by the modifying colours of imagination'. The enterprise was symbolized for them by what they saw as they ranged about the country-side. Such things as 'the sudden charm which . . . moon-light or sunset diffused over a known and familiar landscape. . . . These are the poetry of nature.' The two kinds of poetry which were to share this common principle were, first, the 'supernatural', or 'at least romantic', of which *The Ancient Mariner* was the living, growing exemplar when these ideas were taking shape: secondly, the 'matter-of-fact', whose 'subjects were to be chosen from ordinary life, the characters and incidents were to be such as will be found in every village and its vicinity, where there is a meditative and feeling mind to seek after them'. It was Wordsworth who supplied the 'meditative and feeling mind' for these 'matter-of-fact' poems.

In the short 'Advertisement' which Wordsworth wrote for the *Ballads* he says that 'the majority of the following poems are to be considered as experiments'. There is no reason to suppose that either Wordsworth or Coleridge thought that all poetry should henceforward be written in the style of the boldest of the *Ballads*; indeed, both poets were engaged at the same time in other kinds of composition which they regarded as equally, if not more, important. Wordsworth had begun *The Recluse* and finished *The Ruined Cottage*. Soon afterwards he wrote *Tintern Abbey*. Coleridge wrote *France: An Ode* and *Fears in Solitude*— his two greatest poems whose inspiration is political and national—in this very month of April. *Lyrical Ballads* is an experiment of a strictly limited kind; it was undertaken, say the 'Advertisement', 'to ascertain how far the language of conversation in the middle and lower classes of society is adapted

[1] *B.L.*, ch. xiv.

to the purposes of poetic pleasure'. When he revised and enlarged the 'Advertisement' into the preface to the second edition
in 1800, he altered the phrase 'the language of conversation' to
'the real language of men in a state of vivid sensation'. But the
'middle classes' by 1800 have faded away in favour of 'low and
rustic life', and the language of such people is chosen 'because,
in that condition, the essential passions of the heart find a better
soil in which they can attain their maturity . . . and speak a
plainer and more emphatic language'. Also (and here Wordsworth voiced a doctrine dear to him but most unacceptable to
the critics) 'because in that condition the passions of men are
incorporated with the beautiful and permanent forms of nature'.
This social intercourse with Nature, said Wordsworth, enabled
the poor to use 'simple and unelaborated expressions' to convey
their feelings; of recent years poetry had been bound within a
convention of so-called poetic language which bore no relation
to the 'real language of men', and was consequently of little
value save 'to furnish food for fickle tastes and fickle appetites'.

   In the original advertisement he did not insist on these doctrines of the superiority of the 'rustic' classes and their language.
Rather, the reader was invited to shake off his preconceived
ideas as to what constituted 'poetry' and to judge of it from a
new angle. As the 'Advertisement' is much less well known than
the prefaces of 1800 and subsequent editions, it is not inappropriate to quote the main part of it here.

   Readers [says Wordsworth] accustomed to the gaudiness and
inane phraseology of many modern writers, if they persist in reading
this book to its conclusion, will perhaps frequently have to struggle
with feelings of strangeness and aukwardness [*sic*]: they will look
round for poetry, and will be induced to enquire by what species of
courtesy these attempts can be permitted to assume that title. It is
desirable that such readers, for their own sakes, should not suffer the
solitary word Poetry, a word of very disputed meaning, to stand in
the way of their gratification; but that, while they are perusing this
book, they should ask themselves if it contains a natural delineation of
human passions, human characters, and human incidents; and if the
answer be favourable to the author's wishes, that they should consent
to be pleased in spite of that most dreadful enemy to our pleasures, our
own pre-established codes of decision. Readers of superior judgment
may disapprove of the style in which many of these pieces are executed;
it must be expected that many lines and phrases will not exactly suit

their taste. It will perhaps appear to them, that wishing to avoid the prevalent fault of the day, the author has sometimes descended too low, and that many of his expressions are too familiar, and not of sufficient dignity. It is apprehended that the more conversant the reader is with our elder writers, and with those in modern times who have been the most successful in painting manners and passions, the fewer complaints of this kind will he have to make.

It is clear from this modestly worded little preface that Wordsworth knew well enough that the *Ballads* were not likely to be acceptable to everybody. Later, in response to much criticism, some of it unjust enough, he expanded and hardened his original contention, adding to it much that was and must remain controversial and exaggerated, besides much that is of the highest importance in the definition and understanding of his own and of all true poetry.

Of what was Wordsworth thinking when he spoke of 'the gaudiness and inane phraseology of many modern writers'? 'Gaudiness' might be said to describe Darwin's *Loves of the Plants* and some of Gray's odes. The absurd personifications and refinements of classical periphrasis of Darwin's poem had had their attractions for him when he wrote *Descriptive Sketches*, but he had long outgrown the taste for them. Gray he was coming to regard as one of the chief 'of those who, by their reasonings, have attempted to widen the space of separation betwixt Prose and Metrical composition, and was more than any other man curiously elaborate in the structure of his own poetic diction'.[1] An exception would of course always be made for the *Elegy*. As for 'inane phraseology', he may perhaps have been thinking of the 'Della Cruscans'; Robert Merry, 'Perdita,' and their followers. In Germany in October he speaks of some gardens at Hamburg imitating English gardens 'as Della Crusca might imitate Virgil'. The 'elder writers' would include Chaucer and above all the ballad-makers; by the moderns who have successfully painted 'manners and passions' he no doubt meant Burns, Crabbe, Goldsmith, Langhorne, and Cowper.

Although the *Lyrical Ballads* have all of them the strong originality which is one of the marks of genius, and which made them for long unpopular with the critics, they were by no means beyond the range of the taste of the day in their subjects

---

[1] Preface to *Lyrical Ballads*, 1800, *P.W.* i, p. 391.

and in their appeal to the gentler passions. *The Ancient Mariner* was first thought of as a magazine poem, and magazine poetry, though still dominated by what Wordsworth would have called the 'inane' echoes of the classical school, also contained numerous examples of poems of which the theme was either the charms of Nature or the sufferings or misfortunes of humanity. Bereaved mothers, deserted women, and beggars abound in it, and Wordsworth's poems in this kind were new rather in their language and in their psychological and emotional power than in their subject.[1]

It has been well said that the *Lyrical Ballads*, as far as Wordsworth is concerned, are 'stray leaves' or 'fragments' torn from his own profound study of human emotion and human suffering.[2] They are not to be regarded as a complete testament to these things. *The Recluse* would be that; for *The Recluse* was still Wordsworth's dominating aim although he had reached a pause in its composition which was destined to be a long one. It was in *The Recluse* that he intended to 'convey most of the knowledge of which I am possessed', and this 'knowledge' would be mainly knowledge of the 'primary passions' of men and their results in human character, as he had already drawn them in *The Ruined Cottage* and *The Old Cumberland Beggar*.

What is remarkable about the *Ballads* is their bald objectivity, their penetrating scrutiny of the speech, the appearance, the feelings, and the hardships of those who were born to a 'poor and humble lot'. It is as though, as has been said, 'he had turned his back on his personal life and made something like a strenuous voyage of discovery—a sort of arctic expedition—into a region where life was reduced to its elements, the outward trappings to their simplest'.[3] Wordsworth was not, in the *Ballads*, glorifying poverty as such, or calling on the public to admire people because they were poor. It is indeed clear, especially from *The Last of the Flock*, that he recognized the moral dangers of extreme poverty, though he would not now have ascribed them, as he had three years before, simply to 'ignorance'. He was no advocate of the oppressive poverty which robs the poor man of all 'freedom in his love' and causes 'constriction of the

[1] R. Mayo, 'The Contemporaneity of the Lyrical Ballads', *P.M.L.A.*, June 1954.
[2] T. Hutchinson, *Lyrical Ballads*, 1898, p. xlvi.
[3] H. Darbishire, *Wordsworth*, 1950, p. 61.

heart' to his wife and children. In a blank-verse fragment probably meant for inclusion in *The Recluse*, he puts the problem of poverty in a new light:

> What then can we hope
> From one who is the worst of slaves, the slave
> Of his own home? The light that shines abroad,
> How can it lead him to an act of love?
> Whom can he comfort? Will the afflicted turn
> Their steps to him, or will the eye of grief
> And sorrow seek him? Is the name of friend
> Known to the poor man? Whence is he to hear
> The sweet creative voice of gratitude?[1]

The dates on which Wordsworth wrote or began to write many of the *Lyrical Ballads* are known or can be conjectured with a fair amount of accuracy. It is unlikely that he wrote many of them before that second week in March when Coleridge came to stay and the German plan was first discussed, for up till then he had been busy with the expansion of *The Ruined Cottage*, the lines that were to stand as a prologue to *The Recluse*, and plans for *The Recluse* itself. But on March 8th 1798 —the day before the Coleridges came and two days after Wordsworth had told Losh that he had written 1,300 lines of *The Recluse*—Dorothy noted in her Journal: 'Walked in the Park in the morning. I sate under the fir-trees. Coleridge came after dinner so we did not walk again. A foggy morning but a clear sunny day.' And the next day she wrote: 'A clear sunny morning, went to meet Mr. and Mrs. Coleridge. The day very warm.' Surely it was to celebrate this first burst of spring warmth— soon to give way again to cold windy weather—that William wrote the *Lines written at a small Distance from my House*, and sent them by the hand of little Basil, *to the Person to whom they are addressed*, that is to Dorothy. Later this long title was changed to the simpler one of *To my Sister*.

> It is the first mild day of March:
> Each minute sweeter than before,
> The red-breast sings from the tall larch
> That stands beside our door.

[1] See also *Prel.* XIII, ll. 198–200:
> When poverty and labour in excess
> From day to day preoccupy the ground
> Of the affections . . .

This lyric is probably the 'singular but fine little poem of Wordsworth's' which, says James Losh, Southey repeated to him in Bath on April 3rd. Southey may have obtained it through Cottle, to whom perhaps Coleridge sent a copy. Two others, which resemble it in spirit, *Expostulation and Reply* and its companion poem *The Tables Turned* were written as a result of a conversation with young William Hazlitt, who visited Coleridge at the end of May, and are therefore the last of the poems to be written for *Lyrical Ballads*.[1] They are also the first of the cycle of 'Matthew' poems which Wordsworth completed in Germany in the following winter: since 'Matthew' is a character founded mainly on Wordsworth's 'packman' friend at Hawkshead, the poems are an indication of Wordsworth's return in imagination to the scenes of his boyhood, which were to absorb him so completely in the months spent in Germany.

Though separated by some two months in composition, *Expostulation and Reply* and its sequel are so closely related in thought and feeling to the lines *To my Sister* that the three are almost like one poem. The advice given respectively to Matthew and to Dorothy is essentially the same. To Dorothy he had said:

> My Sister! ('tis a wish of mine)
> Now that our morning meal is done,
> Make haste, your morning task resign;
> Come forth and feel the sun.
>
> Edward[2] will come with you, and pray,
> Put on with speed your woodland dress,
> And bring no book, for this one day
> We'll give to idleness.

And to Matthew:

> Up! up! my friend, and clear your looks,
> Why all this toil and trouble?
> Up! up! my friend, and quit your books
> Or surely you'll grow double. . . .

---

[1] See below, p. 399.
[2] i.e. young Basil Montagu.

> Books! 'tis a dull and endless strife,
> Come, hear the woodland linnet,[1]
> How sweet his music; on my life
> There's more of wisdom in it.

To Dorothy he had declared that

> One moment now may give us more
> Than fifty years of reason;
> Our minds shall drink at every pore
> The spirit of the season.

And to Matthew that

> One impulse from a vernal wood
> May teach you more of man,
> Of moral evil and of good
> Than all the sages can.

Was it to mere idle outdoor rambling that Wordsworth was inviting his listeners? He would most strenuously have denied it. Rather it was to a new ethic; to an experience of joy, serenity, and love itself, which would inevitably, he believed, flow into and forth from the human heart if only it would give itself up to the observation and contemplation of 'Nature's' treasures. The soul would find itself rewarded and enriched through the eye, the ear, the touch. This was Wordsworth's own personal doctrine of 'necessity'. It sprang from the very roots of his own experience, and it still, through his poetry, 'speaks to the condition' of many human spirits. Yet in these lyrics did he not claim too much for the all-sufficiency of 'Nature'? In *Expostulation and Reply*, Matthew remonstrates with Wordsworth for 'dreaming his time away' and neglecting literature:

> Where are your books?—that light bequeathed
> To Beings else forlorn and blind!
> Up! up! and drink the spirit breathed
> From dead men to their kind.

And to this Wordsworth replies, first, that

> we can feed this mind of ours
> In a wise passiveness,[2]

[1] Wordsworth knew little about the names and species of birds. Linnets are not 'woodland' birds at all, and they are here merely symbols of all the smaller singers who inhabit trees and bushes.

[2] *For note see opposite page.*

and secondly, that listening to a bird singing was to be preferred to the 'dull and endless strife' of books.

No candid student of Wordsworth can suppose that he is here declaring himself an enemy to literature. We have to consider first what books they are to which he is taking exception. Hazlitt, whose conversation, as we have seen, gave rise to these two poems, was just then engaged in writing his *Essay on the Principles of Human Action*, an uncompleted and ambitious work for which he had overworked himself in studying all the modern philosophers from Hobbes to Hartley. 'The lines', said Wordsworth in the Preface to *Lyrical Ballads*, 'entitled Expostulation and Reply, and those which follow, arose out of conversation with a friend who was somewhat unreasonably attached to modern books of moral philosophy.' It was these 'sages' whom Wordsworth had come to regard as dangerous guides, mainly because he felt they ignored or even disapproved of what he called the 'primary passions' of men—affection, pity, gratitude, kindness. The pure sensationalism of Hartley, the cold intellectualism of Godwin, led men away from these into an arid desert of mechanical rationalism.

The joyousness—the lilting gaiety almost—of these lyrics is something new and different from anything Wordsworth had hitherto written. Yet he had not forgotten to be sad. In the *Lines written in Early Spring*, while the same faith is testified with even greater vehemence in the joy and 'pleasure' of living Nature, a shadow lies over the spring landscape.

> Through primrose tufts in that sweet bower
> The periwinkle trail'd its wreaths;
> And 'tis my faith that every flower
> Enjoys the air it breathes. . . .

> The budding twigs spread out their fan
> To catch the breezy air;
> And I must think, do all I can,
> That there was pleasure there.

[2] The phrase 'wise passiveness' occurs also in a blank-verse fragment of this period:

> They rest upon their oars,
> Float down the mighty stream of tendency
> In a calm mood of holy indolence
> A most wise passiveness.
>
>   *P.W.* v, p. 413.

If I these thoughts cannot prevent,
If such be of my creed the plan,[1]
Have I not reason to lament
What man has made of man.

The painful sense of contrast between the loveliness of the living universe and 'what man has made of man' had been described by Coleridge in *Religious Musings*, when he

Cast a sad eye to earth and inly mused
Why there was misery in a world so fair.

If we want a particular as well as a general reason for this sadder mood we can find it in the French invasion of Switzerland which took place this spring. On April 16th Coleridge's *France: An Ode*, appeared in the *Morning Post*, renouncing his faith in revolutionary France on account of this act of aggression. Wordsworth afterwards said that his own views underwent a change at the same time and for the same reason.

Some of the *Lyrical Ballads* are critical illustrations of particular doctrines detrimental to the 'feelings', put forward by Godwin in *Political Justice* and in his novel, *Caleb Williams*.[2] The *Anecdote for Fathers*—a real incident which, as already related, took place between Wordsworth and young Basil—by showing that a child will quite naturally and rightly tell a lie if pressed too much for an answer, was a reply to Godwin's doctrine that lying is unnatural and only the result of civilization. *The Last of the Flock* is also founded on a real incident, which 'occurred in the village of Holford, close by Alfoxden', and is a direct contradiction of Godwin's attack on property as the cause of vice. The poor man's little property, says Wordsworth, is the source of all his best virtues, his affection for his home and his animals; its dissipation in face of the threat of starvation is the reason why 'wicked fancies' entered his mind and why he seemed even to cease to love

---

[1] These lines were later altered to the less dogmatic:

If this belief from heaven be sent,
If such be Nature's holy plan. . . .

[2] *L.*, pp. 309–15. Legouis was the first to draw attention to this aspect of *Lyrical Ballads*.

his children. To this theme of the impoverished smallholder Wordsworth returned two years later in *Michael*.[1]

Simon Lee, the Old Huntsman,[2] one of the ballads most frequently laughed at because of the extreme baldness of its style, is also a 'true story' of one of Wordsworth's neighbours, the old retired Alfoxden huntsman, though Wordsworth removes the scene to Wales, 'in the sweet shire of Cardigan'. It is a poem in praise of the virtue of gratitude—again a quality much looked down upon by Godwin, who had said that 'if by gratitude we understand a sentiment of preference which I entertain towards another, upon the ground of my having been subject of his benefits, it is no part of justice or virtue'. It was simply the result of cringing to wealth and power. Poor old Simon, bursting into tears because Wordsworth split his log for him, sent Godwin's theories whistling down the wind. And the comment that Wordsworth made still brings a lump into the throat:

> I've heard of hearts unkind, kind deeds
> With coldness still returning.
> Alas! the gratitude of men
> Has oftener left me mourning.

Goody Blake and Harry Gill, with its Dorsetshire setting and vivid portrayal of the passions engendered by poverty, shows Wordsworth's growing interest in the psychology of fear. It belongs to the 'curse-cycle' of poems which included *The Ancient Mariner*, *The Three Graves*, and *Peter Bell* of which it is in a sense a forerunner. It was probably written very shortly before *Peter Bell*, early in April 1798.[3]

We are Seven, founded on his conversation with the little girl at Goodrich Castle in 1793, is one of the poems about whose composition Wordsworth has left us full details. It was written

[1] 'I am persuaded', wrote Hannah More in 1795 from Somersetshire, 'that no labouring man, even if he be healthy and sober, can maintain a family of any size, and find them clothes and pay rent. . . Hardly any poor man can now get a bit of land for a cow, as all the land in a parish is swallowed up by a few great farmers.' Chatterton, *Memoir of Admiral Gambier*, i, p. 296. The shepherd in *The Last of the Flock* is by no means an exaggerated example of what was happening on a tragically large scale all over the country.

[2] The full title is *Simon Lee, the Old Huntsman, with an Incident in which he was Concerned*.

[3] See above, p. 284, and *L.T.* iii. 78, p. 1339. W.W. to Cottle, May 9th 1798, where he says he is *returning* Darwin.

'in the Grove at Alfoxden', but the last line of the last stanza was composed first, and the scene of its completion is so characteristic of the proceedings of the Alfoxden party that it must be told yet again.

When it was all but finished [says Wordsworth] I came in and recited it to Mr. Coleridge and my Sister, and said, 'A prefatory stanza must be added, and I should sit down to our little tea meal with greater pleasure if my task were finished.' I mentioned in substance what I wished to be expressed, and Coleridge immediately threw off the stanza thus:

> 'A little child, dear brother Jem.'

I objected to the rhyme 'dear brother Jem', as being ludicrous, but we all enjoyed the joke of hitching-in our friend, James Tobin's name, who was familiarly called Jem.[1]

So the line stood (save for the substitution of 'simple' for 'little' when the *Ballads* were published) and so it remained until Wordsworth published his collected poems in 1815. Then the words 'dear brother Jem' were dropped, and not replaced, so that the opening line stands for ever incomplete—

> A simple child. . . .

We are Seven is thus introduced to us by Coleridge. But it is doubtful how far his 'prefatory stanza' really expresses the teaching Wordsworth wished to convey. For Wordsworth's aim in writing this poem was to show 'the perplexity and obscurity which in childhood attend our notion of death, or rather our utter inability to admit that notion'.[2] He had himself experienced that 'utter inability', and in his comments on the *Ode: Intimations of Immortality* he added: 'But it was not so much from feelings of animal vivacity that my difficulty came as from a sense of the indomitableness of the spirit within me'. His little heroine strikes the reader as in some sense akin to Wordsworth in temperament rather than simply full of 'animal vivacity'.[3] This perhaps is why he had originally felt such an interest in her, and why, when Tobin, having seen the *Ballads* as they were going to press in Bristol, 'with a grave

---

[1] James Tobin was a friend of the Pinneys, son of their father's partner in business. His brother John Tobin was the author of several plays.

[2] Preface to *Lyrical Ballads*, 1800, *P.W.* ii, p. 388.

[3] 'The first stanza attributes the child's replies to "animal vivacity" simply, yet her behaviour rather suggests a reflective little girl.' A. C. Bradley.

face' advised him to cancel *We are Seven* because it would make
him 'everlastingly ridiculous', Wordsworth replied: 'Nay, that
shall take its chance, however.'

Two poems, *The Mad Mother* and *The Complaint of a Forsaken
Indian Woman,* are 'studies' in natural grief and love. How
deeply Wordsworth entered into the sentiment of motherhood,
how vividly the movements and emotions of even infants
appealed to him, is apparent throughout his poetry; we see it
first in the description of the Beggar-woman and her children
in *An Evening Walk.*[1] No doubt the thought of Annette and his
own desertion of her, and of his unknown child, gave to these
poems, and to many others, a sharpness of realism that they
would not otherwise have possessed. There is even a similarity
between the language of some of the stanzas of *The Mad Mother*
and that of Annette's letters.[2] But neither poem is an invention of
Wordsworth's based on his own experience. The *Indian Woman*
is taken from an account which he had read in Hearne's *Journey
from Hudson's Bay* of how American Indians treated their sick
comrades, and in the preface of 1800 he spoke of it simply as an
example of the psychology of the mind in extremity, 'cleaving
in solitude to life and society on the approach of death'. *The Mad
Mother* was a story told him by 'a lady in Bristol'—one wishes
he had told us who she was—who had herself seen such a
woman as he described.

The *Idiot Boy* was always one of Wordsworth's favourite
poems. 'I have never written anything with so much glee', he
said; and like *The Waggoner* and parts of *Peter Bell,* it reveals
him in a frolic mood; rather heavy-handed mirth, perhaps, it is;
and it may be impossible to feel as pleased with the poem as did
Wordsworth himself; it has been said that 'it is the frolic of

[1] See above, p. 117.
[2] Thus Wordsworth makes the woman say:

> Thy father cares not for my breast,
> 'Tis thine, sweet baby, there to rest;
> 'Tis all thine own!—and if its hue
> Be changed, that was so fair to view,
> 'Tis fair enough for thee, my dove!
> My beauty, little child, is flown,
> But thou wilt live with me in love.

Annette had written: 'Behold your wife . . . sorrow has altered her much. Do
you know her? If her features are altered . . . her heart is unchanged', &c.
Wordsworth never received this letter but there were others doubtless much the
same in tone. *A.V.,* p. 128.

good spirits in one habitually grave', and is at times rather an awkward affair. Yet it is doubtful whether it would have been a better poem if Wordsworth had kept it entirely pathetic and solemn. He had a deep veneration for the way in which poor people loved their idiot children. 'It is there', he said afterwards, 'that we see the strength, disinterestedness and grandeur of love; nor have I ever been able to contemplate an object that calls out so many excellent and virtuous sentiments without finding it hallowed thereby, and having something in me which bears down before it, like a deluge, every feeble sensation of disgust and aversion.'[1] Perhaps he has not quite succeeded in communicating this feeling to his readers. What chiefly impresses in the poem are certain magical phrases of description, like the opening stanza:

> 'Tis eight o'clock—a clear March night,
> The moon is up—the sky is blue,
> The owlet in the moonlight air,
> He shouts from nobody knows where;
> He lengthens out his lonely shout,
> Halloo! Halloo! a long halloo.

and

> The streams with softest sound are flowing,
> The grass you almost hear it growing,
> You hear it now if e'er you can.

The Thorn is the only poem in the *Lyrical Ballads* which owes its origin to a 'natural object' seen in a moment of visionary excitement. On March 19th Dorothy, William, and Basil were walking in a hail-storm on the top of the Quantock ridge when says Wordsworth, he saw 'a thorn which I had often passed in calm, bright weather without noticing it. I said to myself "Cannot I by some invention do as much to make this Thorn permanently an impressive object as the storm has made it to my eyes at this moment?"' And so 'William wrote some lines describing a stunted thorn'.[2] We cannot help being reminded

---

[1] He even said that he applied to idiots 'that sublime expression of Scripture that *their life is hidden with God*'. It is possible that he owed this attitude in part to his early reading of Coxe's *Travels in Switzerland*, where the peasants of the Valais are described as calling idiot children 'Souls of God without sin'.

[2] *P.W.* ii, p. 511. *D.W.J.* i, p. 13, Mar. 19th.

of that other wet day, long ago, when he waited for the ponies
in the mist, and the objects near him,

> the single sheep and the one blasted tree,

became transformed by

> all the business of the elements

and by his own feverish mood into sources of imaginative
power.[1] The reason why *The Thorn* just fails to be one of his
greatest poems lies in those words 'by some invention'. He was
obsessed by his theory of poetic language and with the necessity
of telling everything in the language of 'the middle and lower
classes of society'. So, we are informed in the 'Advertisement',
'the poem of the Thorn . . . is not supposed to be spoken in the
author's own person; the character of the loquacious narrator
will sufficiently show itself'. And in the second edition in 1800 he
further enlarged upon this dim character as being 'A Captain of
a small trading vessel, for example, who . . . had retired upon
an annuity and . . . having little to do, became credulous and
talkative'. The fiction is not a success. Though the essential
beauty and passion of Wordsworth's poetry often breaks
through, the language is too often trite. As Coleridge later said,
'it is not possible to imitate truly a dull and garrulous discourser
without repeating the effects of dullness and garrulity'.[2] It is in
the description of the little grave and the mysterious happenings
by the 'little muddy pond' that we recognize the authentic voice,
and above all in those two lines about poor Martha herself:

> And she was known to every star,
> And every wind that blows.

Had Wordsworth avoided the captain of the small trading
vessel, *The Thorn* might have been a ballad as moving as the
one in Herd's *Ancient and Modern Scottish Songs* on which he
probably based his simple tale of desertion, infanticide, and
madness. Not long afterwards he copied some lines from this
ballad into a Commonplace Book.[3]

---

[1] See above, p. 69.
[2] *B.L.* ch. xvii. He is really here almost quoting a sentence from Southey's
review of the *Ballads* in the *Critical Review*, Oct. 1798.
[3]
> And there she's lean'd her back to a thorn
> Oh! and alas—a day oh,

The Three Graves, a poem until recently attributed entirely to Coleridge, but now known to have been begun by Wordsworth at Racedown in the spring of 1797, was not included in the *Lyrical Ballads.* Most of it is by Coleridge, who wrote it during this spring at Alfoxden.[1] Wordsworth said long afterwards to Barron Field: 'I gave him the subject of his *Three Graves*: but he made it too shocking and painful, and not sufficiently sweetened by any healing views.' As Wordsworth's own portion of it is conspicuous for the absence of any such 'views', one wonders what he would eventually have made of it. Neither Coleridge nor Wordsworth anywhere gives any hint that Wordsworth was in part the author. Of the four poems on the theme of a curse, *The Three Graves* is chronologically the earliest to be begun, although it was not continued until the spring of 1798. This time it is the curse of a mother laid on her own daughter, with whose affianced lover the mother is herself in love. The story, says Coleridge, is in outline true, and he chose it 'from finding in it a striking proof of the possible effect on the imagination from an idea violently and suddenly impressed on it'. He added that he had been at the same time much fascinated by reading of the like effects of curses on Red Indians in Hearne and Bryan Edwards. These words are closely similar to Wordsworth's account of his motives for writing the tale of *Goody Blake.* 'I wished to draw attention to the truth that the power of the human imagination is sufficient to produce such changes even in our physical nature as might appear almost miraculous.' No

> And there she has her baby born
> Ten thousand times goodnight, and be wi' ye . . ., &c.

Bürger's ballad of *Die Pfarrer's Tochter,* translated by William Taylor with the title *The Lass of Fair Wone* had appeared in the *Monthly Magazine* for 1796 and was probably known to Wordsworth. But he is more likely to have been thinking of the Scottish ballad.

It has often been remarked upon as strange that Wordsworth should have used the name of Basil Montagu's murdered mother, Martha Ray, for the heroine of *The Thorn.* Although it is scarcely possible that he did not know the story, there is another possible origin for at least the surname 'Ray'. There were Rays at Racedown, as we know from Joseph Gill's Diary: Mar. 6th 1796: 'Bob Ray and the Gardener at the Hedge.' As Wordsworth borrowed the name 'Gill' from Racedown, he may also have borrowed 'Ray'. But 'Martha' remains, in tactless prominence, where 'Mary' would have done as well.

[1] *P.W.* i, pp. 308–12 and 374. Coleridge published Parts III and IV in *The Friend,* 1809. Parts I and II, by Wordsworth, were printed from a manuscript copy in Coleridge's hand in Coleridge's *Poems,* 1893, and were thought to be by him until the discovery of the MS.

doubt, with *The Ancient Mariner* in course of composition, the theme of curses was being talked about by both poets, and so the fragment of *The Three Graves* was hunted up and given to Coleridge to finish, while Wordsworth made a ballad out of the story in the *Zoönomia*. *The Three Graves* has not much poetic merit; Coleridge himself claimed that its only merit was psychological. It obviously owes something to the translations of Bürger's German ballads which were appearing in the *Monthly Magazine*. But its interest for us lies in the picture it draws in the last few verses of the late spring which in *Christabel* came 'slowly up that way', and of the way in which the three spent a Sunday morning at Alfoxden. The foggy days early in March and the sudden burst of warmth on Easter Sunday, April 8th, are recorded by Dorothy in her Journal, and the verses probably describe that Sunday when they 'walked in the morning in the wood and half way to Stowey; found the air oppressively warm, afterwards very pleasant'. The tale is being told by an old Sexton:

> 'Twas such a foggy time as makes
>   Old Sextons, Sir! like me,
> Rest on their spades to cough; the spring
>   Was late uncommonly.
>
> And then the hot days, all at once,
>   They came we knew not how:
> You looked about for shade, when scarce
>   A leaf was on a bough.
>
> It happened then, ('twas in the bower,
>   A furlong up the wood:
> Perhaps you know the place, and yet
>   I scarce know how you should.)
>
> No path leads thither, 'tis not nigh
>   To any pasture-plot;
> But clustered near the chattering brook,
>   Lone hollies marked the spot.
>
> Those hollies of themselves a shape
>   As of an arbour took,
> A close, round arbour; and it stands
>   Not three strides from a brook.

Within this arbour, which was still
  With scarlet berries hung,
Were these three friends, one Sunday morn,
  Just as the first bell rung.

'Tis sweet to hear a brook, 'tis sweet
  To hear the Sabbath bell,
'Tis sweet to hear them both at once,
  Deep in a woody dell.

His limbs along the moss, his head
  Upon a mossy heap,
With shut-up senses, Edward lay:
  That brook e'en on a working day
Might chatter one to sleep.

          .   .   .   .   .

The Sun peeps through the close thick leaves,
  See, dearest Ellen! see!
'Tis in the leaves, a little sun,
  No bigger than your ee;

A tiny sun, and it has got
  A perfect glory too;
Ten thousand threads and hairs of light,
  Make up a glory gay and bright
Round that small orb, so blue.

And then they argued of these rays,
  What colour they might be;
Says this, 'They're mostly green'; says that
  'They're amber-like to me.'

There perhaps we come as near as we ever can come to
overhearing the talk of William and Dorothy and Coleridge as
they sat together in the dell of Alfoxden in the first glory of
that long-awaited spring.

XII

FROM *PETER BELL* TO *TINTERN ABBEY*
April–July 1798

> *They wandered away and away,*
> *With Nature, the dear old nurse.*

LONGFELLOW

Eᴀʀʟʏ in April Coleridge walked down into Devonshire to
see his brother the Rev. George Coleridge, with whom he was
anxious to keep on good terms; the Wordsworths spent a night
at Stowey while he was away, keeping Sara company. They
read Godwin's life of his wife, Mary Wollstonecraft, at about
this time and Wordsworth read Henry Brooke's tragedy, *Gustavus Vasa*, lent him by Tobin, 'a strange composition of genius
and absurdity', which made some impression in his mind, for in
The Prelude we find him contemplating Gustavus as a possible
subject for an epic poem.[1] On April 15th they walked to 'Crook-
ham', that is, Crowcombe, a large house and grounds where,
says Dorothy, 'Nature was very successfully striving to make
beautiful what art had deformed—ruins, hermitages, etc. . . .
Happily we cannot shape the huge trees or carve out the valleys
according to our fancy.'

On April 26th an unusual event occurred: 'William went to
have his picture taken.' This was the painting by William
Shuter, best known for his still-lifes of fruit. He was staying at
Stowey; Coleridge, who may have asked for it to be done, gave
it, apparently, to Cottle, who liked to collect portraits of his
literary friends. A little later during this summer Cottle employed Robert Hancock to do a drawing of Wordsworth; and
for some time both the Shuter painting and the Hancock drawing
were in Cottle's possession. The Shuter is interesting because
it shows Wordsworth in a characteristic attitude—the left
hand thrust inside the breast of the coat—and also because it
shows him smiling broadly, his teeth showing. It was Hazlitt
who noticed the 'convulsive inclination to laughter about the

---

[1] See below, p. 609, and *E.L.* 74, p. 187.

mouth' in Wordsworth's countenance. The Hancock drawing
—a profile, whereas the other is three-quarter face—is much
more sedate; Cottle describes both as good likenesses although
they bear little resemblance to one another owing to the difference of position and mood.[1] Years afterwards Crabb Robinson saw the Hancock drawing and wrote to Wordsworth: 'You
have taken abundant care to let the world know you did not
marry Mrs. Wordsworth for her beauty. Now this picture will
justify the inference that she too had a higher motive for her
acceptance of you.'

On April 20th, 'William', Dorothy wrote in her Journal, was
'all the morning engaged in wearisome composition. The moon
crescent. *Peter Bell* begun.' This extraordinary poem is better
understood and admired now than it has ever been since its
publication, which took place under somewhat unfortunate circumstances in 1819.[2] It is Wordsworth's reply or rival to *The
Ancient Mariner*. Like the Mariner, it is the story of the redemption of a human soul. But, whereas the Mariner, for the
one sin of his pride and callousness in shooting the albatross
suffers adventures and 'spectral persecutions' that must set him
apart among men for ever, 'Peter Bell the Potter' is an ordinary
coarse brute of a sinner who is at last frightened into becoming
'a good and honest man' by a process of purely natural visitations—the instruments of his salvation being a dead man, an
ass, a little boy, a withered leaf, a woman, and finally some
Methodist hymn-singers. It has never been loved in the way
that *The Leech-Gatherer* and *Michael* have been loved, yet no
student of Wordsworth can afford to ignore it, for it is of the
very essence of his genius. Not only does it reveal Wordsworth's intense interest in the workings of the human mind—
in what we should call psychology—but it is also a testament
to his central faith: that 'nature' is capable of influencing for
good even one of her more rebellious and insensitive children.
For Peter is the very opposite of Wordsworth's other heroes

---

[1] The Hancock is now in the National Portrait Gallery; the Shuter is in
Cornell University Library, U.S.A. A good reproduction of the Shuter is the
frontispiece to Harper's *William Wordsworth*, 1916, vol. i.

[2] J. H. Reynolds's naughty skit on it and other poems of Wordsworth's appeared
in Hunt's *Examiner* just before its publication, and Shelley's satire *Peter Bell the
Third* immediately after it. How Reynolds obtained knowledge of it is a mystery,
but it is the name only of which he makes fun, not the contents of the poem.

up to this time, the Sailor, the Pedlar, or Marmaduke. It is his
insensitiveness to beauty, his brutality and selfishness, that are
emphasized. And yet Peter was a child of Nature too:

> Though Nature could not touch his heart
> By lovely forms or silent weather,
> And tender sounds, yet you might see
> At once that Peter Bell and she
> Had often been together.
>
> A savage wildness round him hung
> As of a dweller out of doors,
> In his whole figure and his mien
> A savage character was seen
> Of mountains and of dreary moors.
>
>   .   .   .   .
>
> There was a hardness in his cheek,
> There was a hardness in his eye,
> As if the man had fix'd his face,
> In many a solitary place,
> Against the wind and open sky!

Peter is not proof against superstitious fear, and when things
begin to go wrong with him, when he loses his way, when the
ass will not move for all his beatings, and, finally, when the
mysterious appearance in the water proves to be the body of a
drowned man, the process of inward change has begun, though
at first the only manifestations are panic fear and violence. As
soon as he is mounted on the ass and allows the animal to take
charge of the situation, his redemption begins. The mounting
on the ass is for Peter Bell what his blessing of the 'slimy things'
had been for the Ancient Mariner. In each case the victim of their
cruelty becomes the instrument of their redemption. *Peter Bell*
is the last in the cycle of poems founded on the 'idea of a curse'—
that is to say of a vivid impression made upon the imagination
by a sudden and painful idea resulting in a change of the physical
or moral nature. Into it Wordsworth wove many memories and
every-day incidents, from the donkeys who roamed in the woods
at Alfoxden and who, he said, 'put him upon writing the poem',
to the drowned man raised out of the water 'like a ghost'. This
was a memory of his first days at Hawkshead when he had seen

a body so raised out of Esthwaite. Peter, in outward appearance
at least, was a 'wild rover with whom I walked from Builth on
the river Wye downwards nearly as far as the town of Hay', in
1793.[1] Peter's son, Benoni, the 'child of sorrow' whom he
remembers in his remorse, 'I knew', says Wordsworth, 'when
I was a school-boy', and old Ann Tyson had told him the story
of the child's mother. Peter's superstitious fears are in part those
of Wordsworth himself in boyhood. As Peter is chased by a
'dancing leaf'—

> The very leaves they follow me,
> So huge hath been my wickedness—

so had the young Wordsworth been followed by 'low breathings'
when he stole the woodcock.

The long prologue to *Peter Bell* is best understood as a good-
natured joke aimed at Coleridge. In *The Ancient Mariner* Coleridge had plunged into a world of dream, nightmare, and fantasy
on a vast scale; he had as it were written the charter of English
romantic poetry. Wordsworth, in the prologue, imagining himself borne away from the earth in a silver boat shaped like a
crescent moon, soon tires of the stars in their courses and per-
suades his barque to return

> back to Earth, the dear green Earth,

and when the boat protests, he dismisses her with the injunction:

> Take with you some ambitious Youth!
> For, restless wanderer, I, in truth,
> Am all unfit to be your mate.

So he hints at the difference between his poetic calling and that
of his friend. The image of the 'silver boat' like a crescent moon
was no doubt selected because the moon was new that week
when he was writing the poem.[2]

At the end of April the weather grew warm again: Dorothy
noted on May 6th: 'heard the nightingale; saw a glow-worm'.[3]

[1] See above, pp. 237–8.

[2] The famous lines, 130–55, beginning 'Long have I loved what I behold',
were not part of the original poem. They were added between 1805 and the publication of the poem in 1819. The text underwent many changes in the various revisions
that Wordsworth made in 1799, 1800, and 1802.

[3] This was her second glow-worm, the first being the one that William had so
carefully carried home to Racedown. See above, p. 320. It was perhaps the first she
had seen unaided.

On May 14th a second son was born to the Coleridges, and named Berkeley, he being the philosopher now chiefly in favour. According to Coleridge, Sara had 'a remarkably good time', so on the 16th, says Dorothy, 'Coleridge, William and myself set forward to the Cheddar rocks. Slept at Bridgewater.'

The next entry in her Journal is also the last. It reads: 'May 22nd, Thursday. Walked to Cheddar. Slept at Cross.' May 22nd was not a Thursday, but a Tuesday, but apart from this inaccuracy we are faced here with a chronological puzzle. Were there two expeditions to Cheddar? Perhaps the most likely solution is that on the first occasion they completed their walk to Cheddar, returning on the 18th. Coleridge was certainly at Stowey on the 20th, as on that day he addressed thence a letter to Poole whose brother Richard had just died and whose affliction was such that even Coleridge felt diffident about calling on him. Then on Thursday, May 24th (adopting Dorothy's day of the week but not her date), they set off again for Cheddar, but this time with the further purpose of going on to Bristol.[1]

Charles Lloyd, Coleridge's former lodger and pupil, was in Bristol, and Coleridge was anxious if possible to get hold of him and try to put an end to the unhappy quarrel which Lloyd had made between them. Lloyd was an epileptic and mentally very unstable.[2] His former veneration for Coleridge had been turning to dislike and suspicion since the publication, in the previous November, of Coleridge's three sonnets, signed 'Nehemiah Higginbottom', in which he had parodied the style of his own poems, and those of Lloyd and Lamb as well. Dorothy had met Lloyd in London in December, and he had tried to enlist her sympathies, writing to her afterwards a letter of abuse of Coleridge which caused her much distress and which she had shown to Coleridge 'with tears'.[3] Lloyd had also succeeded in estranging Lamb from Coleridge, and Coleridge afterwards said that the whole business preyed so upon him that it made him ill and 'prevented my finishing the Christabel'.[4] This latter complaint need not be taken too seriously, but there was quite enough to be disturbed about, so it was agreed that Words-

---

[1] For the chronology of the last month at Alfoxden see *N. & Q.*, Aug. 1953, 'Wordsworth and Coleridge, Dates in May and June 1798', by H. M. Margoliouth.
[2] Eventually he became insane.
[3] See *R.E.S.* xi, p. 78, quoting a note of S.T.C.'s written in 1811.
[4] Ibid.

worth should go on alone to Bristol from Cheddar and endeavour to 'bring back poor Lloyd, whose infirmities have been made the instruments of another man's darker passions'.[1] This 'other man' was Southey, who also fancied himself attacked by the Higginbottom sonnets, and remained hostile in spite of Coleridge's sincere denial of having included Southey in his parodies.[2] Coleridge wanted to confront Lloyd with his calumnies in the presence of 'all whose esteem I value',[3] in the hope of bringing him to reason. Fortunately (for no good could have come of such a meeting) Lloyd had already left Bristol, but Wordsworth stayed there a few days with Cottle, who drove him back in his gig.

This indeed seems to be the occasion of the famous 'bread and lettuce' dinner described by Cottle in his *Reminiscences*,[4] although his vague dating of it, 'soon' after he became acquainted with Wordsworth, must be rejected. Cottle and Wordsworth called at Stowey to pick up Coleridge with Dorothy, the maid Peggy, and Basil, who had been staying there while Wordsworth was away. On arriving at Alfoxden, the large cheese which had been brought from Bristol was found to have been stolen from the back of the gig by a tramp; the bottle of brandy was broken on the stones of the stable-yard as the party alighted, and neither Wordsworth nor Coleridge knew how to remove the collar from the horse—Peggy had to come to their aid. There was nothing in the house except a loaf of bread, with 'plenty of lettuces from the garden'; even salt had been forgotten. But they feasted happily enough. On this visit of Cottle's, as already described,[5] the plan of the *Lyrical Ballads* was discussed on a walk to Lynton, and Cottle returned, after about a week, to Bristol with *The Ancient Mariner* and some of Wordsworth's ballads in his pocket.

Immediately afterwards, probably on Sunday, June 3rd, Wordsworth went to Bristol again. He wished to see Cottle once more about the printing of the poems, and to reiterate his objections to Cottle's preference of 'Poems in Two Volumes'. But probably his main reason for going was his desire to see 'Monk' Lewis's melodrama, *The Castle Spectre*, performed at

---

[1] *S.T.C.* i, p. 246. S.T.C. to Estlin, May, 1798.
[2] Ibid., p. 251, n.   [3] Ibid., p. 253. S.T.C. to Charles Lamb.
[4] *Cottle*, i, p. 320.   [5] See above, p. 373.

the Theatre Royal.[1] The success of this play aroused Wordsworth's amused contempt, and, perhaps, a touch of jealousy as
well. 'I am perfectly easy about the theatre', he told Tobin in
March: 'if I had no other method of employing myself Mr.
Lewis's success would have thrown me into despair. The Castle
Spectre is a spectre indeed.' He returned probably on June 6th
to Coleridge's cottage, where he found young William Hazlitt
paying his long-projected visit to Coleridge. Hazlitt had arrived
on Monday, June 4th.

Hazlitt was then only twenty years of age. He had not yet
become the formidable critic who in later years aroused Wordsworth's prolonged disapproval and dislike. He had heard Coleridge preach at Shrewsbury in January, and had straightway
become his worshipper. An invitation to Stowey was eagerly
accepted, and on his arrival (on foot) Coleridge took him immediately to Alfoxden, being unaware apparently of Wordsworth's absence. Dorothy, however, made them welcome,
showed them manuscripts of the *Lyrical Ballads* which Hazlitt
'dipped into with the faith of a novice'. They stayed there for
the night, Hazlitt sleeping 'in an old room with blue hangings,
and covered with the round-faced family portraits of the age of
George I and II'.

Next morning, sitting on the trunk of an old oak-tree, Coleridge read aloud *The Idiot Boy*, 'with a sonorous and musical
voice'. *The Thorn*, *The Mad Mother*, and the *Indian Woman*
were also read, and, says Hazlitt, 'the source of a new style and
spirit in poetry came over me. It had to me something of the
effect that arises from the turning up of the fresh soil or the
first welcome breath of spring.' Coleridge, it should be noticed,
read Wordsworth's poems, not his own. This may have been
partly because there were none of his own manuscripts at
Alfoxden, but it is highly characteristic of his modesty about
his own poems and of his absorption in Wordsworth.

On the way back to Stowey Coleridge discoursed to Hazlitt
on the subject of Wordsworth. 'He lamented that Wordsworth
was not prone enough to believe in the traditional superstitions
of the place'—an interesting indication of Coleridge's own

---

[1] *N. & Q.*, ibid. It was performed for a five-weeks' season from April to June
1798, after its successful run in London. Coleridge had written Wordsworth a
long critical description of it from Shrewsbury in January. *S.T.C.*, i, p. 234.

delight in folk-lore and all supernatural happenings. 'In consequence', he said, 'there is a something corporeal, a matter-of-
factness, a clinging to the palpable, or often to the petty, in his
poetry.' This is exactly the criticism Coleridge made of the
Ballads twenty years later in *Biographia Literaria.* 'But', he
went on, 'this objection must be confined to his descriptive
pieces: his philosophic poetry has a grand and comprehensive
spirit in it so that his soul seems to inhabit the universe like a
palace, and to discover truth by intuition, rather than by de-
duction.' Such was the impression made on Coleridge by the
Pedlar's character and soliloquies. Then he gave a description
in simile of the character of Wordsworth's genius. 'His genius',
he said, 'is not a spirit that descends to him through the air;
it sprung out of the ground like a flower, or unfolded itself from
a green spray on which the goldfinch sang.'[1]

Hazlitt's description of Wordsworth as he sat in Coleridge's
cottage devouring bread and cheese and describing his visit to
the theatre, must be given, for all its familiarity.[2]

He answered in some degree to his friend's description of him, but
was more gaunt and Don Quixote-like. He was quaintly dressed . . .
in a brown fustian jacket and striped pantaloons.
There was something of a roll, a lounge in his gait not unlike his
own Peter Bell. There was a severe worn pressure of thought about his
temples, a fire in his eye (as if he saw something in objects more than
the outward appearance), an intense, high, narrow forehead, a Roman
nose, cheeks furrowed by strong purpose and feeling, and a convulsive
inclination to laughter about the mouth, a good deal at variance with
the solemn, stately expression of the rest of the face. . . . He sat down
and talked very naturally and freely, with a mixture of clear gushing
accents in his voice, a deep guttural intonation, and a strong tincture
of the northern *burr*, like the crust on wine.

He talked of *The Castle Spectre*: 'it fitted the taste of the
audience like a glove', he said. But it had not suited his. The
next day the Stowey party again went to Alfoxden, and Wordsworth read *Peter Bell* aloud out of doors. Hazlitt thus heard both
Coleridge and Wordsworth read aloud. 'There is a *chaunt*', he

---

[1] While admitting that Wordsworth's genius was 'no spirit which from Heaven
hath flown' (in the ordinary sense of the word 'Heaven') it is well to remember
Wordsworth's own invocation of the 'gentle breeze', and the strong symbolic
affinity between the wind that blew about him and the 'corresponding mild, creative
breeze' within. See above, p. 273.   [2] Hazlitt: *My First Acquaintance with Poets.*

says, 'in the recitation of both Coleridge and Wordsworth, which acts as a spell upon the hearer and disarms the judgment. . . . Coleridge's manner is more full, animating, and varied; Wordsworth's more equable, sustained, and internal. The one might be termed more *dramatic*, the other more *lyrical*.'

On the walk back in the evening from Alfoxden to Stowey there took place between Hazlitt and Wordsworth the conversation which resulted in the two lyrics on the receptive spirit, *Expostulation and Reply* and *The Tables Turned.* 'I got', says Hazlitt, 'into a metaphysical argument with Wordsworth while Coleridge was explaining the different notes of the nightingale to his sister, in which we neither of us succeeded in making ourselves perfectly clear and intelligible.' Coleridge's 'explanations' about the nightingale have unfortunately not been recorded; of the argument with Wordsworth and of its results enough has already been said.[1]

The Wordsworths' days at Alfoxden were now drawing to a close. Richard Wordsworth was applied to at the end of May and again on June 13th for £30 to pay the rent and Peggy's wages. The remaining part of Calvert's legacy had not yet been paid over, so that they were obliged still to use the strictest economy. 'Our expenses', said Dorothy, 'last year £23 for rent, our journey to London, clothes, servant's wages, etc., included, only amounted to £110.'

Two sad partings had to be made before leaving Alfoxden. Their 'good and dear' Peggy found leaving them a hard trial. 'She would have gone to the world's end with us. I believe she was much more attached to us than to any other beings in the world.' About the time of their leaving Racedown she had imprudently married a rough and, as it proved, cruel man and was now with child, so that her departure would in any case have been necessary. Her husband, who was a blacksmith, does not figure in the story and evidently did not live at Alfoxden. They eventually settled at Hawkchurch in Devon and poor Peggy was condemned to the bitter life of frequent child-bearing and poverty in times made hard by war and high prices. Dorothy sent her money and clothes from time to time and always remembered her with affection.[2]

---

[1] See above, p. 379.   [2] *E.L.* 81, p. 197, *et alia.*

Basil, for whom his father could no longer pay board and lodg-ing, went to live with a sister of his mother's near Huntingdon. In any case, as Dorothy said, it would have been a 'hazardous experiment' to have taken him to Germany. He was now of an age when he should be associating more with other children. She consoled herself somewhat for his loss by considering his great improvement in temper and health. 'Much of his good temper', she said, 'must be owing to our regularity of temper, and the consequent equable treatment which he received from us'—an illuminating revelation of the happiness of the house-hold at Racedown and Alfoxden.

About June 10th Wordsworth went to Bristol for the third time, probably carrying with him the last two poems for in-clusion in the *Ballads*, the fruit of Hazlitt's visit: *Expostulation and Reply* and *The Tables Turned*. On the 12th he and Cottle's brother Amos, the poet, went out to Shirehampton where James Losh, who was now married to Cecilia Baldwin,[1] had taken a house for the summer. A glimpse of Wordsworth as he appeared to his friends at this time is afforded by Losh's Diary.[2] 'June 12, Supper. W. and Mr. A. Cottle. W. pleasant and clear but too earnest and *emphatic* in his manner of speaking in conversation.' Next day Wordsworth became the Loshes' guest, remaining with them until the 16th. Each day there was 'conversation with W.' and 'hearing his poems'. The air was indeed resounding to the *Lyrical Ballads*.

Between June 16th and 23rd, Wordsworth returned to Al-foxden; on the 25th, a Monday, he and Dorothy left 'that dear and beautiful place' for ever.[3] They spent a week in Coleridge's cottage at Stowey, and arrived in Bristol on July 2nd. Here they stayed for a few days with Cottle in Wine Street. 'After three years residence in retirement', said Dorothy, 'a city in feeling, sound and prospect is hateful.' Their hope was to go to Germany 'in two or three months', but Dorothy expected delays, 'as I have no doubt many things will delay the Coleridges which they

[1] See above, p. 257.
[2] In the Tullie House Library, Carlisle.
[3] Dorothy, in a letter to Richard on June 13th, says, 'we shall leave Alfoxden on Saturday the 23rd of this month'. Wordsworth, however, in the note on his journey to Tintern, quoted below, says 'We left Alfoxden on Monday morning, the 26th of June, stayed with Coleridge till the Monday following, then set forth on foot towards Bristol.' *Mem.* i, p. 116. Monday was, however, the 25th.

TINTERN ABBEY, 1794, FROM A WATER-COLOUR BY EDWARD DAYES

have no idea of at present!'[1] In the event, however, their estimate proved accurate enough.

Coleridge was not at Stowey during the Wordsworths' stay there in June. He left it on Sunday, June 24th, to pay a visit to Poole's friend Purkis at Brentford, and to Josiah Wedgwood in Surrey. He came to Bristol on August 3rd, having decided in the meantime on a major alteration in the German plan; namely to leave behind 'Mrs. C. and the little ones', at any rate for the first three months, on account of the expense and the uncertainty of maintaining a family both cheaply and in reasonable comfort in Germany. But before his arrival the Wordsworths had been away on an unpremeditated and, as it proved, a most memorable tour.

Wordsworth felt a longing to see once more the valleys and hills of Wales, through which he had wandered five years before in the summer of 1793, and where he had met the prototype of 'Peter Bell'. On July 9th they spent a night with the Loshes at Shirehampton;[2] the next day they crossed the Severn, probably by Aust Ferry, and spent three days walking up the Wye valley as far as Goodrich Castle and back again.

The details of their tour are preserved in a detached note by Wordsworth made apparently for his nephew, Christopher Wordsworth, who inserted it in his *Memoirs* in 1851. 'We crossed the Severn Ferry', he says, 'and walked ten miles further to Tintern Abbey, a very beautiful ruin on the Wye. The next morning we walked along the river through Monmouth to Goodrich Castle, there slept, and returned the next day to Tintern, thence to Chepstow, and from Chepstow back again in a boat to Tintern, where we slept, and thence back in a small vessel to Bristol.' The return from Chepstow by boat to Tintern in order to spend a second night there is characteristic. As they re-entered Bristol on the evening of July 13th and walked down the road leading from the Downs into the city, he composed 'the last 20 lines or so' of that poem whose full title is *Lines Composed a Few Miles above Tintern Abbey, on revisiting the Banks of the Wye during a Tour, July 13, 1798.*

'No poem of mine', he said, afterwards, 'was composed under circumstances more pleasant for me to remember than this. I

---

[1] *E.L.* 81, p. 196. D.W. to Mrs. Rawson, July 3rd 1798.
[2] James Losh's Diary.

began it upon leaving Tintern, after crossing the Wye, and concluded it just as I was entering Bristol in the evening, after a ramble of four or five days, with my sister. Not a line of it was altered, and not any part of it written down till I reached Bristol.' When he did reach Bristol it was written down at once and taken to Cottle, to be included in *Lyrical Ballads*, at the end of the volume. Not a line of it ever was altered, and the *Tintern Abbey* that we know today is identical with that composed on the Wye's banks—an unusual occurrence in Wordsworth's poetry.

There are several matters of interest connected with the tour, and with the poem and its title. In the first place, the tour was one of the most energetic ever undertaken by William and Dorothy together. In three days they walked over fifty miles —a feat which for Dorothy must have required some endurance. Further, they seem to have taken with them Gilpin's *Tour of the Wye*, which had first appeared in 1771 and had often been reprinted. The opening lines of the poem, describing the Wye scenery, owe a distinct though unobtrusive debt to Gilpin.[1] And, for all the 'impassioned music of the versification', which in Wordsworth's view made it comparable to an Ode, *Tintern Abbey* is, at least in its beginning, a 'landscape-poem' in the eighteenth-century tradition. Finally, the title of the poem is not quite accurate. If it was composed, as Wordsworth says, 'upon leaving Tintern' on July 13th, the scene of its composition must have been not 'above' Tintern Abbey, but below it. In fact, it must have been composed largely on board the 'small vessel' which took them back to Bristol. Much more probably, however, it was begun on the first day at Tintern when they were walking up the river towards Monmouth, and simply completed on the 13th.

It is a curious fact that nowhere in the poem does Wordsworth mention Tintern Abbey itself, though we know that he must have admired it, for they returned from Chepstow to spend a second night there. Gilpin describes its condition; the grass in the ruins was kept mown, but it was a dwelling-place of beggars

---

[1] The following passage in Gilpin should be compared with *Tintern Abbey* ll. 8–18. 'Many of the furnaces, on the banks of the river, consume charcoal, which is manufactured on the spot; and the smoke, which is frequently seen issuing from the sides of the hills; and spreading its thin veil over a part of them, beautifully break their lines, and unites them with the sky.' Gilpin also mentions the absence of arable land and the predominance of wood and pasture.

and the wretchedly poor. The river was then full of shipping, carrying coal and timber from the Forest of Dean. This also Wordsworth does not mention, though he does notice, in a foot-note to the phrase 'a soft, inland murmur', the change from tidal to non-tidal waters not far above Tintern.

Tintern Abbey partakes of the nature of a hymn of thanks-giving for all past and present experiences. It comes fittingly at the end of an extraordinarily happy year, when for the first time he had felt himself in full and articulate control of his genius.

He gives thanks first for what the memory of landscape beauty does for the soul. The affection with which, in the first twenty lines, he greets once more the scenery of the Wye—

> These hedge-rows, hardly hedge-rows, little lines
> Of sportive wood run wild; these pastoral farms
> Green to the very door; and wreathes of smoke
> Sent up in silence from among the trees—

reveals the power and intensity of delight with which he seized on and retained a landscape even when he had only seen it once, for a few passing moments. To the Wye and its banks, seen once five years before, he believed he owed three blessings—apprehended

> oft, in lonely rooms, and mid the din
> Of towns and cities.

There was first a 'tranquil restoration' of tired faculties which was both physical—

> Felt in the blood, and felt along the heart—

and mental—

> passing even into my purer mind.

Secondly, there were feelings 'of unremembered pleasure' from which sprang the impulse to do good:

> little, nameless, unremembered acts
> Of kindness and of love—

such, for instance, as the splitting of a log for old Simon Lee. The third was the most important of all. Wordsworth felt that he 'may have' owed to these 'forms of beauty' imprinted upon his

mind, his deepest experience of all, that of the mystical vision
'into the life of things'.

> Nor less, I trust,
> To them I may have owed another gift
> Of aspect more sublime; that blessed mood,
> In which the burthen of the mystery,
> In which the heavy and the weary weight
> Of all this unintelligible world
> Is lighten'd:—that serene and blessed mood,
> In which the affections gently lead us on,
> Until, the breath of this corporeal frame
> And even the motion of our human blood
> Almost suspended, we are laid asleep
> In body, and become a living soul:
> While, with an eye made quiet by the power
> Of harmony, and the deep power of joy,
> We see into the life of things.

The moment of silence before vision has modes of preparation
varying with each individual soul to whom it is granted: and with
Wordsworth himself it was not always produced in the same
way. But usually what he called 'the affections' played an important, indeed, a decisive part, in 'leading' him to that moment.[1]
And by 'the affections' he meant that intimate delight in the
familiar objects of landscape which had been from early childhood so intense and so persistent. In *The Prelude* he was to
describe such moments in his early morning walks at Hawkshead
in language very similar to that here used.[2]
  And what was that 'life of things' into which he 'saw'? Surely
that unity of all creation in an infinitely joyous being which was
also the vision of his boyhood. A few months earlier, Wordsworth had written in *The Ruined Cottage* some lines descriptive
of his Pedlar's feelings in boyhood, which had been also his own

> With bliss ineffable
> He felt the sentiment of being, spread
> O'er all that moves, and all that seemeth still,

---

[1] Havens, *The Mind of a Poet*, p. 166, points out that the moments of vision
after crossing the Alps (*Prel*. VI, ll. 592–616) and entering for the first time into
London (*Prel*. VIII, ll. 539–59) are not connected with delight in the landscape, but
with an idea—in the first, of having crossed the Alps; in the second, of having for the
first time entered the world's metropolis.
[2] See above, p. 81.

O'er all which, lost beyond the reach of thought,
And human knowledge, to the human eye
Invisible, yet liveth to the heart . . .
                              Wonder not
If such his transports were; for in all things
He saw one life, and felt that it was joy,
One song they sang, and it was audible,
Most audible then, when the fleshly ear . . .
Forgot its functions, and slept undisturbed.

A year afterwards, he took these lines just as they were and incorporated them into the 'poem on his own life' which became *The Prelude*, simply altering the pronouns from the third to the first person, and so removing the thin disguise.[1] The kinship between them and the lines in *Tintern Abbey* shows that the experience they describe was not simply one of boyhood, but was continually repeated in adult life. It had probably been particularly strong during the last happy year.

Biographically, *Tintern Abbey* is important, because it is Wordsworth's own testimony to the change in his feelings and in his outlook since he first came that way five years before. As he looked again on the 'steep woods and lofty banks' of the Wye he saw the image of himself as he was then, flinging himself into delight in nature as though he were slaking an intolerable thirst; seeking in her a refuge from his tormenting mental conflict, and, because his need was so violent, his enjoyment was— or so he thought afterwards—entirely sensuous and devoid of that deeper pleasure 'by thought supplied':

                    I cannot paint
What then I was. The sounding cataract
Haunted me like a passion: the tall rock,
The mountain, and the deep and gloomy wood,
Their colours and their forms, were then to me
An appetite: a feeling and a love
That had no need of a remoter charm
By thought supplied, or any interest
Unborrowed from the eye.[2]

But now
          That time is past
And all its aching joys are now no more
And all its dizzy raptures.

[1] *P.W.* v, p. 385, ll. 241–56.   [2] See above, pp. 232–3.

The loss, however, had been compensated by 'other gifts' more precious. Of these, he dwells particularly on two: one, his new and gentler outlook on the tragedy of humanity; the other, that frequent sense of the presence in him and around him of a universal, illimitable spirit, vague indeed in its definition, but sublime in its grand and all-embracing movement, of which he had been conscious in boyhood, but of which his pre-occupation with human problems had for a time deprived him:

> I have learned
> To look on nature, not as in the hour
> Of thoughtless youth, but hearing oftentimes
> The still, sad music of humanity,
> Not harsh nor grating, though of ample power
> To chasten and subdue. And I have felt . . .
> A motion and a spirit, that impels
> All thinking things, all objects of all thought,
> And rolls through all things.[1]

In those five years in fact Wordsworth had learnt that it was not necessary to divorce nature and humanity in his affections, and that his deepest intuitions which he had known in boyhood, of the unity of all life in one joyous being, were still valid.

And so his eyes came to rest at last on that being who had been the chief human agent in the reconciling work, and the end of the poem is a thanksgiving and a prayer for Dorothy. As we notice how Wordsworth speaks of Dorothy in this poem, we learn what is the particular cause of his thankfulness for her:

> For thou art with me, here, upon the banks
> Of this fair river; thou, my dearest Friend,
> My dear, dear Friend, and in thy voice I catch
> The language of my former heart, and read
> My former pleasures in the shooting lights
> Of thy wild eyes. Oh! yet a little while
> May I behold in thee what I was once,
> My dear, dear Sister!

---

[1] Wordsworth's use of the verb 'roll' is significant. In *To my Sister* he had spoke of

> the blessed power that *rolls*
> About, below, above.

He used it in *A Slumber did my Spirit seal* ('Rolled round in earth's diurnal course' and in *Prel.* I, l. 459: 'as if the earth had *rolled* with visible motion her diurn round'.

To Dorothy still belonged that untamed, primitive delight in natural things which was the inheritance of her childhood. She had as yet undergone no disillusionment or conflict as her brother had, and therefore her enjoyment was not the result of thought or of any process other than the going-forth of pure affection in unsullied joy. Although Wordsworth did not 'murmur' at his own change, and recognized it as gain for which thanks must be given, he knew that a particular form of happiness most pure and precious could be his no more. But in Dorothy he could re-live the past. He could both re-live it through her, and pray that

> When these wild ecstasies shall be matured
> Into a sober pleasure,

her mind, like his, might be full of lovely images:

> a mansion for all lovely forms,

such as should sustain her in future years

> If solitude, or fear, or pain, or grief
> Should be thy portion.

Nor was his prayer unanswered. Even in the years when mental disaster had overtaken her, she never failed, especially when he was with her, to draw delight from the memories of their early years. It was a faculty which they each possessed and which never deserted them; a power greater than ordinary memory, for by it they were enabled not merely to recall, but to recreate, the happy past, as though it were still a present reality. With William this faculty played an increasingly important part in his poetic life; with Dorothy, it was a chief source of comfort throughout a life tried to the uttermost by its own capacity for love and suffering.

XIII

THE BEGINNINGS OF *THE PRELUDE*
GERMANY, 1798–9

In the bleak mid-winter
Frosty wind made moan;
Earth stood hard as iron,
Water like a stone.

CHRISTINA ROSSETTI

O N returning from the Wye the Wordsworths took lodgings at Shirehampton, which was more congenial to them than Bristol itself. This was their headquarters for the next five weeks. Coleridge's arrival in Bristol early in August was the signal for another impromptu excursion into Wales. 'Mr. Coleridge', said Wordsworth, 'proposed it to us one evening and we departed the next morning at six o'clock. We had a very pleasant tour along the banks of the Usk and the Wye into Brecknockshire.'[1] During this tour they called on John Thelwall, who had settled at Liswyn Farm on the Wye near Brecon.[2] Not long after their return they departed for London, where they stayed until the middle of September making arrangements for the German trip. The journey from Bristol to London was characteristic of their habits: it was made 'on foot, per waggon, per coach, per postchaise, having expended, each passenger £1. 18. 6d. and been admitted to the presence-chamber at Blenheim and seen the University of Oxford'. Cottle saw to the dispatch of their luggage. As usual they were short of money. They had borrowed from Cottle before leaving Bristol, and Wordsworth now asked him to help him to dispose of his two 'Gilpin's tours', 'into Scotland one, the other among the Lakes', in order to raise a guinea or two: he also tried to draw on Montagu for £23—a sum which was really only the repayment of a debt Montagu owed to Richard Wordsworth, who had assisted him with his expenses in being called to the Bar. But Montagu was out of

[1] *E.L.* 87, p. 201. W.W. to H. Gardiner, Oct. 3rd 1798.
[2] *L.T.* ii, p. 1281. W.W. to Mrs. Thelwall, Nov. 16th 1838.

town, staying with his brother in Huntingdonshire, and Wordsworth's application was not accepted.[1]

Money for the journey was provided eventually by Richard, who still had control of all William's financial affairs and himself prudently invested the last instalment of Raisley Calvert's legacy (£270) in Consols in December; but the German expedition, both for Wordsworth and Coleridge, was really made possible by Tom and Josiah Wedgwood, Coleridge's benefactors. They arranged that both poets should draw on their Hamburg firm, Von Axen, but it was not simply a question of Von Axen acting as the poets' bankers; the Wedgwoods actually advanced money to Wordsworth to the extent of £110, which Wordsworth did not repay until July 1800, when he at length received the repayment of his loan of £100 to Charles Douglas. Meanwhile James Losh had read 'Wordsworth's and Coleridge's Poems' in Bath on September 19th. This gives us a date before which the *Ballads* must have been published in Bristol.[2]

On September 15th 1798 a party consisting of Coleridge, William and Dorothy Wordsworth, and a young friend and disciple of Coleridge's, John Chester of Stowey, sailed in the Hamburg packet from Yarmouth. Bonaparte's armies had already overrun most of western Europe. Germany was now the only country, except the Scandinavian states, still open to English travellers. Our command of the sea, and the absence yet of submarines and mines from sea warfare, made the voyage perfectly safe from all human interference. But it was a rough passage; 'Chester', wrote Coleridge cheerfully, 'was ill the whole voyage; Wordsworth shockingly ill; his sister worst of all, and I neither sick nor giddy but gay as a lark.'[3] When they reached Cuxhaven Dorothy emerged from the horrible cabin and began her Journal; on the 18th they reached Hamburg, where they found lodgings in a poor inn called 'Der wilde Mann'. Here they stayed a fortnight while they discussed the plans for their future movement. Hamburg was dirty and full of evil smells[4]—obviously it compared unfavourably with English cities in these respects—nor was the country-side around it of

---

[1] *E.L.* 83, p. 198. W.W. to Cottle, Aug. 28th 1798.
[2] Diary of James Losh.   [3] *S.T.C.* i, p. 259. *B.L.*, *Satyrane's Letters*, I.
[4] Dorothy testifies to the decent appearance and behaviour of the inhabitants. 'I have never seen a drunken man', she says, 'nor a woman of the lower orders who was not perfectly decent and modest in her appearance.' *D.W.J.* i, p. 25.

much interest. They made acquaintance, however, with old Klopstock, the 'father of German poetry', a kindly and hospitable, though sublimely ignorant, old man, with whom Wordsworth, talking French—for Klopstock knew no English—exchanged views on English and German poetry.[1] Klopstock's views both on English and German literature were certainly unexpected. He thought the blank verse of Glover superior to that of Milton (whom he had read in a prose translation): Schiller, he said, would soon be forgotten, and fortunately the reputation of Kant (whom he found incomprehensible) was, he said, on the decline in Germany. He would have been horrified to know that Wordsworth's friend, when he left Germany, would take with him £30 worth of the works of Kant. Coleridge, however, was for once obliged to keep silence, for he did not speak French.

Wordsworth had read a good deal of German poetry in translation, for this was the era of William Taylor's translations of Bürger's ballads, while Schiller's *Robbers* had been read in English since 1792. Coleridge himself had begun to translate Wieland's *Oberon*, but he had been anticipated by William Sotheby, whose text had just appeared. Of this poem Wordsworth observed to Klopstock 'that it was unworthy of a man of genius to make the interest of a long poem turn entirely upon animal gratification. . . . "Well, but", said he, "you see, such poems please everybody." ' To this Wordsworth made the crushing reply 'that it was the province of a great poet to raise people up to his level, not to descend to theirs'. Wordsworth further recorded: 'He complained of the Fool in *Lear*. I observed that he seemed to give a terrible wildness to the distress; but still he complained. . . . We talked of tragedy. He seemed to rate highly the power of exciting tears—I said that nothing was more easy than to deluge an audience, that it was done every day by the meanest authors.'

But, although Wordsworth was not able to discover in the countenance of Klopstock 'the marks either of sublimity or enthusiasm', though he was quite incapable of instructing or informing them, though the situation of his house was dull and formal so that in choosing it 'the poet does not seem to have been influenced by poetic ideas', his simple kindness and

---

[1] Wordsworth's records of his meetings with Klopstock were printed by Coleridge in *The Friend*, and also in *Satyrane's Letters*, at the end of *B.L.*, in 1817.

innocence made a pleasant impression. 'He expressed himself', said Wordsworth, 'with the liveliness of a girl of 17.' When they talked of Admiral Nelson's 'rumoured Victory' off the Nile, 'he was all faith. I had my doubts.' 'Poor old man!' wrote Dorothy in her Journal: 'I could not look upon him, the benefactor of his country, the father of German poetry, without the most sensible emotion.'

Apart from such intellectual advantages as the conversation of Klopstock afforded, Hamburg held no attractions for the travellers. Wordsworth was much distressed by the dishonesty of inn-keepers and shop-keepers towards foreigners; in spite of the political popularity of the English in Germany at this time, on account of the war and particularly of Nelson's victory at the Nile, English tourists, even those as obviously poor as the Wordsworths, were cheated without mercy, and sometimes with rudeness as well. Both the Wordsworths and Coleridge fought many a battle over prices with bakers, porters, hosiers, and drivers of diligences, and were by no means always losers. 'It is a *sad* place', said Wordsworth to Poole; 'in this epithet you have the soul and essence of all the information which I have been able to gather.' Remnant's English book-shop was a pleasant oasis in this desert; here they often rested and read, and here they bought Bürger's poems and a copy of Percy's *Reliques*.[1]

While they were at Hamburg an important and in some ways surprising alteration was made in their plans. They agreed to separate; Coleridge and Chester would go to Ratzeburg, a small town near by, much frequented by aristocrats and intellectuals, and then to a university: William and Dorothy were to 'speculate further up in the country'. Unfortunately, Coleridge's letter to Poole in which he explained the reasons for this change has not survived, but we have Poole's reply which shows pretty well what they were. 'The Wordsworths have left you', he wrote on October 8th from Stowey; 'so there is an end of our fears about amalgamation etc. I think you both did perfectly right. It was right for them to find a cheaper situation; and it was right for you to avoid the expense of travelling, provided you were where *pure German* is spoken.' By 'our fears about amalgamation' Poole meant that if the Wordsworths and Coleridge continued

[1] *D.W.J.* i, p. 31.

together they would have difficulty in learning German. He was most anxious that Coleridge, while in Germany, should become thoroughly acquainted with the language. 'Speak nothing but German', he urged. 'Live with Germans. Read in German. Think in German.' Somewhat surprisingly, Coleridge followed this advice with unwonted diligence, and became as proficient in German as Wordsworth was in French. Ratzeburg, where he lived for three months, was exactly suited to his purposes; he became a favourite with educated Germans who furnished him with introductions to the professors at Göttingen, whither he migrated early in February, and where again he was lionized and where he worked very hard collecting material for his projected life of Lessing. But the Wordsworths had no idea of spending their time in Germany in a round of social engagements. For one thing, they could not afford it. A man and woman, they found, travelling together, would be expected to return all the hospitality they received, and this was out of the question. Besides, Wordsworth was not, like Coleridge, bent on mastering German philosophy and science—on repairing in fact the gaps left by an English classical education. Both William and Dorothy wished to acquire such a knowledge of German as would enable them to augment their income by translating, for translating German was at this time popular and profitable. They thought they could combine this with living very cheaply and quietly, while their natural love of wandering drew them towards the more picturesque country to the south. When, therefore, Coleridge went to Ratzeburg, on October 3rd, they took places in the Brunswick diligence, in which they had 'reason to lament' the good roads and well-built stage-coaches of England. Dorothy was soon ill; they took two days to reach Brunswick, and twelve hours to travel from Brunswick to Goslar, a distance of only twenty-five miles, where they arrived on October 6th, and where they stayed for the next four months, though they had had no intention, when they arrived, of living there so long.

    At Brunswick, a tiny incident recorded by Dorothy in her Journal throws light on the familiar nicknames used by the friends in their daily talk. After a cheap picnic breakfast of apples and bread bought by William, 'I', says Dorothy, 'carried Kubla to a fountain in a neighbouring market-place, where I drank some excellent water'. 'Kubla' was surely not, as usually

supposed, a manuscript copy of *Kubla Khan*, but a *can* for drinking, humorously named after Coleridge's builder of the pleasure-
dome.[1]

Goslar, once the imperial home of the Hohenstaufen em-
perors, lies at the foot of the Harz mountains, and this is probably why the Wordsworths chose to stay in it; they hoped to
see something of the country-side—'we have plenty of dry
walks', wrote Dorothy soon after their arrival—and before long
to move on to some other small town among the hills. But an
unusually severe winter kept them frost-bound where they were
until the end of February. Travelling in Germany this winter
was practically equivalent to being frozen to death, for there
were no means of conveyance except uncovered carts over roads
that scarcely merited the name. And the cold was intense. 'The
cold of Christmas day', said Dorothy, 'was so excessive that
when we left the room where we sit we were obliged to wrap
ourselves up in great coats etc. though we only went into the
next room.' Wordsworth invested in a fur gown and a black
fur cap such as the peasants wore, 'in which he looks like
any grand Signior', and Dorothy likewise wrapped herself
in furs.

A little picture of Dorothy and William as they sat beside
their black iron stove—'this comfortless oven'—is afforded by
Wordsworth's lines *Written in Germany on one of the coldest
Days of the Century*, as he watched a fly, half-stupefied with the
cold, crawling about in search of the warmth that had awakened
him.

> No Brother, nor Friend has he near him—while I
> Can draw warmth from the cheek of my Love;
> As blest and as glad in this desolate gloom
> As if green summer grass were the floor of my room,
> And woodbines were hanging above.[2]

Their progress in learning German was disappointing. 'My
hope', wrote William to Coleridge in February 1799, 'was that
I should be able to learn German as I learn'd French, in this I
have been woefully deceived. I acquired more French in two
months than I should acquire German in five years as we have
lived.' The reason for this failure was really the poverty of the

[1] H. M. Margoliouth, *Wordsworth and Coleridge, 1795–1834*, p. 49.
[2] *P.W.* iv, p. 64.

Wordsworths. They had intended to live as Wordsworth had lived in Orleans and Blois, *en pension* with a family, sharing their meals and enjoying full social intercourse with them, but in Germany, or at least in Goslar—for Coleridge had succeeded in finding suitable quarters in a pastor's family at Ratzeburg— such a mode of living was unknown except at a price the Words- worths could not afford to pay. They were obliged therefore to take ordinary lodgings, which they found with a tradesman's widow in the Breite-Strasse, where they lived indeed in 'comfort and quietness', but entirely cut off from any society but that of one another.[1] There was a French *émigré* priest also in the house, and a young apprentice who occasionally visited them in the evenings. There was in any case hardly any society in the town more cultivated than that of 'grocers and linen-drapers', and they, according to Wordsworth, were but 'a wretched race, the flesh, blood and bone of their minds being nothing but knavery and low falsehood'. Even their landlady, who was a decent woman, cheated them of 'halfpence and farthings' at first. There was one 'dear and kind creature', however, whom they could not help loving, though he was little enough help to them as a teacher. 'He is so miserably deaf', wrote Wordsworth, 'that we can only play with him games of cross-purposes, and he like- wise labours under a common German infirmity, the loss of teeth, so that with bad German, bad English, bad French, bad hearing, and bad utterance, you will imagine we have had very pretty dialogues, but the creature is all kindness and benevolence, and I shall never forget him.'[2] He was indeed a figure worthy to stand beside Simon Lee in the *Lyrical Ballads*.

Goslar was as deficient in books as it was in opportunities for conversation. It contained no library. They were obliged to be content with the few books they had brought with them, which included Bürger's poems and Percy's *Reliques* bought in Hamburg; his old favourite, Coxe's *Travels in Switzerland* in the French edition, and, probably, a Theocritus and a copy of Bartram's *Travels through North and South Carolina*, one of Coleridge's tributaries for *The Ancient Mariner*. Most of these

---

[1] This full explanation of their situation has only recently come to light in a letter from Wordsworth to Josiah Wedgwood dated Feb. 6th 1799, in the Wedg- wood Museum at Etruria.

[2] W.W. to Josiah Wedgwood, Feb. 6th 1799 (Wedgwood Museum, Etruria).

books had some part, small or great, in the output of poetry which was the fruit of these strange, isolated months in the little snow-bound German town. For, as he said to Coleridge: 'As I had no books I have been obliged to write in self-defence.' Coleridge said on January 4th:

He seems to have employed more time in writing English than in studying German. No wonder! for he might as well have been in England as at Goslar, in the situation which he chose and with his unseeking manners. . . . His taking his sister with him was a wrong step. . . . Sister here is considered as only a name for mistress. Still, however, male acquaintances he might have had, and had I been at Goslar I would have had them; but W., God love him! seems to have lost his spirits and almost his inclination for it.

Wordsworth indeed was not in a state where company could have been welcome. He was again possessed by the 'creative breeze', and it was blowing now, not gently, but as

A tempest, a redundant energy,
Vexing its own creation.

'Reading', he told Coleridge, 'is now become a kind of luxury to me. When I do not read I am absolutely consumed by thinking and feeling and bodily exertions of voice or limbs, the consequence of those feelings.' The 'feelings' were forcing themselves into poetry at a rapid rate, but there was likewise a hindrance—not new, but perhaps more troublesome than heretofore, which Wordsworth thus analyses:

'I should have written five times as much as I have done, but that I am prevented by an uneasiness at my stomach and side, with a dull pain about my heart. I have used the word pain, but uneasiness and heat are words which more accurately express my feeling—at all events it renders writing unpleasant.' Dorothy, watching him anxiously, wrote 'William is very industrious; his mind is always active; indeed, too much so; he overwearies himself, and suffers from pain and weakness in his side.' Now this was an old trouble: Dorothy had first noticed his 'violent head-aches and a pain in his side' while he was still a schoolboy,[1] when it was considered bad enough to prevent his taking up work as a lawyer. Again in 1794 he had spoken of 'nervous headaches' so severe as to 'deprive me of all recollections'.[2] At

[1] *E.L.* 2, p. 7. D.W. to J.P., Aug. 1787.
[2] Ibid. 45, p. 130. W.W. to William Mathews, Dec. 1794.

Alfoxden three times Dorothy recorded in her Journal that William was unwell or 'very ill'[1]—apparently with short and violent attacks—and when he began *Peter Bell* she noted that its composition was 'wearisome'. The trouble was serious in the summer and autumn following their return to England, so much so that it brought Coleridge hastening north.[2] There seems no doubt at all that by this time the pain in the side and stomach was connected with the effort of composition. It continued to be a plague through all the creative years that lay ahead, and was one of the main reasons why Dorothy, and later Mary and Sara Hutchinson, were so much employed in copying and taking down poems from his dictation; more than mere convenience was involved. At what point the uncomfortable symptoms became associated with the act of writing we do not know, but certainly from the German time onwards they have to be reckoned with as an enemy against which Wordsworth waged a continual and very courageous and exacting warfare.

Of the many 'long and affectionate'[3] letters written to Coleridge from Goslar only two have survived. Of these the first, undated, but written probably late in December, contained three blank-verse extracts from what Dorothy described as 'the mass of what William has written', and versions, afterwards considerably altered, of two of the 'Lucy' lyrics—*She dwelt among the untrodden Ways*, and *Strange Fits of Passion I have known*. Two of the blank-verse pieces, one the description of skating by starlight, the other the adventure of the stolen boat on Ullswater, are found with very few important alterations in Book I of *The Prelude*: Dorothy transcribed them for Coleridge because he had been skating on the lake at Ratzeburg, with the comment: 'A race with William upon his native lakes would leave to the heart and the imagination something more dear and valuable than the gay sight of ladies and countesses whirling along the lake of Ratzeburg.'[4] The third passage (the first, however, in the

---

[1] *D.W.J.* i, pp. 8, 9, 12. Feb. 14th, 19th, Mar. 16th 1798.

[2] See below, p. 447.

[3] *S.T.C.* i, p. 268. S.T.C. to Poole, Jan. 4th 1799. See also Coleridge's verses written in homesick mood from Ratzeburg: 'William, my teacher and friend! etc.' S.T.C. *Poems*, i, p. 304.

[4] Coleridge had written a description of his skating in a letter to his wife and also to the Wordsworths. No letters of his to the Wordsworths during the German time have survived.

letter) is that description of his nutting expedition in the hazel-woods lying to the south of Esthwaite which was never incorporated in *The Prelude*, but was published as a separate poem in the second edition of *Lyrical Ballads* in 1800, with the title *Nutting*. Of 'the mass of what William has written' there was thought to be no contemporary manuscript, until the discovery by de Selincourt, just in time for insertion as an appendix into his edition of the early text of *The Prelude* in 1926, of a note-book, of which the contents all belong to the German period, except some pages in the middle in which Dorothy afterwards entered her Journal for the spring of 1802.[1] Wordsworth's methods of writing first drafts have proved puzzling to editors. In this book he began at the last page and worked backwards. What he wrote was in fact an almost complete text of the first book of *The Prelude*, though in a somewhat different order from the final arrangements, and without the first 270 lines. In order to understand what Wordsworth was trying to do it is necessary to go back to the early months of the year 1798, to the start of *The Recluse*, and the state of mind and feeling which resulted from it.

He had begun *The Recluse* sometime in the new year of 1798 in confidence and an eager optimism: 'I know not anything which will not come within the scope of my plan.' Its purpose was 'to give pictures of Man, Nature, and Society', of Beauty also, 'a living Presence of the earth'; above all, the 'individual Mind', in its mysterious affinities, feelings and powers, was to be 'my haunt, and the main region of my song'.[2] As we know, he had not progressed far with this great plan. He had written the preface or preamble setting forth what he conceived his task to be; the rest consisted mainly of *The Ruined Cottage* as he had enlarged it with the Pedlar's story and soliloquies. Then he had become absorbed in the short pieces which form the bulk of the *Lyrical Ballads*, and in *Peter Bell*, which in itself is a fairly profound study of one sort of 'individual mind'. In a holiday of the spirit he had written his thanksgiving for his return to Nature and to joy in the *Tintern Abbey* lines. *The*

---

[1] Some pages have been used by Dorothy for German exercises, and the note-book also contains the record of his talks with Klopstock and the fragment of an essay on the political philosophy of Godwin and Paley.

[2] See above, p. 363.

Recluse had not been continued, but it was never far from his thoughts. Was there any reason why now, in the solitude of Goslar, he should not take it up again? Yet instead, we find him writing what was in effect his spiritual autobiography; his own personal intercourse with Nature and—to a lesser degree— with man. If we seek an explanation of this change we have first of all his own apology, written many years later when he published *The Excursion.*

Several years ago [he tells us then], when the Author retired to his native mountains with the hope of being enabled to construct a literary Work that might live, it was a reasonable thing that he should take a review of his own mind, and examine how far Nature and Education had qualified him for such employment. As subsidiary to this preparation, he undertook to record, in verse, the origin and progress of his own powers, as far as he was acquainted with them.

This record was in fact begun, not at Grasmere, but in Germany, although the greater part of it was written at Grasmere. We thus have in these sentences a fairly accurate account of the origin and purpose of *The Prelude.* Wordsworth's postponement of *The Recluse* has as its root cause his pre-occupation with his own fundamental experience. He had given a hint of this in the lines written as a preface to *The Recluse*:

> And if with this [that is, with the theme of *The Recluse*]
> I mix more lowly matter; with the thing
> Contemplated, describe the Mind and Man
> Contemplating; and who, and what he was—
> The transitory Being that beheld
> This Vision; when and where and how he lived;—
> Be not this labour useless.

Already many of the fragments of blank verse written at Alfoxden during that spring were concerned with the early experience of his boyhood, that fountain of living waters to which his mind was constantly repairing. The four hundred or so lines which he entered in the note-book at Goslar represent his final yielding to the lure of contemplative memory. He did not know that in doing so he was really sounding the knell of *The Recluse.* The 'poem on his own life' became more and more absorbing in its interest, so that even when he tried to take up *The Recluse* again in the early months of 1800 it was only possible to write a fragment.

When he wrote *We are Seven* he composed, he tells us, the last line of the last verse first, and came for an opening stanza to Coleridge for inspiration. This method of working had also been adopted in *The Ruined Cottage*, where the end of Margaret's story was the first part of the poem to be written down.[1] It is a method which presupposes that the story or pattern of the poem is clear in the poet's mind before actual composition begins. The verse written in the Goslar note-book is of this description, and begins as follows:

> Was it for this
> That one, the fairest of all rivers, lov'd
> To blend his murmurs with my Nurse's song,
> And from his alder-shades and rocky falls
> And from his fords and shallows, sent a voice
> To intertwine my dreams?

The question, 'For this', or 'Was it for this', is repeated four times, each time recalling a scene of early happiness in childhood. But what 'this' was is nowhere indicated. It is explained, of course, in the first 270 lines of *The Prelude*, a passage difficult to date of which no manuscript exists earlier than 1804. It is now believed that Wordsworth did not write down this beginning at all until the summer or the early autumn of 1803 when he told Coleridge he had made 'a beginning to The Recluse'. For both he and Coleridge then considered the 'poem on his own life' as a part of *The Recluse*.[2] But the Goslar note-book does not make sense unless what Wordsworth meant by 'this' in his rhetorical questions had already received mental existence. We must therefore conclude that although he did not commit it to paper (perhaps because of these painful sensations that came upon him so often in the act of writing) he had already thought through and mentally composed that description of his frustrated, uncertain search for a subject for an epic poem, which eventually came to occupy the beginning of *The Prelude*. The state of disappointment in which he found himself because of the failure of that search was not altogether done away even when

---

[1] See above, p. 316, and n.
[2] H. Darbishire, *Wordsworth*, 1950, pp. 93–95. See below, p. 604.

he began to write *The Recluse*. True, he had found a subject, a combination of two of his aspirations, a

> tale from my own heart . . .
> Lofty, with interchange of gentler things,

and a

> philosophic song
> Of Truth that cherishes our daily life,

such as he meant *The Recluse* to be. But was he fit to undertake it? He had turned aside from it to write the *Lyrical Ballads*—why? Was it because of the

> over-anxious eye
> That with a false activity beats off
> Simplicity and self-presented truth?

Or simply his inexperience—a hope that

> Mellower years will bring a riper mind?

The true answer is given in the combination of the first lines of the Goslar note-book, with what immediately precedes them in *The Prelude*; together they form the key to the understanding of the first book of *The Prelude*.

> I recoil and droop, and seek repose
> In listlessness from vain perplexity,
> Unprofitably travelling towards the grave
> Like a false steward who hath much received
> And renders nothing back.—*Was it for this*
> *That one, the fairest of all Rivers, lov'd*
> *To blend his murmurs with my Nurse's song* . . .[1]

The 'listlessness' may well have been heightened by the attacks of headache and pain in the side which so often crippled him, and which, being most severe when he tried to write, at times made him wonder whether he would after all be able to carry out his vocation as a poet. References to this fear are not uncommon in his letters and those of Dorothy during the next few years.[2] In this mood he had recourse to a poet who had suffered from the same sense of frustration and powerlessness—Robert Burns. 'His Ode to Despondency', he told Coleridge at the very time he was writing these early drafts of *The Prelude*, 'I can

[1] *Prel.* I, ll. 265–71.
[2] e.g. W.W. to Miss Taylor, Apr. 9th 1801.

never read without the deepest agitation'.[1] It is easy to see why
it 'agitated' him:

> Happy, ye sons of busy life,
> Who, equal to the bustling strife,
> No other view regard!
> Even when the wished end's denied,
> Yet while the busy means are plied,
> They bring their own reward:
> Whilst I, a hope-abandon'd wight,
> Unfitted with an aim,
> Meet every sad returning night
> And joyless morn the same;
> You, bustling and justling,
> Forget each grief and pain;
> I, listless, yet restless,
> Find every prospect vain.

Under these circumstances, he decided that his real need was
for an exploration of the growth of his own being; the intercourse of his own 'mind' with that of 'Nature'; the rich and
varied character of his total experience, both bodily and mental,
from the earliest dawn of memory to the present day. Circumstances favoured this blessed retreat into the past. For one
thing, Coleridge was not at hand. Coleridge had not entirely
approved of all the *Lyrical Ballads*. He wanted him to write
a great poem; he had been delighted with the idea of *The Recluse*. Nothing but a great 'philosophic song' could do justice to
the genius of 'the *giant* Wordsworth—God love him'. It is not
probable that he would have approved entirely of Wordsworth's
absorption with his own story if he had been present to discuss
day by day what was done. 'Of nothing but The Recluse can I
hear patiently' was the burden of his letters in the following
summer, when Wordsworth endeavoured to propitiate him
by making the growing 'poem on his own life' a personal
offering to him, and promising to make it 'a tail-piece of the
Recluse.'

Coleridge's absence, the isolation of his daily life in the little
German city, the presence of Dorothy, herself a link with his
earliest days, lack of books and outside interests, all alike combined to make his mind a more than usually clear mirror of his

---

[1] *E.L.* 92, p. 222.

own experience. In some such manner, we may conclude, *The Prelude* began to be written.

The two other poems in the letter to Coleridge were described by Wordsworth as 'little Rhyme poems which I hope will amuse you'. We are not accustomed to look for 'amusement' to the 'Lucy' poems of Wordsworth. But, as with the early drafts of *The Prelude* later in the year, Wordsworth is here approaching Coleridge in what he intends to be an apologetic manner. He felt that Coleridge would probably be disturbed at the appearance of more short poems instead of *The Recluse*. So he tried to represent them as of no very serious moment.

The two poems sent in the letter were, as has been said, versions of *She dwelt among the untrodden Ways* and *Strange Fits of Passion I have known*. The first consists of five verses in the letter; it was cut down to three for publication in 1800 and certainly lost nothing thereby.[1] To the second he added a first stanza and dropped the last—that in which he tells 'Lucy' his fears about her death.

> I told her this; her laughter light
> Is ringing in my ears;
> And when I think upon that night
> My eyes are dim with tears.[2]

In another letter to Coleridge which has not survived but which was probably written soon after the first he sent a third poem of this cycle, that 'sublime epitaph' as Coleridge called it, *A Slumber did my Spirit seal*. Yet another, *Three Years She grew in Sun and Shower*, was written when at length spring had come and he and Dorothy had left Goslar and were walking through the Harz forest to Nordhausen. A fifth, *I travelled among unknown Men*, was written two years later in April 1801 and sent in a letter to Mary Hutchinson with instructions that it was to be 'read after She dwelt among'. In feeling and language it belongs as closely to the other four as though it had been written at the same time.

---

[1] The lines in the fourth verse,

> And she was graceful as the broom
> That flowers by Carron's side,

show that Wordsworth had in his mind the ballad of *Owen of Carron*, by his old favourite Langhorne.

[2] See above, p. 319.

The identity of 'Lucy' has been the problem of critics for many years. But Wordsworth is a poet before he is a biographer, and neither 'Lucy' nor her home nor his relations with her are necessarily in the strict sense historical. Nevertheless, as the *Lyrical Ballads* were all of them 'founded on fact' in some way, and as Wordsworth's mind was essentially factual, it would be rash to say that Lucy is entirely fictitious. The idea that she represents some early and unknown love of Wordsworth who died has been frequently rejected—perhaps too hastily—for lack, it is supposed, of evidence of any such person. The love of his youth, so far as he had any, was Mary Hutchinson. Not much is to be gained by straining geographical exactitude out of 'the springs of Dove'. Wordsworth had visited the Derbyshire Dovedale during a college vacation, but not for any length of time, and a stream of that name flows down into Patterdale from Helvellyn; there is another in the Cleveland hills of Yorkshire, not far from Sockburn where he had spent some time with Tom Hutchinson during his college days. An actual Lucy might of course have been met with in one of these dales, but the convenience of rhyme must also be considered. There is, however, definite evidence that the name 'Lucy' is connected with Dorothy. In other poems, known to be concerned with Dorothy, the name 'Lucy' is used: notably in *The Glow-Worm*, and in the early, unpublished version of *Nutting*, which was written in Germany. The poem that became *Strange Fits of Passion I have known* is probably a memory of Racedown, and there may also be a hint in Dorothy's own words in the letter to Coleridge, before copying it out: 'The next poem is a favourite of me—Dorothy.' If she knew that the poem concerned herself, she would certainly be inclined to call it 'a favourite'. Yet the name 'Lucy', though undoubtedly sometimes used for Dorothy, is not exclusively hers. She is sometimes 'Emma' or 'Emmeline', and 'Lucy' belongs also to 'Lucy Gray', whose tragic history was written also in this German time. And an early poem by Rogers, *A Wish*, certainly known to Wordsworth, and almost certainly in his mind when he wrote *I travelled among unknown Men*,[1] is about a 'Lucy'; the name is also used by other poets.

But if 'Lucy' is Dorothy, or if at least Dorothy is the inspira-

---

[1] Cf. 'And Lucy, at her wheel, shall sing . . .': Rogers.
    'And she I cherished turned her wheel . . .': Wordsworth.

tion of the poems, why is she represented as having died? Coleridge's guess about *A Slumber did my Spirit seal* may, of course, be right. 'Whether', he wrote to Poole, 'it had any reality I cannot say. Most probably, in some gloomier moment he had fancied the moment when his sister might die.' On this supposition Wordsworth must have had several 'gloomier moments', as Lucy is thought of as actually or potentially dead in each poem.

But it is not habitual with Wordsworth, when writing to or about Dorothy, to think of her as dead or going to die. Twice, once in *Tintern Abbey* and once in the poem written at Grasmere in 1800, *'Tis said that some have died for Love'*, he seeks to comfort her in case of his own death, but in the poems in which she appears, such as *To a Butterfly, Among all lovely Things*, and the various addresses in *The Prelude*, she is a most living figure. We may perhaps conclude that if the incident recorded in *Strange Fits of Passion* is a genuine reminiscence, probably of Racedown, this poem was composed first of the cycle (it is placed first in all the editions published by Wordsworth) and the rest followed not because they were 'about' Dorothy, but simply as a continuation of the idea of Lucy's death suggested in that first poem. It may also be added that the description of Lucy in *Three Years She grew* is not in any identifiable way a description of Dorothy, or indeed of any woman known to Wordsworth.[1]

Some critics, in view of the fact that *I travelled among unknown Men* was sent in a letter to Mary Hutchinson with instructions to read it 'after She dwelt among', have surmised that the whole series was intended for her.[2] Again, we are faced with the question, 'If Lucy is Mary, why should she be dead'? More recently[3] it has been pointed out that Wordsworth had indeed known a girl who had died, and that he had perhaps, in early youth, loved her. She was Margaret, the second of the Hutchinson sisters, who had died of a consumption in the spring of 1796. Dorothy, writing to Jane Marshall at the time of her death said: 'I have had a melancholy letter from Mary Hutchinson; I fear

---

[1] To mention only one detail, Lucy is described as having a form 'of stately height'. Dorothy was neither tall nor stately.

[2] So A. Beattie, in *Representative Poems of William Wordsworth*.

[3] H. M. Margoliouth, *Wordsworth and Coleridge*, pp. 52–56.

that Margaret is dead before this time, she was then attending her at Sockburn, without the least hope of her recovery from a confirmed consumption. This account has affected me very much —last year at this time we were all together and little supposed that any one of us was so near death.'[1] Wordsworth would have known Margaret as a child and during his first long vacations at Penrith in 1788 and 1789; and again at Sockburn in the early spring of 1794 when he and Dorothy probably paid a visit there. But, as we have seen, his early love in that family was for Mary. Nevertheless, the thought of Margaret's early death and the sorrow it had brought to Mary and Dorothy may well have been an element in the poetic creation of Lucy. Further than that it does not seem possible to go.[2]

One thing is certain about the 'Lucy' poems: the woman whom Wordsworth saw in imagination and called Lucy is not Caroline's mother. And in the last of the poems, written two years later in England, the rejection is even more complete, not merely of Annette, but of all that lay outside England.

> I travelled among unknown men
> In lands beyond the sea,
> Nor, England, did I know till then
> What love I bore to thee.
>
> Among thy mountains did I feel
> The gladness of desire
> And she I cherished turned her wheel
> Beside an English fire.

Of greater interest than the identity of Lucy is the revelation

---

[1] *E.L.* 52, p. 152. D.W. to Jane Marshall, Mar. 1796. In the spring of 1795 Dorothy paid a visit to Sockburn. See her letter thence, *E.L.* 47, p. 132.

[2] In the original version of *She dwelt among* it is said that

> Slow distemper checked her bloom
> And on the heath she died.
> Long time before her head lay low
> Dead to the world was she. . . .

Wordsworth, in his letter to Coleridge, made a curious comment on these lines, telling him that the words 'Long time' were to be considered 'as put in merely to fill up the measure but as injurious to the sense'. It is difficult to see in what way the words are 'injurious to the sense' unless Wordsworth had in mind some real human being who had died, not from a 'slow distemper' but rapidly and unexpectedly. See H. M. Margoliouth, op. cit., p. 55.

in the poems of the mental condition in which they were composed.

> In one of those sweet dreams I slept,
> Kind Nature's gentlest boon,

he says of his ride to 'Lucy's cot', while in the 'epitaph' the first two lines describe with a serene simplicity this creative sleep of the senses when the 'soul' and imagination are most alive:

> A slumber did my spirit seal;
> I had no human fears. . . .

He was still experiencing that condition which he had described in *Tintern Abbey*, when

> we are laid asleep
> In body, and become a living soul.

Lucy Gray—that most haunting of all his ballads of childhood —was the offspring of the snow-bound landscape around him, and of Dorothy's memories of a real incident of her own childhood at Halifax. Echoes of his old favourite *The Babes in the Wood* sound in it;[1] for he had with him a copy of Percy's *Reliques*. 'The solitary child' steps out of the snow-drifts into the growing procession of Wordsworth's poetic children, and she was soon joined by *Ruth*.[2] *Ruth* is a story of desertion, though there is no child to enhance the tragedy or comfort her in her solitude, as in *The Thorn* and *Her Eyes are Wild*. And in this poem we hear a good deal about the deserting husband. The 'Youth from Georgia's shore' who woos and wins Ruth and then deserts her to return to his life 'with roving bands of

---

[1]
> The storm came on before its time;
> She wandered up and down,
> And many a hill did Lucy climb
> And never reached the town.
> > *Lucy Gray.*
> These pretty babes, with hand in hand
> Went wandering up and down;
> But never more could see the man
> Aproaching from the town.
> > *The Babes in the Wood.*

[2] Professor Garrod, in his essay on 'Wordsworth's Lucy', says of Lucy, and Lucy Gray and Ruth that they seem all to belong 'to an order of beings who have lapsed out of nature . . . into human connections hardly strong enough to hold them'. He points out that in *A Slumber* Wordsworth refers to Lucy as 'a *thing* that could not feel the touch of earthly years'. H. W. Garrod, *Wordsworth*, 1927.

Indians in the West', is Wordsworth's picture of what he himself might have been if he had grown up in a savage society.
Outwardly he is the frontispiece of Bartram's *Travels*;[1] in soul
he is a gay and attractive Peter Bell.

> The wind, the tempest roaring high,
> The tumult of a tropic sky,
> Might well be dangerous food
> For him, a Youth to whom was given
> So much of earth—so much of heaven,
> And such impetuous blood.
>
> .　　.　　.　　.　　.
>
> Yet in his worst pursuits, I ween
> That sometimes there did intervene
> Pure hopes of high intent:
> For passions linked to forms so fair
> And stately, needs must have their share
> Of noble sentiment.
>
> But ill he lived, much evil saw,
> With men to whom no better law
> Nor better life was known;
> Deliberately, and undeceived
> Those wild men's vices he received,
> And gave them back his own.

Ruth in her solitude and madness is like another Margaret of
The Ruined Cottage or 'Female Vagrant' of *Salisbury Plain*. She
led

> An innocent life, yet far astray.

Is there perhaps a memory of Wordsworth's own childhood in
the picture of Ruth

> Setting her little water-mills
> By spouts and fountains wild—
> Such small machinery as she turned
> Ere she had wept, ere she had mourned,
> A young and happy Child?

The last verse, visualizing a Christian funeral 'in hallowed mould'
for the poor vagrant, strikes a new note in Wordsworth's

----

[1] Depicting a chieftain with a feather head-dress, like the 'Youth's'. The
description of the American scenery is also taken from Bartram.

poetry. The dead Lucy had been consigned, without apparent concern for her 'immortal part', to be

> Rolled round in earth's diurnal course,
> With rocks and stones and trees.

Perhaps the solitude and wretchedness of Ruth created in him a reaction towards the comfort and kindness which Christian humanity can offer even to a poor dead body.

Did Wordsworth write *The Reverie of Poor Susan* in Germany and not in 1797, as he himself dated it in 1836?[1] The title is an exact translation of Bürger's *Das Arme Süsschen's Traum*, which we know to have been his favourite poem of Bürger's: 'it is the most perfect and Shakespearean of his poems', he said to Coleridge.[2] 'As to Bürger', he wrote to Coleridge, 'I am yet far from that admiration of him which he has excited in you; but I am by nature slow to admire. . . . I remember a hurry of pleasure, but I have few distinct forms that people my mind, nor any recollection of delicate or minute feelings.'[3] Wordsworth well describes here what he sought for in poetry, 'distinct forms' and 'feelings'. He felt that Bürger's poems lacked descriptive force in delineating what he called 'manners'—that is behaviour— 'manners reflecting not the wearisome unintelligible obliquities of city life, but connected with the permanent objects of nature and partaking of the simplicity of those objects'.[4] In Burns, on the other hand, 'everywhere you have the presence of human life. The communications that proceed from Burns come to the mind with the life and charm of recognitions.' *Poor Susan* is almost an answer to this defect in Bürger. She turns from the 'obliquities of city life' to behold in imagination, through the window opened by the thrush's song, 'the permanent objects of nature':

> A mountain ascending, a vision of trees. . . .[5]

---

[1] Altering it afterwards to '1801 or 1802'—a mistake, as the poem was published in 1800.

[2] *U.L.* I. 67, p. 134. Quoted in S.T.C.'s letter to William Taylor, Jan. 25th 1800.

[3] Ibid., 67, p. 133.   [4] *E.L.* 92, p. 221. W.W. to S.T.C., Feb. 1799.

[5] Susan's vision may be compared with Ruth's state when she was insane:

> Yet sometimes milder hours she knew
> Nor wanted sun, nor rain, nor dew
> Nor pastimes of the May:
>   They all were with her in her cell
> And a clear brook with cheerful knell
> Did o'er the pebbles play.

Ellen Irwin or the Braes of Kirtle[1] is another poem influenced by Bürger. It has been well described as 'a mistake'; Wordsworth tells us that he deliberately avoided writing it in the 'simple ballad strain', as it already existed in that form, and chose instead the form of Bürger's *Lenore*. The only question of interest connected with it is—where did Wordsworth read the ballad? For it was not in Percy's *Reliques*, and Scott's *Minstrelsy of the Scottish Border*, in which it was included, was not published until 1802. Ritson's *Scottish Songs* had, however, been published in 1794 in London by Johnson, containing a version of the ballad, and appended to it in a note was a quotation from Pennant's *Tour in Scotland*, in which 'Helen' is called 'Ellen', and which also speaks of 'the banks of Kirtle' on which the tragedy took place. Wordsworth's knowledge of the river name, about which he appends a footnote, must be based on Pennant.

The poems of the 'Matthew' cycle, *A Poet's Epitaph* and *The Danish Boy* complete the output of poetry for the German period. The *Epitaph* is an unsuccessful essay in sarcasm, very rightly criticized by Lamb.[2] *The Danish Boy* is a fragment intended as a prelude to a ballad about a murdered Danish prince. It is interesting as being one of the few poems of Wordsworth which refer to the folk-tales of his own country of West Cumberland. These tales of ghostly Danish harpers still lingered among the fells. John Wordsworth said afterwards of it: 'It is meant as a wild story and dream of fancy.'[3]

The 'Matthew' poems show his mind busy with his schooldays, though the identification of Matthew with William Taylor has been much too readily assumed. He is, as has been already argued, based more on Wordsworth's memories of his old 'Packman' friend.[4] The six poems,[5] though elegiac in character, have a certain quiet cheerfulness and serenity about them; Matthew's life had not been embittered by life's sorrows, although he had lost a daughter; he had lived beloved, the friend

---

[1] Published in 1800 and almost certainly written in Germany.
[2] *Lamb*, i, p. 239. Its resemblance to the 19th Epigram of Theocritus has been pointed out.
[3] *D.C.P.* J.W. to M.H., Feb. 25th 1801.
[4] See above, p. 52.
[5] Two were never published by Wordsworth. They are to be found in *P.W.* iv, 451. They have lines and verses overlapping with the published poem, *Address to the Scholars of the Village School of* ——.

of all the neighbourhood. Again, as in *Ruth*, a Christian image is introduced at the end.

> Such solace find we for our loss;
> And what beyond this thought we crave
> Comes in the promise from the Cross
> Shining upon thy happy grave.

At Goslar Wordsworth also employed himself in writing the beginnings of an essay against the 'sages', particularly Godwin and Paley; it seems from its style to have been intended for publication, though only a fragment of it exists. In it he denied the power of moral philosophy

to melt into our affections, to incorporate itself with the blood and vital juices of our minds, and thence to have any influence worth our notice in forming those habits of which I am speaking. . . . Can it be imagined by any man who has deeply examined his own heart that an old habit will be foregone or a new one formed by a series of propositions which, presenting no image to the mind can convey no feeling which has any connection with the supposed archetype or fountain of the proposition existing in human life. . . . They contain no picture of human life; they *describe* nothing.

This outburst contains several phrases very characteristic of Wordsworth's thought. The strange expression, 'the blood and vital juices of our minds', has a likeness to such lines in his poetry as

> Felt in the blood and felt along the heart,

or the 'vital feelings of delight' which fostered the growth of Lucy.

From a letter from Coleridge to Thomas Longman, the publisher of the second edition of *Lyrical Ballads*, written in December 1800, we learn a tantalizing fact—that the Wordsworths kept a journal while they were in Goslar which Coleridge wanted to incorporate in his projected book about Germany.[1] Dorothy had kept a record of their doings up to their arrival in Goslar, on October 6th; nothing could be more natural than that she should continue it. She had little else to do. But from Coleridge's phraseology it looks as though Wordsworth himself were the author. Part of Dorothy's Hamburgh Journal had in fact been

---

[1] *U.L.* I, p. 164. S.T.C. to T. Longman, Dec. 15th 1800.

written by him, so the Goslar Journal was probably a descriptive
journal written by Dorothy and William together. Its loss is unfortunate for it would have thrown light on the 'lost' two months
from the end of February to April 1799 when their whereabouts
are largely conjectural. Coleridge's book did not materialize,
and when at length his letters from Germany appeared as *Satyrane's Letters* in 1817, they did not include anything by Wordsworth except the account of his conversations with Klopstock.

On February 27th Dorothy and William addressed a long
letter to Coleridge (who was now at Göttingen) from Nordhausen. They had left Goslar at last, on foot, on Saturday the
23rd, as soon as a fine, mild morning gave them leave. They
walked through the Harz forest, enjoying the 'brilliant green of
the earth—moss under the trees', the strange shapes of the
fir-trees, the first song of the lark, 'a sweet, heavenly, liquid
melody', and 'forest views of hill and valley'. They slept first at
Clausthal and the second night at Osterode, where poor Dorothy
was 'stared out of countenance' by the inhabitants who unfortunately were just coming out of church as the English
travellers entered the town. She had to wait in the guard-room
of the gate-house while William was hauled off to the burgo-
master and questioned about passports. At length they obtained
lodging for the night and departed unmolested the next morning, sleeping at Schazefeld, and the next night at a country inn
where the landlord was an old soldier of kindly and contented
manners. 'We were struck', says Dorothy, 'with the extreme
folly of people who draw conclusions respecting national character from the narrow limits of common observation. We have
been much with German hosts and hostesses and notwithstanding the supposed identifying tendence of national manners . . .
these persons appeared in every respect as if made in contrast to
each other.' At Nordhausen they found long-delayed letters from
Coleridge: 'I burst open the seals and could almost have kissed
them in the presence of the post-master', said Dorothy. They
immediately sat down to answer them. William described his
most recent poetical labours before leaving Goslar. 'Wishing',
he said, 'not to be in debt when I return to England I have
lately been employed in hewing down Peter Bell.' The publication of *Peter Bell* was thus still his intention and the earning
of money an overriding motive. 'With another dressing', he

says, 'I think he will do. He has risen in my esteem. Heaven knows there was need.' Some of the parts of *Peter Bell* which were 'hewn' away are still traceable. One of them, with a first and last stanza added, and the name of 'Peter Bell' changed, became a separate poem, namely, *Andrew Jones*, and was published in the second edition of *Lyrical Ballads*. Another is probably to be identified with a charming fairy poem which may at first have formed part of the prologue. It is in the same metre. The first two verses are pure Wordsworth:

> I love upon a stormy night
> To hear these fits of slender song
> Which through the woods and open plains,
> Among the clouds or in the rains
> The loud wind bears along.
>
> Then do I love to stand alone
> By some huge rock or tree defended
> To stand like one that's blind, and catch
> Of those small strains the last faint snatch
> For human ears intended.

The resemblance of these lines to the blank-verse fragment beginning 'There was a spot' is remarkable.[1] They are probably contemporary with it. The rest is a charming description of fairies, and shows that Wordsworth was quite as capable as Coleridge of using 'the supernatural' as the material of poetry.

Wordsworth also told Coleridge that he had devoted 'two days (O Wonder) to the Salisbury Plain. I am resolved to discard Robert Walford and invent a new story for the woman.' This statement is elucidated by one of the manuscripts in which a character appears, an old soldier, who proves to be the father of the sailor's unfortunate wife. He is not, however, given the name 'Robert Walford' or any name at all. The name 'Walford' takes us to an incident in Wordsworth's life at Alfoxden recorded by Thomas Poole.[2] Poole was walking with Wordsworth and Coleridge near Alfoxden, and when they were near the remains of an old gibbet Poole told them the sad story of John Walford, a labourer, who had been hanged there for the murder of his wife. It was a 'hard case', as he had been separated from his true love and forced into marriage with a woman of bad character.

---

[1] *P.W.* v, p. 342. See above, p. 80.   [2] *T.P.* ii, pp. 234–7.

From the cart he said that he was truly sorry for his crime, and that it was not 'fore-intended'. His real sweetheart was standing in the crowd; she climbed into the cart and kissed her lover farewell. The resemblance between John Walford and his own sailor evidently struck Wordsworth deeply. Not only does it account for his intention of introducing the name 'Walford' into *Salisbury Plain*, but he began to write a poem on the subject of this 'Somersetshire Tragedy'. Through some curious and regrettable feeling that the poem was too gruesome and painful to be printed, the manuscript was cut out of the note-book in which it stood and destroyed by the poet's grandson, Gordon Wordsworth, usually so zealous a preserver of all his grandfather's papers. Wordsworth did not complete his new intentions about *Salisbury Plain* and did not write 'a new story for the Woman'. He became absorbed in the 'poem on his own life', and then in the work that led to the second edition of *Lyrical Ballads*. It was fortunate for him that this was so, for *Salisbury Plain*, in thought and feeling, belonged to the past; to have returned to it now would have been to delay and perhaps deflect the new stream of his genius.

XIV

SOCKBURN-ON-TEES

May–December 1799

Then the oak, and the ash, and the bonny rowan tree,
I shall see them at home in my own countrie.

ANON.

From the date of their arrival at Nordhausen on February 27th 1799 until they reached Göttingen about April 20th on their way back to Hamburg and England, the movements of the Wordsworths are unknown. They probably continued to wander about on foot. At Göttingen they did not even stay the night, for Coleridge says: 'I walked on with them five English miles and spent a day with them'.[1] They were in fact determined to get back to England as soon as possible, but the anxious thought of separation from Coleridge for perhaps a long time preyed upon them. 'They were', says Coleridge, 'melancholy and hypped.'[2] For some months past the north of England had been so much in William's mind that they had begun to think of going thither, at least temporarily, and also of persuading Coleridge to come there also. Dorothy, in her letter to him of the previous Christmas spoke of the 'North of England, whither, wherever we finally settle you must come to us at the latter end of next summer, and we will explore together every nook of that romantic country'. Coleridge could join them 'in the County of Durham', where the Hutchinsons lived, 'and I', she added, 'would follow at your heels and hear your dear voices again'.[3] Nowhere better than in that sentence does Dorothy reveal the tenderness, the fidelity, and the innocence of her love for these two unusual beings.

Their plan of spending the summer in the north came true, but it did not seem likely that Coleridge would follow them. On the contrary, the possibility had to be faced of a permanent separation from him, which made Wordsworth in particular very unhappy. 'W. was affected to tears', said Coleridge of the

[1] *S.T.C.* i, p. 296. S.T.C. to Poole, May 6th 1799.
[2] Hypped = depressed. (*O.E.D.*)   [3] *E.L.* 89, p. 210.

Göttingen meeting, 'at the thought of not being near me—wished me of course to live in the North of England near Sir Frederick Vane's great library.'[1] Coleridge, however, was adamant. He still felt he must live near Thomas Poole. 'Finally', he says in his letter to Poole, 'I told him plainly that *you* had been the man in whom *first* and in whom alone I had felt an *anchor*.' The Wordsworths went on their way disappointed and unconvinced, remembering perhaps that it was not long since he had told William 'how you are incorporated into the better part of my being; how whenever I spring forward into the future with noble affections, I always alight by your side'.[2] No doubt, had a suitable house been available, they too would have returned to the neighbourhood of Stowey. Their plans were still quite unfixed. But there seems to have been a real shortage of houses at Stowey, for Poole was trying in vain to find for Coleridge something rather better than the cottage with its lamp and its mice.[3] It was partly owing to such prosaic facts as this that Somersetshire ceased to be the home of either.

Wordsworth had complained for some time of 'the want of books' at Stowey: now at Göttingen he seems to have declared that he must live near a large library. He thought he might get a house in the neighbourhood of his old home at Cockermouth, near Brayton Hall, where Sir Wilfrid Lawson had a large collection. He still thought that he needed reading as a relief from the intensity of his feelings, but Coleridge believed it was congenial company that he needed, and particularly, of course, Coleridge's own. To Poole Coleridge wrote: 'I still think that Wordsworth will be disappointed in his expectation of relief from reading without society; and I think it highly probable that where I live, there he will live, unless he should find in the North any person or persons, who can feel and understand him, and reciprocate and react on him.' Coleridge did not believe that Wordsworth should be in actual fact a 'recluse' and he feared that by retiring to the north he would become so. 'My many weaknesses', he said, 'are of some advantage to me; they unite me more with the great mass of my fellow-beings—but dear

---

[1] This was at Hutton Hall, five miles from Penrith.
[2] *Mem.* i, p. 138.
[3] *S.T.C.* i, p. 297. B.M. Add. MSS. 35343. T. Poole to S.T.C., Jan. 24th 99.

Wordsworth appears to me to have hurtfully segregated and isolated his being. Doubtless his delights are more deep and sublime; but he has likewise more hours that prey upon the flesh and blood.'[1] Many an entry in Dorothy's Journals bears witness to the truth of this last part of Coleridge's diagnosis.

Wordsworth and Dorothy went back to England, and made straight from Yarmouth for Sockburn-on-Tees, where they spent the next seven months with the Hutchinsons.[2] Sockburn had been described by Leland in the sixteenth century as 'a mile compass of exceeding pleasant ground, almost made an Isle as Tees Ryver wyndeth about it'. It was a place having its roots deep in ancient feudal England; there the Conyers family had had their fortified manor house; there tradition told how one of them had slain a 'wyverne', and the falchion with which the deed was done was presented by the owner of the manor to each successive Bishop of Durham on his arrival in the diocese and received back from him again. In the seventeenth century the Conyers family began to die out; the house was abandoned and fell into ruins. Then came Thomas Hutchinson, the yeoman farmer of Whitton, great-uncle of Mary and her brothers and sisters, and looked on 'the pastures of Sockburn covered with that close, rich herbage which clothes our few old fields and demesnes which have been saved from the plough'.[3] He was a pioneer in the breeding of cattle and sheep, and, having taken the estate on tenancy from the Blacketts of Northumberland who were now lords of the manor, he built there a commodious brick house, 'better and worse than a farm-hold' as Surtees contemptuously described it,[4] and proceeded to breed there his famous Sockburn sheep and short-horns. Being unmarried, he adopted his great-nephew Thomas Hutchinson, third brother of Mary, as his heir, and, after his death in 1789, all the young Hutchinson sisters of Penrith, and George, the youngest brother had likewise come to share Tom's home. Dorothy Wordsworth

---

[1] *S.T.C.* i, p. 297. S.T.C. to T. Poole, May 6th 1799.
[2] *E.L.* 97, p. 227. D.W. to T. Poole, July 4th 1799.
[3] Surtees, *History of Durham*, ii, p. 246.
[4] Ibid. In 1777 he produced a sheep weighing 17 st. 8 lb., each shoulder of which weighed 25 lb. 'I willingly pass over in silence', says Surtees 'a modern brick house, which it is said the Blacketts had intended for a residence of a younger son. It is certain, however, that the house was built by Thomas Hutchinson.

who had stayed there in the spring of 1795, has left us a description of the farm and its occupants. The house was

built by their uncle, who left them the furniture and eighteen hundred pounds, which with what they had makes them very comfortable. It is an excellent house, not at all like a farm-house, and they seem to have none of the trouble which I used to think must make farmers always in a bustle, for they have very little corn and only two cows. It is a grazing estate, and most delightfully pleasant, washed nearly round by the Tees (a noble river) and stocked with sheep and lambs which look very pretty, and to me give it a very interesting appearance.[1]

The only approach to Sockburn by road was from the north; but a ford across the Tees gave access to the Northallerton road and was the chief means of communicating with the outside world. The house somewhat resembles Racedown in general appearance, but on each side of the main building is an additional wing, so that in size it is equal to a small country house. The little church, now in ruins, stood a few yards away, and in it was the effigy of the 'armed knight', in chain mail with his legs crossed, trampling on a 'wyverne', which Coleridge used in his poem *Love*, the fruit of his visit to Sockburn in November.

In this secluded and prosperous place Wordsworth renewed his acquaintance with Mary Hutchinson, and Coleridge, when he too came there in the autumn, found in Mary's sister Sara the understanding which his own Sara could not give him and which aroused in him the great devotion of his life. It is not, however, possible to suppose that a formal engagement took place between William and Mary at this time. Long afterwards, when describing to a friend how his affairs stood in 1800, he said that he then, in 1800, 'had no thoughts of marrying'.[2] Nor had he as yet any home, however humble, to which he could invite a bride. He turned to Sockburn, not because he was in search of a wife, but because it was a natural refuge for him and Dorothy in their homeless condition—the home of the family with whom since childhood they had been most familiar and most at ease. More than two years were to pass before William and Mary were betrothed. Meanwhile Sockburn provided a con-

[1] *E.L.* 47, p. 132. D.W. to J.P., Apr. 1795.
[2] Ibid. 205, p. 463. W.W. to James Losh, Mar. 16th 1805.

genial environment in which he could continue to write those poetic recollections of his boyhood which he had begun in Germany, giving them at the same time a more definite place in the pattern of his writings.

The family at Sockburn, when William and Dorothy arrived there at the beginning of May 1799, consisted of Mary Hutchinson, her two sisters, and two younger brothers. All their relatives of the older generation were either dead, or living in Stockton or Penrith, so that they enjoyed complete freedom, entertaining their own friends and deciding their own destinies. They were an industrious, affectionate, sensible clan, loyal to one another in their friendships and interests. 'They are perfectly independent', Dorothy had written when she stayed there in 1795, 'and have not a wish ungratified.' Mary, who was now twenty-nine, kept house with her sisters Sara and Joanna, now aged respectively twenty-four and nineteen. John, the eldest brother, was in business in Stockton. He was at this time Mary's particular confidant, and he was now a young widower, his wife Jane Wilkinson of Penrith having died six years before. Henry, the second brother, was at sea; Thomas, the third, was in possession of the farm; and George, the youngest, was probably assisting him. Of Tom Hutchinson, Dorothy wrote that he was 'a very amiable young man, uncommonly fond of his sisters, and in short everything that they can desire'. It proved, however, that this was to be the last year of the Hutchinsons' occupation of Sockburn; in the following spring Tom migrated into Yorkshire and the brothers took separate farms.[1]

Wordsworth's first weeks at Sockburn were largely occupied with corresponding with his brother Richard and with Cottle on business matters. Richard, when Wordsworth left England had been left in charge of his brother's financial affairs but it was not until after his return that he sent him any news of what had occurred. On May 15th, however, Richard wrote him a long letter, containing nothing but bad news. 'Since you left England', he said, 'I have felt very great anxiety on account of your pecuniary transactions with Montagu and

---

[1] But see Whalley, *Coleridge and Sara Hutchinson and the Asra Poems*, 1955, pp. 35–36, for a slightly different view of their movements. But George mentioned as being at Sockburn at this time in *E.L.* 105, p. 238.

Charles Douglas.[1] With respect to Montagu I have not received a farthing from him. . . . You may have heard that Douglas is in the West Indies. He paid me £10 before his departure but it was totally out of his power to pay the £100 as he had engaged.'

Montagu was in fact now working hard at his profession, that of the Bar, and was on the Norfolk circuit. He was so poor that he had applied to Richard Wordsworth for a loan to pay for his expenses in being called to the Bar, and Richard had lent him 'near fifty pounds' which he had not yet repaid. He was, however, sincerely anxious to repay his debts to Wordsworth, whom he regarded as a perfect type of humanity—poor, good, and able. John Pinney, who had already lent Montagu £500, was again applied to in October for £100, for Montagu was now in serious danger of being sent to gaol as a result of Richard Wordsworth's threats. When Pinney demurred, and suggested that Montagu might endeavour to repay something of what he owed to him, Montagu was furious. 'If I comply with your request', he wrote, 'I must render Wordsworth miserable. I love Wordsworth more than any human being . . . he is and I am in poverty, you are in affluence: I will not therefore occasion uneasiness to that good and able man.' This was a thoroughly Godwinian piece of morality in its distinction between debts to the rich and to the poor: for in spite of Sir James Mackintosh, Montagu remained in some respects, where his emotions were involved, a Godwinian in fact though not by profession, to the end of his days.[2]

Pinney, though exasperated with Montagu, was ready to help Wordsworth. Desperate for money, Wordsworth wrote to Pinney in December 1799 asking him to 'exert himself with Montagu for the repayment of the Principal'.[3] This was perhaps a suggestion that Pinney might advance the sum himself, Wordsworth being unaware that Montagu already owed Pinney £500. Though he could not comply with that suggestion, Pinney did undertake, in the early spring of 1800, to pay to Wordsworth the annuity which had been in abeyance now for some two years. Montagu, in an angry letter to Pinney, says

[1] Charles Douglas had borrowed £100 from Wordsworth when Montagu had borrowed £200. See above, p. 297.
[2] *D.C.P.* and *P.P.* Letters of R.W. to Montagu, May 14th 1799, and Montagu to John Pinney, Apr. 2nd 1800.
[3] *E.L.* 104, p. 234. D.W. to R.W., Dec. 14th 1799.

that he 'did not accept' this offer; but, however it was arranged, the payment of the annuity was renewed at this time. In June 1800 Douglas repaid half his share of the principal; for the other half Montagu became responsible. As Montagu advanced in his profession he gradually paid off the arrears of the annuity[1] and at last the principal itself.

Wordsworth was also in debt to Josiah Wedgwood, on whom he had drawn throughout his stay in Germany. He had thought that Richard would have refunded at least part of this sum (which now amounted to over £100) during his absence, but owing to Montagu's default, Richard was unable to do so. Josiah very kindly did not press him for payment, and it was not until July 1800 that Wordsworth was able to discharge this obligation. He then applied the £100 which he had lent to Douglas, and which Douglas now repaid, to this purpose. It was of course part of his slender capital, but there was no other means of getting out of debt. The letter he wrote to Josiah Wedgwood on July 13th 1800, apologizing for the delay, shows his anxiety to be independent and owe no man anything.

The silence which I have been obliged to keep [he wrote] concerning the sum I am indebted to you has cost me much anxiety. I had £270 in the stocks and consequently by selling out I could have repaid you immediately, but as this sum was the only part of my little property which I could command as my own, and as ill health has for some time rendered literary labour inadviseable for me, I was not without hope that my friends, informed of these circumstances and knowing the delicacy of my situation with respect to you, would exert themselves to repay me so much of my money, then in their possession as would enable me to discharge the debt I owed to you. I hoped also that this knowledge would be a means of my recovering so much of my property out of what I have reason in the common language of the world, to regard as bad hands. Till within this week past I have been disappointed in this expectation. It now however gives me great pleasure to repay you the amount of the several sums which you were so good as to advance me. . . .[2]

His reference to his health and to its effect on his 'literary labour' is significant.

The months at Sockburn were actively productive, but by

---

[1] *E.L.* 138, p. 316, and 145, pp. 326–7. W.W. to R.W., Feb. 23rd and June 26th 1803.

[2] In the possession of Sir Ralph Wedgwood at Leith Hill Place.

September he was feeling strained and ill. Financial anxiety and the worry of the progress of the *Lyrical Ballads*, which for Wordsworth was mainly also a worry about finance, were incessant and tormenting.

Before leaving for Germany he had written to Cottle asking him to transfer the *Lyrical Ballads* and the copyright to his old publisher Johnson, who had evidently expressed an interest in them. It was obviously to Wordsworth's advantage, as he said, to have the *Ballads* on sale in London. Cottle, however, for his own reasons, had already sold the edition, but not the copyright, to Arch, a London bookseller, before he received Wordsworth's letter. The *Ballads* were advertised in the London papers on October 4th 1798. Why Cottle suddenly decided to rid himself of them is not entirely clear, but he had probably been alarmed by Southey, who saw them while they were in the press and, being still out of love with Coleridge, may have told Cottle that they would not sell. Cottle kept the copyright, however, in case after all they proved a success and a second edition was called for. Wordsworth knew nothing of all this until after his return. He then wrote to Cottle, mildly rebuking him for not transferring the *Ballads* to Johnson and reminding him that he still owed him £21. 10s. for the copyright. Cottle sent the money, and offered to pay interest as well, but this Wordsworth refused. 'I am not poor enough yet', he said, 'to make me think it right that I should take interest for a debt from a friend, paid eleven months after it was due.'

Apart from the disappointment about Johnson, Cottle's transactions did the *Ballads* no harm for they eventually sold well and by 1800 the edition was exhausted. Although Cottle had behaved both casually and disingenuously towards Wordsworth, there was no personal quarrel between them and they always remained on the most friendly terms.[1]

Wordsworth felt rather bitterly Southey's review of the poems in the *Critical Review* for October 1798 which he now saw for the first time. *The Idiot Boy* (Wordsworth's favourite), said Southey, 'resembles a Flemish picture in the worthlessness of its

---

[1] *E.L.* 94 and 95, pp. 224–5. W.W. to Cottle, May 1799. *D.C.P.*: R.W. to W.W., May 15th 1799: Letters from Cottle to Johnson and Tobin, Oct. 1798. R. W. Daniel, 'The Publication of the *Lyrical Ballads*', *M.L.R.*, 1938. T. Hutchinson, *Lyrical Ballads, 1798*, 1898, preface.

design and excellence of its execution'; but the other ballads, he complained, were not even well executed. 'He knew', wrote Wordsworth, 'that I published these poems for money and money alone. He knew that money was of importance to me. If he could not conscientiously have spoken differently of the volume, he ought to have declined the task of reviewing it.' And he added, 'I care little for the praise of any other professional critic but as it may help me to pudding.'[1]

But before he wrote this letter, Wordsworth had formed the opinion that the chief obstacle to the successful sale of the *Ballads* was *The Ancient Mariner*. 'If the edition should sell', he told Cottle on June 2nd, 'I shall probably add some others in lieu of The Ancyent Marinere.' Three weeks later he wrote: 'From what I can gather it seems that The Ancyent Marinere has upon the whole been an injury to the volume, I mean that the old words and the strangeness of it have deterred readers from going on.'[2] It was the reviews that caused Wordsworth to make *The Ancient Mariner* the scapegoat for the volume's unpopularity. Southey had called it 'a Dutch attempt at German sublimity', and had been rebuked by Lamb for so doing,[3] and none of the other reviews so far, in the *Monthly Review* in June or the *Analytical* in the previous December, had had a good word to say for it, whereas several of Wordsworth's poems, particularly *The Mad Mother*, *The Idiot Boy*, and *Tintern Abbey* had been pronounced in some degree at least admirable and interesting. Wordsworth's concern that the *Lyrical Ballads* should be, if possible, a financial success, and justify a second edition, stands in curious contrast both to his own dislike of the toil of publishing (which made him exclaim to Cottle 'that no motives whatever, nothing but pecuniary necessity, will, I think, ever prevail upon me to commit myself to the press again') and to Coleridge's apparently complete indifference to public opinion. Nowhere does Coleridge refer to *The Ancient Mariner* or to any of his poems after their publication; they might as well have had no existence for all the attention he pays to their reception. His mind was always more than occupied with projects and dreams

---

[1] *E.L.* 99, pp. 229–30. W.W. to Cottle, n.d., but addressed 'Sockburn'.
[2] Ibid. 95, 16, pp. 225–7. W.W. to J. Cottle, June 2nd and June 24th 1799.
[3] 'I call it a right English attempt, and a successful one, to dethrone German sublimity.' Lamb to Southey, Nov. 8th 1798. *Lamb*, i, p. 136.

innumerable; it seldom dwelt on what was already done. Nor did he regard poetry as his only vocation; moral philosophy, the lives of moral philosophers; the writing of school-books; preaching, teaching, talking; journalism, criticism—there was almost no known form of intellectual communication which Coleridge did not attempt or plan to attempt or imagine that he had attempted. He was now indeed turning away from poetry towards the production of 'the one work', on metaphysics, 'to which I hope to dedicate in silence, the prime of my life'. He was 'not in a poetical mood'; he would publish 'nothing with my name till my Great Work'.

The Wordsworths heard nothing from him since parting with him at Göttingen until after his return in July; this added to their anxieties. At last, however, he turned his attention once more to his friend and his friend's work. The fragments of three letters survive which show clearly, though all too briefly, what Coleridge wanted Wordsworth to do, and something of what Wordsworth had in fact been doing.[1] 'I am anxiously eager to have you steadily employed on *The Recluse*', he said, but he added a suggestion of his own: 'I wish you would write a poem, in blank verse, addressed to those, who, in consequence of the complete failure of the French Revolution, have thrown up all hopes of the amelioration of mankind, and are sinking into an almost epicurean selfishness, disguising the same under the soft titles of domestic attachment and contempt for visionary *philosophes*'. He was thinking perhaps mainly of his brother-in-law Southey, with whom he had sought and made a reconciliation and whom he had accompanied on a tour in Devonshire. Such a poem, he said, 'might form a part of "The Recluse", for in my present mood I am wholly against the publication of any small poems'. It is clear from this that Coleridge still saw in Wordsworth the writer of the 'one work' of universal proportions in the field of poetry, which he himself intended to be in the field of metaphysics.

To this appeal Wordsworth must have replied describing his work after his return to England. What that was is partly to be inferred from Coleridge's letter dated October 12th 1799.

[1] *Mem.* i, p. 159, The manuscripts of these letters were unfortunately destroyed, probably immediately after the extracts were made from them. None of Wordsworth's letters to Coleridge this summer have been preserved.

I long to see [he says] what you have been doing. O let it be the tailpiece of 'The Recluse'! for of nothing but 'The Recluse' can I hear patiently. That it is to be addressed to me makes me more desirous that it should not be a poem of itself. To be addressed as a beloved man, by a thinker, at the close of such a poem as 'The Recluse' . . . is the only event, I believe, capable of inciting in me an hour's vanity.

Obviously Wordsworth had been telling Coleridge that he intended to write—or was already writing—a poem addressed to him. This poem was the 'poem on his own life' which he had begun in fragmentary fashion in Germany, and was now continuing. The idea of dedicating it to Coleridge is the most important event in Wordsworth's poetic life at this time. By so doing he was able to give it a status in his own mind, a purpose and point which it might not otherwise have had. It would thus become a personal offering, full of his own heart's affection as well as his mind's achievements. And by acquiescing in Coleridge's plea that it should be regarded as 'a tail-piece of "The Recluse" ' (though eventually he assigned it the position of a 'prelude', not a 'tail-piece' to the unwritten *Recluse*), he secured Coleridge's approval and interest. But as time went on it became clear that this poem and *The Ruined Cottage* were likely to be all or almost all that Coleridge would ever see of *The Recluse*. 'I grieve', said Coleridge a few months later, 'that "The Recluse" sleeps.' Coleridge in his letters always speaks of *The Recluse* and what we know as *The Prelude* as interchangeable, and this has led to some confusion in interpreting some of his comments.[1] But if his original plea that 'the poem to Coleridge' should be a part of *The Recluse* is borne in mind, these difficulties disappear.

What Wordsworth wrote this summer at Sockburn, and completed there in December just before his removal to Grasmere, was in effect what we know as the second book of *The Prelude*. Two manuscripts exist, one copied by Dorothy, the other by Mary Hutchinson, containing the passages about his boyhood which he had written in Germany, and some five hundred further lines. Both were probably written at Sockburn.

---

[1] e.g. when in 1803 he congratulated Wordsworth on at last making 'a beginning to The Recluse', what he meant was 'a beginning' to *The Prelude*, for it was then that Wordsworth in all probability wrote the first 270 lines leading up to the question 'Was it for this', &c. H. Darbishire, *Wordsworth*, 1950, pp. 93–95. See above, p. 419, and below, p. 604.

The lines are not arranged always as in their final order, and some passages are present which were afterwards transferred to later books of *The Prelude*.[1] The chief boyhood incidents recounted in these manuscripts are the ride to Furness Abbey, and the boating on Windermere; the adventure with the gibbet on Penrith Beacon and the 'wait for the ponies' at Hawkshead. He also included thirteen lines of which the phraseology is based very obviously on the words in Coleridge's letter suggesting a poem on the despair following the failure of the French Revolution.[2] But the main part of Book II consists of very intricate and complicated descriptions of the origins and growth of consciousness from infancy to adolescence, based all the time on his own mental experiences in boyhood and youth. Some of this material is of earlier origin than the summer of 1799. For instance, the twenty-two lines beginning:

> From Nature and her overflowing soul
> I had received so much that all my thoughts
> Were steeped in feeling . . .[3]

are lifted bodily out of *The Ruined Cottage*, where they were descriptive of the Pedlar's youth. Another passage describing his nocturnal wanderings in search of 'the visionary power', beginning

> For I would walk alone
> In storm and tempest, or in starlight nights . . .

was also intended originally for the Pedlar and is found in an early note-book.[4] We thus see Wordsworth collecting material already more than a year old and synthesizing it with what was now written for the first time. Upon the whole we may say that the older material is descriptive of actual states and feelings in boyhood; the newer is reflection upon these states, and an attempt to draw from them some conclusions on the nature of the essential spirit or being of man. Here the influence of Coleridge is perhaps to be discerned, and twice does Wordsworth turn directly to him, first to confirm his faith in the essential

---

[1] *Prel.*, p. xxii. The manuscripts have been named U and V.
[2] Ibid. II, ll. 432–44.
[3] Ibid., ll. 397–419. *P.W.* v, p. 385. See above, p. 405.
[4] Ibid. (1805), ll. 321–41. They are in the Alfoxden note-book, which contained the beginning of Dorothy's Alfoxden Journal, and drafts of *The Old Cumberland Beggar* and other lines descriptive of the Pedlar.

oneness of all experience, and to justify his belief that science was 'a prop to our infirmity', rather than 'our glory and our absolute boast',[1] and finally to claim him as his fellow worshipper and seeker after the truth of their great mistress, Nature.

> For Thou hast sought
> The truth in solitude, and Thou art one,
> The most intense of Nature's worshippers,
> In many things my Brother, chiefly here
> In this my deep devotion.[2]

Wordsworth was indeed thinking much of Coleridge at this time and longing for the great encouragement which Coleridge's presence gave to his creative faculties. Six lines have recently been found in an early note-book, following a draft of the last lines of Book I of *The Prelude*, and headed '2nd Part'—showing that Wordsworth was already thinking of his poem as consisting of several parts or books—and undoubtedly meant as a beginning to 'Book II'. They must belong to this summer.

> Friend of my heart and Genius, we had reach'd
> A small green island which I was well pleased
> To pass not lightly by, for though I felt
> Strength unabated, yet I seemed to need
> Thy cheering voice, or ere I could pursue
> My voyage, resting else for ever there.[3]

Coleridge was as anxious for a meeting as was Wordsworth; it was a question chiefly of times and seasons, and of expense. Wordsworth wrote that his health was not good. 'He is ill and seems not happy', wrote Coleridge to Poole on September 10th, and ascribed it to worry about his financial affairs. In the same letter he mentioned the possibility of himself taking Alfoxden, and, speaking of Wordsworth, he added: 'He renounces Alfoxden altogether.'[4] This is important, for it shows that since July, when Dorothy told Poole that their plans were still quite unfixed, they had determined to settle permanently in the north. Some further light on their reasons for this decision is given in a

---

[1] *Prel.* II, ll. 210–32.
[2] Ibid. (1805), ll. 475–9.
[3] See H. Darbishire, *Wordsworth*, 1950, p. 91. The 'green island' is doubtless a symbol for Sockburn.
[4] B.M. Add. MSS. 35343.

letter of Coleridge to Poole written in March 1800, when the
Wordsworths had already been settled at Grasmere for three
months. 'I would to God', he exclaims, 'I could get Wordsworth to retake Alfoxden. The society of so great a being is of
priceless value: but he will never quit the North of England.
His habits are more assimilated with the inhabitants there; there
he and his sister are exceedingly beloved, enthusiastically. Such
differences do small sympathies make, such as voice, pronunciation, etc.'

But for the present, a meeting between them must be arranged.
In October Coleridge was really alarmed by accounts of Wordsworth's health.[1] Fortunately a means of travelling in comfort
and probably without much expense now became possible.
Cottle, who had also been invited by Wordsworth to visit him
at Sockburn, now decided to go, and take Coleridge with him.
They set forth on October 22nd, travelling luxuriously in a
post-chaise, no doubt at Cottle's expense. On October 26th they
reached Sockburn. 'Few moments in life', confided Coleridge
to his note-book, 'are so interesting as those of our affectionate
reception from a stranger who is the dear friend of your dear
friend! How often you have been the subject of conversation,
and how affectionately!' This 'stranger' must be Mary Hutchinson whom Coleridge had never yet seen. Sockburn, as it proved,
held a still more attractive 'stranger' for him than Mary, in
Mary's sister Sara. But his interest in her was not awakened
during this very brief visit, for the very next day, October 27th,
Wordsworth set forth with Coleridge on foot, and Cottle
'hugely muffled up' about his rheumatic legs, on the mare Lily,
to introduce his friends to the Lake Country. Cottle, however,
only got as far as Greta Bridge. Either he did not like the prospect of long days out of doors in worsening autumn weather,
or he felt that Wordsworth was after all disappointed about the
Lyrical Ballads and would rather not discuss them with him;[2]
at any rate he left the two poets together at Greta Bridge and
departed homewards. It was a tactful departure. Wordsworth
and Coleridge wanted to be by themselves.

---

[1] *S.T.C.* i, p. 313. S.T.C. to Southey, Nov. 10th 1799.
[2] 'The Lyrical Ballads was mentioned but once, and that casually, and only to
account for its failure!' which Wordsworth ascribed to *The Ancient Mariner* and the
unfavourable reviews. *Cottle*, ii, p. 26.

From Greta Bridge (where Coleridge leaned over the para-
pet and watched the 'white rose of eddy foam' and thought 'what
would it be if I had the eyes of a fly!'), they took the coach over
the moorland road across Stainmore and arrived at Temple
Sowerby on the 29th. Here they were unexpectedly joined by
Wordsworth's brother John, who was a much more acceptable
companion than Cottle. He was on leave between two East India
voyages, and was in fact come north to attend the funeral of
Christopher Crackanthorpe—'Uncle Kit', whom Wordsworth
had disliked so much in boyhood, and who had died rather suddenly at Newbiggin Hall, the fine old red sandstone castle on
the Eden which he had inherited from his mother only seven
years before. Uncle Crackanthorpe, said John, had left his niece
Dorothy £100 in his will. This most welcome gift was a proof
of his affection for her—she had received a very kind welcome
from him at Newbiggin four years before[1]—and was soon to
prove of the greatest value, for out of it they were able to furnish
the cottage at Town End, Grasmere, into which they were to
move at Christmas. But Wordsworth noted with some displeasure that 'no one else was named in the will'.

Wordsworth, it is clear, did not call at Newbiggin Hall to
pay his respects to his widowed aunt.[2] She was not a pleasant
woman, but it would have been courteous to have done so. But
both now and always he bore a deep grudge against his uncle
for what he considered his unjust behaviour to his nephews in
their youth. He had also, he thought, given in to the greed and
jealousy of his wife in pecuniary affairs, so that the Wordsworths
were deprived of certain sums of money which would more
properly have gone to them.[3]

The walking-tour now began in earnest. Wordsworth
was determined above all to show Coleridge the scenes of
his boyhood which lately had been returning so vividly upon
his mind. Coleridge kept in his note-book a diary of their
movements and of the landscapes that especially excited him.
Of their talk—which must have been endless and momentous—

---

[1] In Apr. 1795. *E.L.* 47, p. 134.
[2] *E.L.* 103, p. 233. 'I learned from the woman (at the Inn) that John was at
Newbiggin: I sent a note; he came, looks very well.'
[3] *M.Y.* ii. 539, p. 698. Wordsworth was particularly angry that Mr. Crackanthorpe had permitted his mother, old Mrs. Cookron, 'to make a present to his
wife of £500', money which should, he felt, have gone to the Wordsworths.

he unfortunately records nothing, but we may surmise that it ran on Wordsworth's determination to live at Grasmere, and Coleridge's doubts and regrets at his removing himself so far from society, and on the paramount necessity of going on with *The Recluse.*

They set off,[1] William and John Wordsworth and Coleridge, on Thursday, October 31st, from Temple Sowerby, and walked to Barton, the parish in which lay the small family property of Sockbridge of which Richard Wordsworth was the owner. At Barton they dined with the Rev. Thomas Myers, the widowed husband of the Wordsworths' aunt, Ann Wordsworth; thence they walked to Bampton, the village at the foot of Haweswater, where they slept. Next day they walked up the lake, over into Longsleddale and so to Kentmere where the second night was spent; then next day to Troutbeck by the Garburn Pass, down to the shores of Windermere at Rayrigg, the home of Wordsworth's old schoolfellow John Fleming, and crossed the ferry to Hawkshead. It was, Wordsworth told Dorothy, 'a rainy and raw day, a cold passage', and he added: 'much disgusted with the new erections and objects about Windermere'. Rich men were already beginning to build villas on its shores.

It was in all probability ten years since William had seen Hawkshead. The last visit of which there is any record was in the long vacation of 1789. 'Great change', he noted in his letter to Dorothy, 'among the people since we were last there.'[2] The greatest change was one that concerned a cottage at Colthouse. Three years before, on May 26th 1796, Ann Tyson had died.[3] She was eighty-three years old.

There was a change, too, in the village of Hawkshead itself. In the little market square, close under the hill where the church stood, now rose a 'smart Assembly-room', built over the very

---

[1] The chief source of information about this tour is Coleridge's Diary, kept probably with a view to writing an account of it for publication, as all the notes are descriptive of the landscape. It is published under the title 'Samuel Taylor Coleridge discovers the Lake Country', by G. H. B. Coleridge, in *Studies in Honour of Harper*, ed. E. L. Griggs. There is also Wordsworth's letter to Dorothy, written from Grasmere, on Nov. 7th 1799. *E.L.* 103, p. 232.

[2] Whether by 'we' he means himself and Dorothy, or simply himself and John, is not clear. There is no record of Dorothy ever going to Hawkshead, though she may have done so with William during the spring of 1794 when they were staying at Windy Brow.

[3] Hawkshead Parish Registers.

rock where the old lady had displayed her wares for the delight of Wordsworth and his schoolfellows. Wordsworth looked at it with distaste, as it

> perk'd and flar'd
> With wash and rough-cast elbowing the ground
> That had been ours.[1]

It still stands there, with the date 1790 in Roman figures over the windows.

And there was another change, an unexpected one, which was a change not in the valley but in Wordsworth himself. He had, he tells us, approached his old haunts with some dread, fearing that

> Remembrance of myself and of my peers
> Will press me down; to think of what is gone
> Will be an awful thought, if life has one.

But the reality was the reverse of alarming:

> But when into the Vale I came, no fears
> Distressed me; from mine eyes escaped no tears;
> Deep thought, or dread remembrance, had I none.
> By doubts and thousand petty fancies crost
> I stood, of simple shame the blushing Thrall;
> So narrow seemed the brooks, the fields so small!
> A Juggler's balls old Time about him tossed;
> I looked, I stared, I smiled, I laughed; and all
> The weight of sadness was in wonder lost.[2]

They spent but one night at Hawkshead, leaving it on the morning of November 3rd for Rydal and Grasmere. At Rydal Hall they were reproved by a servant for walking past the front of the house—a trespass, in Coleridge's opinion, just about equalled by the 'Trespass on the eye' committed by the owner by 'his damned whitewashing'. The whitening of the larger houses in the Lakes was regarded by the poets as an outrage,

---

[1] *Prel.* II (1805), ll. 39–41. This opening of Book II (ll. 1–55) which is present in one but not both of the early manuscripts, must have been written after the return to Sockburn, and probably before the departure for Grasmere, that is, in Dec. 1799.

[2] *P.W.* iii, p. 2. *Miscellaneous Sonnets*, III. Written probably in 1802: published in *Poems in Two Volumes*, 1807. The experience here described is a familiar one to many who are not poets.

probably because it called too much attention to these new
'erections'; they were quite ready to approve of the whitewashing of the statesmen's farms.

In the evening of November 3rd they entered Grasmere.
Many years before, the boy Wordsworth had looked down into
its jewel-like depth from the top of the pass that leads into
Loughrigg with a shock of delight which had never been forgotten.[1] Now they lingered there for five days, staying at
Robert Newton's village inn, opposite the church, and ex-
ploring in a week of bad weather the recesses of Easedale
and Rydal, with one glorious day when 'light and darkness
co-existed in contiguous masses and the earth and sky were
but one': they spent it accompanying John over the Grisedale Pass on his way back to Newbiggin. On the 7th William
and Coleridge walked on over 'the inverted arch' of Dunmail
Raise to Keswick, through country already darkening to winter
severity: 'savage and hopeless, obstinate sans-culottism', Coleridge called it. From Keswick they both wrote to Dorothy,[2]
Coleridge excited and poetical with the beauty of 'a world of
scenery absolutely new to me': William quite prosaic, but with
a note of suppressed excitement at the end of the letter as he
made a suggestion that must have caused Dorothy a stirring of
the heart: 'I have much to say to you. . . . You will think my
plan a mad one but I have thought of building a house there
by the lake side [at Grasmere]. John would give me £40 to
buy the ground and for £250 I am sure I could build one as
good as we can wish. . . . There is a small house at Grasmere
empty which we might take, but of this we will speak.' Nothing
more is heard of the building plan; no doubt even £250 was too
large a sum for them to raise out of their very slender capital.
But before the end of the year 'the small house' was taken and
William and Dorothy had realized their dream.

They next went to Buttermere, approaching it round the
outer edges of the hills, down Bassenthwaite, and then to Cockermouth and up the Cocker to Lorton and Crummock. No doubt
Wordsworth chose this route because of his desire to see
Cockermouth again. Next day they walked to Ennerdale, where
they met a farmer who told them tales of mountain tragedies,
in particular of the shepherd, Jerome Bowman, who 'slipped

[1] See above, pp. 58–59.   [2] *E.L.* 103, p. 232. *Mem.* i, p. 147.

and broke his leg on the fells a little beyond Scale Force', dying
soon after, and of his son who 'before this took place broke his
neck by falling off a crag. He is supposed to have lain down and
slept—walked in his sleep, and so came to this crag and fell off.'
This story caught Wordsworth's imagination, and a few months
later, as the story of James Ewbank, he made it a part of his
pastoral tale, *The Brothers*, one of the first poems written after
settling at Grasmere.

From Ennerdale they went to Wasdale Head, and so back
to Keswick by Borrowdale, sleeping on November 15th at
Threlkeld. Next day brought them by Matterdale to the shores
of Ullswater, where, on a day of dazzling winter sunshine they
walked down the eastern shore to the foot of the lake.

There the joint holiday came to an end. Coleridge had received
while at Keswick an offer from Stuart of the *Morning Post* that
he should write regular political and literary articles for that
paper: London therefore was his immediate destination. But he
would return first to Sockburn, improve his acquaintance with
the Hutchinsons, and say farewell to Dorothy. He went therefore alone, leaving Wordsworth still in the Lakes, and there,
during an evening of 'Conundrums and Puns and Stories and
Laughter', 'the 'poisoned thorn' of an implacable love pierced
him as he stood before the fire with Sara Hutchinson's hand
pressed within his own.[1] That was on November 24th. The next
day he started for London, and in December appeared a poem in
the *Morning Post* called *Introduction to the Tale of the Dark
Ladie*. It was a version of the poem which he afterwards called
Love and which begins:

> All thoughts, all passions, all delights,
> Whatever stirs this mortal frame,
> All are but ministers of Love,
> And feed his sacred flame.

Wordsworth reached Sockburn the day after Coleridge left it.
His movements during the previous week are unknown, but it is
probable that he returned to Grasmere to arrange about taking
the cottage at Town End. For only three weeks elapsed after
his return to Sockburn before he and Dorothy set forth for
Grasmere. The momentous decision was at last taken—they

[1] T. M. Raysor, *S.P.*, 1929, 'Coleridge and Asra'.

were to live 'in retirement' among their native mountains, far
from Coleridge (unless indeed he were to follow them) in a
vale chosen for its loveliness alone. Gone were all the projects
for living near a great library; there would be no books there
except their own. The sight of Grasmere had stirred memories
from 'hiding-places ten years deep' that were irresistible in their
vividness.

When he came back to Sockburn he found only Mary at
home, 'a solitary housekeeper', but 'overjoyed' to see him;[1]
Dorothy and Sara had gone away on a visit probably to brother
John Hutchinson. On her return important conversations took
place; with what exquisite feelings Dorothy listened to her
brother's account of his house-hunting may be imagined. In a
very few days all was settled, and on December 17th William
and Dorothy set forth from Sockburn on the eighty-mile journey
to Grasmere. The first plan had been to go by coach to Brough
and then by post-chaise to Kendal, but this was rejected, probably
on account of the expense, and they started on horseback,
Dorothy behind George Hutchinson, who went with them eight
miles beyond Richmond, and William on Lily, Sara's mare.
After that they went nearly all the way on foot.

The three days' journey was described in a long letter from
William to Coleridge, written from Grasmere on Christmas
Eve,[2] and also in the long fragment of *The Recluse* (*Home at
Grasmere*) which William wrote in the ensuing months there.
The short days, the 'driving snow-showers that disappeared by
fits', the hard-frozen roads that made walking difficult, had no
terrors for them; rather they felt excited and exhilarated, being
in that delightful mood that makes the body respond willingly
to austere conditions, and the long miles of wild road through
lonely places only served to enhance their joy in each other, in
their freedom and happy solitude. Their way lay by Richmond
into Wensleydale. Near Richmond an incident occurred which
William has recorded in a manner highly characteristic of the
author of *We are Seven*:

Before we entered this venerable town [Richmond] . . . in a beautiful bottom beside the Swale, we saw a mansion of antique appearance
which excited our curiosity. I met a little girl and pointing toward

---

[1] *E.L.* 105, p. 234, W.W. to S.T.C., Christmas Eve, 1799.
[2] Ibid.

the place I asked her who lived in that house. 'Oh Sir we lives there'—
her own Dwelling was at a small distance between me and the great
mansion. 'But the house in the valley overgrown (perhaps I said
covered) with ivy, what is it?' 'Oh Sir, them's only old Bules.' 'Old
Bules' said I, 'what are they?' 'Old buildings Sir' answered the girl
smiling. This little incident put us in good humour with Richmond, and
perhaps the ghostly arch at the bottom of its tall friarage steeple, a
single tower that stands in a green by itself, appeared more interesting
than it really is.[1]

A few miles beyond Richmond, after George Hutchinson had
left them, they reached a spot on the roadside which again
aroused their romantic curiosity. Their experience there proved
the gateway to one of those profound moments of vision, of
seeing 'into the life of things' which from time to time, with
mysterious suddenness, came over William, and into this vision
Dorothy also entered, so that the experience was common to
them both. When they had settled at Grasmere, one of William's
earliest tasks was to record both the adventure and a part of the
visionary experience in the poem *Hart-leap Well*; and also in
some lines which were intended for *The Recluse* but were never
incorporated into that poem.[2]

What they saw was a square grassy mound, and a few yards
away a spring of water, and above the spring, in a line leading
up to the top of the ridge, a succession of three standing stones
obviously placed there by man. Fortunately, an aged man was
at hand, and told them of the great chase in bygone days,
when the exhausted hart, after an all-day flight from its pur-
suers, leapt in three great bounds from the top of the ridge to the
spring, where it lay down and died. Its pursuer, a dissolute
knight, in commemoration of so memorable a chase, proceeded
to build beside the spring a 'bower', in which to entertain his
mistress and his friends, and erected the standing-stones to
mark the poor hart's death-leap. The house had crumbled to
ruin, so that nothing but a grassy square remained, and the
stones, to tell the story of Hart-leap Well. But, said the old
man, to this day it was noticed that no sheep or cattle would
drink from the well;

Something ails it now: the spot is curst.

---

[1] *E.L.* 105, p. 238. The child may possibly have used the north-country word 'bields',
meaning 'houses'.   [2] See the note to *Hart-leap Well* in *P.W.* ii, pp. 514–15.

As William and Dorothy heard the tale they felt themselves standing on the threshold of another world.

> The trance
> Came to us, as we stood by Hartleap Well,
> The intimation of the milder day
> Which is to be, the fairer world than this.

They had been overcome with dejection by the man's story, but, by a process not uncommon in Wordsworth's imagination, depression and disappointment preceded vision. 'The awful trance' into which they entered was a complete experience of successive visions. First of all there was 'the vision of humanity' —no doubt in its darker aspects, callous and acquisitive, like the huntsman. Then came a new and more profound revelation:

> Of God
> The Mourner, God the Sufferer, when the heart
> Of his poor Creatures suffers wrongfully.

Thence hope for the earth that was both the object of the divine compassion and the victim of man's cruelties sprang up within them, taking the form of a vision of an Earthly Paradise, 'the coming of a milder day', in which, as might be expected, 'Nature' would play her beneficent part: the gloomy monuments of human callousness and of the suffering of the innocent would 'all be overgrown', and the deserted spot would revive to cheerfulness.[1] A personal hope for themselves also took shape alongside of the universal vision. They felt their own destiny to be in some way an earnest of that fairer and more merciful world which they desired for all the earth.

> Both in the sadness and the joy we found
> A promise and an earnest that we twain,
> A pair seceding from the common world,
> Might in that hallow'd spot to which our steps
> Were tending, in that individual nook
> Might, even thus early, for ourselves secure,
> And in the midst of these unhappy times,
> A portion of the blessedness which love
> And knowledge will, we trust, hereafter give
> To all the vales of earth and all mankind.[2]

[1] See the last four stanzas of *Hart-leap Well*.
[2] Lines rejected from *The Recluse*, *P.W*. ii, p. 515.

In thus appropriating for themselves a life of peace, by 'seceding from the common world', they believed themselves to be called to an exemplification of 'natural piety', of that life which is happy because it is founded on essential simplicities; humility, hospitality, kindness, and on that intuitive 'knowledge' of their own hearts and of the character of man which was of more value than the doctrines of 'the sages'. As they turned from Hart-leap Well to pursue their road towards the 'individual nook', they felt their purpose strengthened and as it were blessed by the strange experience they had undergone. The good news they had learnt there that

> The Being, that is in the clouds and air,
> That is in the green leaves among the groves,
> Maintains a deep and reverential care
> For the unoffending creatures whom he loves,

was something they could pass on to men. And consciously or unconsciously, they had been drawn nearer than ever to the mind of their great friend. The teaching of Coleridge, who ended *The Ancient Mariner* with the words

> He prayeth best who loveth best
> All things both great and small,

receives a living echo in the last lines of *Hart-Leap Well*, in the lesson:

> Never to blend our pleasure or our pride
> With sorrow of the meanest thing that feels.

The passion for the picturesque was strong in both of them, and at Askrigg where they spent the night they turned aside, just as they were setting forth the next morning, to see the waterfall, and then visited another at Hardraw four miles farther on. This detained them some time, for it was a place of great magnificence, made even more wonderful by the winter pageantry of ice and icicles that festooned the walls of the hollow limestone rock behind the fall. The colours of the rock—'deep black, yellow, white purple violet and dove coloured', the vivid green of the water-plants, and the blue opening of sky above made them feel themselves in a fairy world. 'I cannot express to you the enchanted effect produced by this Arabian scene of colour as the wind blew aside the great waterfall behind which we stood. . . .[1] In the luxury of our imaginations we could not help feeding on the pleasure which in the heat of a July noon this cavern would spread through a frame exquisitely sensible.' They tore themselves away at last and addressed themselves to their walk. 'We were in high spirits and off we drove, and will you believe me when I tell you that we walked the next ten miles, by the watch over a high mountain road, thanks to the wind that drove behind us and the good road, in two hours and a quarter, a marvellous feat of which D. long will tell.'[2] It was this part of the walk, from Hawes to Sedbergh by Garsdale, that he afterwards described in *The Recluse.*

> The frosty wind, as if to make amends
> For its keen breath, was aiding to our steps,
> And drove us onward like two ships at sea,
> Or like two birds, companions in mid-air,
> Parted and re-united by the blast.
> Stern was the face of Nature. We rejoiced
> In that stern countenance, for our souls thence drew
> A feeling of their strength.

William, in the exhilaration of his spirit, heard the voice of his own heart echoed back to him in the voices of the wild:

> The naked trees,
> The icy brooks, as on we passed, appeared
> To question us, 'Whence come ye? to what end?'
> They seemed to say. 'What would ye', said the Shower,
> 'Wild wanderers, whither through my dark domain?'
> The sunbeam said, 'Be happy.'

They spent the second night at Sedbergh and arrived in Kendal about noon on December 20th. Here they spent the rest of the day in the important task of buying furniture, and the next day they drove up to the door of their cottage in a post-chaise just as dark was falling. Old Molly Fisher, who lived in one of the little group of cottages on the other side of the road, had been engaged to light fires in the house before their arrival. She gazed with wonder at her new neighbours as they stood together

---

[1] It is still possible to walk behind the waterfall at Hardraw which consists of a single column of water falling sheer from the top of the cliff into a pool a hundred feet below.　　　　　　　　　　　　　　[2] *E.L.* 105, pp. 234–42.

in the little dark-wainscoted parlour (where, alas, only 'a handful of reddish cinders' glowed in the fire-place!): 'I mun never forget 't laal striped gown and 't laal straw bonnet as ye stood here', she used to say to Dorothy afterwards.[1] Outside, the solemn glow of a winter sunset faded over Silver How. They had gazed at it as they approached in the chaise over White Moss Common and it continued to glow in William's memory:

> When this Vale
> We entered, bright and solemn was the sky
> That faced us with a passionate welcoming,
> And led us to our threshold. Daylight failed
> Insensibly, and round us gently fell
> Composing darkness, with a quiet load
> Of full contentment. . . .[2]

[1] *E.L.* 239, p. 558, and *M.T.* ii. 537, p. 687. D.W. to Catherine Clarkson, Christmas Day, 1805 and Dec. 23rd 1815. 'Laal' means 'little'.

[2] *P.W.* v, p. 319–20. *The Recluse.* Dorothy gives the time of their arrival as five o'clock; William as half past four. *M.T.* ii. 537, 687. *E.L.* 105, p. 242. W.W. to S.T.C., Christmas Eve, 1799.

XV

'A POET LIVING IN RETIREMENT'
GRASMERE, *December 1799 – December 1800*

The mountain said: 'Here is our child come home
To stream and fern, and rock and green growing.

MARGARET CROPPER

Dorothy, writing many years afterwards to her friend
Catherine Clarkson of their first arrival at the cottage, of the
uncurtained beds upstairs and the 'dying spark in the grate of
the gloomy parlour', said: 'We were young and healthy and had
obtained an object long desired, we had returned to our native
mountains, there to live; so we cared not for any annoyances
that a little exertion on our parts would not speedily remove.'
They had come at last to that very cottage which had been
beckoning them from the horizon of their lives for so many
years.

It lay at the foot of the hill where the old road from Ambleside
descends from White Moss Common to the side of Grasmere
lake. The present main road through the wood and along the
margin of the lake had not yet been made. At the top of the
hill was a farm called How Top; at the bottom, on the opposite
side of the road from the cottage, was another called Sykeside,
no doubt because of the little 'syke' or beck which here ran
down into the lake.[1] Four other small cottages stood just above
Sykeside at right angles to the road. The Wordsworths' cottage
had been an inn called The Dove and Olive Branch, which accounts
perhaps for its being slightly different in appearance from the
small farm-houses which were its neighbours. It had latticed
windows, and a wainscoted ground-floor room, which must
have been the bar of the inn. The house had no name when the
Wordsworths took it and they never gave it one. The present
name of Dove Cottage is of more recent date, and seems to
be a reminiscence of the name of the inn. The Wordsworths'

---

[1] 'The little syke murmurs.' *D.W.J.* i, p. 80. Nov. 16th 1801. The barn of
Sykeside is now the Wordsworth Museum. How Top is still a working farm.

address was simply 'Town End, Grasmere', Town End being the name of the hamlet at this (southern) 'end' of the township of Grasmere, as Town Head was of that to the north under Helm Crag. The cottage had two rooms downstairs, the wainscoted room which Dorothy used as a kitchen, and a room leading out of it which, having laid matting over the stone flags, she made her bedroom. There was also a sort of back-kitchen or wash house. Upstairs, the larger of the two front rooms became the 'living room'; the other, in which the chimney 'smoked like a furnace', became William's bedroom. Two other small rooms on this floor completed the accommodation. One of these was 'unceiled', and Dorothy papered it with newspapers. In these humble premises the brother and sister lived for nearly three years alone; and here, after William's marriage in 1802, his three elder children were born. At all times one or other of the Hutchinson sisters, or Coleridge, was to be found there on visits long or short, so that, as Dorothy said, they were sometimes 'crammed edge-full'.

When they first came to Grasmere the cottage lay open to the road, and they enclosed the few yards between it and the roadside with the upright stone flags that still, in a few parts of Westmorland, line the lanes and road-sides.[1] Here was their garden, where peas and scarlet-runner beans (trained up to the house-wall on strings) gave them 'immense' produce in their first summer, and for whose furnishing Dorothy scoured the fells in search of mosses and rock-plants, or brought home gifts of London pride and periwinkle, daisies, and 'white and yellow lilies' from the gardens of friendly neighbours. They also planted honeysuckle and roses against the house.

But the real joy of Dove Cottage was the 'little nook of mountain-ground' which rose steeply behind the house, contained a few fruit-trees, and was always called 'the orchard'. William, writing to Coleridge on Christmas Eve, three days after their arrival, said: 'D . . . in imagination has already built a seat with a summer shed on the highest platform in this our little domestic slip of mountain. The spot commands a view over the roof of our house, of the lake, the church, Helm Crag, and

---

[1] *E.L.* 110, p. 248. D.W. to J.M., Sept. 10th 1800. See the drawing, reproduced as the frontispiece to the first volume of *D.W.J.*, 1941. The flags have now been replaced by an ordinary stone wall.

two thirds of the vale.' This summer-house, or 'moss hut' as
they called it, was not in fact built until 1804, when it served the
purpose of an extra sitting-room in days when the cottage was
full to overflowing.[1] But when Coleridge was at the cottage
at the end of August 1800 he 'discovered a rock-seat in the
orchard' and there was a great clearing-away of brambles. The
ground in the orchard sloped so steeply that they eventually
cut a doorway straight out into it from the staircase landing.
Above the orchard stretched the wild fell-side of rock and turf
and bracken, climbing up and up to Butter Crags and beyond
to the grassy ridges of Fairfield. Part of the fell here was called
the Hollins, for it was wooded with scattered holly-trees. Here
William and Dorothy often sat to look and meditate, and here
William wrote part of his *Celandine* poem.

The cottage at Town End then enjoyed an uninterrupted view
from its windows to the lake.[2] Dorothy thus describes the scene
from their windows on a snowy moonlight winter night: 'The
moon shone upon the water below Silver-How' (the name of the
fell on the west side of the lake), 'and above it hung, combining
with Silver-How on one side, a bowl-shaped moon, the curve
downwards; the white fields, glittering roof of Thomas Ashburner's house, the dark yew-tree, the white fields gay and
beautiful. William lay with his curtains open that he might see
it.' So he had lain in boyhood in Ann Tyson's cottage, watching
the moon 'in splendour couched among the leaves' of the ash-
tree as it swayed to and fro in the wind.

Besides the Sykeside group, there were only two other cottages
at Town End, both of them a little north of Dove Cottage and
on the opposite side of the road. Just beyond them a lane
branched to the left from the main Keswick road, leading
across flat fields to the central part of Grasmere village, with
the rugged square-towered church beside the bridge over the
Rothay, Robert Newton's inn beside the diminutive school-
house at the churchyard gate, and, a little farther to the
west and north, the ancient farm-steads of Pavement End,
Underhowe, and Dockray. From the village a lane led up again

---

[1] *E.L.* 186, p. 425. D.W. to Lady Beaumont, Dec. 25th 1804. The present
summer-house is on the same site as that built by the Wordsworths.

[2] The Prince of Wales Hotel, and the houses of Lake Terrace, built in late
Victorian times, entirely shut out the lake from the cottage at the present day.

to a point about a mile beyond Town End, where the main road began to mount the great Dunmail Raise Pass at the northern end of the valley. This pass is Coleridge's 'inverted arch' and leads to Wythburn and, ten miles farther on, Keswick. On this road lay the Swan Inn, and, farther up, Broadrain, the home of the Wordsworths' friends, the Sympsons. To the east a mountain track led over the Grisedale Pass to Ullswater. These two passes, Dunmail Raise and Grisedale, were traversed over and over again in the ensuing years by William and Dorothy, on their way to and from Coleridge at Keswick, or the Clarksons at Pooley Bridge.

North of the church, and cut off from the lake by some rocky spurs of Silver How, lay that farther part of Grasmere Vale which was called Easedale.[1] A road ran up it past the rocky outcrop of Butterlip How and over Goody Bridge, past the little farm called Blintarn or Blentarn Gill, and then—only a mountain track now—past the waterfall to Easedale Tarn. To the east, another branch of the valley, Far Easedale, led over into Borrowdale. Easedale was called by the Wordsworths in their first year at Grasmere 'the Black Quarter', because, lying to the north-west and surrounded by the high fells, it seemed to be the gathering-place of cloud and storm. They had a particular love for that retired valley, and in later years Wordsworth said that he had composed 'thousands of lines' beside the Easedale Beck.

Southwards from Town End the road to Ambleside mounted the hill and went across White Moss Common, down to the shore of Rydal Water. Just beyond How Top it ran past a grove of Scotch firs, 'thickly planted', which became, in this first year, the favourite haunt of their brother John during his long stay with them from January to September. There he, the 'silent poet', wore a path through the trees by constant walking to and fro, and ever after the wood was 'John's Grove' to William and Dorothy.[2] Opposite the grove was a gate into a field which they came to call the Wishing Gate, or 'Sara's Gate' after Sara Hutchinson, and below the road, running down to the shore of the lake, was Bainriggs, a wood of oak and beech with many rocks in it. At the foot of the lake, the river flows through a

---

[1] The old pronunciation of Easedale was 'Yasdale'.
[2] See the sixth of *Poems on the Naming of Places*, begun on Aug. 30th 1800. *P.W.* ii, p. 118.

narrow pass, before opening out again into Rydal. Some stepping-stones crossed it where the small foot-bridge now is, leading to Loughrigg Fell and the beautiful lifted path called Loughrigg Terrace which runs from Rydal village to join the Langdale road at the top of Red Bank.

Grasmere Lake itself was rich in fish, particularly pike. William and his brother John obtained the use of a boat belonging to Mr. Gell who had built a cottage above the lake on the western side.[1] This was a place of some notoriety with ornamental grounds and was visited by tourists. In Mr. Gell's boat all three spent much time in this first summer setting floats for pike. The island in the lake was uninhabited except by sheep; it became a favourite hermitage of Wordsworth's. Upon it was an out-house to shelter the sheep that pastured there.

> And hither does one Poet sometimes row
> His pinnace, a small vagrant barge, up-piled
> With plenteous store of heath and withered fern,
> (A lading which he with his sickle cuts
> Among the mountains) and beneath this roof
> He makes his summer couch.

And so, lying in 'the open door-place', looking out on the lake, he could allow his mind to form

> Creations lovely as the work of sleep—
> Fair sights, and visions of romantic joy.[2]

There were few spots in the vale with which they had not established familiar and affectionate relations before their first summer was over. The series of blank-verse poems called *Poems on the Naming of Places* was written between December 1799 and September 1800. All except one (*To Joanna*) recall actual walks and places and incidents that became dear through association. The second in the series, *Our Walk was far among the ancient Trees*, was the first poem to be completed at Town End, on December 28th 1799, and was an offering to Mary Hutchinson; it described a walk among the beech-trees of Rydal Park and the finding of a little pool of water in a clearing. Another, about a ramble up Easedale beck on an April morning (*It was*

---

[1] Referred to in the Journal as 'Gell's Cottage'; now called Silver How. Mr. Gell became Sir William Gell; he was an early pioneer of Greek archaeology and lived mostly abroad. He is only once recorded as visiting his cottage during the Wordsworths' time, in June 1800. *D.W.J.* i, p. 48.   [2] *P.W.* iv, p. 198.

an April morning: fresh and clear) shows William in one of his
holiday moods of total abandonment to the abundant life of
nature and spring.

> The spirit of enjoyment and desire
> And hopes and wishes, from all living things
> Went circling, like a multitude of sounds. . . .
>   Up the brook
> I roamed in the confusion of my heart,
> Alive to all things and forgetting all.

In another (*There is an Eminence*) he tells of Stone Arthur,
the rocky peak above the vale on the eastern side, which Dorothy,
with a sure instinct, named after him. How right she was may
be felt by lovers of Wordsworth as they read the poem:

> this Peak, so high
> Above us, and so distant in its height,
> Is visible, and often seems to send
> Its own deep quiet to restore our hearts. . . .
>   'Tis in truth
> The loneliest place we have among the clouds.
> And She who dwells with me, whom I have loved
> With such communion, that no place on earth
> Can ever be a solitude to me,
> Hath to this lonely Summit given my Name.

Scarcely of less interest than the heights and hollows of
Grasmere to the brother and sister were their human neighbours. Not only were these neighbours kindly people with
strongly-marked individuality, but their lives, their economic
and social circumstances, their joys and their sorrows, were
exactly such as to appeal to Wordsworth's sympathy and compassion and justify his conception—formed many years earlier
among similar people at Hawkshead—of the best kind of life
for men. Years afterwards, in *The Excursion*, he told the stories
of some of these, his rural neighbours: Dorothy in her Journal
gives us glimpses of their racy talk and the 'familiar matter'
of their daily lives. It was no Utopian or Arcadian community
in which the Wordsworths had made their home. The shadow
of debt and poverty hung over many of the little farms in the
vale, for these were hard times. The decline of the rural industries of spinning and weaving, because of the growth of the

GRASMERE, FROM THE ROAD THROUGH BAINRIGGS, FROM A WATER-COLOUR BY
PAUL SANDBY

'manufacturing towns', was already having a serious effect upon the small statesman-farmer of the dales, whose livelihood had depended almost as much on the sale of homespun yarn and cloth as on the cultivation of his few acres and the produce of his few cows. 'Subsistence agriculture' was barely sufficient now to support a large family, and richer men were not lacking to buy up small estates and add field to field. The story of *The Last of the Flock* was re-enacted in various ways under the eyes of the Wordsworths at Town End in the persons of their neighbours, the Fishers and the Ashburners.

John Fisher of Sykeside was earning his living as the village cobbler when the Wordsworths came, and he often helped them in the garden. But he owned some land as well, and through some 'mishap' early in his married life had been obliged to mortgage it. His wife, Agnes, was a woman of remarkable personality whom poverty had made the victim of 'avaricious thrift'.[1] She was evidently gifted by nature with powers of intellect above her station.

> Nothing could subdue
> Her keen desire of knowledge.

Her determination to get free of debt at length earned its reward, but too late to bring contentment to that mind 'intolerant of lasting peace'. When she lay on her death-bed the thought that her husband's sister, old Molly Fisher, the Wordsworth's faithful 'daily', would have to take her place in the house, troubled her:

> And must she rule and reign,
> Sole Mistress of this house, when I am gone?

Molly was as stupid as her sister-in-law was clever, which was perhaps a cause of Agnes' jealousy. She came across to the cottage for two or three hours a day, and was paid two shillings a week; 'we could', says Wordsworth, 'have had this attendance for eighteen pence a week, but we added the sixpence for the sake of the poor woman, who is made happy by it'. 'She was very ignorant,' says Dorothy, 'very foolish, and very difficult to teach, so that I once almost despaired of her, but the goodness of her disposition . . . induced me to go on. . . . She is

---

[1] See Wordsworth's description of her in *Excursion*, VI, ll. 675–778. *P.W.* v, pp. 207–11.

much attached to us, and honest and good as ever was a human being.' 'A drollery belonging to the Cottage' was Coleridge's description of her; she stayed with them till 1804, when her sister-in-law's death obliged her to 'rule and reign' at Sykeside. When at length she died, in 1808, Dorothy wrote: 'Poor old Molly Fisher is at rest in the quiet grave. . . . Many a pensive thought have I in my walks to and from Town End, of her and her cheerful happy ways. . . . It goes through my heart to see her empty chair, and a hundred little things that she prized, remaining just as she left them, only dull and dusty.' She left Dorothy her best gown.

Thomas Ashburner, who lived in one of the houses just north of Dove Cottage, was a poor statesman who had fallen on evil days. Eventually, when mortgaging proved of no avail, he sold his land. His delicate wife Peggy, a favourite neighbour of Dorothy's, once told her how much they had loved their little estate and how hard they had struggled to save it.

'Ay', says she, 'I said many a time he's not come fra London to buy our land, however.' Then she told me with what pains and industry they had made up their taxes, interest etc. how they all got up at 5 o'clock in the morning to spin and Thomas carded, and that they had paid off a hundred pounds of the interest. She said she used to take such pleasure in the cattle and sheep. 'Oh how pleased I used to be when they fetched them down, and when I had been a bit poorly I would gang out upon a hill and look ower 't fields and see them, and it used to do me so much good you cannot think.'

But the cottage, even after the land was gone, was a pleasant sight. The family of 'lasses' kept the garden neat, and one of them, a 'hardy girl who mounts the rocks' brought down pieces of quartz to set upon the wall, and even made a little garden up on the fell-side for gooseberry bushes, which Wordsworth discovered one day on one of his rambles. At night he would sometimes pause by the 'blazing window' to look at the picture within of the girls spinning and sewing round the fire.[1] Thomas Ashburner fetched the Wordsworths' monthly cart of coals from Keswick, and little Sally, the youngest of the 'lasses clean and neat and rosy', sometimes helped in the garden, weeding or picking apples, and, later, in the house looking after the children.

[1] *D.W.J.* i, p. 83, and appendix I, p. 433. *Excursion*, VI, ll. 1115–91. *P.W.* v, pp. 223–7 and note.

The Greens of Pavement or Padmire End at the head of the lake were a more prosperous family; two of their seven sons were later ordained.[1] One, Daniel, became perpetual curate of Langdale; Isaac was for many years second master at Sedbergh School. This man left many records of the Grasmere people of his day. John Green, the father, was a butcher and cattle-dealer, 'like Wolsey', as one of his sons said afterwards; he employed a farm-manager and another farm-servant. He was born in the vale, and as a lad fothering sheep on Silver How he would often listen 'if the Lord of Baysbrown's hounds were out', and if he heard them would leave his sheep to join them.[2] Like Simon Lee, 'he dearly loved their voices'.

High in Easedale lived another family of Greens at Blentarn Gill, holding on to the very edge of existence on a tiny mort-gaged estate, on which George Green was now beginning to rear a second family, his first wife having died leaving him with five children. It was these Greens who met their death in the snow on Langdale Fell in 1808 and for whose eight young children the Wordsworths opened a relief fund. They were universally respected for their scrupulous honesty and courage in facing poverty without complaint; their only fault was that they were 'too stiff'—too unwilling to receive help from their neighbours.

The Dawsons of Ben Place (near the Swan Inn on the Kes-wick Road) were an interesting family. Mr. Dawson, says Wordsworth, was 'a man of literary education, and of experience in society much beyond what was common among the inhabit-ants of the Vale'. He had been away for many years at Bunawe on Loch Etive as manager to the Knott Ironworks, and had also been clerk to the Distributor of Government Stamps in the district in days when all the money had to be collected in coin and kept in an iron chest. His son, young George Dawson, whom Wordsworth described as 'Pan or Apollo veiled in human form' was the athlete and champion fox-hunter and sportsman of the vale. He died suddenly in 1807 from cramp after bathing.[3]

[1] For the story of the Greens of Pavement End and their little girl see *Excursion*, VII, ll. 632–941 and note.
[2] All fell-hunting is still done on foot. Baysbrown is the chief farm in Langdale, which had its 'Lord' just as Patterdale then had its 'King' at Patterdale Hall.
[3] *Excursion*, vii, ll. 714–890 and note. *P.W.* v, pp. 254–9.

Up at 'Gell's Cottage', but after Mr. Gell had sold it to Samuel Barber, lived a woman who, though she is not mentioned in Dorothy's Journals or letters, or in *The Excursion*, seems a particularly appropriate figure in the Wordsworthian landscape. She was Aggy Sutton, Mr. Barber's housekeeper and caretaker, and also the devoted nurse of the Green children of Pavement End. This woman, living entirely alone in the woods of Silver How, made companions of the birds, who all came at her call, entered the cottage, and perched on her head and hands.[1]

The parson of the parish (which then included Langdale and Rydal) when the Wordsworths came was one Edward Rowlandson who was curate for the absentee and insane rector, John Craik. Mr. Rowlandson was a heavy drinker; seeing him at a funeral in their first summer Dorothy noted: 'he did not look as a man ought to do on such an occasion—I had seen him half-drunk the day before in a pot-house.' He lived not in the Rectory which was ruinous, but at a house next the school-house which has now disappeared.[2] He owned some land in the parish, the fields known as Beck Islands, in which he earnestly but vainly desired to be buried. His only son, Michael, was an able man, well known as a preacher; he became headmaster of the school at Warminster at which Dr. Arnold of Rugby received his early education. Parson Rowlandson was somewhat of a miser as well as a tippler. He often, Wordsworth tells us, was to be seen gathering the hay in his fields in November by moonlight, because he could not bring himself to hire labour earlier. Yet this man somehow held the respect of his neighbours and the church in his time was always well attended.[3]

There were a few families of 'gentry' in the vale. The Wordsworths' nearest neighbours were the Oliffes of Hollins above the Keswick road, between Town End and the Swan Inn. In one of their fields, it seems, William and Dorothy at one time planned to build their own house. For the cottage, much as they loved it, never quite dismissed from their minds their

---

[1] Memoirs of Isaac Green, in the possession of Mrs. Rawnsley of Allan Bank, Grasmere.

[2] It stood in what is now the garden of the Rothay Hotel. On the death of Mr. Rowlandson in 1811 it was inhabited by some of the Greens of Pavement End who named it Moss Head.

[3] See Wordsworth's description of him in the note to the *Epistle to Sir George Beaumont*, *P.W.* iv, p. 434.

original plans of building a house to their own taste entirely.[1]

The family with whom the Wordsworths were most intimate were the Sympsons, who lived about half-way up the Dunmail Raise road, at a house which still stands, called High Broadrain. Mr. Sympson had been vicar of Wythburn, the parish on the other side of the Raise, for forty-three years when the Wordsworths came to Grasmere; he was a hale old man of eighty-five, a keen fisherman, artist, and engraver,

> an active, ardent mind,
> A fancy pregnant with resource and scheme
> To cheat the sadness of a rainy day.

He had, it seems, in the early years of his priesthood consorted with the nobility, and often talked

> Of long-past banquetings with high-born friends;

complained too of their failure to provide him with a good living, so that he had been forced to accept the poor one of Wythburn. He performed his duties as priest with decent, though not enthusiastic, zeal; he had to travel over the bleak, wind-swept Raise every time he visited church or parish; he was never weaned from the ways of the world to a perfect contentment with his lot. His wife was of a serener, more spiritual frame of mind,

> Far nearer, in the habit of her soul
> To that still region whither all are bound.

For her Dorothy had a great affection. 'She was', she wrote, 'an affecting picture of patient disappointment, suffering under no particular affliction.' With their daughter Margaret and son Bartholomew, who farmed the little glebe, they were also on friendly terms; many were the exchanges of garden produce; calls, walks, tea-drinkings, fishing-expeditions, and picnics which passed between the households. Indeed, judging by the entries in Dorothy's Journal, Mr. Sympson seems to have spent a good deal more time in Grasmere Vale than in his own parish of Wythburn. Considering his age, however, and the situation of his house, this was hardly blameworthy.

And besides the residents, there was the constant floating population of wayfarers—pedlars, discharged soldiers and

[1] *D.W.J.* i, p. 66. Oct. 11th, 1800: 'Mr. Oliff's field, where our house is to be built.'

sailors, gipsies, beggars, and crazy folk—who passed by the door of the cottage. They were a source of interest and often of compassion to the Wordsworths; Dorothy's descriptions of them in her Journal not infrequently were used by Wordsworth as the material for a poem. In this manner *Beggars* was written, and *The Sailor's Mother*, while the meeting with the old Leech-gatherer on September 26th 1800 furnished the theme two years later of *Resolution and Independence*. Once a woman came who might have been William's own 'Female Vagrant.'

'Aye', says she, 'I was once an officer's wife, I, as you see me now. My first husband married me at Appleby; I had £18 a year for teaching a school, and because I had no fortune his father turned him out of doors. I have been in the West Indies. I lost the use of this finger just before he died; he came to me and said he must bid farewell to his dear children and me. I had a muslin gown on like yours—I seized hold of his coat as he went from me and slipped the joint of my finger. He was shot directly.'

Then there was the old man who had been a servant of the Marquis of Granby.

William said to him—'You are a very old man?' 'Aye, I am 83.' I joined in, 'Have you any children?' 'Children? Yes, plenty. I have children and grand-children and great grand-children. . . .' I then said 'What, they take care of you?' He replied, half offended, 'Thank God, I can take care of myself. . . . I brought up my family under the Marquis. . . . O he was a good man, he's in heaven—I hope he is.'

Sometimes they had a glimpse of more terrible things.

A sailor . . . called; he was faint and pale when he knocked at the door—a young man very well dressed. We sate by the kitchen fire talking with him for two hours. . . . His name was Isaac Chapel. He had been at sea since he was 15 years old. . . . He had been on board a slave-ship, the captain's name Maxwell, where one man had been killed, a boy put to lodge with the pigs and half eaten, one boy set to watch in the hot sun till he dropped down dead. . . . He had twice swum from a King's ship in the night and escaped. He said he would rather be in hell than be pressed. . . . He was excessively like my brother John.[1]

William and Dorothy never refused hospitality or money to such people. Long after, in his old age, he exhorted his cook at Rydal Mount who was complaining of the ingratitude of some of the beggars, to 'go on giving, and some day the right

[1] *D.W.J.* i, pp. 85, 165, 148: Nov. 27th 1801; June 30th and Mar. 15th 1802.

beggar will come',[1] and once when a beggar accosted him in
the road, 'he thrust his hand into his pocket as if instinctively
acknowledging the man's right to beg', and when he found no
coin, 'he said in a sort of soliloquy "I have given to four or five
already to-day," as if to account for his being then unprovided'.[2]

Almost from the moment of their arrival in the vale the
Wordsworths had the cottage full of visitors. Brother John
arrived in January and stayed until September. 'We did not know
on what day he would come', wrote Dorothy after his death,
'though we were expecting him every hour, therefore he had no
reason to fear he should surprise us suddenly; yet twice did he
approach the door, and lay his hand upon the latch, and stop,
and turn away without the courage to enter (we had not met
for several years)—he then went to the Inn and sent us word
that he was come.'

Now was formed that precious intimacy between the brothers
and sister that gave them all so much delight. John rejoiced
that the long years of waiting for a home of their own were at
last over for William and Dorothy. 'He loved this fireside,' said
Dorothy, 'he paced over this floor in pride before we had been
six weeks in the house, exulting within his noble heart that his
father's children had once again a home together.'[3] John was
waiting until the ship, the *Earl of Abergavenny*, of which he had
just been appointed Captain, returned from her East Indian
voyage; then he was to begin making those voyages to the
East from which he hoped to make a fortune large enough to
support himself and his brother and sister without anxiety for
the rest of their days. His death by shipwreck in 1805 was the
greatest shock William and Dorothy ever experienced. His
character, and their devotion to him, receive a sad memorial
in the letters they wrote after his death. 'Meek, affectionate,
silently enthusiastic, loving all quiet things, and a Poet in
everything but words', said Wordsworth of him, and Dorothy
recalled how he shared all their tastes and habits, particularly
their love of the night. 'Many a time has he called me out in an
evening to look at the moon and stars, or a cloudy sky, or this
vale in the quiet moonlight—but the stars and moon were his

[1] Batho, *The Later Wordsworth*, p. 45.
[2] Ellis Yarnall, *Wordsworth and the Coleridges*, p. 48.
[3] *E.L.* 235, p. 545. *D.W.* to Lady Beaumont, Nov. 29th 1805.

chief delight, he made of them his companions when he was at sea, and was never tired of those thoughts which the silence of the night fed to him.'[1] It was his intention, when he had made enough money, to build a cottage for his brother and sister, and another for himself, at Grasmere. Like Raisley Calvert, John Wordsworth felt that William had a destiny to fulfil, and he desired nothing more than to assist in that fulfilment. 'He encouraged me', said William afterwards, 'to persist in the plan of life which I had adopted; I will work for you, was his language, and you shall attempt to do something for the world. Could I but see you with a green field of your own and a Cow and two or three other little comforts, I should be happy.'

While he was with them, Mary Hutchinson came and stayed six weeks at the cottage, from the end of February until early in April. Between her and John Wordsworth a close friendship sprang up. 'John used to walk with her everywhere, and they were exceedingly attached to each other', wrote Dorothy after his death. Throughout the autumn of 1800 and the early spring of 1801 he wrote to her frequently, and with warm affection, often addressing her as 'thou' and calling her 'my dearest Mary'. One might take them for love letters, save that the main subject of them is William's second edition of the *Lyrical Ballads* with its new volume of poems which appeared in January 1801. Whatever he may at one time have felt, however, John had no thought of coming between William and Mary when it became clear that they wished to marry. William, indeed, had in 1800 'no thoughts of marrying',[2] nor was he engaged to Mary until the autumn of 1801. When at length their marriage drew near, in the autumn of 1802, a sort of farewell message, scribbled as postscript on a letter of Dorothy's to Mary, revealed the depth of John's feeling. 'I have been reading your letter', he writes, 'over and over again, my dearest Mary, till tears have come into my eyes and I know not how to express myself—Thou art a kind and dear creature. But whatever fate befal me I shall love thee to the last, and bear thy memory with me to the grave. Thine aff^t. John Wordsworth.'[3] The last sentence of this letter is a quotation, word for word, from his brother's poem, *Michael*.

---

[1] *E.L.* 206, p. 468. D.W. to J.M., Mar. 16th 1805.
[2] Ibid. 205, p. 463. W.W. to James Losh, Mar. 16th 1805.
[3] Ibid. 134, p. 309.

John, like many others after him, found the poems the best vehicle for his own deepest feelings. And it was as he said; for he never saw Mary or any of those dear to him again.

John, however, was not left broken-hearted. It seems that a general expectation was formed in the family that he would eventually marry Mary's sister Sara Hutchinson. Wordsworth, writing after John's death, says that during his long stay at Grasmere in 1800 'he found in his Sister and me and Coleridge and in my Wife and a Sister of hers whom at that time he had an opportunity of seeing much of, all that was wanting to make him completely happy.'[1] His intention when he had made his own and his brother's fortunes was, as we have seen, to live at Grasmere, not with William and Dorothy, but in his own house, the site of which he had chosen in a field nearby.[2] This suggests strongly that he was looking forward to marriage. Finally, we have Coleridge's statement to Daniel Stuart in 1808: 'Had Captain Wordsworth lived, I had hopes of seeing her [that is, Sara] blessedly married, as well as prosperously.'[3] That Coleridge could look forward, apparently with pleasure, to his beloved Sara becoming the wife of another seems at first surprising, but the relations between him and Sara were never those of lover and mistress; such a thing would have been impossible for either of them, and completely alien to the sentiments of both the Wordsworths and Hutchinsons on such matters. On the contrary he was most anxious that his own wife should look upon Sara as a friend, and it seems that he told Mrs. Coleridge early in 1803 of the hoped-for marriage. No doubt he felt that Sara, by marrying William's brother, would be no further lost to him than if she were to remain single.

The only difficulty in the matter is the apparent lack of occasions for John to become closely acquainted with Sara. She did not come to Grasmere while he was there, but he must have seen her when he and William paid their visit to the Hutchinsons in Yorkshire in May 1800.[4] He probably saw her again after leaving Grasmere at the end of September, for Dorothy says in her Journal: 'I could not help thinking we should see him again,

---

[1] Ibid. 205, p. 463. W.W. to James Losh, Mar. 16th 1805.
[2] *M.Y.* i. 428, p. 425. D.W. to Mrs. Clarkson, Feb. 23rd 1811.
[3] *U.L.* i. 178, p. 405. S.T.C. to Stuart, n.d. (1808).
[4] See below, p. 476.

because he was only going to Penrith.' At Penrith lived the Hutchinsons' cousins, the Monkhouses, with whom Mary and Sara often stayed. Sara was probably visiting them, and this was the cause of his breaking his journey there. There is no indication that John was ever in the north after this, though it is possible that Sara went to London in the winter of 1802, when he was there in the intervals between voyages. Whatever the degree of intimacy between them may have been, there seems no doubt that their eventual marriage was looked forward to by Coleridge and William and Dorothy as a natural result of the communion of spirit which bound together the two families in so close a union.[1]

By the end of September 1800, the *Earl of Abergavenny* had returned from her voyage, and John must prepare to go. On the 29th William and Dorothy accompanied him to the top of the Grisedale Pass, past the tarn where he had so often fished, until they were within sight of Ullswater. There they parted, and William and Dorothy 'stood till we could see him no longer, watching him as he *hurried* down the stony mountain'.[2] He never returned to Grasmere again.

In the autumn a somewhat unwelcome addition to their neighbours was made by the arrival of Charles Lloyd with his wife and little boy at Brathay near Ambleside. 'We are by no means glad', wrote Dorothy, 'that they are to be our neighbours . . . because Charles Lloyd is . . . perpetually forming new friendships, quarrelling with his old ones, and upon the whole

---

[1] Coleridge's letter to his wife, Jan. 5th 1803, contains mysterious references to Sara's state of health and mind which may refer to her having been asked in marriage by John who was then in England. *U.L.* i. 110, p. 239.

[2] *E.L.* 220, p. 501. D.W. to Lady Beaumont, June 11th 1805. In his *Elegiac Verses* written after John's death, Wordsworth wrote of that parting in a stanza never published:

> Here did we part, and seated here
> With One he loved, I saw him bound
> Downwards along the rocky ground
> As if with eager cheer.
> A lovely sight as on he went,
> For he was bold and innocent,
> He lived a life of self-command;
> Heaven, did it seem to me and her
> Had laid on such a Mariner
> A consecrating hand.
>
> *P.W.* iv, p. 264, app. crit.

a dangerous acquaintance.' However, things in the main went better than might have been expected during the first few months. They met frequently, indeed in that first autumn almost daily, and evidently not always with reluctance on the Wordsworths' part. On October 2nd Dorothy recorded: 'We had a pleasant conversation about the manners of the rich, avarice, inordinate desires, and the effeminacy, unnaturalness, and the unworthy objects of education.' That little bit of indulgence in censoriousness seems to have given them all satisfaction.

Their most intimate friends were the Clarksons at Pooley Bridge. There, at the foot of Ullswater, Thomas Clarkson who, as Dorothy said, 'took such pains about the slave-trade', built a house called Eusemere, where he and his wife Catherine lived until 1804. They soon became intimate with William and Dorothy, who found in Eusemere almost a holiday home. Thomas Clarkson was an enthusiast for the Lake District, and used to go about exclaiming aloud at its beauties. His wife became Dorothy's most intimate friend and correspondent. They first visited Town End in September 1800: in the same week James Losh and his wife and Mr. Marshall of Leeds, the husband of Dorothy's old friend Jane Pollard, also found their ways thither. And they were closely followed by Robert Jones who stayed a week and then went on with Coleridge to Keswick. All this visiting took place in the midst of a busy time of writing the preface to the *Lyrical Ballads*, but the Wordsworths never allowed their literary activities to make them inhospitable.

Coleridge's first visit to Town End took place in April 1800. We know nothing of it beyond the dates.[1] He stayed about a month. He had been working hard in London all winter for Stuart of the *Morning Post*, and was still without a settled home. While at Grasmere he saw a house which was to let at Keswick, called Greta Hall, high up above the river 'with such a prospect that . . . I shall have a tendency to become a god, so sublime and beautiful will be the series of my visual existence'. At Stowey Thomas Poole was still vainly looking for a house for him. Poole, it is clear, was afraid of Wordsworth's influence; he felt that it would, sooner or later, draw Coleridge to the north. 'You charge me', wrote Coleridge to Poole at the end of March

---

[1] *U.L.* i, 69, p. 138. S.T.C. to Godwin, May 21st 1800: 'I left Wordsworth on the 4th of this month.' *E.L.* 107, p. 242. W.W. to R.W., Apr. 11th 1800.

1800, just before his visit to Grasmere, 'with prostration in regard to Wordsworth. Have I affirmed anything miraculous of W? Is it impossible that a greater poet than any since Milton may appear in our days? . . . What if you had known Milton at the age of thirty, and believed all you now know of him?'[1]

While John was at Grasmere, and shortly after Coleridge's departure, the two Wordsworth brothers set off, 'cold pork in their pockets', to walk through the Yorkshire dales on a visit to the Hutchinsons who had now left Sockburn. Tom Hutchinson had taken a farm called Gallow Hill, not far from Scarborough; George, the younger brother, one at Bishop Middleham. Mary and Joanna kept house for Tom; Sara for George; but the sisters migrated a good deal between the two households. We know little of the visit of the Wordsworth brothers, but they explored the Yorkshire caves on the way, and Gordale Scar,[2] and from Gallow Hill Wordsworth called one day at Hunmanby Vicarage, where his old friend Francis Wrangham was living; he was, however, from home. The expedition is of importance because it was the occasion of Dorothy beginning her Journal—the 'Grasmere Journal' from which we draw so much of the knowledge of their daily lives during the next two years. It was, like the Alfoxden Journal, completely informal and intimate, written for no eye but her brother's.

William and John were away three weeks and three days, from May 14th to June 7th—a long absence during which Dorothy was alone at the cottage.

'I felt myself very lonely while I was within doors,' she wrote to Jane Marshall, 'I wanted my little companion Basil, and poor old Molly did but ill supply to me the place of our good and dear Peggy' (their maid of Racedown and Alfoxden days) 'who was quite as a friend to us.'[3] Out of doors she was less melancholy, and it was a sweet and flowery spring, yet there too sadness would overtake her as she sat looking at Rydal on a still evening. 'I sate till I could hardly drag myself away, I grew so sad.' And she comforted herself with her brother's verses:

> In that sweet mood when pleasant thoughts
> Bring sad thoughts to the mind.[4]

[1] *T.P.* ii, p. 8.
[3] Ibid.
[2] *E.L.* 110, p. 251. D.W. to J.M.
[4] *D.W.J.* i, p. 41. May 26th 1800.

Dorothy's love for her brother was at all times accompanied by an undercurrent of anxiety, for his health, which was precarious, and for his achievement as a poet, which was her life's hope. When the stimulus of his presence was withdrawn, anxiety would often predominate, making her sad with that sadness which often overwhelms those whose youth has been disturbed and insecure.

Her chief occupations in her solitude were to cherish house and garden, to walk to Ambleside every post-day for letters, which she seldom found, and to begin her Journal, 'because I shall give William pleasure by it when he comes home again'. One of the tasks she undertook while they were away was to correspond further with Mr. Jackson, the owner of Greta Hall, about letting it to Coleridge.[1] And by the end of June Coleridge said he was 'now finally determined on the North'. Wordsworth had defeated Poole. On June 29th Coleridge, with Sara and Hartley, arrived at Town End and stayed nearly a month with the Wordsworths. During that time Coleridge was prostrated with a cold so violent as to amount almost to rheumatic fever. It was 'from wet' and was the first of the many attacks which eventually made life in the Lake District impossible for him. Wordsworth too was suffering from his old complaint, and Coleridge wrote a description of it to his medical friend in Bristol, Thomas Beddoes, of the Pneumatic Institution, in which he ascribed it to an association of ideas and feelings with 'a particular pain probably in the right hypochondrium'. Dr. Beddoes sent prescriptions, but Wordsworth would have none of them. 'I saw his countenance darken', wrote Coleridge, 'and all his hopes vanish, when he saw the prescriptions. His *scepticism* concerning medicines!'[2] Just before the departure of the Coleridges for Keswick, they all had a picnic on the island of Grasmere Lake, and Coleridge thus describes the scene:

Our kettle swung over the fire hanging from the branch of a fir-tree, and I lay and saw the woods, and the mountains, and lake all trembling, and as it were *idealized* through the subtle smoke which rose up from the clear red embers of the fir-apples, which we had collected; afterwards we made a glorious Bonfire on the

---

[1] Ibid., pp. 44–45. June 4th and 5th 1800.
[2] *S.T.C.* i, p. 338. S.T.C. to Humphry Davy, Oct. 1800, and *U.L.* i, p. 148. S.T.C. to Humphry Davy, July 25th 1800.

margin, by some elder-bushes, whose twigs heaved and sobbed in the uprushing column of smoke—and the Image of the Bonfire, and of us that danced round it—ruddy laughing faces in the twilight—the Image of this in a Lake smooth as that Sea to whose waves the Son of God had said, *'Peace'*.[1]

And now began the endless series of journeys from Greta Hall to Town End, or from Town End to Greta Hall, a sort of shuttle-service of unheralded visits which recall the Alfoxden days. But now thirteen miles separated the two households, instead of three. This, however, does not seem to have troubled them in the least. Between the end of July and the end of December 1800 Coleridge came eight times to the cottage, and Wordsworth visited Keswick five times, Dorothy twice. Coleridge generally stayed three or four days; in August the Wordsworths spent more than a week at Keswick, and another in the middle of November. Often they started on these journeys at dusk or later, arriving at each other's houses about midnight. Thus Dorothy writes on November 15th: 'I walked with W. over the Raise. It was starlight. I parted with him very sad, unwilling not to go on. The hills, and the stars, and the white waters, with their ever varying yet ceaseless sound, were very impressive.' Or 'At 11 o'clock Coleridge came, when I was walking in the still clear moonshine in the garden. He came over Helvellyn. Wm. was gone to bed, and John also, worn out with his ride round Coniston. We sate and chatted till half past three, W. in his dressing-gown.'[2]

The matter of many of these conversations was poetry, and chiefly their own poetry. They were in fact engaged in preparing a new volume of *Lyrical Ballads* for the press.

Wordsworth was writing poetry almost from the very day of his arrival at the cottage, as his poem to Mary, written on December 28th, shows. It was a severe winter and the first two months were months of incessant storm. On 'the first mild

---

[1] It is clear from Dorothy's Journal that there were really two picnics, one on the island, on Friday, July 18th, and one 'in Bainriggs with the Sympsons' on Sunday the 20th, when they made a bonfire. The Coleridges left on Thursday, July 24th. Dorothy was evidently too busy during the Coleridges' stay to keep a daily journal, and wrote a brief summary afterwards. On Sept. 14th a son was born to Coleridge. He called him Derwent, after the river that flowed past the house at Keswick..

[2] *D.W.J.* i, p. 58. Aug. 31st 1800.

ay of March', the day on which he began once more to work
t *The Recluse,* he wrote

> It loves us now, this Vale so beautiful
> Begins to love us! By a sullen storm,
> Two months unwearied of severest storm,
> It put the temper of our minds to proof,
> And found us faithful through the gloom, and heard
> The Poet mutter his prelusive songs
> With cheerful heart, and unknown voice of joy
> Among the silence of the woods and hills.[1]

Of these 'prelusive songs' (prelusive, that is, to *The Recluse*),
he first to be begun was 'the pastoral of Bowman', which he
amed *The Brothers* and which was the first poem in the new
olume of *Lyrical Ballads* published in January 1801.[2] It was
egun on or just before Christmas Eve, 1799, and was intended
o be 'the concluding poem of a series of pastorals, the scene of
vhich was laid among the mountains'. The project for this
eries must have been discussed with Coleridge on their walking
our. Only one other, *Michael,* was completed; though three
ther short poems, *The Oak and the Broom, The Idle Shepherd
Boys,* and *The Pet-Lamb,* bear the sub-title *A Pastoral.* They
re, however, of a less exalted nature and can scarcely have been
hought of as belonging to the 'series'.

The Brothers, 'that model of English pastoral', as Coleridge
alled it, is based on the story told to him and Coleridge by the
hepherd in Ennerdale during their walking tour in November
799. It was composed largely in the wood by the margin of
Grasmere Lake, and so the wood was named after it 'Brothers'
Wood'.[3] It is a simple tale, told in very restrained language,
et it possesses dramatic pathos of a high order. The return of
Leonard Ewbank from sea to his native village, to find his
rother dead and himself unrecognized, and his departure
without revealing his identity to the kind old priest, has some-
hing of the quality of Greek tragedy. It is impossible not to

---

[1] *The Recluse,* ll. 179–88. *P.W.* v, p. 320.
[2] *E.L.* 105, p. 237. W.W. to S.T.C., Christmas Eve, 1799: 'I have begun the
astoral of Bowman'—the name of the shepherd whom he and Coleridge heard of
a Ennerdale. In the poem it is changed to Ewbank. See above, pp. 451–2.
[3] Not to be confused with 'John's Grove', the fir-wood above the road in which
ohn loved to walk. *P.W.* v, p. 457, note to *Excursion,* VI.

feel, moreover, that in writing of the sailor returning to his
native valley in search of his brother,

> With a determined purpose to resume
> The life he had lived there; both for the sake
> Of many darling pleasures, and the love
> Which to an only brother he had borne
> In all his hardships,

Wordsworth was thinking of his own John. John arrived at the
cottage, as we have seen, at the end of January, after the poem
was begun, but probably some time before it was finished. The
description of Leonard's return, and how

>   his heart
> Failed in him; and not venturing to enquire
> Tidings of one so long and dearly loved,
> He to the solitary church-yard turned,

may well be a paraphrase of the shy and anxious John's arrival
at the door of the cottage when he dared not knock and stole
back to the village inn.

These poems differ in one important respect from the narrative poems written at Alfoxden; there is in *The Brothers* no concern with the derangement produced by grief as in *The Thorn* and
The Mad Mother: we have moved away from the moonlight
world of *The Idiot Boy* and *Peter Bell* into the light of common
day. The same normality characterizes all the poetry of this year.

Hart-leap Well was begun 'one winter evening in the cottage
when, after having tired myself with labouring at an awkward
passage in The Brothers, I started with a sudden impulse to
this to get rid of the other, and finished it in a day or two'. The
two fables, *The Oak and the Broom* and *The Waterfall and the
Eglantine* were 'suggested' on the mountain path under Nab
Scar between Rydal and Grasmere. There can be little doubt
that they are conscious reminiscences of Langhorne's *Fables of
Flora*, one of which bears the title *The Wilding and the Broom*.
Except for the series of *Poems on the Naming of Places* already
referred to, Wordsworth wrote few other short poems this
year. One, *Song for the Wandering Jew*, deserves to be better
known than it is, if only for the last two lines:

> Night and day I feel the trouble
> Of the Wanderer in my soul;

while the unnamed poem, *'Tis said that some have died for Love*, contains one of his tenderest outbursts to his own 'gentle Love', Emma, one of his names for Dorothy, imploring her not to grieve overmuch if he should die. *The Childless Father* is a reminiscence of customs with which he had been familiar as a child at Cockermouth; *Rural Architecture*, which was liked by the charitable Lamb, must be dated after Coleridge's arrival, as it is set in the scenery of the road from Grasmere to Keswick.

Two poems, which have never been widely read but which are eminently characteristic of Wordsworth's mind, belong to this summer: *The Farmer of Tilsbury Vale* and *The Two Thieves*. They are both about slightly disreputable characters in whom, nevertheless, Wordsworth saw much to love. Wordsworth was never among the 'unco guid' in his judgements of people; he enjoyed the oddities and even the weaknesses of human nature, and often sought in them the matter of poetry. Of *The Two Thieves*, which is based on a memory of Hawkshead, something has already been said.[1] The story of *The Farmer* was told him by Thomas Poole at Nether Stowey. An old farmer lost his fortune, begged or borrowed from his neighbours, and decamped to London with the money. There he lived by casual labour, but his heart remained young, for every time he saw the fruit and flowers in Covent Garden, or the cows in Smithfield, or a wagon of hay passing up Haymarket Hill, the days of his prosperity in Tilsbury Vale come back upon him, not so much with regret as with happiness.

> Up the Haymarket hill he oft whistles his way,
> Thrusts his hands in a waggon, and smells at the hay;
> He thinks of the fields he so often hath mown,
> And is happy as if the rich freight were his own.

The Farmer is in fact a masculine counterpart of *Poor Susan*, and the poem is written in the same metre. Wordsworth realized the affinity between them, which is perhaps the reason why he did not include *The Farmer* in any collection of his poems until 1815. It appeared in the *Morning Post* in July 1800.

After they had been rather more than two months at the

---

[1] See above, p. 34. Lamb, writing to Wordsworth in 1815, spoke of 'that delicacy towards aberrations from the strict path which is so fine in the Old Thief and the boy by his side, and always brings water to my eyes'.

Cottage, Wordsworth turned his mind once more to *The Recluse*.[1] This was no doubt in response to Coleridge's reiterated pleadings. The fair copy, written partly in Wordsworth's own hand and partly in that of Mary Hutchinson, is entitled: *The Recluse Part First. Book First. Home at Grasmere*. It is impossible to approach this little-known poem[2] without the keenest interest. How would Wordsworth tackle the work on which Coleridge placed such hopes, and which he himself had begun so joyously at Alfoxden two years before? There is first a description of Grasmere, of Wordsworth's early love for it, of his satisfaction in settling there, of the quality and character of the vale, its inhabitants, human and animal; then a most interesting description of what he felt to be the character of his own genius, and for what kind of work it was fitted. Finally, having renounced the writing of an epic, he exclaims:

> A Voice shall speak and what shall be the theme?

The answer is the lines already written at Alfoxden,

> On Man, on Nature and on Human Life, &c.

So, after all, the new beginning to *The Recluse* was only a prelude to this earlier fragment, not a development from it, showing how unsettled Wordsworth still was as to the ultimate character and form of the poem.

There are signs that in *The Recluse* Wordsworth was seeking to reassure both himself and Coleridge that in settling at Grasmere he was fulfilling, and not shirking, his true destiny. This, there can be little doubt, had been Coleridge's fear in Germany, a fear which he must have expressed to Wordsworth, and which Wordsworth felt deserved an answer. He himself was not in love with solitude and retirement for its own sake. Throughout the following years, faithful though he was to

---

[1] Some lines not included in the completed version give the date of composition as not earlier than Mar. 10th:
> Thrice hath the winter moon been filled with light
> Since that dear day, when Grasmere, our dear Vale,
> Received us.

The moon was full for the third time since their arrival on Mar. 10th.

[2] *The Recluse* was printed by Knight in his *Life of William Wordsworth*, vol. iii, in 1889, having been published by Macmillan in a separate volume in 1888. It was never reprinted until 1949 in *P.W.*, v where it appears as appendix A, pp. 313–39.

Grasmere, he often chafed against the lack of books and the difficulty experienced in seeing friends. He told Sir George Beaumont in 1804 that he thought solitude and seclusion from the world 'a great evil'. Nevertheless, there was something about Grasmere which for him was irresistible: it was 'Nature's invitation' in the first place, which he of all people felt bound to accept. So he began his poem by recollecting his first sight of the vale when

> Once to the verge of yon steep barrier came
> A roving School-boy;

when he had felt such perfect contentment in the scene that ever since it became

> As beautiful to thought as it had been
> When present, to the bodily sense; a haunt
> Of pure affections, shedding upon joy
> A brighter joy.

Yet in spite of his love for it, the final decision to live there, far from books, from his friends, from Coleridge even, had not been easily made. But it was justified in the perfect happiness which ensued.

> And did it cost so much, and did it ask
> Such length of discipline, and could it seem
> An act of courage, and the thing itself
> A conquest? Shame that this was ever so—
> Not to the Boy or Youth, but shame to thee
> Sage Man, thou Sun in its meridian strength, . . .
> Thy prudence, thy experience, thy desires,
> Thy apprehensions—blush thou for them all . . .
> What once was deem'd so difficult is now
> Smooth, easy, without obstacle, what once
> Did to my blindness seem a sacrifice,
> The same is now the choice of my whole heart.
> If e'er the acceptance of such dower was deem'd
> A condescension or a weak indulgence
> To a sick fancy, it is now an act
> Of reason that exultingly aspires . . .
> On Nature's invitation do I come
> By reason sanctioned.

And what was it in Grasmere that made it so entirely satisfying?

'Tis, but I cannot name it, 'tis the sense
Of majesty, and beauty, and repose,
A blended holiness of earth and sky,
Something that makes this individual spot,
This small abiding-place of many men,
A termination and a last retreat,
A Centre, come from wheresoe'er you will,
A Whole without dependence or defect,
Made for itself; and happy in itself,
Perfect Contentment, Unity entire.

With an engaging candour he faced the poetic duties which he felt were laid upon him in this dear retreat. The word 'duty' had not yet entered his poetic vocabulary, but its reality was present in his heart. He had something to give to mankind:

to me I feel
That an internal brightness is vouchsafed
That must not die, that must not pass away . . .
Something which power and effort would impart,
I would impart it, I would spread it wide,
Immortal in the world which is to come.

He had for long imagined that this 'something' would be a poem on some heroic theme. There was that in him still which responded to the life of adventure and action; that spirit which in boyhood had driven him to climb crags alone after the eagle's eyrie, and in youth had called forth his devotion to Beaupuy.

Yea to this hour I cannot read a tale
Of two brave Vessels matched in deadly fight
And fighting to the death, but I am pleased
More than a wise man ought to be. I wish,
Fret, burn, and struggle, and in soul am there.

But he had learnt that as a poet his calling was not there. All the poetry of the last three years, the story of Margaret and of the Pedlar, of his own boyhood, of Peter Bell and Leonard, told him that less spectacular but more profound themes were reserved for him. He fully recognized now that this was so, and in his own peculiar way acknowledged it:

But me hath Nature tamed, and bade me seek
For other agitations, or be calm;

Hath dealt with me as with a turbulent Stream
Some nursling of the mountains, whom she leads
Through quiet meadows, after he has learnt
His strength, and had his triumph and his joy,
His desperate course of tumult and of glee.
That which in stealth by Nature was performed
Hath Reason sanctioned. Her deliberate Voice
Hath said, 'Be mild and cleave to gentle things,
Thy glory and thy happiness be there . . .
All that inflamed thy infant heart, the love,
The longing, the contempt, the undaunted quest
All shall survive—though changed their office, all
Shall live,—it is not in their power to die.'

Wordsworth was approaching that synthesis of the homely, the prophetic, and the contemplative spirit which made possible the work of the next eight years.

In July of this year, somewhat surprisingly, the question of producing *The Borderers* was once more brought forward. Coleridge, writing to Stuart of the *Morning Post*, said 'With regard to the Play business, W. has a tragedy by him. . . . This he would transmit by you to Mr Sheridan. . . . Sheridan would advise him on its defects etc.' Coleridge had no love for Sheridan who, after encouraging him to write a tragedy, had never returned the copy of *Osorio* sent him in 1797 and had even made fun of it in conversation. Now, through Stuart, he was 'making all his old offers over again . . . damned impudent dog'.[1] Coleridge would have nothing to do with him, but there is some indication that Wordsworth and Sheridan did correspond, for in a letter to Josiah Wedgwood in November Coleridge says: 'Sheridan has sent to *him* [meaning Wordsworth] too, requesting him to write a tragedy for Drury Lane. But W. will not be diverted by anything from the prosecution of his great work.' By 'his great work' Coleridge meant *The Recluse* which was now in abeyance but which Coleridge was always hoping he would resume. In any case Wordsworth could not contemplate writing another play.

But he failed to go on with *The Recluse*, either in the spring or after the publication of *Lyrical Ballads*. Coleridge's visit in

[1] *Letters from the Lake Poets to Daniel Stuart.* S.T.C. to Stuart, July 11th 1800. *U.L.* i. 72, p. 147. S.T.C. to Poole, July 24th 1800.

April may have had the undesired effect of interrupting his labours: it is even possible that Coleridge may have expressed some disappointment with what had been already written. He had no doubt been hoping for something more of a 'philosophic song'; something less purely descriptive of Grasmere and of Wordsworth's own feelings. Whatever the cause, Wordsworth never wrote any more of *The Recluse* proper. Its place was taken first by *The Prelude* and then by *The Excursion*, both of which were considered to be closely related to or even integral parts of it. In later years Dorothy and Mary often urged him to return to his task, but in vain.[1]

Instead his attention this summer was turned to the welcome and unexpected success of the *Lyrical Ballads*, and to the preparation of a second edition, with an additional volume, containing all the short poems written in Germany and since his return. The *Lyrical Ballads*, in spite of Wordsworth's apprehension, were all sold by the beginning of June 1800. Perhaps their ultimate success was in part due to an excellent review which appeared in October 1799 in the *British Critic*, and which was probably written by Wordsworth's old friend of his London days, Francis Wrangham. He, however, knew nothing of Wordsworth's authorship and confidently ascribed the whole volume to Coleridge. This was the only review which came near to appreciating and reciprocating the purpose of Wordsworth and Coleridge in the *Lyrical Ballads*, although most critics had given the volume a tolerably kind welcome. 'It is not by pomp of words', said this reviewer, 'but by energy of thought, that the sublime is most successfully achieved; and we infinitely prefer the simplicity even of the most unadorned tale in this volume to all the meretricious frippery of the Darwinian taste.' Although neither here nor in any review was the full significance of the achievement understood, and although here as elsewhere *The Ancient Mariner* was still a stumbling-block, nevertheless the Wordsworths had modest cause for satisfaction. The way was now clear for a second edition. On June 8th William informed Richard that 'another edition is called for by the Booksellers', and that Longman had offered

---

[1] *P.W.* v, p. 367, where many of the later references to *The Recluse* by Dorothy, Mary, and others are collected, showing how anxiously those who knew him best longed for him to take it up again.

him £80 'for the right of printing two editions of 750 each
of this vol. of poems and . . . one of 1000 another of 750 of
another volume of the same size'. Cottle, when he gave up
publishing in the autumn of 1799, had disposed of all his copy-
rights to Longman. That of the *Lyrical Ballads*, however, had
been valued by Longman at 'nothing', whereupon Cottle asked
for it back and made a present of it to Wordsworth, who was
thus in 1800 the owner of it. The Bristol connexion was, however, still kept up, as the new edition was printed there by the
firm of Biggs & Cottle. No doubt it was the final success of the
Ballads which caused Longman to change his mind.[1]

Thus the new edition was written in Westmorland, printed in
Bristol, and published in London. Coleridge showed an unexpected practicality in all the details connected with its production.
While he was in Bristol, in June 1800, he had become intimate
with young Humphry Davy, the famous chemist, who was
working with Dr. Beddoes at the Pneumatic Institution for
treating patients with gases. Coleridge gave Davy many of the
manuscripts of Wordsworth's most recent poems, and either
then, or soon after his arrival at Grasmere, prevailed on
Davy to see the new edition through the press at that end. On
July 28th the Wordsworths received a letter from Davy enclosed
in one from Coleridge, 'about the Lyrical Ballads', no doubt
undertaking this task, for on the same day Wordsworth wrote
to him enclosing some manuscript poems and asking him to
correct the punctuation, 'a business at which I am ashamed to
say I am no adept', and 'to look over the proof-sheets of the
2nd volume before they are finally struck off'. He added that
he would send off poems 'every post-day, viz. three times a week,
till the whole is completed', and asked Davy to arrange for
printing to start at once.[2] The promise to send poems 'every
post-day' was not kept, and Wordsworth told Wrangham when
the poems were finally published in January 1801 that he had
been 'three months behind hand in fulfilling my engagement
with Longman'.[3] The reasons for this delay will be seen presently. It was decided to abandon anonymity and to publish the

---

[1] W. Hale White, *Wordsworth and Coleridge MSS. in the possession of T. N.
Longman.*
[2] *E.L.* 109, p. 244. W.W. to Humphry Davy, July 28th 1800.
[3] Ibid. 117, p. 263. W.W. to Francis Wrangham, Feb. 1801.

new edition with the title, *Lyrical Ballads, by W. Wordsworth*. Coleridge's name was omitted from the title-page, though all his poems in the first volume still stood there, with one new one, *Love*, added. Almost certainly, Coleridge was mainly responsible for this curious arrangement. Wordsworth in the previous December had said to Coleridge—'Take no pains to contradict the story that the Lyrical Ballads are entirely yours. Such a rumour is the best thing that can befall them.'[1] This was no doubt being said because of the review in the *British Critic*. But Coleridge's modesty about his own poetry amounted almost to a disease. It was Wordsworth who was 'the greatest poet since Milton', and he must become known. Coleridge still regretted that so many short poems were holding up the progress of *The Recluse*; nevertheless, Wordsworth's name must no longer be concealed. 'I am especially pleased', he wrote to Longman on December 15th 1800, 'that I have contributed nothing to the second volume, as I can now exert myself loudly and everywhere in their favour without suspicion of vanity or self-interest.' And to Wrangham a few days later he wrote: 'Wordsworth is a great, a true Poet—I am only a kind of a Meta-physician.'[2] All that he would allow was the insertion of a short paragraph in the preface to the effect that *The Ancient Mariner* and the other poems of which he was the author were written by 'a friend'.

Indeed, Coleridge could not have worked harder for the *Lyrical Ballads* if they had been his own 'great work' instead of a small work by his friend. The manuscripts of the poems and the letters about their publication which have survived show how much of the labour of correspondence and preparation he undertook. Some of the poems and all the directions to the printer, the contents table and corrections to the first volume, and even Wordsworth's letter to the printer of December 23rd are in his hand.[3]

It is possible that Coleridge's activity was in part due to the fact that at this time his own health was tolerably good while Wordsworth was constantly suffering from fatigue and attacks

---

[1] *E.L.* 105, p. 242. W.W. to S.T.C., Dec. 24th 1799.
[2] *U.L.* i. 79, p. 164, and 80, p. 165.
[3] W. Hale White, op. cit., passim. Most of the copying of the poems was done by Dorothy; towards the end Sara Hutchinson assisted her.

of pain. In July Wordsworth himself told Josiah Wedgwood that 'ill health has for some time rendered literary labour inadviseable for me', while Coleridge wrote to Stuart on July 11th that 'Wordsworth's state of health at this present time is such as to preclude all possibility of writing for a paper'. Early in October Coleridge became even more anxious. 'Wordsworth's health declines constantly', he wrote on October 2nd, and on the 7th 'The illness of my dear friend Wordsworth called me peremptorily to Grasmere.'[1] There is, curiously, no mention in Dorothy's Journal of Wordsworth being ill before Coleridge came over on the 4th. He stayed till the 7th: on the 5th Dorothy reports indeed that 'William went to bed, very ill after working after dinner'. In the following spring of 1801—a period not covered by Dorothy's Journal—we find brother John writing: 'I do not know what to think or say about William's health—I only hope he will have good spirits and bear up under the pain he may suffer as much as possible.' John thought that his brother's health might be affected by anxiety about finance. Montagu had indeed resumed payment of the annuity and the arrears owing since he stopped payment in 1797, but his instalments came rather irregularly and not always with the full amount. 'I hope', wrote John, 'William suffers nothing from lowness of spirits in consequence of *Montagu*.' And he added: 'I am placed in such a situation that I can always have it in my power to assist him, but the longer I keep back the better it will be for us all.' By this John meant that he was anxious to save as much money as possible for investment in his voyages, from which eventually he hoped to secure the independence and prosperity of himself and his brother and sister.[2]

Up till the first week in October 1800 it was the intention of the three to include Coleridge's *Christabel* in the new volume. He brought over the newly-written second part of it to Grasmere on October 4th and read it to William and Dorothy, who were 'exceedingly delighted' with it. William's admiration was, however, tempered, at least afterwards, with some criticisms and regrets. In the first place, he did not believe the story was meant to have an end, and therefore came in time to prefer it

---

[1] *Letters of the Lake Poets to Daniel Stuart*. S.T.C. to Stuart, July 11th and Oct. 2nd and 7th 1800.

[2] *D.C.P.* J.W. to D.W., Apr. 7th 1801. See above, p. 471.

without the second part—'inasmuch as the second part creates an expectation [of an end], and the daylight—at least so abrupt and so short a notice of them in that state—divests the persons of much of their charm'. 'If', he said, Milton 'had only just brought Satan out of hell to this earth and there left him, he had much better have kept him in hell, where he showed to so much more advantage.' Coleridge did not allow enough time in *Christabel* for the change in atmosphere between the first and second parts to become familiar.[1] The soundness of Wordsworth's criticism here will be felt by most people.

After two days of discussion and deliberation they came to a unanimous decision 'not to print Christabel with the L.B.'[2] It was a sensible decision. The poem was, for one thing, very long: Wordsworth, says Coleridge, 'thought it indelicate to print two volumes with his name, in which so much of another man's was included'. Then it was not, even yet, completed. Besides, *Christabel*, like *The Ancient Mariner*, was 'in direct opposition to the very purpose for which the *Lyrical Ballads* were published';[3] the experimental purpose, that is, of showing 'incidents of common life' in the light of 'primary passions'. For Wordsworth was as insistent as ever on this aspect of things. Life at Grasmere, among the shepherds and states-men, had increased and confirmed his belief in ordinary experi-ence as the all-sufficient material for conveying poetic feeling and poetic truth. *Michael*, which he began on October 12th, is his chief testimony to that conviction. *Christabel*, in the mean time, was to be published separately along with *The Pedlar* (that was the title by which the Wordsworths now spoke of *The Ruined Cottage*); a plan which was never carried out. 'I assure you', Coleridge told Davy, 'I think very differently of *Christabel*. I would rather have written *Ruth* and *Nature's Lady*,[4] than a million such poems. But why do I calumniate my own spirit by saying "I would rather"? God knows it is as delightful to me that they *are* written.'

Coleridge's enthusiasm for Wordsworth's poetry and appar-ent indifference to his own may partly account for his acquiescence

[1] *Life of Dr. Henry Alford*, 1873, p. 61. The conversation quoted took place in the year 1830.
[2] *D.W.J.* i, p. 64. Oct. 6th 1800.
[3] *S.T.C.* i, p. 337. S.T.C. to H. Davy, Oct. 9th 1800.
[4] Coleridge's name for *Three Years She grew*.

in the extraordinary fate which befell *The Ancient Mariner* in the new edition. Wordsworth's original plan of omitting it altogether was not pursued.[1] Instead it was removed from its original position at the beginning and placed at the end of the first volume; the archaic spellings were altered and a long note, written by Wordsworth, was attached. This note was never reprinted in any subsequent edition of the poems; perhaps Wordsworth was ashamed of it; perhaps Dorothy or Lamb pleaded for its abolition. The only excuse that can be made for it is that it was an attempt, though a very clumsy one, to meet what Wordsworth believed was the public's dislike of the poem by admitting that it had defects as well as merits. Coleridge, moreover, must have seen the note and given his full consent to its inclusion. Never did his worship of Wordsworth and his own self-abasement before him have more curious results. The note is in spirit very like the note to *The Thorn*, written at the same time. There he had called upon his readers to imagine the story to be narrated by a superstitious and talkative retired 'Captain of a small trading vessel'. In the note to *The Ancient Mariner* he regretted that the Mariner had no regular profession or place in society. Why he should have thought that the professionalizing of the Mariner would have made him more acceptable to the public is a mystery. But he had complained of the poem's 'strangeness'. Coleridge ought not to have made it so strange. That Wordsworth should have so utterly misunderstood the quality of his friend's genius can only be attributed to his own obsession with the 'incidents and situations of common life'. So far as is known Coleridge never complained of the note, nor so much as mentioned it in his correspondence.

After the decision on *Christabel*, it was hoped for some time that Coleridge would write some shorter pieces for the new volume. He promised some contributions towards the *Poems on the Naming of Places*.[2] But on October 17th Wordsworth returned from a short visit to Keswick and reported that 'Coleridge had done nothing for the L.B.', the excuse being that he was

---

[1] See above, p. 442.
[2] *E.L.* 112, pp. 255–6. W.W. to Biggs & Cottle, Oct. 10th 1800. This was the letter in which Wordsworth gave orders that 'such Pages of the Poem of Christabel as have been printed, (if any such there be), be cancelled'.

'working hard for Stuart', and had not had time.[1] On the 22nd Coleridge himself arrived to confirm these tidings. They were not perturbed. 'We were very merry,' says Dorothy. 'Wm. read after supper *Ruth* etc; Coleridge *Christabel.*'

On August 14th 1800 Coleridge had told Poole that 'the two volumes of the *Lyrical Ballads* will appear in about a fortnight or three weeks'. They did not appear until January 1801. The main cause for the long delay was the writing, first, of the preface, and, secondly, of *Michael.*

The preface, which was a much longer document than the advertisement of 1798, was, Wordsworth maintained to the end of his life, written 'solely to gratify Coleridge'. He had, himself, 'never felt inclined to write criticism', but, in view of the poems being 'materially different' from what was commonly admired, he consented to supply what he called 'a few words of introduction', which became an essay of some six thousand words. 'The Preface', he said years afterwards, 'was written at the request of Mr. Coleridge out of sheer good nature. I recollect the very spot, a deserted quarry in the vale of Grasmere, where he pressed the thing upon me and but for that it would never have been thought of.'[2] It is, however, difficult to believe that he 'never cared a straw about the theory', for however disinclined he may have been to begin it, he certainly became deeply interested in it as he wrote it. 'He talked much', said Dorothy on October 3rd, 'about the object of his essay for the second volume of L.B.' It was completed before September 30th, for on that day Dorothy 'wrote the last sheet of Notes and Preface'.

Coleridge afterwards said that 'it was at first intended that the preface should be written by me'.[3] Had he undertaken it it is unlikely it would ever have been finished. As it was, he remained its chief instigator, but, though every sentence was discussed between them, it was emphatically Wordsworth's composition, and contained some opinions which Coleridge did not share. 'Although Wordsworth's Preface', said Coleridge in 1802, 'is half a child of my own brain, and arose out of conversations so frequent that, with few exceptions, we could scarcely either

[1] *D.W.J.* i, p. 67.
[2] *L.Y.* ii. 1244, p. 910. W.W. to W. R. Hamilton, Jan. 4th 1838. Ibid. 1565, p. 1248. W.W. to E. Moxon, Apr. 10th 1845; Barron Field, MS., i, p. 111.
[3] *S.T.C.* i, p. 373. S.T.C. to W. Sotheby, July 18th 1802.

of us, perhaps, positively say which first started any particular thought . . . yet I am far from going all lengths with Wordsworth.'[1] Many years later he wrote a reasoned critique of Wordsworth's style in poetry and of his ideas.[2] But even now he was conscious of certain disagreements which by 1802 made him 'suspect that somewhere or other there is a radical difference in our theoretical opinions respecting poetry'. He could never quite approve of the 'daring humbleness of language and versification', and the 'strict adherence to matter of fact, even to prolixity', of some of the ballads. The preface itself was, he felt, (and here most modern readers will agree with him) 'in parts obscure beyond any necessity, and the extreme elaboration and almost constrainedness of the diction contrasted (to my feelings) somewhat harshly with the general style of the Poems to which the Preface is an introduction'.[3]

In the preface Wordsworth for the first time attempted to give his own definition of the nature of poetry, its origin, and purpose. As we should expect, he traced its true source in the feelings. 'All good poetry', he said, 'is the spontaneous overflow of powerful feelings'—feelings, however, which had been 'modified and directed by our thoughts, which are indeed the representations of all our past feelings'. According to this definition the poet was simply a man who, 'possessed of more than usual organic sensibility, had also thought long and deeply'. If this is not a description of universal application, it certainly defines very clearly the kind of poet Wordsworth himself was. But to this description he added a yet more interesting piece of self-investigation.

Poetry [he said] takes its origins from emotion recollected in tranquillity: the emotion is contemplated till, by a species of re-action, the tranquillity gradually disappears, and an emotion, kindred to that which was before the subject of contemplation, is gradually produced, and does itself actually exist in the mind. In this mood successful composition generally begins . . . but the emotion, of whatever kind from various causes is qualified by various pleasures, so that in describing any passions whatsoever . . . the mind will, upon the whole, be in a state of enjoyment.

The biographical interest of this passage is obvious. This is

---

[1] Ibid., p. 386. S.T.C. to Southey, July 29th 1802.   [2] B.L., chs. xiv and xvii.
[3] S.T.C. i, p. 387. S.T.C. to Southey, July 29th 1802.

how *The Prelude* was written; the first two books of it recording the 'emotions' of his boyhood were already in existence. The writing of them must have caused Wordsworth to meditate on his own mental processes; for so exact and scientific a description must have been the outcome of long meditation on experience. What he describes in the preface is, in part, the contemplative state which can exist without 'overflowing' into poetry. His own 'Poor Susan' relived in a moment of intense feeling the scenes of her childhood with a physical vividness and so entered into a contemplative vision; but it was only a momentary, a passing ecstasy; it left a blank sensation of homesickness when the vision was over. Wordsworth's imagination could carry the process on into the creative sphere. We should note the phrase, 'the tranquillity gradually disappears'. Wordsworth, in common with other poets, composed in a state of intense excitement. We have heard him describe to Coleridge the uncontrollable gestures and exclamations which accompanied composition. Dorothy, watching him once in such a moment, wrote in her Journal: 'William kindled, and began to write the poem'.[1] It was no doubt partly on account of this intense excitement that he generally composed out of doors, and in motion, walking up and down between two fixed points. But with the excitement came the joy of creation. If composition was often 'wearisome' and difficult, the ultimate achievement was a joyous experience, which no sadness of the thing contemplated could destroy.

This meticulous description of the creative process was something which had never before been attempted in English literature. It remains Wordsworth's contribution to the psychology of poetry, of great practical value not only to poets, but to all who would use and understand their faculties of imagination, recollection, and contemplation.

The rest of the essay was concerned with more controversial matters, particularly with the question of the 'language' of poetry and prose. Wordsworth's declaration that there was no essential difference between the language of poetry and prose,

---

[1] *D.W.J.* i, p. 125, Mar. 17th 1802. The poem was *The Emigrant Mother*, partly written on the previous day and finished by moonlight in the orchard at Town End. In Sept. 1800, at the very time *Lyrical Ballads* was going to press, she wrote to Jane Marshall: 'He writes with so much feeling and agitation that it brings on a sense of pain and internal weakness about his left side and stomach.' *E.L.* 110, p. 251.

save in the use of metre and rhyme, was his apology for what
he had tried to show in the *Lyrical Ballads*. He was still at
war with the personificators, and all their stock-in-trade of
'poetic diction'. Here Coleridge whole-heartedly agreed with
him; but he never accepted Wordsworth's contention that the
language of 'low and rustic life' was best suited to poetic
writing, because it was the language of men who 'hourly
communicate with the best objects from which the best part of
language is originally derived'; and who from their social
circumstances 'convey their feelings and notions in simple and
unelaborated expressions'. What did he mean, asked Coleridge
afterwards, by 'the best objects'? Was he speaking of natural
objects, or of such an influence, for instance, as the Bible, which
was well known to the dalesmen? Good speech is the result of
'good sense and natural feeling' rather than of 'the best objects'.
And here Wordsworth was not very consistent, for he admitted
that even rustic speech needed to be 'purified . . . from all lasting
and rational causes of dislike and disgust'. Here he may be
referring to dialect, which he never used in his poetry, although
he loved northern speech and himself pronounced words with a
'Cumberland burr'. Dialect, however, would have tended to
make his poetry obscure. He had complained of the 'old words'
making *The Ancient Mariner* difficult. But, although Wordsworth may not have been entirely happy in his choice of
expressions to convey the importance of the change he was
trying to make in 'poetic diction', it is impossible to quarrel
with his insistence that poetry must concern itself with reality,
and that its language must therefore be 'a selection of language
really used by men'. Here he was, as he himself insisted, following the example of Shakespeare and Chaucer whose language
was 'pure and universally intelligible even to this day'. Poetry
must not be separated from 'the sympathies of men' either by
'triviality and meanness' or by 'false refinement'.

There is more in the preface than a criticism of bad poetry.
In it we see Wordsworth the man of action, the social reformer,
and critic of the bad customs of his day. In his poems, he tells us,
'it is the feeling which gives importance to the action and
situation, and not the action and situation to the feeling'.
Ordinary incidents, 'great and simple affections', are his subject-
matter. And this was something of general and not merely

literary importance. Wordsworth was the first poet to see the dangers which were threatening the mind and spirit of man in his generation. His prophetic warning, solemnly uttered, is no whit less appropriate in our own.

The human mind [he says] is capable of being excited without the application of gross and violent stimulants. . . . A multitude of causes, unknown to former times, are now acting with a combined force to blunt the discriminating powers of the mind, and, unfitting it for all voluntary exertion, to reduce it to a state of almost savage torpor. The most effective of these causes are the great national events which are daily taking place, and the increasing accumulation of men in cities, where the uniformity of their occupations produces a craving for extraordinary incident, which the rapid communication of intelligence hourly gratifies.

War and industrialization, said Wordsworth, were blunting the spirit of man. What further can we say a hundred and fifty years after, save that where Wordsworth lamented the 'frantic novels, sickly and stupid German tragedies, and deluges of idle and extravagant stories in verse', which were driving out the study of the great poets, we can point to even more meretricious forms of pseudo-culture? Wordsworth in this catastrophe placed his hopes in 'certain indestructible qualities of the human mind', and in his belief that 'men of greater powers' would 'systematically oppose' these evils more effectively than he could do by the 'feeble endeavour' of the *Lyrical Ballads.* No doubt he was here indicating Coleridge and his 'great work', constantly talked about and as constantly postponed. It was not destined that English taste should be purified by any 'system' of philosophical criticism, nor even by a new 'Divine Comedy' called *The Recluse.* After all it was the 'feeble endeavour' of the *Lyrical Ballads,* and their successor the *Poems* of 1807, and *The Excursion* and the 'poem to Coleridge' finally called *The Prelude,* which kept the springs of English poetry fresh and sweet and became the nourishment of many hungry hearts.

Into *Michael,* begun on October 12th and not finished until December 9th 1800, went all his faith in the shepherd-statesmen of the fells whom from boyhood he had loved,

> not verily
> For their own sakes but for the fields and hills
> Where was their occupation and abode.

Coleridge, replying to Davy's remark that the poem was 'full of
just pictures of what human life ought to be', said: 'Believe me,
that such scenes and such characters really exist in this country'.[1]
Wordsworth, writing to Poole, described his own purpose as
being 'to give a picture of a man, of strong mind and lively
sensibility, agitated by two of the most powerful affections of
the human heart; the parental affection, and the love of property,
landed property including the feelings of inheritance, home, and
personal and family dependence'. He also said that 'in writing
it I had your character often before my eyes, and sometimes
thought I was delineating such a man as you yourself would
have been under the same circumstances'.[2] The story of *Michael* is
a fusion of two local traditions. 'The character and circumstances'
of Luke, Michael's son who leaves home and takes to bad courses,
were, he tells us, 'taken from a family to whom had belonged,
many years before, the house we lived in at Town-End, along
with some fields and woodlands on the eastern shore of Grasmere'. Michael himself was drawn from an old shepherd who
had been 'seven years in building up a sheepfold in a solitary
valley'. In the introductory lines of the poem Wordsworth
hints that such a story had been known to him in boyhood and

> led me on to feel
> For passions that were not my own, and think . . .
> On man, the heart of man, and human life.

And he adds:

> Therefore, although it be a history
> Homely and rude, I will relate the same
> For the delight of a few natural hearts;
> And, with yet fonder feeling, for the sake
> Of youthful Poets, who among the hills
> Will be my second self when I am gone.

Wordsworth may have disliked the toil of publishing, but there
is no doubt that he now and always prayed, 'Fit audience let me
find, though few'.

The sheepfold of the poem was near at hand,

> Up the tumultuous brook of Greenhead Ghyll—

---

[1] *U.L.* i. 82, p. 169. S.T.C. to H. Davy, Jan. 11th 1801.
[2] *E.L.* 119, p. 266. W.W. to T. Poole, Apr. 9th 1801.

that deep cleft in the 'forest-side of Grasmere Vale' a little north-east of the village. Hither, on October 11th 1800, came William and Dorothy 'in search of a sheepfold'. The theme of the poem had evidently already been decided upon.

It was a delightful day [says Dorothy], and the views looked exceedingly cheerful and beautiful, chiefly that from Mr. Oliff's field, where our house is to be built. The colours of the mountains soft and rich, with orange fern; the cattle pasturing upon the hill-tops; kites sailing in the sky above our heads; sheep bleating and in lines and chains and patterns scattered over the mountains. . . . The sheepfold is falling away. It is built nearly in the form of a heart unequally divided. Look down the brook, and see the drops rise upwards and sparkle in the air in little falls, the higher sparkles the tallest. We walked along the turf of the mountain till we came to a cattle track made by the cattle which come upon the hills. We drank tea at Mr. Simpson's, returned at about nine—a fine mild night.

William began writing the poem on the next day. They called it at this stage 'The Sheepfold', and many are the entries in Dorothy's Journal in the next two months of its toilsome advance:[1] 'William worked all the morning at the sheepfold, but in vain. . . .' 'William had been unsuccessful in the morning at the sheepfold. . . .' 'Wm. could not compose much, fatigued himself with altering.' Several times he was 'very sick and very ill', or 'not well', and the poem could not proceed at all. There were interruptions too. Thomas Clarkson called and stayed a night on October 29th. At the same time John Stoddart, Coleridge's journalist friend, came and 'talked all day' with William; on November 15th William, hearing that Coleridge was ill, went to Keswick and stayed a week. Dorothy walked over to join him there on the 17th, and Sara Hutchinson, who arrived at Keswick during Wordsworth's visit, returned with him and Dorothy to Grasmere for a long stay. She helped Dorothy in getting the poems copied for Longman. The Keswick visit seems to have done Wordsworth good, for by November 26th he was 'very well and highly poetical', and on December 9th the poem was finished.[2]

Various note-books testify to the labour bestowed on *Michael*. Many passages exist which were not finally included in the

---

[1] *D.W.J.* i, pp. 66–71. Oct. 11th, 21st, 31st, Nov. 7th *et al.*
[2] Ibid., i, pp. 73–76. Nov. 15th, 17th, 26th, Dec. 9th 1800.

poem; others are to be found in the eighth book of *The Prelude*.[1] Some of these take us deep into Wordsworth's thought about man and Nature, and man *in* Nature, and the subtle, inarticulate 'affinities' which bind man to his native earth, and make of his life a unity and a thing of grandeur and significance. So he ruminates on discovering during a mountain walk the ruins of a sheepfold:

> For me,
> When it has chanced that having wandered long
> Among the mountains, I have waked at last
> From dream of motion in some spot like this,
> Shut out from man, some region—one of those
> That hold by an inalienable right
> An independent Life, and seem the whole
> Of Nature and of unrecorded time;
> If looking round I have perchance perceived
> Some vestiges of human hands, some stir
> Of human passion, they to me are sweet
> As lighter sunbreak, or the sudden sound
> Of music to a blind man's ear who sits
> Alone and silent in the summer shade.
> They are as a creation in my heart;
> I look into past times as prophets look
> Into futurity. . . .

Another of these rejected passages, describing the old shepherd, gives us a glimpse into Wordsworth's own methods of conversing with the people of the fells and drawing from them utterances worthy of their surroundings:

> No doubt if you in terms direct had ask'd
> Whether he lov'd the mountains, true it is
> That with blunt repetition of your words
> He might have stared at you, and said that they
> Were frightful to behold, but had you then
> Discoursed with him in some particular sort
> Of his own business, and the goings on[2]
> Of earth and sky, then truly had you seen
> That in his thoughts these were obscurities,
> Wonders and admirations, things that wrought

---

[1] *P.W.* ii, pp. 479–84.

[2] 'Goings on'—a phrase beloved by both Wordsworth and Coleridge. See *Prel.* I (1805), l. 616 and VI (1805), l. 350. The phrase was omitted in the 1850 text.

Not less than a religion in his heart.
And if it were his fortune to converse
With any who could talk of common things
In an unusual way, and give to them
Unusual aspects, or by questions apt
Wake sudden recognitions that were like
Creations in the mind, and were indeed
Creations often, then, when he discoursed
Of mountain sights, this untaught shepherd stood
Before the man with whom he so convers'd
And look'd at him as with a Poet's eye.

The poem itself has always been one of the best loved of all
Wordsworth's writings, not only because of the pathos of the
story, but because of the profound yet extraordinarily simple
statements of thought and feeling, arising from the power of
Wordsworth's ethical discovery that suffering, when illuminated
by love, creates its own nobility of heart. So, when the tragedy
of his son's bad way of life bursts upon Michael:

There is a comfort in the strength of love;
'Twill make a thing endurable, which else
Would overset the brain, or break the heart. . . .
     Among the rocks
He went, and still looked up to sun and cloud
And listened to the wind . . .
And to that hollow dell from time to time
Did he repair, to build the Fold of which
His flock had need. 'Tis not forgotten yet
The pity which was then in every heart
For the old Man—and 'tis believed by all
That many and many a day he thither went
And never lifted up a single stone.

NOTE

A letter from Wordsworth to Longman dated December 18th 1800 h
recently come to light, showing that Wordsworth had, besides the Preface, near
completed an 'introductory Essay to prefix to the second volume'. He foun
however, that 'it required so many quotations to illustrate the argument' that
would have been too long. I am indebted to the Henry W. and Albert A. Be
Collection of the New York Public Library for permission to quote from th
hitherto unpublished letter.

XVI

FROM *LYRICAL BALLADS*, 1800, TO *THE LEECH-GATHERER*

January 1801 – July 1802

THE second edition of *Lyrical Ballads*, with the second volume containing all the new poems, was published about January 25th 1801, although the date on the title-page was 1800.[1] The volumes could be bought separately and the second sold much better than the first.[2] On the title-page appeared a somewhat mysterious motto:

> Quam nihil ad genium, Papiniane, tuum!

Wordsworth had taken it from Selden's foreword to Drayton's *Polyolbion*, printed in Anderson's *British Poets*, which John Wordsworth had with him at Grasmere and gave to his brother when he left. It is meant as a joke against Sir James Mackintosh, the distinguished lawyer, whom Coleridge did not much like. Papinianus was a Roman lawyer, and the motto has been freely translated:

> How absolutely *not* after your liking, O learned jurist![3]

John Wordsworth, who was waiting in London to be sworn in to the command of the *Earl of Abergavenny* in succession to his cousin the elder Captain Wordsworth, wrote to Mary Hutchinson on December 5th 1800, 'O those vile L.B.! Why do they not come out? I think it is a great pity that William should be losing so much time.'[4] The delay was now with the

---

[1] *D.C.P.* J.W. to M.H., Jan. 31st 1801. 'They have been out now about 5 days.'

[2] Ibid., J.W. to D.W., Feb. 21st 1801. 'Arch has had a great sale of the 2nd volume, though I was surprised to find he had sold but few, very few, of the 2nd edition' (i.e. vol. i).

[3] T. Hutchinson, *Lyrical Ballads 1798*, 1898, p. lix. W. Hale White, op. cit., p. 13. That the reference is to Mackintosh is certain from an entry in one of Coleridge's note-books. He has a nightmare and then, quoting the motto, comments: 'This [i.e. the nightmare] Mackintosh would prove to be nonsense with a Scotch smile.' *A.P.*, Mar. 4th 1805.

[4] *D.C.P.* J.W. to M.H., Dec. 5th 1800.

printers in Bristol, who, he thought, could have had the first volume in the hands of the booksellers before now. However, on January 30th in the new year he wrote joyfully to William: 'I cannot express how much everyone that I have seen appears to be delighted with some *one* of your poems, and more particularly *The Brothers.*' Even the publisher, Longman, of whom John did not entertain a very favourable opinion, 'could not help expressing how high Mr. Wordsworth's character stood in the poetical department, and showed by his looks that he expected to gain a great deal by the book'.[1] John thought Longman 'a Jew' for not giving William more than £80 for the poems: 'he will clear at least £400 or perhaps £500'.

John had been employed by William on a mission of some importance in connexion with *Lyrical Ballads*. At Coleridge's suggestion letters were written to several prominent men and women describing the purpose and character of the new poems. These letters John delivered to Longman who undertook to send them out with presentation copies to each person addressed. The list of recipients is a curious one. They were Mrs. Jordan, the actress ('who intended to sing stanzas of The Mad Mother in *Pizarro* if she acted Cora again') ;[2] Mrs. Barbauld, formerly Lucy Aikin, the poet ; the Duchess of Devonshire; Sir Bland Burgess, whose poem, *Richard Cœur de Lion*, Wordsworth evidently admired; William Wilberforce; and Charles James Fox. Coleridge dictated all the letters over Wordsworth's signature, except that to Fox. This was Wordsworth's alone. His letter to him, and Fox's reply, have fortunately been preserved, as has also Coleridge's letter to Wilberforce.[3]

Wordsworth's feeling for Fox is known to the world from the lines he wrote in 1806 'when the Dissolution of Mr. Fox was hourly expected'. In youth, Fox had appeared to him and his friends as the champion of liberty in evil days, because of his opposition to the war with France. Wordsworth's own views on the war had now undergone a considerable change since the invasion of Switzerland in 1798 and the elevation of Bonaparte soon afterwards to a virtual dictatorship based on military

[1] *D.C.P.* J.W. to W.W., Jan. 30th 1801.
[2] *U.L.* i. 79, p. 163. S.T.C. to T. N. Longman, Dec. 15th 1800.
[3] *E.L.* 116, p. 259. W.W. to C. J. Fox, Jan. 14th 1801. Coleridge's letter is in the British Museum. Griggs, *Collected Letters of S. T. Coleridge*, ii, p. 666 James Hutton, *Letters of Sir Bland Burgess*, p. 308.

force.[1] It is unlikely that, as late as 1801, he still held 'Foxite' views on the possibility of a peace. It was more Fox's personal reputation that drew his regard, as one who in his essential character thought and felt for his fellow-beings in a human-hearted way. The letter itself is a revelation of Wordsworth's own social faith. That he connected that faith so closely with Fox at this time is a point of some interest to those who would follow the development of his thought.[2] It may profitably be compared with his *Letter to the Bishop of Llandaff* written just nine years before. The revolutionary destructiveness is gone, but the glowing concern for human ills is still there, enriched by compassion and knowledge.

In common with the whole English People [he says] I have observed in your public character a constant predominance of sensibility of heart. Necessitated as you have been from your public situation to have much to do with men in bodies and in classes . . . it has been your praise that you have not thereby been prevented from looking upon them as individuals, and that you have habitually left your heart open to be influenced by them in that capacity. This habit cannot but have made you dear to Poets; and I am sure that, if since your first entrance into public life there has been a single true poet living in England, he must have loved you.

He next enumerated what he believed to be the chief social evils of his day, and the effect of these evils on the lives of poor people. Here we see Wordsworth as the enemy of industrial change, not because it was change, but because it was, he believed, destroying the best things in English life. This conviction, which he held with passionate intensity, is the foundation of his later political conservatism, which had less a party than a social cause.

'By the spreading of manufactures through every part of the country', he wrote, 'by the heavy taxes upon postage, by work-houses, Houses of Industry,[3] and the invention of Soup-shops etc.

---

[1] In 1821 Wordsworth told James Losh that his views on the war had changed about the time of the invasion of Switzerland. *L.Y.* i. 674, p. 57.

[2] The letter was first printed, without Wordsworth's permission, by Sir Henry Bunbury in the *Correspondence of Sir Thomas Hanmer, Bart.*, in 1838. Wordsworth's letter to Bunbury disapproving of its publication makes amusing reading. *L.Y.* ii. 1278, p. 957.

[3] Cf. *The Old Cumberland Beggar.*

      May never House, misnamed of Industry, &c.

superadded to the increasing disproportion between the price of labour and that of the necessities of life, the bonds of domestic feeling among the poor . . . have been weakened, and in innumerable instances destroyed.' He even described in detail the plight of two of his neighbours, an old couple[1] who would soon be unable to look after themselves. The woman

told my Servant two days ago that she was afraid they must both be boarded out among some other Poor of the parish . . . but she said, it was hard, having kept house together so long, to come to this, and she was sure it would 'burst her heart'. I mention this fact [said Wordsworth] to show how deeply the spirit of independence is, even yet, rooted in some parts of the country. These people could not express themselves in this way without an almost sublime conviction of the blessings of independent domestic life.

He then invited Fox to the perusal of *The Brothers* and *Michael*. 'You have felt that the most sacred of all property is the property of the Poor. The two Poems which I have mentioned were written with a view to shew that men who do not wear fine clothes can feel deeply.' He poured out once more all his feelings about the statesmen of the dales. 'Their little tract of land serves . . . as a tablet upon which [the domestic feelings] are written. . . . It is a fountain fitted to the nature of social man from which supplies of affection, as pure as his heart was intended for, are daily drawn.'

Fox's reply was long in coming. 'I suppose', said John Wordsworth in February, 'he is thinking and most likely interesting himself in the Ministerial changes.' For this was the time of Pitt's resignation and the formation of Addington's Ministry. At length, however, in May, he wrote a kind reply which showed that he had really read the poems; it must, however, have been disappointing to Wordsworth as far as it concerned *Michael*.

The poems [said Fox] have given me the greatest pleasure; and if I were obliged to choose out of them, I do not know whether I should not say that 'Harry Gill', 'We are Seven', 'The Mad Mother', and 'The Idiot', are my favourites. I read with particular attention the two you pointed out; but whether it be from early prepossessions,

---

[1] The couple have not been identified. They may have lived in one of the four cottages just above Sykeside.

or whatever other cause, I am no great friend to blank verse for sub-jects which are to be treated of with simplicity. You will excuse my stating my opinion to you so freely, which I should not do if I did not really admire many of the poems in the collection, and many parts even of those in blank verse. . . . 'The Nightingale' I understand to be Mr. Coleridge's, who combats, I think, very successfully, the mistaken prejudice of the nightingale's note being melancholy.[1]

Fox was the only one of those written to who sent more than a formal reply. The others were 'all respectful and polite, but all written immediately on the receipt of the Poems, and con-sequently expressing no opinion'.[2]

The opinions of their friends and of the public about the *Lyrical Ballads* caused much amusement at Dove Cottage. The poems usually aroused either strong admiration or distaste, and people differed widely in their preferences. Sometime in the early spring of 1801 Wordsworth sent what he called some 'harmonies of criticism' in tabulated form to Coleridge at Keswick.[3]

Nutting	*Nutting*
Mr. C. Wordsworth	Mr. Stoddart[4]
worth its weight in gold.	can make neither head nor tail of it.
Poet's Epitaph	*Poet's Epitaph*
Mr. Charles Lamb	Mr. Stoddart
the latter part eminently good and your own.	The latter part I don't like, it is very ill written.
Idiot Boy	*Idiot Boy*
Mr. John Wordsworth	Mr. Stoddart
(A Lady, a friend of mine:) Could talk of nothing else.	Thrown into a *fit* almost with disgust, cannot *possibly* read it.

[1] *Mem.* i, p. 17.
[2] *U.L.* i. 84, p. 173. S.T.C. to T. Poole, Feb. 13th 1801.
[3] *E.L.* 121*a*, p. 276.
[4] See above, p. 498. Stoddart wrote a very favourable review of the poems in the *British Critic* for Feb. 1801. This was probably because of his admiration for Coleridge. John Wordsworth thought the review 'too indiscriminately flattering'. It has been thought to have been by Wrangham, but John's letter proves it to be by Stoddart. *D.C.P.* J.W. to M.H., Feb. 25th 1801. Stoddart's remarks were probably made orally during his visit to Grasmere.

Wordsworth himself believed that *Joanna* and *Nutting* 'show the greatest genius of any poems in the second volume',[1] though he directed people to *Michael* as that which contained his most important 'views'.

Fortunately for posterity, Lamb's first letter to Wordsworth about the *Lyrical Ballads* has survived together with another to a friend about the result of his criticisms on the poet. Lamb disappointed Wordsworth—one hesitates to say 'offended'—by saying nothing about *Michael*. He spoke warmly of the 'Song of Lucy' and *The Old Cumberland Beggar*, though that was, he said, 'too like a lecture'; he broke a lance for Coleridge by protesting against Wordsworth's apologetic note on *The Ancient Mariner*; and finally said in general of the new poems; 'I do not feel any one poem in it so forcibly as the Ancient Marinere, the Mad Mother and the Lines at Tintern Abbey in the first.' This letter was written on January 30th 1801. Wordsworth replied to it; his reply has not been preserved, but on February 15th Lamb wrote to Manning one of his classically amusing letters, which more than supplies the loss of Wordsworth's own.

I had need [he says] be cautious henceforward what opinion I give of the 'Lyrical Ballads'. All the North of England are in a turmoil. Cumberland and Westmorland have already declared a state of war. I lately received from Wordsworth a copy of the second volume . . . with excuses for not having made any acknowledgment (of my play) sooner, it being owing to an 'almost insurmountable aversion to letter-writting'. This letter I answered in due form and time . . . adding unfortunately that no single piece had moved me so forcibly as the *Ancient Mariner, The Mad Mother*, or the *Lines at Tintern Abbey*. The Post did not sleep a moment. I received almost instantaneously a long letter of four sweating pages from my Reluctant Letter-Writer, the purport of which was, that he was sorry the 2nd vol. had not given me more pleasure (Devil a hint did I give that it had *not pleased me*), and 'was compelled to wish that my range of sensibility was more extended, being obliged to believe that I should receive large influxes of happiness and happy Thoughts' (I suppose from the L.B.)—With a deal of stuff about a certain Union of Tenderness and Imagination, which in the sense he used Imagination was not the characteristic of Shakspeare, but which Milton possessed in a degree far exceeding other Poets: which Union, as the highest species of poetry, and chiefly deserving that name, 'He was most proud to aspire

---

[1] *D.C.P.* J.W. to M.H., Feb. 25th 1801.

to'; then illustrating the said Union by two quotations from his own 2d vol. (which I had been so unfortunate as to miss). . . . After one has been reading Shakspeare twenty of the best years of one's life, to have a fellow start up, and prate about some unknown quality, which Shakspeare possessed in a degree inferior to Milton *and somebody else*!! This was not to be *all* my castigation. Coleridge . . . starts from his bed of sickness to reprove me for my hardy presumption: four long pages, equally sweaty and more tedious, came from him. . . . What am I to do with such people? I certainly shall write them a very merry Letter.[1]

The 'merry Letter', if it ever was written, has not survived— withered perhaps in the wrath of the outraged poets. But nobody could quarrel long with Lamb.

After his favourable report from London in January, John was obliged to confess a month later that: 'even I scarce hear [the poems] mentioned, except I *lug* them in myself'.[2] 'Most of William's poetry', he truly remarked, 'improves upon 2nd 3rd or 4th reading—now people in general are not sufficiently interested with the first reading to induce them to try a second.' A typical opinion, said John, was that of one of his acquaintances, who 'read the [Old Cumberland] Beggar—"Why", says he, "this is very pretty, but you may call it anything but poetry."'[3] There was evidently much need for Wordsworth's preface to explode the popular fallacies with regard to 'poetic diction'.

He received a few letters of unsolicited interest and approval. Among them was one from Lewis, the author of *The Monk* and *The Castle Spectre*, who also sent a poem, which, said John, 'is the most funny I have ever read: it is quite a caricature of its kind: they ought to have made a parson of him instead of a M.P.' (Lewis was at this time member for a Wiltshire constituency). John added: ' "The Convict" of William's is nothing compared to Lewis's.' From this remark it appears that by now *The Convict* was regarded as something of a joke by the family.[4]

Another letter was from a Miss Taylor, who perhaps had some inklings of the influence of environment on the formation of personality, and asked for some account of Wordsworth's life in so far as it had tended to form his 'present opinions'.[5] The

---

[1] *Lamb*, i, pp. 245–7.
[2] D.C.P. J.W. to M.H., Feb. 25th 1801.
[3] D.C.P. J.W. to M.H., March 9th 1801.
[4] D.C.P. J.W. to M.H. and D.W., Mar. 9th and 10th 1801.
[5] *E.L.* 120, p. 268. W.W. to Miss Taylor, April 9th 1801.

author of *The Prelude*, however, refused to be drawn. He gave
her a very bare outline of his education and added 'my opinions
have grown slowly, and I may say, insensibly'. Had he, she
asked, always 'thought so independently'? He replied by
referring her to his early poems, *An Evening Walk* and *Descriptive Sketches*, which would show her 'how very widely different
my former opinions must have been from those which I hold at
present'. He thought these poems must be still lying somewhere
in Johnson's warehouse, 'for I have reason to believe that they
never sold much'. She complimented him on the simplicity of
his style. This drew from Wordsworth a strong criticism of one
of his own poems, *The Female Vagrant*, the earliest poem in the
book, in which, he said, he was now conscious that he had not
adhered to his own rule of 'looking steadily at his subject'. 'The
diction of that Poem is often vicious, and the descriptions are
often false, giving proofs of a mind inattentive to the true nature
of the subject on which it was employed.' And he appended a
number of corrections to the text. All these were embodied in
the next edition of the *Lyrical Ballads*, which appeared in 1802.
In them can be traced the first signs of that softening process
which eventually transformed *Salisbury Plain* into *Guilt and
Sorrow*. Above all, the stanza in which he had described British
soldiers as a brood

That lap (their very nourishment) their brothers' blood,

was entirely omitted. The days were approaching when he would
entertain very different ideas of the army.

The alterations to *The Female Vagrant* were also sent about
this time to brother John in London, and with them some 'corrections' to 'the poem to Coleridge'. What these 'corrections'
were it is not possible exactly to know, but a little earlier Sara
Hutchinson had copied and sent to John 'two whole sheets' of
unpublished poetry. 'I shall keep them for ever for her sake',
said the faithful John.[1] What was this poetry? The year 1801
was not a productive year for Wordsworth. He was often
unwell, to such an extent that he seems even to have doubted
whether it would be possible for him to go on writing at all.[2]

[1] D.C.P. J.W. to M.H., Apr. 11th 1801.
[2] 'I am sorry to find that Wm ... finds himself unable to go on with any work.'
Ibid.

Except for the lyric *I travelled among unknown men*, which was sent to Mary in April, we know of no new poetry written since John's departure which he had not already seen in *Lyrical Ballads*—except some fragments rejected from *Michael*. What Sara sent therefore must have been some earlier material, most probably part of the 'poem to Coleridge' which he had not yet seen. This would explain the arrival of the 'corrections' a few days later from Dorothy. Dorothy, describing William's poor health at this very time, said 'he is always very ill when he tries to alter an old poem, but new composition does not hurt him so much',[1] implying that he had recently been engaged in alterations.

William was often unwell, but Coleridge's health was giving them all the greatest possible concern. On December 20th 1800 he had walked to the cottage, only to be stricken with a violent attack of rheumatic fever, the result of getting wet through on the walk. It was the culmination of months of minor ill health, and although after about a fortnight he returned to Keswick, he did not recover quickly and was unable to complete the book on Germany which he was writing for Longman. During the spring and early summer it became obvious that he would never be well if he stayed in the damp climate of the Lakes. In April William and Dorothy went to Keswick for a week—'a melancholy visit', said William. Their anxiety about him was intense. 'We both trembled, and till we entered the door we hardly durst speak', said Dorothy in describing their arrival.[2] It was not only Coleridge's physical condition that distressed them, but the even more harrowing sight of his now permanent unhappiness in marriage. There was scarcely a pretence of affection now on the part of Sara Coleridge, who spent all her time nursing her children. 'Her radical fault', wrote Dorothy, 'is want of sensibility, and what can such a woman be to Coleridge?' Coleridge, with little Hartley, paid another visit to the cottage early in May, and Hartley stayed behind for some weeks attending the Grasmere village school. By July plans were forming to get Coleridge out to St. Michael's in the Azores for the winter— a suggestion made by John Wordsworth who knew the islands well. The difficulty of course was money. Coleridge for nine months had been too ill to work: he was in debt to tradespeople,

[1] *E.L.* 121, p. 274. D.W. to M.H., Apr. 27th 1801.   [2] Ibid., p. 272.

to various friends including Poole, and to Longman, who had advanced him £30 on the security of his promised book about Germany. This debt Wordsworth insisted upon taking upon himself for the present,[1] because, he said, Coleridge 'had put himself to great expense in order to come and settle in this country on my account'. It was a generous act, for Wordsworth could ill afford to lend money. In July Wordsworth and Coleridge agreed each to write to Poole about the situation. Wordsworth refused to let Coleridge tell him beforehand what he meant to say, 'so that', said Coleridge, 'he might write with his opinions unmodified by mine'. Coleridge's letter[2] ended in an elaborate and rather disingenuous refusal to apply to Poole for the necessary money for his journey, at least unless 'the booksellers' completely failed him. Wordsworth, more realistically, asked Poole straight out whether he could lend Coleridge £50. The plan of raising money from the booksellers on the security of yet unwritten books he entirely disapproved, 'as I am sure it would entangle him in an engagement which it is ten to one he would be unable to fulfil'. Poole had at this time many claims on his help, for it was a time of great distress among the poor, and he was the prop and comforter of his country-side. He replied, unfortunately, to Coleridge, not to Wordsworth, offering to lend him £20, and advising him to raise the rest from other friends. This Coleridge regarded as a refusal. It at once aroused his resentment and the letter he wrote to Poole shows how difficult a thing it was sometimes for his friends to bear with him. He said that he had not wished Wordsworth to write—'I have such an utter dislike to all indirect ways of going about anything, that when Wordsworth mentioned his design of writing to you, but would not explain to me, even by a hint, what he meant to write, I felt a great repugnance to the idea, which was suppressed by my habitual deference to his excellent good sense. I wish I had not suppressed it.'[3] This was not the version of the story he had given Poole in his earlier letter. He reproached Poole with being unfeeling in pecuniary affairs; he himself would never have refused such a sum to

---

[1] *E.L.* 118, p. 265. W.W. to Longman and Rees, Mar. 27th 1801. Ibid. 145, p. 327, W.W. to R.W., June 26th 1801 (wrongly dated 1803).
[2] *U.L.* i. 85, p. 174. S.T.C. to Thomas Poole, July 1801.
[3] *T.P.* ii, p. 63. S.T.C. to T.P., Sept. 7th 1801.

anybody if he had had it; but how could Poole be expected to share his own and Wordsworth's feelings about money, since he was a member of the propertied class? That Poole could forgive such a letter as this speaks highly for his tolerance and affection: he was deeply hurt, but in a month or two the waters were calm once more; Coleridge had himself asked for a loan of £25 which Poole had sent, and plans were made for Coleridge to visit Stowey in the winter. The Azores were given up—the climate there, Coleridge discovered, was after all too damp, though the real reason probably was financial. Instead he went off on a visit to the Hutchinsons in Yorkshire and bathed in the sea at Scarborough. By the autumn he was somewhat better in health. A little later Coleridge, filled with wrath at his own country 'where the laborious poor are dying with grass in their bellies', was once more considering emigration to America, 'if Wordsworth would go with me'. Or they might all go and live in the Pinneys' large house in the Isle of Nevis.[1] In the meantime he worked out mentally a counterblast to the Hartleian doctrine of association, which tired him so that Wordsworth had to beg him to desist. They seem to have talked much of philosophy at this time. Coleridge said that he had analysed the causes of the 'unmerited reputation' of Locke, Hobbes, and Hume, 'entirely to Wordsworth's satisfaction'. They were still busy freeing the new century from the rationalism of the old.

It is clear, however, that after the strenuous autumn of writing *Michael* and preparing the *Lyrical Ballads* for the press, Wordsworth was very tired. Few poems can with certainty be ascribed to the year 1801. At the end of April he sent, in a letter to Mary Hutchinson, the lyric *I travelled among unknown Men*, which belongs to the 'Lucy' cycle, all the rest of which had been written two years before in Germany. It is a good example of his habit of re-living a long-past experience and transmuting it into poetry. There is also *The Sparrow's Nest*, a lyric at once light in style and profound in feeling, inspired by the recollection of Dorothy in childhood. It is impossible to say whether a real finding of a real sparrow's nest preceded it, or whether, as with the parallel poem *To a Butterfly*, written a year later, he was simply 'kindled' by some chance remark of Dorothy.

Two other lyrics, which he said were 'designed to make one

---

[1] *S.T.C.* i, p. 350. S.T.C. to Southey, July 25th 1801.

piece', also belong to this year: *Louisa*, written in the same metre as *Three Years she grew* and afterwards placed by Wordsworth next to *Strange Fits of Passion*; and *To a Young Lady who had been reproached for taking long Walks in the Country*, founded probably on a recollection of the occasion when, eight years before, their aunt Mrs. Crackanthorpe had rebuked Dorothy for 'rambling about the country on foot'. But the 'dear child of Nature' is not Dorothy in actuality any more than Lucy or Louisa is, for she is thought of as a happy mother of children. The last verse, prophesying

> An old age serene and bright
> And lovely as a Lapland night,

if it is to be taken as a benediction on Dorothy, is inexpressibly moving when we think what her old age was like. This poem was published in the *Morning Post* in February 1802.[1]

Meanwhile life at Grasmere and in the cottage pursued its quiet course. Some fir-trees, high on the fell above John's Grove were cut down: John wrote wrathfully to Mary: 'I wish I had the *monster* that cut them down in *my* ship, and I would give him a tight flogging.'[2] Money was still hard to come by at Dove Cottage. John did what he could to replenish his brother's wardrobe. 'You may tell William I shall send him down a new silk hat and the old one I had at Grasmere . . . and all the old clothes I can muster.' He also had thoughts of sending them his old telescope (what had become of the telescope in use at Racedown?), but 'I will see first whether I shall want it'. John was above all anxious to make money by his voyages so as to set up his brother and sister and himself with modest comfort. For this purpose that part of Wordsworth's capital which was 'in the funds' was sold and put at his disposal to invest in the voyage. At length, in May, he set sail from Portsmouth and was away for fifteen months.[3] Before he sailed he arranged for an allowance of £20 a year to be paid to Dorothy from the India House out of his own pay.

From John Wordsworth's letters to Mary Hutchinson it appears that William and Dorothy visited the Clarksons at

---

[1] For 'Lapland night' see above, p. 165.
[2] D.C.P. J.W. to M.H., Feb. 26th 1801.
[3] E.L. 145, p. 327. W.W. and D.W. to R.W., June 26th 1801.

Eusemere, and Coleridge at Keswick during the month of February 1801. Writing to Mary on February 16th he says: 'By this time *they* [meaning William and Dorothy] are at Grasmere. I received a letter from William this morning. He tells me that they walked from Mr. Clarkson's over the mountains and they are now going to Keswick.' This was the first of many visits to the Clarksons. At Keswick they seem to have stayed about a fortnight, for on the 25th John wrote again: 'I suppose by this time *they* will be thinking of returning to Grasmere.'[1] The underlined pronoun indicates that within the little circle that Coleridge called 'the concern', William and Dorothy were recognized by the others as holding the place of honour.

A curious light on one aspect of their life is afforded by a letter of Wordsworth's to Wrangham in early February 1801. 'We live', he said, 'quite out of the way of new books; I have not seen a single one since I came here, now 13 months ago.' They were thrown back on old favourites and in the autumn were reading a great deal of Spenser and Chaucer both aloud and to themselves. In March 1803 Charles Lamb copied out for Wordsworth in a letter a very long poem called *Winter* by Cotton, the editor of Walton's *Angler*, another 'on the inconveniences of old age', and Cowper's *Loss of the Royal George*, with the apology: 'In your obscure part of the world, which I take to be Ultima Thule, I thought these verses out of books which cannot be accessible would not be unwelcome.'[2] Of periodicals, they took the *Morning Post*, for which Coleridge fitfully wrote political articles and in which Wordsworth's earliest sonnets were to appear. Dorothy once spoke of his 'wasting his mind in the magazines'.[3] There are even indications of other indoor pursuits besides reading. In a letter to his publisher, Longman, dated March 27th 1801, Wordsworth says: 'Mr. Coleridge and I are conjointly in your debt for two copies of Withering's Botany, and two botanical microscopes.' The microscopes remind us of Wordsworth's lines about Coleridge in the 'Castle of Indolence' stanzas, written in the following spring:

> Glasses he had, that little things display,
> The beetle panoplied in gems and gold,
> A mailèd Angel on a battle-day.

---

[1] *D.C.P.*   [2] *Lamb*, i, p. 343.
[3] *D.W.J.* i, p. 103. Jan. 27th 1802.

Coleridge, whose capacity for new interests was limitless, was trying to arouse Wordsworth 'to have some intellectual pursuit less closely connected with deep passion than poetry', and Wordsworth was not unwilling. A plan had been discussed a few weeks earlier of moving to Keswick, where William Calvert, Raisley Calvert's brother, had been rebuilding the house at Windy Brow. He suggested that William and Dorothy should come and live in it with him, and he would then build on to it a little chemical laboratory where they and Coleridge and Humphry Davy—if he could be persuaded to visit them—would study the new science of chemistry. Nothing came of the plan: perhaps Wordsworth felt that sharing a house with Calvert, who cared not a straw for poetry, might prove difficult. As for the botany book, Dorothy had often been at a loss, before it came, as her Journal shows, for the name of a flower, and once exclaimed: 'Oh! that we had a book of botany!'[1]

In September 1801 Wordsworth paid his first visit to Scotland.[2] He went in order to attend the wedding of Basil Montagu, who was now rising to eminence at the Bar, and once more regularly paying Wordsworth's annuity. He was engaged to Laura, daughter of a wealthy Suffolk landowner, Sir William Rush. The entire Rush family, Sir William, his wife, their six daughters, and Montagu determined to mark the occasion by making a tour to Scotland. On the way they picked up Wordsworth, and the party travelled to Glasgow by way of Longtown and Hamilton, where they visited the Duke of Hamilton's picture gallery. The marriage took place in Glasgow on September 6th 1801. It proved a most happy union, but tragically short. Laura Montagu died in 1806, at the age of twenty-four, leaving to her friends a memory of loveliness of person and character which was not soon forgotten.[3]

From October 10th 1801 we are again able to follow the

---

[1] D.W.J. i, p. 38, May 16th 1800. The full title is: *The Arrangement of British Plants according to the latest Improvements of the Linnaean System.* 4 vols. London, 1796. The book, after more than a century's interval, has returned, through the kindness of its possessor, to its original home at Dove Cottage, its margins filled, here and there, with notes in Wordsworth's hand about the flowers they found among the fells.

[2] There are very few references to this visit. Dorothy mentions it twice in her *Recollections of a Tour of the Highlands,* 1803: *D.W.J.,* i, pp. 217, 230. See also Kegan Paul, *William Godwin.* S.T.C. to Godwin, Sept. 22nd 1801.

[3] *M.Y.* i. 262, p. 40. D.W. to Mrs. Clarkson, June 30th 1806.

Wordsworths' doings from day to day, for Dorothy's Journal is once more our guide.[1] William's long holiday from writing poetry continued. It was not until December that he began to write once more; and then it was but to try his hand at modernizing Chaucer. He started with *The Maunciple's Tale*, which Dorothy calls the 'Tale of Phoebus and the Crow', but soon he changed to *The Prioress's Tale*, which he completed, and then went on to *The Cuckoo and the Nightingale* which was then thought to be by Chaucer. The text which he used was that of Dr. Anderson's *Works of the British Poets*, which John Wordsworth had taken with him on his early voyages and which he had left behind him at Grasmere when he went away in September 1800. 'From these volumes', says Wordsworth, 'I became first familiar with Chaucer', and he added: 'so little money had I then to spare for books, that, in all probability, but for this same work, I should have known little of Drayton, Daniel, and other distinguished poets of the Elizabethan age, and their immediate successors, until a much later period of my life.' Anderson's text was defective in many respects and Wordsworth's translations suffer somewhat from the mistakes of Dr. Anderson. On his second visit to Scotland in 1814 he met Anderson, then an old man, at the Manse of Traquhair, and thanked him for the value his collection had been to him. *The Prioress's Tale* was published in 1820; very much later, in 1839, he sent *The Cuckoo and the Nightingale* and part of *Troilus and Cressida* to Thomas Powell for inclusion in his *Poems of Chaucer Modernised*. His love for Chaucer was great, and he thought that he ought to be made 'tuneable to modern ears'. When some of his friends complained of Chaucer's indecency, Wordsworth admitted that he was so in his 'comic tales' but said that 'he was never openly or insidiously voluptuous', and 'had towards the female sex as exquisite and pure feelings as ever the heart of man was blessed with'.[2]

On December 21st 1801 *The Ruined Cottage*, or *The Pedlar* as they now generally called it, was taken out and read through: 'he was full of hope what he should do with it': two days later

---

[1] The Journal recommences on Oct. 10th 1801 and runs until Jan. 16th 1803. It is clear that a volume linking it with the 1800 Journal has been lost, for the latter ends on Dec. 22nd 1800 in the middle of a sentence.

[2] *L.Y.* ii. 1323, p. 1002. W.W. to I. Fenwick, 1840.

he 'made himself very ill' with attempts to alter it.[1] He did not touch it again until the end of January.

November 1801 saw Coleridge's departure for a long absence in London and Somersetshire, and Mary Hutchinson's arrival for a two months' stay at the cottage. The Journal, which starts on October 10th, shows Coleridge walking backwards and forwards from Keswick, and a succession of other visitors. Tom Hutchinson, Mary's brother for whom she kept house at Gallow Hill, near Scarborough, came on October 16th and his visit was made the occasion for an excursion to Penny Bridge and Coniston with a night away from home and an adventure on Windermere in which they were 'in danger of being cast away'. At the end of the month Tom left, and the Clarksons came for a visit which lasted for several days.

On October 25th Mary was expected at Greta Hall, but she did not arrive until some days later.[2] By November 9th she had arrived at Grasmere and on that day the three walked over to Keswick. Coleridge was about to leave. He dared not risk another winter in the lakes. He was going first to Eusemere where the hospitable Clarksons were already entertaining his wife and the two boys. Coleridge was thus alone at Greta Hall when the Wordsworths and Mary came. Dorothy's description of their night's stay is significant: 'We enjoyed ourselves in the study and were *at home*.' But next day, when 'poor C. left us' and they themselves returned to Grasmere, the thought of his unhappiness, of his perhaps long absence, and of all their past companionship and joy, overwhelmed her and on the way home she broke down. 'Every sight and every sound reminded me of him—dear, dear fellow, of his many walks to us by day and by night, of all dear things. I was melancholy and could not talk, but at last I eased my heart by weeping—nervous blubbering, says William. It is not so. O! how many, many reasons have I to be anxious for him.' William's harshness is strange, but probably for him too the strain of parting had been almost more

---

[1] *D.W.J.* i, pp. 92 and 95.

[2] The entry for Oct. 25th is 'Rode to Legberthwaite with Tom, expecting Mary', but whether she actually arrived is not clear. She is not mentioned again till Nov. 9th, but there is a gap of five days from Nov. 4th to 9th. She probably came in this interval, when the Clarksons certainly departed. Dorothy speaks in a letter of her having stayed 'seven weeks' with them. As she departed on Dec. 28th this would place her arrival about Nov. 8th.

than he could bear, and for Mary's sake he had held back his own grief. By the next day they were calmer. 'Baked bread and giblet pie—put books in order—mended stockings. Put aside dearest C's letters, and now at about 7 o'clock we are all sitting by a nice fire. Wm. with his book and a candle, and Mary writing to Sara.'[1]

Coleridge's letters from London were always a source of anxiety; if his news of himself was bad, it threw them all into a state of wretchedness. Mary seemed almost as much affected as William and Dorothy. Thus on the evening of December 6th: 'Mary and I walked to Ambleside for letters—reached home by 11 o'clock. . . . We opened C.'s letter at Wilcock's door. We thought we saw that he wrote in good spirits, so we came happily homewards, where we arrived 2 hours after we left home. It was a sad melancholy letter, and prevented us all from sleeping.' The burden of answering these 'melancholy letters' fell mainly on Dorothy, who was only too willing to spare William the fatigue of writing. She carried the thought of Coleridge about with her in all her walks and rambles. Thus, on a December day when the snow hid all the grass and the ashes were 'glittering spears with their upright stems', she made an encounter with a hip-laden rose-bush the occasion for a little sacramental act on his behalf: 'The hips very beautiful and so good!! and, dear Coleridge! I ate twenty for thee, when I was by myself.'

On November 24th a strange adventure befell William, walking by himself in the road beside John's Grove. 'I went to meet him', says Dorothy, '. . . He had been surprised and terrified by a sudden rushing of winds, which seemed to bring earth and sky and lake together, as if the whole were going to enclose him in; he was glad he was in a high road.' It is difficult to judge whether this was a real hurricane or a subjective experience. It had been a windy, showery day, with rainbows, and white waves on the lake; now it was moonlight and raining a little, but evidently nothing unusual had been noticed at the cottage, and he was some distance above the lake when it occurred.

There are hints in the Journal this autumn of increasing pleasure between William and Mary in each other's company. Dorothy speaks of them coming in one evening 'chearful, bloom-

_____
[1] *D.W.J.* i, p. 79. Nov. 9th, 10th, 11th 1801.

ing and happy', and on another occasion 'fresh and well' after
an evening walk; she likewise reports a conversation of a
humorous kind with old Molly, who evidently thought she knew
what was in the wind. 'Molly was very witty about Mary all
day', she writes on November 16th. 'She says: "ye may say what
ye will, but there's naething like a gay auld man for behaving
weel to a young wife".' William was notorious for looking a
great deal older than his years. They probably became formally
engaged during this period, for in February 1802 Coleridge
wrote from London to his wife: 'Wordsworth will marry soon
after my return', and he went on to describe another of the
many plans that were destined never to be fulfilled, namely, that
the two households, William, Mary, and Dorothy Wordsworth,
and his own family, would 'set sail about July from Liverpool to
Bordeaux', there to spend two years in a warm climate. By the
new year, therefore, their marriage was fixed on, but it did not
take place until October 1802. There were difficulties which
needed much careful handling before Wordsworth felt himself
conscientiously free to marry. A long exchange of letters with
Annette Vallon occupied the spring months, culminating in the
journey of William and Dorothy to France.[1]

At the very end of December 1801, Wordsworth suddenly
turned to the 'poem to Coleridge'. He wrote 'some lines of the
third part', that is of Book III of *The Prelude*, on December 27th,
and continued absorbed in composition the next day when they
were all walking along the shore of Thirlmere to Keswick. 'We
[that is Mary and Dorothy] parted from Wm. upon the Rays.
He joined us opposite Sara's Rock.[2] He was busy in composition
and sat down upon the wall. We did not see him again till we
arrived at John Stanley's.'[3] But it was only a brief stirring. The
'poem to Coleridge' 'slept' again almost undisturbed until
February 1804, though there was a return to it on at least one
occasion in January 1803.[4]
The walk to Keswick was a prelude to a winter holiday. They

---

[1] *S.T.C.* i, p. 367. See below, p. 553.
[2] The 'Rock of Names' on which, the year before, they had all carved their
initials. See below, p. 551.
[3] *D.W.J.* i, p. 96. Dec. 28th 1801.
[4] Ibid., p. 188. Jan. 11th 1803. 'William was working at his poem to C.'

stayed one night at Greta Hall—'dear Coleridge's desert home' as Dorothy called it, for Coleridge had already left for London— and next day walked in frost, wind, and showers of hail, by the exposed road over the moors to Ullswater, where they spent nearly a month with the Clarksons at Eusemere. Mary left them there after a day or two to visit her aunt, Elizabeth Monk-house, in Penrith, but she returned for a few days in the middle of January 1802 to be escorted as far finally as Stainton Bridge by William and Dorothy—a pretty place which reminded them of Sockburn. 'Dear Mary!' wrote Dorothy, 'there we parted from her. I daresay, as often as she passes that road she will turn in at the gate to look at this sweet prospect.'

While with the Clarksons they saw a good deal of Thomas Wilkinson, the Quaker who lived at Yanwath, on the Eamont between Pooley Bridge and Penrith. He delighted in gardening and laying out his grounds by Eamont's banks; it was to his spade that Wordsworth later addressed some verses that have, perhaps, met with more ridicule than they deserve.[1] But Wilkinson had also travelled a good deal, and had written an account of his visit to the Highlands of Scotland which, though not published till 1824, was circulated in manuscript among his friends. It is a curious fact that one of Wordsworth's most famous lyrics, *The Solitary Reaper*, was inspired, not so much by a personal recollection of a Highland girl 'reaping and sing-ing by herself', as by Wilkinson's description of one seen by him, whose strains 'felt delicious long after they were heard no more'.[2]

On January 23rd 1802 William and Dorothy left Eusemere to return to Grasmere. Like the good mountaineers they were, they went by the mountain route over Grisedale Pass; it was 'difficult with snow', and by the tarn at the top the mists came down so that for a time they were uncertain of their way, 'but thanks to William's skill we knew it long before we could see our way before us'. And then, when at length they reached home, 'O how comfortable and happy we felt ourselves, sitting

[1] *To the Spade of a Friend. P.W.* iv, p. 75 and p. 416 n. The lines were written in 1806.

[2] *D.W.J.* i, p. 380. Wilkinson wrote on Feb. 15th 1801: 'I had lately a young Poet seeing me that sprung originally from the next village'; i.e. Sockbridge, the patrimony of Wordsworth's father. *D.C.P.*

by our own fire, when we had got off our wet clothes and dressed ourselves fresh and clean. . . . We talked about the Lake of Como, read in *Descriptive Sketches*, looked about us and felt that we were happy.'[1] Their home-coming was enlivened too by finding ' £5 from Montagu and £20 from Christopher', the latter a present now made yearly to Dorothy by her youngest brother, 'until he marries'. He was now a Fellow of Trinity, and had been engaged since 1800 to Priscilla, sister of the Wordsworth's difficult neighbour Charles Lloyd, and was waiting until he could obtain an appointment to a living, which would make marriage possible.

From January until early March 1802 Wordsworth was much engaged with 'altering *The Pedlar*'. What he wanted to do was to publish it as a separate poem, and not as part of *The Recluse*. In the last copy that had been made of it by Dorothy, probably in 1799, the long section added to the poem in the early spring of 1798, describing the boyhood and character of the Pedlar in terms which were really descriptive of Wordsworth's own boyhood, had been omitted and placed in a separate 'addendum'.[2] Evidently Wordsworth felt that this section was scarcely part of the story of Margaret and her cottage, yet felt its importance in the development of his work as a whole. But he was still fascinated by the Pedlar, and wanted to make him the dominating character in the poem. Not much was done, however, until January 26th, when 'Wm. wrote out part of his poem and endeavoured to alter it and so made himself ill.' From then until March 7th the references to *The Pedlar* are very numerous, to copying, 'altering and refitting', and to dissatisfaction because it was 'uninteresting'.

The pain, weariness, and sleeplessness which his labours brought on are also minutely recorded by Dorothy. On January 31st 'Wm. had slept very ill—he was tired and had a bad headache.' On February 10th he 'got to some ugly place [in the poem] and went to bed tired out'. Two days later 'I recopied The Pedlar, but poor Wm. all the time at work . . . wore himself and me out with labour. We had an affecting conversation. Went to bed at 12 o'clock.' Dorothy often sat at his bedside reading aloud to him until the small hours in an endeavour to get him to sleep. Thus on May 4th she recorded: 'I repeated

---

[1] *D.W.J.* i, p. 101. Jan. 23rd 1802.   [2] *P.W.* v, pp. 404–8.

verses to William while he was in bed; he was soothed and I left him. "This is the spot" over and over again.'[1]

   And it was not only *The Pedlar* and the series of lyrical poems that followed it in the spring that destroyed his rest. Coleridge was in London, and his letters, with their detailed accounts of his ill health and other miseries, made both William and Dorothy wretched. 'A heart-rending letter from Coleridge', she wrote on January 29th, 'we were sad as we could be.' On February 8th they walked to Rydal for letters and in the chilly dusk 'we broke the seal of Coleridge's letter and I had light enough just to read that he was not ill'. In the evening William wrote to him and became 'very unwell' as a result. Dorothy sat up writing to Mary Hutchinson, Montagu (who had just sent them £8 of his debt), William Calvert, and Sara Coleridge. At two o'clock she crept out to put the letters under Fletcher the carrier's door. 'I never felt such a cold night. . . . I collected together all the clothes I could find, (for I durst not go into the pantry[2] for fear of waking William). . . . I could not sleep from sheer cold.'

   At the end of February a note in the margin of the Journal records 'Disaster Pedlar.' This must mean the virtual destruction of one of the copies, for three days later on March 3rd she says: 'I was so unlucky as to propose to rewrite the Pedlar. Wm. got to work and was worn to death.' However, on the 6th she completed her fair copy and at last on March 7th: 'I stitched

---

[1] These lines, called *Travelling* in the manuscript, were never published by Wordsworth. They record yet another hour of happy companionship with Dorothy.

> This is the spot:—how mildly does the sun
> Shine in between the fading leaves! the air
> In the habitual silence of this wood
> Is more than silent; and this bed of heath—
> Where shall we find so sweet a resting-place?
> Come, let me see thee sink into a dream
> Of quiet thoughts, protracted till thine eye
> Be calm as water when the winds are gone
> And no one can tell whither. My sweet friend,
> We two have had such happy hours together
> That my heart melts in me to think of it.   *P.W.* iv, p. 423

The lines about the look in Dorothy's eyes are also found in a draft of *Nutting*, written long before in 1798 (*P.W.* ii, p. 505), and years later, in 1817, he used them again in the second of the two poems to 'Lycoris' (Dorothy), *P.W.* iv, p. 97.

[2] 'The pantry' must have been the 'sort of lumber-room' upstairs which she had earlier described, next to William's bedroom, and in which extra bedding must have been kept. *E.L.* 110, p. 248. D.W. to J.M., Sept. 10th 1800.

up the Pedlar.' It was not for nothing that Wordsworth spoke of his poetry as 'my toilsome songs', and no wonder that he wrote, probably not many months after this exhausting spring, three sonnets, *To Sleep*.[1]

The character of the alterations can be inferred from two manuscripts, in Dorothy's hand, in which a new origin and name are given to the Pedlar. Instead of being called Armytage and being a native of Cumberland, his name is now Patrick Drummond, and he is a Scotsman, bred on Perthshire hills as

A herd-callan for forty pence a year.

This change was made, apparently, after receiving a letter from Sara Hutchinson on January 27th. It was, says Dorothy, 'a sweet long letter, with a most interesting account of Mr. Patrick'.[2] Mr. Patrick was James Patrick, known as 'the intellectual Pedlar' of Kendal, a Scotsman with whom Sara had passed several years of her childhood; he had married Sara's cousin Margaret Robison. Wordsworth himself tells us that his 'Wanderer' in *The Excursion* is partly a picture of Patrick, and there can be little doubt that it was now, in this winter of 1801–2, that he began to meditate upon him. He had probably heard Sara describe her old friend in conversation, and now wrote to her for fuller information; the 'sweet long letter' was the result.[3]

On March 10th, when at last the alterations were finished, Wordsworth spoke of 'publishing the Yorkshire Wolds poem' (that is *Peter Bell*) 'with *The Pedlar*'. This shows conclusively that *The Pedlar* was now thought of as a completely separate poem, no longer related to *The Recluse* as in its first inception it had been. It must always be a matter of regret that he did not carry out this project. Although *The Pedlar* became eventually the first book of *The Excursion*, it is upon the whole a more impressive poem in the earlier versions, whether we choose the original *Ruined Cottage* of 1798 or *The Pedlar* of 1802, than it became when it was altered again for *The Excursion*.

---

[1] The date of the 'Sleep' sonnets is not exactly known, but as they were among the poems sent to Coleridge in Mar. 1804 they were probably written in 1803.

[2] *D.W.J.* i, p. 102.

[3] The description in this new part of the poem of the little 'fair-haired, fair-faced' girl, 'tiny for her years', is probably a description of Sara, who was small and fair. *P.W.* v, p. 406.

As for *Peter Bell*, its long–delayed publication in 1819 was attended by so many unfortunate circumstances that it has taken more than a century to recover from its entry into the world. But still he hesitated, and soon was deep in a new tide of lyric poetry, of great variety and range, so that the spring months of 1802 can be compared with those of 1798. The actual dates of many of the poems with minute details, sometimes, of the circumstances of their composition, are known to us through Dorothy's Journal; we are able to follow from day to day her brother's second great period of lyrical creation.

It began on Thursday, March 11th, with *The Singing Bird*, published later under the title of *The Sailor's Mother*. Next day he wrote *Alice Fell* and *The Beggar-Woman*—called simply *Beggars* when it was published. All these poems were about poor people whom he or Dorothy had met on the roads near the cottage, or of whom, as of Alice Fell, they had been told by some acquaintance. The story of Alice Fell was told them by a Mr. Graham, a Quaker, a friend of Thomas Clarkson, who begged Wordsworth to make a poem of it 'for the sake of humanity'.[1] These three poems are all in the severest style of the homeliest of the *Lyrical Ballads*: Coleridge would have pulled a long face had he been by, and many years later he did indeed say that they 'would have been more delightful to me in prose'.[2] He had not yet, however, returned from his winter in the south, though a week later he was with them again. It may well be that Wordsworth was attracted once more to *Lyrical Ballads* subjects and style because he was or had recently been engaged in revising the *Ballads* for a new edition, which appeared in April.[3]

Wordsworth had met the 'Sailor's Mother' about a year earlier 'by the wishing-gate', and he prided himself on having reproduced her story 'nearly to the letter'. If we had Dorothy's Journal for the year 1801 we should probably find it there; there is in fact a reference to it in a letter from John to Dorothy dated April 7th 1801. 'Your story of the Seaman's mother', he wrote, 'was affecting, just what human nature is and ought to be. The sailors are allowed, and particularly in merchant ships, to carry birds, and they are more fond of them than other men.'[4]

[1] *P.W.* i, p. 359.   [2] *B.L.*, ch. xviii.
[3] *E.L.* 127, p. 285. D.W. to R.W., Apr. 6th 1802.
[4] *D.C.P.*

Dorothy had written about 'the Beggar woman' in her Journal in May 1800. Now on March 13th 1802 William 'half cast a poem on the subject' while he and Dorothy were walking back from Rydal. After tea she got out her Journal and read him her own account, 'and an unlucky thing it was, for he could not escape from those very words and so he could not write the poem. He left it unfinished and went tired to bed.' It is a curious instance of her words blocking instead of releasing his inspiration, for *Beggars* is in no way superior in imaginative treatment to Dorothy's portrait, although on two other occasions when he certainly relied on her Journal to assist his own memory, he produced two of his greatest poems: *Resolution and Independence* and *I Wandered lonely as a Cloud*.[1]

But on March 14th Wordsworth struck a rarer vein; he wrote the first of his three 'Butterfly' poems: *To a Butterfly*:

> Stay near me—do not take thy flight!
> A little longer stay in sight!
> Much converse do I find in thee,
> Historian of my infancy!
> Float near me; do not yet depart!
> Dead times revive in thee:
> Thou bring'st, gay creature as thou art!
> A solemn image to my heart,
> My father's family!
>
> Oh! pleasant, pleasant were the days,
> The time, when in our childish plays,
> My sister Emmeline and I
> Together chased the butterfly!
> A very hunter did I rush
> Upon the prey:—with leaps and springs
> I followed on from brake to bush;
> But she, God love her! feared to brush
> The dust from off its wings.

It was a recollection of childhood and must always be linked—as he himself linked it in publication—with *The Sparrow's Nest*, written in the previous spring. Dorothy shows us exactly how it was written.

. . . While we were at breakfast that is (for I had breakfasted) he, with his basin of broth before him untouched, and a little plate of

---

[1] See below, pp. 534–5, 538.

bread and butter he wrote the Poem to a Butterfly! He ate not a morsel, nor put on his stockings, but sat with his shirt-neck unbuttoned and his waistcoat open while he did it. The thought first came upon him as we were talking about the pleasure we both always feel at the sight of a butterfly. I told him that I used to chase them a little, but that I was afraid of brushing the dust off their wings, and did not catch them. He told me how they used to kill all the white ones when he went to school because they were Frenchmen.[1]

The recollection of the delight of childhood which is the inspiration of the poem was thus prompted not by seeing a butterfly but by talking about butterflies with Dorothy. Her detailed description of the circumstances is a sign that she took a special delight in having been unknowingly its inspiration. For the second time—*The Sparrow's Nest* being the first—he had paid her a magnificent compliment, showing her as the possessor in childhood of feelings that only came to him at a later stage.

March 16th and 17th saw the writing of *The Emigrant Mother*, a poem much in the style of *The Mad Mother* of the *Lyrical Ballads*; on the 23rd, 'a mild morning, William worked at *The Cuckow* poem'. It should be noted that this most famous lyric was not prompted by *hearing* the cuckoo. It was in any case far too early in the year. In the Lakes the cuckoo is not about until the end of April and in fact was first heard this year by William and Dorothy on the first of May.[2] The 'Butterfly' poem had started a train of recollections of which *To the Cuckoo* is the climax. It was recollection in Wordsworth's own peculiar vein, not merely of sights and sounds but of the whole complex of emotions and mental experiences which these sights and sounds awakened. The thought of the butterfly had called up the 'solemn image' of 'my father's family'—before death had broken it up. So Wordsworth called the butterfly 'historian of my infancy'. The cuckoo was an even more significant symbol. Its call, remembered, not physically heard, brought up into consciousness the 'visionary hours' of boyhood, when the earth seemed no longer earth but 'a prospect in the mind', or, as he says in the

---

[1] *D.W.J.* i, p. 123. Mar. 14th 1802. The uniform of the French army before the Revolution was white, faced with green. Coleridge, in a letter to Poole dated May 7th 1802, copied out *To a Butterfly* and *The Sparrow's Nest*. The first verse of *The Sparrow's Nest* differs considerably from the published version. *U.L.* i. 94, p. 195.

[2] *D.W.J.* i, p. 142. 'Heard the Cuckoo to-day this first of May.' The sentence was written large, across the entire page.

poem, 'an unsubstantial faery place'. The names he gives to the cuckoo in the poem make it something not of earth, a herald from a spiritual world. It is

> No bird, but an invisible thing,
> A voice, a mystery.

It is

> that Cry
> That made me look a thousand ways . . .
>
> a hope, a love,
> Still longed for, never seen.

Wordsworth himself said later that his 'concise interrogation'—

> Shall I call thee Bird
> Or but a wandering Voice?

'dispossesses the creature almost of a corporeal existence'. This was exactly what Wordsworth, by the alchemy of his imagination, from his earliest boyhood had been doing with the world of sense. He gazed on it until it 'revealed the invisible world'.[1]

From *To the Cuckoo* it was but a short step, both in time and in thought, to *The Rainbow*, and to the beginnings of the *Ode: Intimations of Immortality*. On March 26th he 'worked at *The Cuckow*' and also *The Rainbow*.[2]

> My heart leaps up when I behold
> A Rainbow in the sky:
> So was it when my life began;
> So is it now I am a man;
> So be it when I shall grow old,
>   Or let me die!
> The Child is father of the Man;
> And I could wish my days to be
> Bound each to each by natural piety.

Again, there is no reason to suppose that Wordsworth saw a rainbow on that day—Dorothy would have mentioned it in her Journal if he had. But the rainbow, like the cuckoo, was a symbol for Wordsworth just as it had been for Noah. He had once seen in boyhood, on a day of wild storm, in the vale of Coniston, a rainbow, which

> Immoveable in heav'n, kept standing there,
> With a colossal stride bridging the vale,

---

[1] *Prel.* vi, l. 601.   [2] *D.W.J.* i, p. 128. *P.W.* ii, p. 25.

> The substance thin as dreams, lovelier than day—
> Amid the deafening uproar stood unmoved,
> Sustain'd itself through many minutes space;
> As if it were pinned down by adamant.[1]

Perhaps the remembrance of that rainbow and its strange persistence was the reason why he now chose the rainbow to symbolize the continuity of his imaginative life. For that was a tenet of his faith which was now being put to the test.

For with this uprush of 'emotion recollected in tranquillity' and transmuted into poetry came some sadness and self-questioning as well as delight. The cuckoo's voice, heard in imagination, could re-create for him 'that golden time again'; could bring into existence once more the 'visionary hours' when

> the sky seemed not a sky
> Of earth,

when the Universe was apprehended 'with bliss ineffable' and in all things he

> saw one life and felt that it was joy.

But when he had written those words in 1798[2] he was describing an experience which was already in some sense past. The earth was still a place of wonder and delight, but it was earth, not heaven. Now, four years later, the problem came upon him with tremendous force—why was this so? Why was it that, with the passing of the years, the glory which had transfigured all things for him in boyhood had faded, and he no longer saw the earth 'apparelled in celestial light', except when meditation on the cuckoo's cry brought him temporarily once more into that 'faery place'? The problem formed the subject of his next poem. On March 27th, 'a divine morning, at breakfast William wrote part of an Ode'. It was this poem which became the *Ode: Intimations of Immortality from Recollections of Early Childhood.*

> There was a time when meadow, grove and stream,
> The earth, and every common sight,
>   To me did seem
> Apparelled in celestial light,
> The glory and the freshness of a dream.

---

[1] *Prel.*, p. 601. A passage not included in the printed text.
[2] They were part of the description of the Pedlar's boyhood in *The Ruined Cottage*. Later they were incorporated into *Prel.* ii, ll. 416–34 (1805).

> It is not now as it has been of yore;
> Turn whereso'er I may,
> By night or day,
> The things which I have seen I now can see no more.

So he put the problem, continuing it through three more stanzas, completed with the question:

> Whither is fled the visionary gleam?
> Where is it now, the glory and the dream?

And there, for the present, the poem ended, with a question unanswered, a problem unsolved. Some two years later he took it up again and completed it. For the present we are concerned only with the first four stanzas. These must have been finished in some form on the day they were begun, for on the next day William and Dorothy departed for Keswick to see Coleridge, who had returned from London in the middle of March and had already spent two nights at Grasmere; and on April 4th, a Sunday, while the Wordsworths were still at Keswick, Coleridge wrote between sunset and midnight the 'Letter' in verse to Sara Hutchinson which, much pruned and with the name 'Sara' changed to 'Edmund', was published in October in the *Morning Post* under the title *Dejection: an Ode*.[1] That Coleridge had read Wordsworth's *Ode* before writing his 'Letter' is clear enough. First, in his own last stanza he gives his answer to Wordsworth's question. The soul herself, he says, is the origin of the 'glory' with which the earth is enveloped: addressing Sara, he exclaims:

> O pure of Heart! thou needst not ask of me
> What this strong music in the Soul may be,
> What and wherein it doth exist,
> This Light, this Glory, this fair luminous Mist,
> This beautiful and beauty-making Power!
> *Joy*, innocent Sara! Joy, that ne'er was given
> Save to the pure, and in their purest hour,
>   *Joy*, Sara! is the Spirit and the Power,
> That wedding Nature to us gives in Dower
>   A new Earth and new Heaven,
> Undreamt of by the Sensual and the Proud!
> Joy is that strong Voice, Joy that luminous Cloud—
>   We, we ourselves rejoice!

[1] For the original text see H. House, *Coleridge*, 1953, pp. 157–65.

> And thence flows all that charms or ear or sight,
> All melodies, the Echoes of that Voice,
> All Colors a Suffusion of that Light.

How different from Coleridge's purely subjective solution was Wordsworth's, two years later, with its magnificent incursion into the realms of pre-existence, its glorification of childhood as a beatific state, its acquiescence in a loss that could never be made good, its sublime thankfulness for the beauty that yet remained! The difference lies no doubt in the personal experience and history of each poet. Coleridge, faced with the misery of a home from which love had fled, might well feel that

> we receive but what we give
> And in *our* life alone doth nature live.

Wordsworth, who had suffered no such disaster and in a few months' time was to enter into a happy marriage, could not be so easily satisfied, and sought a more far-ranging answer.

There are other lesser indications that *Dejection* was written after reading Wordsworth's stanzas and in consequence of them. Wordsworth had written, after describing the joyous behaviour of nature on a bright spring morning:

> My heart is at your festival,
> My head hath its coronal.

Coleridge, looking forward to the day when Sara, Mary, Dorothy, and William would live together in 'one happy home', had exclaimed that then, rejoicing in their happiness,

> I too will crown me with a coronal.

But, if *Dejection* is in some ways an answer to Wordsworth's *Ode*, the *Ode* itself owes much to an earlier and little-known poem by Coleridge. Wordsworth had never previously used the ode form. Yet, in vigour, freedom, and majestic dignity it flows along, as though all came 'as naturally as leaves to a tree'.[1] Coleridge had published in the *Morning Post* in October 1800 a poem called *The Mad Monk: An Ode in Mrs. Ratcliff's Manner.* The second stanza contains the following lines:

> There was a time when earth, and sea, and skies,
> The bright green vale, and forest's dark recess,

[1] Forman, *The Letters of John Keats*, p. 108. 'Poetry should come as naturally as leaves to a tree or it should not come at all.'

With all things, lay before mine eyes
In steady loveliness:
But now I feel, on earth's uneasy scene,
Such sorrows as will never cease:—
I only ask for peace;
If I must live to know that such a time has been!

The resemblance to the opening stanza of Wordsworth's *Ode* is too striking to be accidental. But there is nothing more in common between the two poems, and it is a little strange that Wordsworth should have been thinking of it so closely. It may be, however, that it had come into his mind a few days before, in quite another context. On March 18th Wordsworth went to Keswick to see Coleridge on his return from London, and the next day Coleridge himself arrived at the cottage. Dorothy's record of that arrival is significant. 'His eyes', she says, 'were a little swollen with the wind. I was much affected with the sight of him, he seemed half stupefied. William came in soon after. Coleridge went to bed late, and William and I sate up till four o'clock. . . . They disputed about Ben Jonson. My spirits were agitated very much.'[1]

Coleridge's 'half stupefied' appearance may have been due to opium. During the previous year he had certainly become more dependent on it, finding in it the only relief from his many physical sufferings. But Dorothy may have known nothing of it as yet, and perhaps in the long nocturnal conversation William first disclosed to her this fatal habit in their great friend.[2] In any case their conversation must have ranged back and forth over Coleridge's troubles—his ill health, his unhappy home, his failure to write books, his devotion to Sara. And as they talked those lines of his may have been remembered and repeated as sadly appropriate to his case. Only a week later William began to write the *Ode*.

In the *Ode*, as in the *Cuckoo*, Wordsworth anticipates the landscape of late spring. What he describes is a 'sweet May morning'; 'the heart of May', not the end of March. Lambs, which leap about in the pastures of the *Ode*, are not born in the

---

[1] *D.W.J.* i, p. 127.
[2] For a curious incident that must have its origins in opium and of which Dorothy was a witness see a letter of S.T.C. to Godwin, June 23rd 1801, Turnbull, *Biographia Epistolaris*, i, p. 249.

central part of the Lake District in any numbers until the middle
of April. He was still hearing in imagination the cuckoo's
'twofold shout', and thus seeing the landscape in which alone
the cuckoo's cry is appropriate.

In the third stanza occurs a puzzling line:

> Now, while the birds thus sing a joyous song,
> And while the young lambs bound
> As to the tabor's sound,
> To me alone there came a thought of grief:
> *A timely utterance gave that thought relief,*
> And I again am strong.

What was the 'timely utterance' which rescued him from his
melancholy mood? It can scarcely have been anything else than
The Rainbow, written only the day before the *Ode* was begun.
We must suppose that the mood of regret for vanished 'splendour in the grass and glory in the flower' had been with him for
some time. The thought of the rainbow—the 'bridge' symbol—
had come 'timely', to reassure him that, after all, and in spite
of appearances, there had been no violent breach with the past.

The question is bound to be asked, in considering the *Ode*
from a biographical point of view: How long had Wordsworth
been aware that he no longer saw Nature 'apparelled in
celestial light' as he had seen her in boyhood? And also, at what
period and why, whether he was aware of it or not, had the
vision begun to fade? The second question is perhaps easier to
answer than the first. In the uneasy years following his return
from France, his vision of Nature had certainly darkened. The
undisturbed 'intercourse with Beauty' was now all too frequently
a restless, 'greedy' indulgence of the outward senses, a striving
no doubt to recapture the old peace, which bitter human experience had set at a distance, and mental conflict made un-
attainable. Such was his mood when he first visited the Wye
and Tintern. The gloom, although it was not unrelieved by
happier moods, was still with him for some time at Racedown;
the first beginnings of *The Ruined Cottage* were, as we have seen,
the fruit of gloomy, not happy, communings with moonlight on
a solitary heath.[1] And then gradually

> Nature's self, by human love
> Assisted, through the weary labyrinth

[1] See above, p. 286.

> Conducted me again to open day,
> Revived the feelings of my earlier life.[1]

It is difficult to believe that at Alfoxden Wordsworth was not just as 'happy' in his intercourse with Nature as he had been at Hawkshead; moreover, he felt and gave voice to what he believed to be Nature's own 'pleasure' and enjoyment in her own ineffable and overflowing Life:

> And I must think, do all I can,
> That there was pleasure there.[2]

Similarly in *Tintern Abbey* he speaks of the 'serene and blessed mood' in which the senses are left behind in quietness and 'we see into the life of things', as though it were a not uncommon experience at that time. Whether or not his vision of Nature at this time was as brilliant as it had been in boyhood it is impossible to say with accuracy, but at least there was no sense of departed glory; he would not have said, in the Alfoxden days,

> The things which I have seen I now can see no more.

The experience which he describes in the *Ode*, the awareness of loss of vision, must have been of more recent occurrence; his full consciousness of it was, perhaps, not very much earlier than the actual writing of the *Rainbow* poem. To account for the change is another matter. It may be explicable perhaps in physical terms of the decline of his very acute 'organic sensibility'—his extreme sensitivity to sights and sounds—as he approached middle life. For his visionary experience, as we have seen, was always the result of the perception of some event in the world of sense, such as the sight of the gibbet on Penrith Beacon, or the solitary climb to the eagle's eyrie, or an early morning walk round Esthwaite, or the cuckoo's cry. In boyhood his faculties of perception had led him naturally and almost inevitably over the border into the 'visionary' world. That this now seldom happened may simply have been due to the gradual decline of these faculties into something less abnormally receptive. This process—perhaps itself natural and inevitable—may have been hastened by physical pain and weakness, from which he had suffered much during the last two or three years, and by the intensity with which he had laboured at his appointed task.

---

[1] *Prel.* X (1805), ll. 922–6.
[2] *Lines written in Early Spring.* See above, p. 381.

He had become a great poet. In doing so he had paid a price for that achievement—he no longer beheld the earth with the colours of heaven. But it was only this particular kind of vision which was withheld. He was still, as will be seen in considering *The Leech-Gatherer*, capable of passing into the 'visionary world' when deeply moved by certain kinds of human experiences.

Coleridge's lines to Sara were evidently not shown to the Wordsworths before they left Keswick next day (April 5th) for Eusemere, for Dorothy wrote on April 21st, after their return to Grasmere: 'Coleridge came to us and repeated the verses he wrote to Sara. I was affected with them. . . . The sunshine, the green fields, and the fair sky made me sadder; even the little happy, sporting lambs seemed but sorrowful to me.' She might well be 'affected'. The good times with Coleridge were fast drawing to a close. Nevertheless, his April visit to Grasmere was a happy one; they all seem to have made it a holiday time, and to have laid aside sad thoughts in the delight of each other's company. They walked into Easedale on a day when the streams were roaring after a night of rain; William and Coleridge amused themselves by throwing stones into the beck while Dorothy sat under 'the single holly behind that single rock in the field'. William's lyric mood was strong upon him and he came up to her repeating the lines which he had written shortly before while lying in bed one morning at the cottage:

> I have thoughts that are fed by the sun.
>> The things which I see
>> Are welcome to me,
>> Welcome every one:
> I do not wish to be
>> Dead, dead,
> Dead without any company;
>> Here alone on my bed
> With thoughts that are fed by the Sun,
> And hopes that are welcome every one,
>> Happy am I.

> O Life, there is about thee
> A deep delicious peace,
> I would not be without thee,
>> Stay, oh stay!

> Yet be thou ever as now,
> Sweetness and breath with the quiet of death,
> Be thou ever as now,
> Peace, peace, peace.[1]

It was, he said, recalled to his mind 'by the dying away of the stunning of the waterfall as he came behind a stone', the sudden quiet seeming like the quiet in which the poem was written. Light-hearted lyric though it is, it is shot through with the fascination of the idea of death, which Wordsworth as a boy had been unable to conceive as a possibility:

> I do not wish to be . . .
> Dead without any company.

Yet life must have 'sweetness and breath *with* the quiet of death'. We are reminded of a little incident which Dorothy recorded only a week later,[2] after a visit to John's Grove. 'William lay, and I lay, in the trench under the fence—he with his eyes shut and listening to the waterfalls and the birds. . . . William heard me breathing and rustling now and then, but we both lay still and unseen by one another; he thought that it would be sweet thus to lie so in the grave, to hear the *peaceful* sounds of the earth, and just to know that our dear friends were near.' In such a way had the little 'cottage-girl' of *We are Seven* spoken of death, and so had the ballad-makers of old time.

Such a mood of contentment and overflowing happiness is visible in other poems written in this month of April. *The Tinker*, written a few days afterwards, is one, and the lines which he inaccurately called *Written in March while resting on the Bridge at the Foot of Brother's Water* is another. They were in fact written on April 16th, as he and Dorothy were walking back from Eusemere after their April visit to the Clarksons. That visit was memorable in many ways: from Eusemere William had gone to Yorkshire to visit Mary and had written the 'Glow-worm' poem for Dorothy on the way back:[3] and on this very walk homewards they had seen the daffodils by the shore of Ullswater—'a long belt of them, about the breadth of a country turn-pike road'.[4] William's poem about them, *I wandered lonely as a Cloud*, was not written until two years later,

---

[1] *D.W.J.* i. April 25th 1802. *P.W.* iv, p. 366.
[2] *D.W.J.* i, p. 139. Apr. 29th 1802.   [3] See below, pp. 556-7.
[4] *D.W.J.* i, p. 131. Apr. 15th 1802.

and, drawing freely as it does on Dorothy's description of them in her Journal, is a typical instance of a poem written in a state of 'recollection in tranquillity'. The Brother's Water lines, on the contrary, were spontaneous and immediate, and Dorothy's description of the same scene was written after they reached home, with the poem as a model. She had left William sitting on the bridge and had walked up the lake side, repeating to herself the precious 'Glow-worm' poem. When she returned she found him 'writing a poem descriptive of the sights and sounds we saw and heard. There was the gentle flowing of the stream, the glittering, lively lake, green fields without a living creature to be seen on them, behind us a flat pasture with 42 cattle feeding.'[1] So in the poem:

> The Cock is crowing,
> The stream is flowing,
> The small birds twitter,
> The lake doth glitter,
> The green field sleeps in the sun;
> The oldest and youngest
> Are at work with the strongest;
> The cattle are grazing,
> Their heads never raising;
> There are forty feeding like one!

Not all even of these lighter poems were completed without toil and effort. Dorothy recorded that on April 28th he worked away at *The Tinker* 'though he was ill and tired. . . . He promised me he would get his tea and do no more, but I have got mine an hour and a quarter and he has scarcely begun his.'

He also wrote at this time several poems about wild flowers. The two 'Celandine' poems were written on April 30th and May 1st, while sitting on the fell-side above the cottage.[2] *Foresight*, about the wild strawberry, was written after a chance remark of Dorothy's,[3] and two poems about the daisy show how determined he was to celebrate the humbler works of Nature just as much as the humbler ranks of human society—his little girls and beggars. The first stanza of the first 'Daisy' poem is a

[1] Ibid., p. 133. Apr. 16th 1802.
[2] Ibid., pp. 140–1. Apr. 30th and May 1st 1802.
[3] Ibid., p. 139. Apr. 28th. 'I happened to say when I was young I would not have pulled a strawberry blossom. . . . At dinner time he came in with the poem . . . but it was not quite finished, and it kept him long off his dinner.'

picture of himself in that unquiet period of his youth when, as he said again later in *The Prelude*, he was under the domination of 'the bodily eye' without being able to exercise the imaginative faculty; then in the serener mood of the more recent years:

> In youth from rock to rock I went,
> From hill to hill in discontent
> Of pleasure high and turbulent,
>   Most pleased when most uneasy;
> But now my own delights I make,
> My thirst at every rill can slake,
> And gladly Nature's love partake
>   Of Thee, sweet Daisy.

Unlike *To the Cuckoo* and *To a Butterfly*, the flower poems do not proceed from the deepest levels of his experience and when he came to classify his poems in his own highly individual way some years later, he placed them, rightly, among *Poems of the Fancy*, and not among *Poems of the Imagination*.[1]

A little later, on June 8th, he wrote a lyric which catches the spirit of a summer evening with the same vividness as 'The Cock is crowing' had caught the mood of a spring morning, and which, like that poem, is an immediate transmutation of mood into poetry with no intermediate process of 'recollection'. Dorothy relates the circumstances. 'After tea' (that is to say, late in the evening, for 'tea' was then the last meal of the day) 'William went out and walked and wrote that poem, "The sun has long been set", etc. He first went up to G. Mackereth's with the horse, afterwards he walked on our own path' (that is the path bordering John's Grove) 'and wrote the lines; he called me into the orchard, and there repeated them to me—he then stayed there till 11 o'clock.'

> The sun has long been set,
> The stars are out by twos and threes,
> The little birds are piping yet
>   Among the bushes and trees;

---

[1] The metre of the 'Daisy' poems is the same as Ben Jonson's *Underwoods* and Drayton's *Nymphidia*. He had lately been reading Jonson, but the poems are also closely akin to Burns', *To a Mountain Daisy*, with which he had been long familiar. A third 'Daisy' poem, in a different metre, was written in 1805 after the death of John Wordsworth, as a memorial to him.

There's a cuckoo, and one or two thrushes,
And a far-off wind that rushes,
With a noise of water that gushes,
And the cuckoo's sovereign cry
Fills all the hollow of the sky.
   Who would go 'parading'
In London, and 'masquerading',
On such a night of June,
With that beautiful soft half-moon,
And all these innocent blisses?
On such a night as this is![1]

A few nights later they walked together on the same path and Dorothy, with William's lines in mind, observed: 'It was a silent night. The stars were out by ones and twos, but no cuckoo, no little birds, the air was not warm, and we have observed that since Tuesday, 8th, when William wrote "The sun has long been set", that we have had no birds singing after the evening is fairly set in.' The poem, which was published in 1807, was for some reason omitted from all subsequent editions until 1835, when 'at the request of the Friend in whose presence the lines were thrown off'—that is of Dorothy—it was at length reprinted.

Another poem which can now with confidence be assigned to this spring[2] (though Dorothy does not mention its composition) is the first of the two poems *To a Skylark*—'Up with me! Up with me into the clouds'. Its joyous style and the flowing freedom of its metre—a wonderful paraphrase of the lark's singing —relate it closely in spirit to such lyrics as 'The cock is crowing' and 'The sun has long been set.' Coleridge, said Wordsworth long afterwards, used 'severely to condemn and treat it contemptuously', and when it appeared in the *Poems* of 1807 it received very severe treatment from the reviews, but Wordsworth always liked it though he altered some of its expressions in later editions.

The most important poem (except for the *Ode*) of this wonderful spring was begun on May 3rd, in the evening, continued the next day, and finished, in its first form, on May

---

[1] The lines about 'parading' and 'masquerading' refer to Burns's poem *The Twa Dogs*:

    At operas and plays parading,
    Mortgaging, gambling, masquerading.

[2] *Poems in Two Volumes*, ed. T. Hutchinson, 1897, pp. 185–6. G. Whalley, *Coleridge and Sara Hutchinson and the Asra Poems*, 1955, p. 25.

7th. This was *Resolution and Independence*, or, as they always called it among themselves, *The Leech-Gatherer*.[1] It is perhaps the poem in which we see more of Wordsworth than in any other single poem: here are many of his most characteristic moods and states of soul; joy and despondency; trance and vision; here too are stanzas and lines almost as 'homely' in style as some of the *Lyrical Ballads*, side by side with tones of deepest passion. The history of the poem is somewhat curious. On October 3rd 1800 William and Dorothy met an old man in the road who told them that he was a leech-gatherer. Dorothy's description of him in her Journal gives us the groundwork of the poem. He was 'almost double', wore 'an apron and a night-cap', besides two coats; he had had a wife, 'a good woman, and it pleased God to bless us with ten children'. 'All these were dead but one, of whom he had not heard for many years, a sailor. His trade was to gather leeches, but now leeches are scarce and he had not strength for it. He lived by begging and was making his way to Carlisle, where he should buy a few godly books to sell. . . . He had been hurt in driving a cart, . . . his body driven over, his skull fractured.'

It will be noticed that nearly two years elapsed between meeting the leech-gatherer and writing the poem. And the old man of the poem is not a retired, but a working leech-gatherer, and Wordsworth meets him, not in the road, and in Dorothy's company, but alone on a moor, beside a mountain pool. *The Leech-Gatherer* is, indeed, an example of a new picture created by Wordsworth out of old materials drawn from the 'hiding-places' of the past, united to more recent experiences and moods. Of these, the most striking in the poem is the mood of exaltation with which the poem opens, followed immediately by one of depression and gloom at the thought of 'mighty poets in their misery dead'.

> But, as it sometimes chanceth, from the might
> Of joy in minds that can no further go,
> As high as we have mounted in delight
> In our dejection do we sink as low;
> To me that morning did it happen so. . . .

---

[1] The references to the writing of the poem in Dorothy's Journal are as follows: *D.W.J.* i, p. 142, May 4th; p. 144, May 7th; p. 145, May 9th; then a long gap, and p. 166, July 2nd and July 4th.

Then comes the stanza about the poets, 'Chatterton, the marvellous Boy', and Burns, so glorious in youth, so disastrously dead in his prime, and the conclusion:

> We poets in our youth begin in gladness,
> But thereof come in the end despondency and madness.

Of what nature was the dejection which Wordsworth experienced and from which, in the poem, he is rescued by the conversation with the old man? The key to its cause lies probably in the word 'thereof' in the last line of the third stanza. The very gladness which poets experience in such a high degree contains in itself the seeds of their own undoing. Conscious of immeasurable creative powers, endowed with unusual capacities of understanding and joy, they are also, for all their gifts, strangely vulnerable. Chatterton's 'pride', which would not suffer him to ask for help, even when he was starving, drove him to suicide. Burns's conviviality killed him. Collins, a poet deeply beloved by Wordsworth, went 'melancholy mad'. And what of two poets yet more closely known—himself and Coleridge? There can be little doubt that Wordsworth's physical sufferings during the last two or three years—his prostrating headaches, the pain in his chest and side, and above all perhaps his sleeplessness—were arousing in him fears that he would not be able to continue with his poetic vocation. The very act of writing was in itself the sure prelude to physical and nervous exhaustion, as many an entry in Dorothy's Journal during this spring had testified. As long ago as the Goslar winter of 1799 he had told Coleridge how much his health limited his writing.[1] More recently he had told Miss Taylor, his unknown correspondent, that he intended to devote his life to literature 'if my health will permit me'. In May 1801 Dorothy had written to Coleridge: 'Poor William! His stomach is in bad plight. We have put aside all the manuscript poems, and it is agreed between us that I am not to give them up to him even if he asks for them.' Where almost every act of concentrated poetic composition— at least if accompanied by writing—led to this sort of thing, the future may well have looked black, and depression have been a frequent companion. For to Wordsworth poetry was life. Coleridge also must have been among the poets doomed to

---

[1] See above, p. 415.

disaster in Wordsworth's thought. The events of the past six or seven weeks had been closely concerned with him: with his health, his domestic problems, his poetry, and his future. What Wordsworth himself tells us about some of the origins of *The Leech-Gatherer* seems to lead naturally enough to Coleridge. 'I was', says Wordsworth, 'in the state of feeling described in the beginning of the poem [that is in a mood of exaltation quickly followed by depression] while crossing over Barton Fell from Mr. Clarkson's, at the foot of Ullswater, towards Askham.' That may have been on April 7th 1802 (his thirty-second birthday) when he left the Clarksons on foot to go into Yorkshire to visit Mary Hutchinson. Only two days earlier he and Dorothy had parted from Coleridge, and three weeks before that Coleridge had walked into their cottage 'half-stupefied', and William and Dorothy had sat up till four o'clock talking about him. Then on April 21st he had come again and had read them his verses to Sara, and Dorothy and (can we doubt it?) William also, had felt the joy fade from the spring landscape as he read. It is difficult not to feel that one stanza of *The Leech-Gatherer*, although Wordsworth is speaking of himself, is not even more descriptive of Coleridge than it is of Wordsworth.

> My whole life have I lived in pleasant thought,
> As if life's business were a summer mood;
> As if all needful things would come unsought,
> To genial faith, still rich in genial good; . . .
> But how can he expect that others should
> Build for him, sow for him, and at his will
> Love him, who for himself will take no heed at all?

Coleridge's craving for love, understanding, and approval led him as we have seen sometimes to demand almost superhuman forbearance from his friends. And he certainly took even less effective heed of his personal affairs—though constantly talking about them—than did Wordsworth who managed somehow to live within his tiny income and even to take over some of Coleridge's debts.

The poem goes on to describe his encounter with the leech-gatherer, and here we meet for the first time with a word new in Wordsworth's vocabulary—one which was to play an increasingly important part in the poetry of the years to come. It is the word 'grace'. The sudden sight of the old man is thus introduced:

> Now whether it was by peculiar grace,[1]
> A leading from above, a something given,
> Yet it befell that, in this lonely place,
> When I with these untoward thoughts had striven,
> Beside a pool bare to the eye of heaven
> I saw a Man before me unawares. . . .

Henceforward the poem, as far as Wordsworth is concerned, becomes visionary in quality. The strange conversation between the two moves onward, during which Wordsworth twice fell into a sort of trance;

> But now his voice to me was like a stream
> Scarce heard; nor word from word could I divide:
> And the whole body of the Man did seem
> Like one whom I had met with in a dream;
> Or like a man from some far region sent,
> To give me human strength, by apt admonishment.

And the second time:

> In my mind's eye I seemed to see him pace
> About the weary moors continually,
> Wandering about alone and silently.

He was in the world of vision once more, the same world into which he had entered that day on Penrith Beacon years before when he had fled in terror from the gibbet.[2] It can scarcely be by chance that the landscape of *The Leech-Gatherer* is almost identical with that of the incident on Penrith Beacon—a wide and desolate moor, with a mountain tarn, and, in each case, one solitary human figure. The leech-gatherer himself is likewise closely akin to two other figures who had helped to shape Wordsworth's soul—the blind man seen in the streets of London on whom he had gazed

> As if admonished from another world,[3]

and the discharged soldier whom he had met in the moonlight

---

[1] The phrase 'a peculiar grace' is used in *The Happy Warrior*, written in 1805.
[2] See above, p. 11.
[3] *Prel.* VII, l. 649. The similarity between this line and the description of the leech-gatherer as

> a man from some far region sent
> To give me human strength by apt admonishment

is very striking.

on the road at Sawrey during his first long vacation, who told his soldier's tale and answered Wordsworth's questions with

> a strange half-absence, as of one
> Knowing too well the importance of his theme,
> But feeling it no longer.

All these figures, and the leech-gatherer himself, are invested with the atmosphere of what he called 'visionary dreariness', from which he was able to draw a strange inward strength and peace.

The Leech-Gatherer is of personal importance in the life of Wordsworth because it shows that he was still, in spite of the loss of his vision of the glory of Nature lamented in the *Ode*, capable of passing into the visionary state when deeply moved by human encounters. It took a year and a half for the vision to mature. The great significance which the old man came to have for him was the result of the accumulated fears and hopes of his creative years. Yet it was in the end a simple moral experience. He felt himself rebuked, admonished, cheered. The last stanza carries us deep into Wordsworth's real humility of heart:

> And soon with this he other matter blended,
> Cheerfully uttered, with demeanour kind,
> But stately in the main—

(again, we are reminded of the discharged soldier's 'stately air of mild indifference')—

> and, when he ended,
> I could have laughed myself to scorn to find
> In that decrepit Man so firm a mind.
> 'God', said I, 'be my help and stay secure,
> I'll think of the Leech-gatherer upon the lonely moor!'

The Leech-Gatherer was originally a longer poem than any text of it which now exists.[1] It was sent, in its original form, about the end of May, to Mary and Sara Hutchinson for their perusal. We do not possess the letter in which they offered certain criticisms, but we have William's and Dorothy's replies

---

[1] Coleridge, enumerating the poems written by Wordsworth during this summer, in a letter to Southey in July, says that they were 'Thirty-two in all' and that one of them contained 'one hundred and sixty lines'. This must be *The Leech-Gatherer* of which the present text is 140 lines.

to them,[1] documents highly characteristic of the writers and revealing in a quaint manner the intensity of Wordsworth's views about his own poetry. The poem had evidently, in its first form, contained an account of the leech-gatherer's former life, his marriage, and his ten children. This Mary and Sara had had the temerity to criticize as 'tedious'. Wordsworth wrote to Sara:

You say and Mary (that is you can say no more than that) the Poem is *very well* after the introduction of the old man; this is not true, if it is not more than very well it is very bad, there is no intermediate state. You speak of his speech as tedious; everything is tedious when one does not read with the feelings of the Author—*The Thorn* is tedious to hundreds; and so is the *Idiot Boy* to hundreds. It is in the character of the old man to tell his story in a manner which an *impatient* reader must necessarily feel as tedious. But Good God! Such a figure, in such a place, a pious self-respecting, miserably infirm Old Man telling such a tale!

My dear Sara [he went on], it is not a matter of indifference whether you are pleased with this figure and his employment . . . it is of the utmost importance that you should have had pleasure from contemplating the fortitude, independence, persevering spirit, and the general moral dignity of this old man's character. Your feelings upon the Mother,[2] and the Boys with the Butterfly,[3] were not indifferent: it was an affair of whole continents of moral sympathy.

To this lecture Dorothy also added a postscript:

Dear Sara—when you happen to be displeased with what you suppose to be the tendency or moral of any poem which William writes, ask yourself whether you have hit upon the real tendency and true moral, and above all never think that he writes for no reason but merely because a thing happened—and when you feel any poem of his to be tedious, ask yourself in what spirit it was written—whether merely to tell the tale and be through with it, or to illustrate a particular character or truth etc.

Dorothy's advice is, in fact, the best possible for most people embarking on the study of Wordsworth's poetry.

The end of this episode is the most amusing part of it. When *Resolution and Independence* appeared in print in the *Poems in Two Volumes* in 1807, all Sara's and Mary's criticisms had been adopted and the necessary alterations made, even to verbal

---

[1] *E.L.* 132, pp. 304–7. D.W and W.W. to M.H. and S.H., June 14th 1802.
[2] i.e. *The Emigrant Mother.*   [3] i.e. *Beggars.*

details.[1] It is probable that their views were upheld and rein-
forced by a more powerful critic—Coleridge himself. *The Leech-
Gatherer*, or as much of it as then existed, was read or repeated
to him, probably on that very May 4th when it was first composed. It was a hot day: they met Coleridge on the Wythburn
side of Dunmail Raise, and went with him to 'a moss-covered
rock, rising out of the bed of the river', where, in an immortal
vignette, Dorothy recorded: 'William and C. repeated and read
verses: I drank a little brandy and water and was in Heaven.'
Many years afterwards, Coleridge used *The Leech-Gatherer* to
illustrate what he called Wordsworth's 'inconstancy of style'—
his sudden sinkings from the sublime to the commonplace.[2] In all
probability the parts of the poem which concerned the old man's
former life were in the more 'matter-of-fact' Wordsworthian
manner which Coleridge always disliked, and which Mary and
Sara found 'tedious'. Their ultimate omission shows that Wordsworth was by no means as impervious to argument as he
seemed. Nor of course was this the only occasion on which he
yielded to the opinions of others on points of style. Lamb's
criticisms of *A Poet's Epitaph* were all adopted in later editions,
and so were some of Coleridge's on the *Ode*.

Besides Coleridge, Mary, and Sara, *The Leech-Gatherer*,
while yet in manuscript, had another, humbler auditor whose
opinion of it is not recorded. On this same June 14th, while
Dorothy was writing the first part of the joint letter to Mary
and Sara, the hair-cutter, Williamson, came to cut Wordsworth's
hair. 'William', wrote Dorothy, 'is reading the Leech-gatherer
to him'. One of the Wordsworth's neighbours at Town End—
probably Peggy Ashburner—was 'well acquainted with The
Thorn';[3] so they were evidently in the habit of reading the
poems to their village friends as well as to their own intimate
circle.

On May 9th, the same day that he finished *The Leech-Gatherer*
in its first form, Wordsworth began another important poem,
which he called *Stanzas written in my Pocket-copy of Thomson's
'Castle of Indolence'*. It was about himself and Coleridge.

---

[1] Mary had objected to the word 'view' used as a verb, and to the expression
'sickness had by him'. In the printed text there is no verb 'view' and 'had' is
changed to 'felt'.   [2] *B.L.*, ch. xxii.
[3] *M.Y.* i. 275, p. 64. W.W. to Sir G. Beaumont, Sept. 1806.

'William', says Dorothy, 'worked at The Leech Gatherer almost incessantly from morning till tea-time. I copied The Leech Gatherer and other poems for Coleridge. I was oppressed and sick at heart, for he wearied himself to death. After tea he wrote two stanzas in the manner of Thomson's *Castle of Indolence* and was tired out.' Next day: 'William is still at work, though it is past ten o'clock—he will be tired out I'm sure. My heart fails me.' Finally, on the 11th: 'William finished the stanzas about C. and himself.' These stanzas form one of Wordsworth's most delightful poems. It must always remain a mystery that Matthew Arnold in his notes on the poem made an erroneous identification; saying that the first four stanzas describe Coleridge, and the next three Wordsworth. It is of course the other way round. First there is his own self-portrait; his happiness; his restless comings and goings; his frequent fits of depression, illness, and exhaustion; his hours of silence and contemplation; his siestas in the orchard; his possession by his muse as by a daemon.

> Here on his hours he hung as on a book,
> On his own time here would he float away,
> As doth a fly upon a summer brook. . . .[1]

> Ah! piteous sight it was to see this Man
> When he came back to us, a withered flower—
> Or like a sinful creature, pale and wan.

> Down would he sit, and without strength or power
> Look at the common grass from hour to hour:
> And oftentimes, how long I fear to say,
> Where apple-trees in blossom make a bower,
> Retired in that sunshiny shade he lay;
> And, like a naked Indian, slept himself away.

The poem seems to represent him as rather more restless than he actually was.

> Thus often would he leave our peaceful home,
> And find elsewhere his business or delight,
> Out of our Valley's limits did he roam:
> Full many a time, upon a stormy night
> His voice came to us from the neighbouring height . . .

[1] Cf. the first of the sonnets *To Sleep*, ll. 6–8. *P.W.* iii, p. 8.

Some thought he was a lover and did woo:
Some thought far worse of him and judged him wrong;[1]
But verse was what he had been wedded to;
And his own mind did like a tempest strong
Come to him thus, and drove the weary Wight along.

Wordsworth did not in fact often leave the valley under the impulse of his muse. More often it was to visit Coleridge at Keswick, though he would often return, as described, at an unexpected hour. Poetic inspiration indeed often 'kindled' out of doors, but frequently no further from home than 'John's Grove', or Easedale beck, or the fell above the house. But the 'driving' nature of the visitation when it did come, allowing no rest and frequently reducing him to complete exhaustion, is testified to often enough by Dorothy in her Journal.

How tender and whimsical are the verses about Coleridge!

A noticeable man with large grey eyes
And a pale face that seemed undoubtedly
As if a blooming face it ought to be.

Unfortunately the most living line of all,

A face divine of heaven-born idiocy,

was cut out and something less vivid substituted, although Coleridge had once described himself as having a face of 'great, indeed, almost idiotic good-nature'. Then,

Noisy he was, and gamesome as a boy;
His limbs would toss about him with delight
Like branches when strong winds the trees annoy.

Justice Coleridge, when Wordsworth read the poem to him in 1836, wrote: 'Wordsworth and Mrs. W. both assured me the description at that time was perfectly accurate; that he was almost as a great boy in feelings and had all the tricks and fancies there described.'[2] All Coleridge's many-sided 'goings-on' are there; his 'devices' and 'inventions rare', musical and scientific.

Long blades of grass, plucked round him as he lay,
Made, to his ear attentively applied
A pipe on which the wind would deftly play;
Glasses he had, that little things display,

[1] Presumably this means that some people thought him insane.
[2] *Mem.* ii, p. 309.

> The beetle, panoplied in gems and gold,
> A mailèd angel on a battle day. . . .

Coleridge is represented as 'enticing' 'that other Man' 'to view his imagery', and the last stanza shows them in all the happiness of their great companionship before they were forced apart by Coleridge's vain search for health in a foreign climate, and by all the unhappiness that followed his return.

> There did they dwell—from earthly labour free,
> As happy spirits as were ever seen,
> If but a bird, to keep them company,
> Or butterfly sat down, they were, I ween,
> As pleased as if the same had been a Maiden-queen.

It is the privilege of poets to enter more completely into the beauty and interest of the passing moment than can most other men, and this poem of Wordsworth's—so skilfully imitating in its style the poetry of an earlier generation, yet remaining entirely original—has preserved for us their frequent and intense enjoyments, so eagerly shared, which were as real a part of their friendship as the communication of sorrow and 'dejection'.

The spring of 1802 was a time of lyric creation never again equalled by Wordsworth. That is not to say that he never again wrote lyrics as great as those of this spring, for *The Solitary Reaper* and *I wandered lonely as a Cloud* and the rest of the *Ode* were yet to come, and several besides of a high order. Nor had he even reached the highest point of his creative activity, for *The Prelude* was yet unwritten save for the first two books, and so were all the sonnets. But the months from March to early June 1802 were unsurpassed for the frequency with which poem followed poem, as well as for their quality. In a period of about ten weeks he had written over thirty poems,[1] nearly all of high, many of supreme, interest and excellence. It is, however we look at it, a remarkable achievement. Curiously, yet characteristically, he took no steps about publication, although *Lyrical Ballads* appeared in another edition (the third of the first volume) in this very summer. The reason was partly his great dislike of 'the toil of publishing', and partly his feeling that his next

[1] 'Thirty-two', says Coleridge. *S.T.C.* i, p. 386.

publication ought to be *The Recluse*. Eventually, however, when it was clear *The Recluse* would not be forthcoming, they appeared, with many sonnets, as *Poems in Two Volumes*, in 1807.

The greatest of the poems had been the product of a strong uprising of his power of imaginative recollection combined with the depth and passion of his feeling about Coleridge and about his own poetic vocation. Nothing in any of them betrays his pre-occupation with another matter which was in fact demanding at this very time much expense of thought and emotion. He was about to marry Mary Hutchinson, and in order to do so without reproach, he felt that with the advent of peace between England and France, he must first bring to an end in honourable fashion his connexion with Annette Vallon. The spring and summer of 1802 were filled with intricate negotiations to this end. Unfortunately we are obliged to rely largely on conjecture where Annette is concerned, for all letters from her have been lost, and only the broad outlines of what occurred are certainly known.

XVII

MARRIAGE, 1802-3

By the end of 1801 William and Mary had determined to marry. There can seldom have been a more unobtrusive wooing. Not a single poem of this most prolific spring of 1802 was addressed to Mary or was even remotely concerned with her, except *A Farewell*, the poem written about the cottage at the end of May 1802, in anticipation of leaving Grasmere to marry Mary and fetch her home. And in that he seems rather to recommend Mary to the 'little nook of mountain ground' as a suitable inhabitant, rather than to offer the cottage to Mary as a wedding gift. Addressing the cottage, he says:

> A gentle Maid, whose heart is lowly bred,
> Whose pleasures are in wild fields gathered,
> With joyousness, and with a thoughtful cheer,
> Will come to you; to you herself will wed;
> And love the blessèd life that we lead here.

Had Wordsworth chosen Mary Hutchinson to be his wife chiefly because she loved the kind of life that he and Dorothy led together? Such a conclusion would not be far from the truth. His love for Mary was as different from his love for Annette as love can be, and yet remain love. It was, for one thing, the result of long familiarity, whereas his passion for Annette had swept him off his feet in a few weeks. In the five periods which he had spent in Mary's company—at Racedown in the spring of 1797, at Sockburn in 1799, at Gallow Hill in 1800, and twice at Grasmere in the spring of 1800 and the last two months of 1801, he had learnt to love what from boyhood he had recognized in her—her 'perfect happiness of soul'.[1]

The part played by the sisters, Mary and Sara Hutchinson, in the lives of Coleridge and Wordsworth is remarkable just because it is so undramatic. Coleridge had fallen in love with Sara at Sockburn in 1799 and thenceforward she was his good angel, helper, and confidante. It is doubtful how far his wife

---

[1] See above, pp. 78-79, for the description of Mary in *Prel.* XII, ll. 151-73.

ever realized the extent of his love for the other Sara, who certainly never gave Sara Coleridge cause for ordinary jealousy, nor, it seems, did Coleridge ever endeavour to make her do so. Sara Coleridge was in fact more jealous of the Wordsworths than of Sara Hutchinson, probably because, as Coleridge himself told her,[1] the Wordsworths in their habits and conversation were more remote from her than either of the Hutchinsons. They moved in what to her was an uncivilized world, into which they were continually drawing her husband. Their immense walks, which were often nocturnal, and in all weathers; their carelessness about times of arrival and departure; the ruin of clothes and footwear which resulted from their rambles;[2] their complete lack of conventional 'gentility' were a sore trial to a woman to whom convention meant everything.

Mary and Sara, on the other hand, while all their sympathies and tastes lay with the poets and Dorothy, somehow contrived to be less 'wild'. They had, both of them, a certain steadying, soothing power, and this perhaps was what made them both such acceptable companions to three people as storm-tossed with emotion as Coleridge, William, and Dorothy.

Mary was only less dear to Coleridge than Sara. How Mary's gentleness soothed and comforted him in his distress is revealed in the original version of *Dejection: an Ode*. It is probably a memory of his visit to the Hutchinsons in the summer of 1801. Addressing Sara, he says:

> It was as calm as this, that happy night
> When Mary, thou and I together were,
> The low decaying Fire our only Light,
> And listen'd to the Stillness of the Air!
> O that affectionate and blameless Maid,
> Dear Mary! on her Lap my head she lay'd—
> Her Hand was on my Brow,
> Even as my own is now;
> And on my Cheek I felt the eye-lash play.
> Such joy I had, that I may truly say,
> My spirit was awe-stricken with Excess
> And trance-like Depth of its brief Happiness.

---

[1] *U.L.* i. 110, p. 238. S.T.C. to Mrs. Coleridge, Jan. 5th 1803.

[2] 'I have now no clothes but what are patched at the elbows and knees and in the seat', wrote Coleridge to Sara Hutchinson after his descent from Sca Fell in Aug. 1802. See below, p. 576.

Two memorials, one in stone, and one on paper, remained to bear unconscious witness to the interlocking friendship of Coleridge, the Wordsworths, and the Hutchinson sisters. One was a rock on the road to Keswick, which they called 'Sara's Rock', on which they carved their initials on their many journeys to and from each other's homes:

W.W., M.H., D.W., S.T.C., J.W., S.H.

On the day when *The Leech-Gatherer* was first read to Coleridge on the other side of Dunmail Raise, Dorothy recorded: 'We parted from Coleridge at Sara's crag, after having looked at the letters which C. carved in the morning. I kissed them all. William deepened the T. with C's pen-knife.' The rock was blasted away when the new road was made along Thirlmere.[1] The other memorial, a frail sheet of blotting-paper, has survived the rock. It lies opposite the date May 15th 1802, in Dorothy's Journal and on it is written:

S. T. Coleridge

Dorothy Wordsworth. William Wordsworth

Mary Hutchinson. Sara Hutchinson.

William. Coleridge. Mary.

Dorothy. Sara.

16th May

1802

John Wordsworth.

One name is conspicuous by its absence—that of Sara Coleridge.

Every week in the spring months of 1802 and sometimes oftener, Dorothy wrote to Mary Hutchinson, and as often Mary wrote to her. Sometimes Dorothy wrote to Mary and Sara together, for it seems that from February to the end of April Mary was staying at Bishop Middleham, near Bishop Auckland in Durham, where George, her youngest brother, was farming and Sara keeping house for him. Tom Hutchinson was established as a tenant-farmer at Gallow Hill near Scarborough: normally Mary was his house-keeper, but as Joanna lived there also Mary was able to move about from one brother to another, and to make her visits to Grasmere and Penrith. Dorothy's

---

[1] The late Canon H. D. Rawnsley vainly endeavoured to prevent its destruction. Some fragments of it have been built up near the spot. A most interesting water-colour sketch of it in its original setting on the road by the lake is in the possession of Mrs. Rawnsley at Allan Bank.

letters seem to have been mainly of the diary-type; an account of their daily doings.[1] Sometimes William added a postscript, but the main burden of the correspondence fell on the indefatigable Dorothy, so that it is scarcely an exaggeration to say, as De Quincey afterwards did, that she wrote his love-letters for him all through this spring of his strange courtship.

Wordsworth's marriage entailed bringing his wife into an already existing household. That Dorothy would share their home and their life was accepted as a matter of course from the first. But Dorothy would not have been human if she had not looked forward to so important an event as her brother's marriage with a measure of 'agitation' and suffering. This, as she knew and said, was not due to any forebodings about her own or her brother's happiness, but to the uncontrollable force of her 'tender feelings'. Mary, except for Jane Marshall, was her oldest friend; their contrasting temperaments made each an object of interest to the other, while their fundamental feelings and enjoyments were the same. It was not likely that Dorothy, who had unhesitatingly welcomed the unknown Annette as a sister simply because William loved her, would shrink from accepting Mary at the cottage as William's bride. On September 29th, a few days before the wedding, she wrote to Jane: 'I have long loved Mary Hutchinson as a sister, and she is equally attached to me; this being so, you will guess that I look forward with perfect happiness to this connection between us, but, happy as I am, I half dread that concentration of all tender feelings, past, present and future which will come upon me on the wedding morning.' And, as we know, she did suffer on that day. But neither before nor after the wedding, nor through all the long years of close companionship that lay ahead, is there any trace, in letter or journal, or from the observations of any third person, of strain or impatience or jealousy between the two women upon whom the happiness of Wordsworth's life depended. Here, indeed, lay the great motive of their concord. They were both necessary to William. And to anyone familiar with the ecstasies and depressions which succeeded one another from

---

[1] *E.L.* 129 and 132 are the only letters surviving of the correspondence of this spring and summer. In the second (written on Monday June 14th 1802) Dorothy says: 'Now for a little history of what has passed since I wrote last to you, which was on Wednesday, a long time for me, I have seldom been so long lately.'

day to day at the cottage, it must appear that the presence
there of so 'benign' a being as Mary Hutchinson could only
have exercised upon the brother and sister a calming and
beneficent power.

Mary's appearance and manner are best known to us through
De Quincey, who saw her first in 1807, when, with Sara
Coleridge and her children, he arrived at Town End on his first
visit to the poet whom he had long all but worshipped. She was
not beautiful in any conventional sense; tall, dark-haired, and
with a fair and blooming skin, she had a most pronounced
'obliquity of vision'—probably a cast—which *ought* to have
been displeasing', but was not, because of that 'supreme expression of her features . . . a sunny benignity, a radiant
graciousness, such as in this world I never saw surpassed'. She
was not, like Dorothy, talkative; Clarkson used to say that she
'could only say, "God bless you!"' But it would be a mistake to
think of Mary as a mere statue of benevolence. She was deeply
sensitive; her tenderness of heart made her so, and she could be
physically affected by her feelings just as Dorothy and William
could be. Dorothy wrote to her on April 16th 1802, just after
returning with William from their visit to the Clarksons at
Eusemere:

> My dear, dear Mary! I am deeply concerned to hear that you
> are so thin. . . . I cannot doubt but that you *will endeavour* to take
> care of yourself, yet I am very fearful that your ardour of mind
> may lead you to do imprudent things. . . . Take no more exercise
> than would be proper for the regaining of your strength supposing
> that you were nearly as *weak* as you are *thin*—above all, my dearest
> Mary, seek quiet or rather amusing thoughts—Study the flowers, the
> birds and all the common things that are about you. O Mary, my dear
> Sister! be quiet and happy. Take care of yourself—keep yourself
> employed without fatigue, and do not make loving us your busi-
> ness, but let your love of us make up the spirit of all the business
> you have.

Mary's anxiety is better understood when some of the events
of this spring of 1802 are realized. On December 21st 1801,
while Mary was staying at the cottage, there came a letter 'from
France'.[1] It was, of course, from Annette Vallon. The negotiations which resulted in the Peace of Amiens in March 1802 were

---

[1] *D.W.J.* i, p. 92.

already in progress, and it was once more possible to exchange letters. Wordsworth answered it on January 26th 1802. Between then and the beginning of July six letters were received from Annette—one of them was from Caroline also, now nearly ten years old—while William wrote three times to Annette, and Dorothy twice.[1] The dates of some of these letters are interwoven with sundry journeyings of William to visit Mary, and with an important decision taken at the end of March, that William and Dorothy should visit Annette.

Whether Annette's letter was a reply to an earlier one from Wordsworth we do not know. Dorothy's Journal records nothing previous to this letter from Annette; as all subsequent correspondence between them is recorded, it seems probable that Annette was the first to write. Her letter naturally gave rise to many anxious considerations, which may account for the delay in answering it. There was Caroline to be considered; some financial provision for her might be asked which Wordsworth could ill afford to make on the eve of marriage. That Annette was still suggesting marriage between herself and William is improbable. She was known as 'Madame Williams', or even 'Veuve Williams' among her friends, and evidently considered this as a sufficient protection of her name. She is much more likely to have felt anxiety for her daughter's future than for her own. In any case she was now deeply involved with the 'underground' Royalist movement in France, and could scarcely have contemplated leaving her country. Her life since 1792 had been one of danger, secret intrigue, and all that we associate nowadays with the word 'resistance'. Her brother Paul Vallon had very nearly lost his life during the Terror and was in hiding in Orleans for many months. Annette and her sisters lived together in Blois, which was a centre of counter-revolutionary activity and of Chouan resistance. The house of the Vallon sisters was known to the Government, throughout the years of the Directoire and Consulate, as a place of refuge for Chouans, emigrants, and priests who refused to take the 'constitutional' oath and were consequently proscribed. In January 1800 the house was ordered to be searched and Annette herself was described by the govern-

---

[1] *D.W.J.* i. Feb. 16th, 22nd, 24th; Mar. 22nd, 26th; May 15th; June 7th, 12th, 14th; July 3rd, 5th. The letters of June 14th and July 5th were written by D.W., those of Feb. 24th, Mar. 26th, and May 15th by W.W.

ment police as 'Widow Williams at Blois; gives shelter to Chouans'. The sisters remained, however, personally unmolested, though they were never reconciled to the régime of Napoleon, as many of their friends were. At the Bourbon Restoration Annette's unfailing courage and devotion to the Royalist cause was the subject of a petition from many leading Royalists to the king for a pension in her favour—a recognition which was somewhat tardily granted. From that time onwards she appears to have lived entirely in Paris.[1]

On February 14th, a fine winter morning, with snow on the hills, Wordsworth decided to go on horseback to Penrith, to see Mary who was staying there with her aunt Elizabeth Monkhouse. 'Off he went', says Dorothy, 'in his blue spencer, and a pair of *new* pantaloons fresh from London. He turned back when he had got as far as Frank [Baty]'s to ask if he had his letters safe then for some apples, then fairly off.' He stayed, apparently, with the Clarksons, and only saw Mary 'for a couple of hours between Eamont Bridge and Hartshorn Tree'.[2] They discoursed, no doubt, chiefly about Annette. It is even possible that William now for the first time told Mary the story, though it is far more likely that she had known about it almost from the first, for Dorothy had made no secret of it to her other friend, Jane Marshall. But a new situation had arisen which required her co-operation. The strangeness and pathos of it all could not but have affected her and perhaps contributed to the 'thinness' which two months later gave Dorothy so much concern.

While Wordsworth was at Penrith a reply came from Annette. Its contents cannot have been displeasing, for Dorothy recorded that she and William 'spent a sweet evening' on his return, which must mean one tolerably free from anxiety. Annette's next letter, received on March 22nd, is described as being from 'poor Annette'; possibly because it contained an account of the dangers and privations she had suffered in recent years; but whatever its contents it had important consequences. 'We resolved', says Dorothy, 'to see Annette, and that William should go to Mary.'

---

[1] *A.V.* passim.
[2] Hartshorn Tree was an ancient oak on the road from Penrith to Appleby, the scene of a medieval hunting adventure. It was still standing in a decayed state for some years after 1802.

This second journey to see Mary took place at the beginning of April while they were staying with the Clarksons.[1] He set out on April 7th, his thirty-second birthday, Dorothy accompanying him for six miles. It was probably on this walk that he experienced those moods of exaltation followed by depression which he later commemorated in *The Leech-Gatherer*.[2] Going across country to Askham, where Dorothy probably left him, he would have taken coach from Penrith over Stanemoor, and reached Bishop Middleham, near Bishop Auckland, where Mary was staying with Sara and George, the next day. On the 12th Dorothy received a letter from himself and Mary. She had walked over snow-covered roads to Thomas Wilkinson's, at Yanwath on the Eamont, and received her letter while there, but as she was not alone she only glanced at it. The good Quaker insisted on accompanying her on her homeward walk when she would rather have been alone. He 'questioned me like a catechizer all the way. Every question was like the snapping of a little thread about my heart—I was so full of thought of my half-read letter and other things. I was glad when he left me. Then I had time to look at the moon while I was thinking over my own thoughts.' Next day, while she was out, William returned. A maid was sent to summon her. 'The surprise shot through me.'[3] 'I believe I screamed.'[4] She was always excited by his appearance, but her unusual agitation on this occasion must have been connected with her anxiety as to how Mary had received William's decision to visit Annette. Such a visit would involve a postponement of the date of their marriage (which had been originally designed to take place in the spring) until after it had been paid. And the date of the visit would depend on Annette and her movements.

Wordsworth brought back with him to Eusemere a poem. It was *The Glow-worm*, written as he was riding back from Middleham on a horse belonging to William Calvert.[5] 'Between

---

[1] See above, p. 519.   [2] See above, p. 540.
[3] *D.W.J.* i, p. 131. Apr. 13th 1802.
[4] *E.L.* 129, p. 290. D.W. to M.H., Apr. 16th 1802.
[5] Ibid. 128, p. 286. W.W. to S.T.C., Apr. 16th 1802. In this letter Wordsworth describes how the horse fell with him and was found to need shoeing. 'I was so ignorant as not to know that a horse might stand in need of new shoes though the old ones might not be loose.' He wished Coleridge to buy the horse, 'and I will make up any loss if he should not happen to suit you'.

the beginning of Lord Darlington's park at Raby and two or three miles beyond Staindrop' he became so absorbed in writing that he did not even notice the jogging of the horse.[1] *The Glow-worm* recorded 'an incident which took place about seven years ago between Dorothy and me'—that is, it was a memory of Racedown, and its opening line is

Among all lovely things my Love hath been.

'My Love', is not Mary, from whom he had just parted in 'an ugly storm of sleet and snow', but Dorothy, waiting anxiously at Eusemere for his return. Her notes about this poem are unusually full, a sure sign that she felt particular pleasure in it, as well she might.[2] He could not have devised a better means of assuring her that his love for her was unchangeable and unchanged.

During May and June the question of leaving Dove Cottage and going to live at Keswick again arose. Coleridge was most anxious that after William's marriage the Wordsworths should all come and live in the unoccupied rooms at Greta Hall. This plan was of course most unwelcome to Mrs. Coleridge, and fortunately Dorothy saw at once that it would not do. On June 7th she wrote to Mrs. Coleridge setting her mind at rest on the subject, and when Coleridge came over on the 10th, still hoping to persuade her, she remained firm. Even to live in another house at Keswick would, she thought, probably be unwise: to live at Greta Hall 'would do nothing but harm'.[3] By the middle of June they had decided to leave for Gallow Hill 'before the next full moon', and did actually depart on July 9th. By this time the plan for going to France had been fixed for August; they would spend a fortnight at Gallow Hill first, and the marriage would take place on their return.

It may here be asked, how could Wordsworth possibly contemplate marriage on an income of about £70 a year and the occasional earnings of his pen? Mary had only £400 of her

[1] *D.W.J.* i, p. 35. Apr. 20th 1802.
[2] For the poem see above, pp. 319–20. D.W. calls it *The Glow-worm*. *D.W.J.* i, p. 135.
[3] *E.L.* 132, p. 303. W.W. and D.W. to M. and S. Hutchinson, 14 June 1802. Dorothy's solitary visit to Keswick on May 17th was probably connected with this scheme (*D.W.J.* i, p. 148), as was Coleridge's letter of May 20th (ibid.) 'telling us not to go to Keswick'. He was evidently temporarily discouraged, but hopeful again a fortnight later.

own[1] and Dorothy, who would live with them, nothing at all, beyond the small allowance given her by her brothers John and Christopher. The question had, however, been carefully examined by the brother and sister, and Dorothy had come to the wise and unselfish decision which we should expect of her. At Richard's request she wrote to him in June stating what she considered to be an adequate allowance for herself, to be provided for her by her other three brothers, who were all hitherto unmarried, and earning reasonably good incomes.

I shall continue [she said] to live with my brother William,—but he having nothing to spare, nor being likely to have, at least for many years, I am obliged (I need not say how much he regrets this necessity) to set him aside, and I will consider myself as boarding through my whole life with an indifferent person. Sixty pounds a year is the sum which would entirely gratify all my desires.[1]

This, she said, with her 'habits of frugality' would enable her to 'exercise her better feelings in relieving the necessities of others. I might buy a few books, take a journey now and then.'[2] Christopher and John were already making her an allowance of about £20 a year each, so that all she was doing was to ask Richard to supply her with another £20 to free her from living on William's income. Richard would certainly have done as she asked, but these arrangements were in fact made unnecessary by the happy ending to the story of the Lowther debt.[3]

On May 24th 1802, James Lowther, Earl of Lonsdale, died.[4] His immense wealth and all his landed property were left by will to his distant cousin, Sir William Lowther of Swillington in Yorkshire, who was also one of his 'nominated' M.P.s. The viscounty was continued, but not the earldom. The great question for the Wordsworths—and indeed for many other people—was: Would Lord Lowther pay his predecessor's debts? Wordsworth himself was even doubtful whether their claim was

[1] *E.L.* 199, p. 451. W.W. to Sir G. Beaumont, Feb. 20th 1805.

[2] Ibid. 131, p. 299. D.W. to R.W., June 10th 1802.

[3] It used to be said that Wordsworth's marriage was only made possible by the settlement of the Lowther debt, but this is obviously not so, for the arrangements for his marriage were well in hand before the death of Lord Lonsdale. It was Dorothy's determination no longer to be dependent on him which made the marriage a financial possibility.

[4] 'Lord Lonsdale is no more. Improve this information if you can to your and your family's advantage', wrote Captain John Wordsworth of Whitehaven to Richard on May 25th 1802.

still good in law, after the conclusion of the great lawsuit in 1791, which had indeed gone in their favour but had left the amount actually owing undetermined and unpaid. He began, in June, a long correspondence with his brother Richard in London, which reveals not only his anxiety to obtain the money due to the family, but also his desire to approach the matter in a spirit of equity, 'betwixt man and man'. His uncle William Cookson was also of this opinion. 'Try', he wrote to Richard on June 22nd, 'what an appeal to Lord Lowther's Honour and Conscientiousness may produce', adding that Mr. Wilberforce was willing to help if he could do so with propriety. Wordsworth was terrified that his brother, who regarded everything from a purely legal point of view, would set on foot another lawsuit, which would again lead to no result. While still uncertain whether Lord Lowther would make himself responsible for the earl's debts, he wrote to Richard proposing to draw up a memorial for presentation to Lord Lowther, stating their case, and in particular, 'the utter destitution of my sister on account of the affair'. He must have discussed this suggestion with his friends, for on June 18th Luff[1] came over from Patterdale to announce the glad news of an advertisement in the *Cumberland Paquet* inviting all those who had claims against the late earl to send in their statements as soon as possible, and brought with him from Mr. Clarkson a paper which was apparently a sort of draft memorial on the lines suggested by Wordsworth. William immediately forwarded this paper to Richard who was already advising caution and delay. Following the lines of Clarkson's memorial, he begged Richard not to antagonize Lord Lowther by demanding the repayment of the interest as well as the principal of the debt, as this might lead to legal proceedings, which William was determined to avoid.

Should Lord Lowther reject the payment of this debt of ours . . . from their enormous amount, with what greater success could you carry on a suit against him, with his immense Fortune than against his predecessor? . . . What success was a poor man ever known to have against a very rich one in a Law Suit? [Here we seem to hear echoes of the Wordsworth of the *Letter to the Bishop of Llandaff*!] In whatever manner you proceed in the business, let me earnestly

[1] Captain and Mrs. Luff, friends of the Clarksons, lived on the south side of Patterdale, where the Wordsworths sometimes stayed with them. *D.W.J.* i, pp. 413–19.

exhort you to avoid everything which may appear like a manifestation
of a disposition to challenge Lord Lowther to try the affair in a court
of justice.

To this letter Richard seems to have replied with something
of a snub, rejecting any such idea as the presentation of a
memorial to Lord Lowther in person. At any rate he made
William very angry.

I feel it proper to inform you [William wrote on July 3rd] that I
must disapprove of the tone which pervades your second Letter.
Many parts of it are totally deficient in that respect with which Man
ought to deal with man, and Brother with Brother. You seem to speak
to me as if you were speaking to a Child: this is very unbecoming on
your part; and it is not fit that I should hear it without informing you
that it is your duty to guard against anything of the kind in future.

Having thus rebuked his brother, he went on in a quieter tone
on the old danger of approaching the affair too much in a purely
legal manner. Wordsworth, if he had become a lawyer, would,
one feels, have been happiest in Equity.

Depend upon it [he says], if you proceed according to the Letter in
this track we are ruined. Though the affair must be bottomed no doubt
upon a right in Law, that right will be lost to us, . . . if we do not
constantly bear in mind that our hopes of success . . . must depend
entirely upon our combining with this right certain principles of natural
justice, and considering the affair as an affair betwixt man and man.

He protested against Richard's exhortations to delay.

You must know as well as I that such exhortations are the common
Language of hackney men of business . . . a sort of mechanic rule which
they lay down, easy to adhere to, and thus they cheaply purchase to
themselves the applause of being mechanical, circumspect and temperate
men. But if ever there was a case that called aloud for promptness and
decision, it is the present: it must be plain to common sense that Lord
L. will be most likely to act worthily and justly, I will not say nobly
and generously, while the freshness of his new situation is upon him,
while he is *studious* of popularity, and before he is tired out by the
burthen of his duties. . . . No step of the nature of a proceeding in Law
shall be taken with my approbation. If without consulting me such
step be taken. . . . I appraise you that I immediately divide from you
upon the business and shall act singly upon my own judgment.[1]

So William fulminated, and Richard replied upon the whole

[1] D.C.P.

in a conciliatory tone. He insisted that 'meddlesome persons' (by whom he no doubt meant chiefly Mr. Clarkson) must not interfere in an affair which required caution and experience: everything must be done 'under inspection of Messrs. Graham, Lord Lowther's solicitors'. He promised, however, to avoid litigation, and assured him that he was proceeding as expeditiously as circumstances would permit. To William's threat of acting separately from him he replied that he had 'no desire to act in a matter where my exertions are thought nothing of', and appealed to him to keep the family united. The storm appears then to have died down, and the negotiations for the payment of the debt proceeded smoothly enough. By the beginning of 1803 an agreement was arrived at on the basis of a payment of a sum in the region of £8,000. Wordsworth expressed himself as satisfied with this offer, although it was less than the real amount of the debt, which, with the interest, amounted to £10,380. However, as he said, 'no money can ever make us complete amends for the loss which we have sustained', and Lord Lowther's solicitors might easily have tried to obtain greater reductions. With a sly reference to his earlier letters he added: 'it is evident he [Mr. Graham] does not consider the case merely as a man of business; . . . but with the feelings also of a just man, attending the claim which we have in moral equity'.[1]

Meanwhile, on July 9th 1802 William and Dorothy had left Grasmere on their long journey to Gallow Hill. On the evening before they left they had walked backwards and forwards on their path on White Moss Common, reading a batch of letters—'one was from M.H., a very tender affecting letter, another from Sara to C., from C. to us, and from my Brother Richard'. In the morning Dorothy wrote a last farewell in her Journal: 'William is eating his broth. I must prepare to go. The swallows, I must leave them, the well, the garden, the roses, all. Dear creatures!! they sang last night after I was in bed—seemed to be singing to one another, just before they settled to rest for the night. Well, I must go. Farewell.'[2]

[1] E.L. 138, p. 315. W.W. to R.W., Feb. 23rd 1803.
[2] D.W.J. i, p. 168. The swallows had built a nest in the eaves outside her bedroom window.

The journey was made largely on foot. They walked first to
Keswick where they spent two nights, then walked with Coleridge some miles on the way to Eusemere. 'He was not well,
and we had a melancholy parting after having sate together in
silence by the road-side.'

They arrived late at Eusemere, 'having lingered and loitered
and sat down together that we might be alone'. The days when
they would have such frequent opportunities of being 'alone'
were growing few. After two nights with the Clarksons, they
took coach from Brougham over Stainmore to Leeming Lane
on the Great North Road. On Stainmore a shower came on, 'but
we buttoned ourselves up both together in the Guard's coat, and
we liked the hills and the rain the better for bringing us so close
to one another—I never rode more snugly'.[1] From Thirsk they
walked the rest of the way, over the Hambledon Hills past
Rievaulx Abbey, where 'thrushes were singing, cattle feeding
among green-brown hillocks about the ruins', as yet unex-
cavated and untrimmed. They slept at the pleasant inn at
Helmsley, and walked the next day, by Kirby Moorside and
Sinnington, to Gallow Hill, being met, characteristically, by
Mary and Sara, when they were still seven miles from the
house. After ten days there, William and Dorothy set forth
once more, this time in a post-chaise, on their way to London
and France. They went by Hull, Lincoln, and Peterborough,
arriving in London on July 29th.

From the day of their departure from Grasmere until their
return to Gallow Hill in October, Dorothy's Journal takes on a
subtly different character. It reads more like her *Recollections of
a Tour in Scotland in* 1803, which was written not during, but
after the tour, and was intended for circulation among her friends.
In the 'Calais' Journal there are no longer the brief daily entries,
but a number of descriptions of places and incidents which might
be of general interest, while the four weeks' stay at Calais is
condensed to less than five hundred words. The conclusion that
this part of the Journal was written with a view to sending it
to one or two friends is strengthened by the existence of a
separate sheet containing the description of Calais, with a few
alterations in the text. Annette and Caroline are mentioned,
but not described, and no hint is given anywhere of conversations

---

[1] *D.W.J.* i, p. 169.

that passed between them. The probability is that she intended
to show it to Mrs. Clarkson who later copied out the Scottish
Journal, and who certainly knew the outline of the story of
Annette in later years,[1] and probably knew it now.

Dorothy speaks of 'various troubles and disasters' during the
two days they spent in London; what these were we do not
know, but they received 'kind attentions' from William Sotheby,
a distinguished man of letters (he was the translator of Wieland's *Oberon*) and friend of Coleridge whom he had visited at
Keswick earlier in the summer.

Early in the morning of July 31st they crossed Westminster
Bridge on the top of the Dover coach. Dorothy wrote in her
Journal afterwards. 'The city, St. Paul's, with the river and a
multitude of little boats made a most beautiful sight. . . . The
houses were not overhung by their cloud of smoke, and they
were spread out endlessly, yet the sun shone so brightly, with
such a fierce light, that there was even something like the purity
of one of nature's own grand spectacles.' William, deeply
moved, let the sight sink deep, and when they returned a month
later, wrote that sonnet which still makes us catch our breath as
he caught his that July morning:

> Ships, towers, domes, theatres and temples lie
> Open unto the fields and to the sky;
> All bright and glittering in the smokeless air.
> Never did sun more beautifully steep
> In his first splendour, valley, rock or hill . . .[2]

There are many unanswered and unanswerable questions

---

[1] See D.W.'s letters to her about the time of Caroline's marriage in 1816.
M.Y. ii, pp. 600, 725.

[2] He called the sonnet: *Composed upon Westminster Bridge. September 3, 1802.*
By Sept. 3rd they had been back in London for three days. It may be that he had
indeed composed it on the outward journey and did not 'write' it until afterwards.
The closeness of the thought of the sonnet to Dorothy's description is very noticeable. It may well be that she wrote up her Journal at the same time. In John Thelwall's *Peripatetic*, published in 1793, there is a curious passage describing the
view of London from Highgate Hill, which it seems probable Wordsworth must
have read and perhaps recollected when he composed the sonnet. 'No sooner did
I behold the vast metropolis expanding beneath my feet . . . see turrets spires and
cupolas thronging in pompous vassalage round the still more magnificent dome,
than wonder and delight rushed immediately to my heart. Nature—Nature perhaps
was knocking at my bosom, and hard indeed must have been that heart that did not
beat at the prospect of a place where it had so many inducements.'

about the sojourn in Calais, which had been appointed as the
meeting place with Annette. In the first place, why Calais, and
not Paris, or Blois? Paris, as the seat of a government detested
by Annette, would not have been acceptable to her and perhaps
not even safe. Nor would Wordsworth have wished to be
caught up in the crowd of English visitors, of whose tolerance
of Bonaparte he could not approve. And Wordsworth would
certainly not have been very welcome at Blois among Annette's
relations, as her former lover or supposed husband, who was
now about to marry someone else. Indeed, it seems probable
that they both wished for as much privacy as possible. Another
curious feature of the affair is the length of the Wordsworths'
visit. They stayed for four weeks in Calais, in rather unattractive
lodgings, with nothing to do but walk on the sands with Annette
and Caroline. Dorothy mentions no sight-seeing or expeditions
to other places; she describes only the sunsets, the distant views
of the English coast and the phosphorescent lights in the water
at night. At this, 'Caroline', she says, 'was delighted'. That is
her only comment on their companions. Yet no doubt the visit
was friendly. If it had not been, they would have parted sooner.
'We walked by the sea-shore almost every evening with Annette
and Caroline, or William and I alone.' The weather was hot,
and they bathed. When, on August 30th, they arrived back again
at Dover, they 'sate upon Dover Cliffs, and looked upon France
with many a melancholy and tender thought'. Melancholy, no
doubt, because Annette's life was a dangerous and difficult one
and they could do little to assist her in it; tender, because of the
past, and, perhaps, because of Caroline, the 'dear child, dear
girl', of the sonnet—one of several—that William brought back
with him.[1]

That sonnet indeed shows that he was by no means indifferent
to his lively little French daughter. He had evidently hoped to
find in her some repetition of his own or Dorothy's mystical
ecstasies when brought into communion with Nature. He found
it not, but his disappointment was tender and fatherly, as he
listened to her screams of delight as she watched the phosphorescent waves, and, assuming his most priest-like tones, he
uttered his benediction upon her:

---

[1] *P.W.* iii, p. 17, *Miscellaneous Sonnets*, XXX, *It is a beauteous Evening, calm
and free.*

> Dear Child! dear Girl! who walkest with me here,
> If thou appear untouched by solemn thought
> Thy nature is not therefore less divine:
> Thou liest in Abraham's bosom all the year;
> And worshipp'st at the Temple's inner shrine,
> God being with thee when we know it not![1]

We do not know whether he undertook to make Caroline an allowance as soon as the Lowther money was paid over. The resumption of the war in the following year would have made its payment impossible. But on Caroline's marriage, the year after Waterloo, he settled £30 a year upon her until 1834, when he gave her a lump sum of £400. The parting with Annette must have been a friendly one, for their correspondence was resumed during the autumn, as Dorothy's Journal shows, and doubtless would have continued had not war once more closed all communications.

Wordsworth wrote seven sonnets while he was at Calais. All, except the one already quoted, were concerned with his feelings and fears about England and about France. Just as in the spring he had written no poems about Mary and his immediate concerns, but had drawn his inspiration from 'hiding-places' of long ago, so now he wrote not about Annette but about the public events which so deeply moved him. He was, as a poet, capable of a remarkable detachment from his immediate circumstances. Until now he had written no sonnets,[2] and said afterwards that he used to think that form of composition 'egregiously absurd'. His change of feeling came about through Dorothy reading aloud to him one day in May 1802, the sonnets of Milton. With them, of course, he had long been familiar. But on this occasion he was 'particularly struck by the dignified simplicity and majestic harmony that runs through most of them. . . . I took fire . . . and produced three Sonnets the same

---

[1] Other manuscripts show the following variants:

> Dear Child! dear happy Girl! If thou appear
> Heedless—untouch'd with awe or serious thought . . .
>
> . . . .
>
> Thou dost not seem to heed these things one jot,
> I see it, nor is this a grief of mine;   *P.W.* iii, p. 17.

[2] Except a few written in early youth, of which the best is the one to Dorothy written in 1792, beginning 'Sweet was the walk along the narrow lane'. *P.W.* i, p. 296.

afternoon. . . . Of these three, the only one I distinctly remember is "I grieved for Buonaparté".'[1]

The impact of Milton was like a match to tinder. For, far from being completely absorbed by the 'moods of his own mind', or by the significance of the cuckoo and the rainbow, Wordsworth was passionately alive to the great drama of the struggle with France, and his feelings about it were now poured forth in a torrent of verse, at once rugged and stately, that continued to flow long after his return from France. The rise of Bonaparte and the establishment of the Consulate, based on military force and government by decree, had destroyed all Wordsworth's hopes of France's recovery after the fall of Robespierre. Against Bonaparte he felt a strong revulsion, though at first it was a half-pitying revulsion—'I *grieved* for Buonaparté'. He was a man who, because he had had only a military education, had missed all the best blessings of existence.

> The tenderest mood
> Of that man's mind—what can it be? What food,
> Fed his first hopes? what knowledge could he gain?[2]

At Calais he felt the sinister atmosphere of the new revolution all around him; the death of liberty tainted the air. So Milton also had felt, when the Scottish Presbyterians came to London. And he was haunted by the contrast between 1790 and 1802. He thought of Robert Jones, and of their walk through the rejoicing crowds twelve years before, when

> a homeless sound of joy was in the air[3]

the voice of the new freedom. Now the French no longer felt free. The old greeting, 'Good-morrow, citizen', sounded hollow, 'as if a dead man spake it'. The public holiday for 'young Bonaparté's natal day', when he was proclaimed Consul for life, was treated more as a day for following individual pleasures than as a great act of national rejoicing.

---

[1] *P.W.* iii, p. 417. Note to Miscellaneous Sonnets. The seven Calais sonnets are I, II, III, V, VI, and VIII of *Poems dedicated to National Independence and Liberty*, ibid., pp. 109–12, and *It is a beauteous Evening, calm and free*, ibid., p. 17.

[2] Ibid, p. 110, *I grieved for Buonaparté*.

[3] Ibid., p. 110, *Jones when from Calais southward you and I*. This sonnet was composed 'on the road leading to Ardres', the road along which Jones and Wordsworth had started when they left Calais in July 1790.

> Far other show
> My youth here witnessed in a prouder time;
> The senselessness of joy was then sublime.[1]

His sorrowful mood changed to one of indignation as he watched the crowds of English visitors who, taking advantage of the peace, were coming over in the Dover packet and hastening to Paris to survey the Louvre stacked with the spoils of Italy and if possible catch a glimpse of the First Consul. For the war against the French Republic had not been popular and had quite failed to make the English anti-French, nor did they yet realize the significance of Bonaparte. So

> Lords, lawyers, statesmen, squires of low degree . . .
> Post forward all. . . .[2]

Among the 'squires' was Thomas Poole himself, who had crossed in June and was still in Paris. His letters to Coleridge testify to the accuracy with which Wordsworth had sensed the political atmosphere. 'Since I have been here a revolution has passed in France; very quietly, I assure you, for no one says anything— a very bad symptom of its popularity. Those who do speak, speak as you may suppose men would, who had hopes of being free.'[3] And, among the 'statesmen', Charles Fox was there, living near the Bibliothèque Nationale, in which he read daily for his *History of James II*. But he also attended Bonaparte's levées, thereby calling down the wrath of Coleridge in the *Morning Post*.[4] Poole, in describing Fox's activities, wrote: 'It is curious that I should write to you about an Englishman from Paris; but there are few subjects so interesting as Fox to be found in France.'[5] Wordsworth could not be so dispassionate; he called his fellow countrymen 'men of prostrate mind', and 'feeble Heads, to slavery prone'. But he must have forgiven Fox, or he would not have written the great *Effusion* on his death four years later.

The sonnet to Toussaint L'Ouverture, the captured leader of the insurgent Negroes of St. Domingo, who was now in prison

---

[1] Ibid., p. 111, *Calais, August 15, 1802*.
[2] Ibid., p. 109, *Calais, August, 1802*.
[3] *T.P.* ii, p. 87. T.P. to S.T.C., Aug. 22nd 1802.
[4] *Essays on His own Times*, by S. T. Coleridge, edited by his daughter (1850), ii, pp. 552–85. The articles, in the form of open letters to Fox, appeared in Nov. 1802.
[5] *T.P.* ii, p. 89. T.P. to S.T.C., Aug. 22nd 1802.

in a fortress in the Jura, where he died a few months later, shows,
better than any other written in France, the link between
Wordsworth's passionate demand for political and personal
liberty, and his other passion, for 'air, earth and skies'—the
elements of the natural world which symbolized freedom in his
mind. To Toussaint he says:

> Live and take comfort; thou hast left behind
> Powers that will work for thee; air, earth and skies;
> There's not a breathing of the common wind
> That will forget thee.

And not only the 'common wind', but all the emotional content
of the being of man:

> Thy friends are exultations, agonies,
> And love, and man's unconquerable mind.[1]

They returned to England with pleasure and relief. Wordsworth declared that it was the happiest home-coming he had
ever had. Church bells, some boys playing cricket, the sound of
the waves beating on 'the chalky shore'—'all, all are English'.[2]
In London they spent three weeks, staying in Paper Buildings
in the Temple, in the rooms occupied during law terms by the
Basil Montagus. At present, however, the Montagus were in
Cambridge. For the Wordsworths this was a happy time of
family reunion with all their brothers, for Christopher came up
from Cambridge and John, to their great delight, arrived home
from his East Indian voyage while they were there. They also
spent two days at Windsor visiting the Cooksons, Uncle
William being then in residence as a canon of St. George's
Chapel, Windsor. His displeasure over William's conduct in
early days was evidently a thing of the past and the visit was a
happy one. In London they saw much of the Lambs, who lived
close by and were just returned from a visit to Coleridge at
Keswick, where they had climbed Skiddaw, and even spent a
couple of nights in the cottage at Town End with the Clarksons,
who were occupying it during the Wordsworths' absence.[3]
Lamb had satisfied himself 'that there is such a thing as that

---

[1] *P.W.* iii, p. 112, *To Toussaint L'Ouverture.* The phrase 'unconquerable mind'
is an echo of Gray, in *The Progress of Poetry.*

[2] Ibid., p. 114, *Composed in the Valley near Dover on the day of Landing.*

[3] *Lamb,* i, p. 315.

which tourists call romantic, which I very much suspected before'. He now took the Wordsworths to 'Bartelmy Fair', thereby supplying Wordsworth with material for a yet un-written part of *The Prelude*.[1]

Wordsworth's meditations, however, during these three weeks, were about the state of England's 'soul'. He could not feel happy about it. The English, he noticed, were suffering, at least in London, from too much prosperity and 'undisturbed wealth'. 'I could not but be struck', he said afterwards, 'with the vanity and parade of our own country, especially in great towns and cities, as contrasted with the quiet, and I may say the desolation, that the revolution had produced in France.'[2] In our own day we are accustomed to associate war with heavy taxa-tion, the loss of overseas trade, steep rises in wages, offset by restrictions on spending of all kinds; but in Wordsworth's England income tax never rose above two shillings in the pound, wages remained disastrously low, and our command of the sea kept the Atlantic trade routes open and our West Indian possessions secure. The land-owners and the middle class continued to flourish and to increase their wealth as corn prices rose and the demands of the war for the army and navy filled the pockets of the industrialists. Wordsworth, a poor man who had earlier suffered injustice from a rich man and was in any case most frugal in his private habits—'a simple, water-drinking bard'—broke forth into verse which has something of the ring and sting of Old Testament prophecy. He wrote two sonnets: *O Friend! I know not which way I must look*, and *Milton! thou should'st be living at this hour*.[3] His habit of looking into the past is here applied not to his own life but, for the first time, to the history of his country. He saw a vision of what seemed to him a worthier England, whose heroes were the leaders of the Puritan Revolution and their Whig successors. Another sonnet, written probably but a few weeks later, celebrated by name the seventeenth-century revolutionaries:

---

[1] *Prel.* VII. Lamb, writing to Coleridge in November, says that he is sending off to Keswick a box containing various books and some 'strange, thick-hoofed shoes' belonging to Wordsworth, which he had evidently left behind. The shoes were, said Lamb, 'very much admired at in London'. *Lamb*, i, p. 328.

[2] *P.W.* iii, p. 455. W.W.'s note to Sonnet XIII of *Poems dedicated to National Independence and Liberty*.

[3] Ibid., pp. 115–16.

The later Sidney, Marvel, Harrington
Young Vane, and others who called Milton friend.[1]

For above them all towered the figure of Milton:

Thy Soul was like a Star, and dwelt apart.

Compared with that heroic age of 'plain living and high thinking', England was now 'a fen of stagnant waters'. It is curious to
note how Wordsworth's historical imagination was steeped in
the Republican and Whig tradition. This was due not to teaching
in childhood but to his association with the English Jacobins
and the French Girondins in early youth, to whom Vane and
Algernon Sidney were heroes. The visit to Calais had stirred
up his memories of France, and of his reading and discussion there
of Roman and English political ideals.[2] But the English Puritans
were more than political theorists. The Puritan ideal of life,
austere and simple, had a natural attraction for Wordsworth.
To this he added his own devotion to Milton, the prince of
Puritans, as well as of poets.[3]

Compared with the Puritan heroic age, what had France to
show? With somewhat pharisaical wonder, Wordsworth turned
his eyes once more across the Channel:

France, 'tis strange,
Hath brought forth no such souls as we had then.
Perpetual emptiness! unceasing change!
No single volume paramount, no code,
No master spirit, no determined road;
But equally a want of books and men!

If he could not regard Bonaparte as a 'master spirit', and his
policies as a 'determined road', the picture is perhaps not
inaccurate. Books in plenty and men in plenty there had been
in the years before the Revolution and until the advent of the
Terrorists. But since Robespierre there had been too much
bloodshed and too much turmoil to give encouragement to men
of letters. There was no Milton of the French Revolution.

While he was in London Wordsworth sent his sonnet on
Bonaparte to the *Morning Post*, where it appeared on September

---

[1] *P.W.* iii, p. 116, *Great men have been among us.*   [2] See above, pp. 207–8.
[3] It is curious to turn from these sonnets to the *Ecclesiastical Sonnets* of twenty
years later. There only Milton survives to be celebrated: his comrades have
become 'a madding faction', and Laud and Charles the First take their places.

6th, curiously signed with initials W.L.D.[1] 'It comes upon my feelings', said Coleridge, 'as in the spirit of the best of Milton's sonnets.' Coleridge, who was writing articles on political subjects for the *Morning Post* all this autumn, including an attack on Fox for his visit to Paris, may have suggested to Wordsworth that he should endeavour to have more of his political sonnets published in that periodical, for on Christmas Day, 1802, the day after Coleridge and Tom Wedgwood had called at the cottage on their way back to Keswick from London, Dorothy wrote to her brother John: 'William has written some more sonnets; perhaps you may see them in the *Morning Post.*' On January 13th 1803, *Is it a reed that's shaken with the wind* appeared there, and on January 29th an editorial paragraph of considerable interest appeared under the heading 'Poetry'.

We have been favoured [it ran] with a dozen Sonnets of a Political nature, which are not only written by one of the first Poets of the age, but are among his best productions. Each forms a little Political Essay, on some recent proceeding. As we wish to publish them in connection with each other, we now reprint No. 1 and No. 2, the first from our Paper of September 6th, the second from our Paper of the present month. The other numbers shall follow in succession.

One suspects the hand of Coleridge in this editorial. It was followed by *I grieved for Buonaparté* and *Is it a reed*; in February appeared three more, *To Toussaint L'Ouverture* on February 2nd, *We had a female Passenger* on the 11th, and *Festivals have I seen* on the 26th. Then there was a pause till April when *It is not to be thought of that the Flood* appeared on the 16th. There was then a still longer pause until September 17th when *When I have borne in memory what hath tamed* was printed. After that there were no more of the political series, perhaps because Stuart about this time sold the *Morning Post*; but in October two other sonnets by Wordsworth, *I find it written of Simonides,* and a translation of one of Milton's sonnets,[2] appeared in it, so that it is difficult to account for the failure to print the other five political sonnets making up the dozen. It is not difficult to

---

[1] The meaning of these initials is obscure. The suggestion of Hutchinson was that they stand for 'Wordsworth Libertati Dedicavit'.

[2] *P.W.* iii, pp. 408 and 577. Coleridge, writing to Poole on Oct. 14 1803, mentions 'that sonnet of his about Simonides and the Ghost' as one of 'a multitude of small Poems' which were 'hurtful' to his genius. *U.L.* i, p. 291.

surmise what they were, for there are only six remaining of a strictly political character which could have been written by January 1803. These are: *Great men have been among us; Milton; O Friend! I know not which way I must look; Fair Star of Evening, Splendour of the west; On the Extinction of the Venetian Republic;* and *England! the time is come when thou should'st wean.*

Speaking of England in this sonnet, Wordsworth complains:

> at this day
> If for Greece, Egypt, India, Africa
> Aught good were destined, thou wouldst step between.

He might well feel that our failure to abolish the slave-trade was a great wrong to Africa, and he probably took the view that Warren Hastings had oppressed India, but it is surprising to find Egypt and Greece included. We had just driven Bonaparte from Egypt, an action which Wordsworth could hardly have criticized, and the 'Greek question' had not yet arisen as a serious issue. The Venetian Republic had, of course, been 'extinguished' five years before, but for Wordsworth this would make no matter; his habit of 'recollection' would have brought the event before him with all the poignancy of the original tragedy. The same characteristic applies to the sonnet which he himself believed to be the best he ever wrote—*Thought of a Briton on the Subjugation of Switzerland.* He wrote it in 1806, but Switzerland had been 'subjugated' in 1798.

Coleridge's comparison of Wordsworth's 'Bonaparte' sonnet with 'the best of Milton's' anticipated the judgement of later generations. Never since Milton had the sonnet spoken to the world with such a trumpet voice as did Wordsworth's in 1802 and 1803. Yet there is no evidence that the world took much note of them. The austerity and ruggedness of their style, and the severity with which they criticized England's faults, could scarcely have gained them popularity. To most readers they must have seemed harsh and strange.

William and Dorothy arrived once more at Gallow Hill on September 24th. It was harvest time and Tom Hutchinson 'was forking corn, standing upon the corn-cart'. October 4th was the day fixed for the wedding of William and Mary at Brompton Church. Their wedding was as quiet as their courtship had been. All was planned in consideration for Dorothy, whose feelings were wrought up to an almost unbearable pitch. The brothers Jack and George Hutchinson came over for it, but of the whole household, only Jack, Tom, and Joanna accompanied the bridal couple to church as necessary witnesses to the ceremony, which took place early in the morning. Dorothy remained upstairs, trying to keep calm, while Sara prepared the wedding breakfast. When Dorothy saw 'the two men running up the walk, coming to tell us it was over', she could do nothing but lie almost insensible on her bed till Sara came to rouse her with the news that 'They are coming'. 'This forced me from my bed where I lay, and I moved, I knew not how, straight forward, faster than my strength would carry me, till I met my beloved William and fell upon his bosom. He and John Hutchinson led me to the house, and there I stayed to welcome my dear Mary'—who, it seems, had been almost forgotten while Dorothy was being revived!

'Whether', said Mary long afterwards, dictating memories of her youth for her children, 'it was in consequence of our friends' thinking us an improvident pair, I do not know—but it is a fact that we did not receive a single *wedding-present*.' There had been some hopes of a silver coffee-pot from Mary's cousins the Scurfields, 'as that was the marriage present they sent to my cousins Hutchinson', but no coffee-pot arrived. Mary's bachelor Uncle Henry Hutchinson of Stockton, with whom she had passed part of her childhood, had 'designated' Wordsworth as 'a Vagabond', because he had no regular profession; 'I knew', said Mary, 'it would be useless to ask his consent.'[1] The marriage was therefore solemnized without the blessing of any of Mary's older relations.

The wedding journey back to Grasmere was made in a chaise, by the same route traversed by William and Dorothy three months before. They had 'sunshine and showers, pleasant talk, love and chearfulness'. As they passed over the Hambledon Hills by Sutton Bank, they were treated to a great sunset

---

[1] Old Uncle Henry softened somewhat towards Wordsworth as the years went by. 'I knew he had read *some* of his Poems, the Happy Warrior being his favourite', said Mary in her memoirs. Mary is not quite correct in saying they received no wedding presents, for John sent her a new gown and wrote on Oct. 22nd: 'I am glad and rejoiced to hear that my *sister* Mary likes the *choice* of my new gown. May she long wear it and I see it.' J.W. to D.W., Oct. 22nd 1802, *D.C.P.*

spectacle on the far side of the Plain of York. 'Far, far off us, in
the western sky, we saw shapes of castles, ruins among groves,
a great spreading wood, rocks and single trees, a minster with its
tower unusually distinct, minarets in another quarter, and a
round Grecian Temple also; the colours of the sky of a bright
grey, and the forms of a sober grey, with a dome.' So wrote
Dorothy after they reached home, but Wordsworth had already,
on the same evening, put the vision into a sonnet, to which no
doubt she turned as she wrote, for her prose largely follows his
verse.[1] As they gazed, they realized what is a common experience with those who contemplate sunsets, that they would
forget the glories they had seen:

> they are of the sky,
> And from our earthly memory fade away.

Again some months later he emphasized this thought in a curious
sonnet in which he seems to repudiate sky-scapes as suitable
objects of recollection:

> Grove, isle with every shape of sky-built dome
> Though clad in colours beautiful and pure,
> Find in the heart of man no natural home:
> The immortal Mind craves objects that endure.[2]

Yet the description of the cloud-city in the second book of *The
Excursion*[3] has strong affinities with the *Hambledon Hills* sonnet,
and he there shows no disposition to exclude clouds from praise.

On October 9th the following curious announcement of the
wedding appeared in the *Morning Post*.

Monday last, W. Wordsworth, Esq. was married to Miss Hutchinson, of Wykeham, near Scarborough, and proceeded immediately,
with his wife and his sister, for his charming cottage in the little
Paradise Vale of Grasmere. His neighbour, Mr. Coleridge, resides in
the Vale of Keswick, 13 miles from Grasmere. His house, (situated
on a low hill at the foot of Skiddaw, with the Derwent Lake in front,

---

[1] *P.W.* iii, p. 25. The sonnet is XI of Miscellaneous Sonnets.

> there stood Indian citadel,
> Temple of Greece, and minster with its tower
> Substantially expressed. . . .

[2] Ibid., p. 26, *Those words were uttered in a pensive mood.*
[3] Ibid. v, pp. 71–72.

and the romantic River Greta winding round the hill) commands, perhaps, the most various and interesting prospects of any house in the island. It is a perfect *panorama* of that wonderful vale, with its two lakes, and its complete circle, or rather ellipse, of mountains.

This paragraph, written obviously by someone who knew both the poets and who had also visited the lakes, might possibly emanate from Charles Lamb, who had visited Keswick and the cottage at Town End while Wordsworth and Dorothy were in France and had written with enthusiasm to his friends about the scenery of Keswick. Or is it one of Coleridge's jokes? The Wordsworths were evidently somewhat annoyed at being thus advertised as though they and Coleridge were among the attractions of a tourist resort, for John Wordsworth wrote to Dorothy: 'It [meaning the notice] is not quite so bad as I thought it would have been from what you said.'[1]

On the wedding day itself the *Morning Post* had printed a version of Coleridge's *Dejection: an Ode*. It was a touching and memorable wedding gift. Wordsworth's happiness at this time could only have made Coleridge feel more acutely than ever his own domestic miseries, and indeed he had had a terrible summer of storms and discords, followed at length by a somewhat more tranquil period. The Ode, as it appeared in the *Morning Post*, was addressed to 'Edmund'—who is Wordsworth—wherever 'Sara' had been named in the original version, and the most poignant lines of personal suffering were omitted. That Coleridge should have chosen this time for publishing the poem is a measure of how constantly his mind ran on Wordsworth and his affairs. Another and less noble indication of the same interest is to be found in the epigram—one of many—called *Spots in the Sun* which appeared on October 11th. It is a mischievous jest at Wordsworth's visit to Annette.[2] For Coleridge could jest as well as lament, though his poetical reputation was never enhanced thereby.

On arriving at Grasmere the old life of walks and reading, expeditions to Keswick to see Coleridge and visits of Coleridge to the cottage, was taken up again. Dorothy kept a journal,

---

[1] *D.C.P.* J.W. to D.W., Nov. 7th 1802. Wordsworth himself sent a short announcement to the *Yorkshire Herald*, where it appeared on Oct. 9th. *D.W.J.* i, p. 176 and n.
[2] *S.T.C. Poems*, ii, p. 909.

rather irregularly, until January 1803; after that we hear no
more from her in this way of their daily doings. At the end of
the year we find her making a resolution to keep it 'regularly,
and if I can, legibly', but after January 16th 1803 there is
silence.[1] Henceforward her long letters to Mrs. Clarkson and
Lady Beaumont become the chief source of our knowledge of
their family life. She continued to keep journals of their tours
and expeditions. The cessation of her daily record of life at the
cottage leaves a blank that nothing can fill. It may be attributed
perhaps to the presence of Mary to whom she could now confide
her anxieties about William or her delight in some beautiful or
curious sight, more readily than to her Journal. For Dorothy
had been, ever since the days when her brother described her as
'a little prattler among men', a great talker, in need of some
companion to take the overflow of her nervous enthusiasm and
all her concern for the things and people that she loved. Her
Journal had supplied that need during the time when, alone with
William, she had been absorbed in his welfare. Now she shared
that absorption with Mary, without jealousy and without
reserve. She was happier, calmer, and better in health as a
result, as her letters prove, and we, who lose so much by the
change, must not grudge her the blessing of a more peaceful
spirit.

Coleridge came over on October 11th and they all went back
with him to Keswick, 'Mrs. C. not being at home', for a three-
day stay. He had, while they were away, performed what was
probably the most remarkable feat of solitary mountaineering
yet achieved by anyone who was not a mountain shepherd. He
had left Keswick on August 1st and was away for ten days on a
tour which took him over to the sea at Egremont, and up to
Wastdale Head, whence he had climbed to the summit of Sca
Fell. Following his usual rule of 'where it is first *possible* to
descend, there I go', he had descended the entire face of Broad
Stand, 'dropping' from one ledge to the next 'without the least
influence of fear', until he reached the bottom, whence he
continued downwards till he reached John Towers' farm at
the head of Eskdale. All this he had described in a long journal-

---

[1] The last entry describes an expedition to Matthew Newton's to buy some
gingerbread for which 'William had a fancy'.

letter to the Hutchinsons and Wordsworths.[1] True to a favourite pastime of theirs, he told them how he 'shouted out all your names in the sheepfold where echo came upon echo, and then Hartley and Derwent, and then I laughed and shouted Joanna'.[2] And on the summit of Sca Fell he had burst forth once more into poetry—the great song of praise to the God of Nature, which he called *Hymn before Sunrise in the Vale of Chamounix*. Coleridge had never been to Chamounix or seen Mont Blanc. The poem is certainly consciously indebted to Frederica Brun's *Chamounix beim Sonnenaufgange*, but he must also often have heard Wordsworth talking about his visit to Chamounix with Robert Jones in 1790.[3] The poem was published in the *Morning Post* on September 11th with a long introductory note speaking of the vale of Chamounix and its beauties exactly as though he had visited them.[4] Wordsworth never liked this poem. Coleridge afterwards said that he condemned it 'in toto, as a specimen of the mock-sublime'. Its picture of Nature proclaiming aloud the praises of the God of Nature is certainly too simplified to agree with Wordsworth's vision of Nature itself as 'relationship and love'; yet surely he must have felt the splendour of the description—especially of Mont Blanc 'visited all night by troops of stars'.

Early in November Coleridge departed for London and the west, returning with Tom Wedgwood on Christmas Eve to the cottage, where he learnt of the birth of his daughter, Sara, on the previous day,[5] and hurried on to Keswick. That evening Dorothy recorded a little description of the interior of the cottage:

William is now sitting by me, at ½ past 10 o'clock. I have been beside him ever since tea, running the heel of a stocking, repeating some of his sonnets to him, reading some of Milton's, and the *Allegro* and *Penseroso*. It is a quiet keen frost. Mary is in the parlour below attending to the baking of cakes, and Jenny Fletcher's pies. Sara[6] is in

---

[1] 'Coleridge Discovers the Lake Country', in *Wordsworth and Coleridge, Studies in Honour of G. M. Harper*, Princeton, 1939. Part of the letter was written on the summit of Sca Fell itself.

[2] In reference to Wordsworth's 'echo' poem, *To Joanna*.

[3] *Prel.* VI, ll. 528–40. [4] S.T.C., *Poems*, i, pp. 376, 377.

[5] *D.W.J.* i, p. 186.

[6] Sara Hutchinson had been staying at Keswick during Coleridge's absence and had come to Grasmere probably early in December. She went back to Keswick, with Coleridge, on Jan. 7th.

bed in the toothache. . . . My beloved William is turning over the leaves of Charlotte Smith's sonnets, but he keeps his hand to his poor chest, pushing aside his breastplate. Mary is well and I am well, and Molly is as blithe as last year at this time.

Except for the writing of a few more sonnets and the translation of some of Ariosto's *Orlando Furioso*, this was not a poetical autumn. In the new year Wordsworth began once more 'working at the poem to Coleridge', but again this was but a momentary attempt. *The Prelude* was not continued with any success until the following January, that of 1804, although important additions were made to the first book probably during the late summer of 1803.

On June 18th 1803 Mary gave birth to a little boy.[1] He was christened John at Grasmere Church on July 15th; Coleridge and Richard Wordsworth were godfathers; Dorothy, godmother. Old Mr. Sympson was proxy for the absent Richard, and they all returned for 'christening cake, tea and coffee' at the cottage. Although Dorothy's way of mentioning the christening— 'To-day we have all been at church; Mary was *churched*, and the babe christened'—perhaps indicated the unusualness of their 'all' being at church, there is no reason to suppose that the christening itself was anything but quite naturally regarded by them all. They would never have scandalized their neighbours by omitting so important a ceremony. Coleridge, whose strong Unitarianism had prevented his having his children baptized in infancy, was moving rapidly towards orthodoxy in this respect. Hartley and Derwent were baptized in the November of this same year 1803, while Sara was christened shortly after her birth.[2]

Coleridge's health was still very precarious, and at Christmas 1802 he was again making plans for going to a warm climate. For a time he thought of going with the even more invalid Tom Wedgwood as his companion, but the outbreak of war again in May 1803—'this damned War business', as he called it—caused him for a time to give up the plan. He was very ill at Keswick throughout April and May 1803, with the influenza which

---

[1] His birth had not been expected until July. *E.L.* 144, p. 325. D.W. to R.W., 18th June 1803.

[2] *E.L.* 154, p. 347. D.W. to Catherine Clarkson, Nov. 13th 1803. *U.L.* i, 112, p. 245. S.T.C. to S. Purkis, Feb. 1st 1803. Derwent had in fact been privately baptized in infancy when very ill with croup. That the ceremony was repeated or at least completed publicly was another sign of Coleridge's changing theology.

afflicted the whole country, and his recurrent rheumatic fever. Afterwards, in a long letter to Thomas Poole written in October, he complained that Wordsworth had neglected to come and see him during this illness, and added to this complaint an analysis of Wordsworth's own state, in which we can see, besides much shrewd insight, the beginning of that envy of Wordsworth's domestic happiness in contrast with his own misery which grew painful and dangerous after his return from the Continent in 1806.

'I saw him', he says, 'more and more benetted in hypochondriacal Fancies, living wholly among *Devotees*—having every the minutest Thing, almost his very eating and drinking, done for him by his Sister, or Wife—and I trembled, lest a Film should rise, and thicken his moral Eye.'[1] That there was danger for Wordsworth in the loving régime of his household is undeniable, but his 'hypochondriacal Fancies' and 'self-involution' were not in fact nearly as dangerous to his powers of work as was Coleridge's own weakness of will to him, which prevented him from writing regularly even when he was physically capable of it. Wordsworth had his own share of illness in this sickly spring and was still strongly affected by the nervous pain which writing brought. A 'Fancy' it may have been, by Coleridge's standards, and perhaps Mary and Dorothy paid too much attention to it— but he struggled against it to such an extent in the autumn as, to Coleridge's delight, to write 'a beginning to his *Recluse*', or, as Wordsworth would have called it, 'the poem on my own life', and in the following winter to take up the poem where he had left it at the beginning of the third book and continue it to its completion.

Meanwhile there were signs that what he had already published was having extraordinary influence on the minds of some. At the end of July Wordsworth received a strange letter from a young man called Thomas De Quincey. It was sent through Longman, the publisher of *Lyrical Ballads*, who delayed forwarding it for nearly two months.[2] De Quincey, who was not yet eighteen, was at this time at Liverpool, recovering from his

---

[1] *U.L.* i. 129, p. 291. S.T.C. to Poole, Oct. 14th 1803.
[2] This letter, together with the early draft which the anxious boy made before sending it, is now in the Dove Cottage collection at Grasmere. It was until recently considered lost and its discovery is one of the most important additions to our knowledge of De Quincey. It is printed in E. Sackville West's life of De Quincey, *A Flame in Sunlight, 1936*.

extraordinary and terrible adventure in the underworld of London, during which he had nearly starved to death. In the following autumn he went up to Oxford. His letter to Words-worth reveals not only the tense emotions of his own being, but the effect which *Lyrical Ballads* and their obscure author could have on the younger generation of readers. William Hazlitt had been similarly affected four years before by hearing the poems read aloud in 1798, though he had not given himself up to hero-worship of the author. But De Quincey's letter is one of worship—the worship of a very young, self-conscious, lonely, and sensitive soul—issuing in an urgent prayer for the friendship of the adored object.

My object in troubling you, Sir [he writes], is that hereafter I may have the satisfaction of recollecting that I made one effort at least for obtaining your notice, and that I did not, through any want of exertion on my own part, miss that without which what good can my life do me? I have no other motive in soliciting your friendship than what (I should think) every man, who has read and felt the 'Lyrical Ballads' must have in common with me. . . . I may say in general . . . that the whole aggregate of pleasure I have received from some eight or nine other poets that I have been able to find since the world began falls infinitely short of what these two enchanting volumes have singly afforded me; —that your name is with me for ever linked to the lovely scenes of nature;—and that not yourself only but that each place and object you have mentioned, and all the souls in that delightful community of your's—to me

'Are dearer than the sun'.

He went on to say, in language of unashamed passion, that only the hope of Wordsworth's friendship had for nearly two years past rescued him from despair. Yet 'what claim can I urge to a fellowship with such a society as yours, beaming (as it does) with genius so wild and so magnificent?' He could only plead 'that my life has been passed chiefly in the contemplation and altogether in the worship of nature', that he was 'but a boy', and could not therefore 'draw you one step farther from the sweet retreats of poetry to the detested haunts of men', and, finally, that Wordsworth would never find any 'more ready (I speak from my heart) to sacrifice even his life whenever it would have a chance of promoting your interest and happiness—than he who now bends the knee before you'.

Wordsworth replied to this epistle with great wisdom and

kindness. Gently he warned De Quincey that 'my friendship is not in my power to give; this is a gift which no man can make; it is not in our own power. A sound and healthy friendship is the growth of time and circumstance; it will spring up like a wild-flower when these favour, and when they do not it is in vain to look for it.' He warned him, too, that he was setting a 'very unreasonable value upon my writings compared with those of others. You are young and ingenuous, and I wrote with a hope of pleasing the young, the ingenuous and the unworldly above all others; but sorry indeed should I be to stand in the way of the proper influence of other writers.' Finally, he warned De Quincey not to expect a regular or frequent correspondence. 'You probably would never guess from anything you know of me that I am the most lazy and impatient letter-writer in the world. You will perhaps have observed that the first two or three Lines of this sheet are in a tolerably fair, legible hand, and now every Letter, from A to Z, is a complete rout, one upon the heels of another.' He added a brief invitation to De Quincey to visit Grasmere. Then, in a postscript, he reiterated the invitation with more warmth: 'I seem to have expressed myself absolutely with coldness. This is not my feeling, I assure you. I shall indeed be very happy to see you at Grasmere.'

Nearly three years were to pass before De Quincey, still trembling with awe, made his first attempt to call at Dove Cottage. From Coniston he advanced 'to the very gorge of Hammerscar,[1] from which the whole vale of Grasmere suddenly breaks upon the view'. He saw the 'ark-like island', the 'opposite shore revealing all its little bays and wild sylvan margin', and 'just two bowshots from the water, a little white cottage gleaming from the midst of trees', and knew it to be the home of his god. But then he was overcome with self-conscious fears. 'I retreated like a guilty thing, for fear I might be surprised by Wordsworth, and then returned faint-heartedly to Coniston and so to Oxford, *re infecta*.' That was in the summer of 1806. It was not until the Christmas of 1807 that he at last managed to reach the cottage and meet Wordsworth, having been requested by Coleridge, then in Bristol, to escort Mrs. Coleridge and the children back to Keswick.[2]

---

[1] i.e. to the neck of fell between Grasmere and Langdale at the top of Red Bank.
[2] De Quincey, *Works*, ii, p. 231.

Lyrical Ballads had come out in a new edition in April 1802. Copies did not arrive at Grasmere until June. There were no new poems; Coleridge's *Dungeon* and Wordsworth's *A Character* were omitted, and there were alterations in *Ruth* and some other poems. There was, however, a long addition to the preface, of nearly three thousand words, in which Wordsworth discoursed at length on the question, 'What is a Poet?', on the definition of 'pleasure' as a poet experiences it, and on the contrasting functions of the poet and the scientist, in which the scientist certainly got the worst of it. Wordsworth's distrust of science arose from his suspicion that the scientists were tampering with the 'living universe', and making of 'this beauteous world' a mere laboratory of unrelated studies. Not all Coleridge's microscopes could convince him that this was not so. It was not long since in *A Poet's Epitaph* he had castigated the 'philosopher'—that is, the scientist—who

> would peep and botanize
> Upon his mother's grave,

and earlier still he had declared that

> Our meddling intellect
> Misshapes the beauteous forms of things—
> We murder to dissect.

In the first book of the 'poem to Coleridge' he had appealed to him as one who assigned to scientific inquiry its proper limits, regarding it

> Not as our glory and our absolute boast
> But as a succedaneum and a prop
> To our infirmity.

Now in the preface he showed that he thought most scientists too absorbed in the pursuit of some particular truth to be concerned, as the poet must be, with all that affected his fellow men. 'The Poet', he declared in a passage of great and eloquent power, 'is the rock of defence of human nature; and upholder and preserver, carrying everywhere with him relationship and love. . . . Poetry is the breath and finer spirit of all knowledge; it is the impassioned expression which is in the countenance of all science.' But science was still remote and unfamiliar. Let it but put on 'a form of flesh and blood', and 'the Poet will lend his divine spirit to aid the transfiguration'.

Wordsworth was here undoubtedly showing a lack of imagination about the scientist's task, but to one as conscious as he of the unity of all life, of a spirit 'that rolls through all things', and of the 'mind of man' as the seat of visionary and creative power, interpreting and sanctifying the Universe which is at once its home and its field of spiritual discovery, the inevitable tendency of scientists to divide and classify and label the world of Nature seemed presumptuous. He mentions three kinds of scientists—chemists, botanists, and 'mineralogists'—who ought to make 'these respective sciences manifestly and palpably material to us as enjoying and suffering beings'.[1] It is difficult to know exactly what Wordsworth expected them to do, beyond what they were already doing. His silence about Newton, for whom he felt of course the deepest veneration, perhaps indicates that for him Newton had done what these failed to do: he, in the abstract world of mathematics, to which Wordsworth had often repaired for relief from the torment of feeling, had laid down principles which seemed to give unity and coherence to the whole physical world.

Coleridge saw the great importance of Wordsworth's vision of Nature as one of 'relationship and love', and knew better than most people what he had gone through to preserve and sustain it. Nevertheless, he thought him unfair to the scientists, and saw that the whole process of his approach to Nature by way of the feelings rather than the intellect might, if pressed too far, lead to a repudiation of our powers of understanding and knowledge. The whole matter came to a head in a three-cornered argument which took place in October 1803 between Coleridge, Wordsworth, and William Hazlitt, who was making a stay of several months at Keswick during which he painted portraits of both Coleridge and Wordsworth which unfortunately have not survived.[2] Strangely, Coleridge found himself in a minority of one against the other two. Writing his account of the dispute in his note-book late that same night, sore from

[1] See *Excursion*, III, ll. 172–94, for a slightly disparaging description of a geologist's activities.

[2] Southey reported that someone, seeing the portrait of Wordsworth, remarked: 'At the gallows—deeply affected by his deserved fate—yet determined to die like a man.' Wordsworth afterwards said that 'the unfinished work was destroyed', 'as he did not satisfy himself or my friends'. But young Hartley said: 'It is very like— but Wordsworth is far handsomer.' *U.L.* i, p. 265.

what had evidently been an unexpected revelation of Wordsworth's less tolerant temper, he wrote what amounts to a tender
appeal to his friend to be less critical of others.

The dispute turned on the 'argument from Design'; the
common conviction both of scientists and philosophers of the late
seventeenth and early eighteenth centuries that because 'Nature'
followed certain laws and because animals were endowed with
instinct which perfectly adapted them to their environment, the
natural world gave forth unmistakable evidence of a divine and
benevolent Creator.

A most unpleasant dispute with Wordsworth and Hazlitt. I spoke,
I fear, too contemptuously; but they spoke so irreverently, so malig-
nantly of the Divine Wisdom that it overset me. Hazlitt, how easily
raised to rage and hatred self-projected! but who shall find the force
that can drag him up out of the depth into one expression of kindness,
into the showing of one gleam of the light of love on his countenance.
Peace be with him! But *thou*, dearest Wordsworth—and what if Ray,
Derham, Paley[1] have carried the observation of the aptitude of things
too far, too habitually into pedantry? O how many worse pedantries!
how few so harmless, with so much efficient good! Dear William,
pardon pedantry in others, and avoid it in yourself, instead of scoffing
and reviling at pedantry in good men and a good cause and *becoming*
a pedant yourself in a bad cause—even by that very act becoming one.
But surely, always to look at the superficies of objects for the purpose
of taking delight in their beauty, and sympathy with their real or
imagined life, is as deleterious to the health and manhood of intellect
as, always to be peering and unravelling contrivance may be to the
simplicity of the affection and the grandeur and unity of the imagination. O dearest William! would Ray or Derham have spoken of Nature
as you spoke of God?

In the course of this argument Hazlitt no doubt 'scoffed' at
every kind of religious approach to a philosophy of the Universe,
being a disciple of Godwin and his necessitarian rationalism.
But Wordsworth's objections to the 'argument from design'
arose from his profound empirical conviction that God was one
with the Universe, not external to it. Of Deity external to
Nature, 'making' it as a watch-maker makes a watch, he was

---

[1] John Ray's *Wisdom of God in the Creation* and Derham's *Physico-Theology* were
standard works dealing with the 'argument from Design'. Ray's book was published
in 1691 though it was written a generation earlier. Paley's *Natural Theology: or
Evidence of the Existence and Attributes of the Deity collected from the Appearances of
Nature* had appeared in 1802.

suspicious and critical. 'There is nothing', he wrote later, in answer to some criticisms of *The Excursion*, 'in the course of the religious education adopted in this country, and in the use made by us of the Holy Scriptures, that appears to me so injurious as perpetually talking about "making" by God'.[1] It was not long since he had written of

> the one interior life
> That lives in all things, sacred from the touch
> Of that false secondary power by which
> In weakness we create distinctions, then
> Believe that all our puny boundaries are things
> Which we perceive and not which we have made;
> In which all beings live with god, themselves
> Are god, Existing in the mighty whole. . . .[2]

Now, in 1803, he would perhaps have modified that language somewhat; whatever he may have said in 1798, he did not now regard Nature and God as interchangeable, and he had allowed himself to call upon the name of 'God' in many of his recent sonnets; he had informed his daughter Caroline that 'God was with her when she knew it not'; and he was about to speak of combating

> in the sight
> Of a just God for liberty and right.

Nevertheless, God was not Paley's creator-mechanic, and in argument with Hazlitt Wordsworth no doubt reverted to an almost completely pantheistic attitude.

Coleridge, listening to some such outpouring, felt that Wordsworth was in danger of becoming a 'pedant' in the cause of beauty divorced from intellectual knowledge, the 'bad cause' of what Coleridge, who loved philosophic accuracy, afterwards called 'the vague, misty rather than mystic, confusion of God with the world, and the accompanying nature-worship', which appeared in Wordsworth's poetry and which, said Coleridge, 'is the trait in his poetic works which I most dislike as unhealthful'.[3] Coleridge longed to make Wordsworth the king of

---

[1] *M.Y.* ii. 511, pp. 618–19. W.W. to Catherine Clarkson, Dec. 1814.
[2] *Prel.*, p. 512. The lines occur in an early note-book and were not included in the final text of *The Prelude*. They are connected with Book II, ll. 216–19.
[3] Allsop, *Letters etc. of S. T. Coleridge*, 1836, i, pp. 105–7.

philosophers as well as poets, and often spoke of him as such, but Wordsworth would not be crowned. He remained a poet, one who had had his vision and must speak of it and let others philosophize about it if they could.

Coleridge held up his portrait of Wordsworth the philosopher to two other visitors to Keswick who from this summer onwards were to play an important part in the lives of the Wordsworths. They were Sir George and Lady Beaumont. Beaumont was an amateur landscape-painter of moderate attainments, and a great patron of art. He was a wealthy country-gentleman with an estate at Coleorton in Leicestershire where he was building a mansion, another (his birth-place) at Dunmow in Essex, and a house in Grosvenor Square. Writing of him after his death, Sir Walter Scott described him as 'by far the most sensible and pleasing man I ever knew; kind, too, in his nature, and generous; gentle in society, and of those mild manners which tend to soften the causticity of the general London tone of persiflage and personal satire'. He also said of him that he was 'the man in the world most void of affectation', and, regarding Wordsworth, that 'he understood Wordsworth's poetry, which is a rare thing'.[1] Wordsworth was already known to him and his wife by his poetry when they came to Keswick. We turn to Coleridge for a description of its effect upon Lady Beaumont. She, he said, was 'a miniature Madame Guion, a deep Enthusiast, sensitive, trembles and cannot keep the Tears in her eye'. After reading one of Wordsworth's *Poems on the Naming of Places* she declared that had the poet entered the room at that moment, she would have fallen at his feet.[2] They both saw Hazlitt's portrait of Wordsworth and told Coleridge that it gave them an idea of Wordsworth 'as a profound, strong-minded Philosopher, not as a Poet'. This pleased Coleridge who told the Beaumonts that Wordsworth was 'a great Poet by inspirations, and in moments of revelation, but . . . a thinking, feeling Philosopher habitually —that his Poetry was his Philosophy under the action of strong winds of Feeling—a sea rolling high'.[3]

Sir George lost no time in lavishing sympathetic benevolence

---

[1] Scott's *Journal*, Feb. 14th 1827 *et al.*

[2] *U.L.* i. 121, p. 266. She also told Coleridge that 'when she was a child, previously to saying her prayers, she endeavoured to think of a mountain or great river . . . in order to raise up her soul and kindle it.' *A.P.*, Feb. 13th 1804.

[3] *U.L.* i. 121, p. 266.

on Wordsworth. Before he had seen Wordsworth at all, he determined to make him a valuable present. Having learnt from Coleridge of the inconvenience of the distance between Keswick and Grasmere now that Coleridge's health was so poor, Sir George determined to make it possible for them to live nearer each other. Without saying anything to Wordsworth he bought the little estate of Applethwaite, close under Skiddaw at the head of Bassenthwaite, and presented it, through Coleridge, to Wordsworth, so that he could build a house there for himself. Wordsworth, when he learnt from Coleridge what Sir George had done, was somewhat embarrassed. It was probable that Coleridge was going abroad for a considerable time, and he himself could scarcely afford to build a house. Even if Coleridge stayed at Keswick, there was the difficulty of Mrs. Coleridge and her dislike of the Wordsworths. He finally asked Sir George to let him keep the estate for the present, and 'lay out the rent in planting', until such time as he might be able to build. If that time never came, he would hand back the deeds to Sir George.

Sir George's reply to this suggestion admitted of no argument. 'Never mention another word about returning Applethwaite to me', he wrote. 'Plant it, delve it and build on it or not as it suits your convenience, but let me live and die with the idea the sweet place, with its rocks, its banks, and mountain stream are in the possession of such a mind as yours, and moreover', added this charming and modest benefactor, 'let the particulars of the transaction remain unkown to all but you, Coleridge, Lady Beaumont and myself.' He even tried to show that Coleridge was more worthy of thanks in the matter than himself.

Indeed indeed you overrate my share in the little transaction, you will recollect when the business was settled I never had seen you, and tho' I felt deeply indebted for pleasure received and had had a character of you from Coleridge which I could not but admire, yet whatever thanks are due ought to be paid to him, and I soon found there was no means of doing this so effectually as by accommodating his friend. I had moreover a most ardent desire to bring you nearer together . . . and that this would be a means of contributing to the pleasure and improvement of the world, by stimulating you both to poetical exertions. This you see was selfish, so talk no more of obligations.[1]

Thus did the good Sir George excuse his own benevolence,

[1] *D.C.P.* Sir G. Beaumont to W.W., Oct. 24th 1803.

and Wordsworth was fain to submit. He never parted with the estate and never built a house there. But the gift was of value from another point of view. Writing to Richard in the following December Wordsworth thus described the estate—somewhat cavalierly, it must be admitted. 'Sir George Beaumont', he said, 'made me a present last summer of a few old houses with two small fields attached to them in the Vale of Keswick, value £100, it was for me to patch up a house there if I liked to be near Mr. Coleridge. But this I decline, though he insists on my keeping the land, so you see I am a freeholder of the County of Cumberland.' In the years to come, politics became of more and more absorbing interest to Wordsworth, and his political rights as a freeholder of his native county with a vote at election-time became of some importance.

Sir George, meanwhile, became an intimate and devoted friend of Wordsworth by correspondence, as did Lady Beaumont of Dorothy. The generosity of such people as the Beaumonts was so tactfully exercised as to be acceptable without embarrassment. Twice they lent the Wordsworths a house on their Leicestershire estate of Coleorton when the cottage was becoming too small for their increasing family. But there was one aspect of their friendship which affected Wordsworth in an unexpected, some would say an unfortunate, way. Sir George was a high Tory in politics, and his kindness to Wordsworth, combined with that of another distinguished patron and helper of the same political persuasion, Lord Lowther, subtly assisted Wordsworth's progress towards political conservatism, and especially towards faith in the landed gentry as a class, which is so marked a development of his middle life. But in every private aspect, the friendship of the Beaumonts is yet another example of the extraordinary good fortune which attended Wordsworth at intervals throughout his life.

XVIII

THE SCOTTISH TOUR AND AFTER
August – December 1803

> *On the idle hill of summer,*
> *Sleepy with the flow of streams,*
> *Far I hear the steady drummer*
> *Drumming like a noise in dreams.*
>
> A SHROPSHIRE LAD

MARY had recovered so well after John's birth that in August Wordsworth, Dorothy, and Coleridge felt justified in carrying out a six weeks' tour in Scotland. Joanna Hutchinson came to keep Mary company while they were away. 'Do not', said Wordsworth to his brother Richard, 'imagine we are going to launch out in expence, we expect it will do our health good, and shall travel with one horse only. We do not expect to go into a more expensive house for some time than the one we now occupy and therefore can afford to take this recreation.' Nevertheless, money was borrowed for the tour. Four years afterwards we hear from Coleridge of some confusion about the repayment of a loan of some £50 from Daniel Stuart to Wordsworth for the purposes of the tour.[1]

In one respect the tour differed from all others previously made—they bought a horse and an Irish car in which to make the journey. Coleridge thus describes their equipage.

We have bought a stout horse, aged but stout and spirited, and an open vehicle called a jaunting car. There is room in it for three on each side, on hanging seats, a Dicky box for the driver, and a space or hollow in the middle for luggage, or two or three bairns . . . Your feet are not above a foot, scarcely so much—from the ground, so that you may get off and on while the horse is moving without the least danger. There are all sorts of conveniences in it.

There was also the very great inconvenience that it provided no shelter whatsoever against bad weather. However, the car served them well enough on their tour and was for long

[1] *U.L.* i. 166, p. 375.

afterwards a useful addition to the Wordsworths' household. Coleridge was not very hopeful of any benefit from the tour for himself. He tried to think that 'the exercise and excitement will be of so much service as to outweigh the chances of injury from wet and cold', but confessed that 'I never yet commenced a journey with such inauspicious heaviness of heart before.'[1] They set out from Keswick in their curious conveyance on August 15th, intending to make for Glasgow by the same route which Wordsworth had travelled with Montagu and the Rush family two years before; from there they were to explore the Highlands.

'We were very happy during our tour,' wrote Dorothy afterwards, 'particularly the last month, for at first we were but half weaned from home and had not learnt the way of enjoying ourselves—we seemed to consider the whole tour as a business to be by us performed for some good end or other, but when we had fairly got forward the rambling disposition came upon us and we were sorry to turn back again.' On the whole, the health of both William and Dorothy benefited by the tour, though Dorothy found her strength taxed to the utmost by its exertions, so that she was glad to 'loll in indolence before the fire' in the rough Highland inns and cottages where they stayed, unable even to write letters to her friends. On her return she began to write her *Recollections of a Tour in Scotland*. It is not a journal, for she took no notes at the time, and did not begin it until after her return.[2] And it was written 'for the sake of my friends, who, it seems, ought to have been with us', and is thus not of a private and intimate nature like the Grasmere Journal. She gives no hint of any difficulties of adjustment with Coleridge and it is from his own letters that we surmise that, for the first time, he found himself unable to find complete enjoyment in the Wordsworths' company. 'Somehow or other', he wrote to his wife, 'I have not been quite comfortable.' And to Tom Poole, after his return home, he wrote: 'I soon found I was a burden on

---

[1] *U.L.* i. 122, p. 269. S.T.C. to Southey, Aug. 14th 1803.

[2] She began it in Sept. 1803, continuing it until December when it was interrupted by Coleridge's arrival and his serious illness; resumed it in Feb. 1804 and was again interrupted; the last part (she divided her story into three parts) was not begun until 1 April 1805, when William persuaded her to resume it to afford some distraction from her grief at the death of John Wordsworth at sea in February.

them, and Wordsworth himself a brooder over his painful hypochondriacal sensations, was not my fittest companion.' These 'sensations', Coleridge complained, 'kept him silent and self-centred'. William was certainly in poor condition at the beginning of the tour, sometimes unable to eat, and easily exhausted, but he was not always silent. The poet Rogers, whom they met at Dumfries, and who had recently been staying at Keswick, reported that Coleridge and Wordsworth were so absorbed in 'talking about poetry' that 'the whole care of looking out for cottages where they might . . . pass the night, as well as seeing their poor horse fed and littered, devolved upon Miss Wordsworth'. This, however, is a very misleading description of their methods. Dorothy's *Recollections*, besides showing that they were only in Rogers' company for a quarter of an hour, makes it clear that the care of the horse was throughout entirely William's business, and that he used to inquire of the ostlers at the various inns about accommodations at the next stage.[1] Talk there was, however, in plenty, whether it was defining the 'precise meaning of the words grand, majestic, sublime, etc.' or of the field 'regularly covered' with ragwort, as though it had been sown as a crop, which made William laugh, while 'C. was melancholy upon it, observing that there was land enough wasted to rear a healthy child.'[2]

Wordsworth, for his part, long afterwards said that Coleridge was 'in bad spirits, and somewhat too much in love with his own dejection'.[3] Their moods made them out of tune for perfect mutual enjoyment, and Wordsworth made the wise suggestion, when they returned to Luss on Loch Lomond after visiting Loch Katrine, that Coleridge should walk back to Stirling, get the coach from there to Edinburgh and so return home. While they were making their excursion to Loch Katrine on foot, the weather broke and showed no signs of recovery. Coleridge preferred walking in rain to an open carriage or a boat—he had walked all the way down Loch Katrine while William and Dorothy went by water—and so the parting was decided upon, and on August 29th he went on his way. 'We portioned out the contents of our purse before our parting', says Dorothy, 'and after we had lost sight of him, drove heavily

[1] *D.W.J.* i, p. 235 *et al.*   [2] Ibid., pp. 223, 218.
[3] *P.W.* iii, p. 438. Note to *Memorials of a Tour in Scotland, 1803*.

along. . . . Our thoughts were full of Coleridge. . . . I shivered
at the thought of his being sickly and alone, travelling from
place to place.' She need not have distressed herself. Coleridge
found himself 'so happy alone', and instead of proceeding to
Edinburgh, struck north to Glen Coe and Fort William and
walked for eight days at the rate of rather over thirty miles a
day, was arrested at Fort Augustus as a spy, and finally arrived
in Edinburgh on September 12th. Thence he returned to Keswick by coach, where he found the Southeys in great grief at the
sudden death of their little girl, 'the unexpected gift of a long
marriage'. Very soon afterwards the Southeys became permanent
inhabitants of Greta Hall. William and Dorothy proceeded in
their jaunting car to Dalmally, Loch Awe, and the Appin shore
of Loch Linnhe, then through Glen Coe to the King's House on
Rannoch Moor—the wildest of all the wild inns at which they
stayed—on to Loch Tay, Killiecrankie, and Blair Atholl, and so
back by Crieff, Strathyre and Callander to Stirling, and at last,
on September 15th, they entered Edinburgh, only two days
after Coleridge had left it.

There is no purpose in recounting again the tour so well
described by Dorothy; but here and there an incident can be
picked out which sheds light once more on Wordsworth's
enthusiasms, tastes, and habits of mind. At the beginning of
the tour, they visited the grave of Burns at Dumfries, and his
house there in which his widow was still living, and passed near
his earlier home at Ellisland. 'We were glad to leave Dumfries',
wrote Dorothy, '. . . we could think of little else but poor Burns,
and his moving about on that "unpoetic ground". . . . We passed
Ellisland at a little distance on our right, his farmhouse. We
might there have had more pleasure in looking round . . . but
there is no thought surviving in connection with Burns's daily
life that is not heart-depressing.' As they looked across at their
own Cumberland mountains from near Ellisland 'we talked of
Burns, and the prospect he must have had, perhaps from his own
door, of Skiddaw and his companions, indulging ourselves in the
fancy that we *might* have been personally known to each other,
and he have looked upon those objects with more pleasure for
our sakes'. They thought of Burns' sons, left fatherless as they
themselves had been; one of them, Francis Wallace, already lay
beside his father in Dumfries kirkyard. 'We talked of Coleridge's

children and family, then at the foot of Skiddaw, and our own new-born John a few miles behind it; while the Grave of Burns' son, which we had just seen by the side of his father, and some stories heard at Dumfries respecting the dangers his surviving children were exposed to, filled us with melancholy concern, which had a kind of connection with ourselves.'

Wordsworth afterwards wrote three poems about this visit to Burns' grave.[1] Of these, the first, *At the Grave of Burns*, was partly written before 1807, though not published until 1842; the second, says Wordsworth, 'though felt at the time, was not composed till many years after'. It is an address to Dorothy, recalling their first early acquaintance with Burns's poems as they walked together in the Lowther woods:[2]

> When side by side, his Book in hand,
>   We wont to stray,
> Our pleasure varying at command
>   Of each sweet Lay.

In both poems the strength of the feeling actually experienced at the time overflows in what Dorothy would call many 'affecting lines'. And, among some more commonplace stanzas, one celebrates in prophetic splendour the fame of Burns:

> Through busiest street and loneliest glen
> Are felt the flashes of his pen;
> He rules 'mid winter snows, and when
> Bees fill their hives;
> Deep in the general heart of men
> His power survives.

The third of these poems, *To the Sons of Burns*, was written in its first form probably late in 1805, and published in 1807. It is a warning to the poet's sons not to follow in their father's footsteps, but Wordsworth is never at his best when he is preaching and admonishing.

The tour which began with the dead Burns ended with the living Walter Scott. On September 17th they walked out early from the village inn at Roslin, east of Edinburgh, to Lasswade, where Scott was then living, and found him and his wife not yet stirring. They stayed to breakfast, however, and Scott 'limped by our side through the groves of Roslin', and promised to meet

---

[1] *P.W.* iii, pp. 65–71. *Memorials of a Tour in Scotland, 1803*, II, III, and IV.
[2] See above, p. 73.

them again two days later at Melrose, whither he was going on his way to Jedburgh, to the Assizes, for he was then Sheriff of Selkirk. They had no formal introduction to Scott, but the link between them was Coleridge's friend John Stoddart, who had lately written a handsome guide-book to Scotland[1] and had visited Scott at Lasswade. Scott was now engaged in composing the *Lay of the Last Minstrel*, and at Jedburgh he dined with them at their lodging and there 'partly read and partly recited, sometimes in an enthusiastic style of chant, the first four cantos'.[2] The scene is precious to imagination. But the Wordsworths, even while they listened with delight to the 'easy, glowing energy of much of the verse' (not, one notes, quite all of it!) noticed with some dismay the strong resemblance of some parts of it to Coleridge's yet unpublished *Christabel*. Scott had heard *Christabel* recited by Stoddart, who had 'a very wicked memory',[3] and having just begun to write the *Lay*, he was delighted to find in *Christabel* 'so happy a specimen of the same kind of irregular metre which he had adopted'. His delight led him to learn *Christabel* by heart, and unconsciously to imitate it in style and phraseology. 'We were both equally convinced', says Dorothy, 'from the frankness of Walter Scott's manner that it was an unconscious imitation.' William was doubtful whether he should point out to Scott that he was plagiarizing; he decided that it could not be done with propriety on so slight an acquaintance, but afterwards, when the *Lay* was published, he regretted that he had not done so. He feared that the *Lay* would 'tarnish the freshness of *Christabel* and considerably injure the first effect of it'. Dorothy, however, was so convinced of the superior originality of *Christabel* that she did not much fear the effect of the *Lay*.

The rest of their time with Scott was delightfully spent. He showed them Melrose Abbey, and he and William shared a bedroom at the inn there.[4] From Jedburgh he walked with them

---

[1] *Remarks on the Local Scenery and Manners of Scotland*, 1801. On p. 230 is a quotation (unacknowledged) from Wordsworth's *Ruth* in a description of the islands on Loch Lomond.

All the fairy crowds
Of islands that together lie, &c.

[2] Lockhart, *Life of Scott*, i, p. 352.

[3] Rogers, *Table Talk*, p. 209, n.

[4] 'I could not persuade the woman to show me the beds, till she was assured from the Sheriff himself that he had no objection to sleep in the same room with William.' *D.W.J.* i, p. 395.

up the Jed Water as far as Ferniehurst, which reminded them of Alfoxden, and after the Assizes were over at Jedburgh, he travelled with the Wordsworths in their car up the vale of Teviot to Hawick where they slept. Next day he bade them farewell. 'We wished', said Dorothy, 'we could have gone with Mr. Scott into some of the remote dales of this country, where in almost every house he can find a home and a hearty welcome.' 'His local attachments', she afterwards wrote, 'are more strong than those of any person I ever saw—his whole heart and soul seem to be devoted to the Scottish Streams, Yarrow and Tweed, Tiviot and the rest of them, of which we hear in the Border Ballads, and I am sure that there is not a story ever told by the fire-sides in that neighbourhood that he cannot repeat. . . . He is a man of very sweet manners, mild, cordial and cheerful.'[1]

Wordsworth was deeply attracted; on returning home he wrote almost at once to Scott, sending him his sonnet on Neidpath Castle, and begging him to come to Westmorland. 'Scotland and England', he said, 'sound like division, do what we can, but we really are but neighbours; if you were no farther off and in Yorkshire, we should think so.' And he signed himself 'Your sincere Friend, for such I will call myself, though slow to use a word of such solemn meaning to any one'.[2]

One remark of Scott's caused Wordsworth some surprise. Scott said that he felt sure 'he could if he chose, get more money than he should ever wish to have from the booksellers'. His actual profession, the law, he said, was not profitable. Wordsworth, who was unable to make money by his own writings, and whose brother Richard and friend Basil Montagu were prospering as lawyers, was surprised. The years to come proved Scott to be perfectly right. But yet Scott did not impress Wordsworth primarily as a man of letters. It was 'his bodily sports, exercises and social amusements' that seemed to interest him most—fishing, duck-shooting, and riding about the country-side—his 'Liddesdale raids' as he called them, when he explored every ruined peel-tower and was welcomed at every remote farm-house in all the wide Border.

Except for the sonnet on Neidpath Castle,[3] which was written

[1] *E.L.* 217, p. 493. D.W. to Lady Beaumont, May 4th 1805.
[2] Ibid. 152, p. 344. W.W. to Scott, Oct. 1863.
[3] *P.W.* iii, p. 83. *Degenerate Douglas! oh the unworthy Lord.* Scott often recited

in view of the castle and its fallen woods, Wordsworth's poems arising from the Scottish tour were all written after his return home—some as much as two or even three years afterwards. Once he did kindle, while contemplating Kilchurn Castle at the head of Loch Awe, but he only got as far as the third line. 'At the sight of Kilchurn Castle', he wrote to Sir George Beaumont, '. . . I felt a real poetical impulse: but I did not proceed. I began a poem (apostrophizing the castle) thus:

> "Child of loud-throated war! the mountain stream
> Roars in thy hearing; but thy hour of rest
> Is come, and thou art silent in thine age:"

but I stopped.'[1] He did not complete it until many years afterwards.

The best of the poems, which he called 'Memorials' of the tour, celebrate some incident in which a human figure, seen in the context of the Highland landscape and being a part thereof, becomes charged with imaginative or visionary significance. Such are *Stepping Westward* and *The Solitary Reaper*, both of which were written in 1805, the latter, as has been noted, being suggested more by a passage in Thomas Wilkinson's *Tour in the Highlands* than by the recollection of a particular incident in their own tour. Dorothy copied it in a letter to Lady Beaumont on November 7th 1805, two days after it was written, and remarked: 'There is something inexpressibly soothing to me in the sound of those two lines

> "Oh listen! for the Vale profound
> Is overflowing with the sound,"

I often catch myself repeating them in disconnection with any thought, or even I may say recollection of the Poem.' *To a Highland Girl*, on the other hand, was written very soon after his return home. It lacks the magic of the *Reaper*, but it contains some very explicit affirmations of Wordsworth's most characteristic processes. The girl and her surroundings make one image, and it is a dream-image, like the vision of the leech-gatherer on the moor.

> In truth together do ye seem
> Like something fashioned in a dream;

this poem in the original form in which Wordsworth sent it to him in his letter of Oct. 1803.

[1] *E.L.* 151, p. 342. W.W. to Sir George Beaumont, Oct. 14th 1803.

> Such Forms as from their covert peep
> When earthly cares are laid asleep.

Yet she was a human reality.

> But O fair creature! in the light
> Of common day,[1] so heavenly bright,
> I bless Thee, Vision as thou art,
> I bless thee with a human heart.

He blessed her, as he had blessed his daughter Caroline, and also the memory of her which would cause her to be a living reality to him for ever.

> For I, methinks, till I grow old
> As fair before me shall behold,
> As I do now, the cabin small,
> The lake, the bay, the waterfall;
> And thee, the Spirit of them all.

The Scottish tour indeed was a holiday full of their own peculiar type of romantic pleasure. 'Scotland', said Dorothy, 'is the country above all others that I have seen, in which a man of imagination may carve out his own pleasures; there are so many *inhabited* solitudes, and the employments of the people are so immediately connected with the places where you find them.'

But of all the poems resulting from the Scottish Tour, *Yarrow Unvisited* is most truly Wordsworth's.[2] It is an exercise in his favourite habit of 'recollection', but as it were in reverse, for he and Dorothy did *not* visit Yarrow: they decided still to draw on their anticipations of its beauties, on what they knew of it in poetry and ballad. 'At Clovenford', says Dorothy, writing of September 18th, their last Sunday in Scotland, 'being so near to the Yarrow, we could not but think of the possibility of going thither, but came to the conclusion of reserving the pleasure for some future time.'[3]

---

[1] It is perhaps worth noting that here Wordsworth first used the phrase 'the light of common day', which appears in a more famous context in the later stanzas of the *Ode*, written in the spring of 1804.

[2] Of this poem T. Hutchinson wrote: 'The great subject of the poem—the duty of spiritual frugality, of laying up in the heart stores of meditative joy from which one refrains from drawing all that might be drawn of present delight—is the only idea left on the mind.' *Poems in Two Volumes 1807* (1897), ii. p. 185.

[3] Wordsworth afterwards said that their reasons for passing it by were not quite the same as those given in the poem. He does not say what they were. Perhaps he and Dorothy were simply rather tired.

The poem (which was written 'soon' after their return home, sometime therefore in the autumn of 1803) is closely associated with their acquaintance with Scott. When Wordsworth sent a copy of it, many months later, to Scott, he said: 'I wrote the stanzas, not without a view of pleasing you. . . . They are in the same sort of metre as the *Leader Haughs,* and I have borrowed the name *Burn-mill* meadow from that poem, for which I wish you would substitute something that may really be found in the Vale of Yarrow.' Scott in reply suggested 'Broad Meadow', but Wordsworth never altered it.[1] By *Leader Haughs* Wordsworth means a poem by the 'Minstrel Burn', one of the last true wandering minstrels of the Border, like the one whom Scott celebrated in his *Lay.* Scott loved to repeat this old poem and must have done so to Wordsworth who was scarcely likely otherwise to be acquainted with it.[2] Its last two verses run as follows:

> Sing Erceldoun and Cowdenknowes,
> Where Homes were ance commanding,
> And Drygrange, wi' the milk-white ewes,
> 'Twixt Tweed and Leader standing.
> The bird that flies through Redpath trees
> And Gledswood banks each morrow,
> May chant and sing—*sweet Leader Haughs*
> And *Bonnie Howms of Yarrow.*

> But Minstrel Burn cannot assuage
> His grief while life endureth,
> To see the changes of this age
> Which fleeting time procureth;
> For mony a place stands in hard case,
> Where blythe folk kent nae sorrow,
> With Homes that dwelt on Leader side,
> And Scotts that dwelt on Yarrow.

Of these last four lines, Scott told Wordsworth that they had 'from early youth given my bosom a thrill'. Other ballads contributed to *Yarrow Unvisited,* particularly Hamilton's great poem, *Busk ye, busk ye, my bonnie, bonnie bride.* It is curious

---

[1] *E.L.* 191, p. 436. W.W. to Scott, Jan. 16th 1805. *Letters of Sir W. Scott,* ed. H. C. Grierson, i, p. 239. Scott to W.W., Mar. 16th 1805.
[2] The poem is, however, in Allan Ramsay's *Tea-Table Miscellany.*

to remark how here, by drawing on real balladry under the immediate inspiration of Scott and Scott's country-side, Wordsworth produced one of his best poems, whereas five years earlier, in *Ellen Irwin*, where he had deliberately avoided the ballad convention, he signally failed.

Apart from the Scottish poems, the poetry of this autumn of 1803 is the outcome of his extreme excitement about the danger of invasion, which was now thought by almost everyone to be imminent. His anxiety about it was already intense while he was still in Scotland, as the *Killiecrankie* sonnet written in October after his return, shows—

> O for a single hour of that Dundee
> Who on that day the word of onset gave!
> Like conquest would the men of England see;
> And her foes find a like inglorious grave.[1]

In his letter to Sir George Beaumont of October 14th 1803, three weeks after his return to Grasmere, Wordsworth wrote: 'My Sister will transcribe three sonnets, which I do not send you from any notion I have of their merit, but merely because they are the only verses I have written since I had the pleasure of seeing you and Lady Beaumont.' The three were the sonnet on Neidpath Castle which he also sent to Scott, the sonnet *To the Men of Kent*,[2] and the one which he called *Anticipation*, in which he calls everyone to rejoice without stint in the imaginary defeat of the invading army, and ends with the extraordinary lines:

> Clap, infants, clap your hands. Divine must be
> That triumph, when the very worst, the pain,
> And even the prospect of our brethren slain,
> Hath something in it which the heart enjoys:—
> In glory will they sleep and endless sanctity.

[1] *P.W.* iii, p. 85. It bears the subtitle 'An invasion being expected, October, 1803'. The exclamation 'O for one hour of Dundee' was made on the field of Sheriff-muir by a veteran chieftain exasperated by the dilatoriness of Mar. The story was told by Scott in his *Border Minstrelsy*, from which Wordsworth must have learnt it.

[2] The raising of 10,000 volunteers in the Cinque Ports by Pitt who was their Warden (being out of office at the time) during this summer had made a great impression on the country. Wordsworth was not the only person to write poems on the subject: the popular magazines contain other examples, e.g. the *Anti-Gallican* It has been suggested that Wordsworth had been reading Drayton's *The Baron's Wars*; the magazine ballads also contain references to the legend of the men of Kent resisting William the Conqueror.

The Wordsworth of *Salisbury Plain* and *The Ruined Cottage,* who had cursed governments because they taught young men habits of bloodshed and violence, seems very far away. Yet we are looking, as it were, only at the reverse of the coin. Eleven years before his heart had glowed with a like passion as he watched the young men of France volunteering for her defence against the 'coalesced kings' who threatened her frontiers. It was not the fault of the Beaupuys of the Revolution that France had become an aggressor and an invader in her turn. Something very deep and fundamental in Wordsworth's nature reacted, not grudgingly, or reluctantly, but with whole-hearted enthusiasm, when the great symbols of his faith were threatened. England had now become a symbol of liberty and 'national independence', closely akin to what France had stood for in his youth. There was much that was bad in her national life—his sonnets of the previous year had not spared her—nor was he ever a disciple of Pitt, who, he believed, was too much inclined to cling to power and office for his own sake rather than his country's;[1] but the condition to which first Robespierre and then Bonaparte had reduced France made hesitation futile. One thing only mattered now—a 'united front' against France. With his thoughts still running on the Royalists and Puritans, he wrote some very indifferent *Lines on the Expected Invasion,* pleading for the union of potential 'Pyms and Miltons' with those who would have followed Falkland and Montrose.

> Come ye—whate'er your creed—O waken all,
> Whate'er your temper, at your Country's call;
> Resolving (this a free-born Nation can)
> To have one Soul, and perish to a man,
> Or save this honoured land from every Lord
> By British reason and the British sword.

Three other sonnets quickly followed those he had sent to Sir George Beaumont. They were a lament over the temper of France (*One might believe that natural miseries*), an attack on the rich (*These times strike monied worldlings with dismay*), much in

---

[1] When Pitt died in 1806 Wordsworth wrote to Sir George Beaumont: 'His first wish (though probably unknown to himself) was that his Country should prosper under his administration; his next, that it should prosper: could the order of these wishes have been reversed, Mr. Pitt would have avoided many of the grievous mistakes into which, I think, he fell.' *M.T.* i, p. 7. W.W. to Sir G. Beaumont, Feb. 11th 1806.

the spirit of *O Friend! I know not which way I must look* of the previous autumn, and a meditation on the rise of Bonaparte (*When, looking on the present face of things*) in which the idea of 'Providence' and of men as the 'Instruments' of that Providence is bowed to in face of an almost overwhelming sense of despair.

> I find nothing great:
> Nothing is left which I can venerate;
> So that a doubt almost within me springs
> Of Providence, such emptiness at length
> Seems at the heart of all things. But, great God!
> I measure back the steps which I have trod;
> And tremble, seeing whence proceeds the strength
> Of such poor Instruments, with thoughts sublime
> I tremble at the sorrow of the time.[1]

For it was sorrow, rather than anger, which underlay Wordsworth's patriotic fervour—sorrow at the disgrace of France and at the imperfections of his own country. The same feelings were shared by Coleridge, with an even more strongly religious bent. To Coleridge, the notion of the invasion as a judgement for national sins and particularly for the slave-trade was vividly present.

If it be God's will that the commercial Gourd should be canker-filled—if our horrible iniquities in the West Indian Islands and on the coasts of Guinea call for judgment on us—God's will be done! . . . But I seriously think that this invasion if attempted . . . by the Corsican Tippoo Sahib, will be a blessing to this country and to Europe. Let us be humble before our Maker, but not spirit-palsied before our blood-thirsty enemies. We will tremble at the possible punishment which our national crimes may have made us worthy of, from retributive Providence: we will tremble at what God may do; but not at what our enemies can do of themselves. When were we a more united people? When so well prepared?

So wrote Coleridge to his brother on October 2nd 1803.

Thomas Poole, who was in London temporarily engaged in assisting Joseph Rickman in the government inquiry into the state of the Poor Laws, shared Coleridge's feelings, and added: 'You ask me what part I have taken in this business. Nothing, as aforesaid, but stirring myself about the Volunteers. . . . What

[1] *P.W.* iii, p. 119.

have you done? Could you not give us more of the men and the times? What has Wordsworth done in this or *any other way?*'

Wordsworth could have answered that, besides writing sonnets, which, through Sir George Beaumont, were sent to the press,[1] he also had 'stirred himself about the Volunteers'. The Government had issued orders in July for the enrolment in each parish of all able-bodied men (the Quakers alone being exempted on conscientious grounds) in the militia. If, however, Volunteer Corps were formed locally in satisfactory numbers, the call-up of the Militia would be postponed. The response throughout the country to the call for volunteers was immediate and over-whelming. In the north-west, Lord Lowther, as Lord Lieutenant of both Cumberland and Westmorland, set about organizing Volunteer Corps in every part of his Lieutenancy from Carlisle to Kendal. When Wordsworth returned from Scotland one of his first acts was to go to Ambleside with 'the greatest part of the men of Grasmere' to enrol himself with them in the Grasmere Volunteers. That was on October 3rd. On Sunday, the 16th, they went again to Ambleside to put on what Wordsworth called their 'military apparel'. Grasmere was a model parish. 'We have turned out', wrote Wordsworth, 'almost to a man', whereas at Keswick 'they are sadly remiss', having been 'thwarted by the orders and counter-orders of the Ministry and their servants.'[2] Mary and Dorothy were at first a good deal alarmed, but Dorothy, seeing that her brother was really enthusiastic, decided that 'if he really enters into it heart and soul and likes it, that will do him good', and she added: 'surely there never was a more determined hater of the French nor one more willing to do his utmost to destroy them if they really do come'.[3] Yes, Wordsworth was now 'a hater of the French', as represented by Bonaparte, though it was a hatred tempered by a deep and mournful pity as he contemplated the senselessness of French aggression.

[1] 'I am delighted with your patriotic lines, they are animating to a degree', wrote Sir G. Beaumont to W.W. on Oct. 24th 1803. (*D.C.P.*) He sent the *Men of Kent* and *Anticipation* to the papers; only *Anticipation*, however, was printed in the *Poetical Register* and again in 1804 in a patriotic digest called the *Anti-Gallican*. They eventually appeared in the *Poems* of 1807, long after the danger which inspired them had passed away.

[2] *E.L.* 151, p. 341. W.W. to Sir G. Beaumont, Oct. 14th 1803.

[3] Ibid. 150, p. 335. D.W. to C. Clarkson, Oct. 9th 1803.

How piteous then that there should be such dearth
Of knowledge; that whole myriads should unite
To work against themselves such fell despite:
Should come in phrensy and in drunken mirth,
Impatient to put out the only light
Of Liberty that yet remains on earth.[1]

By the new year invasion was no longer daily expected, but the Grasmere Volunteers still marched twice a week to Ambleside 'to be exercised'.[2] This, however, is the last we hear of them. It does not appear that Wordsworth obtained a commission. On the other side of Helvellyn, in Patterdale, Tom Wedgwood, unable through his chronic bad health to volunteer himself, raised, equipped, and paid a company of some eighty men from among the statesmen of the surrounding dales. He spent £800 out of his private fortune on this enterprise, clothing and arming the enthusiastic farmers as riflemen. They called themselves 'Wedgwood's Loyal Mountaineers', and wore felt hats, ornamented with brass strips engraved with their title.[3] Tom Wedgwood made Luff their Captain, and it is in a letter from him to Tom in May 1804 that we have a picture of Wordsworth visiting them after a day of strenuous 'exercises'. 'A very severe day it was', says Luff, 'but an excellent dinner of Beef and plum pudding to which 120 sat down, recruited their exhausted strength. . . . The gratitude of the men was unbounded. William Wordsworth dined with us on the lawn before the house and declared it to be the most interesting day he ever witnessed, such as he should long remember; and said he almost envied you your feelings on the occasion.'[4]

'Such things' [as military exercises] wrote Sir George Beaumont to Wordsworth, 'suit not poets or painters, but I am afraid we must all come to it at last.' Fortunately for posterity, Wordsworth's military enthusiasm did not interrupt the main flow of his poetry or limit it to the writing of patriotic sonnets. The spring of 1804 saw the resumption of the 'poem on his own life', and he continued it, letting it grow to more than twice its

---

[1] *P.W.* iii, p. 118. *One might believe that natural miseries.*
[2] *E.L.* 158, p. 358. D.W. to Mrs. Clarkson, Jan. 15th 1804.
[3] One of these strips is now in the possession of Sir Ralph Wedgwood of Leith Hill Place, Surrey.
[4] R. Litchfield, *Tom Wedgwood*, p. 152. The house where the dinner took place was probably 'Lyulph's Tower', a mansion on the western shore of Ullswater.

intended length, until its completion in May 1805. But even before he gave himself up to his task, he had done something which brought to Coleridge great relief and happiness. He had made what Coleridge called on October 14th 1803, in a letter to Poole, 'a beginning to his Recluse'.

Bearing in mind that Coleridge always called 'the poem to Coleridge' or 'the poem on my own life' *The Recluse*, and insisted on regarding it as an integral part of the great 'philosophical poem' which he continued to implore Wordsworth to get on with, it seems probable that we have here the clue to the filling-in of the first two hundred lines of *The Prelude* leading up to the question 'Was it for this . . .?' with which he had begun to write the first book in Germany four years before.[1] From the tense of Coleridge's sentence it looks as though the work were recent; and we are naturally inclined to conclude that it was begun between Wordsworth's return from Scotland on September 26th and his visit to Keswick on Sunday, October 9th, when he would have told Coleridge what he was doing. But Wordsworth himself had told Sir George Beaumont on October 14th that the three sonnets he enclosed were 'the only verses' he had written since he saw Beaumont just before leaving for Scotland. Dorothy also, writing to Mrs. Clarkson on November 21st, says: 'William has written two little poems on subjects suggested by our Tour in Scotland—that is all that he has actually done lately.' Was the 'beginning' to *The Recluse* then made sometime in the summer, before the departure for Scotland? If so, it was probably no more than a beginning, perhaps simply the writing down of the fifty-four lines from 'Oh there is blessing in this gentle breeze', which now stand at the opening of *The Prelude*, but which hitherto had been 'floating loose about' in fragmentary form since their composition in September 1795, after he left London for the West Country. Or Coleridge's words may mean no more than that Wordsworth had discussed with him the 'beginning' to *The Recluse*, and promised that henceforward *The Recluse* would be his main concern. Coleridge often referred to schemes of his own as though they were at least partly written works and he may well have spoken of *The Recluse* in the same way. Such a conclusion could be drawn from the continuation of his remarks in his letter to Poole of

[1] See above, p. 419.

October 14th. 'I rejoice therefore with a deep and true joy', he says, 'that he has at length yielded to my urgent and repeated—almost unremitting—requests and remonstrances—and will go on with The Recluse exclusively.' By February 1804 we know that he was indeed hard at work; by the end of March five books, including the 'beginning', had been copied for Coleridge to take abroad. Whether the 'beginning' had in fact been written before February must remain uncertain, but on the whole it seems unlikely that much progress had been made with it, for from December 20th to January 14th Coleridge was at the cottage seriously ill, and soon after his departure a severe illness of Dorothy's for a time threw William into a state of acute anxiety.[1]

Coleridge was elated at having at last reawakened *The Recluse*. He discoursed to Poole on Wordsworth's genius and on *The Recluse* in delighted tones: 'A great Work, in which he will sail on; an open Ocean and a steady wind; unfretted by short tucks, reefing and hawling and disentangling the ropes—great work necessarily comprehending his attention and feelings within the circle of great objects and elevated Conceptions that is his natural Element. The having been out of it has been his Disease—to return into it is the specific Remedy, both Remedy and Health. It is what Food is to Famine.' Most readers of Wordsworth will scarcely go so far with Coleridge as to call his lyrical genius 'disease' and the absence of a great work 'famine', and indeed Coleridge is here exaggerating even his own feelings, or rather perhaps deliberately allowing them to be worked into a state of exaggeration. 'I have seen enough', he goes on, 'positively to give me feelings of hostility towards the plan of several of the Poems in the L. Ballads: and I really consider it a misfortune that Wordsworth ever deserted his former Mountain Track to wander in Lower valleys; tho' in the event it may prove to have been of great Benefit to him. He will steer, I trust, a middle course.'[2]

This was indeed what Wordsworth did. Henceforward he made the completion of the 'poem on his life' his main task, but he did not cease to write shorter poems. Coleridge believed that the writing of short poems was 'hurtful to him—such things as

---

[1] *E.L.* 162, pp. 367–8. W.W. to S.T.C. Mar. 6th 1804. *L.Y.* iii, p. 1346. D.W. to C. Clarkson, Feb. 26th 1804.
[2] *U.L.* i, p. 291. S.T.C. to T. Poole, Oct. 14th 1803.

that Sonnet of his in Monday's Morning Post, about Simonides and the Ghost'.[1] Hurtful, presumably, because they dissipated his powers instead of concentrating them on *The Recluse*. And Coleridge had another quarrel with Wordsworth's shorter poems. They had caused him to acquire a 'sectarian' reputation; 'to be called the Head and founder of a *Sect* in Poetry'. This had reference no doubt to the remarks in the first issue of the *Edinburgh Review* in October 1802. Here, in a review of Southey's *Thalaba*, unfavourable criticism had been made of the 'fraternity' which was supposed to be responsible for *Lyrical Ballads*, and in particular of the 'effusions of that poet who commemorates with so much effect the chattering of Harry Gibbs's [*sic*] teeth', &c. But it is more difficult to understand why Coleridge should have singled out Wordsworth's sonnets as 'sectarian'. 'Assuredly', he wrote, 'he has written and published in the Morning Post, as W.L.D. and sometimes with no signature, poems written with a sectarian spirit and in a sort of Bravado.' The 'W.L.D.' sonnets were the seven published sonnets of 1802, in which he voiced his feelings about Bonaparte, England, and Liberty.[2] One of them, *I grieved for Bonaparte*, Coleridge had already compared with Milton. They were not written in the language of 'the lower orders of society', as the *Lyrical Ballads* were supposed to have been, and 'bravado' seems the last word to apply appropriately to their spirit. Had Coleridge referred to the 'Invasion' group of sonnets, his criticism would have had more validity. But these were not yet published.

The 'beginning' to *The Recluse*, or rather to *The Prelude*, is really an apology to Coleridge for not having written more of *The Recluse* hitherto. It may be divided into two parts. The first 113 lines are a telescoped, rather than an historical, version of his autobiography from his arrival at Racedown in September 1795 until his settlement at Grasmere at the end of 1799.[3] The second part of the passage (from l. 114 to l. 271 of the first book of *The Prelude*), in which he describes his unsuccessful attempt to write either an epic or a philosophical poem, presents us with a picture of Wordsworth's mental ambitions as they existed now, in the winter of 1803–4 (for the present tense is used throughout) rather

---

[1] *P.W.* iii, p. 408. *I find it written of Simonides.* This sonnet was never included by Wordsworth in any of his collected editions.

[2] See above, pp. 570–1.   [3] See above, pp. 272 ff.

than as they were in the spring of 1798 when, filled with a sudden access of confidence which did not last, he had begun to plan *The Recluse*. What is most striking is his concern with an epic subject, and the particular colour which that subject would obviously have received had he eventually settled upon one, and, secondly, his failure to so settle and his strange confession of defeat.

> If my mind
> Remembering the sweet promise of the past
> Would gladly grapple with some noble theme
> Vain is her wish; where'er she turns she finds
> Impediments from day to day renewed.

No less than eight themes for an epic are enumerated. They throw much light on his thought, his reading, and his imaginative musings. First, there was the possibility of

> some British theme, some old
> Romantic tale, by Milton left unsung.

Wordsworth probably knew that Milton had contemplated an epic on King Arthur; he may even have seen the manuscript in the library of Trinity College, Cambridge, in which a scheme is elaborately drawn up for a poetic history of Britain before the Norman Conquest. Significantly, he aims at completing Milton. Milton, with Shakespeare, Spenser, and Chaucer, formed the great 'square' of his master-poets and exemplars, whom he had set himself to 'study and equal *if I could*'.[1] So Spenser is the inspiration of his next theme—a sort of knightly pastoral—

> I pipe
> Among the Shepherds with reposing knights
> Sit by a Fountain-side and hear their tales.

Then other themes, drawn from his reading of Plutarch, Gibbon, Hakluyt, and more obscure histories, attracted him. First comes Mithridates, an opponent of Roman tyranny, whom Wordsworth, quite independently of any previous author, identifies with Odin himself, the founder of the Gothic race who eventually overran the Roman Empire.

> I would relate
> How vanquished Mithridates northward passed
> And, hidden in the cloud of years, became

[1] *Mem.* ii, p. 470.

> That Odin, Father of a race by whom
> Perish'd the Roman Empire.

He then speaks of Sertorius, another refugee from Roman tyranny, who, according to Plutarch, 'found shelter in the Fortunate Isles', which were, according to later geographers, the Canaries. And he again seems to have modified this legend in his own original way. Sertorius' followers, he says,

> left their usages, their arts and laws
> To disappear by a slow gradual death;
> To dwindle and to perish one by one,
> Starved in their narrow bounds: but not the Soul
> Of Liberty, which fifteen hundred years
> Surviv'd, and, when the European came
> With skill and power that could not be withstood
> Did, like a pestilence, maintain its hold,
> And wasted down by glorious death that Race
> Of natural Heroes.

How did Wordsworth come to the knowledge of so obscure a subject as the difficult subjugation of the Canary Islands by the Spaniards in the fifteenth century? There was only one book in English that dealt with the subject, George Glas' translation of Abram de Galindo's unpublished account in Spanish called *The History of the Discovery and Conquest of the Canary Islands*, published in 1764. There the prolonged difficulties encountered by one Spanish governor after another in subduing Canaria, Tenerife, and other islands because of the 'strength, courage and number' of the inhabitants was fully set forth. About a year before, at Christmas 1802, Coleridge had played with the idea of going to 'Tenerife or Gran Canaria' for his health. He, with his insatiable thirst for knowledge, probably obtained a copy of Glas' book and lent it to Wordsworth. Wordsworth's contention that 'the Soul of Liberty' in the islands was a survival from the days of Sertorius was, however, his own personal interpretation of the story.

The same grand theme of liberty pervades the four other subjects which he tells us suggested themselves to him. There was the 'unknown man' who 'in tyrannic times'

> Suffer'd in silence for the love of truth.[1]

---

[1] *Prel.* I, ll. 202–5. 'unknown' becomes 'high-souled' in 1850 text.

There was Dominique de Gourges, 'that one Frenchman', whose story was told in Hakluyt, who went alone to Florida to avenge the massacre of the French settlers by the Spaniards,

> not to comfort the oppressed,
> But, like a thirsty wind, to roam about,
> Withering the Oppressor.[1]

Then there was Gustavus Vasa, the deliverer of Sweden, of whom Wordsworth had read at Alfoxden in Brooke's play.[2] And finally there was Wallace who left his name

> to be found like a wild flower
> All over his dear country, left the deeds
> Of Wallace like a family of ghosts
> To people the steep rocks and river banks,
> Her natural sanctuaries, with a local soul
> Of independence and stern liberty.[3]

He had found plenty of Wallace's traces during the Scottish tour lately ended, and they linked themselves in his mind with the tales and ballads of Wallace told by his old 'Packman' friend at Hawkshead.

These legendary or heroic themes, all concerned with the 'motif' of liberty, did not, in spite of his absorption in the thought of invasion, and the near presence of an oppressor in the form of Bonaparte, result in any one of them being selected for an epic. Yet during the next two years Wordsworth did indeed write an epic, of which the 'hero' is himself and the story that of his own spiritual adventures, discoveries, and sufferings. *The Prelude* is the only kind of epic that he could ever successfully have written, for, had he chosen any other 'hero' that person would inevitably have become himself. Wordsworth was not without the gift of creating living beings and entering objectively into their experience. It is seen in many of his shorter poems, and is at its best in the figure of Margaret in *The Ruined Cottage* and that of the old shepherd Michael. But such people could never have risen to epic stature. A sustained and prolonged theme for him would have to be one arising directly out of his own experience, for here and only here could he appraise and criticize,

---

[1] Ibid., ll. 206–12.   [2] *E.L.* 74, p. 187. W.W. to James Tobin, 6th May 1798.

[3] Ibid., ll. 214–20. The lines about Wallace are in themselves an indication that this part was written after the return from Scotland. Cf. Dorothy's *Recollections. D.W.J.* i, p. 228.

select and unify, with an objectivity and accuracy of under-standing which he could never have given to an imaginary or even historical hero.

There was one subject which might have recommended itself to him for epic treatment but which he does not mention; one of which Coleridge some years before had entreated him to write and with which his own experience and sympathies were closely entwined—the French Revolution. Coleridge's plea that he should write 'a poem in blank verse addressed to those who, in consequence of the complete failure of the French Revolution, have thrown up all hopes of the amelioration of mankind', although it did not lead to an epic or even to a poetical 'Essay on the French Revolution', was not forgotten.[1] As he advanced in writing the 'poem on his earlier life' he found that he could not end it, as he had at first intended, simply at his first long vaca-tion from Cambridge, but that he must go on and speak of those exciting and shattering years in which he was caught up in the Revolution and all but destroyed by it and its repercussions. The theme of the Revolution enters *The Prelude* in the sixth book, and in a sense is always present thenceforward until the end. But it is of the Revolution as Wordsworth experienced it and suffered from it that we read, not an epic with Danton and Robespierre, Brissot and Bonaparte as its heroes or villains.

The continuation of *The Prelude* proper did not begin until the new year, 1804. In the meantime the close of the year 1803 brought two events with it: one, a sudden visit, obscure in its origins, from Hazlitt; the other, Coleridge's last stay at Town End at Christmas, a sorrowful visit anyhow because the time had come when he was really going to leave them in search of health in a warmer climate, and made doubly distressing by his falling into one of his violent attacks of illness.

Hazlitt had been spending the autumn of 1803 mainly at Keswick. There he had indulged in some sort of escapade involving a girl, which had brought down upon him the wrath of some of the young men of the neighbourhood and he had only just escaped being ducked in the river. He fled to Grasmere, where he arrived at midnight at the door of the cottage and was taken in by the Wordsworths. Wordsworth supplied him with clothes and money and he departed from the Lake District for

[1] See above, p. 443.

ever. Many years later, in conversation with Crabb Robinson in 1815, Wordsworth, who was by that time decidedly cool towards Hazlitt, and had been so for several years, told him that his dislike of Hazlitt had begun at the time of the Keswick incident. This, however, cannot be accepted, for in March 1804 he wrote to Hazlitt a perfectly friendly letter about Hazlitt's portrait of little Hartley Coleridge. The latter part of it runs as follows:

Nobody durst venture to seize your clothes or box. . . . We mean to go to Keswick as soon as the weather improves, and I shall take particular pains to hunt after it. In the meanwhile it shall be mentioned to Mrs. Coleridge. . . . I have been tolerably busy this last month having written about 1200 lines of the Poem on my own life. I should have liked to shew you 200 yards or so of mountain brook scenery which I found out yesterday above Rydale. They are some of the finest old stumpified staring trees I ever saw, with a small waterfall, rocks of all shapes, etc. I passed also under Nab Scar at Rydale which you sketched a part of: it is infinitely finer in winter than in summer time; and indeed is a noble place. We are all pretty well—and desire best remembrances;

> I am very affectionately yours,
> W. Wordsworth.[1]

If Wordsworth had been feeling out of love with Hazlitt at this time he would not have promised to look for his box, or told him of the progress of *The Prelude*, or signed himself 'very affectionately yours'. Yet by 1808 his feelings had undergone a change, for in that year, when on a visit to London, Wordsworth had called on Lamb with the intention of reading to him his newly-completed *White Doe of Rylstone*; but finding Hazlitt there, he wrote to Coleridge 'I of course refused'. They had not met in the interval, but in 1806 Hazlitt had published his strange political pamphlet, *Free Thoughts on Public Affairs or Advice to a Patriot; in a letter Addressed to a Member of the Old Opposition*, in which he attacked those who, like Wordsworth and Coleridge, had changed their attitude to France and the Revolution after the rise of Bonaparte. At the end of it he had appended a short essay on the 'character of Mr. Pitt', which was based on 'the masterly and unanswerable essay' of Coleridge in the *Morning Post* two years before, in which Coleridge had

[1] *L.T.* iii. 161, p. 1949. P. P. Howe, *William Hazlitt*, pp. 99–101.

attacked Pitt savagely. This essay Hazlitt advised everybody to read. Coleridge was still abroad when *Free Thoughts* appeared; he would certainly have resented Hazlitt's use of his essay, and Wordsworth no doubt resented it for him, for clearly Hazlitt wanted to show up Coleridge as a political apostate. Nor could Wordsworth forgive Hazlitt's open admiration of Napoleon, or his sneer at those who had changed their opinions about the war. In time of war men are easily incensed against each other if their opinions differ. When in 1815 Hazlitt began to criticize Wordsworth's poetry in Leigh Hunt's *Examiner*, Wordsworth dragged in the 'scapes of the great god Pan', as Lamb called the Keswick episode, as further justification for his disapproval of Hazlitt, although they had had nothing to do with the origins of his hostility.[1]

Hazlitt's affair at Keswick apparently took place early in December; on December 20th 1803, Coleridge arrived and stayed until January 14th 1804. A summer and autumn of wrecked health and continued unhappiness at home had determined him to delay no longer in going abroad in search of health at least, but he was as yet undetermined where to go; it would be either to Malta or Madeira, and eventually, through Stoddart, who was King's Advocate there, it was to Malta. He was determined to take with him one helper at least—one unfailing and fatal assistant. 'You will oblige me', he wrote to Thelwall who passed through the Lakes this autumn, 'by going to the best druggist in Kendal for me and purchasing an ounce of crude opium, and nine ounces of Laudanum, the latter put in a stout bottle and so packed up as that it may travel a few hundred miles with safety.'[2]

Money was also a necessity. Except for the Wedgwood pension, Coleridge could have had no income at this time, for he was not producing anything, and such an expense as a voyage abroad could only be met out of borrowed money. It was Wordsworth who supplied it. 'Wordsworth', wrote Coleridge, 'had, as I may truly say, *forced* on me a hundred pounds.' But Wordsworth himself was obliged to resort to borrowing, and the

---

[1] *Lamb*, ii, p. 146. Lamb tried to make light of the incident, of which Wordsworth had evidently told him in a letter not now extant. See also Coventry Patmore, *My Friends and Acquaintance*, iii, pp. 140–54. Patmore believed the estrangement to be entirely due to political differences and Hazlitt's bitterness.

[2] *U.L.* i. 131, p. 297. S.T.C. to Thelwall, Nov. 26th 1803.

money was advanced by William Sotheby, the kind friend in London who had looked after William and Dorothy on their road to France.[1]

Coleridge spent three weeks at Grasmere, most of the time in the grip of violent illness. Dorothy and Mary nursed him devotedly, and in real alarm at the extremity of his sufferings. Yet, with the extraordinary resilience that was always astonishing his friends, as soon as he had gained some release from internal pain, he got up and walked the nineteen miles to Kendal, 'through mud and drizzle, fog and stifling air, in four hours and thirty-five minutes'. His sudden recovery astonished himself and everyone. 'I could not expect anyone to believe it who had not seen it', said Wordsworth.[2]

So he went on his way. The Wordsworths did not see him again for nearly three years. He was never out of their thoughts. During the three months which elapsed before his final departure from England all the literary output of the cottage was in one way or another inspired by him. William went on rapidly with the 'poem on his own life' which was also the 'poem to Coleridge', while Dorothy and Mary set to work to make a complete copy of all William's unpublished poetry, including *The Ruined Cottage,* and the 'poem on his life', so that Coleridge could carry them with him on his travels. This was a tremendous task, not only for its length but because of the difficulty of transcription, for as Dorothy said: 'they are scattered about in this book and in that, one Stanza on one leaf, another on another, which makes the transcribing more than twice the trouble'. Coleridge had been very insistent about having a copy of the poems, and it was indeed fortunate that he was so, otherwise, said Wordsworth, 'one half of these last three books' of the 'poem on his own life' might have been lost for ever through illegibility. 'I shall never, I hope', said he, 'get into such a scrape again.'[3] And not only did they make a copy for Coleridge, but

[1] R. B. Litchfield, *Tom Wedgwood,* p. 167. S.T.C. to T.W., Jan. 24th 1804. *E.L.* 164, p. 371. W.W. to W. Sotheby, Mar. 12th 1804.

[2] *S.T.C.* ii, p. 451. S.T.C. to R. Sharp, Jan. 15th 1804. Was Coleridge making the weather seem worse than it was? In the next sentence he ascribes his recovery to a change in the weather, and Dorothy says that he departed 'on a fine sunny morning'. *E.L.* 158, p. 356. D.W. to C. Clarkson, Jan. 15th 1804.

[3] *E.L.* 167, p. 380. W.W. to S.T.C., Mar. 29th 1804. The 'last three books' are Books III, IV, and V of *The Prelude*: all that had been written up to the end of Mar. 1804. Dorothy says that the copying required 'William's almost constant

another for themselves. For the women of the cottage, therefore, the spring of 1804 was a time of unremitting labour at 'an intricate and weary job'; with much of the work of the house to do as well—for poor old Molly was failing in health and unable to be of much assistance—and Johnny to nurse, it is small wonder that Dorothy was obliged to interrupt the writing of her *Recollections*. But the copying was also a labour of love and a means of comforting themselves for the blank left in their lives by Coleridge's departure. Dorothy not only copied poems but wrote him long letters about their doings. 'Farewell, my beloved Friend', she wrote at the end of one of these. 'William, who is sitting beside me reading *Hamlet*—(we are both at the little green round table by the fire side, the watch ticking over our heads. Mary is with the sleeping Baby below stairs, writing to Sara)—William exhorts me to give over writing: so farewell, my dearest Coleridge. May God bless you, and your faithful and affectionate, Dorothy Wordsworth.'[1]

Dorothy's picture, with which she sought to comfort Coleridge, is happy and peaceful. And for all his seriousness, and his desire that people should read his poetry only in the spirit in which it was written, and in spite of times of depression and disappointment about his own work, Wordsworth was now essentially, as Coleridge had remarked, a happy man. A glimpse of how he appeared to others is afforded by Samuel Rogers, who about the year 1812 met both Wordsworth and Southey at Lowther Castle. Here it was Southey, not Wordsworth, who appeared the 'recluse'; for he scarcely ever left the library. '"How *cold* he is", was Wordsworth's exclamation—himself so joyous and communicative.'[2]

These are not adjectives which are normally associated with Wordsworth, yet when the years which culminated in the completion of *The Prelude* are passed in review, there seems much to justify them. The life of Wordsworth up to 1804 indeed presents something of a paradox. He 'retired to his native mountains' in order to write a poem called *The Recluse*, which originally had the unrecluse-like alternative title of 'Pictures of Man, Nature and Society'. He failed to write it, but what he did write

attendance', and adds, 'I think William would never have had the resolution to set us to work again.'
[1] *E.L.* 162, p. 367. Mar. 6th 1804.   [2] Rogers, *Table Talk*.

concerned at every point man's mind and heart, his 'imagination' and 'affections'. He lived in happy comradeship with his family and chosen friends; his children, his neighbours, and the floating population of the roads were sources of inspiration and delight to him. His house was often overflowing with visitors. There was, indeed, a sense in which he was a 'recluse'; though always hospitable, he was glad enough to have his fireside to himself again. As he said:

> I am not one who much or oft delight
> To season my fireside with personal talk—
> Of friends who live within an easy walk,
> Or neighbours, daily, weekly, in my sight . . .
> Better than such discourse doth silence long
> Long, barren, silence square with my desire;
> To sit without emotion, hope, or aim
> In the loved presence of my cottage-fire,
> And listen to the flapping of the flame,
> Or kettle whispering its faint undersong.[1]

But enough has been said to show that the balance between solitude and society in Wordsworth's life was well maintained; that the 'rock with torrents roaring' which he felt his 'soul' essentially to be had had its crevices well planted with flowers; that he, like his own Happy Warrior,

> though thus endued as with a sense
> And faculty for storm and turbulence,
> Is yet a Soul whose master-bias leans
> To homefelt pleasures and to gentle scenes.

During the past seven years this harmonious tension had enabled him to become one of that company whom he so dearly loved—

> The Poets, who on earth have made us heirs
> Of truth and pure delight by heavenly lays.

[1] *P.W.* iv, p. 73, *Personal Talk*. The date of this sonnet-sequence is uncertain but it belongs to the Dove Cottage years.

INDEX

WILLIAM WORDSWORTH'S WORKS

PRINTED IN GREAT BRITAIN
AT THE UNIVERSITY PRESS, OXFORD
BY CHARLES BATEY, PRINTER TO THE UNIVERSITY